Concessions of a Serial Campaigner

ROBERT SHRUM

No Excuses

SIMON & SCHUSTER

NEW YORK   LONDON   TORONTO   SYDNEY

SIMON & SCHUSTER

Rockefeller Center
1230 Avenue of the Americas
New York, NY 10020

For information regarding special discounts for bulk purchases,
please contact Simon & Schuster Special Sales
at 1-800-456-6798 or business@simonandschuster.com.

Designed by Dana Sloan

Manufactured in the United States of America

10 9 8 7 6 5 4 3 2 1

Library of Congress Cataloging-in-Publication Data is available.

ISBN-13: 978-0-7432-9651-9
ISBN-10: 0-7432-9651-6

To Marylouise,
My Wife, My Life

CONTENTS

Footfalls echo in the memory
Down the passage which we did not take
Towards the door we never opened
Into the rose-garden.

— T.S. Eliot, *Four Quartets*

The Democratic Party has never been invested with power on the basis of a program which promised to keep things as they were.

We have won when we pledged to meet the new challenges of each succeeding year.

We have triumphed not in spite of controversy, but because of it; not because we avoided problems, but because we faced them.

We have won, not because we bent and diluted our principles, but because we stood fast to the ideals which represent the most noble and generous portion of the American spirit.

—Robert F. Kennedy

INTRODUCTION: THE "SHRUM CURSE"

Shortly past 7 P.M. on November 2, 2004, I got onto a freight elevator at the end of a closely guarded hotel corridor with John Kerry, his Secret Service detail, and campaign manager Mary Beth Cahill. The candidate had just completed a long afternoon of last-minute get-out-the-vote calls. A network journalist had called me a short time before to confirm that given the exit polls, there was no way we could lose; the polls would just have to be wrong in too many places. Now we were heading back to Kerry's home on Beacon Hill a few blocks away to go over the victory statement that he would soon deliver to a crowd of tens of thousands in Boston's Copley Square. I broke the silence, looked over at Kerry, and just said: "Mr. President."

"Not yet, not yet," he cautioned, although it became clear over the next hour or so that he believed it, too. For me, it was the triumph of hope over experience. I should have known better than to presume victory or believe exit polls after 2000, when there were at least three different moments when we were sure Al Gore had won. But as the elevator descended, I was thinking back to something else—those lonely nighttime rides from New Hampshire to Boston less than a year before, when Kerry had been written off, even scorned, and the press was picking regularly at the carcass of the campaign. We had few reporters in tow, no entourage to speak of, just an anonymous blue Suburban van speeding through the cold—and when we got to the house, Teresa, standing on the porch, would say: "Come on in and have something to eat. I have a nice glass of wine for you." And now, as I thought we were standing on the mountaintop, I remembered the valley.

At his home, Kerry was anxious to review and polish the victory speech. For almost twenty-five years, I'd been trying to stop being a speechwriter. But at moments like this—for acceptance speeches at a national convention, announcements of candidacy, or State of the Union addresses—I tended to be pressed back into service. The truth was I enjoyed it, as long as I didn't have to do it all the time, and I enjoyed mentoring new generations of speechwriters. Actually, I had no choice, since I couldn't and can't type. So, in addition to contributing their eloquence, they had to deploy their laptops to keep a constantly rewritten text in coherent shape.

The young speechwriter Josh Gottheimer, who had traveled with Kerry for months, was there, laptop ready. So were the podium and prompters set up for practice in the large entry foyer of John and Teresa's redbrick town house, a former convent on Boston's posh Louisburg Square. There were Dutch and Flemish masters on the walls, including a chilling painting called *Vanitas,* which features a skull amid books, food, and flowers, a symbol of the futility of all human ambition. We got a call: the Bush campaign had been working that afternoon on a concession statement. We never knew if it was true. We were just getting ready for a run-through when the phone rang again and Mary Beth's BlackBerry began to beep. We were told we had better get back to the war room in the hotel.

As we left, Kerry's daughter Alex, who had followed and filmed the campaign for months for a documentary, was sitting on the front steps. She looked at me and in a voice that was close to tears asked: "Everything's going to be all right, isn't it?" The only thing I could say to the intense, fragile, aspiring filmmaker and actress who'd gone to Brown with my stepson Michael, was: I think so. And then, when I saw the look on her face, I added: Yes, yes, I'm sure it is.

Our pollsters and number crunchers were calling into the war room on a speakerphone from Washington. Florida was closer than we thought; it would be tight, but we'd probably be okay there. Ohio, on the other hand, was secure. Mary Beth, someone I'd had run-ins and disagreements with, but who'd come in when the campaign was coming apart a year before and kept it together, said as we sat on a couch in the hotel suite: "Shrum, on a personal level, I just want you to know how happy I am for you." She smiled and said: "You made the difference; the debates made the difference. All the crap you took—it's over."

The number crunchers called again. Florida, well, Florida now looked bad; too many votes in the I-4 corridor, a stronghold of the religious right. Ohio was narrowing, but we'd make it there. I could feel where the evening was heading, even if I was trying to hope against hope. Through a guarded stairwell, I walked downstairs one floor to the room where my wife Marylouise had retreated from an A-list party for the big Kerry fund-raisers. She was sitting on a king-sized bed, watching the returns on television with two young assistants from my firm, Jon Herczeg and Greg Minoff. Greg was crying and she was holding him in her arms. I said it wasn't over, there was still Ohio, and I'd come back every 15 minutes or so.

But now, every 15 minutes or so, it was Kerry who was calling both Mary Beth and me. He was checking on the numbers; in truth, he desperately wanted reassurance. The reports from Ohio grew steadily bleaker: to overcome the Bush lead, we'd have to carry a daunting proportion of the outstanding ballots, including the contested provisional ballots. There was talk about the Diebold voting machines—the company was owned by one of Bush's biggest contributors; about the lack of a paper trail, and about the long waiting lines to vote in African-American precincts in Cleveland.

I walked out of the dining room, where we were all gathered around the speakerphone, crossed the rest of the gigantic suite, and looked out the window at the lights of Boston twinkling far below as the crowd at our victory party left for home. Kerry called on my cell phone about 2:15 A.M. Before he could ask, I said: "It's less than a fifty percent chance this is going to work out." He called back on the speakerphone in the dining room to talk out the options in Ohio one more time: he knew that if he didn't contest the results, there'd be some angry Democrats. Teresa thought then—and believed increasingly in the coming months—that Ohio and perhaps other states had been stolen. I'm not sure she was wrong. The lawyers were prepared to challenge the results; the planes were chartered and ready to fly. But Ron Klain, the former Gore chief of staff who'd worked with me on the Kerry debate preps and was honchoing the legal team, glumly advised the candidate, as he'd already said to us, that there was no realistic chance we could succeed in court. Kerry said he'd wait until next morning to decide what to do. He ended the call and a few seconds later my cell phone rang again: "Can you be at my house about nine A.M.?"

Marylouise and I walked arm-in-arm the few blocks from our headquarters hotel to the Four Seasons. I was paying for us to stay there because the last year had been hard for her, too. Now we could celebrate. Instead, I pulled my chair up to the desk in our room and wrote a concession speech.

In my own mind, I conceded something else. I knew how I would be portrayed, now more than ever—as the black cat of American politics, someone who had connived, confused, consulted, and condemned no fewer than eight Democratic presidential candidates to defeat. Now that's quite a record.

That would mean that I, as a twenty-eight-year-old speechwriter, hired six months before the election, brought down George McGovern—with no help from Richard Nixon, dirty tricks, Watergate, a flubbed vice-presidential choice, and the Vietnam War. That all on my own, again a speechwriter, I caused the candidacy of Edward Kennedy to falter, even as he ran against a sitting president from his own party. Never mind that his announcement coincided with the fifty-two American diplomats being taken hostage in Iran. That, as a consultant, I took on the long-shot campaign of a largely unknown congressman named Dick Gephardt, who won an upset victory in Iowa, and then brought him to rack and ruin. This is where my devotion to "populist" Democratic Party values also came into play. Not satisfied, just five weeks before the 1992 New Hampshire primary, I was hired to undertake a political rescue mission for presidential hopeful Bob Kerrey. I managed not to be able to save him.

Hard to believe I did this all by myself—or that anyone ever hired me to try again. But someone did. And what is real is that I played a big hand in the election of Al Gore as president—then watched his win be stolen away by a butterfly ballot and the battering ram of the Republican machine in Florida.

Then, of course, I lost the White House for John Kerry. I'll take my share of the blame. I made mistakes. So did all of us; you always do in campaigns. I also know that voters out there were swayed by the memories and manipulation of 9/11 and the last-weekend Osama bin Laden tape. I got some credit when my much-criticized strategy helped propel Kerry from a pre-primary collapse to a sweep of almost every primary and caucus. But now—as much as or more than anyone else—I was seen as responsible for his near miss against George W. Bush.

All this was summed up in the "Shrum Curse," a phrase bannered on the front page of the *New York Times* as the clammy darkness of impending defeat seemed to be settling over Kerry's campaign for the nomination in late 2003.

Now, the "Shrum Curse" is not to be confused with the "Shrum Primary." Political junkies anywhere in reach of cable TV knew the "Shrum Primary" as a contest in which many potential 2004 presidential candidates pursued and courted me, battling for my services as strategic consultant, ad maker, and speechwriter. It may seem contradictory that the persona of the "Shrum Curse" was also the persona of the "Shrum Primary," but it's true. It happened. I read it in the papers and heard it on TV—again and again, sometimes from the same observer.

What also happened in my career was that I had a great run in politics—in thirty winning Senate campaigns, twenty for Congress, and eleven for governor; the election of mayors across America, including the first African-American mayor of New York; and even though it was the only sheriff's race I ever enlisted in, the victory of the first African-American sheriff in a majority white county in the

Deep South since the Civil War. I was privileged to help elect progressive leaders in Britain, Israel, Ireland, and a war-torn Colombia. "Help" is the operative word. Candidates win elections; consultants "lose" them.

Along the way, I quit Jimmy Carter as he was speeding toward the White House. I fought with—and for—Bill Clinton. I had loyalty given to me by clients, partners, friends, and other consultants. I even had friendship extended by members of the media. And I had done my best to change my country for the better.

In the weeks that followed Kerry's defeat, I decided that it was time to move on with my life—that if all my years in national politics had involved more than personal ambition, it was time to step back, to reflect on what I had witnessed and done, on the victories, the defeats, and the larger purposes that have driven me on. Some of what I write here will differ from what's been reported or published elsewhere, but it's what I know and remember from across the years. In 1970, *Life* magazine had called me a "wunderkind"; now I truly was what the media most frequently called me—a "senior" strategist. I had worked for some dogs—and some of the candidates I had worked for probably thought I wasn't much good, either. But I had also stood with good and sometimes great leaders, discovered their strengths and flaws and my own, fought in the front lines of battles I really cared about, and experienced the truth of what I once said to my stepson Michael: "If you go into politics, just remember that every two years, you can get your heart broken."

But I wouldn't have chosen any other life. In an essay I wrote as a sixteen-year-old, which my sister Barbara found years later and framed, I looked ahead: "I will hold myself remiss if my personal ambition lacks certain basic ideals. I will know the poet's kind of life"—which in retrospect I guess meant attempting to weave some poetry into politics. "I have aspirations; I have aimed high. And if I fail, I will still have succeeded, for I will have striven to accomplish high aims." Looking back, I have known both the hurt of defeat and many happy returns.

This book is not just the story of that journey, but of the events I have witnessed, the candidates who have been my clients and often my friends; the crises, the battles, and the history I have been part of. In it, there are proud and painful moments to be remembered; insights, conviction, and maybe even some wisdom; progress made and lost; and sometimes even laughter. I hope, to paraphrase a line Ted Kennedy and I both love, that I have learned to take issues seriously, but never to take myself too seriously.

1

A FORTUNATE YOUTH

My parents were part of that extraordinary World War II generation who joined the great westward migration of the 1950s. I was eight, my sister Barbara was six, when they piled us into their 1948 Chevy coupe for the cross-country drive toward the better life offered by this new America—booming growth and perpetual sunshine.

It was a big decision. My father's family had settled in western Pennsylvania before the American Revolution, stayed there and eked out a life, generation after generation. When he was six years old, my grandfather went to work, winding up as a lineman for West Penn Railways. For most of their lives together, my grand-parents lived on the wrong side of Connellsville, across the Youghiogheny River, in the working-class west side, where soot fell from the smoldering coke ovens that rose across the tracks and up the hill from their house.

My mother was far better off, the child of first-generation Irish-Americans, a family that achieved small-town economic and politi-cal heights in a matter of years. Her father, a prominent Catholic and decorated Spanish-American War veteran, was a member of the state legislature.

When Clarence Shrum married Cecilia Welsh—the pretty Catholic girl and her Protestant tool-and-die beau—the difference in backgrounds meant something, and that something was that their "mixed marriage" bent the rules. Their wedding took place on Christmas afternoon, in the rectory attached to the Church of the Immaculate Conception. It was a lonely event; the priest forbade their families to attend.

More than a decade later, the Korean War was on and Hughes Aircraft was recruiting. My dad came home one night and abruptly and bravely announced that we were moving to California. They were making this move for us, their son and daughter. They wanted more for us than the scarred and stratified western Pennsylvania region could offer. My mother had taught me to read from the funny pages when I wasn't yet four years old; in the first grade at my parochial school, I got in trouble because I could already read and balked at tracing letters in order to learn how. My father wanted the best education he could find for us. He often said I'd go to Pitt—and after we moved to California, Stanford. Of course, every year during football season, we still rooted our hearts out for Notre Dame to beat USC. It was the Catholics versus the Protestants; but Dad had now converted as a gift to my sister and me.

In California, there were many dinners alone with my mother and sister while my Dad worked two back-to-back shifts. It got even more hectic when he left Hughes and became one of the first employees of a new company called Paper Mate Pen. He was now something of a self-taught engineer who helped design ballpoint pens so they'd write without smudging, for which he got a thankyou. Inventing was covered by his hourly wage.

In the 1950s, Culver City, California, was a soundstage for the American Dream, home to aerospace workers and skilled craftsmen from our neighbor, MGM. The movies were everywhere. A friend and I would climb the fence around the RKO backlot, and play near a set for Tara, the antebellum southern mansion from *Gone With the Wind*. It was thrilling and disappointing, so very Hollywood, a glorious front with nothing behind it.

I missed my cousins so much that I even nagged my parents into briefly moving back to Pennsylvania. We stayed exactly six weeks. Fortunately, Paper Mate was happy to take my father back. Los Angeles, with its sunshine and the trips to Venice Beach at Christmas time, was a magical place for most kids, but I didn't entirely fit in. They were plunging into California's newest sport, surfing. But not me. My father was a superb athlete; I was a klutz. I was diving—but into books, biography, history, and politics. Every month, my parents gave me money to buy books; I still have some of them. My mother wrote a note to the Culver City Public Library giving me permission to read "adult" books like Carl Sandburg's multivolume *Lincoln*. My first job—I was only twelve or thirteen—was in a local bookstore run by a self-taught polymath named Stanley Brile. He tried to convince me there was no God. "Just read Schopenhauer," he said. I tried.

My Democratic leanings came from my mother, who went with her father to Franklin Roosevelt's second inaugural, but my political passion from my father, who broke with his family's long Republican tradition during the New Deal. My first political memory is of them joyously banging pots and pans in the middle of the night when Truman came from behind to beat Dewey in 1948. I loved politics: I even persuaded my parents to let me stay home from school to watch Douglas MacArthur's speech to Congress—"old soldiers never die, they just fade away"—after Harry Truman fired him for insubordination during the Korean War.

Truman was second best; Roosevelt was the hero. Back in Connellsville, when FDR became president, my dad had helped organize a union at the mine supply shop where he worked after graduating from high school. The New Deal's labor laws protected the workers who signed on—and my father's wages went from two dollars to four dollars a day. Our family believed in unions. Every night at dinner our radio was tuned to "Edward P. Morgan and the News" presented by the AFL-CIO.

In 1952, I watched the Democratic Convention gavel to gavel on our new television. Afterward, I went down to volunteer at the Culver City Democratic Headquarters. I made phone calls—and because I had a nine-year-old's voice, got used to people on the other end of the line addressing me as "Yes, ma'am."

The Eisenhower landslide stunned me—I didn't yet understand

that some elections are unwinnable; but Stevenson's concession speech deepened my nascent appreciation for the power of words. I can still hear him quoting Abraham Lincoln's line: "It hurts too much to laugh, but I'm too old to cry." Earlier, the power of words had impressed me in a different way when Ike's running mate, Richard Nixon, delivered his "Checkers speech" supposedly explaining the slush fund his contributors had set up for him while actually delivering a cloying piece of demagoguery about not returning the "little dog" that someone had given his two young daughters. Even to a nine-year-old, it was a phony speech, a bad speech—and worse, for most of the country, it worked.

Uncle Tom and Aunt Kit and their family followed us to California. Tom was a postman, and gave me a priceless introduction to a world of information, thanks to the undeliverable magazines from his route, magazines like *The Atlantic* and *Newsweek*. At St. Augustine School, some of the Irish nuns regarded Joe McCarthy as close to a saint—and were still rooting for Franco in the Spanish Civil War. The magazines armed me for arguing; and the sisters were good enough to engage in a give-and-take that forced me to find other sources of proof for this debate. I read Whittaker Chambers's *Witness*, a brilliant, baroque piece of writing, even though I rebelled against its thesis that liberalism inexorably led to communism. But it whetted my appetite to hear from the other side. I searched out the new conservative *National Review* and was appalled by the magazine's defense of segregation. My father had grown up in an integrated neighborhood and my parents had no prejudice. One of the few times in my life that he spanked me was when I'd come home from the first grade and used the "N" word.

We were Californians in all things—except the ultimate California dream, owning our own home. Too concerned about financing a good education for their son and daughter, my parents deferred buying a house until I graduated from Georgetown.

Our vacations focused on the West: San Francisco, Carson City, and a dude ranch outside Las Vegas that we returned to for three summers, with its big pool and cheap rates. One year, one of the larger cabins was occupied by a man who looked to me like Sumner

Welles, FDR's under secretary of state. I'd seen his picture in my Roosevelt books, and, without much hesitation, I approached him and asked if he was Sumner Welles. He seemed surprised that a fourteen-year-old knew or cared. I didn't know then that Welles had left the State Department in the midst of World War II because he had supposedly propositioned a sleeping car porter. The man who might have been Welles—to this day I'm not sure, but he sounded real—sat and talked with me day after day about Roosevelt, Churchill, Stalin, and Harry Hopkins, FDR's right-hand man.

This was magic, like the movies, this man talking about FDR, who, he said, was silver on the surface and quicksilver underneath—hard to pin down, always maneuvering; even when FDR made up his mind and was moving in a definite direction, he was often getting to a place which only he knew. And FDR had few illusions about Stalin; Yalta wasn't a sell-out; it was the best deal Roosevelt and Churchill could make under the circumstance. It was a fascinating tutorial and Welles, if that's who he was, said he would see me next summer. But when we came back the next year, he wasn't there.

I took the entrance exam to get into Loyola High School, the Jesuit prep school eight miles away, a long bus ride or hitchhike from Culver City. The nuns said I would win a scholarship—but I missed it, so my parents just paid the $250 a year, an amount that actually meant something to them in 1957.

At Loyola, I finally found a competitive sport I was good at: speech and debate. There were tournaments every week, and I started winning. Debaters collected evidence "cards" in recipe boxes, to be used in alternate rounds as we debated both sides of the yearly topic. Both the evidence and the issues were heavy slogging, with topics like "Resolved: that the United Nations should be significantly strengthened," a question the country is still debating half a century later. Arcane and all-consuming, debate fit right in with the venerable Jesuit curriculum that ranked rhetoric as a central academic discipline along with Latin and Greek. (I can still recite the opening lines of the *Odyssey* in the original, but that's about it.) Debate became the school of my life. It was about public policy and the political process; more often than one would expect, the history I knew could come in handy, too.

In the summer of 1960, real politics was coming to Los Angeles. I yearned to be part of the Democratic National Convention. I even briefly joined the Young Democrats, who, it turned out, were not so young—more like thirty, very old to me, and still trying to find their first rung on the political ladder. Since I really was young, I would be picked to help lower the American flag from the rafters to fly over the convention the first night.

In May, at age sixteen, I turned up at the headquarters of Citizens for Kennedy, housed in an office building near MacArthur Park, and met a kind and efficient Liz Russ, in charge of organizing the volunteer effort. She let me stuff envelopes and run errands and then, as the Kennedy team began to arrive, sent me to press secretary Pierre Salinger's office in the Biltmore Hotel to do the same kind of grunt work. I picked up sandwiches and coffee, mimeographed and carried messages. After Salinger's deputy Andy Hatcher found out I could write, at least presentably, I even tried my hand at the first draft of decidedly unimportant press releases.

In the days leading up to the convention, my other assignment was to escort visitors from the press office upstairs, to the candidate's supposedly secret suite. Kennedy was actually staying at a private home, but he used the Biltmore Hotel's Suite 9300 for meetings. I was supposed to walk the guests to the door and then leave. But one afternoon, when I took former New York governor Averell Harriman up, he asked if I'd ever met Senator Kennedy. I said no; he knocked; the candidate opened the door, greeted Harriman, and then with a smile asked him who he'd brought along.

I told Senator Kennedy I was working in Pierre Salinger's office and what I did there. He asked when I came to work and when I went home. "On the first bus in the morning and the last bus at night, around midnight," I managed. JFK said he assumed I wasn't being paid anything and asked how old I was. "Sixteen, but soon I'll be seventeen." I thought to myself I'm going to get killed by Salinger for being in the suite, but we were just standing there, and Kennedy seemed in no hurry. Where, the senator asked, was I thinking of going to college? My high school was really pushing a Catholic college, I answered. How about Georgetown? he asked, adding that's where his brother-in-law Steve Smith went. Kennedy shook my hand, said good-bye, and guided Harriman toward the couch.

I was a starry-eyed kid then and John Kennedy was a luminous presence in that room, a presence tempered by his easy manner and ironic smile—just how ironic I found out when I got back to Salinger's office. The candidate had called him. "You're supposed to be taking people up there, not going in and talking to him," I was told. What was my mother's phone number? If it was all right with her, I could have meal money and a hotel room—a room that I shared with a Coke machine and a stack of paraphernalia for "The Kennedy Girls," the ubiquitous cheerleading sidelight at the convention. I think JFK was teasing Salinger, who was being good-natured about it, and my convention got even better.

On Wednesday night, I went to the Sports Arena for the nominations. Minnesota governor Orville Freeman's TelePrompTer broke as he nominated Kennedy. I was worried, especially after Senator Gene McCarthy's eloquent nomination of Adlai Stevenson, the defeated Democrat of 1952 and 1956, as "not the favorite son of any one state but the favorite son of fifty states"; an enormous demonstration engulfed the convention. McCarthy, I was told years later, was acting at the behest of Lyndon Johnson, who had to stop Kennedy on the first ballot if his own candidacy stood a chance. There was also McCarthy's resentment of the Kennedys; he saw himself as the better Catholic—and, if there was going to be one, he should be the first Catholic president. As the demonstration intensified, seemingly out of control, I retreated to one of the VIP lounges to which I had a pass. Chicago mayor Richard Daley and a clutch of Illinois delegates were briefly there. "The favorite son of fifty states," one of them quipped; "he didn't carry very many of them." I timidly asked one of Daley's pals if we should be worried. The mayor, who'd abandoned Stevenson for Kennedy, looked up and said: "It's done—first ballot," and left the lounge.

He was right. Afterward, I was on an elevator back at the Biltmore when two Texans, Senator Lyndon Johnson and House Speaker Sam Rayburn, got on. No one noticed me. Rayburn was swearing a blue streak telling Johnson he could not, no matter what, accept the vice presidency from that "goddamned Kennedy machine." It happened, of course, the next afternoon, starting decades of controversy about whether Kennedy really wanted Johnson.

Long afterward, when I was working for Ted Kennedy, he told me that well before the convention, he'd been with his father and JFK when they decided between themselves that Johnson was the strongest choice. They didn't tell anyone in advance because the liberals and labor would be upset. The conventional wisdom is that the Johnson pick was not only chaotic, but half accidental; the truth may be that it was a fine piece of calculation that had to be executed in a messy way, with JFK intervening calmly at the most perilous moments in the process to reassure Johnson that he really was the choice. The Kennedys often disagreed with their controversial father on policy, but they loved him absolutely and valued his political advice. For JFK and Joseph P. Kennedy, the bottom line in 1960 was winning—and the ticket had to have a real shot at the South.

In the fall of my senior year, I volunteered at the Kennedy-Johnson headquarters in Culver City; covered the Kennedy and Nixon appearances at the University of Southern California's first voter events for the *Loyalist*, our high school magazine (not an unbiased reporter, but I gave Nixon a fair shake); and argued the Kennedy side in Loyola's presidential debate. My team won the debate. Nixon won the mock vote at a school where Kennedy's Catholicism mattered less to most students than the fact that they were from wealthier, largely Republican backgrounds, like the sons of Bob Hope and character actor Pat O'Brien.

That fall, the admissions director from Georgetown visited Loyola and told me I was being awarded the Ignatian Scholarship—one was given in each of the regional Jesuit provinces in the United States. It would pay my Georgetown tuition for four years. I gave it back when I later won a National Merit Scholarship—which, combined with my record in speech and debate and my grades, led to my selection as valedictorian. You didn't have to be first in the class; I wasn't. The Jesuits wanted a good speech.

There was a bump on the road to graduation day. Father McFadden, Loyola's principal, called me in one day that spring. Why, he asked, did I want to go to Georgetown? Obviously, Georgetown was not Father McFadden's choice for me. Bob Mathewson, the young Jesuit scholastic who was my debate coach early on, had stayed in touch with me after he left for his Jesuit-mandated theological study, and was the person who had encouraged me to pick Georgetown, the "best Catholic college in the country." I wasn't squealing on Mathewson. Father McFadden had a habit of piling one question on another: "You don't have to be valedictorian, you realize? Why not Loyola of Los Angeles—if our best graduates don't go to our Jesuit colleges on the west coast, how will we improve those schools?" I remember my answer as clearly as if it were yesterday: "But Father, I'm not going to a college to improve it by my presence. I'm going there to have it improve me." Father McFadden's gruff exterior concealed—and when you were a freshman, not a senior, the disguise was very convincing—a decent man with a soft spot for the high school students who were his lifelong vocation. After I got out my impertinent response, he stared for a second and then laconically told me to just go back to class. I never heard another word about the issue he'd raised.

Before graduation, we had a spiritual "retreat" conducted by a forbidding Jesuit straight out of *A Portrait of the Artist as a Young Man*. The Second Vatican Council was about to bring the Church into the twentieth century, but fire, brimstone, and fear still radiated from the pulpit. At the retreat we were subjected to vivid Joycean descriptions of the everlasting torment of sinners, capped by the story of the Student Body President (a boy) and the Sodality President (a girl) who'd committed "serious acts of indecency" in the backseat of his car after the senior prom. There was a car wreck on the way home; the girl was killed; and when the boy hobbled up the aisle on crutches at her wake, she sat bolt upright in the coffin and screamed: "Don't pray for me. I'm in Hell." It was a standard story, but we didn't know it. We were also shaken during a graphic retelling of the clinical details of the crucifixion when the retreat master suddenly whirled around and slowly clanged out the words: "Someone in this chapel is in the state of mortal sin." Given the standards of that day, in a roomful of high school seniors, it was almost certainly true.

Then came a sunny graduation day in 1961, the same day President Kennedy was holding his summit meeting with Nikita Khrushchev in Vienna. I'm not sure that's what my classmates wanted to hear about, but they did—from me. My speech began: "This is the hour of crisis, the year of challenge, the decade of decision." I still have the text; it was more like a speechwriter's tryout than a high school senior's fond farewell. Still, my parents were proud, the Jesuits were pleased, and my classmates—well, they probably expected it, and most of them shook my hand or clapped me on the shoulder afterward.

That summer, I traveled to the national speech tournament in Pittsburgh. I'd missed qualifying in debate or extemporaneous speaking, so I went in something called Student Congress. I didn't do well. I think I believed the way to win was to be a know-it-all. I just plain talked too much. So I decided not to debate in college—a decision that didn't outlast my first week at Georgetown.

I had never seen the campus until we drove through the front gates after a cross-country trip with some fellow Loyola graduates who were sophomores and juniors; in those days, you didn't—most of us couldn't afford to—go on "college tours" to check out different campuses before you applied. As we passed the circle in front of the neo-Gothic Healy Tower, the first thing that struck me was that most of the buildings were really old—an impression that was almost instantly reinforced when I was assigned to a dorm room just down the hall from "Old North." From its porch, George Washington had spoken to the student body in 1797.

For some reason, maybe just curiosity, I did go to the first meeting of what was called the Philodemic Debating Society. That evening set the course of my college career—and much of my life. Not because of the trappings or traditions of the Philodemic, but because a young Ph.D. named Bill Reynolds, a nattily dressed intellectual in his second year as director of debate at Georgetown, decided I was going to debate.

The competition was fierce. In the final round of the Dartmouth tournament in 1963, the Harvard team accused us of making up our evidence. After a withering, sarcastic assault, my partner and I decided to break the format and ignore the time limits, reading at length from our sources, telling the audience we didn't care whether we won or lost, but we were determined to convince them that we hadn't betrayed their trust. The two of us agreed that when the timekeeper stood up during the last rebuttal, my partner would tell him to sit down while he finished reading out the original sources. We won the round and the tournament, and my friendship with Larry Tribe, the graduate student who was coaching the Harvard team, survived my angry reaction afterward.

Debate was a nonstop battlefield of ideas and stratagems, my training ground for the back-and-forth of politics. It also gave me many of my closest friendships: Tribe, who became a professor at Harvard Law School and a path-breaking constitutional scholar; John Sexton, the future dean of NYU Law and then president of NYU; Lee Huebner, Nixon's speechwriter when I was McGovern's, who went on to become publisher of the *International Herald Tribune*; Bob Bennett, the Washington lawyer who would represent Bill Clinton and Reagan's defense secretary Caspar Weinberger; my debate partner John Koetl, now a federal judge; and generations of younger people I would come to know who would make their marks in politics, government, and business.

One of those young people did not debate, but I met him because of debate. In my senior year, I was named the outstanding college debater in the country and someone on the freshman team told me he had a classmate who wanted to meet me. It was the spring of 1965. At Teehan's, a student hangout a block off campus that served ten-cent beers, I had several while chatting with a boyish, impressive Bill Clinton. I don't remember all of the three-hour conversation except that we talked about JFK, Robert Kennedy, and Lyndon Johnson—who, despite all the legislation he was passing, didn't have remotely the same appeal to either of us as his predecessor. Bill talked about his fellow Arkansasan, Senator J. William Fulbright, who would become Clinton's mentor as he moved toward a Rhodes Scholarship. I told Bill I thought he would make a hell of a debater. He replied that he didn't have time to do the research—he was already in elective politics, president of the freshman class—but if someone else could do it, maybe he could debate.

I didn't see Clinton for years after that, although we all heard the news that he had won a Rhodes. Then in 1972, George McGovern made one of his rare campaign stops in the South. After the plane door opened, Clinton, who was managing Texas for us, bounded up the stairs, saw me as he entered the front cabin, gave me a hug and a big hello—"Bob, how are ya?"—as if we'd last seen each other only last week.

The real gift of debate was the way it taught clarity and conciseness; what mattered was not oratory, but analysis. I often thought about that working with John Kerry in the 1996 Senate and 2004 presidential campaigns. He's a naturally gifted debater who was on the team at Yale when I was at Georgetown. But we never met— none of us ever debated Yale—because Rollin Osterweiss, the Yale professor who had also coached the prophet and polemicist of the new conservatism, William F. Buckley, Jr., disdained the emphasis on evidence and rapid-fire delivery that characterized the activity at most colleges. At least as we heard about him, he valued rhetorical skills and flourishes, complication, and, yes, nuance. And John Kerry, I was told years later, was one of his best students.

John Kennedy's assassination in 1963 was an unthinkable and terrifying clap of thunder in our college lives. Presidents just didn't get shot, not in our country; that happened in "banana republics" or the Soviet bloc. When I first heard the news from a fellow student who burst into my room, I thought maybe it was a bad joke, but the stricken look on his face told me otherwise. Students by the hundreds gravitated to the brick courtyard outside Old North, where several of the Jesuits said an impromptu mass. Some of us were off to the side of the porch listening to a radio with the volume turned very low. As the mass was ending, we slipped a note to one of the Jesuits, who suddenly intoned, "May his soul and the souls of all the faithful departed rest in peace." People swayed and then began to cry. That weekend, with two friends, I waited in line in the November cold for eight hours and then, for a few seconds, passed by the casket in the Capitol rotunda.

Academics were not my priority at Georgetown. At the end of my freshman year, I scraped into the honors program, which put about twenty-five of us into a separate and, in theory, more advanced curriculum. We promptly mounted the first—very mild—student revolt of the 1960s on the Georgetown campus. Our American Civilization professor, Father Durkin, a venerable Jesuit steeped in the pre–Vatican II Church, argued that Herman Melville and a number of other great American writers—"almost everyone," we joked— were secret Catholics. We petitioned the dean to have him removed. The dean summoned us to a meeting: "This is my university. If you don't like it, leave." None of us did; this was the *early* sixties. I had been away at a debate tournament when the plot was hatched, but Durkin blamed me for it. It was only with difficulty that another Jesuit persuaded him not to flunk me.

I majored in history because I loved it—and because I loved it, I had conveniently already read most of the assigned books. But there was a bump along that road, too. Bill Clinton's favorite teacher, the historian Carroll Quigley, praised me and asked me to stand up in class after I'd been named the nation's top debater. The problem was I had skipped class that day; my roommate ran back to wake me and tell me what had happened. I rushed over to see Professor Quigley, who was a fanatic about class attendance. He stared at me for a minute and told me to be there the rest of the semester. I made sure I was—and he was on the committee that voted me high honors in history.

Even though my scholarship paid my tuition, Georgetown was a financial stretch for my parents, who had to come up with the money for room and board. I didn't have much spending money. Bill Reynolds went beyond the normal debate coaching duties and bought me a better suit to wear to debate tournaments. Each summer, I went home to Los Angeles and took a job, any job, to save up for school. For two summers, I worked for the bankruptcy law firm run by the father of someone on our debate team; my job was to clean out, catalogue, and move whatever was left in the latest business that had gone belly up. Once, I was told to drive a sixteen-wheel truck back from San Luis Obispo to Los Angeles. It was bad enough that I was a bad driver to begin with; but I didn't even know how to drive a stick shift—and I got lost, suddenly finding myself driving a giant rig through the posh residential streets of Montecito, a suburb of mansions outside Santa Barbara.

The summer before my senior year, the only job I could get was at Farmer John's slaughterhouse on the far east side of L.A. Work started at 6 A.M., so I was on the bus at four thirty every weekday morning. My job was to wheel barrels of fresh-cut pork from the cutting table to the weighing station. No matter how crowded the bus became on the way home, no one was ever brave enough, or desensitized enough, to sit down next to me. I was surrounded by a protective cone of odor. When I got home, I would undress in the garage and my mother would wash my clothes out. After five weeks, my father told me to quit; somehow we'd find the extra money for me to go back to school. It was the Goldwater summer, and some of my classmates had come to California to volunteer at the Republican Convention in San Francisco and then spend a month and a half in L.A. One of them, George Thibault, the smartest person in our class, today the director of the Academy of Harvard Medical School, wasn't for Goldwater. He just wanted to see what a convention was like. He ended up helping to escort Goldwater's moderate rival Nelson Rockefeller safely off the podium as the angry delegates screamed out their fury.

Just before I left L.A., I got my Law Board scores. I applied to two places: Harvard and Yale. I got into both, a tribute to my board scores, not my grades, but chose Harvard because I could get a job coaching debate at Brandeis. A scholarship paid my tuition—which, unbelievably today, was all of $1,500 a year. But my parents were finally going to buy their own home and I had to come up with my living expenses on my own. The Brandeis job paid me just enough.

I went to law school based on what was, for me at least, a false assumption—that it was the best preparation for politics. Six weeks in, as we were learning medieval forms of civil procedure and old English land law, I simply stopped going to class and focused on coaching debate. I didn't go back to the classroom at all that year. I survived academically because his wife Carolyn persuaded Larry Tribe, who was graduating and leaving to clerk for the California Supreme Court, to postpone his departure for a week, take me to the library every morning, and make me study into the night. He also gave me his notes, which reduced most courses to twenty or twenty-five very neatly written pages. For the next two years, if Larry hadn't taken the course, I tried not to because I needed those notes.

My first year, Larry and I did something else together. Don Hewitt, producer of the first Kennedy-Nixon debate and soon to be the creator of *60 Minutes,* came to Harvard to recruit two students and Henry Kissinger to debate the Vietnam War against the British Labour politician Michael Foot and a team from Oxford. This would be the second transatlantic live broadcast on the Telstar satellite; CBS was calling the series *The Town Meeting of the World*. It was December 1965. I was still for the war—after all, as far as I knew, so was Robert Kennedy. Hewitt and several other CBS executives interviewed dozens of students. Larry and I were selected, although I don't think he much likes to remember the whole episode. We were told to go off and see Professor Kissinger, who promptly informed us that we'd have to help him get ready since he was an expert on Europe and nuclear diplomacy, not Southeast Asia.

Larry and I spent a lot of hours with each other—and fewer hours with Professor Kissinger—throwing arguments back and forth, anticipating responses, and plotting strategy. When I glance at the tape today, I'm amazed by two things: how young we look, even Kissinger, and how wrong we were.

A year later, I was against the war—but a year after that, when the presidential primaries rolled around, I was still out of step with the majority of my classmates. They were for Gene McCarthy, the first to challenge President Johnson; I was one of the few Harvard Law students for Robert Kennedy. I think one reason was that I wanted a Kennedy restoration, but I also admired RFK's idealism and intensity. I saw McCarthy as a John the Baptist figure: he had prepared the way, but he couldn't be nominated.

As law school was drawing to a close, the country seemed to be coming apart. Martin Luther King, Jr.'s, assassination was followed by Robert Kennedy's. In spring 1968, I was trying to figure out how to work for him, but only for the summer. Beyond that, if I didn't teach, I'd be drafted. And I knew that if I was drafted, I wouldn't go. I was the part-time debate coach at Boston College, which now offered me a full-time teaching position. I assumed that this was going to be my career. I wasn't about to be a lawyer; I didn't even take the bar exam. I had half earned only one distinction at Harvard Law School. My name was inscribed on the wall of the library alongside other luminaries like Alger Hiss because, with seven other team members, I won the Ames Competition in appellate advocacy. But in doing so, I was a little like the Bill Clinton I met at Georgetown: I contributed ideas and arguments, but I didn't have time to do the research.

I settled in at BC, was elected to the board of directors of the National Debate Tournament, and began teaching courses in freedom of speech for which Larry Tribe, now a professor at Harvard Law, was once again my tutor. One day he called and asked me to dinner. He loved debate, and so did I, but he didn't think I should spend my life as a debate coach. I wanted to be in politics, I said, but I didn't know how. I'd written a lot of speeches in the form of opening arguments for my debate teams and, hard as it may be to believe, on that basis, Larry thought I had the talent to be a speechwriter. And we aimed high because we didn't know enough to know how far we were reaching. Who would I want to work for? Ted Kennedy? Larry knew someone there. And he knew someone with John Lindsay, the liberal Republican mayor of New York. He offered to write to both. It sounded like a long shot, but I said yes. It was February 1970, and I returned to the BC campus to get my teams ready for the Dartmouth debate tournament.

2

"COME HOME, AMERICA": WRITING THE WORDS THAT MOVED ONE STATE

The Kennedy office wasn't hiring, so for the only time in my life, I went to work for a Republican.

For me, it was a rapid transformation—a couple of meetings, a trial speech, and I went from college debate coach to speechwriter for the mayor of New York, John Lindsay. I was replacing Jeff Greenfield, who had written speeches for RFK before signing on with Lindsay after the assassination. Greenfield was heading off to be a media consultant—briefly—with David Garth, one of the pioneers of turning the techniques of Vance Packard's "hidden persuaders" into political advertising. My entire tryout was a half-hour talk with Lindsay's press secretary, Tom Morgan; an assignment to write a speech on any topic I chose; and a week later, a rapid-fire series of meetings with Morgan; Greenfield, who rushed in and asked, "Did you write this?"; Deputy Mayor Dick Aurelio; and finally Lindsay himself. I was hired on the spot. I had to start immediately, in the middle of the semester, so I commuted between New York and my classes in Boston.

I remember only the first line of my tryout speech, tying the war in Vietnam to the violence that increasingly stalked America—"No moment in our time—and no place on our planet—is safe from the stain of violence." A little overblown, certainly, but John Lindsay appreciated rhetoric and he was playing two parts: filling what he'd called "the second toughest job in America," and claiming an increasingly prominent role as a national leader of the anti-Nixon, antiwar forces.

To Lindsay's regret, he had some backtracking to do. He had given the speech seconding Spiro Agnew's nomination for vice president at the 1968 Republican Convention. Agnew, the mild-mannered moderate from Maryland, emerged after the election as the conservatives' favorite pit bull; the speechwriters figured out he would read anything they put in front of him. They plied him with alliterations on steroids. For example, those who opposed the war were "nattering nabobs of negativism." Lindsay was now an Agnew target as the mayor gave a steady stream of speeches that laid out a progressive and, yes, presidential agenda. In the spring of 1970, he flew to Berkeley to denounce the Nixon administration's assault on civil liberties as "repression . . . with a quiet voice in a business suit." A few weeks later, I drove with him to the University of Pennsylvania. His speech there scorned the Nixon administration's "decision to spend more money on war than on people" and denounced the rise in "polarization. . . . You can hear it in a Governor's call for a bloodbath on college campuses. And in the [radical] Weatherman's rhetoric of violence that threatens New Haven tonight," where the trial of the Black Panthers was sparking an upheaval at Lindsay's alma mater, Yale. But his message was overshadowed by his response to a student's question about draft evaders. "The ones I have unending admiration for," he said, "are the guys who will not serve . . . in Vietnam . . . and take the consequences for it. These are the guys who are heroic." Forgiveness for resisters was still controversial when President Carter granted them amnesty in 1977. Lindsay's admiration for them in 1970 was incendiary.

As we headed back to New York late that night in the mayor's limousine, we listened to the playoff game between the New York Knicks and the Los Angeles Lakers. We were interrupted by the buzzing of the large clunky car phone. I remember Lindsay's answer: "Well, I said it, I believe it, and we'll just have to make the best of it." The press office scrambled to make it clear that he regarded our soldiers as heroes, too. The Knicks won the game in overtime.

The episode was a first-hand lesson in the humanity and character of politicians. Despite all the talk about handlers and strategy, what leaders actually think they sometimes actually say, even if by conventional standards it's a mistake.

Maybe I was infected by Lindsay's candor. A month or so later, my own words caused a riot. The Nixon administration's sudden invasion of Cambodia had sparked a nationwide strike on college campuses; the Ohio National Guard killed four Kent State students; two others were killed at Jackson State in Mississippi. I was ordered to draft a proclamation declaring a day of mourning in New York City. I'd never written anything like that, so I opened the file drawers and looked up some past examples. With them in mind, I concluded the proclamation with a flourish—a directive to lower to half-staff the flag that flew over City Hall in order to honor the dead students. Within hours, thousands of construction workers marched up Broadway, surrounded City Hall—there was no security zone around the building then—and demanded that the flag be returned to the top of the pole. The mayor was uptown. City Councilman Matt Troy, who ironically would later become an early backer of George McGovern's antiwar campaign, climbed to the roof and raised the flag. The hardhats roared their approval. A police officer pulled me away from the flying bricks hurtling toward the windows.

The uprising showed how tough Lindsay's job was: the city and country were divided over race as well as the war, and the Nixon White House was exploiting the discord as a conscious political strategy. Before I arrived, Lindsay had held New York together while other cities were burning in the race riots of the 1960s. He did it by walking all but alone into the tinderbox of angry crowds and persuading them to go home. I witnessed a memorable reprise in the fall of 1970, when the city's jails were seized by the inmates and guards were held hostage. The staff moved into Gracie Mansion for all night meetings. I drafted appeals to the prisoners to be broadcast on radio by the mayor, and caught catnaps on a sofa in the first-floor ballroom.

Corrections Commissioner George McGrath argued the only choice was an all-out armed assault on the prisons. Lindsay refused; he wasn't going to kill the inmates and see the guards get killed, too. Instead, he issued an ultimatum demanding the release of the hostages but promising that as soon as that happened, he would go to the jails personally to discuss the inmates' grievances. McGrath was appalled: What if the mayor was taken hostage or shot? Lindsay said he'd take that chance—and, if it went wrong, he didn't want anyone negotiating for his release.

He was driven to the Tombs, the city's most notorious prison; he was inside from shortly after midnight until 3 A.M. As prisoners yielded at jails across the city, some force was used but with no loss of life. Then, while Lindsay was inside the Queens House of Detention, the enraged police and correction guards conducted their own riot, clubbing and kicking the surrendering inmates. The spectacle was brutal—and shocking. Afterward, Lindsay was as angry as I ever saw him, even though he had averted the kind of tragedy that a few months later left twenty-nine inmates and ten hostages dead when Governor Nelson Rockefeller ordered an all-out attack, shotguns literally blazing, in reaction to an inmate takeover of the Attica State Prison.

John Lindsay had courage, both the courage of his principles and genuine physical courage. But there was one step that for a long time he couldn't summon the will to take—leaving the Republican Party.

In late October, just before the 1970 midterm elections, Lindsay gave a widely reported speech denouncing Spiro Agnew and the Nixon White House for a campaign of fear and smear. David Garth and I discussed language announcing that Lindsay was becoming a Democrat—or at least, that he no longer considered himself a Republican. Lindsay rejected it outright.

There may have been a calculation that it would be better for him to change parties later. If so, the calculation was about as wrong as it gets in politics. When he finally switched to the Democrats in the summer of 1971, just days before he launched his unofficial but obvious quest for the Democratic nomination for president, he looked cynical and self-serving; changing parties could only work if it looked like what I believe it was for him, a decision driven by conviction. What held Lindsay back for so long was his genuine sense of identification as a liberal Republican. He had deep antipathy toward the Democratic "bosses" he disdained for sullying New York City politics. But as mayor, he had to make deals with them, or I assumed he did. As I remember it, Brooklyn boss Meade Esposito, later indicted and convicted for corruption, secured a contract to re-carpet City Hall. Despite the lapses and deals, Lindsay never stopped seeing himself as a reformer—*his* Republicans were the party of civil rights. Back when he was a congressman, he and Jacob Javits, New York's progressive Republican senator, pushed for civil rights legislation when President Kennedy was still reluctant to introduce it. Lindsay was determined not to see that Republican tradition overwhelmed by Nixon's Southern Strategy.

Lindsay was, in a classic sense, a tragic figure, undone politically by his own choices. In 1968, he decided not to take what Governor Rockefeller didn't want to give him, but had to if Lindsay asked for it—the appointment to the U.S. Senate after Robert Kennedy's assassination. But he was at a high point in his first term; it was easy, if ahistorical, to assume that any mayor's popularity could last, especially in the turbulent sixties. Lindsay's young aides, who viewed themselves as remaking the world's greatest city, were opposed to the Senate option; the job in New York City, they argued, was more important and had to be finished. David Garth told me that he had lobbied Lindsay to go to the Senate, where he would have had a secure platform and a longer time horizon for national leadership. Garth could be a tough customer in any internal battle, but he lost that one. Ironically, Lindsay would run for the Senate in 1980—and finish third in the Democratic primary.

I was obsessed with beating Nixon in 1972, and by the late spring of 1971, I didn't see how Lindsay, still a Republican, could do that. But I wasn't looking to join another campaign; then a friend of a friend, a direct-mail specialist from California, Chuck Winner (what a name for a political consultant—it suggested that nomenclature was destiny), called and invited me to dinner. At the end of the evening, he asked if he could drop by the office the next day and pick up a packet of speeches I'd written. He just wanted to read them on his way to Washington.

A few days later, my secretary buzzed and told me there was someone named Bob Squier on the phone. He introduced himself—he was Ed Muskie's media adviser. Chuck had passed on the speeches I'd given him. They wanted to hire me. Could I come down to Washington and meet Squier, Berl Bernhard, the campaign manager, and Senator Muskie?

Muskie had shone as Hubert Humphrey's VP choice in 1968; he'd made an almost Lincolnian impression on a bitterly divided America when he had calmly invited an antiwar heckler onstage to have his say and then responded in a strong but respectful way. He seemed to be a voice of reason in a season of madness. He'd done it again on national television the night before the 1970 midterm elections. His speech was crafted by Dick Goodwin, an aide to both JFK and RFK, who had also written Lyndon Johnson's famous speech on voting rights in which LBJ claimed for himself and proclaimed for America the anthem of the civil rights movement: "We Shall Overcome." The memorable words Goodwin drafted for Muskie denounced the Nixon charge that the Democrats were soft on crime: "That is a lie—and the American people know it is a lie." If you believed the polls, Muskie was the strongest Democratic candidate in 1972, assuming that Ted Kennedy would hold to his decision not to run. I told Squier that I probably wasn't ready to leave Lindsay. He pressed hard—just come down and talk. I said I'd get part of a day off and take the early shuttle to Washington.

Bob picked me up at National Airport in a two-seater convertible with the roof down on a sparkling spring day. As the wind ran through my hair—I had a lot more then—he raced toward the first Muskie campaign headquarters in a suite on L Street next to Bernhard's law offices. Bob was funny, irreverent, smart; years later, he and Roger Ailes, the Nixon consultant who became famous for the selling of the president in 1968, would team up to do political commentary on *The Today Show*. Squier had a face made for television. And he had produced both Muskie's election eve broadcast and Hubert Humphrey's speech in September 1968, when he separated himself from Johnson's war policy and then came back from a 15-point deficit to almost win the election. On the first take, Humphrey muted his tone when he pledged to halt the bombing of North Vietnam, while raising his voice as he made the concession conditional and reserved the right to resume the air offensive. Bob asked him to go through the speech again, this time really hitting the first part, the bombing halt, and softening his tone for the rest—just in case they needed an alternative take. Bob promptly sent the alternative to the networks, and when it was shown to the reporters, they trumpeted that at last there was a clear Humphrey break with Johnson on Vietnam. The words on paper weren't that clear; but in this case, the medium really was the message. That day, by in effect manipulating his candidate, the press, and the public, Squier became a media consultant who almost changed the course of history.

I met with him, Berl Bernhard, and other staff members. They filled me in on the campaign, the role they wanted me to play, and described the endorsements they'd lined up. Their bottom line was that Muskie had a foothold on both sides of the ideological street. He was now against the war, but he could appeal to regulars convincingly; he was acceptable to liberals looking desperately for a winner. The campaign had lined up big names on both sides of the divide. This endorsement strategy, which perfectly portrayed Muskie as the establishment choice he was, would prove to be one of the campaign's fatal mistakes in a year when angry antiwar Democrats wanted a new politics and a different kind of nominee. We had a late lunch—and then Bob drove me back to the airport so I wouldn't miss my plane. As I was getting out of the car in front of the Eastern Airlines terminal, I said: "But I didn't meet Muskie." Bob responded: "Oh, you'll love him"—just come back and meet him next week.

I was at my desk in New York when Sam Roberts, then the City Hall reporter for the *Daily News* who would go on to a long career at the *New York Times,* called and asked me if I was going to work for Muskie. I was stunned. I hadn't made up my mind. But I knew enough not to mislead Sam. So I made an off-the-record deal with him: If it were true—and it could be—I would tell him first. As I hung up, I knew what I was going to do. I phoned Squier, who to this day I think was Sam's source, described the conversation, and said I'd take the job but I needed a few days to get my ducks in a row.

The next person I told was the *Village Voice* journalist Jack Newfield—of all places, on the lawn at his wedding reception. His reaction was instantaneous: He was disillusioned with Lindsay, but I should work for George McGovern, not Muskie. Jack told me McGovern was a candidate I could really commit to. He wanted to put me on the phone right away with McGovern. I said no. The last thing I needed was three potential candidates for president.

I told Morgan and then the mayor about my decision. Tom was sad but not visibly angry, and asked if there was anything that could change my mind. Lindsay was decent, even gracious. I thought maybe it was out of WASP self-discipline. But the few times I saw him over the next twenty years, it was always like meeting an old friend again. In this small matter, as in so many great ones, he was a class act. I went back to my cubbyhole office, called Sam Roberts, and said he could write the story. It was a small one.

I had to get rid of my rent-stabilized apartment—$213 a month—in a modern building with a doorman and a swimming pool around the corner from a restaurant named Elaine's, which I frequented before it became a celebrity hangout. But I was twenty-seven, not very practical, and moving my furniture was just beyond me. I packed my clothes, told a friend she could have the furniture if she picked it up, and took the train to Washington, where I moved in with friends from college debate who were renting a house in Georgetown.

I finally did meet Muskie the next day. He was a looming, angular presence, with a dry sense of humor. His trademark expletive, which I heard several times in that first session, was "shit a goddam." His top Senate assistant, John McEvoy, warned me that "the Senator" had a towering temper that could be ignited by almost anything at almost any time. Muskie told me he mostly hated his speeches and hoped we could do better.

The first trip I took with him was to the Vermont Democratic dinner. We flew up on a small charter plane-—Muskie, his wife Jane, his old friend and "body man" Charlie Lander, his press secretary, and me. In the hotel room before the dinner, Jane surprised Muskie with a painting for their wedding anniversary. He looked at it and without saying a word turned back to his speech text. She asked if he liked it and he said no. In front of Charlie and me, their initially testy exchanges escalated into a furious battle. I left as Jane told him he could spend their anniversary night alone.

My own honeymoon with the candidate lasted several months. He liked the speeches and the campaign compiled a speech packet to hand out to prospective recruits. At the Liberal Party Dinner in New York, Muskie's performance bested both George McGovern and John Lindsay, who had been expected to carry the night. Anne Wexler, a veteran of the 1968 "Dump Johnson" insurgency who ultimately would become an assistant to President Carter and a consummate K Street lobbyist, signed on with Muskie. A few months later, when the campaign seemed to lack direction and message, Anne burst into my office, brandishing the speech packet: "I didn't go to work for him. I went to work for your speeches."

But one of the best of the speeches was Muskie himself at his best—the flinty man of integrity from Maine who detested injustice. He was scheduled to address the National Governors Conference in Puerto Rico; the draft printed for distribution focused on the dry subject of federal revenue sharing with the states. The afternoon before the speech, Muskie, one of the architects of revenue sharing, called me and ordered up a stark alternative. Nelson Rockefeller had launched his attack at the Attica prison, the country was reeling from scenes of the carnage, and Muskie was determined to denounce it. I thought I had to point out a couple of problems, got hold of Bernhard, and we called Muskie back. The audience was, after all, governors likely to be sympathetic to Rockefeller. And while we believed Attica was appalling, even cowardly, the majority of the country might approve of the attack (as it turned out, they did), just as a majority had supported the Chicago police when they battered the antiwar demonstrators at the 1968 Democratic Convention.

"I don't care," Muskie responded. "I know what I want to say; I know what I have to say." I sat down, dashed off the words, and dictated them to a staffer who was traveling with the candidate. A few hours later, in a speech that elicited sparse applause, he starkly criticized one of their own to the assembled governors: "Now we have to ask ourselves how and why we have reached the point where men would rather die than live another day in America." The Attica prisoners had taken hostages and threatened lives. Muskie didn't defend them, but he did assail the loss of hope, the complacency of power, the culture of violence, and the toll it was taking on the national character.

The speech made headlines and one of the networks actually broadcast several minutes of it uninterrupted on the evening news. But there was a backlash, not just from the usual Nixonian practitioners of the politics of division but from a whole segment of our own supporters. Moderates and southerners complained the speech was bad politics: Muskie was being pushed, or was pushing himself, too far to the left. The reaction revealed the weakness at the heart of the campaign. Muskie was a serious man torn between the passion of antiwar and liberal Democrats and the practical cautiousness of the party establishment.

He was against the Vietnam War and for withdrawal, but he also felt an almost disabling sense of responsibility because he had supported the war until 1969. And he had constant political pressure from Washington "wise men" not to talk too much about Vietnam—at a time when it was the consuming concern of primary voters. I felt that pressure in the fall of 1971, when I was sent to see former Defense Secretary Clark Clifford and his law partner Paul Warnke. Clifford was a legend: he'd been Truman's strategist in the come-from-behind 1948 campaign; he'd run JFK's transition team; and the newly elected president had joked afterward at the Gridiron Dinner that Clifford wouldn't agree to take an administration job— all he wanted in return for his transition work was his name on the dollar bill. Clifford was the hawk who had succeeded Robert McNamara as secretary of defense and then, much to Lyndon Johnson's surprise, orchestrated an end to the endless escalation of American troop levels in Vietnam. As courtly as his double-breasted suits and his leather-clad office, Clifford was one of those individuals who convince the world that they're not just intelligent, but also gifted with a depth of judgment and wisdom by simply talking very slowly and caressing every syllable. His deliberate way of gesturing—forming an open triangle with his two hands and slowly raising and lowering his fingers—perfectly matched the pace of his speaking.

Muskie, he said, could and should continue to push for withdrawal from Vietnam within a certain time, while still favoring continued military aid and combat air support for South Vietnam forces. How was this fundamentally different from where Nixon was heading with Vietnamization? I asked. Clifford answered by saying it would be irresponsible not to continue helping the South Vietnamese—and how could this position hurt Muskie in any event? McGovern wasn't a problem; he was at 2 or 3 percent in the polls.

This central issue never got definitively settled until McGovern was not only a threat but the Muskie candidacy was crashing. It was a tactical candidacy and Muskie lacked a core rationale other than winnability. "Muskie, he can beat Nixon" was actually one of the campaign's slogans. "But for what?" the voters ultimately asked. That was the question posed by Mark Shields, an antiwar ex-Marine and a veteran of RFK's 1968 campaign, when we convened in early December 1971 to plan Muskie's formal announcement, scheduled for right after the New Year. About ten of the top campaign staff were with the candidate in SB-4, his windowless Senate hideaway office buried in the bowels of the Capitol Building near the steam pipes. As we discussed the announcement speech, Shields looked at Muskie and asked: "But Senator, what's in your gut? What is it that you want to say? Why are you doing this?" Barely missing a beat, Muskie roared back: "Well, that's what I hired all of you for. That's what I hired Shrum for," as he shot a glance at me. Muskie was sure of one thing, the location of the announcement—Kennebunkport, Maine, where he had a summer home; from there, a year before, he'd delivered the 1970 midterm election speech. That was the best reason not to go back, several of us argued. That earlier speech was now a celebrated event; why invite comparisons? The candidate left for the Christmas break. I went to Squier's ski-chalet in Bryce Mountain, Virginia, where I gave his two sons a springer spaniel puppy. They promptly named the puppy "Shrummie." They didn't know it, but it was an old family nickname—my father, my uncles all had it.

The next few days, all we heard from Muskie in snowy Maine were the sounds of silence. We hoped that he was basically satisfied and tinkering with the speech—or, we feared, he just hadn't decided what he wanted to say.

Fear won out. The night before the announcement, we gathered on the icebound Maine shore in a hotel with no guests except our staff and members of the national press. Muskie locked himself in his hotel room and about one in the morning, long legal pad sheets started sliding out from under his door. We had them typed up and then read over a script that mostly consisted of the obligatory assaults on Nixon's failings. That was fine as far as it went, but that's as far as it went. It didn't meet Mark Shields's test: while the speech said why Nixon shouldn't be president, it didn't say why Muskie should. The refrain of the draft was: "It's not good enough."

I have a theory—back in 1971 it was just an instinct; I didn't articulate it until the 1980s—that there are two streams of rhetoric in the Democratic Party: the hopeful approach of FDR and JFK, who, even in the darkest moments, conveyed a sense of purpose and optimism; and the gloomier, if sometimes eloquent language of Adlai Stevenson and the intentionally prosaic Jimmy Carter, both of whom were superb at describing how bad things were. Think of Carter's scolding speech in the summer of 1979 about the depressed mood of America, and the grim tone of his 1980 campaign against Reagan, which emphasized how difficult the problems were and how dangerous his opponent was. Or read Stevenson's 1952 acceptance speech: "The ordeal of the twentieth century, the bloodiest, most turbulent era of the whole Christian age, is far from over." This is a long way from "The only thing we have to fear is fear itself."

Muskie's doom-and-gloom draft was firmly in the Stevenson tradition. In the morning, he announced that he and I would have breakfast in his room; everybody else would go downstairs and read the two drafts—his and mine—and then come back. When the others returned, the candidate put the question: Which speech is better? George Mitchell, who would succeed Muskie in the Senate and then serve as Majority Leader, was a trusted, longtime adviser. He cleared his throat and said that well, they were both good—but on balance, for the purposes we were trying to achieve, they thought, well, that Bob's was preferable. Muskie shot back: "Shit a goddamn, who's running for president—Shrum or me?"

The upshot of that post-breakfast discussion was a dog's breakfast of a speech. We spent hours trying to put the drafts together. Muskie told us we had to keep the "not good enough" refrain. The speech wasn't inspirational, it had no appeal that could galvanize voters; it was a downer. And when things go bad in politics, they get worse. Muskie's Kennebunkport house wasn't winterized. The advance team found another house, also not winterized, but with room for giant heating fans. The press waited in a cold side room while Muskie continued editing, revising, and moving paragraphs around as the fans whirled away. When he finally sat down for the taping, the noisy fans had to be turned off. We all shivered through several takes of the speech, including the reporters still huddled in that nearby room. They paid us back with their stories.

In retrospect, Muskie's candidacy, like those of most candidates, depended on being who he really was instead of listening to too many advisers, trying to split the difference and trying to have it both ways. For example, I'm convinced Muskie was genuinely, even strongly, opposed to the Vietnam War. Occasionally, he overcame his own healthy sense of guilt about having been for it all the way through the '68 campaign. Seven weeks after the announcement, when he was already in trouble, he delivered a blunt antiwar speech to a church group in Washington. Tony Lake, a deputy to Henry Kissinger in the Nixon White House who'd resigned to protest the invasion of Cambodia, worked with me on the speech. He also persuaded the "wise men," like Clifford and Warnke, to advise Muskie to give it.

We had been apprehensive about his reaction, but he seemed almost relieved to be unequivocal. But right afterward, a call came in from Texas lieutenant governor Ben Barnes, our informal liaison with Lyndon Johnson, warning us that the former president was mighty displeased with what Muskie had said. So while McGovern was running hard on the war issue, Muskie again retreated from it—not by changing his position, but by speaking less about it.

Muskie somehow had to reach the liberals in the party. Mike Barnicle, the future columnist, a larger than life personality who had worked for California senator John Tunney, wrote a speech on political reform, taking the Nixon administration to task for its ethical lapses, specifically citing its increasingly suspect dealings with the communications giant ITT, International Telephone and Telegraph. Muskie read the speech on the plane to California. In his hotel room there, the candidate irritably told Barnicle and me he wouldn't give it. He offered no explanation. We tried to persuade him. He turned to Tunney, his Senate colleague, who was there to campaign with him, and asked what he thought. Tunney said it was exactly the right speech for this audience, which was largely composed of wealthy liberal activists; if Muskie wasn't going to focus on the war, then give this speech. In response, Muskie slowly tore up the speech, then threw the pieces of paper in our general direction and yelled at Tunney: "If you like it so much, then give it yourself."

What Muskie did say left the California crowd divided between those who were disappointed and those who were ready to defect. As smart as he was, as effective as he could be debating on the Senate floor, his extemporaneous speeches almost never worked on the campaign trail in 1972 the way they had in 1968. By far the most memorable one was delivered in front of the offices of New Hampshire's ultra-right-wing newspaper, the *Manchester Union Leader*. Muskie cancelled his Florida schedule, and flew to New Hampshire to defend his wife from the paper's charge that she had invited the female reporters on her press bus to swap "dirty jokes." The *Union Leader*, whose late publisher William Loeb ran a jihad against every faintly progressive Democrat or moderate Republican—and the paper still does—had also just run a story claiming that Muskie had referred to French Canadians as "Canucks," an ethnic slur against a critical voting bloc in New Hampshire. The letter in which Muskie supposedly did this was a forgery, one of a long list from the Nixon dirty tricks factory; the slur was even misspelled. I was still in California, on a break at my parents' home, when Berl Bernhard called:

The press is saying Ed cried in New Hampshire. He explained the circumstances. Muskie, standing on a flatbed truck in a driving snowstorm in Manchester, had choked up while talking about the attack on his wife, and the whole episode was on film.

I took the red-eye to Washington. Muskie always insisted that he hadn't cried; the snowflakes had gotten into his eyes and melted as they hit his cheeks. The almost uncontested criticism that followed is probably inconceivable now. Today a candidate could cry, if it was about the right thing. Muskie hardly looked weak in the footage. But it came to symbolize his downfall and afterward was seen as the turning point.

In reality, McGovern was already gaining in the polls in New Hampshire. He was campaigning hard against the war; he had an army of young volunteers on the ground. He was becoming *the* peace candidate, the nonestablishment choice, the kind of new politics maverick New Hampshire voters are drawn to.

To make matters worse, our local campaign chair, Maria Carrier, told the press that she would shoot herself if Muskie didn't get 50 percent of the vote. Tony Podesta, the operative we'd sent in from Washington, exploded in frustration; he gave Carrier a squirt gun. In the end, Muskie won, but with "only" 48 percent. The campaign was in trouble. In politics, what counts is not where you are at any given moment, but where you're headed. And our direction was decisively downward.

The breakwater was supposed to be Florida, where virtually every important party and elected official was with us. The dark side of the Nixon campaign was a looming presence there, too. Voters were phoned between 3 A.M. and 5 A.M., the callers saying they were organizers for Muskie. A fake Muskie letter was circulated about the segregationist Alabama governor George Wallace, running in the Democratic primaries appealing to resentment and anger, on the slogan "Send Them a Message." The forged letter served to confirm the notion that we were "Them" when it compared Wallace to Hitler.

But that wasn't what destroyed our campaign; we self-destructed. Muskie still had no big theme, no coherent message, no consistent appeal. So for Florida, we simply and explicitly argued winnability: this to a southern Democratic electorate, drawn to Wallace's call to lash out against "the establishment." Mark Shields captured the futility of the approach in his reaction to one Muskie slogan: "President Muskie! Don't you feel better already?" No, they don't, Mark said; there is no emotional connection with Muskie, they don't really know him, and they don't want to be told how they feel or that they only have one choice.

As the returns rolled in, with Wallace carrying every county and Muskie headed for fourth place, he started talking about dropping out. He had no interest in even looking at the election night statement I'd prepared, which had to be rewritten because its tone sounded incongruous in light of Muskie's crushing defeat. He wouldn't reveal what he intended to say downstairs at our "victory" party in the ballroom. As he headed out the hotel room door, George Mitchell made one last effort. "Ed, what are you going to say?" Muskie shot back, "Wouldn't you like to know?" He and his wife rode down in the elevator with Alan Baron, a cherubic, savvy strategist who'd managed our Florida campaign. He reported to us afterward that as the elevator descended, Jane Muskie told her husband that it was all right if he quit the campaign; maybe they could go home and have another baby. Muskie didn't reply. He walked off the elevator, onto the stage—and announced he was in the race to stay. And that wasn't all he said. He denounced Wallace for appealing to people's worst instincts and playing on racial prejudice. It was true and brave, even if it was an expression of his frustration. It was also bad politics: Muskie was universally portrayed as a "sore loser."

There was a scapegoat pushed off the cliff after the defeat. Bob Squier was fired. It was a classic case of shooting the message meister; maybe Bob's commercials weren't effective, but that reflected the reality of a candidate who didn't have a persuasive rationale, a compelling case to make to voters. Strategists can sculpt messages and media advisers can make ads, but they can't make up for a candidate who doesn't want to say something, can't figure out what to say, or won't say it consistently. But somebody has to be blamed, somebody has to be dispensed with—it's just human nature; and until the final defeat, the fault is never the candidate's.

Bob's career was almost ruined, but he held on the next few years, working out of a small basement apartment on Capitol Hill where video gear occupied more space than the furniture. He gradually rebuilt his reputation and his firm into a leading force in Democratic politics. We remained close until I went into the same business in the 1980s. For my thirty-fifth birthday, he had a big sign made and framed. It was a play on both Barry Goldwater's 1964 slogan, "In your heart, you know he's right," and McGovern's, "Right from the start." My sign read: "Shrum for President: In Your Heart, You Know He Can Write—from the Start." It still hangs in my office.

As the Muskie campaign lurched on to Wisconsin, the emerging front-runner was George McGovern. He'd finished fifth in Florida, but his campaign had all but explicitly conceded the state to Wallace in advance. No one in the press treated Florida as a defeat for him, and McGovern's brilliant pollster Pat Caddell, a Harvard senior whose graduation now hinged on his finding time to take and pass a required swimming test, had identified a hot-button issue in Wisconsin to broaden McGovern's appeal. McGovern now proposed a national plan to relieve the pressure of local property taxes. He became both the antiwar and the anti–property tax candidate.

The Muskie campaign was dispirited and the candidate's temper was dry tinder; almost any comment could spark a flare-up. One day, as our chartered Electra turboprop, an aircraft with a history of 1950s crashes, lumbered across the sky, Hadley Roff, the deputy press secretary, came into Muskie's compartment where several staff were briefing the candidate. He told Muskie that the press had a question about something. I don't remember what it was, only that it was fairly routine. But I've never forgotten Muskie's reaction. He slapped Hadley across the face with a hot towel. Hadley, stunned, walked out without saying a word. Muskie was persuaded that he had to apologize; we left the compartment as Hadley was being asked to return.

I had a similar experience during the same period when I went to

Muskie's home to discuss a speech draft. He asked why we wanted to say "this"—I think it was about the war. As I was answering, he hurled something in my general direction, a lead crystal donkey that dispensed cigarettes out its rear end. It missed, but I was stunned. I just got up and went home. Berl Bernhard called and said, "Ed's sorry." That night, I had dinner with Muskie and his wife at his favorite restaurant, Moon Palace, an old-fashioned Cantonese place on Wisconsin Avenue. Muskie said nothing about what had happened that afternoon and neither did I. Over egg rolls, we had a warm, often funny conversation, where he reminisced about his early days in politics, when Maine was a rock-ribbed Republican state and he got himself elected governor and then became the first Democrat popularly elected to the Senate in Maine's history. He was looking beyond the defeat that was staring him in the face, back to earlier races where he had beaten the odds.

He was crushed again in Wisconsin, finishing fourth; McGovern won the primary. The campaign decided not to contest Massachusetts. Pennsylvania, held on the same day, would be the battleground. But Muskie ran fourth there, too. Hubert Humphrey won that one, and the race was now between him and McGovern. Right afterward, about ten of us were asked to a meeting in the candidate's Senate hideaway. The campaign didn't have the money to go on, but Muskie wasn't ready for an unequivocal withdrawal. He would announce he was "suspending" his campaign. We would be the skeleton staff that was kept on, and, George Mitchell said, we had to focus on helping Humphrey. Our only hope was that he would stop McGovern, but fall short himself; the McGovern people would never come to Humphrey, but a deadlocked convention could turn to Muskie. It was a long-shot scenario, but it was the only shot.

I climbed into a cab with Jim Johnson, a good friend who'd actually managed to carry a parcel of delegates for Muskie in the Illinois primary where there was no presidential contest at the top of the ballot; by then, that was an advantage for our campaign. Johnson had a program to educate people to vote for individual delegates—and it worked. Now with that lonely victory a distant memory, the two of us were on our way back to the big Muskie headquarters we'd moved into a few months before—an aging brick office building on K Street that the McGovern campaign would later take over, proving an iron law of campaign staff: It expands to fill the space allotted. Jim and I both knew that we couldn't help Humphrey. If it was between him and McGovern—and it was—then we wanted McGovern to win. This was a tougher call for Jim than for me: he was from Minnesota and his father had been the speaker of the state legislature. Jim knew Humphrey well and was close to Walter Mondale (he would run his 1984 presidential campaign); but he was also strongly against the war. Jim is one of the most judicious people I know; even though he had come out of the National Student Association, a leading force in the student movement of the 1960s, he dressed more like a young Republican, almost never raised his voice, and operated with a Norwegian sense of self-containment. But his mind was made up and so was mine: If we were going to try to help anyone, it was McGovern; we'd have to quit the Muskie operation. I went to see the candidate a day or two later and told him I was leaving and why. He asked if I'd work for anyone else and I answered honestly that I was for McGovern, but hadn't been asked.

Not everyone who ultimately went to McGovern—and a lot of Muskie's staff did—told him where they were heading. It wasn't easy, and not just because Muskie was a formidable figure. For me, the problem was that whatever had happened in the year I was with him, I respected his talent, his integrity, and his achievements. He was a legislative main force in the nascent environmental movement. In the years following the presidential campaign, he was the architect of wholesale reform in the federal budget process. But that, like another of his trademark issues, revenue sharing, wasn't the kind that captured headlines or the public imagination. In his presidential bid, Muskie had too many interlocutors: senators, politicians across the country, staff studded with future stars from George Mitchell to Jim Johnson, Tony Podesta, Anne Wexler, and Tony Lake. The whole was less than the sum of the parts. The cascade of advice created a whirlpool, not a direction; it tended to breed inconsistency and drive toward the lowest common denominator.

In politics, if you offend no one, you persuade no one.

Muskie never was himself in 1972 and the question Mark Shields asked before the announcement was never answered: What was in his gut? At the Democratic Convention that summer, Shields told me, "If all the Muskie staff had worked for McGovern and all the McGovern staff had worked for Muskie, McGovern would still be the nominee." In the end, the candidate is not a product of the campaign; the campaign is ultimately a reflection of the candidate.

In May, the race was transformed again when George Wallace was shot after a speech in a Maryland shopping mall outside Washington, D.C. Wallace never could have won the nomination, but he might have mounted a third-party challenge, as he had in 1968, drawing votes away from Nixon. More than ever now, the argument against McGovern was that he couldn't win. Probably no Democrat could have by this point in 1972.

The 1972 primaries weren't easy for traditional Democrats, who couldn't credit, and to a damaging degree would never accept, the nomination of an insurgent like McGovern. And the McGovern forces, while determined ultimately to make peace with the establishment, had to fight every inch of the way to the nomination. On all sides, there was plenty of bitterness to go around. Frank Mankiewicz, Robert Kennedy's former press secretary who was one of the co-captains of the McGovern campaign, expressed both sides of the coin. He wanted to bring people in, but in the sometimes bitter day-to-day exchanges that the ongoing contest provoked, he could and did give better than he got. When Senator John Tunney endorsed Muskie, Mankiewicz had derided him as "the lightweight son of the heavyweight champion"—Gene Tunney, who had pounded Jack Dempsey in their 1926 title fight. Ditto for Indiana senator Birch Bayh, who announced for Muskie just as public support for the candidate was tanking: "It's the first time I've ever heard of a rat jumping on a sinking ship," Mankiewicz said.

It was also Mankiewicz who called me after I'd left Muskie. During the Pennsylvania primary, McGovern had seen a last-gasp Muskie television address on Vietnam:

The Scriptures tell us: "Which of us, if his son asked him for bread, would give him a stone?" Our sons have asked for peace, and we have sent them off to war. Our sons have asked for jobs, and we have sent them to an Asian jungle.

Mankiewicz had been told I'd written this; was that right? If so, could I come in and see him and talk about working for McGovern? Two days later, I was on the plane to California, the site of the decisive primary.

As I was about to discover, resentment toward those who hadn't been with McGovern from the start was rife. After I arrived in California, I was mostly ignored. One person, who was later to become a friend, scornfully told me off about my Muskie connection. I wasn't assigned a hotel room, so I stayed at a friend's apartment and she gave me a ride to the McGovern headquarters every day. But I didn't have much to do other than look at and edit some of our printed handouts and talk to no discernable purpose about what was happening with some of the staff I already knew. Mankiewicz finally put me on the road with the by now massive McGovern entourage of press and campaign aides. I met the candidate for the first time—for about ten seconds.

The weekend before the primary, from a press viewing room at a television station, I watched the candidates debate, and saw McGovern pummeled for his welfare plan, $1,000 a year for every person in America—not just every needy person, but literally every American. The tax system would claw back the extra money and then some from those who didn't need it. To a liberal economist, it might be a theoretically elegant system; to voters, it sounded ridiculous. Humphrey was relentless in prosecuting the attack. McGovern wasn't prepared for it. Later, he told me he was surprised by the behavior of his old friend, who, in the 1930s, had judged his high school debates and who'd found a home in the Maryland suburbs next door to his own for the McGoverns when George was first elected to Congress. By primary day, the margin had narrowed; McGovern beat Humphrey by just 5 percent. But under California's winner-take-all system at the time, McGovern now had all the state's delegates, and the nomination—or so it seemed. The emerging ABM movement—"Anybody But McGovern"—would challenge the delegation on the convention floor.

Back in Washington, I still had almost nothing to do. McGovern was in New York for a primary that was all but conceded to him in advance. I decided I needed to get on with my life. I had no savings; I'd gotten no paycheck. I had to start looking for something, even if I had no idea what it was. I walked over to Frank Mankiewicz's office. I went in, sat down, and started to say that I really wasn't doing anything in the campaign when the phone rang. It was a press call. I waited until it was finished and then started up again. But the phone kept ringing and I never got out more than my first couple sentences. So I went to the office next door and called Frank myself. We were well into the conversation when he said, "Wait a minute, weren't you just here?" I said it looked to me like we had a better chance to talk if we were on the phone.

I went back to Frank's office. He said he was sorry things had been so chaotic, but I couldn't leave the campaign. He had an immediate assignment: McGovern was about to appear at a union convention. I should sit down with Lester Spielman, our labor liaison, get briefed on the event, and draft a speech. I called Lester, but he said he already had a draft; he'd show it to me later that day. I read the draft and told him it was terrific. Well, he allowed, it had already worked pretty well; it was adapted from a speech Ted Kennedy had given to another labor convention. "Adapted" turned out to be a mild term: the two speeches tracked each other all too closely. We can't give this, I said; the almost certain Democratic nominee for president couldn't just lift someone else's words. He wouldn't do it if he knew about it—and if he did it, he'd get caught.

I stayed up through the night to write a new draft. Because I couldn't type, Frank's secretary tapped it out while I stayed around to help her decipher my handwriting. Then I went home to get some sleep. A few hours later, my phone rang. I was groggy as a vaguely familiar voice asked for me, slightly mispronouncing my name. It was George McGovern. Had I written this speech? It was good. He really liked it. Could I come up to his Senate office in the next couple of days, sit down, and talk with him? He wanted to start on the acceptance speech.

Over a cup of coffee a few days later, I began to get to know someone who was to become a lifelong friend. He had that flat midwestern accent that people sometimes hear as tentative or soft. In fact, McGovern, for all his decency, had an unyielding inner core on issues he cared about. He understood the Nixon strategy to position him as weak on national defense, un-American in his opposition to the war, not tough-minded enough to lead in a dangerous world. He was a World War II bomber pilot who resented the attacks. He saw the acceptance speech, which in that pre-cable era would have an almost universal audience, as his best chance to let Americans see him for who he really was.

Also there was John Holum, McGovern's legislative aide and longtime speechwriter, who was to prove a generous and ungrudging partner for me, someone wholly committed to getting his candidate elected rather than protecting his own turf. In the fall, we'd add a third speechwriter named Sandy Berger. I didn't know it then, but I'd spend the next three decades in politics, while Sandy and John soon went straight, serving in the State Department in the Carter years. Eventually, Sandy would become national security adviser to President Clinton and John the director of the U.S. Arms Control and Disarmament Agency.

When McGovern and I next sat down, we discussed the notes I'd written and he outlined some of his own ideas. We weren't finished when his administrative assistant, a crusty, no-nonsense South Dakotan named George Cunningham, came in and said McGovern had to move on to the next meeting. That's okay, McGovern said, we'll pick up on this on the plane to Miami, the site of the national convention. But I'm not going on the plane, I replied; I'd been told I had to go on a bus, which was taking some of the staff on the 24-hour ride down to Miami. It was time I'd rather use to work on the speech, I said. I'll just stay in Washington, send the drafts by Thermofax (then the newest technology—a primitive, creakily slow, and literally smelly transmission system that took 8 minutes to transmit each page). We could talk on the phone. McGovern called Cunningham back in. Why, he asked, wasn't Bob on the plane? Because, Cunningham said, preference had been given to those who'd been with McGovern from early on. The candidate was silent for a few seconds and then said, "That's not the purpose of the plane. We're trying to win an election. It's a big plane. Take somebody off and put Bob on so we can get some goddamn work done."

McGovern didn't share his staff's resentment toward newcomers. He understood that he needed all the help he could get, a united party, all the Democrats he could enlist, no matter who they'd supported before. At the same time, he did have a persistent, wistful, even charming sense that those closest to him had always been with him. In the years since, he's often harkened back to something "we"—he and I—experienced in New Hampshire or somewhere else along the early primary trail. For a while, I reminded him I wasn't there then; he looked so unhappy that I just stopped correcting him and let the conversation move on.

On the flight to Miami, we did have a session with Holum and a few others. As the staff stepped off the plane, we were handed our hotel assignments and room keys. The McGovern headquarters was the ultramodern, high-rise Doral; I was assigned to a low-rise hotel forty-five blocks away in South Beach, back then a run-down area very different from the glitz of today. I don't remember the name of the hotel. I do remember that it didn't have air-conditioning, that my first paycheck wasn't coming until next week, and that I had only a few dollars, which I spent on food over the next day. It was a sweltering 24 hours. I was determined to finish the draft and stayed up almost all night. By the next afternoon, I had a folder full of yellow legal pages blotched with drops of perspiration. Now I had to get to the Doral.

I decided to walk through the late afternoon heat. After a few blocks, I spotted a man who was wearing convention credentials around his neck and a delegate badge on his suit. I said something like, "You're not going to believe this, but I'm one of McGovern's speechwriters. I don't have any money with me and I have to get to the Doral." What made this seem even more implausible was that my bag hadn't been delivered to my hotel; I looked even more rumpled than my usual disheveled self. For some reason, the neatly pressed delegate chose to believe me. He said he was just about to take a cab and he'd be happy to drop me off. On the ride, he introduced himself as Herschel Laskowitz, the mayor of Fargo, North Dakota—and a Humphrey delegate. In the fall, when we stopped in Fargo to refuel the campaign's 727 on a trip to the west coast, I looked for Mayor Laskowitz to thank him for believing the ridiculous notion that the apparition he'd encountered at a Miami bus stop really was who he said he was.

When I walked into the Doral lobby, I ran into Mankiewicz. The candidate, he said, had been looking for me: no one seemed to know what hotel I was in; why wasn't I in the Doral? Before I could answer, an advance man was taking me up to McGovern's suite on the seventeenth floor. He gave me a quizzical glance and asked what had happened. I did have a draft of the speech, I said, and then told him where I'd been. He invited me to sit down and offered me a vodka martini. After sending the handwritten yellow pages down the hall to be typed, he phoned Tony Podesta, another Muskie refugee, now deputy director of the McGovern scheduling and advance team, and told him to find my bag and get me a room on the sixteenth or seventeenth floor of the Doral even if he had to move someone else.

It was clear after Monday night that McGovern had enough votes to secure the nomination. We would keep the California delegates we needed after winning a credentials challenge—the last-ditch maneuver of the anti-McGovern forces. They had been outmaneuvered with a parliamentary tactic devised by Rick Stearns, who'd come from his Rhodes Scholarship at Oxford, where Bill Clinton was his classmate, to serve as our chief delegate counter.

A lot was now riding on the acceptance speech. McGovern said he would make some edits while Holum and I kept working on the draft. Two legends, the witty and heterodox economist John Kenneth Galbraith and the historian Arthur Schlesinger, Jr., had submitted their versions and we incorporated a few sentences from them. But only a few: Galbraith's draft proclaimed that McGovern was proud to be "radical," and would have proved that McGovern was as far left as the Nixon campaign alleged. McGovern regarded Schlesinger's draft as too professorial. I was in awe of Schlesinger; my graduation present from high school had been his three-volume *Age of Roosevelt*. His achievements were matched by his magnanimous and picaresque spirit. After the convention, he told me what he thought about my role in the acceptance speech. With a gentle jibe, he said: "Bob, I just want you to know that some young kid will come along someday and they'll decide he's a better speechwriter—and you'll only get a line or two in the acceptance speech."

McGovern, a literate, frequently eloquent writer, made his edits and then asked us to edit him. For the first time in American history, an acceptance speech made a major issue of tax loopholes, tax reform, and a fairer tax system. McGovern would flesh out the details during the general election campaign; ironically, his plan—closing loopholes while sharply lowering tax rates—was remarkably close to the landmark reform Ronald Reagan would sign into law in 1986.

The speech was designed to achieve one overriding objective: while calling for withdrawal from Vietnam within ninety days, it would reassure voters about McGovern's patriotism and strength on national security. A battle to include more than an elliptical reference to his heroic service as a bomber pilot in World War II was lost; other advisers opposed it on the grounds that we were "the antiwar campaign." I blame myself for not appealing this issue to McGovern, who agreed afterward that it was unbelievable that he didn't talk about his service; he finally did in the fall.

The most noted passage in the acceptance speech, the ending, would be caricatured and distorted for decades ahead, cited as the essence of "McGovernism," a phrase the right wing—and his enemies in the Democratic Party—treated as synonymous with national weakness. In a powerful litany, McGovern issued a call to "come home, America"—of course from Vietnam, but not from the nation's global role; the speech explicitly summoned Americans home "to the belief that we can seek a newer world." In essence, "come home, America" was an appeal not to retreat to our shores, but to return to our best ideals. McGovern asserted that current policies of secrecy, deception, and intervention in Vietnam actually "weaken our nation." It was a case the country had to hear.

At the end of the draft, McGovern inserted a quote from Ralph Waldo Emerson that not only broke the rhythm of the speech but sounded forced and academic. We discussed it, but he wouldn't budge. We had to enlist another ally. So I went to see Warren Beatty, someone I'd just met a day or two before. Not only had I instantly liked him; I realized that this mega-movie star, with his playful sense of the absurd, was a serious figure with a sense of political strategy. I hoped, and assumed, he also had good judgment about the spoken word as I walked down the Doral corridor and knocked on his door. His girlfriend, the preternaturally beautiful Julie Christie, answered it in her bathrobe and invited me in. Warren wasn't there, but he'd be right back. She was British, and wanted to ask me some questions about how the convention worked, and what was happening next. To be honest, I was so distracted looking at her that I'm not sure my answers made much sense. Warren arrived and I explained how I was trying to get Ralph Waldo Emerson out of the speech. He looked at the draft and the two of us headed for McGovern's suite.

Once there, Warren offered a pithier, more persuasive argument than I'd thought of. "Look, George," he said, "you can't do this to this speech. It would be like making love to a beautiful woman—it's wonderful, it's as good as it's ever been—and then at the last minute pulling out and saying, 'I'll let Waldo finish for me.' " McGovern laughed and the Emerson quote was gone.

On Thursday, as we were putting the finishing touches on the speech, I was in and out of McGovern's suite during the vice-presidential selection process. McGovern had assumed almost until the convention that, at the end, Ted Kennedy might reverse his position and agree to be his running mate. But in a preemptive *Boston Globe* story, Kennedy had slammed the door irrevocably shut. The process today—careful vetting, interviews, polling every name on a carefully drawn-up list—is very different than it was then. With time on our hands, Alan Baron and I had written a memo during the

California primary suggesting that McGovern set up what would now be regarded as a primitive form of vetting. Afterward, McGovern said he never saw the memo; when Baron and I had written it, we were barely tolerated refugees from the Muskie camp.

Until 1972, picking a running mate was usually the product of a last-minute deal or an ad hoc afterthought. After 1972, the VP selection would never be left to the convention's final hours—with the exception of Ronald Reagan's foolish flirtation with Gerald Ford in 1980, followed by his quick choice of George Bush.

The traditional way of deciding on the vice-presidential nominee was a train wreck waiting to happen, and it was McGovern, on that Thursday in 1972, who got hit by the onrushing locomotive. The most interesting possibility was derailed by the chaos of that day. The word had been sent through several people that Muskie might be willing to serve as McGovern's running mate. I was one of those who got the message. When it didn't happen, I just concluded that McGovern had rejected the idea. Afterward, McGovern told me that no one had ever informed him that Muskie was a real possibility— which is one reason, aside from my natural tendency to hold and express strong opinions, that ever since then I have tended to speak up even when I believe I'm advocating something a candidate doesn't want to hear. But at the 1972 convention, I was twenty-eight years old. I'd known McGovern for less than a month, and I didn't imagine even trying to reopen a negative decision about Muskie.

A succession of prospective choices, including Walter Mondale and Wisconsin senator Gaylord Nelson, turned McGovern down. Boston mayor Kevin White was eager for the job, but McGovern was told Kennedy was opposed to picking White. Mankiewicz proposed Kennedy brother-in-law Sargent Shriver, the first director of the Peace Corps. But Shriver had assumed he wouldn't be selected and was on a business trip to Moscow. I ventured that taking him would be great television, as the reporters converged on him, followed him to the airport, and monitored his journey across Europe and the Atlantic. So what if he wasn't there to give his acceptance speech? We'd get a great media ride anyway. No one was buying that. We'd had a tough and at times chaotic convention; what would it look like if McGovern couldn't even produce his own running mate on the podium Thursday night?

It was late, and the choice was moving toward a young first-term senator from Missouri, Tom Eagleton—smart, moderate, a name repeatedly suggested by other senators who'd rejected McGovern's overtures. Eleanor McGovern, the candidate's wife, was uneasy with Eagleton, but she couldn't really say why. The decision had to be made. McGovern called Eagleton and told him he was the choice, but he wanted him to talk with Frank Mankiewicz. I was standing just inside the room when Frank asked Eagleton if there was anything in his background that we should worry about. Only a few seconds later, after he presumably said no, Frank started discussing logistical details—Eagleton should come to the Doral now, McGovern would hold a press conference with him, he'd have to get an acceptance speech ready.

Thursday night, exuberant delegates placed other names in nomination for vice president. No one thought Eagleton would lose, but for the first time in history, women constituted almost half of a national convention's delegates, and wanted at least a token nominating speech for one of their own: Sissy Farenthold, a liberal activist who'd almost won the Democratic primary for the governor of Texas. She became part of a spontaneous avalanche that buried the schedule for the acceptance speech. In all, thirty-nine people other than Eagleton—including Walter Cronkite—would register some votes in a roll call extending into the first hours of a new day.

On the floor of the convention, I found Pat Caddell, McGovern's pollster, now just graduated from Harvard College. I'd met him earlier that week. I had an occupational bias that the acceptance speech ought to be heard and seen; but beyond that, Pat and I agreed that it was an absolute strategic necessity. We went to Mankiewicz—or Gary Hart, the young campaign manager who would later become a senator from Colorado and come close to capturing the Democratic nomination for president himself. Could we postpone the acceptance speech until the next night? Pat and I asked. No, most of the delegates were leaving on chartered flights. Couldn't we just let local Democrats in to fill the hall? What mattered was the television. And if that wouldn't work, why not suspend the vice-presidential nominating process, and let McGovern speak before it was too late? That, we were told, was against the party rules. To which my reaction, and Pat's, was, wait a minute, we *are* the party. Our suggestions may have seemed panicked or impetuous; after all, we were "kids." In any case, we were told, there was nothing to do but let the process grind to a finish.

As McGovern strode onto the platform at 2:30 A.M., an exhausted convention, fired up by Ted Kennedy's booming introduction of the nominee, burst back into life. But an exhausted nation had long since switched off the television sets and gone to bed. Standing just below the podium, as waves of applause rolled across the floor and up into the rafters, I thought to myself: The only place that it's prime time is in Guam—which, as they traditionally say during convention roll calls, is "where America's day begins," because it's on the other side of the International Date Line.

Conventions today are precisely orchestrated affairs; there is no gavel-to-gavel network coverage, just an hour or two for three of the four nights. The audience, drawn by the multitude of other channels, has declined sharply. Reporters complain that conventions are boring; political professionals, including me, insist that they be tightly scripted—and that's because they still can matter. Al Gore, for example, registered double-digit gains in the polling after his acceptance speech in 2000. In contrast, the disarray of the 1972 Democratic Convention inflicted deep wounds on McGovern—and not just because of the bitter floor fights like the California challenge, or even the reaction that if the candidate couldn't run his own convention, how could he run the country? Most of all, an America that didn't really know McGovern didn't get to meet him. Eight points behind in May, he was now 14 points behind after the convention that was supposed to showcase him to the nation. Could it get any worse?

The reports about Eagleton's shock treatment for depression broke shortly afterward, while McGovern and Eleanor were on a working vacation in the Black Hills of South Dakota. I had stayed in Washington to put together an "instant book" based on the candidate's speeches; one purpose of the book, McGovern told me, was to modify his now notorious $1,000-a-person welfare reform plan with minimum fuss or notice. Eagleton and his wife flew out to see McGovern, and then held a catastrophic press conference in which the vice-presidential nominee didn't know the name of the medicine he was taking. He could only say it was "a little blue pill." McGovern himself said he was behind Eagleton "one thousand percent"—an unfortunate numerical parallel to his welfare plan that came back to haunt him when he finally had to force his running mate off the ticket. The instantly famous "thousand percent" phrase laid the groundwork for the Nixon campaign's charge that McGovern was, as one of their attack ads graphically showed, a weathervane. That's another reality of American politics: For all the focus on consultants and spin doctors, some of the most consequential moments come when candidates, trying to please the immediate audience, blurt out something that instantly becomes fodder for the national conversation. Very often, it's something they're explicitly advised not to say.

But that day in the Black Hills McGovern had an immediate audience of two—Senator Eagleton and Eagleton's wife—and he was desperate to keep them on his side. Eagleton had offered to leave the ticket, then or later, and make it clear it was his decision if that's what McGovern wanted; Eagleton just asked for the chance to go out there, campaign, and prove he could overcome the problem. The days that followed produced a political meltdown. Caddell's numbers were grim. The dialogue was so consumed by the Eagleton issue that nothing else the presidential candidate said would be heard.

Mankiewicz and Hart concluded that the political nightmare had to be ended—Eagleton had to go. But by now Eagleton's position, too, had changed. He held a high card: there was no way under the party rules to depose a vice-presidential nominee who wasn't willing to abdicate. He'd go, but McGovern would have to say that his health was not the reason. The beleaguered presidential candidate, briefly back in Washington, also understood, better than his campaign staff, that deposing Eagleton wouldn't end the nightmare and might compound it. He'd picked Eagleton; he'd backed him unequivocally; if he changed course now, the political fall-out could be more toxic than if he tried to outlast the controversy. I didn't know he was thinking that way until he called and asked me to draft a statement reaffirming that Eagleton would stay on the ticket. He instructed me not to tell anyone else what I was doing. McGovern barely glanced at the draft I handed him. We wouldn't need it, he soon told me. Not only had the renowned psychiatrist Karl Menninger advised him that "for the interest of the nation," Eagleton should "step down," but McGovern had had long talks with his running mate's doctor in St. Louis and another doctor at the Mayo Clinic. They had said in one way or another that they had grave reservations about putting Eagleton in a position where he might have to face the pressures of the presidency. McGovern announced that he was asking Eagleton to step aside—not because of that, but because the controversy was coming to dominate the campaign.

I don't know if the "Eagleton Affair," as the press oddly named it, would play out any differently today in an America with more enlightened attitudes toward mental health. I don't know the considerations that influenced the doctors' judgments, although they had access to a substantial amount of relevant information. Some files, I believe, were slipped to the campaign by an employee at one of the hospitals where Eagleton had been treated. In any event, the McGovern campaign, while acting pretty much the way presidential campaigns had in the past, had inadvertently provided a textbook case in how not to select a vice president.

Eagleton was off the ticket, but on the public mind for the rest of the campaign. As McGovern's ratings sagged, Eagleton's rose on a wave of sympathy. When the McGoverns went to St. Louis for a "Unity Dinner" that fall, they ate with the Eagletons before the event in a two-story hotel suite. I was in an upstairs office that opened onto a balcony over the dinner party below. The conversation was polite, strained, and punctuated by painful periods of silence. At one point, Barbara Eagleton looked across the table and said: "You know, George, Tom's the most popular political figure in America."

From August on, McGovern certainly wasn't, which made it all the more difficult to recruit a new running mate. The choice would be made at a so-called mini-convention—in reality, a hastily convened meeting of the Democratic National Committee (DNC) in Washington. Muskie, whose staff had tried to send word that he would take the second spot in July—the message that never reached McGovern—was asked to run now and said no. McGovern turned to Hubert Humphrey, who said he had no interest in being vice president again—and who plainly understood that he wouldn't be even if he accepted the nomination. Events continued to unravel until McGovern tapped Sargent Shriver, who would bring a new sense of joy and energy to the campaign. But the damage was done; McGovern's image was in tatters and his standing in the polls was shredded.

On a Texas swing soon afterward, McGovern and his newly minted running mate motorcaded to the LBJ ranch to meet with the former president. Lunch was almost macabre. Johnson, who had a serious history of heart disease that killed him just months later, would cut an individual bite from his steak, pour salt on it, and after chewing and swallowing it, puff on an ever-present cigarette—a ritual he repeated all through the meal. Johnson did issue a pro forma endorsement of the Democratic ticket—and then called the White House with the assurance that he was really for Nixon; after all, some of his closest aides and allies were running Democrats for Nixon.

No one said it, but there was a sense that the campaign was all but over. That reality was brought home to us on our kickoff swing for the general election in early September. Ted Kennedy was with us and the first stop was Minneapolis; 10,000 people jammed into the auditorium. Minnesota's governor Wendell Anderson was introducing Kennedy, who would then introduce McGovern. Anderson ended with a rousing line, or so he thought: "The man who will be back in Minneapolis in 1976 as the Democratic nominee and the next President of the United States, Senator Ted Kennedy." There was a microsecond of silence, a shudder of confusion sweeping across the crowd, and then a roar of cheers for Kennedy. Everyone knew what had happened—except Anderson. Kennedy didn't miss a beat: "Wendell Anderson is right. I will be back in Minneapolis in 1976, campaigning for the reelection of a great Democratic President—George McGovern." The cheers resumed as Anderson's expression revealed a sudden realization of what he had said: McGovern was going to lose.

We saw huge crowds on that initial swing, and the press wondered what would happen when Kennedy wasn't campaigning with us. But after he left, the crowds kept coming, all the way to the end, and they buoyed McGovern's spirit and ours. The candidate decided that he was going to focus on two issues: the war and Watergate. Caddell pushed back. Attacking Nixon on Vietnam and Watergate wasn't working; McGovern had to emphasize the economy and other bread-and-butter issues. And he did discuss jobs, inflation, and economic justice, telling audiences all across the country, "There's something fundamentally wrong when a business executive can deduct the cost of his two-martini lunch, and a worker can't deduct the cost of his baloney sandwich." But the candidate's passion was peace in Vietnam, and to him the issue was not just a failure of policy. He believed the election was above all else a fateful referendum on America's character. In a speech at Wheaton College, a stronghold of evangelical Christianity, McGovern cast the election as a choice about basic values. He was criticized for moralizing—for being too much and too self-righteously the preacher's son he was. (Today, of course, candidates get criticized for not talking values.)

It was hard to convince people of the corruption in the Nixon administration. For a long time, *The Washington Post* seemed to be the only newspaper that took the Watergate break-in seriously; to get the rest of the press to report at least something about it, McGovern took to recounting the latest *Post* story in his stump speeches, which, I was told, discomforted Bob Woodward and Carl Bernstein, who didn't want to be dragged into the partisan warfare.

When Caddell came to the campaign plane for a meeting to reiterate that McGovern was overemphasizing the war and Watergate, I finally looked at him and said, "Pat, we're not going to win anyway. Let's let the guy be who he is, tell the truth. He's running for history now"—an indication of a certain naiveté. I've learned since that losing is a cardinal sin, and you have to wait a long time for history to weigh in.

The doomed but defiant McGovern band crisscrossed three-quarters of the country—we went South only twice—usually making three stops a day. I temporarily got over a fear of flying that would plague me off and on until my mid-forties. The pilots not only let McGovern fly our 727 one day—and as a former bomber pilot, he had some idea how to do it—they also let me sit in the co-pilot's seat, hold the wheel as the aircraft went straight ahead, and then move it to the right to send the plane through a gentle turn. We were remarkably good-spirited for a campaign flying toward defeat. We had learned to live with our frustrations. For example, McGovern was accessible to the press and Nixon wasn't—and, in effect, we were punished for that openness. It was a lot easier for reporters to confront our candidate with a tough question or catch him in a slipup. They thought they had one night near the end of the campaign, when McGovern, shaking hands along a fence in Michigan, encountered a torrent of abuse from a Nixon partisan. He looked at him, leaned over, and said, "Kiss my ass." The press overheard it and the brief exchange was clearly headed for the next day's headlines. Some of the staff called it a catastrophe and said McGovern had to apologize. I thought this was ridiculous; McGovern had shown some Truman-like grit. The candidate had no intention of backing down anyway, and after the story broke, we actually saw a slight updraft in the polling.

Just days before the election, Henry Kissinger made an announcement about Vietnam: "We believe that peace is at hand. We believe that an agreement is within sight." To us, it was the last in a long line of deceptions: the Nixon administration was ready to manipulate and mislead even when they didn't have to; maybe, it occurred to me, Nixon was obsessed with carrying all fifty states. The next night, McGovern responded in a nationally televised speech.

While we were writing it, he had a telephone conversation with someone whose son had been killed in action after Kissinger's announcement. My most vivid memory of that drafting session is that after the phone call, a stricken McGovern just sat there and said nothing. Then he toughened up the language of the speech. I'd never seen him so moved. That night, he told me, wait and see, *if* Nixon wins, they'll be back to the bombing after the election—which is, of course, what happened over Christmas of 1972.

That *if* was bothering Gary Hart and Frank Mankiewicz. Late Sunday afternoon, Frank phoned and said he and Gary were concerned that McGovern actually thought he might win. Someone had to tell him the reality—and I was that someone. After our last event of the day, I wandered into McGovern's hotel room and asked if we could talk for a minute. I don't remember what city we were in—they were all a blur by now. I just remember that the living room of the suite had a garish, mirrored bar. I said that Gary and Frank (I wasn't doing this just on my own hook) were worried that he thought we might win, but it was clear we were going to lose and—I paused—actually lose pretty big. McGovern asked me to sit down on the couch and went over and poured us each a vodka on the rocks. He handed me one, thanked me, and said, "Bob, I know, I know. But I just need to believe for one more day."

Election eve ended with a massive rally that clogged the roads leading to the airport in Long Beach, California. It didn't feel like a loser's crowd. We touched down in Sioux Falls before dawn. I wrote a first draft of the concession speech, and went over it with Sandy Berger and John Holum. Just before the returns started coming in, McGovern took a nap. I went out to a Mexican restaurant with Gary Hart's wife Lee, the writer Pete Hamill, and his girlfriend Shirley MacLaine. Halfway through the guacamole, an advance man approached the table and said Senator McGovern wanted me to come back now.

As I entered his suite, Walter Cronkite was on television: "Pennsylvania for Nixon . . . New York for Nixon . . . Illinois for Nixon . . ." and the list rolled relentlessly on. McGovern was standing in front of a sink in the bathroom shaving. The door was open; Jeff Smith, his assistant who ran the traveling party, was crying. McGovern put his razor down, looked up, and told Jeff: "It's okay. It's okay. We'll wake up in the morning, and our lives will go on." Through his tears, Jeff replied, "That's easy for you to say." The candidate broke into laughter. McGovern asked for the concession speech, reworked it, and added a reference to Adlai Stevenson and the Lincoln quote he'd invoked that had captured my imagination as a child in 1952: "Well, it hurts too much to laugh, but I'm too old to cry." I remembered the quote so well that I was able to supply it to McGovern word for word.

The concession speech was gracious but unusual in that it explicitly reaffirmed the commitments of the campaign and pledged cooperation with President Nixon—but pointedly, in doing what was right for the country. Afterward, we gathered again in the suite. We had lost forty-nine of the fifty states. There's a wonderful picture of John Holum, Sandy Berger, and me sitting with the candidate—two of us cross-legged on the floor next to his chair. He looked down at us, and with a rueful note of affection, said, "There they are—the men who wrote the words that moved one state."

The next morning, we flew back to Washington. We knew that all of us—the candidate, his family, the staff, and the press—would not be together ever again as we had been for the months and miles of the fall campaign. When we landed, Sarge Shriver was at the airport to greet us and to stand with McGovern one last time. The Secret Service agents, many of whom had come to like and even admire a candidate they never thought they would, were suddenly gone.

Within two years, Watergate, which had no effect on the election, would destroy the Nixon administration, drive the president from office, and send many of the architects of his victorious reelection to jail. McGovern, who had been right on Watergate and the war, should have had an easy ride to Senate reelection in 1974. But a few days before the voting, he called me from South Dakota. He was locked in a tight race with a former Vietnam POW and Congressional Medal of Honor Winner, Leo Thorsness; he didn't know if he was going to make it. Could I come out for the last couple of days? On election morning, we walked around his hometown of Mitchell in a sharp, icy wind as he reminisced about his first try for the Senate in 1960 and how he stood with John Kennedy as the patrician presidential nominee spoke about farm policy to a throng of skeptical farmers at the National Plowing Contest. Later, Kennedy told his brother Bobby: "I think we just cost that nice man a Senate seat." Once elected, the new president couldn't give McGovern the job he wanted, secretary of agriculture, because it was already slated for someone else. So Kennedy elevated the Food for Peace Program, moved it into the office of the president, and named McGovern to run it. McGovern left after a year and a half to try for the Senate again. On election night, he won by a narrow margin of only 200 votes. Years later, he told me how Robert Kennedy warned him that the ballot boxes had to be protected so the election wouldn't be stolen. The president got the Senate Rules Committee to send someone in to help McGovern survive the recount process. He recounted the sad coda to the story: only a year later, Senate Majority Leader Mike Mansfield approached McGovern to take over from Ted Kennedy, who was presiding over a humdrum day of Senate business. It was a task assigned to junior senators. As they reached the dais, Mansfield had to tell Kennedy that his brother had just been shot in Dallas.

In a later conversation, McGovern described how he saw the difference between "Bobby and Jack": Bobby was tough and intense, but warmer and easier to know. They'd have lunch together, McGovern trying to keep his weight down by eating fruit and cottage cheese, while RFK ate two cheeseburgers, French fries, and a hot fudge sundae, joking that it was how he stayed thin. JFK was cooler, cerebral, and more reserved; he had a healthy sense of irony about himself and everyone around him. He called his press secretary Pierre Salinger in one day and ordered him to buy up every Cuban cigar he could find in Washington; the next day, JFK signed the embargo on imports from Cuba. McGovern's reaction as the reports about Kennedy's womanizing surfaced was in effect to shrug his shoulders. People just didn't understand, he said, that in the 1950s, the House and the Senate were frat houses; in that respect, there was nothing unusual about Kennedy.

Buoyed by the post-Nixon Democratic tide of 1974, McGovern made it through that Senate race—by 6 percent. The next year, he asked me to write a memo to Hubert Humphrey proposing they run together as a ticket in the upcoming Democratic primaries, with McGovern willing to take the second spot. They discussed it. Humphrey said he'd consider it for a few weeks, that he was genuinely intrigued, but ultimately said no. While McGovern tried to find a way forward, 1972 had put him in a box. There was an iron-clad conventional wisdom that he'd been repudiated because he was too far to the left. Moreover, in the modern history of the Democratic Party, there's ample reason to doubt that any nominee can come back from defeat. The Republicans recycle their losers: Nixon; Reagan, who ran three times before he won; Ford, almost resurrected for a second turn as vice president in 1980; the first George Bush, who was picked after he lost for the presidency; and even this Bush, the presumptive choice in 2000 despite his father's loss eight years earlier and despite his own thin record as the relatively powerless governor of Texas. For Democrats, on the other hand, defeat, no matter how narrow, is usually the equivalent of a political death penalty, with the losers thrown onto the scrap heap of regret and recrimination. Al Gore, the winner who lost, chose not to test this history when he refused to run in 2004. He could think about trying in 2008; but even before John Kerry's malaprop joke during the mid-term elections, he was being discounted and pressured not to run. Both Gore and Kerry got a far higher percentage of the popular vote than Bill Clinton did when he was first elected with less than 43 percent. But McGovern's loss was so devastating that for Democrats, he became a political untouchable.

Nineteen seventy-two was my crash course in the manners, mores, and culture of national politics. I witnessed the power of the conventional wisdom and the ways of the national press, including the inside deals by which an anonymous source could trade information in return for getting a story printed. I first learned it the hard way: one morning shortly after I went to the Muskie campaign, I picked up *The Washington Post* to read an anonymously sourced Evans and Novak column assailing my "superheated style" in "a fighting anti-Vietnam speech" that was "wisely discarded" by the candidate. Bob Novak, who years later became a friend and, in the 1990s, frequently my fierce conservative opponent on talk television, was a great reporter and eventually I, too, would become a source. But in 1971, he didn't know me from Adam. I'm sure Novak's story came from someone in the "moderate" wing of the Muskie operation who assumed, since I'd worked for John Lindsay, that I was ideologically dangerous—and maybe I was.

Someone very different from Novak also became a friend in that '72 campaign: Hunter Thompson. One night in 1973, we had a long dinner at Nathan's, an Italian restaurant in Georgetown; as the clock passed one in the morning and the drinks kept coming, Hunter asked me if I wanted some coke. I knew he didn't mean the soft drink, and I assumed he wanted to go somewhere. But as I was saying no, he simply took a vial out of his pocket and spread lines of white powder across the table as he rolled up a dollar bill. The restaurant was nearly deserted, and he *was* Hunter Thompson, but I said, Look, we just can't do this. He consumed the lines in a flash, looked across the table at me, and said, "There's nothing wrong with having fun." His intoxicant of choice that night was different from mainstream Washington's, but the attitude wasn't as countercultural as he thought. My first Washington lunch with a reporter after I'd joined the Muskie enterprise had come with two martinis and wine; it was then standard operating procedure. People drank, sources spilled or spun, and then everybody went back to the office—and, in theory, back to work. I tried the ritual a few times, then found I couldn't get much done all afternoon. But the day we returned to Washington following McGovern's landslide defeat, there was nothing left to do, so a few of us went out for one of those liquid lunches.

In presidential politics, losing is a short, sharp good-bye.

3

ALMOST TO THE WHITE HOUSE

In 1973, with the help of Senator Edward Kennedy, whom I barely knew, I returned to Harvard as a Kennedy Fellow at the Institute of Politics. This meant a stipend, a university house—far bigger than I needed—and constant interaction with undergraduates, half of whom seemed to be aspiring to run for president themselves some day. The next year, I stayed in Cambridge to write a book with Pat Caddell (we never did) and a column for *Rolling Stone* (we wrote exactly one).

Our class of Kennedy Fellows was an eclectic crew. Our graybeard—he did have one—was Alan Otten, who would return to his column at the *Wall Street Journal*. Bill Spring, an antipoverty crusader, would improbably become a vice president at the Federal Reserve Bank in Boston, where he was a voice for social justice. Our group also included Roy Hattersley, the future deputy leader of the British Labour Party, who never returned after orientation week; and the most intriguing figure of all, Pierre Pelham, a courtly, raffish Alabamian who was a state senator and a top political operative for George Wallace. The younger Institute fellows—and Pierre—gathered with students and friends at least once a week for a bull session in the basement of a now defunct German bar, the Wursthaus. For most of us, Pierre was a rara avis: how could someone this smart, this intellectually engaging, be for Wallace? When I reflected on our reaction, it reminded me of the apocryphal comment attributed to Pauline Kael of *The New Yorker* after the 1972 election: "I don't see how Nixon won; I don't know anyone who voted for him." We offered the expected criticisms and Pierre batted them away: the racist appeals were "crap"; he didn't believe them and Wallace didn't mean them. But us "liberals" better figure out how to talk to Wallace's folks instead of talking down to them. He hoped we would—because, surprisingly, his real favorite for president was Teddy Kennedy.

I also renewed my ties with debate. I team-taught at the Georgetown Summer Debate Institute with John Sexton, who had spent his college years turning St. Brendan's, a blue-collar Catholic girls high school in Brooklyn, into a national debate powerhouse. He didn't attend his own classes at Fordham and his grades suffered. He was and is larger than life, but by now, he was in his thirties and it was time for him to live his own life. So I gave him the same kind of advice Larry Tribe had given me a few years before. He needed to move on—in his case, go to law school. His Law Boards were high, even if his 2.1 college grade point was, to put it mildly, unusual for a Harvard applicant. But Tribe, already on the road to stardom as a constitutional scholar and litigator, vouched for Sexton to the Admissions Committee—and Sexton, as dean of NYU Law School and now president of the university, still delights in saying Harvard was the only law school that didn't summarily reject him. He would become an editor of the *Law Review* and a clerk for Chief Justice Warren Burger; but that would wait, because right after he was admitted to Harvard, he petitioned for a three-year deferment to fulfill his responsibility to the young high school freshmen he'd recruited to the debate team. The dean of admissions was so taken with the reason that she granted the request.

And I met Tom Rollins, the most successful college debater of the 1970s, who had come to my alma mater Georgetown from Texas where his father was in the oil business. Even though he arrived as something of a Republican, he became my closest friend. In the 1980s, he would run the Labor and Human Resources Committee for Senator Kennedy, then go into business, and in 1998 marry his fellow *Harvard Law Review* editor, Vicky Radd, the top aide to chief of staff Erskine Bowles in the Clinton White House. In college, Rollins regularly beat a brainy MIT debater named Larry Summers. Once, at the annual Dartmouth tournament, Summers asked me why he always ended up a quarter- or semifinalist and not a winner. I told him he was really smart—he knew it; he often argued brilliantly; but he didn't really listen to the other side.

The best of the debaters all followed a well-beaten path to Harvard, most of them to the law school, and Summers to graduate school in economics. From Sexton to Rollins and beyond, they often signed on as Larry Tribe's research assistants. (Later on, that role would be filled by Barack Obama.) Larry was generous in giving his assistants credit, even on occasion co-authorship. In the mid 1970s, he was engaged in an intellectual marathon, writing the first comprehensive treatise on constitutional law in almost a century and a half. When he finally finished the first edition, he asked me to read and edit the preface; he probably should have asked Sexton or Rollins. I thought Larry had to be unequivocal, not just about the idea of a living Constitution but about the reality of the judicial branch. So I penned a few lines that, in effect, admitted that liberal judges were "results-oriented," charged that conservatives were, too—and suggested that was not only the way things were but the way they should be. The lines made it into the book and were cited in the years ahead in attacks on Tribe from the Republican right. In subsequent editions, the thought was modified, softened, and finally all but smoothed away.

I stayed in Cambridge after my fellowship because Pat Caddell and I, with the hubris of the young, decided to write a book charting the Democratic Party's path to the future. We had long lunches, random notes, and almost no work product. Other exigencies beckoned. Pat was polling for an array of candidates in the fall of 1974, including Michael Dukakis in his first and successful run for governor of Massachusetts. I was recruited to coach Dukakis for his debate against incumbent Frank Sargent, a solid, polite, moderate Republican, a gentleman of the old clubs and the old school. Dukakis, an immigrant's son who'd earned his way to Swarthmore and Harvard, was absolutely sure of himself and what he already knew. As the prep started, he announced that he would studiously ignore Sargent during the debate and never mention his name. I said that he'd look stiff, unnatural, even arrogant. But JFK, he replied, had never acknowledged Nixon in the 1960 debates. Yes, he had, I insisted—in a variety of ways as "the Vice President," "Mr. Nixon." Dukakis said that I was just wrong; suddenly we were debating each other instead of practicing to debate Sargent. Joe Grandmaison, the young architect of McGovern's 1972 "victory" in New Hampshire, was managing Dukakis's bid. He called a 10-minute break; in the corner, he told me we had to convince the candidate that he'd look terrible if he just treated Sargent like he wasn't there. I asked Joe if someone could go to the apartment I now shared with Caddell a few blocks away and retrieve a green soft-cover volume that contained all the Kennedy and Nixon debates. It arrived just as we were about to resume. Dukakis looked at the transcripts, didn't say a word— and turned on a dime as he prepped in a mock Q and A, invoking Sargent's name so often that we had to nudge him to a middle ground.

I recounted the story to McGovern and Humphrey at a lunch after Dukakis was elected. This set Humphrey off. Dukakis, a cool, almost metallic, self-conscious "reformer," had recently criticized Humphrey as an outworn relic of the old politics. Humphrey's response tumbled out: "I tell you the difference between Dukakis and me. He wants the pipeline to be nice and clean and shiny, and as long as it is, he doesn't care if shit comes out the other end. I don't care if the pipeline's messy and even shitty at times as long as the right result comes out the end." That's the best description I've ever heard of the dividing line between process liberals—reformers—and results-oriented progressives.

McGovern couldn't run in 1976, but I couldn't resist a presidential campaign. The one article Caddell and I actually published in *Rolling Stone* keyed off the post-Watergate disillusionment of Americans with conventional politics and the rising anti-Washington mood in the country. We both foresaw the emergence of "a man on a white horse," a candidate who didn't fit the usual mold, a virtual unknown who could come from anywhere, except Washington, D.C., to win the next presidential election. By late 1975, Pat had found him—a one-term governor of Georgia named Jimmy Carter. Caddell was anxious to enlist me, but I was scheduled to accompany McGovern on a trip that was politically risky in conservative South Dakota—to Vietnam, less than a year after America's humiliating retreat. The most surprising aspect of the trip came during our meeting with Ho Chi Minh's successor, Pham Van Dong. Contrary to the central rationale for the war, he was intent on building good relations with the United States as a counterweight to the Soviet Union and China. Vietnam had no interest in being part of a monolithic Communist bloc.

Months before McGovern had brought me back to Washington as staff director of the Senate Hunger Committee, technically the Select Committee on Nutrition and Human Needs. The truth was that the committee hung by a thread. Its enemies in the Senate included southern Democrats and a majority of Republicans. Their *bête noire* was food stamps, which conservatives turned into the poster program for federal waste, fraud, and abuse. The committee survived because Democrats controlled the Senate, because senators like McGovern and Ted Kennedy fought for it—and because we had an unlikely secret weapon, Bob Dole.

Dole was the second-ranking Republican on the committee and we needed him to survive. He'd been Nixon's hatchet man in 1972, a constant source of vicious attacks on McGovern as radical and unpatriotic. But, talking with Kim Wells, the tow-headed young Kansan who advised Dole on politics and a whole range of issues, I got the sense that Dole could be a champion for food stamps and for the committee. McGovern, Dole, Wells, and I had a wary lunch. Our sell was that food stamps weren't just right for the poor; they were good for Kansas farmers.

But that's not the only reason Dole became a champion of food stamps and a genuine friend of McGovern's. (He would horrify Republicans in 1996 when, as he resigned from the Senate after winning the GOP presidential nomination, he praised McGovern, Hubert Humphrey, and Ted Kennedy in his farewell speech.) There were two sides to Bob Dole. I knew it at the lunch, watching him struggle to cut his food because the wounds that almost killed him in World War II had left him with a withered arm. The experience had also left him resentful and combative. He was so volatile that in partisan warfare he could wound himself; as a vice-presidential nominee in 1976, he cracked that the two world wars and Korea were "Democrat Wars"—and then as a presidential candidate in 1988, he would snarl at the first George Bush: "Stop lying about my record." But his war wounds also helped shape Dole's other side, an instinctive sympathy with the weak and the vulnerable that in the decades to come periodically discomforted the more ideological members of his party. The Bob Dole who joined George McGovern to save food stamps in the 1970s would join Ted Kennedy to save the Voting Rights Act during the Reagan years—and then join Iowa liberal Tom Harkin to pass disability rights.

By the time I returned from my trip with McGovern, the Iowa caucuses had ended. The surprise winner was Jimmy Carter. His antipolitics stump speech, including his promise to *never* tell a lie," was pitch-perfect in a post-Watergate America. But in Washington, there was resistance to Carter because he was a southerner; he was too religious—as he proclaimed "born again"—now a commonplace in presidential politics, but at that time a startling statement to hear from a national candidate.

I resisted the negative reaction. If John Kennedy's Catholicism wasn't a legitimate concern, why was Jimmy Carter's evangelical faith? And a southerner at the top of the ticket could be the ticket to victory—if he had a defensible record and the "right" views on race. I was gradually drawn into the campaign.

I wanted to be convinced because I wanted to win. Besides, I spent time with Carter's campaign manager Hamilton Jordan and his press secretary Jody Powell, who were smart, irreverent, and focused—and I was comfortable with them. They were genuine outsiders primed to run an anti-Washington crusade; but that could make it difficult to navigate Washington after they got there. Carter, as I soon found out, had no ideology, no central informing political ideas. This was an asset, not a liability in 1976, because it let him transcend the polarities of the Democratic Party—and the country. To those who had been driven away by McGovern, he was mainstream, Christian, and reassuring. To me, when I first met him on March 14 in the Madison Hotel, he was reassuring and progressive. He padded in from a connecting room in his bare feet and volunteered his "admiration" for McGovern: "We believe in essentially the same things." The difference, the heart of his appeal, was obvious: his persona, packaging, and provenance made Carter electable. He asked me to sign on with him, "to handle issues and writing on the plane."

Carter nearly lost the Wisconsin primary; Pat's polling in the days leading up to the primary showed that voters saw the candidate as vague, unspecific, trying to have it both ways. Behind the slogans, where was the substance? I made a suggestion unlike any other in all my time in politics—that this time, the best communications medium was not television, but print. The campaign should take out full-page newspaper ads with a headline: "Jimmy Carter on the Issues." The issues should be listed one by one—and the print under each of them should be as small as possible. The point was not to convey a lot of real information; instead, the medium was the message: The closely packed words on the page would convince people that Carter did have positions, in more detail than they conceivably wanted to read. I laughed: "We don't really want them to read it. We just want them to think, my God, Carter's actually got a lot to say on this stuff." It was practical expedient—or a cynical one. But I was willing to play that game as long as I believed Carter was what I thought he was.

I also agreed to draft a speech on health care for a national convention of black medical students. In it, Carter said that those who make governmental decisions about health care aren't the ones who suffer when mistakes are made; they have good health insurance for themselves—an idea that Ted Kennedy would deploy against Carter in 1980. Carter also committed himself unequivocally to comprehensive national health insurance. He delivered the draft while changing very few words—and more important, without building in escape hatches and evasions. For me, it was further proof that Carter was "for real."

I was for him, but wasn't quite ready to leave the Senate. I gave my advice, conferred with Caddell, and wrote memos on my own time. McGovern was skeptical about Carter, and frustrated by his rise. So I soon had to make a choice. Caddell wanted me to go to Atlanta for a weekend strategy session. I said I had to tell McGovern, who responded quietly but in no uncertain terms that I worked for him. He wasn't for Carter and I couldn't go.

Jody Powell called when I didn't show up and pressed me to join the campaign. The next day, I was back at Harvard for a discussion at the Institute of Politics. I was handed a note that Jimmy Carter had called. I called back. He said it was time for me to decide and he hoped I'd make the right decision. I said I had decided, and Carter told me, "It's going to come out all right . . . we're going to win." I'd been at the Hunger Committee a little less than a year. When I informed McGovern the next day that I was leaving and signing on with Carter, he was visibly unhappy, but said he'd always have a place for me if I ever wanted to come back. (And he meant it.)

That next Monday morning, on the inside of the campaign, I encountered someone I hadn't met before: Jimmy Carter. Behind the reflex smile, there was steel—but more about his ambition than his convictions. Atlanta mayor Maynard Jackson wanted help with a highway dispute before he endorsed Carter. Carter responded to the aide who'd relayed the request: "Maynard Jackson can kiss my ass and you can tell him that." Glancing over a list for his foreign policy task force, he singled out my friend Tony Lake, later director of Foreign Policy Planning in the Carter-era State Department, and Bill Clinton's first national security adviser: Isn't he "one of the people mentioned in *Washington Monthly* campaigning for Secretary of State?" Carter was also unhappy that Lake was "the one who quit on Kissinger." Tony had resigned from Kissinger's White House staff to protest the bombing of Cambodia.

I was inside the campaign for only ten days. On that first morning, I realized that Carter, on almost every policy, wanted to make sure "it doesn't commit me to too much." I think this reflected three realities. First, politically he wanted to be as blank a slate as possible except on his overarching anti-Washington theme; he calculated that it was the best way to win, although the sense that he was more empty pieties than specific stances ultimately almost cost him the election as Ford surged in the final weeks. As Stu Eizenstat, his future director of domestic policy, told me: "Jimmy doesn't like to take positions. I'm surprised he went as far as he did on national health insurance." Second, I believe that, for all his religious faith, Carter didn't have deep beliefs about most public policy. He was more an engineer who saw each issue as a discrete question, without an ideological reference point, to be analyzed and considered in what was almost a process of zero-based decision making. (He was running on "zero-based budgeting.") Third, Carter resented the pledges he had to give to make himself nominatable in the Democratic Party. He was for a 5 to 7 percent cut in the defense budget, but he was, the issues staff said, "unsure about opposing the B-1 bomber." When he did come out against it, he scratched out a sentence condemning "overhasty approval of B-1 production" and the statement ended with a loophole that would let him approve the B-1 if a review somehow could "justify" it.

Carter was also upset that he had to make the standard pro-Israel statements. As he said in that Atlanta meeting, referring to Senator Scoop Jackson of Washington State, who was too conservative to get nominated but was running hard: "Jackson's got all the Jews anyway; we get the Christians." Much later, the Carter aide and loyalist Peter Bourne wrote that when I recounted this remark in an article, "Shrum, himself Jewish, clearly intended to foster the image of Carter as anti-Semitic." I think Bourne missed my Catholicism because he made an assumption about my last name. And I was just reporting what Carter had said: it was what it was. In the fall of 1976, in a *Playboy* interview that became famous because he confessed that he had "committed adultery in my heart," Carter rationalized his comment to me about the Jewish vote. It was "a disappointment" that he wasn't doing better, but he was "pro-Israel" anyway: "I guess we'll have to depend on non-Jews to put me in office." He added that

I had treated it as "some kind of racist disavowal of Jews . . . sleazy twisting of a conversation." Based on Carter's statements in the years since, I do think it is fair to say that he is not an enthusiastic supporter of Israel. Carter's frustration at touching the required Democratic bases would slip out inadvertently at the start of his acceptance speech a few months later when he said: "It's a pleasure to be here with all *you* Democrats."

I stayed behind briefly in Atlanta, then left to meet up with Carter in Pennsylvania, where he was supposed to tour a mine and then issue a tough statement on mine safety and black lung disease. In the car at 6:30 A.M. on the way to our first stop of the day, a shift change at a coal plant, he worried about the reaction of the mine operators. He stripped out a provision to extend black lung coverage to all miners who'd worked thirty years before 90 percent of mines met federal dust standards. But at least there were tough new enforcement provisions. I left the campaign caravan, Xeroxed fifty copies of the statement, and caught up with Carter at our photo op coal mine in Finleyville, Pennsylvania. Another staffer pulled me aside and said we weren't going to release the statement: "Jimmy thinks it's too radical." Late that afternoon, on our chartered 727 from Pittsburgh to Wilkes-Barre, we were smashing across the sky through a fierce thunderstorm. Al Hunt from the *Wall Street Journal*, who was even more terrified of turbulence than I was, was my seatmate and we were wrapped around each other in a vain effort to cushion the force of violent ups and downs. I was summoned to the candidate's front cabin, where he was sitting alone, staring out the window, unfazed by the lightning around the plane. He was apologetic about the mine safety statement; but "these things" were too "controversial." Why should he do this for the mineworkers when their union president wouldn't endorse him? Anyway, "I don't think the benefits should be automatic. They chose to be miners."

Yeah, I thought, instead of, say, neurosurgeons. That night, in my motel room, I wrote out the first notes about my doubts. Maybe I should have left then. But what would people say if I did that after only a few days? And even if I didn't say anything and Carter won, I'd be ostracized from Democratic politics. I kept going, and so did

Carter. On a television interview, he answered a question about fair employment by saying there was very little deliberate discrimination. Bob Shogan, a no-nonsense reporter for the *Los Angeles Times* who had a sharp nose for news and a sharper cynicism about politicians, grabbed me and said: "What the hell does he mean by that?" After the candidate and I had dinner with his economic task force, I told him about Shogan's question. "I didn't say that," he insisted. I responded that I'd heard something like it, too. An annoyed Carter gave no ground: "I did *not* say that."

Caddell had arrived with his Indiana primary poll; we sat down with Jody Powell to review it. Voters increasingly doubted whether Carter was taking "clear stands on the issues"—and it showed in the Indiana results, where he was now only 8 points ahead of Jackson. The best antidote was a big Pennsylvania win, which would all but knock Jackson out of the race. After we left Jody's room, Pat and I sat outside in a cool April night on the steps of a Holiday Inn. I told him I wasn't a good fit for Carter; I was thinking about leaving the campaign. I was genuinely torn. I thought Carter was going to win, although I couldn't foresee that he would be one of only two Democrats to gain the presidency in thirty years. But victory wasn't all I cared about—if I went, I'd go quietly, I said to Pat. Pat was agitated. We were good friends, and I also sensed that if I went, he worried he'd be blamed for bringing me in. I didn't want that to happen, either. He asked me not to do anything until the next day—a quick flight to Memphis and back to Pennsylvania.

In the front compartment of the plane on the way to an intermediate stop, Carter rejected a statement drafted by Eizenstat urging Congress to override President Ford's veto of the child care bill: "I would have vetoed it myself." He glanced at me and said that he supposed my "ex-boss"—I assumed he meant McGovern—"thinks the bill is just great." Years later, Tom Donilon, Hamilton Jordan's young assistant in the White House and then the 1980 campaign, told me this was just standard operating procedure for Carter, a way to keep his advisers and staff a little off balance. When we landed, I called Pat and told him I'd had it. He asked me to talk to Jody on the way to Memphis.

I still didn't know Powell well, but I liked him personally, a feeling he certainly wouldn't reciprocate within a few days. Adept with the press, wry about himself, and in private candid about Carter, Powell understood the art of a deal, didn't care much for ideology, and didn't pretend that his boss did, either. It would be "terrible" if I left. He wouldn't tell Carter that I might—it would upset him; but on the first flight back from Memphis, the candidate and I should talk.

I didn't get to say much in the hour we spent together. Carter answered questions before I could ask them. He admired George McGovern; on mine safety issues like black lung and on child care, he just didn't want to talk about congressional legislation "even if I favor it." He was engaging, solicitous, and complimentary. I asked Carter the Mark Shields question: Why did he want to be president? He answered: "Well, let me read your and Pat's memo [on Pennsylvania issues] and we'll talk about it tomorrow."

During dinner in the Pittsburgh Hilton restaurant, Carter sounded exactly like the antipolitician he was running as. On Bob Strauss, the Washington insider and consummate Democratic national chairman who later would become one of Carter's closest advisers, he said: "If we can't remove Strauss [from the DNC], I'll be a pretty pathetic nominee." On potential vice-presidential choices, he dismissed Scoop Jackson, liked populist Oklahoma senator Fred Harris, didn't respond when Caddell brought up Muskie, and winced at the mention of his eventual choice, Minnesota senator Fritz Mondale. He clearly didn't want Ted Kennedy. Jody Powell said: "The smartest thing Lyndon Johnson ever did was not to take Bobby Kennedy." (LBJ and Carter both left a Kennedy out there to challenge them for renomination.)

Monday, the day before the voting in Pennsylvania, Carter was off on a trip to Connecticut and New Jersey. I stayed in Philadelphia to write a victory statement and outline a schedule of speeches for the next two weeks. Still I couldn't overcome my own doubts: I wanted to be in the White House, but I didn't think Carter should be president.

On Tuesday, with the draft of the victory speech finished and

Carter on his way back to Philadelphia, I pulled a chair up to the small desk in my hotel room and wrote my resignation letter in longhand. I put it in an 8-by-11 campaign envelope addressed to Jody and left it, marked, "Personal," at the front desk of the hotel. At 5 P.M., on April 27, as the voters were casting ballots that would bring Carter a landslide primary victory, I took a cab to the train station and bought a first-class ticket on the Metroliner to Washington. It was a small extravagance that I couldn't afford. I had no idea what I was going to do next.

In the small squall that would break days later about my departure from the campaign, the assumption was that I quit because Carter wasn't "liberal" enough. As I look back on it now, that's true—but only to an extent. In my resignation letter to Carter, I not only wrote that "your strategy is largely designed to conceal your true convictions, whatever they may be"; I also expressed what I saw as the essential flaw in the Carter candidacy and a Carter presidency: "I am not sure what you believe in, other than yourself."

I don't doubt that Jimmy Carter is deeply religious, but despite the novelty and political punch of saying that in 1976, especially in the South, it had little or nothing to do with the challenges he'd face in the White House. In a time of great testing, he often tinkered. The exception—the Camp David peace accord between Egypt and Israel—was his finest hour, but it was swept from public consciousness, first by a wave of inflation; then, during a summer of discontent in the third year of his presidency, by a nationally televised speech that sounded as if he was blaming the country for failing him as president; and finally by the Iran hostage crisis, which saved him in the 1980 primaries but doomed him against Reagan.

Carter has largely been an acclaimed ex-president. I just wish he could have skipped the intermediate step. The Roman historian Tacitus wrote of another leader who failed once in office that all would have thought him fit to rule if he never had.

Nearly twenty-five years later, Al Gore decided to give Carter, who had long been consigned to the shadows of Democratic conventions, a prominent place on the 2000 convention platform. At the last minute, someone pointed out that unlike the other first-rank speakers, we had no film to introduce him. I dashed off a treatment and script and agreed that we wouldn't tell Carter that the film had come from me. I'm not sure he would have minded. Four years after that, in the VIP reception at the Unity Dinner after John Kerry had locked up the 2004 nomination, I carefully tried to avoid what I presumed would be an awkward encounter for Carter. But as I turned away from a conversation, there he was. He put out his hand, shook mine, and said: "Bob, thank you for all you did in Pennsylvania in 1976." I was taken aback.

After I left the Carter campaign, there were calls urging me to come back. I told Caddell that I wouldn't change my mind—there was no use arguing about it, and I'd prefer to just fade away. I was good friends with Dick Goodwin and his wife, the historian Doris Kearns Goodwin; I fled to Boston to hide out at their colonial home in Lexington. Dick's reaction to my decision was that he didn't trust Carter, didn't think he was up to the job, and didn't understand why I worked for him in the first place: "You're better off out of there— even if he wins." Jacqueline Kennedy Onassis came by for dinner. I'd never met her before and I've never met anyone else who focused on the person she was talking to with such complete attention. She didn't know that I resigned from the Carter campaign, but I told her about it. What else could I do? She was troubled by him, she said, but she didn't offer conventional political reasons. He sounded too pious; he didn't seem to have any sense of humor—and she didn't see the resemblance others did to Jack. It may be hard to credit now, but in 1976 *Time* magazine compared Carter to JFK.

I was pretty sure I would never work in Democratic politics again. Carter was going to win, and by the time of the Democratic Convention in Madison Square Garden, I had a new career, as a columnist and reporter for *New Times* magazine. It was a sharply edited incubator for young writers like Robert Sam Anson, Frank Rich—who was then the movie critic—Janet Maslin, and Lawrence Wright. Anson, a friend from the '72 campaign, was the reason I was at the magazine. He introduced me to the editor, Jon Larsen, an even-tempered contrarian who prodded the staff about their predictably liberal views. My first piece recounted my days and disillusionment with the Carter campaign. Larsen then asked me if I wanted to co-author Anson's regular political column "Party Lines"; not long after, Anson turned it over to me and Larsen made me the magazine's Washington editor.

As I set out to cover the Carter transition, I was determined to be fair. But the first story I had led to two of the youngest stars in the Democratic foreign policy firmament: Richard Holbrooke and Tony Lake had both left the Foreign Service during the Vietnam War; they were now advising the president-elect.

Holbrooke has never hidden or even shaded his ambition. I was given a tip that he was assuring the pro-detente forces in Carter's divided foreign policy team that he was working to limit the influence of hard-liners like Zbigniew Brzezinski, while telling the hard-liners that he was trying to contain the influence on Carter of those on the other side like Paul Warnke. I called Holbrooke to check on the story. I read it to him. "This will ruin me," he responded. But was it true? He said he'd phone back. Instead, I heard from Lake. Don't do this, he said—if you do, Carter will be furious with Dick, and we need Dick in the administration; you'll hurt the things you and I care about in foreign policy. I killed the item. I don't know what Carter would have done if it had run, but I do know that Holbrooke, who became his assistant secretary of state for Asia, has been one of the country's most effective policymakers and diplomats—in that post, and since then, in the Balkans and at the United Nations in the 1990s.

Spiking the Holbrooke item at Lake's request should have suggested that I wasn't made for journalism. In retrospect, I think it was an early warning sign that somehow I'd go back to politics.

The *New Times* piece I'm proudest of, and the one that seeded a new political commitment for me, focused on the ballot initiative to ban gay teachers in California's public schools. Like most "progressives" in my generation, I'd heard, laughed at, and told my share of "queer" jokes. The political encyclopedist and activist Alan Baron, my friend who forgot more electoral stats than even Karl Rove ever knew, told me after he came out that every time a friend had cracked a "queer" joke in the past, it hurt him—but for so long he couldn't say anything about it. David Mixner, another friend and one of the leaders of the Vietnam Moratorium, had moved to Los Angeles to run Tom Bradley's campaign for mayor. He'd then come out, in a letter sent to hundreds of friends.

Now Mixner and his partner Peter Scott were spearheading a campaign against the antigay initiative, Proposition 6, which would have banned gays and lesbians from teaching in California public schools. To make "No on 6" more palatable to the Democratic establishment, they'd recruited straight men to take the public leadership roles in the campaign. But they were having trouble getting a straight publication to do a serious piece. A Dade County vote that had overturned rudimentary protections for gays had commanded national headlines because Anita Bryant, second runner-up in the Miss America contest and a second-rate recording artist, had headlined the antigay crusade. Now it had come to California. It was a big story because if the crusade succeeded there, it could sweep the country. Jon Larsen immediately signed off on the piece; it fit his vision of *New Times* as a journalistic pathbreaker and provocateur.

In Los Angeles, the "No on 6" headquarters was a barren space. Volunteers were sitting on the floor to make calls and stuff envelopes. Mixner and Scott dispatched two of them to the local office of state assemblyman Julian Dixon to pick up some used furniture. We went off to lunch. When we returned, the volunteers were there, but the furniture wasn't. It was just too ugly, one of them explained.

With a practiced political shudder, Mixner sent them back and asked me: "Please don't write this." He outlined where the campaign was: they had started out far behind, but now the polls were narrowing and they might have a surprise that would make the difference. Ronald Reagan was thinking of publicly opposing the Briggs Initiative on the grounds that the proposition would destroy discipline in the classroom: a student who got punished or got a bad grade could retaliate by alleging that the teacher was gay. The charge all by itself would trigger an investigation. It was a clever argument, one Mixner and Scott advanced in a meeting with Reagan. But I couldn't write about his potential role because he hadn't moved yet.

I wanted to interview the initiative's author, State Senator John

Briggs, a fierce reactionary from Orange County. I flew to Sacramento after calling his office for an appointment. I was told there probably wouldn't be a problem. But when I arrived, the answer was no; he didn't have the time—either in Sacramento or down in Orange County. I assumed his staff had checked out the magazine or me—or both. After a visit with Governor Jerry Brown in the state capitol, I was sitting near the front of a flight to L.A. that was still boarding when John Briggs serendipitously got on. I told him I was writing a magazine piece about the Briggs Initiative and asked if he'd mind chatting for a few minutes. In his words that day and throughout the campaign, he was ultimately his own worst advocate. He explained, for example, that there was a "large, well-financed movement" of homosexuals, one that was concentrated in California. And as for Jerry Brown, still single at forty years of age, Briggs noted that Brown had attended "a Cassius Clay fight"— "Jerry may be accused of having some effeminate qualities, but that isn't one of them."

Briggs's expostulations exposed the initiative as an exercise in barely disguised bigotry. The "No on 6" campaign mass-mailed the *New Times* article to voters. But now a far more powerful voice was heard. Ronald Reagan urged the defeat of the Briggs Initiative in his newspaper column. Mixner mailed out the column and ordered up a statewide television spot. A few months before, the polls had shown 75 percent in favor of Prop 6; on election night, with Reagan's intervention playing a crucial role, the initiative lost by more than 1 million votes.

New Times may have won the National Magazine Award, but it was closed down in the fall of 1978 by MCA Universal, the media conglomerate that had bought it not long before. A decade later, my wife Marylouise and I were having Christmas dinner with MCA's chairman and the king of Hollywood, Lew Wasserman, and his family. He asked me what I'd done in between McGovern and the 1980 campaign. I wasn't going to tell him about Jimmy Carter; pictures of Lew with Carter and Lyndon Johnson were all around his daughter Lynn's house, where we were gathered. I mentioned *New Times*. He said it was one of his favorite magazines—whatever happened to it? "Lew, your company owned it and shut it down." No one ever checked with me about that, he responded.

With *New Times* out of business, I wrote for a brief-lived magazine called *Politics Today*; don't put politics in the title of anything if you want to sell it. I did cover stories for *New York* magazine on Carter's controversial energy secretary James Schlesinger—the art department turned his head into a nuclear cooling tower—and on Edward Kennedy's prospective challenge to Jimmy Carter in 1980. I argued that perhaps the best way for Kennedy to win was not to run; a Democratic Party disappointed in Carter, increasingly alienated from him and fearful of defeat, might draft Kennedy without a bruising internal battle. I was only half-serious. I knew Jerry Brown was going to enter the race: he had all but told me that. But the cover was powerful. This time, the art department devised an illustration that showed Kennedy being sworn in as president with a glowering Carter behind him.

4

THE DREAM THAT WOULDN'T DIE

Among contemporary American political leaders, Edward Kennedy is the best known for the longest time, the best understood, and the most misunderstood.

For more than twenty years, he was a prime entry in the lexicon of the "great mentioner," the culture's mythic but powerful gatekeeper to the list of those routinely described in the media as being "mentioned" for president. After he was elected to JFK's Senate seat in 1962, he was one of the most junior senators but one of the most famous. So in his early days, at President Kennedy's suggestion, he walked the corridors of Capitol Hill, entered the offices of his senior colleagues unannounced, and asked the receptionist if "the Senator" had a few minutes to see him. It was a gesture of respect, seemingly effective, Kennedy told me years afterward—until he sat down with the Senator of Senators, Richard Russell of Georgia, who'd been in office since 1933. Kennedy had read up on each of his colleagues. For Russell, he thought he'd found the ideal grace note. He said he hoped the Georgian would help him learn the ropes; after all, they did share a rare kind of kinship: they'd both come to the Senate shortly after turning thirty. Russell didn't smile. "Senator," he drawled, "there is one difference. By then, I'd been elected Speaker of the Georgia House and then Governor." Ted Kennedy loves to tell the story.

His first chance for the White House came sooner than anyone could have imagined. After RFK's assassination in 1968, there was a sudden movement to draft "Teddy," who had just given a speech pledging to "pick up the fallen standard." How close did he come to a nomination he didn't seek? Bill Daley, who served as secretary of commerce in the Clinton administration, shared with me his insider's perspective as we were embroiled in the 2000 Gore campaign. Just before the '68 convention, Bill walked into his parents' home. His father was Chicago mayor Dick Daley, the last great big-city Democratic boss. Bill found the basement filled with stacks of TED KENNEDY signs. I thought we were for Humphrey? he asked his father. Not if Kennedy will take it, was the answer. But those signs never saw the light of the Convention Hall as the last Kennedy brother shied away from running.

Many years after Chicago, Kennedy told me he worried that he wasn't ready for an all-out campaign in 1968. It was only three months after the trauma of a second assassination—and he was concerned about his brothers' children and his own. He decided he could wait for another time. In one election cycle after another, all the way into the mid-1980s, Kennedy would lead in the polls as the Democrats' choice for their next nominee. It was in the mid-eighties, on a flight from South Africa, that he looked back on it all and said he'd learned that in politics you couldn't necessarily pick your time; when the door was open, you had to go through it. He didn't run in 1972, I'm convinced, not simply because of the accident at Chappaquiddick but because Nixon looked unbeatable. In 1976, Ford, too, was an incumbent and Kennedy would have to forgo a reelection campaign for the Senate. But as 1980 approached, the door seemed to be opening; yes, Carter was the Democratic incumbent, but increasingly beleaguered even within his own party. After what seemed to be the failed presidencies of Lyndon Johnson and Jimmy Carter, Democrats from some of the party's top operatives to the grass roots were beginning to look again to a Kennedy restoration.

* * *

When Carter shut down the process of governing amid the energy and economic woes of the summer of 1979, the nation watched with mingled fascination and apprehension as he retreated to Camp David for a week of séances with philosophers, historians, religious, labor, and business leaders, and a sprinkling of governors and members of Congress. As the president of the United States sat on the floor listening and taking notes, his guests told him what was wrong with America. Vice President Mondale, who had left Camp David early, was convinced, as his top aide Jim Johnson told me, that what was happening was "crazy." Mondale, Johnson said, seriously considered resigning the vice presidency. Coming down from that mountaintop, Carter delivered what would become known as the "malaise" speech. That word wasn't in the text, but it was in an earlier memo from his pollster Pat Caddell and became a trademark phrase as it leaked out of the Camp David sessions. Ironically, though I didn't realize it at the time, the speech's description of a "crisis of confidence" in the country echoed Robert Kennedy's warning amid the turmoil of 1968 that there was "a deep crisis of confidence . . . in our leadership." There was another irony: Carter spoke of a president "who feels your pain"; the line didn't work for him the way it did when Bill Clinton recycled it a decade and a half later.

The suspension of the presidency while Carter was at Camp David, his subsequent nationally televised jeremiad, and then his sudden decision to fire five cabinet members put more pressure on Kennedy to challenge the incumbent. Senate Democrats worried that Carter at the top of the ticket would drag them all down. At the top of the White House, there was a sense of bravado—or maybe it was wishful thinking—that a Kennedy challenge might be good for Carter. Chief of Staff Hamilton Jordan's assistant Tom Donilon remembered Jordan arguing that facing and defeating Kennedy would redeem the president's apparent weakness and strengthen him for the general election. This would prove to be a colossal miscalculation.

Kennedy hadn't announced, but the first confrontation was looming—on his home turf, in Boston, at the dedication of the John F. Kennedy Library in mid-October 1979. It was the prelude to a campaign that would change my life, bringing me back into national politics not for a year but for a quarter century. Kennedy would become a close friend. And it was in that 1980 campaign that I met my future wife.

I was in the crowd on that sunny day as Carter, Kennedy, and the Kennedy family sat with stiff cordiality on the platform in front of the library. No one was prepared for Carter's artful and witty gambit. The president borrowed a riff from JFK and with an uncharacteristically light touch applied it to the otherwise unspoken political drama that was on the minds of everyone in the audience:

> *I never met him, but I knew that John Kennedy loved politics, he loved laughter, and when the two came together, he loved that best of all.*
>
> *For example, in a press conference in March 1962, when the ravages of being president were beginning to show on his face, he was asked this two part question: "Mr. President, your brother Ted said recently on television that after seeing the cares of office on you, he wasn't sure he would ever be interested in being President."*

The audience laughed. Carter smiled, and so did Kennedy—he had to. But Carter was just warming up:

> *And the questioner continued: "I wonder if you can tell us whether, first, if you had to do it over again, you would work for the presidency and, second, whether you can recommend this job to others?" The president replied, "Well, the answer to the first question is yes, and the second is no. I do not recommend it to others—at least for a while."*

The laughter reached a crescendo, but Carter wasn't finished:

> *As you can see, President Kennedy's wit and also his wisdom is certainly as relevant today as it was then.*

The successive waves of mirth that rolled across the lawn were real, but there was an almost palpable sense of unease among those preparing the return to the New Frontier.

I had no doubt I wanted to be part of that journey. But aside from a few perfunctory interactions after I'd met Kennedy on the Mc-Govern plane, the only time I'd spent with him was during a weekend when Sarge and Eunice Shriver had invited me to Hyannisport. It was the first time I got a sense of him as a person. On the patio at the Shrivers' for drinks before dinner, I chatted with Rose Kennedy, who asked me question after question about my background, what my father did, where I'd gone to school. Then she called out: "Teddy, Teddy." He came over. Look at all Bob's done—she recounted it to my chagrin—and he didn't have any of the advantages your father and I gave you. Kennedy was bemused in the easy way I'd get used to in future years, and sat down to ask me more about myself.

I discussed the idea of joining the 1980 campaign with Dick Goodwin. Of course I should do it, Dick said. He was going to Washington for a strategy meeting at Kennedy's McLean home and he'd get it done. Later in the campaign, Goodwin told me it hadn't been all that easy. Steve Smith, Kennedy's brother-in-law and my future good friend, at that point wasn't thrilled about the idea of hiring "Shrum." He had turned on Carter, Steve objected, why not us? According to Dick, Kennedy himself wryly observed that quitting Carter probably shouldn't be a disqualification—after all, he was about to run against him. (And the notion that I'd resign in protest again was far-fetched; you can only do that once in a lifetime unless you're an unguided missile—but maybe Steve worried that I was.) Goodwin took out a checkbook, wrote a check to Steve for $10,000, tore it in half, gave one half to him and kept the other one himself. If Shrum did anything crazy, Dick said, he'd give Steve the other half and he could cash the check. Kennedy said, in effect, let's give it a try—and Dick told me later that the check would have bounced; he didn't have $10,000 in the bank.

In late October, Steve offered me a job. I'd travel with Kennedy—one week on the plane, one week off—an obvious safety valve; if necessary, I could be removed quietly and permanently to the headquarters. I'd be working with Carey Parker, who'd be on the plane all the time. Carey, I'd quickly learn, not only had an incisive, first-rate mind; he also had a rare kind of selflessness that invariably put Kennedy's interests first. For the next nine months, we'd share a hotel room, a row of seats on the plane just behind the candidate, and a dual mission—to find the right words to navigate through a chaotic political season—and at each stop to find a couple souvenirs Carey could take home to his two young children. (Parker has worked in Kennedy's office so long, since 1969, and shaped so much legislation, that one could almost think of him as a 101st senator.)

Stories were swirling around Washington that CBS correspondent Roger Mudd's interview with Kennedy was "godawful." What had happened, as the Kennedy staff recalled it, was that Mudd, an old friend, had said he wanted to talk to Kennedy in Hyannisport just before his annual summer camping trip with his children, nieces, and nephews. Mudd wanted some shots of that, too. The only staffer with Kennedy, as he and Mudd sat on the lawn to videotape their conversation, was his young and inexperienced administrative assistant Rick Burke. Mudd's early questioning didn't focus as expected on what Hyannisport meant to Kennedy and his family—this was no "soft" interview. Instead, Mudd zeroed in on Chappaquiddick, where Mary Jo Kopechne, one of RFK's former campaign workers, had drowned ten years before when Ted Kennedy's car went off a bridge. In response, Kennedy awkwardly described that night as "the incident." He sounded unfeeling, but it was actually a protective shell over the deeply painful feeling of someone who'd seen too many deaths in his life, and could hardly bear to be responsible for one. Small decisions can make a big difference in politics. If there'd been a press secretary at the interview, he might—and should—have interrupted early on, told Kennedy there was a phone call, walked into the house with him, and advised him to call the whole thing off, telling Mudd they'd have to resume at a later date—which would never come.

A second Mudd interview was scheduled to fix the first—this time, in Kennedy's Senate office. But when asked why he wanted to be president, Kennedy lapsed into a shorthand of half-sentences, pauses, and a halting list of issues. He sometimes talked—and still talks—that way. So did JFK and RFK. Edward Kennedy once ruefully said to me, he'd gotten used to it growing up; there were sessions around a crowded dinner table where you had to resort to that kind of verbal shorthand to get a word in edgewise. But even if his two brothers had their own moments of broken syntax, that wasn't how the country remembered them. In 1980, the last Kennedy brother was to be compared not just with Jimmy Carter but with idealized images that had been powerfully imprinted on the national consciousness.

So the overture to his official announcement that he was taking on Carter was an off-key, nationally televised, press-amplified train wreck of an interview that previewed the weakness of a Kennedy strategy based on the premise that since he was far ahead, he should measure his words carefully to avoid sounding too "liberal" or taking sharp issue positions. This strategy didn't fit the candidate; it made someone with strong convictions awkwardly self-conscious about what he could and couldn't say. Edward Kennedy is the worst politician I've ever seen at saying nothing.

In fact, the interview wasn't as bad as the pre-broadcast hype, but that didn't matter; what mattered was the filter through which it was perceived. Yet at least initially, Kennedy's lead in the polls was barely dented. What proved to be far more damaging was something else that occurred just before the announcement: fifty-two American diplomats were seized by "students" loyal to the Ayatollah Khomeini, whose fundamentalist regime had taken over Iran after the fall of the Shah, one of America's closest allies for nearly forty years. At first, what would become the Iranian hostage crisis looked like another headline that might be resolved in a few days. We easily came up with a response for Kennedy: Whatever our other differences, as Kennedy soon said in a speech in New Hampshire, "As a united people, we support our government's efforts to bring the hostages home . . . on this issue, at this hour, we remain one nation, indivisible . . ." Little did we know that what was in store wasn't an hour but a year of crisis; that Carter would invoke the hostages to skip the primary debates and turn the early contests to his advantage by asking Democrats to vote for him to send a clear message of resolve to the Iranians. Ultimately, Carter would pay a high price, but not until the fall.

When Carey and I finished it, Kennedy's November 7 announcement speech was long on rhetoric and short on substance—which only drew more attention to what happened in the question-and-answer period that followed. A reporter asked the candidate if his wife Joan, sitting on stage, was going to campaign with him. She was living in Boston while he was spending most of his time in Washington. The Kennedy partisans booed the question, but he quieted them and she came to the microphone. "I look forward to campaigning for him," she said. "And not only that. I look forward very, very enthusiastically to my husband's being a candidate and the next President of the United States." Her voice, as one wire service characterized it, was "quivering." Joan told us over and over in the following months that she wanted to be out on the trail; but whenever she was, the stories conveyed the impression that Kennedy was forcing her to do it. Larry Horowitz, who ran the Health Subcommittee, was one of the doctors who always traveled with us in case someone made an attempt on Kennedy's life. He was also a valued confidant. After one of Joan's appearances, Horowitz said that he thought her presence was doing us more harm than good. It was a trap we and she couldn't get out of, no matter how hard she tried.

After the announcement, Kennedy barnstormed from Maine to Chicago, to Tennessee and across the South, and then to Hartford, Connecticut. In a booming voice, he delivered a muted message—and the press noticed it. When he could talk about an issue like health care, he went on and on. I told him that one answer he gave, which clocked in around 20 minutes, could best be described as "everything you ever wanted to know about health care—and a hell of a lot more besides." I didn't know how he'd react. He laughed and said, Okay, I'll keep it shorter. As I was to learn, Kennedy was one of those uncommon politicians who genuinely want some people around who say what they think instead of what will please the principal; as he asked me later, "What good does it do to have a bunch of advisers who just agree with you? I can agree with myself if that's what I want."

Carey and I spent the first week working with Kennedy on Q and A and trying to settle on a stump speech. When I told Kennedy I was getting off the plane and would see him again in seven days, he asked why. I replied that was the deal—I'd been slated to spend one week on, one week off. "Well, I'm the candidate," he said, "and the deal is you're staying."

The first contest, where a Kennedy victory could all but knock Carter out, was Iowa. Our polls there were strong, as they were almost everywhere, but our first visits weren't promising. Constrained by a cautious front-runner strategy from saying what he really felt, Kennedy sometimes got distracted and slipped up. He was churning through a stump speech with the amorphous theme of "leadership" when instead of referring to "farm families," he called them "fam farmilies" and talked about the long-defunct "Wabash Railroad." We couldn't get much attention with the hostage story dominating the news, but we broke through this time—all over the national media. On the way back to Iowa for our next visit, I suggested a joke—what Kennedy called an "opener"—for the first stop: "I have returned to Iowa to talk about the important issues of fam farmilies and the Wabash Railroad." The candidate stared at me across the top of his half glasses. No, he wasn't going to do that. Carey Parker warned me that I shouldn't have done it; he was afraid I'd replanted the phrase in Kennedy's mind and we'd hear it that night. Sure enough, that's what happened. Kennedy paused as soon as the words were out of his mouth. The audience laughed nervously. Kennedy broke the tension in the smoke-filled hall: "There must be something in the air out here"—he said as he stretched out his hand and stretched out the words for emphasis. The assembled Democrats roared. Kennedy, expected to be what his brothers were assumed to have been, was an easy target when he made a verbal gaffe. Eventually, the reporters traveling with us, who came to respect him for never complaining about the coverage, relented: One night, after 12 or 14 hours of campaigning, he said "United Notions" instead of "United Nations." The crowd chuckled, but the glitch never made the news.

In November, we flew to Los Angeles to give a speech to a public interest law organization run by Charlie Palmer, a lawyer and former leader in the antiwar movement who'd taken a leave to work on our issues staff. Charlie was with us for the event and Doris Kearns Goodwin was traveling with the campaign for a few days. She and I were planning to have dinner in L.A. together, but Charlie wanted us to have a drink first with him and his wife. I demurred on the grounds that I was tired—and I was. I'll never forget Charlie's response: "You really have to meet Marylouise; you're going to love her." Doris already knew her and it was surprising that I didn't. I was in law school when she'd been Gene McCarthy's deputy national press secretary in the 1968 campaign against Lyndon Johnson. After that, she was a leading force in the Vietnam Moratorium and the National Welfare Rights movement. I should have encountered her somewhere along the way, but I hadn't.

I thought Charlie had said that Marylouise worked for the *Tidings*, the Catholic weekly in Los Angeles, so in the bar of the Bonaventure Hotel downtown, where the seating areas were pods floating far above the lobby floor, I started interrogating her about the new Pope, John Paul II. As we chatted, she figured out my mistake—and she lightheartedly corrected me. She was Catholic, she did have a divinity degree from Yale, but she worked at "the *Times*—the *Los Angeles Times*." She looked tired; Charlie was assigned to the headquarters in Washington and she was driving the carpool for her young son and his classmates while copyediting sections like "Food" with headlines like "Lenten Soufflés Make a Light and Lively Repast." She'd been sent to copyedit on the soft side because she was regarded as too political, "too left," to be a reporter, even though she'd been UPI's youngest national reporter in the 1960s. She would soon end up as the *L.A. Times* society columnist—where of course she wrote more about political events than debutante balls. Despite the tiredness, and the obvious tension between Charlie and her, I found her fascinating, funny, and insightful. After the two of them left, I told Doris I wished I knew Marylouise better. I didn't see her again until she and Charlie had split up three years later. But his initial observation was right: I was going to fall in love with her—and marry her in 1988.

It was an expensive campaign; we had a chartered and specially equipped United Airlines 727, and we had to keep hopscotching from Iowa and New Hampshire to New York, Florida, and California to raise money. We were in San Francisco in early December when Kennedy spoke his mind—and the truth—about the Shah, and the roof caved in. Kennedy had repeated his standard answer about the hostages—on this "we're all united as Americans"—so many times he didn't even talk about it anymore. We'd had a long day and some of us wanted to go out for dinner. Kennedy said fine; all he had left was a run-of-the-mill interview with Rollin Post, a local television correspondent. Most of the senior staff was in a restaurant miles away when Post nudged Kennedy not about the hostages but about the Shah himself. It was Post's last question: Ronald Reagan had said the Shah should be permitted to remain in the United States because he'd been a "loyal ally" for years; what did Kennedy think? He should have refused to be drawn; his mantra about unity wasn't exactly on point, but it was good enough. But Kennedy was frustrated. Carter's approval rating had risen in one month from 32 to 61 percent—not on the basis of something he'd accomplished, but because of a crisis he'd inadvertently provoked by admitting the Shah into the country for medical treatment. That was what had triggered the seizure of the hostages. When we returned to the hotel, a worried advance man rushed up and informed us that Kennedy had told Post, on camera, that the Shah was "violent . . . corrupt"; he'd stolen "umpteen" billions of dollars.

I drafted a statement that night reaffirming the candidate's commitment to national unity regardless of his views of the Shah; the critical line was: "Support for the hostages is not the same as support for the Shah." We convened in Kennedy's room in the morning and conferred on the phone with operatives and advisers back in Washington. They didn't think the episode was such a big deal; if Kennedy issued a statement, he might just ramp up any reaction to his original comment—which, after all, had nothing to do with the hostages. We ought to wait until we got to Reno, our next stop, to see if he needed to say anything more at all. By the time we landed, all hell had broken loose. Carter's press secretary Jody Powell and his campaign chair Bob Strauss had lambasted Kennedy for dividing the country at a time when Americans needed to stand together.

Without quite saying it, they questioned Kennedy's patriotism. I took the clarifying statement out of my briefcase; we made a few changes; Kennedy approved it, and we raced to catch up with the news cycle. But it was too late; the time difference with the east coast was working against us. The networks had already put their packages to bed. Instead of making it harder for the Carter forces to go after him, Kennedy's clarification, although we never called it that, was now just a footnote to a negative story that was all the more memorable because he'd said the Shah had stolen "umpteen" billions—a non-number that stuck in every viewer's mind.

Carter's agents had cleverly exploited our delay. So did Reagan, whose defense of the Shah had inspired Post's question to Kennedy. Reagan, himself an announced candidate, happily weighed in against Kennedy—he preferred to run against Carter, who in this month of the hostage crisis had built a 14-point lead over him. As Reagan's adviser Mike Deaver told me long afterward, their campaign never thought that was more than temporary. We had violated a first rule of politics: When you have a problem, fix it before it gets worse.

By now, Kennedy himself sensed that events had overtaken— and were overwhelming—the campaign's cautious strategy. At least on the surface, on the bubble of the hostage crisis, Carter no longer looked like a certain loser in the fall. With Kennedy's own poll lead among Democrats evaporating, he increasingly chafed against the constraints of his own "message box." He had to draw some real differences with Carter on issues that mattered to him—and the electorate. He couldn't just talk about "leadership"; it was his own leadership that was now in question. One day in mid-December, as we campaigned through Iowa, he said he wanted to toughen up his stump speech. Carey Parker wasn't there—he'd taken a day off. So I came up with some language on oil company profiteering and antitrust action against big conglomerates, along with a tougher critique of Carter on health care. The reaction from our Washington headquarters might have gotten me thrown off the plane, but Kennedy said, look, it was his idea, he wanted to do it and he'd done it. In reality, we couldn't improvise our way out of a downward slide even if we ratcheted up the rhetoric, as Kennedy did again in a speech to the United Mine Workers: "In 1976, we thought we ended 8 years of Republican rule. We were wrong. In 1980, it is time to end 12 years of Republican rule and put a real Democrat back in the White House."

We considered a nationally televised speech on the economy. With the country again facing an energy shortage and long gas lines, with the inflation rate in double digits and rising, I was convinced that we couldn't shy away from Kennedy's belief in government as an instrument of national purpose. Instead of the Carter drift and Reagan's call to laissez-faire and tax cuts, I thought Kennedy should forthrightly offer a plan for gas rationing and wage and price controls. Surprisingly, so did Steve Breyer, the chief counsel of the Senate Judiciary Committee that Kennedy chaired and the intellectual architect of airline and trucking deregulation, the landmark legislation that confounded the cliché that Kennedy always favored "big government." But what could be more "big government" than a wage and price freeze—or controls? As the economy deteriorated, Breyer wrote in a December 22, 1979, memo to Kennedy, we have "to contrast you, as a president with a coherent strategy for dealing with the economy, as against Carter, who does not have one . . . the freeze seems the best of the wage/price alternatives. . . . Most of the economists surveyed would see [gas] rationing as an acceptable way to deal with dependence upon OPEC." The briefing book that Breyer put together then wouldn't be put to use for another month, until after Kennedy was routed in the Iowa caucuses.

We didn't move at this point in part because we thought we had a good chance to get at Carter: the January 6, 1980 *Des Moines Register* debate with him and the other challenger, California governor Jerry Brown, whose only role in the few primaries he participated in would be to siphon anti-Carter votes from Kennedy. We headed to Palm Beach right after Christmas for debate prep. While we were there, Kennedy asked if I'd like to bring my parents to supper; with my father retired, my parents had moved to south Florida. My mother's first reaction was she didn't have time to do her hair. My father didn't care: "We're coming." When they arrived, a couple of advance men carried my mother, who had a broken leg that wasn't fully healed, up the front steps of the Kennedy mansion. Senator Kennedy showed them around, taking my mother's arm, while doing what parents like most, praising their son or daughter. Rose Kennedy was, as she had been the first time I met her, full of questions and interested in the people she met. I could see my family gradually relaxing, and was soon listening to my mother and Kennedy's mother discuss their mutual devotion to the Blessed Virgin Mary. For me, it was a happy evening in a hard season; my mother talked about it for the rest of her life—and we always reminded her that it was all right that she hadn't been able to do her hair.

While we were in Palm Beach, just ten days before the debate, Carter suddenly pulled out on the grounds that he couldn't take time off from the hostage crisis: "I don't think there is any way I can leave Washington," he explained to the editor of the *Des Moines Register*. The *Register* countered by offering a debate in Washington, to be broadcast to Iowa. Carter declined this, too, on the predictable ground that he couldn't spare any time for politics—although he had more than enough time to invite Democrats from Iowa and the early primary states to come to Washington and meet with him in the White House.

Not only had the debate been cancelled, but after the Soviet invasion of Afghanistan in late December, Carter now had a new foreign policy crisis—and was benefiting from it. He addressed the nation on television, slashed grain exports to the Soviets, and took the issue to the UN Security Council. The press was consumed with Afghanistan—and the Iranian threat to try one or more of the U.S. hostages for spying. A Kennedy relaunch, an economic speech, even one with big proposals, would be a blip in the news—and probably would be seen as an act of desperation. But Kennedy was through with temporizing, even if he couldn't refocus the campaign on the economy. He came out against the grain embargo, and was criticized for pandering to Iowa's farmers. He knew that might happen, but didn't care; he was going to say what he thought. He also thought Carter was on the wrong track in Afghanistan. The time to stop the Soviet invasion was before it happened, not by embarking on an election-driven policy of renewed cold war with Moscow and intervention in Afghanistan, which, Kennedy observed to me, led God knew where. (Funding the anti-Soviet guerrilla forces would ultimately give rise to Osama bin Laden and al Qaeda; Kennedy was more right than he knew.)

We saw the trouble we were in—not just in Iowa but every-where—during a side trip the candidate insisted on taking to Indi-anapolis for a dinner honoring his Senate colleague Birch Bayh. The trip made no political sense at this point, but Kennedy had given his word and we flew through an ice storm to get there. After an intro-duction long on praise for Bayh and short on any appeal for his own cause, Kennedy had to sit patiently and apparently unperturbed at the head table as Bayh delivered a speech that all but endorsed Carter. It was so graceless that some of the more boisterous members of the press corps, who couldn't believe we'd knocked around the sky for this, retreated to a corner and popped balloons while Bayh was droning on. Back on the plane, in the front compartment with Kennedy, I said, "What a son of a bitch." No one on the staff dis-agreed. But Kennedy couldn't get mad at Bayh. Sixteen years before, when the small plane carrying him, Bayh, and Bayh's wife to the Massachusetts State Convention had crashed, Bayh had climbed back into the burning fuselage, pulled out a paralyzed Kennedy, and saved his life. Kennedy was constantly reminded of the crash by the continuing back pain that plagued him every campaign day. And it was one of the reasons that he sometimes, as I put it, "biffed and far-bled" when the pain hit while he was speaking—an explanation we weren't going to offer to the press. Kennedy was disappointed in Bayh but he didn't want to hear anyone bitching about him. Bayh, he said, had a pass, and always would.

The day before the Iowa caucuses, Kennedy appeared on *Issues and Answers,* then the ABC network's Sunday interview show. The briefing materials suggested that he lower expectations and refuse to predict he would win: "[I] expect to do well . . . [it's] a long campaign; only just beginning." But despite all the discouraging signs, all the straws in Iowa's wind, and all the polls, we heard a rosier prognosis at lunch on caucus day at Kennedy's McLean, Virginia, home. Steve Smith, Kennedy's longtime political counselor Paul Kirk, and most of the campaign's top echelon were there. Our political director Carl Wagner had given someone else the "honor" of delivering the "good news." The polls weren't looking good, but what mattered in Iowa was intensity and who actually showed up at a caucus. The Kennedy campaign had 30,000 hard identified—"id-ed"—supporters, more than the entire total attendance at the caucuses four years before. There was a strong chance Kennedy would win—or if he didn't, that it would be a lot closer than people were predicting.

After lunch, Kennedy asked me to stay for a few minutes. Casually dressed in slacks and an open shirt, standing in the foyer of his home, he put out his hand, wobbed it toward the floor like a plane falling from the sky, and offered his prediction: "This baby's going down." He's had this experience before, I thought—for real. The tone in his voice suggested he was through with easy reassurance. Whatever he did, he'd do it his way from now on. I didn't know what that was, or would be. He said Carey and I should prepare a concession statement. We'd need it: Kennedy did get his 30,000 "id-ed" caucus goers, but Carter got twice as many in an Iowa Democratic turnout that set a record.

The day after, we cancelled Kennedy's public schedule and began a series of meetings where we analyzed—or argued—the future, if any, of our 1980 campaign. Though I was the newcomer in an enterprise whose central figures had been with Kennedy for years, I was given room to speak my mind. And I did: Kennedy had to stay in, I said. Carter had no idea where to take the country. He was being temporarily propped up by foreign crises he'd caused or didn't know how to cope with. There were strong arguments on the other side coming from others: The polls were bad everywhere, we couldn't raise money, how were we going to win? If Kennedy continued, he'd be beaten again and again until he was destroyed as a national force. After one session, Steve Smith, who was still pretty dubious about me, backed me into a corner and said something like, Do you care about this guy? I do. He's my best friend. And if you keep giving him this kind of advice and he takes it, you're going to ruin him. I responded that I had to tell Kennedy what I thought was right for him.

Two nights after the Iowa defeat, Carter gave his State of the Union address. When we gathered afterward, Kennedy was full of fire. He thought Carter was beating the drums of a phony war with the Soviets by hinting that through Pakistan, we'd aid an Afghan resistance. That country was no more a decisive theater in the cold war than Vietnam, Kennedy said. As for Carter's proposal for draft registration, Kennedy was against it, period; and as for boycotting the Moscow Olympics, we'd be punishing our own athletes more than the Soviets. I said that Carter had decided to ride this crisis and the hostages as his only route to reelection. In the State of the Union, he'd offered nothing on the economy or energy except recycled and token proposals. Kennedy noted wryly that Carter's third big "action to strengthen our nation's economy" was to "continue our successful efforts to cut paperwork."

The eight of us in the room were still split; we had one more go-round. I didn't think arguing the money or the polls mattered anymore. So I cleared my throat and said that in addition to his big differences with Carter, and Carter's bleak prospects in the general election, there was another reason Kennedy had to continue: The rap on him from critics and Kennedy haters was that when things got tough, he ran away. I didn't mention Chappaquiddick; amid the silence in the room, I knew it would have been a step too far—not only needless, but painful. Kennedy had entered the race when it looked easy, I continued. His critics alleged he'd done it just out of ambition. He had insisted and, I believed, there was something more at stake. If he dropped out now, no one would think he had run for president out of principle or for the party; he'd be labeled a quitter forever. I finished and, for a few long seconds, no one said a word as Kennedy just looked at me. He said: "Thank you"—and added that he'd heard enough, it was time to take a vote. Who thought he should withdraw and who thought he should continue? We each gave a one-word answer. The vote, Kennedy said, was 4 to 4—and he was in the race to stay: "Let's get ready and go."

The political waters were rough, but Kennedy was about to become a different kind of candidate—the only kind he was comfortable being—a candidate freed of the cautionary straitjacket of the front-runner. Any strategy designed primarily to hold on to a lead risks losing it, especially in primary contests where voters don't have to cross party lines to switch candidates. But now Kennedy was determined to run, to win or lose, on the basis of what he really believed, in a campaign that would demonstrate his resolve in adversity and the strength of his commitment to progressive values. We scheduled a speech at Georgetown University for Monday, exactly one week after the Iowa caucuses.

The speech was finished in an all-night session at his McLean home. Allard Lowenstein, the spearhead of the "Dump Johnson" movement in 1968, showed up early in the evening. I don't know if he'd actually been invited, but Al could appear at Kennedy's house during the campaign without prior notice. The Secret Service would call from the gate at the top of the driveway; Kennedy would let him in; and Al, with memos, speech ideas, and rolled-up clothes popping out of his bulging briefcases, offered his advice—and was offered a guest room to sleep in overnight.

There were reams of paper, including a draft of the foreign policy section from Arthur Schlesinger, Jr., and memos and notes from Steve Breyer and Paul Kirk. Kennedy sifted through the alternatives and then turned in as we turned to the task of fashioning a semifinal product. We decided that Kennedy ought to begin starkly, with the mistakes in Afghanistan—Carter's statement that he was "surprised" by the invasion, the emptiness of responding with a call for draft registration, and the hyperbole that characterized the Soviet move as the gravest threat to peace since World War II. We crafted six principles that should guide America's response, the first of which would have an eerie resonance a quarter century later in Iraq: "It is impractical to rely on a doctrine that requires us to stand astride the Persian Gulf solely on our own."

There were two passages that Tony Lake later told me especially provoked the president's ire. The first condemned the administration for saying and doing nothing as Soviet forces gathered on the Afghan border, and then drawing "a line in the dust that was already rising from the tread of Soviet tanks." The second offending passage insisted that the cause of nuclear arms control should not be sacrificed in the course of responding to the Soviet invasion. The United States had to be realistic about its own national interests; the issue wasn't whether we liked the Russians: "It is less than a year since the Vienna Summit, when President Carter kissed President Brehznev on the cheek. We cannot afford a foreign policy based on the pangs of unrequited love."

Kennedy had directed us to be blunt about the hostage crisis; he just wasn't interested in safe words that weren't true. And before he delivered the speech, the candidate would strengthen the language: the Carter "policy seems headed for a situation of permanent hostages"—something Kennedy had been aching to say ever since he'd been pilloried for his comments in San Francisco.

It was well past midnight. With the first part of the speech finished, Al Lowenstein went to bed. Carey and I would still be up for hours. We segued from crisis abroad to crisis at home with words I had scribbled on a piece of paper at the start of the drafting process—a pledge to "speak for all the Americans who were ignored in the [Carter] State of the Union address." Kennedy would now coin a phrase that would be picked up by others across the years, and repeated word for word by George W. Bush in 2006: "We must cure our addiction to foreign oil." Breyer had already done the backup work on gas rationing and wage and price controls. Kennedy didn't think a wage-price freeze was an ideal solution; but the shock of a freeze was the only answer to the inflationary spiral other than recession—which would soon hit under Carter and then again under Reagan. No one who would be hearing the speech could doubt at this point that Kennedy was in the race to stay, but I was determined to save the explicit words for the end so that, in a rolling series of pledges—on civil rights and equal rights, on economic fairness and health care, on the environment, and on the central issue of war and peace—Kennedy could repeatedly bring the audience to its feet with a defiant refrain: "I have only just begun to fight."

As we drove onto the campus, we encountered a roiling sea of students. They jammed the stairwells up to the third floor where

Kennedy was to speak on the stage of Gaston Hall, the gilded, fres-coed setting where I had debated as an undergraduate. I found a place to pace, just outside the balcony doors in a secure holding area. On the other side, there were more reporters and television cameras than we had seen since the announcement speech. Kennedy received a thunderous reception, and the story commanded the evening news. Finally, he was running on his own terms.

We had debated whether to address Chappaquiddick directly. John Douglas, a low-key Washington superlawyer and Robert Kennedy's assistant attorney general, had written a memo the day before the speech urging that Kennedy be "personal," explain how "experiences, including Chappaquiddick, have brought you to where you are." This was too pointed, but we all knew what Doug-las meant. Paul Kirk was convinced Kennedy had to confront the issue head-on, but I resisted doing it at Georgetown: it would con-sume the coverage; Kennedy wouldn't be heard on anything else; we'd be centering our relaunch on an argument where our best hope was to limit the damage. Kirk bought that argument—and Ken-nedy himself was determined to take a clear shot at Georgetown at getting the message out. But he also agreed with Paul that he had to try and limit the political fall-out of Chappaquiddick in coming contests in Maine and New Hampshire, where day after day the right-wing *Manchester Union Leader* was delivering a fusillade of al-legations and fabrications about the accident and its aftermath. *Reader's Digest*, at the time a commonplace in American homes, had weighed in with its own Chappaquiddick hit piece.

So we decided to spend precious, dwindling campaign resources to broadcast a half-hour version of the Georgetown speech just in New England. The broadcast would start with Kennedy talking plainly and directly about Chappaquiddick. Paul Kirk drafted and redrafted suggested language. Carey Parker, who was wary of the idea, got a brief handwritten note—I think from Paul: "*All* New England people want reference to Chappaquiddick"—presumably our political people. Kennedy was resigned as he reviewed and re-vised the text with Parker and me and then recorded the speech. He was also fatalistic about yet another attempt to explain Chappaquiddick even if he knew it had to be made. The Kennedy haters wouldn't be swayed, but perhaps he could move the doubters.

I don't know that the speech achieved even that much, but doing it seemed to lift a burden from the candidate. I also knew that he believed that he was telling the truth. Personally, I had no doubt after an earlier, unguarded moment in his office when the *Washington Star* disputed his account of the direction of the tides when, according to his story, he had swum the waters between Chappaquiddick and Martha's Vineyard after the accident. His reaction, when we discussed the *Star*'s report, was adamant: He said he didn't care what they wrote, goddamn it, he had swum across; he knew what the tides had been like that night and he'd never forget it. But how could we respond to the *Star*? Larry Horowitz asked. With the truth, and that's the truth, Kennedy said, whether they believe me or not. As we were talking about how to handle the issue, we learned, from a series of maps and tidal surveys, that Kennedy was right. He had no way of knowing the material would turn up, but he had been unwilling to look for another way to handle the *Star*. The Carter forces would exploit Chappaquiddick, while barely mentioning the word, to stall Kennedy's momentum as he began to come back in the 1980 race two months later. There's no way for the electorate to know a candidate as those around him do. But the tragedy, not just for Kennedy but for the progressive cause, was that he likely would have been president even before 1980—except for Chappaquiddick and the false conspiracy theories it spawned.

As we headed north for Maine and New Hampshire, we left behind our expensive chartered plane. We took with us a stack of large cardboard charts and Kennedy campaigned nonstop by turning his rallies into town meetings where he made the case for gas rationing and wage and price controls. Now that his views weren't cushioned in caution, Kennedy had a lot he wanted to say and plenty of time to say it. By 2004, primaries and caucuses fell like dominoes one right after another. In 1980, three weeks separated Iowa and Maine, with another two weeks after that to campaign in New Hampshire. And we had a constant companion on the bus that rolled day after day across the Maine tundra long into the night—Governor Joe Brennan, a moderate Democrat who'd come out early for Kennedy. He introduced Kennedy with a rousing call for change at nearly every stop. To counter Brennan, the Carter campaign brought in a former governor, Ken Curtis, who took "vacation" time off from his nonpolitical post as ambassador to Canada. Curtis's incursion had little impact on the race, but an unpredictable one on the future of the U.S. Senate. A few months later, when Edmund Muskie resigned his Senate seat to become secretary of state, Governor Brennan got to appoint his successor. He talked with Kennedy about the choice. The one person, they agreed, who wouldn't be picked was Ken Curtis. Instead, Brennan plucked George Mitchell, Muskie's former aide, off the federal bench; his judgeship had been Muskie's reward for years of faithful service, including his obligatory and endless rounds of golf with Muskie. It was a game Mitchell came to detest, I was told. Once on the bench, Maine lore had it, he'd thrown his golf clubs into the sea and concentrated on tennis. The judgeship had not only rescued him from golf but insulated him from taking sides in the 1980 presidential contest. So he now became a senator, and within a few years, Senate Majority Leader. Ken Curtis went into permanent political obscurity. For him, payback came early.

When all the votes were counted and the caucus process completed, the Maine delegation would be evenly split and Carter would lose it on the most crucial roll call at the national convention. But on caucus night, it wasn't reported that way. The state party apparatus, which Brennan didn't control, claimed another Carter victory.

New Hampshire was next. We were far behind there; our state coordinator, an activist in the McGovern and Udall campaigns, a woman with the wonderfully Yankee name of Dudley Dudley, had joined the "Draft Kennedy" movement before Kennedy decided to run. She had told me Carter was going to "get killed" in New Hampshire in the fall. But the primary was now a different story—and she was coldly realistic about how steep the uphill climb was. You could just sense how steep in audiences whose mood was far different than it had been across the border in Maine. A lot of Democrats showed up to see Kennedy but not necessarily to cheer for him. And they were seeing a mighty drumbeat of television news that made it seem unpatriotic not to support Carter, whatever else they thought of him. A few days before the primary, Tom Quinn, Jerry Brown's campaign manager, a long-ago competitor of mine in high school debate, called me and asked if we could meet at one of Kennedy's rallies. So the press wouldn't see us, we stood outside in the cold. He said he was going home to California; he'd told Brown that all he was doing by staying in was helping Carter. Quinn was right about Brown's impact in New Hampshire. Kennedy lost the state, but Carter's margin was 11 percent, a third of what it had been in Iowa, and the president claimed just 49 percent of the vote. Without Brown's 10 percent, New Hampshire would have been closer—and we could have argued that the momentum was inching our way.

We did have a back stop where we had a Kennedy-friendly electorate and the institutional support to win—or so we thought. It was Illinois. But to get there, we had to get by four big southern primaries. Kennedy's chances in all of them looked bleak. Still we had to make an effort, at least in Florida, especially in the Jewish and black communities in the southern part of the state. Under the reform rules of the Democratic nominating process, in almost every state, the number of delegates you received was proportionate to your share of the vote. The math was inexorable: an opponent who already had a lead in delegates could count on 30 percent or 40 percent even in the later primaries that he lost. A challenger who fell too far behind too soon could never catch up; this is pretty close to what ultimately happened to Kennedy. So he was on a quick trip to Florida, trying to salvage some delegates there, when we found out that he now faced the threat of humiliation—defeat in his home state of Massachusetts.

He flew to Boston for two days of frantic campaigning and we scripted a statewide television spot. This signaled starkly how much trouble he was in, but we had no other choice. House Speaker Tip O'Neill had famously said that people had to be asked for their votes; Kennedy took the adage one long step further. He not only asked Massachusetts Democrats for their votes—but then, on his own, before a union audience, added: "I want your support and quite frankly, I feel I deserve your support." Someone yelled out:

"You got it, Ted." And he did, winning by almost 2 to 1, his first out-right victory of the primary season.

A win at home didn't count. After Massachusetts, we headed for Illinois, our one-time safety net, which turned into a near death trap. In the heady days before the announcement, both sides of the Democratic divide in the state were available to Kennedy. On one side were Rich and Bill Daley, the sons of the legendary mayor of Chicago who'd died in late 1976. On the other was the incumbent mayor, Jane Byrne, who'd been elected in a massive voter revolt the year before, when Daley's colorless successor failed to clean up the snow clogging the streets after a 20-inch blizzard. All politics, even presidential politics, is local in Chicago. The Daleys hadn't welcomed the coming of Byrne; whoever she was for, they'd be against—and vice versa. Carter and Kennedy would be divided between them. I wasn't in the campaign when the choice was made; but as Steve Smith recounted it to me in the days before the primary, Byrne was the mayor and she had the patronage power, which was presumably all-powerful in the city; this confused how Dick Daley exercised power and how Jane Byrne frittered it away. As Steve said to me, "Byrne seemed like the smart choice at the time." She could pull Kennedy through if he ever got in trouble—which by now he was. But so was she; the male-dominated political establishment had tolerated her briefly, then shredded her. Her own temperament, or temper, didn't help—she never encountered a fight she didn't wade into. Kennedy's standing in Illinois as the primary neared wasn't primarily Byrne's fault; but now a vote against him could be a "twofer"—a vote against her, too. We talked about keeping her away from Kennedy. Then, suddenly, I was away from Illinois.

Steve Smith told me to leave the plane for a few days and come to New York to work on a new set of ads. The campaign had just hired David Sawyer, another one of the pioneer media consultants. Steve and I—and often Al Lowenstein—met in Sawyer's editing studio in New York to script and cut spots with him. It was the first time I'd ever done it; one of my favorite spots used videotape of Carter at the plate at a staff baseball game swinging and missing repeatedly. Each time he took a swing, the spot referred to some issue like inflation or the gasoline shortage. It ended: "Three strikes and you're out." Carter looked hapless; the spot was funny—and it was negative. But we couldn't keep playing defense. We had to pull Carter out of the penumbra of the hostage crisis, make him the issue, remind Democrats of why they'd turned against him in the first place.

Al popped in and out—and for the first couple days Steve took me across the street for lunch to La Côte Basque, a classic French restaurant with food and prices to match. It was a big change from the burgers and fries I was eating on the road. It was also the time when I came to know Steve, which was not an easy thing to do. He was, as Ted Kennedy would say in his eulogy for Steve years later, not just his brother-in-law but his "other" brother. He was tough, strong-willed, and sometimes abrupt. By now—and I don't know exactly why—he'd changed his mind about me and decided I was loyal, which to Steve was a primary value.

One afternoon, we returned to Sawyer's studio, expecting Lowenstein to show up. He didn't. But as Steve said while we waited, Al was never on time for anything in his life. A call came from Steve's assistant, Pauline. Al had been shot by a mentally deranged former sixties activist. With a practice honed in tragedy, Steve was all action. Make sure Al had the best doctors. How bad was it? he asked. All but hopeless. Find his kids and Jenny, his ex-wife; tell them and take care of them. Kennedy, who was supposed to speak to the American Federation of Teachers in Manhattan the next morning, left Illinois and headed for the New York hospital where Al lay dying.

I was sitting in a corridor there, writing on a legal pad with my briefcase as a laptop desk. With Secret Service and police everywhere, Kennedy went to Al's room. He emerged to say that he didn't want to give the AFT speech that had already been drafted; he wanted to talk about Al Lowenstein. I was already drafting it, I responded. The next morning, we headed for the event—and a brief confrontation with the union's president Al Shanker, who was supporting Kennedy even though Shanker's views on national security were closer to Senator Scoop Jackson, the hard-line Democratic cold warrior, and the emerging neocons. I'd found this out personally earlier in the campaign, when Shanker complained to Kennedy about my McGovern background. Let's talk about my views, not my staff, was Kennedy's response. Shanker had been at odds with Lowenstein—in the way that two people who agreed on a lot could be divided in the intense ideological hothouse of New York City. Shanker now demurred that talking about Lowenstein was the wrong speech for this union crowd, which was scheduled to endorse Kennedy's long-shot candidacy that day. Kennedy replied it was the speech he was going to give, and that was that.

Kennedy entered a ballroom packed with cheering teachers' union activists, but the mood was transformed by the tone of his opening lines: "I had come here today to speak of inflation and the economy, of education and the cities, and of my opposition to the Administration's policies. But this is not the right day and that is not the right speech." He spoke of what he had seen in the hospital: "Even as he lay dying, Al Lowenstein fought fiercely for his life as he had struggled all his life on behalf of others. . . . If no man is an island, then Allard K. Lowenstein was a continent, a universe, a vast expanse of compassion, conviction and courage." At first, the silence in the ballroom was breathless. The audience wanted a way to approve, to applaud, and the activists rose up as one when Kennedy finally gave them the chance: "We will not accept a society in which a handgun can be bought today"—the reaction was sustained, so strong that Kennedy couldn't finish the sentence—"and fired tomorrow to kill a man like Allard Lowenstein." The teachers endorsed Kennedy and stayed with him all the way to the primary and the convention. The union's political director, Rachelle Horowitz, told me how Shanker explained his support: "I trust Kennedy more with a peashooter than Carter with a nuclear missile."

It was Saturday morning and the Illinois primary was only three days away. Kennedy rushed back to the state. On Monday, as the dyed Chicago River flowed emerald green, he walked in the St. Patrick's Day Parade. And he did walk—to the consternation of the Secret Service. With a raw snow whipping the streets, and his wife Joan clinging to his arm, Kennedy and Mayor Byrne were met with block after block of booing and obscenities. Byrne's reaction was to scowl. Kennedy slowed down to shake hands and separate himself from Byrne. She dropped back to seek dubious refuge next to him; and the catcalls intensified. He walked from one side of the street to the other, surrounded by a swarm of Secret Service and reporters, to greet the friendly faces he spied in the crowd—and not incidentally, escape Byrne again. It was almost comic, but it was painful to see the nation's most famous Irishman beleaguered in the city whose votes had made his brother president.

Because Illinois had taken advantage of an exception to the party rules—and awarded delegates in a winner-take-all process in each of the state's congressional districts—Kennedy's 30 percent of the statewide vote was only worth 14 delegates, while Carter chalked up 165. The slope we had to climb was now sheer. To overcome Carter's lead, Kennedy would have to beat him by almost unbelievable margins in the contests ahead. Editors told their reporters to prepare their stories on Kennedy's withdrawal.

New York looked like our last stand. Yet as we pushed ahead despite the bleak polls, we were dogged, if not cheerful, and Kennedy's inexplicable good spirits kept us going. Carey Parker and I briefed him for a meeting with the *New York Times* editorial board. One of the "facts" we gave him was wrong—he put it out there, and the journalists around the tables corrected him. Downstairs, he motioned Carey and me into the limo, told us what happened, and then gracefully let us off the hook with a classic line: "I'll thank you to let me make my own mistakes; as you may have noticed, I'm very good at it."

At a rain-swept airport in Syracuse, Kennedy climbed off the old prop plane we'd chartered, certain he was about to be endorsed by the local congressman, Jim Hanley. But Hanley too had read that morning's *Daily News* poll, which showed Carter with a 2-to-1 lead. Standing with Kennedy in the rain for twenty minutes or so, all he could manage was to damn the candidate with vague praise. Kennedy was "offering an alternative for consideration." Pressed further, Hanley said Kennedy was "opening up the avenue for dialogue." A reporter asked: But was Hanley for Kennedy, was he going to vote for him? A tongue-tied Hanley responded: "I would have to say that I will keep that private." Kennedy put his arm around Hanley and gave it another try: "You can tell these guys, Jim, they won't tell anybody." Amid the laughter, Susan Spencer from CBS, her camera rolling, asked Hanley to go ahead and say it "off the record." But Hanley stood firm in his quagmire of indecision, despite one last jocular nudge from Kennedy: "Come on, Jim, do the right thing." When that didn't work, Kennedy shrugged and called the event off: "Well, Jim, I think they've run out of film." The candidate led a wet gaggle of reporters back to the plane.

So Kennedy, apparently headed for electoral doom in New York and Connecticut, which voted the same day, fought on, with astonishing élan, with persistence but not bitterness. In our TV ads, we were showing Carter striking out—on inflation, energy, health care. But we had only $200,000 to spend on airtime; Carter had more than $700,000—and a new spot to defend himself against a potentially lethal mistake in New York. Nearly three weeks before, his administration had cast a vote at the United Nations referring to Jerusalem as "occupied" territory and condemning Israeli settlements there and in the West Bank. The vote was a first for U.S. diplomacy—and as the anger built, and the politicos inside the Carter campaign weighed in, the White House conceded that vote had been a "mistake." Then had come a Carter ad, broadcast with numbing repetition, reaffirming his support for Israel. But we weren't letting him off the hook. At "all stops in New York City," as our briefing book put it, Kennedy was to denounce "the decision to change [a] long-standing position and vote . . . against our ally and friend, Israel. The buck does not rest on the Secretary of State's desk; it rests on the President's desk."

The polls didn't budge. The Carter forces had a smugness that I thought just might backfire. They were already trumpeting their inevitable triumph, asking why Kennedy was running anymore; he couldn't win enough delegates now anyway. I said, hopefully, to Carey Parker that this was dangerous: the voters didn't like to be told that they didn't count—and maybe underneath the surface, there was a feeling of unease with Carter, that it wasn't time to close down the process and irrevocably settle on him. The last weekend before the primary, we motorcaded to Brooklyn, where Kennedy was scheduled to speak to an ultra-Orthodox group. We expected hundreds of people, a thousand if we were lucky. Instead, the candidate and all of us with him were engulfed by what seemed like an entire community, cheering and pushing forward as the Secret Service struggled to get Kennedy to the stage. One police officer told me he thought there were like 10,000 people there. They weren't buying Carter's excuse for calling Jerusalem "occupied" territory. The crowd was exhilarating, but a little dangerous: at one point, I picked up a youngster who was being pressed under the barricades into the staff and reporters jammed up against a building and handed him back to his father. It was almost possible to believe that we were gaining ground—especially when we encountered another rousing reception from a very different crowd, as we returned to Manhattan and drove past the gay bars on the far West Side. Patrons poured out waving hand-lettered Kennedy signs. It was a nice piece of advance work; but maybe it wasn't just manufactured—maybe the reaction was real. Kennedy just said, well, he hoped more people shared it. It had been an extraordinary day of light in the gathering political darkness. But the glimmers of hope were extinguished on Monday when the last Harris Poll in the *Daily News* predicted a Carter landslide by a margin of 20 points.

Steve Smith told me to come to his office the next morning. If the results were what they looked like, he said, Kennedy had to quit. I didn't argue; what else could we do now? Steve asked me to draft a withdrawal statement. It took me a little over an hour; there were passages in it that later appeared in Kennedy's convention speech. Steve's assistant Pauline, white-haired, omnicompetent, and the soul of discretion, typed up the draft. Steve and I looked it over. Each of us kept a copy. I left mine back in my hotel room and set off on a walk that took me from Fifty-ninth Street to the tip of lower Manhattan and back. I stopped for a cup of coffee and browsed in a couple of bookstores, carefully confining myself to the sections on Greek, Roman, and medieval history—about as far away as I could get from the events unfolding in the polling places I occasionally passed by.

As I came through the revolving doors of the hotel around 6 P.M., a staffer grabbed me and threw me into a car headed for Steve and Jean Kennedy Smith's house on the Upper East Side. I was wanted, urgently, was all the explanation I got. After I walked into the house, Steve asked me where I'd been. Before I could answer, he said it didn't matter; had I heard the exit polls? Kennedy was winning New York—not by a little, but in a landslide—and might even win Connecticut. He did. The candidate who had taken a quick trip to Washington, was hurrying back. Obviously, we needed something different than what we had drafted; we needed a victory statement. When I handed it to Kennedy later—the first time I'd seen him that day—he glanced down at it and then before he started reading looked up and just said: "Thank you." Then he laughed: "Can you believe *this*?"

Out of money and out of chances, we had rented a small ballroom at a modest midtown hotel. As the returns were pouring in, so were the pols; the original Kennedy supporters who'd made themselves scarce in recent weeks were now making an appearance. I stopped to chat with Jimmy Breslin, the fabled columnist who'd come out for Kennedy just before the primary after taking him to Sunday mass at a local parish church in Queens. The mass had been another straw in the wind no one noticed: the congregation—and this never happened in a Catholic church in those days—had actually applauded as Kennedy walked down the aisle. Now, on this victory night, Breslin spotted one of the prodigal pols preening in the hotel lobby before waiting to go upstairs to share in the glow of success. Breslin shouted at him to "get out"; he hadn't been there when it counted; how dare he show "his fucking cowardly face now?" As the profanity rained down on him, the pol retreated, came in another door, and found a back way to the ballroom. The crowd went crazy when Kennedy hit the stage. After a struggle to quiet the applause so he could speak, he set it off again as he began with what was now the city's trademark slogan: "I love New York."

Leaving behind the euphoria of New York, we headed for the liberal Democratic heartland of Wisconsin on our Air New England charter. The boxy, cumbersome commuter plane was supposedly carrying a reborn candidacy on the move, but the ride was nerve-wracking and agonizingly slow; we had to put down every few hundred miles to refuel. On approach to one airport, the pilot, who had never been there before, couldn't find the runway. Larry Horowitz's trademark phrase was "*This* is beyond belief"—and all too often, in 1980, it was. This time, Larry and I, and the anxious lead agents on our Secret Service detail, stood in the passage behind the cockpit staring out the windows to figure out where we were supposed to land. On another flight, Kennedy's twelve-year-old son Patrick, who was "helping" Carey and me with speeches—I saved one set of the index cards he'd written and they still hang framed on the wall of his father's Senate office—had an asthma attack as we lumbered across the sky. We had to land short of our destination. Soon, short of money or not, we were traveling commercially and sometimes in chartered small jets. We'd done that before with the press flying in formation around us in their own planes; we even chartered 727s near the end of the primaries.

No matter how we got to where we were going, April was a cruel month that led nowhere. When a new poll suggested that Kennedy might run strong in Wisconsin, the president appeared on television and announced an imminent breakthrough in the hostage crisis. It was a phony moment—nothing more than an offer by Iran's figurehead president to take "custody" of the hostages, which never actually occurred. But as Hamilton Jordan wrote, it was "good news" for Carter. Watching *The Today Show*, we all knew what that day in Wisconsin would bring: instead of a close race, Carter snatched up another convincing victory.

Then, days later, on April 11, we had a sudden infusion of desperately needed campaign cash thanks to Steve Smith and Miles Rubin, a member of "the Malibu mafia" who'd given or raised hundreds of thousands of dollars for the 1972 McGovern campaign. Miles had come up with a loophole in the $1,000 limit on contributions now set by federal law: artists could produce twenty-five, fifty, or even two hundred lithographs for the Kennedy campaign and the entire edition would be a contribution worth no more than the price of the paper it was printed on—in each case, less than $1,000. The campaign could then turn around and "sell" each lithograph to donors for $250, $500, or $1,000. Andy Warhol, Robert Rauschenberg, Jamie Wyeth, and other artists signed on.

We had just walked into a reception to thank the artists at the duplex apartment of Kennedy's sister Pat Lawford on the East River in Manhattan when Rauschenberg, standing on a landing at the top of a staircase, spotted the candidate, shouted out "Teddy," and promptly plunged headfirst down the spiral marble stairs. Kennedy, the Secret Service, and the rest of us watched transfixed as it seemed to happen in slow motion. Kennedy broke the mood, turned to the doctor who was traveling with us and told him to help. Cleaned up, with bandages on, Rauschenberg seemed no worse for wear and the party went on.

We had enough resources to go on, but like the flying Dutchman of American politics, we were looking for a place to win. And there was one, a big one that might be within reach. It was Pennsylvania. We had an ad featuring the actor Carroll O'Connor, who played Archie Bunker in the landmark sitcom *All in the Family*; on April 14, we put the ad on the air in Pennsylvania. Bunker was a blue-collar, right-wing loudmouth whose stereotypical outbursts exposed intolerance for what it was. O'Connor himself was now one of the most authentic figures in America. Volunteering to help, O'Connor wrote his own script. It was blunter than anything the candidate had said, but maybe only Carroll O'Connor could have said it this way: Carter "may be the most Republican president since Herbert Hoover and he may give us a depression that will make Hoover's look like prosperity." The minute that our media consultant David Sawyer and I saw it, we knew it was dynamite. It could shake up the race anywhere, but it was spot on for Pennsylvania—a perfect pitch to both blue-collar Democrats and progressives in the Philadelphia suburbs.

The next day, the Service Employees Union endorsed Kennedy, and Philadelphia mayor Bill Green, whose father had all but kidnapped the 1960 Pennsylvania delegation for JFK, finally decided to defy the odds and do what he'd wanted to do all along. He, too, came out for Kennedy, whose appearance at a rally the year before had given Green's own campaign for mayor a crucial boost. Suddenly

Pennsylvania was starting to look like Kennedy country. ABC News even reported that some voters were wondering if Carter was using the hostage crisis as a political tool. But the Carter forces had another weapon in their arsenal. Deploying it would poison an already rancid race; but facing the possibility of defeat in another one of the country's largest states, one Carter would have to carry in the fall if he was the nominee, his managers hit the airwaves with a new series of spots attacking Kennedy's character—not by focusing explicitly on Chappaquiddick, but with code words that evoked it like "trust" and "character."

The Carter ads assumed, correctly, that Pennsylvania was really three different states: Philadelphia and the suburbs, where the character attacks didn't resonate; the old anthracite region around Scranton and Wilkes-Barre, where primordial, predominantly Irish loyalty to the Kennedys might blunt the attacks; and the area west of the Allegheny Mountains, including Pittsburgh, where bread-and-butter Democrats were socially conservative. There, the Carter ads stopped Kennedy cold. As the returns were reported long into the night, we could have drawn a line right down a map of the state; the Alleghenies were a breakwater that turned back the Kennedy tide in eastern Pennsylvania and marked the start of a Carter wave from the central to the western part of the state. If Kennedy had swept Pennsylvania, the nominating process would have blown wide open; instead, after endless hours of counting, with Bill Green pacing the floor, oscillating between confidence and doom, we learned that Kennedy had squeaked by with a 9,700-vote margin statewide.

The narrowness of the victory did spawn a quintessentially Philadelphia story. When it came time to formally organize the state's delegation and elect its chairman, the Carter forces tried to seize control. Our choice for chairman was Bill Green. The decision came down to one wavering delegate, who'd been assiduously courted by the White House. As he prepared to announce his vote, we were told, Vince Fumo, a Kennedy backer and powerful state senator from South Philadelphia, with an iron grip on local patronage and a commitment to loyalty as a cardinal virtue, got up, walked across the room, and stood wordlessly in front of the wavering delegate. In another place where all politics is local, the blandishments of the White House were no match for Fumo's glare. The delegate got out one word—"Kennedy"—and we controlled the delegation.

The economy was lurching into "stagflation"—a painful, unprecedented combination of inflation and job losses. With just four days to campaign in Michigan, I block-printed the statistics on yellow pads for Kennedy: "Saginaw—Unemployment Rate 15 to 17%"; "Flint—Unemployment—Over 13%"; "Grand Rapids—GM Plant Layoffs—7200 workers." We weren't seeing places, or crowds, that wanted four more years of Carter. On the eve of the caucuses, however, a U.S. military operation designed to rescue the hostages failed as one helicopter broke down, another got lost in a sandstorm, and a third crashed into a military transport plane in the Iranian desert. Eight U.S. soldiers died. We suspended campaigning, and left for Washington so fast that some of our traveling press corps never got to check out of the hotel and left their bags behind. A lot of Democrats who were moving to us rallied around the flag one last time as they usually rally around presidents in a crisis. JFK had marveled that his approval rating soared to 83 percent after the Bay of Pigs; "The worse you do," he said, "the better they like you." In the Michigan caucuses, we eked out a "victory," taking 71 delegates to Carter's 70.

The failed rescue mission marked the final moment in the primaries when the hostage crisis functioned as a safety net for the president. He apparently sensed that the rationalization for not campaigning had run its course—and holding to it could only hurt him. On April 30, he announced that he was ending his self-imposed moratorium on campaigning, although he still refused to debate Kennedy. His timing was convenient. The next week's contests in the southern states of Texas, Tennessee, and North Carolina—and the precincts of conservative Indiana—weren't contests at all. Carter won them all without campaigning. We were back where we were in March—written off, but this time even further behind in delegates. Week after week, the results were all wrong. We'd land and the advance staff would hand me a page of discouraging numbers: "Maryland 8:45 . . . 41% [for Kennedy]; Nebraska 21% [in] . . . C52 . . . K35." Kennedy would glance at them and then we would go to his hotel room to "go over tomorrow."

After another loss in Oregon, when we had flown low over and around Mount St. Helens to get a better view of the smoldering volcano just days before it exploded, the only tomorrow we had left was Super Tuesday on June 3. California, Ohio, New Jersey, and four smaller states would mark the last and single biggest day of a long primary campaign. Kennedy had to refresh his rationale for running: If he couldn't claim enough delegates to secure the nomination no matter what happened on Super Tuesday, then why was he still in the race? We needed to put down a marker and "commit" news. I suggested we make a public offer to Carter: If he debated Kennedy before June 3, Kennedy would treat the primaries that day as a referendum; if Carter won the most votes on Super Tuesday after a debate, Kennedy would withdraw. If, on the other hand, Kennedy prevailed, he would stay in the race all the way to the convention. Kennedy liked the idea—first, because he resented Carter's use of the hostages as a pretext to avoid debating; and second, because he was convinced Carter would lose in the fall, was ready to engage on the issues while Carter was rusty, and felt that he, the president, and the party had to resolve the contest once and for all. But without a debate and a subsequent Super Tuesday vote to decide the outcome, Kennedy wasn't going to just walk away from the case—and cause—he'd been passionately making since Georgetown. In fact, the speech draft in which he issued his challenge previewed the first line of his convention speech more than two months later: "This is a campaign not for a candidate alone, but for a cause."

We decided to announce the offer at an appearance at the Los Angeles Press Club—an institution housed in a worn building in a run-down section of Hollywood. A day or two before the event, I took both my handwritten and a typed copy of the draft, the only ones we had at that point, into a television studio in San Francisco so Kennedy could review the material in a holding room before we departed for the airport and a quick side trip to Albuquerque. We had just left the studio and our motorcade was approaching the on-ramp of the freeway when I realized that I'd left the drafts behind. Not only could a reporter pick them up off the desk, but we now had nothing more than the original notes I'd made that were stuffed in my briefcase. Against all rules, I ordered the terrified driver of our staff car to pull out of the motorcade. I can't, he said. Just do it, I ordered, with no time to explain why. Carey Parker and Nelson Rising, a young L.A. developer who was raising money for us, sat stunned as the driver did a U-turn and we headed back to the TV station. I told them what had happened, but in the pre-cell phone era, there was no way to contact the motorcade and explain. As we screeched to a halt at the station, I jumped out, huffed and puffed my way past the security guard and across the newsroom, and retrieved my file folder. We then raced toward the airport, hoping to catch up with Kennedy, only to see the campaign charter accelerating down the runway; the Secret Service doesn't let presidents or candidates sit in a plane on the tarmac waiting for the staff.

We couldn't get a commercial flight to Albuquerque that would arrive before Kennedy was finished; we decided to meet up with him in L.A. We had no money to spare, so Nelson broke the federal campaign finance law and paid for the tickets—and then for an expensive lunch in Beverly Hills. Hours later, when Kennedy arrived, he acted surprised to see us and asked: "Where have you guys been?"

As expected, Carter rejected the debate challenge. But the speech did make news and it energized our troops, who were led in California by Clinton's future secretary of commerce, Ron Brown. Most state campaign managers instinctively downplay expectations, but Ron said we had a real chance. The problem, again, was that Carter had the money to blanket California with television ads. We needed at least enough to keep our organization going and our offices open. For obvious reasons, the "smart" money wasn't coming to us. We had some liberal contributors in California. One event was hosted by Frances Lear, then the wife of TV producer Norman Lear, the creator of *All in the Family*. I went outside, and wandering around the grounds, came upon Norman standing alone in the garden. His wife had banished him from the house because he was, for the moment, supporting the emerging third-party candidacy of John Anderson, a moderate pro-choice congressman who'd been trounced in the Republican primary. I invited Norman to enter his own house, but he seemed afraid to go in.

We had one group that was ready to give—the newly assertive gay community.

Gay rights had provoked a brief but intense disagreement earlier in the campaign. Kennedy hadn't been in the forefront of the issue, even though the Senate sponsor of the bill banning employment discrimination against gays was his Massachusetts colleague Paul Tsongas. As the campaign unfolded, gay activists pushed to know where Kennedy stood. Post-Iowa and post-Georgetown, I sensed that he wasn't in the mood to duck tough issues. When we gathered to argue this one out—which ultimately turned on whether we'd propose a gay rights plank in the Democratic platform—some of the most senior political advisers in the campaign were appalled. Paul Kirk reviewed the costs: It could kill us in Ohio; it could make things worse all across the Midwest; Kennedy was already regarded as too liberal—and this issue was way out of the mainstream. And it was—in 1980. I thought that arguing the politics wasn't a promising approach. Instead, I said that when President Kennedy had to confront the question of civil rights, he knew the political price to be paid; Lyndon Johnson had warned that the South could be lost to the Democrats for a generation. But as the crisis mounted in 1963, when the decision couldn't be postponed, Kennedy knew there was only one answer he could give—and in proposing far-reaching legislation, he also became the first president to say that civil rights was "a moral issue." It was one of the great moments of his presidency. Now Edward Kennedy was facing another issue that was a matter of simple justice. Would he oppose discrimination and support a measure of equal treatment for gays? Kennedy said that when it was put that way, he didn't see that he had any other choice. Kirk shook his head. Kennedy responded: "Paul, look at it this way. It's the upside of my downside; nobody thinks I have a self-interest."

On May 21, we were driving toward a gay fund-raising event in the Hollywood Hills. The sponsoring committee had forty-five members, the majority of whom would die from the then unknown disease of AIDS. As we briefed Kennedy in the limousine, he asked where Jim Foster was. Foster was a gay activist from San Francisco who'd kept the local Kennedy headquarters there open with his own money and some off-the-books contributions when the campaign had ordered offices across the country closed to save money after the Iowa defeat. Told that Foster was on the bus with the press and the rest of the staff, Kennedy asked, Why are you guys briefing me instead of Jim? He ordered the motorcade to stop. Foster was plucked from the back of the bus. I squeezed onto a jump seat in the limousine alongside someone else, and Jim sat next to Kennedy as we reviewed the questions the audience was likely to ask.

The national headquarters had ordered the fund-raiser closed to the press. Foster said that this would be a problem for the gay community. Were we embarrassed to be there? In the driveway outside the massive house, Kennedy ordered the event open. If we let the reporters stand outside, they'd just think—and write—that we believed there was something wrong with where we were. During the Q-and-A period, Sheldon Andelson, the first openly gay man on the Board of Regents of the University of California, challenged Kennedy. Why had he come here to collect gay contributions but been too afraid to let the press in? Kennedy, who would deliver Andelson's eulogy a few years later, responded by asking him to turn around and look at the balcony off the second floor, where we'd hastily provided a place for reporters and cameras. Kennedy introduced him with genuine gusto to several of the correspondents: "Sheldon, that's Cassie Mackin from ABC News . . ."—and down the line he went. The crowd laughed and applauded. (In the platform negotiations a month later, the Carter campaign was willing to concede almost anything if Kennedy would just agree to ax the gay rights plank. He would reject the offer outright.)

We had just enough money to run on fumes, keep the plane flying and the political operation going—and attempt something that had never happened in the modern history of California: win a statewide primary with virtually no paid media against an opponent who could afford wave after wave of airtime. Our pollster told us that while California and New Jersey were at least possible, Ohio was too far gone. Kennedy pushed back; he had his own instinct about Ohio—where unemployment was soaring, inflation was double-digit, and mortgage rates were above 13 percent. But the rest of us accepted the polling results, ignoring the reality that we'd only survived to this point by taking risks—and that another one was needed to overcome the long-shot odds for the nomination. The strategy of skipping Ohio sparked a fierce response from our own people on the ground, led by Paul Tully, gruff, passionate, and acknowledged as the best organizer in decades of Democratic politics. The Carter campaign believed the numbers, too, and briefed the national press that they were going to win the state by a big margin. Carter ventured out of the Rose Garden to appear in Columbus and Cleveland, where he was picketed by trade unionists protesting his economic policies. But he had a flood tide of advertising—and until the very end, we overflew Ohio as we shuttled from California to New Jersey, with brief pit stops in other states.

Tully had raised $60,000 in grassroots money to buy Ohio ads for three days. Mark Shields, now a newspaper columnist, had canvassed at one steelworkers' bar and reported that they were voting for Kennedy. Finally, on the last weekend of the primaries, the candidate flatly ordered a last-minute stop in Cleveland. Our rally was at the Arcade, a multi-tiered, indoor Victorian-era kind of mall that then had few if any stores. But that day it had people—thousands of them—and each level echoed with blasts of foot-stomping and applause. In the plane on the way to San Jose, on election eve, Kennedy said he never should have listened to the polling; maybe even now he could win Ohio.

The next morning at 6 A.M., he greeted workers at the Lockheed plant in Burbank—and then headed east for New Jersey and Washington. We were flying in a cone of ignorance with no contact with anyone on the ground about the exit polls. It was just as well, because the first reports we got that afternoon in Newark weren't encouraging. By the time we reached Washington a couple hours later, however, the next wave of exit interviews had been calculated. It looked like we might just pull off a string of victories; even Ohio was close, and Tully had gone into action. He put operatives on the phone to radio stations in southern Ohio, Carter's best area; they said they were calling from the National Weather Service to issue a tornado warning. People should not leave their homes.

Kennedy carried California, New Jersey, New Mexico, Rhode Island, and even South Dakota; he lost Ohio by 7 percent, and with it, the last best chance for the nomination. That state, Carter had touted in advance, was his firewall; and so it became. Politics, in victory or defeat, always echoes with "ifs." If Kennedy had taken all the big states, including Ohio, Carter's position might have crumbled. A discontented party was, at best, resigned to renominating him; he had enough delegates and there was a rule that required them to vote for him. But a defeat in Ohio could have pushed the worried delegates so hard that they might have voted to change that rule.

Carter called Kennedy; we convened in Kennedy's living room in McLean the day after the primary to discuss how to respond. Where could—and should—the Kennedy campaign go from here? Was there any way forward, now that Carter had a clear majority to lock down the nomination? Paul Kirk, someone I'd come to know and respect for his integrity, but who I seemed fated to clash with, surprised the handful of us in the room by suggesting it was time for Kennedy to pack it in. It was dangerous to fight all the way to the convention in August; the party might never forgive Kennedy if a wounded Carter lost to Reagan. Kennedy pushed back: If people wanted to blame him, they could already point to his protracted fight in the primaries. And Democrats stood no chance against Reagan if we didn't offer the country some sense of hope. I believed that Kennedy deserved, and for the sake of any future presidential run needed, a chance for Americans to see him at his best, in a debate or more likely a speech at the convention. So I suggested Kennedy return Carter's call and set up a meeting at the White House—where he could ambush Carter by renewing the debate challenge, not just face to face with the president but to the national press.

Kirk was angry. We couldn't blindside the president of the United States. Carter would assume the meeting was to make peace, not escalate the battle. The conversation started to drift; maybe there was something else we could do. What was it? Kennedy sharply asked. He got up, went into his study, and phoned the White House.

The next day, he was with Carter for almost an hour. Right afterward, Kennedy asked me to record his recollections of the encounter. He opened with a conciliatory tone, telling Carter he was "realistic about the arithmetic." Carter replied: "You've had a lot of hard words to say about me. I know campaign rhetoric, but I've never attacked you personally." Kennedy, who was incensed about the Carter ads questioning his character, interrupted the president: "Those ads of yours didn't handle me with kid gloves." When Kennedy pressed for a debate, Carter didn't respond at first, but then asked whether, if there was a debate, Kennedy would publicly pledge to support the nominee. Kennedy, who had repeatedly refused to give that kind of blank check as long as Carter wouldn't give some on the issues, held his ground: He'd have to see where Carter ended up on the economy. Kennedy in effect was inviting the president to put forward a new economic plan—not just to the convention but to Congress—and to do it now. Carter didn't accept that, or didn't want to. His anger showed in a diary entry that was later made public: Kennedy "seems to be obsessed with the idea of a personal debate." Front-runners never want a debate, but "never" is a dangerous word in politics. This time, the president missed the point—that a debate was now his best way to avoid a convention battle. When politics gets personal, anger clouds judgment.

Kennedy now had a rationale to carry his case to the convention in New York City. And we could file a series of "minority reports" on the platform. They seemed like a fail-safe way to guarantee that Kennedy could speak to the delegates and the country; if worse came to worst, he could take the podium to argue for his minority reports.

For a short while, it appeared we might not have to settle for that. Party leaders who hadn't endorsed either candidate—New York governor Hugh Carey, Senate Majority Leader Robert Byrd, and Washington superlawyer Edward Bennett Williams—called for a rules change so delegates could vote their conscience in an "open convention." Edmund Muskie, who had become Carter's secretary of state a few months before, was suddenly touted as the alternative choice; he didn't discourage the speculation. Neither did we: If

Carter's delegates were freed, we calculated that we were better organized that anyone else to pick up the pieces—and our count
showed that virtually every one of our delegates, who'd stood with
us in the hard months of the primaries, would stick with Kennedy
all the way.

On Monday, August 11, 1980, the opening night of the convention in
New York City, Carey, Ed Williams, and our campaign prosecuted
the fight to repeal what we had named "the robot rule": Delegates
shouldn't be forced to vote for a candidate no matter what the consequences to the party or how circumstances had changed. We finished the fight, the roll was called, and the rule held; there was no
doubt left that Carter would be the nominee. In his hotel suite at the
Waldorf-Astoria, Kennedy matter-of-factly said: "That's it." I hur-
riedly block-printed a brief statement on yellow legal sheets; I
couldn't bring myself to write it until that moment. Kennedy
glanced at them and left, papers in hand, for a hastily convened press
conference in the hotel to announce he was withdrawing from the
race. He refused to say unequivocally that he would support the
nominee. He was waiting for the outcome of the platform debate
and Carter's formal nomination on Wednesday; he returned to the
living room of the suite to rehearse the speech that the Carter people
had agreed, reluctantly, to let him give.

The first notes I had made weeks before reveal that reluctance.
Curiously, I'd scrawled them on a 5-by-8-inch envelope containing a
direct-mail solicitation for the propaganda magazine *Soviet Life* that
had arrived at my house. I hadn't even opened it, but it was the nearest scrap of paper when I suddenly had a burst of thoughts about the
speech. The return address on the envelope was "Pushkin Square,
Moscow." I later wondered how conservatives would have reacted if
they'd known that this was where Kennedy's convention speech
started.

My notes contemplated the one expedient that would allow Kennedy to speak in prime time even if our fail-safe failed and the
president's men moved the platform debate to the afternoon: the

nominating speeches had to be in prime time—and Kennedy could always "second" his own nomination. He could dispose of the awkwardness in a phrase and move on to the message: "I have come here tonight not to second a nomination"—in the final version it became "not to argue as a candidate"—but "because I am committed to a cause," which finally became "to affirm a cause."

But seconding his own nomination felt forced and we didn't want to be forced to do it. In the run-up to the convention, Paul Kirk negotiated with Carter's top command, who wanted an iron-clad guarantee that Kennedy would endorse Carter. But before the rules vote, Paul wouldn't go that far, so he simply told them Kennedy would do the right thing. Our political director Carl Wagner warned Carter operatives that we could distribute "crickets," tiny tin noisemakers, to the delegates, and when the president gave his speech, well, have you ever heard the sound of a thousand crickets chirping? The good cop–bad cop approach did the trick—and we had a deal that Kennedy could speak in a prime-time platform debate. The one thing that wasn't negotiable was that Kennedy had to speak after the debate on changing the robot rule; the Carter forces weren't ready to run the risk that Kennedy might stampede the convention before they had their nominating majority locked in. In any event, I had initially cast the draft as an acceptance speech because I was going to show it to Kennedy over the weekend, and while he almost certainly foresaw the outcome of the rules fight, he was battling hard and didn't need to face defeat before it came.

Before putting pen to pad, I'd asked Joel Perwin, a young Judiciary Committee staffer I'd first known when he was a national championship debater at Harvard, to locate transcripts of Ronald Reagan's syndicated radio show. I'd occasionally heard it, and had a feeling it would provide the fodder for a mocking assault whether Kennedy was nominated or defeated. The most far-fetched and unforgettable sally was Reagan's assertion that "eighty percent of air pollution comes from plants and trees." When I first saw it, I asked Perwin the question Kennedy later asked me: "Did he really say this?" In a federal archive of Richard Nixon's vice-presidential papers, Joel also dug up an intriguing series of letters between Nixon and Reagan, who often wrote his in longhand. We had the Xerox copies and they were amusing: "Under his tousled boyish hair cut [JFK] is still old Karl Marx." There was also a telegram from "Mr. and Mrs. Ronald Reagan" urging Nixon to pick Goldwater for vice president in 1960: "Cannot support ticket if it included Rockefeller." (JFK would have been happy to see Nixon take Reagan's advice; the '60 election wouldn't have been close.) I didn't use any of the correspondence; the radio transcripts were enough and they sounded similar notes: "Fascism was really the basis of the New Deal"; the income tax was "invented by Karl Marx." I had fun stitching all this into the speech. Kennedy—and the convention—would relish it.

I also went through Kennedy's past speeches, marked the best paragraphs, and put them on file cards. From the unused withdrawal statement in New York: "Someone has to speak for those who have no voice, to stand for those who are weak or exploited, to strive for those who are left out or left behind." I redrafted the words: "It is the glory and the greatness of our tradition to speak for those who have no voice, to remember those who are forgotten, to respond to the frustrations and fulfill the aspirations of all Americans seeking a better life in a better land." I slightly amended a passage from another earlier speech to read: "The poor may be out of political fashion, but they are not without human needs."

The first draft was written the Thursday and Friday before the convention opened, in a small study next to Kennedy's Senate office. I wasn't finished when Kennedy was about to depart for New York, so I said I'd just take the shuttle and catch up with him. The campaign was short on cash; Kennedy had accepted federal funding, so he couldn't spend his own money. When I got to the Waldorf, I found that Carey Parker and I were sharing the other bedroom in the candidate's suite. I took the draft into the living room and read it over with Kennedy, Parker, and John Douglas, the trusted veteran of the RFK Justice Department who was invariably present to offer counsel at crucial moments. All good speeches have an inner logic that isn't labored or contrived, but natural and almost instinctive. In his or her head, the writer has to hear not only the speaker's voice, not just the sound of the language, but the flow of the argument.

That's what I thought I had done. I was expecting instant appreciation. It wasn't forthcoming. Douglas said the draft was "excellent"—which was high praise from him. Kennedy dissented: "I'm not sure this does it." I was frustrated and worried; the last thing we needed was to start all over again. I argued back. It was the right speech, it would work; we could tweak it, but it would be a disaster to rewrite it to death. Kennedy raised his voice; he didn't agree and that was that. At that point, I did something I still can't believe. I slammed my briefcase down on the floor, said do whatever the hell you want, and stalked out, slamming the door behind me.

I was sitting in a chair in the next room staring straight ahead—how could I have lost it that way?—when an appalled Carey Parker walked in, accompanied by Douglas. Kennedy had gone off to a meeting but he'd soon be back. Douglas calmly said: Let's go in and start again—and maybe you ought to start by saying you're sorry. When the time came, I did just that. Kennedy told me to forget it, although I had been, he added, "kind of fresh." Douglas commented that the speech was "ninety-five percent there." Kennedy had some edits—and he wanted to send the draft to Arthur Schlesinger and Ted Sorenson, who'd both written speeches for his brothers. Then he asked if we'd all like to have a drink. I was relieved and grateful.

Schlesinger and Sorenson sent edits the next morning and Carey and I incorporated several of them. More important, both Schlesinger and Sorenson signed off on the speech, having resisted every speechwriter's inveterate tendency, including mine, to submit an alternative draft. With me to New York I'd brought *Words Jack Loved*, a privately published collection of JFK's favorite quotes and poems, along with his own best lines, compiled by Ted Kennedy for family and close friends. For the passage at the close of the convention speech, I took liberties with a passage from Tennyson's *Ulysses*; a couple of the phrases were wrong if we won—and too painful if we lost. So I struck out several of them:

> *I am part of all that I have met . . .*
> *Tho much is taken, much abides, ~~and tho~~*
> *~~We are not now that strength which in old days~~*

Moved heaven and earth; that which we are, we are
One equal temper of heroic hearts,
Made weak by time and fate, but strong in will
To strive, to seek, to find, and not to yield.

During practices, when he reached the language on the Tele-PrompTer roll congratulating "President Carter on his victory here," Kennedy, sitting in his bathrobe with Carey and me, waved his index finger in a circle as a signal to skip ahead. He was going to say what he had to—but not over and over.

We still had two hurdles to overcome. First, Kennedy worried that he might lose his voice while he was speaking; it had happened, for no apparent reason, once or twice before. Larry Horowitz, the adviser who was also a Stanford M.D., had come up with a foul-tasting elixir of honey, hot water, and vinegar. There was no scientific basis for it, Larry told us, but Kennedy thought the placebo worked—and so it did. The candidate would gulp down the concoction just before he left for the Convention Hall at Madison Square Garden. Second, because Kennedy was close to convinced that the TelePrompTer would break down, we had to take special precautions—as I discovered a few hours before the speech when I told him I was going to watch it on television in the hotel suite. He responded, Oh no, you're not; if I'm giving this, you're going to be there. And he had an assignment for me. While Carey Parker would be stationed next to the prompter operator to make sure the right text was scrolling on the screens, I was to sit on the steps just to the side of the podium. If the prompter broke, Kennedy would circle his hand behind his back and I'd hold up a sheet with the page number writ large while simultaneously saying, for example, "Seventeen, middle," so he could flip to the right place in the backup typed text in front of him.

As Kennedy mounted the podium on Tuesday and I slid onto my assigned step just feet below it, the floor was engulfed in a sea of blue Kennedy signs. The Carter forces had accorded him 15 minutes. He would take 45. The "opener" was a natural; it conceded defeat, but harkened back to the biggest victory of the primaries: "Well, things worked out a little different from the way I thought, but let me tell you, I still love New York." Kennedy forced his way through the cheers as his voice played rhythmically across the balanced cadences:

I am asking you to renew our commitment to a fair and lasting prosperity that can put America back to work.

This is the cause that brought me into the campaign and that sustained me for nine months across 100,000 miles in 40 different states. We had our losses, but the pain of our defeats is far, far less than the pain of the people that I have met.

We have learned that it is important to take issues seriously, but never to take ourselves too seriously.

The serious issue before us tonight is the case for which the Democratic Party has stood in its finest hours, the cause that keeps our Party young and makes it, in the second century of its age, the largest political party in this republic and the longest lasting political party on this planet. . . .

Now I take the unusual step of carrying the case and commitment of my campaign personally to our national convention. I speak out of a deep sense of urgency about the anguish and anxiety I have seen across America. . . .

The economic plank of this platform on its face concerns only material things, but it is also a moral issue that I raise tonight. It has taken many forms over many years. In this campaign and in this country that we seek to lead, the challenge in 1980 is to give our voice and our vote for these fundamental Democratic principles. . . .

This was the Kennedy forged in the fires of a long primary campaign, but most of the country and most of the convention were seeing him that way for the first time. The Carter delegates were cheering, too, and across the floor I saw people being swept away, standing on chairs, a Democratic Party united at last as Kennedy launched into a master class on how to deal with Reagan:

The 1980 Republican convention was awash with crocodile tears for our economic distress, but it is by their long record and not their recent words that you shall know them.

The same Republicans who are talking about the crisis of unemployment have nominated a man who once said, and I quote, "Unemployment insurance is a prepaid vacation plan for freeloaders." And that nominee is no friend of labor.

[A roar came up from the floor]

The same Republicans who are talking about the problems of the inner cities have nominated a man who said, and I quote, "I have included in my morning and evening prayers every day the prayer that the Federal Government not bail out New York." And that nominee is no friend of this city and our great urban centers across this Nation.

[More rolling thunder as the convention crackled in anticipation of what came next]

The same Republicans who are talking about security for the elderly have nominated a man who said just four years ago that "Participation in Social Security should be made voluntary." And that nominee is no friend of the senior citizens of this nation.

[The response was continually rising—but Kennedy cut through the noise]

The same Republicans who are talking about preserving the environment have nominated a man who last year made the preposterous statement, and I quote, "Eighty percent of air pollution comes from plants and trees." And that nominee is no friend of the environment.

[The convention was simultaneously cheering and laughing—and so was the country. Then the *coup de grace*, and the only time in the speech Kennedy actually mentioned Reagan's name]

And the same Republicans who are invoking Franklin Roosevelt have nominated a man who said in 1976, and these are his exact words, "Fascism was really the basis of the New Deal." And that nominee whose name is Ronald Reagan has no right to quote Franklin Delano Roosevelt.

Now Kennedy truly was the voice of the party—and he argued the case for a new approach to jobs and inflation, energy and tax reform, equal rights and national health insurance. The convention hit another crescendo with a passage that's since been recycled by others, the borrowing glossed with edits:

The President, the Vice President, the members of Congress have a medical plan that meets their needs in full. And whenever Senators and Representatives catch a little cold, the Capitol physician will see them immediately, treat them promptly, fill a prescription on the spot. We do not get a bill even if we ask for it, and when do you think was the last time a member of Congress asked for a bill from the Federal Government?

I say again, as I have before, if health insurance is good enough for the President, the Vice President and the Congress of the United States, then it is good enough for you and every family in America.

At its best, a political speech resembles a symphony, rising and rousing the audience, then falling to a quieter level, transfixing the listeners instead of eliciting applause. Kennedy shifted tone again as he talked personally about the campaign and signaled to a convention that now didn't want him to finish that he was about to:

In closing, let me say a few words to all those that I have met and to all those who have supported me, at this Convention and across the country. There were hard hours on our journey, and often we sailed against the wind. But always we kept our rudder true. There were so many of you who stayed the course and shared our hope. You gave your help; but even more, you gave your hearts.

Because of you, this has been a happy campaign. You welcomed Joan, me and our family into your homes and neighborhoods, your churches, your campuses, your union halls. When I think back on all the miles and all the months and all the memories, I think of you, I recall the poet's words, and I say: What "golden friends" I have.

[On a television monitor below me on a desk to the side of the podium, I saw the cut-aways of people rapt with attention, one of them folding her hands as if in prayer]

Among you, my golden friends across this land, I have listened and learned.

Kennedy now personalized issues in a way that Ronald Reagan subsequently would in his State of the Union messages. Many politicians since then have used the same device. It's grown tired, but it was fresh and powerful in 1980.

I have listened to Kenny Dubois, a glassblower in Charleston, West Virginia, who has ten children to support but has lost his job after 35 years, just three years short of qualifying for his pension.

I have listened to the Trachta family who farm in Iowa and who wonder whether they can pass the good life and the good earth on to their children.

[Couldn't we find a farm family who'd met Kennedy, I had asked the research staff, but whose name didn't sound, in Kennedy's distinctive accent, like "tractor"? No such luck; it was too late, so Kennedy had practiced how to clip the word. It still sounded like "tractor"]

I have listened to young workers out of work, to students without tuition for college, and to families without the chance to own a home. I have seen the closed factories and the stalled assembly lines of Anderson, Indiana and South Gate, California, and I have seen too many, far too many idle men and women desperate to work, I have seen too many, far too many working families desperate to protect the value of their wages from the ravages of inflation.

Yet I have also sensed a yearning for new hope among the people in every state where I have been. I have felt it in their handshakes, I saw it in their faces. And I shall never forget the mothers who carried children to our rallies. I shall always remember the elderly who have lived in an America of high purpose and who believe that it can all happen again.

Tonight in their name, I have come here to speak for them. And for their sake, I ask you to stand with them. On their behalf I ask you to restate and reaffirm the timeless truth of our party.

As Kennedy continued, the monitors showed a woman with tears streaming down her face. Then at last, he uttered the obligatory words:

I congratulate President Carter on his victory here.
I am confident that the Democratic Party will reunite on the basis

of Democratic Party principles, and that together we will march to-
ward a Democratic victory in 1980.

And someday, long after this Convention, long after the signs come
down, and the crowds stop cheering, and the bands stop playing, may
it be said of our campaign that we kept the faith. May it be said of our
party in 1980 that we found our faith again.

Applause, and then the convention became eerily quiet. This was
where Kennedy, who adjured references to his brothers in political
speeches—it was just too painful—invoked them without saying
their names, touched deep chords of memory, inferentially evoking
what might have been as he quoted the truncated Tennyson.

And may it be said of us, both in dark passages and in bright days, in
the words of Tennyson that my brothers quoted and loved, and that
have special meaning for me now:

> *I am part of all that I have met*
> *Tho much is taken, much abides*
> *That which we are, we are—*
> *One equal temper of heroic hearts*
> *Strong in will*
> *To strive, to seek, to find, and not to yield.*

For me, a few hours ago, this campaign came to an end. For all
those whose cares have been our concern, the work goes on, the cause
endures, the hope still lives, and the dream shall never die.

As he finished, he was a young lion in winter. The convention
exploded. When I stood up from my assigned seat on the steps,
Kennedy looked at me and nodded yes. His family came to the
platform—and even after they all left, the demonstration continued
to mount, pause, and resume with even greater force. Kennedy was
now in a holding room behind the podium. When I came in, he said
wryly: "Well, I think it did work."

There were negotiations under way as the Carter operatives assessed their capacity to defeat Kennedy platform amendments. Hamilton Jordan ordered his twenty-five-year-old assistant, Tom Donilon, to phone around. He asked Governor Brendan Byrne how many Carter votes in New Jersey they could hold. One-half vote, Donilon recalled Byrne replying, mine—but he wasn't sure about that one, either. The Carter managers came to terms: All the Kennedy amendments on the economy would pass on a voice vote—except wage and price controls. We might have had the strength to force it through, but Kennedy agreed not to; it would be too stunning a repudiation of Carter.

House Speaker Tip O'Neill tried to gavel the convention to order. The demonstration intensified. Finally, Kennedy reappeared, the rafters shook again, and he extended his arms to quiet the noise and said: "Thank you and let's proceed with the convention." He left for a small party in his hotel suite. I stayed behind on the podium for the votes on our deal with Carter. There to enforce it was the sharp-edged, sharp-tongued New Yorker Harold Ickes, a main player in progressive campaigns from dump Johnson to elect Clinton (either one). When the delegates finally quieted, O'Neill called for a voice vote on the first platform amendments and before the sound even died away declared them passed. The vote for wage and price controls was so much louder than the vote against it that O'Neill hesitated briefly, then gaveled the proposal down.

I hurried through the corridors of Madison Square Garden to find a cab. The cabdriver had the convention coverage on his radio; the commentator was analyzing Kennedy's speech—and reporting that Bob Shrum and Carey Parker had written it. I was panicked; how would Kennedy react to this? Back at the Waldorf, I picked my way through the family and friends gathered in the suite and asked Kennedy if I could talk to him for a minute. We went off to the side. I recounted what I'd heard in the cab and added that I hadn't told anyone. He said: "Oh, I told." A reporter had asked him as he was leaving the convention, he explained. "I'd like to say I wrote it. But if I didn't say anything, everybody else would say they wrote it. So I said you and Carey wrote it." I was struck by his sense of generosity and his security about himself. He's not uptight about who writes a speech. It's not how he measures his achievement; it isn't common in politics, but he gives credit instead of taking it. For Christmas of 1980, he sent friends large reprints of the convention speech. On mine, he wrote: "To Bob—I hope you have another one in you for 198—."

Thursday was Carter's big night. And Kennedy had to perform again. Once Carter finished his acceptance speech, Kennedy would have to join him on the platform and raise Carter's hand into the air. Maybe we could just shake hands, Kennedy suggested Thursday afternoon. No, that wasn't good enough, I said. Kennedy and I practiced several times in his hotel room; I quipped that it wasn't that hard. Maybe not for you, he answered; then he promised that come what may, he'd do it. But things got complicated when we tried to arrange the logistics. Kennedy would come to Madison Square Garden just before the president spoke and wait in a holding room. No, the Carter team said, that wouldn't work; the cameras might cut away from Vice President Mondale's acceptance speech. Okay, we'd go to the Garden just before Mondale spoke. No, the Carter campaign didn't want to risk cutting into the television coverage for the speeches nominating Mondale. It was agreed that Kennedy would leave the hotel for the convention as soon as Carter finished his speech; the balloons would drop during a prolonged demonstration and Kennedy would be there in plenty of time. A debacle was now set in motion.

Kennedy and I practiced again, with the image of Mondale at the podium flickering on the television set we weren't paying attention to. As Carter began his acceptance speech, Kennedy went to take a shower; he left the bathroom door open and we turned the volume up so he could listen. Carter was paying a brief tribute to the late Hubert Humphrey, "who should have been president," when he stunned the convention—and us—by referring to him as "Hubert Horatio Hornblower . . ." Carter suddenly realized what he was saying and rushed to get out—"Humphrey." Kennedy emerged from the bathroom with a towel around his middle: "*What* did he just say?" Caddell told me afterward that in the '76 Carter campaign, "Hubert Horatio Hornblower" had been the derisive nickname for the famously long-winded Humphrey. Carter, perhaps thrown by his Hornblower slip and, Caddell told me right after the speech, the fact that the TelePrompTer malfunctioned, droned through his delivery to a listless crowd.

As soon as he finished, we were downstairs and in the motorcade. The ride to Madison Square Garden should have taken no more than 10 or 12 minutes—if the New York City police provided the intersection control they had before, stopping traffic and moving cars to the side to clear a path. But while there were police with us, there was no intersection control. We were told afterward that we'd been stripped of it at the behest of Mayor Ed Koch, a bitter foe of Kennedy's during the primaries. We crawled toward the Garden. We listened to the convention on the radio as the demonstration was dying out. The balloons wouldn't drop from the rafters. (Someone on the floor shouted out: "Free the Democratic balloons.") To keep the demonstration going, an array of luminaries was ushered to the platform; we were still inching along as lesser lights got their moment in the sun. I said to Kennedy in a kind of lighthearted way, Don't forget to raise Carter's hand.

When we finally entered the hall and reached the stairway to the podium, I again said, "Don't forget," and then went out onto the floor. As I looked up, my heart sank. There were so many people on that stage it looked like Filene's basement in the first crush of the after-Christmas sale. The convention cheered as Kennedy was announced. Next to me in the barely roped off section in front of the platform, I heard a voice on the walkie-talkie in the hands of one of the Carter operatives: "Don't drop the balloons now." I don't know whether it was because the Carter forces didn't want it to happen "for" Kennedy, or didn't want it to distract from the tableau of unity that was finally about to unfold. The balloons hung motionless above as Kennedy and Carter had trouble finding each other on the crowded platform. The president frantically pursued his quarry through a throng of dignitaries and hangers-on. It lasted about two minutes, but it seemed like an eternity, a slow-motion political train wreck played out in front of tens of millions of viewers on television.

Carter and Kennedy finally encountered each other—and then . . . shook hands. What had happened to our choreography? I asked Kennedy afterward. It didn't feel right, he said, in that press of people; if Carter had tried to raise his hand, he wouldn't have resisted, but it just didn't happen.

Thus ended the 1980 Kennedy campaign—and while the moment was instantly notorious, it was also the kind of candid expression of the real feelings on both sides that we hardly ever see in politics. Leaving Madison Square Garden, I bumped into the *Boston Globe*'s Marty Nolan, and repeated what Caddell had said to me a few minutes before: "The prompter," Nolan mocked, "the prompter— that's not all that's broken."

The Monday after the convention, I handed Kennedy a memo that laid out an approach to the general election: "You have to do several events with Carter . . . it is essential for you to be involved without being overenthused—to help Carter without abandoning the principles of your own campaign." Kennedy should fight hard for Democratic Senate candidates even if they hadn't stood with him. He should appear with Carter soon, but not too often. The operating assumption of that August 18 memo to Kennedy was that Carter would lose, maybe even "in Massachusetts."

Kennedy wanted something in return for his help. The president had refused to nominate Archibald Cox to the federal appeals court in Boston. He was the Harvard Law professor and Watergate Special Prosecutor who'd become a household name when Nixon fired him in the "Saturday Night Massacre." Carter claimed he couldn't appoint Cox because of his age and then offered Kennedy another explanation when they met face-to-face before the primaries: Cox had come out for Mo Udall for the '76 Democratic nomination. A standoff ensued. Carter wouldn't name Cox—and Kennedy as chairman of the Judiciary Committee wouldn't approve anyone else. But now Kennedy had maximum leverage—and an alternative in mind. It was a footnote in the agreement we negotiated for the general election, but in a year when we hadn't made a president, it turned out to be the first critical step in the making of a Supreme

Court justice. Carter would nominate Steve Breyer, Kennedy's chief counsel on the Judiciary Committee, to the vacant seat on the Court of Appeals.

Carter's road to defeat culminated when he finally agreed to debate Reagan just a week before the election. Kennedy and I sat at a Beverly Hills debate-watching party with Jerry Brown; former Senator John Tunney, Kennedy's law school roommate; and an array of movie stars and studio chieftains. Reagan's statement at the start of the debate that "the first priority must be world peace" elicited hoots of derision. But after an awkward silence following Carter's comment that he'd discussed nuclear arms control with his thirteen-year-old daughter Amy, people gamely clapped for Carter's other answers. Reagan's most memorable moment, when he reacted to one Carter accusation with a pitch-perfect response—"There you go again"—provoked someone in the room to insist that Carter had been right, Reagan had proposed cutting Medicare. That was true, but it was hardly the point. As the debate ended, the room pronounced Carter the clear winner. We were heading for our mini-motorcade when Kennedy said, "They're crazy," and asked me what I thought. "Carter got killed," I answered. Reagan now seemed more presidential than the president.

I worried about a gathering landslide that could not only bury Carter but cost Democrats ten or twelve Senate seats and control of the Senate itself. It seemed unthinkable, but I outlined how it might happen in a memo to Kennedy. Then came a call from Caddell: Kennedy was scheduled to be in Michigan the day before the election, but he had to get back to Massachusetts right away. The president was in trouble there. Kennedy knew what that meant; if it was a fight to hold Massachusetts, he said, and his voice trailed off. Almost a year to the day after I'd signed on with him, I stood in the back of a room as Kennedy finished out the 1980 campaign speaking too late in the evening to a group of senior citizens at a retirement home next to the expressway that led from Boston to the suburbs. You could see what was coming in this crowd, which cheered Kennedy and sat on their hands when he mentioned Carter. (This had happened before, and when it did, Kennedy had paused and said: "Now the next time I mention President Carter, I want all of you to applaud.")

In the darkness on the way to Hyannisport, I said maybe we'd hold the Senate. Kennedy ribbed me: Had I changed my mind? I really hadn't—and we didn't.

After the election, Kennedy asked me to stay on as his press secretary, and one of my first assignments was to get as little press as possible. He called me into his office the day after Reagan was inaugurated to tell me that he and Joan had decided to get divorced. Paul Kirk had negotiated a statement with Joan's lawyers—and no, I couldn't edit it or change a word. It was straightforward: they had made the decision "together, with the understanding of our children." I was to put it out—and to any and all questions, the answer was to say nothing more. I was a little surprised, but in retrospect I don't know why. Except for one visit to Hyannisport during the 1980 primaries when I'd sat in their bedroom and had coffee with them in the morning, to me they seldom looked comfortable together. I told Kennedy I was sorry and prepared for a barrage of press calls where I wouldn't have anything to say.

I'd get a lot of calls in the next three years about Kennedy and women. The rumors far outpaced the reality. When a *Washington Post* Style columnist reported that Kennedy had spent a weekend in Maine with someone who was supposedly an old flame, he ordered me to call Ben Bradlee, the paper's executive editor. Kennedy had been in Florida that weekend; he hadn't seen the woman in years. Bradlee said he'd check with the columnist and call me back. He was, after Watergate, a legendary editor; irreverent, often brusque, but fair. That's how he sounded when he phoned back. "Are you going to break my balls on this?" I decided a retraction wasn't worth nearly as much as getting him to agree that before the *Post* ran something like this again, someone at the paper would at least check with me. That was a deal, he said; he added, "Thanks, pal," a characteristic Bradlee flourish that had nothing to do with our relationship.

This conversation was an exception; on most of the sensational stories, all I said was something like: "We don't comment on rumors."

As the first year of the Reagan administration unfolded, Kennedy's relationship with the new president could be characterized as civil war when it came to policy and more than civil on a personal level. At a sunlit ceremony in the Rose Garden, Reagan presented Ethel Kennedy with the Congressional Gold Medal for RFK that Jimmy Carter, intentionally or inadvertently, had failed to bestow for two years. Reagan and Edward Kennedy both spoke. Kennedy, who could hardly bear to allude to the assassination of his brothers, spoke of "a special sense of relief this year, Mr. President, at your own recovery from the attack against you"—when Reagan had been shot outside the Washington Hilton. Like House Speaker Tip O'Neill, Kennedy enjoyed Reagan's company. At times, Kennedy was astounded by the president's apparent disconnection. At a meeting with senators on shoe imports, Reagan read his answers from cards and seemed to know none of the senators by name except Kennedy. But Kennedy respected Reagan for restoring the authority of the presidency—and for a sense of grace that culminated in his presence at Kennedy's home to raise money for the JFK Library when it was in financial trouble. Reagan was at his best that night, affable, eloquent, even soaring as he described how swiftly JFK's moment had passed and how long it would last in history and memory.

That Edward Kennedy and Ronald Reagan got along never got in the way when Kennedy decided he had to oppose the president. The big enchilada was the Reagan tax cut. Opposing it was hopeless after the attempt on Reagan's life. So Larry Horowitz, now Kennedy's chief of staff, convened a session in the Senate office to go over the issue one more time. Kennedy came in a little late and asked what this meeting was about. I said we were there to discuss how he should vote on the Reagan tax cut. I couldn't tell if he was annoyed at me or surprised—he knew that I was against it. But Horowitz pressed on. Kennedy had to understand the lay of the land: If he voted no, he might be on the losing end of a 99-to-1 outcome in the Senate. Without missing a beat, he replied: "Well, why don't you guys have your discussion. But I'm voting against it." We got up and left the office. In the end, there were just eight senators who answered no when the roll was called. We noted that several of Kennedy's colleagues, who were also thinking of running for president in 1984, waited in the back of the chamber to see what he did before they cast their votes.

For him, the battle—such as it was—moved to an unfortunate if funny conclusion. The tax bill went to a Senate-House conference committee. The final version would come back to the Senate for approval. Even though the congressional summer recess hadn't started, Kennedy let me accept an invitation from Larry Tribe and his family to go to Italy with them. Tribe had made some money as an advocate in high-profile legal cases, and our first stop was in Venice at the Cipriani Hotel, a glorious, expensive place that had a vast swimming pool supposedly designed by Americans in feet and built by Italians in meters. I'd be back there many times, but I didn't think so then—not on my public sector salary. We returned to the hotel after lunch on a hot August day and I found a note to call Kennedy. When I got through, which in the early eighties took half an hour or more, he told me that when the conference finished approving the Reagan tax cut on Saturday night and the Senate was about to cast a pro forma vote on the bill, he'd objected. He wanted a roll call, so the process had to be delayed until Tuesday. But he'd entered his objection from Cape Cod—and one of the Boston papers had headlined the story: "Senate Swelters While Kennedy Suns." I asked the question I had to: Did he want me to come back? No, he answered with a wink in his voice, he just wanted me to know what I was missing.

Kennedy didn't miss a beat. In short order, he saved the Voting Rights Act from the ideologues in the Reagan administration, including a young Justice Department lawyer, John Roberts, the future Chief Justice. He did it by enlisting Bob Dole, the conservative senator who'd stood with George McGovern to save the food stamp program. On voting rights, all Dole wanted was credit for "the Dole bill." Kennedy handed it to him at a jam-packed press conference.

I was handling a constant stream of press calls seeking interviews with Kennedy. Tom Brokaw, the anchor of *The Today Show* through

1981, had an unusual approach; with Kennedy, Brokaw functioned as his own booker. He'd regularly call me and ask: "Is he ready yet? Just let me know when." Years later, Brokaw told me that he didn't do this with everyone. But his calls were a testament that everyone wanted to hear from Kennedy—not generally about the issues, but about politics and the next campaign.

There was one issue where Kennedy at first had a hard time getting anyone to listen: AIDS, although we didn't call it that at first and no one was sure what it was. Jim Foster, the Californian who'd refused to shut down our San Francisco campaign office in 1980 and would ultimately die of the disease, came to see me along with Larry Bush, a reporter for the national gay newspaper *The Advocate*. Gay men were getting sick, they said, it was an epidemic, and Kennedy had to do something about it. I talked with Larry Horowitz, who said the nature and causes of the problem were a mystery to the medical profession. I took Foster to see Horowitz and then to say hello to Kennedy. Horowitz now had our health staff talking with the National Institutes of Health and the Centers for Disease Control and Prevention.

But even after the disease was identified, it was tough to get Congress or the administration to act. The Reagan Justice Department ruled that private or public sector employees with AIDS could be legally fired. Some Democrats were squeamish about a plague that the far right was blaming on perversity and promiscuity. One breakthrough was cultural, the other political. My future wife Marylouise Oates whose clout came from her society column in the *Los Angeles Times*, was close to David Mixner and his partner Peter Scott, the gay rights activist who was organizing a "Commitment to Life" dinner in Los Angeles in 1985 to raise awareness about AIDS and resources to help those who had it. Scott asked her to help recruit a high-profile co-chair for the event, Wallis Annenberg, the daughter of the publishing mogul who owned *TV Guide* and spent most New Year's Eves with the Reagans. Wallis in turn persuaded former First Lady Betty Ford to co-chair the dinner with her. Marylouise was covering the event for the *L. A. Times*; she had already persuaded her publisher Tom Johnson to contribute $10,000 of the paper's money to AIDS

Project Los Angeles. She was supposed to be writing about this stuff, not fund-raising, Johnson said—and then agreed to ante up.

That night, when Betty Ford called for ending the stigma imposed on people with AIDS, symbolized a transformation of attitudes. Elizabeth Taylor, Shirley MacLaine, and a constellation of stars showed up. President Reagan, who had avoided even mentioning the disease for years, sent a telegram that said his administration had now made stopping AIDS a "top priority." The event and the coverage afterward were proof that culture was more powerful than politics. Kennedy was now making progress on the issue. He worked with Orrin Hatch, a Mormon Republican from Utah, to hold the first Senate hearings on AIDS and push through the first funds for research and care.

In the early 1980s, Kennedy was running a kind of alternative presidency, built on both his capacity to assemble coalitions in the Senate and the power of forceful disagreement with Reagan. As the new administration's arms buildup mounted, he and one of the last liberal Republicans, Oregon Senator Mark Hatfield, called for a freeze on the size of both Soviet and U.S. nuclear arsenals. In two weeks of 14- and 16-hour days, Carey Parker and I wrote a book on the freeze, an instant paperback from Kennedy and Hatfield, that sold 200,000 copies by June 1982. While the freeze resolution never passed the Congress, it did serve three purposes. First, the Reagan administration, which had disdained arms control, publicly announced that it was prepared to negotiate with the Soviets. Second, Kennedy established his own line of communications with Moscow; Horowitz embarked on a series of secret trips to prepare for a Kennedy visit to the Soviet Union. But with one top Soviet leader after another hit with a terminal illness, Larry was now back in the medical business, calling on American doctors and researchers to advise on treating the dying dictators. This would have seemed astounding if it was known. Larry told me that the state of Soviet medicine was, in his signature phrase, "beyond belief"—and he accurately predicted just about how long Gorbachev's predecessors would last (three of them expired in three years). Horowitz briefed the White House whenever he returned from Moscow. Finally, the nuclear freeze strengthened Kennedy's lead for the 1984 Democratic nomination. When he introduced it in the Senate, virtually every Democrat thinking of running for president felt compelled to endorse it.

Kennedy himself was also running for reelection in Massachusetts. Having seen some of his colleagues lose their Senate seats after a failed presidential bid, he was taking his own race seriously. All through 1982, when the Senate wasn't in session, campaigning at home alternated with campaigning for other Democratic candidates as we flew back and forth across the country. We also had a new pollster: Pat Caddell. I'd wanted to bring Pat on board from the time Carter was defeated. He'd told me after the 1980 race that there had been a strategy for Kennedy to win in Iowa that he had discovered in a series of long interviews with voters there. He had asked them to imagine how they would feel four years ahead if Carter was president—or if Kennedy was. As they answered, they had shifted from being 2 to 1 for Carter to 2 to 1 for Kennedy. The key for Kennedy would have been to transcend the tumult of the hostage crisis and pose a bigger choice to the voters. Caddell briefed Carter, who put the report on the interviews in his desk in the Oval Office—and ordered his pollster not to discuss it with anyone else. I was determined to have Caddell on our side this time. In 1982, he polled for us not only in Massachusetts but in Iowa and New Hampshire. He told us that we were secure in the Senate race, and that in Iowa, New Hampshire, and nationally, Kennedy had a decisive lead for the nomination and a realistic chance against Reagan.

My first inkling that Kennedy wasn't so sure about another race for president came on a charter flight after a day of campaigning for Frank Lautenberg, the Democratic Senate candidate in New Jersey. Kennedy said he was amazed at how little anger there was toward Reagan despite the grip and pain of the recession. Everywhere he'd traveled, during the midterm, Kennedy continued, he sensed that people liked the president, that Reagan had a reservoir of goodwill even if they didn't like the job he was doing. The personal liking for Reagan, I argued back, wouldn't translate into Republican votes in 1982 or 1984, when the economy would probably still be in trouble. I was wrong about that, too; but it was what I wanted to believe.

On Election Day, Kennedy went home to Cape Cod to sail with his children. By the time he returned to Boston for the victory celebration, we were pretty confident that he'd get 60 percent of the vote—and he did. I handed him the draft of the victory statement, redolent with nearly explicit references to the coming contest with Reagan. He started crossing them out and then ordered me to rewrite the whole thing; this was a night when he wanted to focus on Massachusetts. His reaction made it clear that he was in no mood for dissent. Horowitz told me that Kennedy's children, especially Patrick, had pressed him during the sail not to run for president this time. They were a united front. Patrick, who feared that someone might shoot his father, was only fifteen and needed his father at home. Larry asked me not to say anything; Kennedy still hadn't made up his mind.

When Kennedy returned to Washington in the first week of December, he called me into his office. He was ready to announce that he wouldn't be a candidate—not in 1984. He said again that he wasn't as optimistic as other Democrats about Reagan's vulnerability. True, you could never know for sure and after 1980 he was inclined to accept the argument I'd made that you ought to take the nomination when you could get it. But the message from his children had carried the day: They would campaign for him if he ran, but please don't. Kennedy told me to prepare a statement right away; he wanted to make the announcement before it leaked. I reached into the inside pocket of my jacket and pulled out some folded legal pages: "It's already done." I hadn't had it typed yet; I didn't want to take the risk. Kennedy, who could read my handwriting—he'd done it often enough as we amended speeches at the last minute—said it was about right, and, with a sideways glance at Horowitz, asked how I'd known what he wanted to say. I'd thought about it since election night, I answered, and decided we ought to be ready.

Kennedy was out of the race, but not the limelight; for example, in 1983, lightning struck accidentally from the religious right. A form letter arrived in the office from Jerry Falwell that was obviously a misdirected part of a mass mailing. Thanks to some computerized list, it was impersonally personalized—"Dear Senator

Kennedy"—and included a "Moral Majority" membership card made out to him, and a call to join in combating the threat of "ultra-liberals like Ted Kennedy." I leaked the letter to the *New York Times*, which reported it in a tongue-in-cheek political note. Cal Thomas, then Falwell's public relations strategist, sent a handwritten note to Kennedy that half-seriously invited him to speak at Falwell's Liberty Baptist College. I suggested that we take it seriously and accept. Larry Horowitz was all for it. Kennedy, who prized the chance to reach out while standing his ground, told us to find a date.

I've seldom enjoyed working on a speech as much as this one. My friends joke that I have more books about popes than presidents—and I have a lot of those. I spent two weekends mostly by myself, researching and writing at a long table in the conference room with piles of notes on 3-by-5 cards and volumes on topics ranging from constitutional law to evangelical texts and the documents of Vatican II, the council that had been called by John XXIII to renew the Catholic Church. I wanted Kennedy to cite the Pope explicitly in the heartland of a fundamentalism that had been hostile to Catholicism long before the new televangelists had taken on political progressives. Falwell himself was something of an exception; he'd been attacked, I discovered, for "yoking together with Roman Catholics, Mormons and others." The ideal quote from John XXIII was his warning to ultra-conservatives in his own Church as he opened the Vatican Council: "We must beware of those who burn with zeal but are not endowed with much sense . . . prophets of doom, who are always forecasting disasters, as though the end of the earth was at hand." Kennedy liked the reference—it was a direct response to the apocalyptic rhetoric on the religious right—and he and I constantly discussed what the speech should say. He wanted to explicitly mention a woman's right to choose and advance an argument that Mario Cuomo would repeat and elaborate on a year later in the heat of the 1984 campaign; as Kennedy put it, banning abortion would be futile "when a majority or even a substantial minority disagrees . . . the proper role of religion is to appeal to the conscience of the individual, not the coercive power of the state."

We flew to Lynchburg, Virginia, on a private jet sent by Falwell, had a nonalcoholic cocktail hour in the backyard, and then ate a multicourse meal in the dining room of his imposing mansion. When we entered the college gym, the atmosphere was respectful— and strained. At the outset Kennedy won over the students, at least personally, with a string of openers. He invited Falwell to pray at the inauguration of "the next Democratic president" in 1985; Falwell "might not appreciate the president, but the Democrats would certainly appreciate the prayer." He asked Falwell to give "all the students an extra hour next Saturday night before curfew"—they laughed and started to applaud—and in return he promised "to watch the Old Time Gospel Hour next Sunday."

Day after day in the Senate, Kennedy was fighting hard: for nuclear arms control; against the covert CIA war to overthrow the left-wing Sandinista regime in Nicaragua; for children's health care and college aid for the middle class; for making Martin Luther King, Jr.'s birthday a national holiday. Most of the battles would ultimately be won. He could run for president someday and I'd be there. But I had the presidential itch now and he indulged that, up to a point, all through 1983 and the 1984 primaries. So while I was working full time as his press secretary, I was also moonlighting—at first fitfully and then more deeply—in the presidential campaign.

Tentatively and privately, I was for Gary Hart, who had managed the 1972 McGovern campaign and was now a senator from Colorado. Hart phoned me the weekend before he announced for president. He had multiple drafts; he didn't like any of them. Could he stop by my condo in Georgetown so I could look at them and maybe help him out? I said I'd have to ask Kennedy, who surprised me by saying if I wanted to do it, I could—but I had to make sure no one else knew about it. Hart and I sat at the dining table with paper spread all around us. He knew what he wanted to say and he showed me what he liked in the various drafts. We threw ideas around. He had to leave and I said I'd get a new version to him.

On February 17, 1983, Hart announced his candidacy and his commitment to "a new vision"—instead of relying on "old remedies

. . . and shopworn policies," it was time to "build a bridge to a new era." (In 1996, I would wonder whether Bill Clinton, who was "building a bridge to the 21st century," had seen this speech.) Hart's message, like Kennedy's in 1980, also affirmed Democratic values: "We must preserve our enduring ideals by replacing tired assumptions with new and fresh ideas." He pledged to be a president who "asks anew what all of us can do for . . . [the] common good"—a phrase we probably should have borrowed for the 2004 Kerry campaign since it summed up, even more in this Bush era than in the Reagan one, what should be distinctive about Democrats.

My copy of the *New York Times* hadn't been delivered the morning after the Hart announcement; I normally read it in the cab on the way to work. When I sat down at my desk, there was a note from Kennedy to come into his office. He was sitting there with a copy of the *Times* in his hands. He read from it: "Today's speech ended with a peroration done in the rolling cadences and parallel constructions favored"—he slowed down—"by Senator Edward M. Kennedy of Massachusetts. Bill Shore, Mr. Hart's political director, said that Robert Shrum, the speechwriter generally credited with providing Senator Kennedy's trademark flourishes, was among those who reviewed Mr. Hart's speech." Kennedy looked at me, paused, and then said: "Well . . ." I didn't know how it happened, I replied; Hart had promised that no one would say anything. Kennedy said we'd hear from the Mondale people for sure; we'd tell them it wouldn't happen again—and I had to stay away from the campaign, at least for a while.

Kennedy never said another word about the episode, but I backed out of the '84 sweepstakes. Meanwhile, Pat Caddell was on his own relentless search for Mr. Right, with a memo arguing that a combination of experience and freshness—a mythical Senator Smith—could prevail in the primaries and against Reagan. The memo, intentionally, fit Senator Joe Biden of Delaware perfectly—as Pat saw him. Another young senator, Chris Dodd of Connecticut, was an imperfect fit. They both read the memo but declined to let Caddell tempt them into the race. Months passed. Over dinner, sometime in December, I said to Pat that the only real alternative was Gary Hart, even though he'd slipped his thematic moorings after his announcement and wandered across the issues landscape; at one point, Hart was going to be the education candidate. Caddell had a hard time settling for less than his ideal; but finally as 1983 ended, he settled on Gary Hart.

He also said we had to talk. He had produced another lengthy memo setting out a strategy to position Mondale as the establishment choice and Hart as the candidate of new ideas. Caddell asked me to work with him on a speech and some concepts for television spots. I gingerly raised the question with Kennedy: After hours, could I talk with Caddell about the Hart campaign? Could I give him some help? Yes, but keep it out of the papers.

The speech Pat and I shaped was, as Hart himself observed, too long; but the speech and the strategy recast the race in Iowa. His assets were his principal opponent's vulnerabilities and the contrast was no longer implicit. It was just two weeks before the Iowa caucuses and Hart was blunt, even brutal, as he spoke in Council Bluffs: "At the very time our nation needs thought and courage, it is being offered a candidacy of the establishment past, a candidacy brokered by backroom politics and confirmed by a collective sense of resignation. . . . The Democratic Party that was once the party of education is in danger of becoming the party of teachers' unions . . . the party that used to ask people only for their idealism too often now asks people only for their price." The answer was "a new generation of leadership"—and Hart didn't just say it, he seemed to embody it. Jim Johnson, now Mondale's campaign chairman, was handed a copy of the speech (he told me after the campaign), read it, and decided my fingerprints were all over it. Larry Horowitz did, too; in Kennedy's Senate office, he warned me to be careful.

Four days later, in the *Des Moines Register* debate, Hart fired the next salvo. The candidates could ask each other questions, and before Caddell headed to Iowa to brief Hart, I suggested that the challenge to Mondale ought to be straightforward. Ask him to name three domestic issues where he disagreed with the AFL-CIO. Hart whittled the question down: "Cite one major domestic issue in the last three or four years where you have disagreed with the AFL-CIO or organized labor." Mondale refused to answer, explaining that the unions supported him because "they trust me." His nonresponse not only proved the accusation but sounded glaringly political.

Caddell's influence in the campaign was now clear—and he wasn't shy about his role. In the Iowa debate, South Carolina senator Fritz Hollings, who had a lethal wit even if he wasn't going anywhere in the primaries, had commented that "poor Gary Hart was locked for two hours with Pat Caddell coming all the way over here from Omaha. Imagine that." The crack annoyed Hart, and the nerve Hollings hit would goad Hart into a mortal blunder down the road, in the Illinois primary. But for now, the comment really didn't cut with voters, who had little or no idea who Caddell was. (I liked Hollings, whose Senate office was one door away from Kennedy's and who'd asked me to leave Kennedy and work for his campaign; he wanted, he said, "my own Shrum," pronouncing it like the second half of mushroom.)

Mondale took just under 50 percent of the vote in Iowa; it was a Pyrrhic win. Hart, with a second place showing of 15 percent, was now the designated challenger, a magnet for the press attention that had eluded him for months. He could appeal to Democrats worried that the good, gray Mondale couldn't compete with Reagan in the fall. In Caddell's office, the overnight polling began tracking a surge for Hart in the New Hampshire primary. In the end, he carried every county but one. A media wave was now bearing Hart along, and Caddell gleefully said that nothing could stop the momentum unless Hart screwed up. By any reasonable reckoning, Hart should have gone on to the nomination; he would have it in hand at least twice and let it slip away or kick it away—once in March 1984, with the help of others, and then in June, entirely on his own.

First, however, came a moment when the Hart campaign was plain outmaneuvered by the other side. With five primaries just ahead, Mondale abandoned Rhode Island and Massachusetts after Kennedy refused to endorse him. His strategists also downplayed Florida, the biggest prize of three southern contests. Instead, they backgrounded reporters that what they had to do was carry Georgia; it would be a bonus if they squeezed out first place in Alabama. And Mondale threw a roundhouse punch of his own in a debate in

Atlanta. Hectoring Hart to explain the substance behind his new ideas, Mondale borrowed what was then the best one-liner in America, from a Wendy's commercial: "Where's the beef?" The audience broke into laughter. Like all political lines that hit home, this one had a plural pedigree. Kennedy had deployed it days before the debate at a roast of the imposingly heavyset Tip O'Neill: "One thing is for sure about Tip O'Neill. You know that no one will ever say 'Where's the beef?'" AFL-CIO president Lane Kirkland was there, picked up the line, and applied it to Hart. Mondale operative Bob Beckel in turn heard what Kirkland had said and passed the line along.

In the debate, Mondale finally seemed to have a spark of life—and he narrowly edged Hart out in Georgia, and had his bonus win in Alabama. They were the only primaries he'd won so far. But his campaign spin had seeded the ground: Georgia was *the* test, never mind Hart's romp in Florida and New England. Yet the nightly numbers from the upcoming contest in Illinois showed Hart ahead by double digits. If he won there, Mondale would collapse. And although we didn't know it at the time, the Mondale managers had concluded that if they lost Illinois, they couldn't go on.

It was the first time a Hart nomination that was all but secured would be thrown away. Caddell decided that the Hart advertising should attack Mondale for his association with the Cook County Democratic chairman, a local alderman named Edward Vrdolyak. Mondale could be tagged as the candidate of the "bosses" and the machine. The polling showed it was a strong argument; but Hart was already thinking beyond the Illinois primary to the general election: he wanted Vrdolyak and the Cook County organization with him in the fall. I was with Caddell on Friday night before the primary, when Chris Dodd, the only senator who'd endorsed Hart early on, called. Dodd was in Chicago with the candidate; Hart was in a cold fury about the Vrdolyak ad. He claimed he'd never seen the script. I've never known if that was true. Now he wanted the ad off the air. Caddell told Dodd that if Hart took it off, he'd look like he was backing down. That wasn't the only issue, I added; the logs at the television stations closed Friday afternoon. No matter what Hart decided, even if he got one or two stations to open up and make a change, the spot was bound to keep running until Monday. The best thing to do now was just take the heat; the worst of it was probably past anyway.

Dodd made the case to Hart, who didn't want to listen. Months later, sitting in the basement of his suburban Maryland home, Hart explained his reaction to me. It was an echo of what I'd heard from Muskie years before and what candidates often say when they feel an adviser is overbearing or over-prominent. Caddell had backed him into a corner, Hart said. Who was the candidate anyway—him or Caddell? I replied that Hart was the only one they were going to call "Mr. President."

After Hart publicly disowned the Vrdolyak ad, it just kept airing and airing, as the press lethally reported. How could someone run the country if he couldn't even control his own campaign spots? Hart's double-digit lead melted away. The process was reinforced with a new Mondale spot that by painful coincidence hit the airwaves on Friday night. It showed a red phone ringing with a red light flashing on it as the narrator intoned: "The idea of an unsure, unsteady, untested hand is really something to think about."

Hart lost the primary by 6 percent. Mondale, who'd been down and almost out, was once again the odds-on favorite. He won New York—big; he carried Pennsylvania and Missouri. Hart was trying to grind his way back with victories in western states as a Harris Poll found him in a tie with Reagan. Then Mondale was hit by a media firestorm: His strategy had been to lock up the nomination early, but when the unexpected onrush of Hart threatened to push his primary spending beyond the limits set by federal laws, unions set up "independent" delegate committees that could spend money on his behalf. Marylouise was now tracking money as well as social power for the *L.A. Times*; where was this pro-Mondale spending coming from? she asked one of his advisers, David Ifshin, a friend of hers from the antiwar movement and a prominent advocate for Israel. Ifshin answered the question and she broke the story; but an editor thought it wasn't important enough for page one, and ran it in a box on page three. A few days later, *The Washington Post* rebroke the news and it was page one everywhere.

Mondale was once again the poster child for the old politics. And Hart was on the move again as the final round of contests neared that year's Super Tuesday. On June 5, 1984, California, New Jersey, and three smaller states would render a final verdict. If Hart won both California and New Jersey, he'd prevail.

With little more than a week to go, Hart was moving fast in California and far ahead in New Jersey. Then Caddell phoned me and said there was a problem; I had to come in. The night before, at a fund-raiser in Los Angeles, Hart had used an "opener" that would close off his march to the nomination: politicians shouldn't tell jokes unless they're naturally good at it. Hart explained that most of the time, he and his wife Lee "campaign separately; that's the bad news. The good news for her is that she campaigns in California and I campaign in New Jersey." It was bad enough, but was about to turn terminal. Lee interrupted him: "I got to hold a koala bear." Hart picked up the riff: "I won't tell you what I got to hold—samples from a toxic waste dump." Paul Maslin, Caddell's young associate, moaned that he didn't even want to read the next tracking poll from New Jersey. On primary night, instead of sweeping New Jersey, Hart lost every delegate but one—and then that one, too, was gone with a recount. In California, Hart's massive win hit the news on Pacific time, three hours later. The Mondale campaign exploited the time zone difference to scoop up undecided delegates. Once again, the nomination that was within Hart's grasp was fumbled away.

A Hart nomination would have shaken up the 1984 race, enough to jostle but not overthrow Reagan. Still, 1984 set Hart up for 1988, especially if Kennedy didn't run. And when that time came, Hart almost certainly would have been the nominee and probably president but for the scandal that engulfed him, fairly or unfairly, when a *Miami Herald* reporter trailed him to a Washington town house—and reported that he'd spent the night inside with a model and actress named Donna Rice. A provocative photo surfaced of her sitting on Hart's lap on a yacht in Florida. He publicly insisted that nothing had occurred, and he stuck to that when we talked about it years later. He was bitter at the press, especially Paul Taylor of *The Washington Post*, who'd cleared his throat and, under instructions from his editors, asked Hart if he'd ever committed adultery. "I don't have to answer that," he snapped. Whatever the truth about Donna Rice, Hart had opened the way to the question. He'd been careless—just as he had in 1984 in dealing with the controversy that cost him Illinois and in joking his way out of a New Jersey win and the nomination. This time he was forced out of the race before it began.

For all his gifts, Hart was an unnatural politician, a cerebral man who forced himself to play a public part. Although he didn't have the standard politician's personality, he had come close to the ultimate political prize. In the end, I believe he was fatalistic about the outcome, reflecting an attitude of political predestination rooted in the hard tenets of the fundamentalist Nazarene faith he'd been raised in. Either he was supposed to be president—or he wasn't.

I was no longer Kennedy's press secretary; in 1984, I had shifted to running his PAC, a political action committee designed to help elect Democratic candidates across the country. One of them was Lloyd Doggett, an Austin liberal who'd won an upset victory in Texas in the Democratic Senate primary, but was now running well behind the Republican nominee, the turncoat conservative Democrat Phil Gramm. On a trip to Austin, I met the Doggett campaign manager, who looked and sounded like a Gothic character out of the pages of *All the King's Men*. His name was James Carville. His swagger, his shaved head, his stories and aphorisms spilling out in a hyperkinetic, sometimes profane geyser of heavily accented phrases and half-sentences—I'd never encountered anyone in politics like this. In the next few years I'd come to appreciate Carville's contempt for the usual kabuki of campaigns, the irrelevant details and proprieties that slow down decision making, and his capacity to cut to the strategic heart of the contest.

He didn't like meetings that lasted longer than 25 minutes; he'd just get up and leave. The first morning at Doggett headquarters, he was circling the floor like a caged lion. There had to be a way to get back in the race, but Mondale on the ticket wasn't helping any. And then there'd been that Doggett fund-raiser at a gay bar, where contributors stuffed money into the jock strap of someone named "The Banana Queen"—or that's what they said—and the Doggett campaign had to give the money back. Doggett had to get away from the social issues; but the economy, that was roaring back. Texas loved Reagan, and Mondale, Mondale—well, Jesus Christ, that was a disaster. This is the closest I can get to re-creating Carville's frustrated energy as he relentlessly grabbed for a strategic lever he couldn't find. But there was one thing that could get done—and if we couldn't get that done, well, screw it. The campaign had hired a young student from the University of Texas, Paul Begala, to write speeches. But Doggett wouldn't stick with a stump speech. Some message, any message, was better than him wandering all over the goddamn lot. So we focused on the speech. The drafts Begala had given Doggett were first rate; we reworked them. I think Carville hoped that if I somehow blessed a version, the candidate would be more amenable to it. I blessed it. Doggett agreed to it; but after I left, he would continue on as he had before. It didn't really matter. There are campaigns that can't be won no matter what the candidate does, or how talented someone like Carville is.

To this point, James had never managed a winning campaign, despite his intensity and intuitive gifts. But he was undaunted. Over margaritas one night on my trip to Austin, we moved on from the search for a strategic frame to what I can only describe as Carville's life maxims. Run 25 minutes every day: he was skinny now in his trademark tight-fitting jeans, but he used to be fat; he liked to drink and eat. So, no matter what else you were doing, you just had to stand up at four thirty or five in the afternoon and go jogging. The meeting, or the candidate, could always wait. James was a bachelor then and he also shared his maxim for finding a date in a bar: "Go ugly early." He wasn't politically correct or conventional, but he was progressive: Kennedy in '80 and Hart in the '84 primaries, after an intervening Senate campaign that almost beat Jesse Helms in North Carolina. There, Carville gleefully recalled, he himself had been compared to Satan. After my time in Austin, I didn't see how Doggett could win. But Carville—somehow, I thought I'd see him again, and Begala, too.

Although I didn't realize it, the fall of 1984 would be the last time I'd travel the country with Kennedy in a presidential campaign—

someone else's or his own. Yet for me, the most memorable moment that fall wasn't political but personal. I ran into Marylouise, who was covering a Kennedy speech in Beverly Hills; sat talking with her in her car afterward; and then we kissed. I told her I had the next day off. Did she want to go to Disneyland? As soon as I got back to my hotel room, I began to worry: she was not only a journalist who was writing about politics as well as the social scene, but a larger than life personality, a force of nature. This couldn't go any further unless I was ready to get serious. And I wasn't. The next day I never even held her hand as I traipsed around Disneyland in a pair of black suit pants and a white dress shirt; amid the tourists in khakis, polo shirts, and Bermuda shorts, she joked that I looked like a priest on his afternoon off. As we waited in line at the "Small World" ride, I was rattling on about conversations with Kennedy, Hart, and Mondale's campaign chair Jim Johnson, when she poked me in the ribs; people around us were staring at me. On the way back to L.A., she invited me to visit over Christmas. I was wary, but drawn to her. Later, I would tell her the thought I had that day—that she was an "E Ticket Attraction." In the book of Disneyland tickets you had to buy back then, the "E"s were the precious few that got you on the best rides. I promised I'd see her over the holidays.

On election night in 1984, it was "morning again in America"— the line from Reagan's most memorable ad—as he swept forty-nine states, with Mondale barely even taking his home state of Minnesota. It wasn't the outcome I'd argued for at the start of the year, when Bill Buckley invited me to join George McGovern for a special edition of Buckley's nationally televised *Firing Line*. It was to be taped at the Yale Political Union, where Buckley had honed his inimitable polemical gifts before putting them on such conspicuous display in the conservative magazine he founded, the *National Review,* whose self-proclaimed mission was to stand "athwart history yelling 'Stop!' "

In the debate, Buckley and George Will would argue that Ronald Reagan, who had at least partially fulfilled that mission, deserved to be reelected. McGovern and I would take the other side. I'd often told Ted Kennedy before tough interviews that the key was to prepare, prepare, prepare, but once in the fray don't strain to remember a series of pre-scripted answers. When the exchange begins, you have to assume you're ready—as ready as you're going to be. Don't hesitate; just "say the first thing that pops into your head." Often it's just naturally the right answer. After I arrived in New Haven, met Buckley for the first time, and huddled with McGovern, I was handed a message to call Kennedy. It was just minutes before we were to go on stage. Kennedy's voice rumbled across the line: "Bob, just say the first thing that pops into your head."

In reality this was, and is, the right advice. Buckley, who repeatedly brought me back to *Firing Line* over the next decade, once confessed that he often gained the advantage when an opponent paused to search for a word or phrase; Buckley would jump in and seize the dialogue. A year after the Yale encounter, Buckley and I were the lead debaters on his show on whether to "go full speed ahead with Star Wars"—Reagan's plan or fantasy about ballistic missile defense. We each headed a debate team that included experts on weaponry and arms control; we certainly weren't. Buckley challenged me during the Q and A: "Now Mr. Shrum, don't try to fool anybody. You don't know the slightest thing about . . . what expenses are required to research this program." I replied with the first thing that popped into my mind: "Do *you*?" Buckley said: "No." I forged ahead: "Which leads, Mr. Buckley, to the question: what are you and I doing up here talking about this?" Buckley, who could take as gracefully as he gave, featured the exchange in his book *On the Firing Line* in 1989.

At one of our subsequent encounters, he recalled the outcome of the debate on the 1984 election. He was still smarting because in the Yale Political Union's vote after the debate, Buckley, Will, and Reagan had lost. He said to me that this proved just one thing: "As Yale goes, so goes Minnesota."

Kennedy had been right to skip the run against Reagan, whatever the reason. He would have lost. But Reagan couldn't run again and I figured the next time Kennedy would have a clear shot at last.

He was picking up where RFK had left off when he took a trip to the apartheid-scarred country of South Africa in early 1985. I went with him, missing Christmas with Marylouise. I didn't tell her why and she found out where I was from *Time* magazine because I said something in South Africa that sparked a brush fire in the media there. It came near the end of a journey that persuaded Kennedy to push for economic sanctions—a policy the Reagan administration stubbornly opposed.

The trip was exhilarating, tense, and at times turbulent. Kennedy, in defiance of South African law, stayed the first night in the black township of Soweto, in the home of Bishop Desmond Tutu. The next morning, in Bishop Tutu's room, I noticed an open box casually placed on the dresser. I asked Tutu if I could pick up what was inside; it was the first and last time I've ever held a Nobel Peace Prize in my hands. The South African press was blistering Kennedy every day as an intruder: He was appealing to "the Negro vote" to run for president in 1988; after Chappaquiddick, he had no credentials to speak about right and wrong. We had to fly hundreds of miles to visit Winnie Mandela, the wife of South Africa's most famous freedom fighter. Nelson Mandela was in prison for life and she was in "internal exile" in a remote corner of the country. Over and over, the apartheid regime, which normally prohibited demonstrations, allowed a black separatist group to disrupt Kennedy's stops. The U.S. ambassador, Herman Nickel, an apologist for apartheid, introduced Kennedy at a speech by criticizing his "whirlwind tour."

It was in Durban, a seaport on the Indian Ocean, that I committed news I didn't intend to. Kennedy was meeting with the Zulu chief Gatsha Buthelezi, who had formed an alliance of convenience with the government because he had no hope of winning power in a South Africa where everyone could vote. In a meeting room at a hotel, Buthelezi attacked the idea of sanctions or disinvestment, and lit into Bishop Tutu. I got tired of hearing his rant, so I slipped out the back door to find refuge in the hotel lobby. A beefy white man—I later found out he was a former city councilman—lumbered toward me. He yelled: "Why don't you go back to your own country instead of coming here? I've been to the United States. I've seen what happens to black people." I responded that at least we were trying to end discrimination and inequality, and that was the difference: "You're running a slave state here." Suddenly I saw the camera from South African television; my protagonist happily departed. He'd done his job; I'd played my part. The outburst would get attention—and it did, in the South African press, then in the AP and the *Time* story that Marylouise read. As we were leaving the hotel, with Buthelezi's two hundred chanting followers finally dispersing, I climbed into the car with Kennedy and told him what happened. "You said *what?*" he asked incredulously. I told him again. "Well," he answered, "I wish I could say that."

After we left, the apartheid regime and its supporters were confident that Kennedy's visit didn't matter. The *Johannesburg Sunday Times* blustered that he was "not even a very important member of the United States Congress." Kennedy joined with the Black Caucus to push for sanctions; he brought along Democrats who'd previously bought the line that some form of "constructive engagement" with South Africa was a better course. Republicans enlisted, and in the fall of 1986, the Senate and the House overrode President Reagan's veto. Four years later, the apartheid government yielded to the unremitting pressure and freed Nelson Mandela. He and Kennedy talked—for the first time ever—the next day. The onetime prisoner for life would become the first black president of South Africa. Mandela traveled to Boston to the Kennedy Library, and thanked Edward Kennedy for trying to visit him in jail. Kennedy had been denied entry, but Mandela knew he was just outside the gates, and "the message of hope, of strength . . . gave us . . . the feeling that we had millions behind us."

For Kennedy himself, the trip to South Africa mattered in another way. Midway across the Atlantic on our return flight, Kennedy expressed his frustration that so much of the press coverage back home seemed to buy the line that he'd gone to South Africa primarily to seize an issue and an advantage with African-Americans for the next presidential campaign. Was every fight on every issue bound to be seen and distorted through that lens? Even my recent decision to move on and, with Kennedy's help, become a political consultant was interpreted as more preparation and maneuver for an '88 run.

He called me in mid-December 1985: Could I fly to Boston? Someone would pick me up and drive me to Hyannisport. It was a cryptic conversation. I told my consulting partner David Doak what I assumed: "Kennedy's not running." As soon as I got to Kennedy's house, the classic waterside structure where he and his brothers and sisters had spent their summers, I ran into Larry Horowitz, who was still Kennedy's chief of staff. (He'd shortly decamp to California to produce television movies and Broadway shows like *Spamalot* and *The Wedding Singer*.) Larry, I said, is this what I think it is? He shrugged—Kennedy wanted to tell me himself—and I went into the living room that overlooked the desolate December seascape of Nantucket Sound. He offered me a vodka—as if I seemed to need one. I took it and said: "I know, you're not going to run for president." That's right—and he didn't want to argue about it. I told him I had to make one point: "This time, you get to run against Bush. And that's the best chance you'll ever have." I realized it wouldn't persuade him, but I had to get it out there. He brushed the argument aside: "I know, and I don't want to run." He couldn't achieve what he wanted in the Senate—on South Africa, on arms control, or in the shaping of a new Democratic domestic agenda—when everything he did was discounted as a 1988 campaign ploy.

It was a different reason than the last time, but I'd heard his ruminations ever since South Africa. I'd also been to this movie before, the last time he'd dropped out. "I got it," I told him. Horowitz came in and we focused on Kennedy's statement. To have credibility, I suggested, he would have to acknowledge explicitly that this decision probably meant a permanent end to his quest for the White House. "Put it in," he said. I had already made out a few notes on the flight to Boston and went into the bedroom right behind the living room, where I'd stayed before, to write the draft. It was the room where JFK had been confined to bed after he returned wounded from the South Pacific: he and the twelve-year-old Teddy had taken turns reading aloud to each other from Stephen Vincent Benét's epic Civil War poem, *John Brown's Body*. I recalled Kennedy telling me about that—and added something to the sentence renouncing his national ambitions: "I know this decision means that I may never be president. But the pursuit of the presidency is not my life. Public service is." This decision was, of course, not just an end but a beginning. In the years ahead, Kennedy would secure his place as the leading senator of his time, one of the great senators in history.

Although I'd left Kennedy's staff by the time he left the presidential sweepstakes for the last time, I've never stopped working with him. At Christmas 1999, he sent Marylouise and me a new biography of him by the *New York Times* reporter Adam Clymer. He'd inscribed it: "We couldn't have taken this voyage without you." In truth, I couldn't have taken my voyage without him—from the 1980 campaign, to the world of political consulting, to national campaigns not only in America but in Britain, Ireland, and Israel. He paid me a fee when I first went into consulting because, he explained, it would take a few months to get started and I needed some money to tide me over. He also knew that for me, consulting, advising on strategy, and making television ads wasn't just a business—that I was determined to play a role in electing a president and fighting for the kind of Democratic Party he and I believed in. For me, the years ahead inevitably would be a mix of ambition and belief; but as Kennedy joked at the surprise fortieth birthday he threw for me in a cavernous Senate Hearing Room crowded with my friends: "I believe this nation should commit itself to achieving the goal, before this decade is out, of landing Bob Shrum a job in the White House." It was a parody of JFK's challenge to land a man on the moon before the end of the 1960s. Kennedy concluded by turning to me: "Look at it this way—sooner or later, your luck is bound to change."

5

THREE PEOPLE AROUND
A TELEVISION SET

■ was drawn to media consulting because television advertising was the rising force in political campaigns. In 1986, John Balzer of the *Los Angeles Times*, one of California's savviest reporters, would ask me why Alan Cranston wasn't holding political rallies during his Senate reelection race and I answered: "A political rally in California consists of three people around a television set." And being paid well as a consultant was a way to live my dream while fulfilling my parents': they'd had to wait until I was out of college to afford a tract home in the San Fernando Valley. They were proud of what I did, but my father gently reminded me that I had no savings. In 1986, the first mid-term election year I was in the business, I made over $400,000, an astounding multiple of what I'd earned in any year before.

Political media began as a sidelight in the early 1950s as television was taking center stage in American life. For the 1952 Eisenhower campaign, the pioneer television producer Robert Montgomery, helped by Madison Avenue execs, created 60-second ads and spruced up Ike's wooden delivery when he was, in the words of a newspaper chain that supported him, "running like a dry creek" early in the fall. In 1960, under the supervision of another ad exec,

Bill Wilson, the Kennedy media team produced a devastating negative ad to counter Nixon's slogan "Experience Counts." The ad showed President Eisenhower answering a press conference challenge to name one major decision his vice president had participated in making. "If you give me a week, I might think of one," an irritated Eisenhower had responded.

But over time political advertising became a distinct enterprise, without all the costly bells and whistles of Madison Avenue. The first political media consultants tended to come from television, not campaigns. This would change, too, and I was an agent of that change. In early 1985, Pat Caddell and I had dinner with David Doak, a burly midwesterner and rising Democratic star who came from a more conservative side of the party than I did; he'd worked for Carter in 1976 and 1980 and managed Chuck Robb's campaign for governor of Virginia at the height of the Reagan ascendancy in 1981. He actually had some media experience; he'd been with Bob Squier—for a year—and then left. He and Caddell were starting a media firm. Would I like to join them?

Pat assumed that I'd agree to be part of it, if at all, on a part-time basis while remaining with Kennedy's political operation. No, I explained, I was ready to move on. That was great, Caddell said, but we couldn't split the money evenly. He and Doak would each receive 40 percent of the profits—and I'd have to settle for 20 percent. I hardly knew Doak, so I was a little surprised when he took me aside in the elevator lobby back at Caddell's office building: he'd give up part of his cut and propose that the two of us get 30 percent; Pat would be shamed into accepting an even split. Instead, Caddell said any deal was fine with him as long as he kept his 40 percent. For me, the episode built an instant bond of trust with Doak.

Doak brought us our first client: Jerry Baliles, running to succeed Robb as governor of Virginia. In 1985 we had to persuade clients to hire us when all we had was our reputations, and none of them centered on making political ads. Our sample reel of spots was drawn from one race, Baliles, that wasn't yet won. So the candidates we tended to get thought they needed us as much as we needed them.

In different ways, their campaigns were precursors of factors that would play an increasing role in American politics for the next twenty years—the fierce clash over abortion rights, the difference between manufactured candidacies and authenticity, the rise of women in American politics, the hot-button issue of sexual identity, and the power of negative advertising.

Bob Casey was a silver-haired, devout Irish Catholic who was thinking about a fourth—a fourth—try for governor of Pennsylvania. In the state's political circles, he was derisively nicknamed "the three time loss from Holy Cross," where he'd gone to college. We didn't seek him out; he called us. His twenty-five-year-old son, Bobby, today a U.S. senator, was with him when he showed up in our office. Bobby was pushing his dad to run again in a primary against former Philadelphia DA Ed Rendell. They'd already seen one pollster who'd bluntly said he wasn't interested, Casey didn't have a chance. But as Casey laid out his story, the three of us cared less and less about the odds. I identified with him as he recounted how his father, a coal miner at the age of ten, had lifted himself out of the mines to become a lawyer at forty. I knew that kind of story; only in our family, it had taken two generations. Months later during the campaign, Casey would call me from Connellsville and happily announce: "I'm in *your* hometown."

In his early thirties, Casey had been elected auditor general of Pennsylvania, then lost one of his three races for governor because another Bob Casey, the owner of an ice cream parlor, had confused voters by putting his name on the ballot for lieutenant governor. And yet another Bob Casey, running on the name, had been elected state treasurer. The real Bob Casey had an iron sense of determination—not just about himself, but about the Pennsylvania he came from and the people he identified with. As mines and old industries closed, whole sections of the state—from his hometown of Scranton to the coal fields of southwestern Pennsylvania and the neighborhoods of Pittsburgh's north side—were being written off. He wanted to run to change that—and he would run if we'd do it with him. He was there, he said, to pitch us, not to have us pitch him.

Casey didn't need consultants to invent a message to justify his ambition. His story, I said in that first meeting, was Pennsylvania's story; he'd been knocked down more than once and so had a lot of hardworking people across the state. Our slogan would consciously play on the congruence of biography and message: "Bob Casey is coming back—and so is Pennsylvania," and we'd name our official campaign committee "The Real Bob Casey Committee."

In that first meeting, Casey told us he was pro-life; we should understand that he'd never change or back down. Caddell, Doak, and I were pro-choice; but for us, and most of the Democratic Party then, there wasn't a litmus test requiring all our candidates at every level to favor abortion rights. And while I disagreed with Casey, I admired the strength of his conviction. Several years later, I would try to persuade him to move a little to open the door to national office for himself. He said he'd think about it; when I got back to my apartment in Washington from the state capital in Harrisburg, my phone was ringing. He appreciated the advice, but wanted to be clear. He wouldn't change, ever, no matter what.

Caddell also had the Senate Democratic whip, Alan Cranston, on the hook. He was in trouble and just might take a gamble on us. Cranston had had an easy time in California until he dyed his hair near-orange and ran for president in 1984; he came across as a hard-left candidate and slightly ridiculous. His implausible campaign quickly faltered, but the damage was considerable in his home state. He seemed old and out of touch—and in 1986 was the Republicans' number one target. He was a consummate health nut and lifelong runner. But our challenge with Cranston would be to disguise him—focus groups called him "cadaverous"—in his own commercials, and destroy his opponent. The one thing he couldn't be was authentic.

I was having discussions with another potential client whose authenticity was her strongest suit, although she didn't know it. Congresswoman Barbara Mikulski was weighing a Senate race in Maryland, where the incumbent, one of the last of a vanishing breed of moderate eastern Republicans, was retiring. I had dinner with Barbara on Capitol Hill. In the Democratic primary, Mikulski would have to run against another sitting member of Congress and the retiring governor. There were no Democratic women in the

Senate and the only Republican was the daughter of a former presidential nominee. Barbara would have to struggle to raise money. What did I think? she asked. I answered that she was likely to win. She had a base in and around Baltimore, where she lived in a nine-foot-wide row house in the old ethnic neighborhood of Fells Point; the Baltimore area accounted for the single largest bloc of voters in the primary. And in the primary, she'd be one woman against two men.

Then I paused. Barbara was not just a potential client but a long-time friend. She wasn't married; she had no children; she prized being in Congress and she was a visible and influential woman in American public life. What would she do with herself, I asked, if at the age of fifty, she gave up her House seat and then lost the Senate race? She should take a weekend and think about it. There were no sure things in politics.

She had one other question; she'd talked with other media consultants and they'd described how they'd smooth and shape her image. Barbara, who stretches her height to 4 feet, 11 inches, was self-conscious about her stature and her feisty temper. "How else," she later explained to me, "did someone my size get heard except by raising her voice?" She was short, plump, loud, and ethnic—not the standard politician for the television age. How would we present her? "As short, plump, loud, and ethnic," I replied. That's what she was, and a lot of Maryland voters could appreciate that. If her consultants didn't get in the way, she'd come across as real.

Mikulski took a weekend by herself to think it through and decided to run. On the phone, she said she was also inclined to hire us—in part because I hadn't just told her to "run, run, run." But there was one obstacle. The model for our firm, as Caddell saw it, was a one-stop shop that integrated poll taking and ad making. Paul Maslin, Caddell's associate, thought the model was driving business away; he abruptly resigned one day, took one of Caddell's top analysts with him, and went into business with Harrison Hickman, a refugee from another established firm. Hickman was Mikulski's pollster—and he was convinced that if we were hired, Caddell would wage a nonstop effort to steal the polling contract. With difficulty, Doak and I persuaded our partner to promise he would not do this—or so we thought. The three of us boarded the Metroliner for a half-hour ride to Baltimore to reassure Mikulski's team that we would never challenge Hickman's role.

In the meeting, Pat grudgingly uttered the necessary words. Then on the trip back to Washington, our partnership effectively ended. Through gritted teeth, Caddell announced that he wasn't entirely giving up on the polling. Hickman wasn't up to the job; Pat would ferret out the weaknesses in his numbers—and the campaign would change its mind. I'd given my word and so had Doak. This was the latest in a string of disagreements with Caddell, most of them about money. It was also the last straw. A letter dissolving the firm was hand-delivered to Caddell's office and Doak and I found temporary refuge with Hickman and Maslin. From their conference room, we phoned our clients. Casey was distraught: all three of us had to work for him and he didn't care how we structured our relationship. Cranston said the same thing. The Mikulski campaign promptly signed us on, but ruled out any role for Caddell. The story of the breakup was in the paper the next day; it was just a political note and most readers wouldn't even know who any of us were anyway. But it mattered in the self-referential orbit of political operatives, and Caddell at first wouldn't speak to Doak or me, let alone collaborate on anything.

The impasse was broken when Joe Biden stepped in. He'd been elected to the Senate from Delaware twelve years before, at the age of twenty-nine. Caddell had been his pollster then; now Biden was preparing a presidential bid for 1988. He wanted Caddell and Doak in his campaign and he wanted me as well. I was back from Hyannisport and Kennedy's announcement that he wouldn't run when Biden summoned Caddell, Doak, and me to his Senate office. Biden pushed us. Could we find a way to work together? Doak and I said yes—as long as we weren't in the same firm with Caddell. We could share clients, but not Mikulski; we couldn't force her to hire someone she didn't want to. Caddell objected that one of our common clients, Steve Pajcic, who was running for governor in Florida, was *his* friend and might want to dispense with us. Biden interrupted: all the clients we shared before the breakup, *all* of them, should continue to be shared—and that included Pajcic. Biden asked us to shake hands on the deal; they were wan handshakes. But I said to Pat, and I meant it, "I'm sorry."

The deal held with Casey and Cranston—and with another woman who was running for statewide office, Jane Eskind, a candidate for governor of Tennessee. She would lose her primary in a way I'd never forget. Caddell would tell her that his election eve poll had her on a clear track to victory. Her election night suite was replete with silver buckets of champagne, the corks ready to pop. As the returns came in, I felt like swapping the bubbles for vodka. The numbers were wrong. Tennessee was no more ready to elect a woman governor in 1986 than it would be ready to elect an African-American senator in 2006.

But the "Treaty of Biden" broke down with Steve Pajcic, who initially said that he wanted to have all three of us, then changed his mind, keeping only Caddell. I would watch from the sidelines as he lost in November when his campaign failed to respond to a barrage of negative attacks. I was taken aback when he called afterward. He said he had some money left, and he was going to send it to Doak and me because we'd never received anything for all the work we'd done with him in the early months of the campaign. I told him that wasn't necessary. He replied that sending us some money was the honorable thing to do—and he did. Nothing else like this would ever happen in all my time as a political consultant.

Doak and I would last as partners for nine years—remarkable in part because we were so different. He preferred to sit in the conference room hour after hour to labor a single phrase. Sometimes it paid off; after tossing ideas back and forth, a process punctuated by long periods of silence for David's ruminations, we hit on a powerful populist frame for Dick Gephardt's 1988 presidential campaign: "It's your fight too." At other times, our long hours in that conference room were frustrating rituals that stifled spontaneity. But 1986 was a remarkable first year for us that propelled Doak and Shrum to the first rank of Democratic consultants. Once there, our visibility and expanding client list also made us a target for competitors, who accused us of minting money in too many races and soon nicknamed us "Soak and Run."

None of our 1986 campaigns was easy, although Mikulski's came closest. I witnessed the power of her authenticity when a day of outdoor filming in Baltimore was rained out. She took me to an indoor market lined with vendors and stalls. Everyone there seemed to know her and they all called this congresswoman by her first name, Barbara, and sometimes Barb. I cut back on the material we'd scripted and the next day filmed Mikulski moving through the market again. The set of spots was as real as anything gets in political advertising. A white-haired woman told her in a distinctive Baltimore accent: "Jeepers, you've lost weight, haven't you?" Mikulski responded with instant panache: "I'm counting my calories, counting my blessings, and counting my votes." In the Democratic primary, she finished 20 points ahead of her nearest rival. Mikulski's campaign was not a case of consultants devising an image, but a classic case for getting out of the way and letting a candidate be herself—of filming a woman for office without trying to pretty her up or soften her edges. Her spots even showed her owning up to her presumed drawbacks; in one of them, she confessed with a smile, "Sometimes I do raise my voice *a little*."

On primary night, she urged the crowd to "make sure the Mikulski victory is not a one-night stand." Who else would or could say something like this on statewide television? Her Republican opponent in the general election was Linda Chavez, a turncoat Democrat I knew from the Kennedy '80 campaign, now a brittle neoconservative who'd served in the Reagan administration. No one gave her much of a chance, so she tried to shake up the race with an innuendo about Mikulski's sexual orientation. Borrowing a phrase coined at the 1984 Republican Convention, she constantly referred to Mikulski as a "San Francisco–style Democrat." Harrison Hickman reported that most voters didn't understand what she was saying— Mikulski was from Fells Point.

Still, in case we had to respond to the smears, we had to ask Mikulski some hard questions. We already had. Wendy Sherman, her campaign manager and in later years the Clinton administration's chief negotiator with North Korea, had driven us to a session with the candidate neither of us wanted to have. The three of us quietly met at Sherman's home. Wendy and I were appalled that we had to discuss something that should have been her business and nobody else's. Mikulski was direct. No, she wasn't a lesbian; she just wished a Prince Charming had come along in her life. She wryly said, looking at me, "There was no Ted Kennedy who ever asked me out." We told her that when the innuendo came, she just had to brush it off. Chavez's code phrase failed; but in the two decades since, gay-baiting has become a staple of Republican tactics.

In Pennsylvania, negative ads determined the outcome in both the primary and the general election—although Casey's stubborn pro-life view almost cost him the governorship. We started out with a positive spot focusing on Casey's personal story that made his message about Pennsylvania's hopes and hurts believable. But positive could only get us so far. We blasted Rendell for fixing parking tickets when he was DA, including his own. In another ad, featuring a series of black-and-white photos accompanied by ominous camera clicks, we criticized Rendell for taking $300,000 in campaign money from executives and associates of a company that he failed to investigate—and which was now the subject of a federal inquiry. The spots kick-started my reputation for slash-and-burn negatives. Over the years, Doak would get less of the blame because he would be less visible and thus less of a lightning rod. But neither of us was bothered by the attacks on Rendell; they were factual, even if we accentuated the impact with music, visuals, and one-liners that cast the facts in the most sinister light. Casey winced at the ads, but said to put them on—as long as they were true.

He took another step on the road to victory when he replaced a campaign manager who'd been with him from the start but was out of his depth. Did we have any suggestions? Yes, someone named James Carville, who after the loss in that Texas Senate race in 1984 was sitting on his couch in Louisiana watching reruns of his favorite television comedy, *The Andy Griffith Show*. As I'd discover, Carville could reprise whole sections of the dialogue and entire plots of individual episodes; his favorite character—and he could sound just like him—was Don Knotts's befuddled deputy sheriff, Barney Fife. James was an alien presence in the world of Pennsylvania political operatives. He didn't know the local players, we told Casey. That, the candidate replied, was an advantage in a place where all the locals were incessantly maneuvering against each other. There was one other thing, said Doak, who'd been the most successful Democratic campaign manager of the early 1980s. He was sure Carville was the best we could get. But he'd lost a lot of races. "So have I," Casey replied; maybe they'd be a good fit. Carville came north, and the straightlaced Irishman and the ragin' Cajun hit it off immediately. Casey was amused by Carville's bad-boy lifestyle and language—and delighted by the pyrotechnic drive he brought to the job.

On primary night, the three time loss from Holy Cross won the Democratic nomination for governor on his fourth try—by a margin of 16 points. But by August, he was running double digits behind the Republican nominee. Before the race was over, we would run the most notorious negative ad of 1986.

Our opponent, Lieutenant Governor Bill Scranton, was the thirty-nine-year-old son of a former governor, a Yale graduate, and a self-confessed 1960s "hippie." Casey's hometown was named for the Scrantons; they'd been the bosses living on the hilltop, while Irish immigrants like the Caseys lived in the valley and worked in the utilities and the railroad equipment factories owned by the Scrantons. Casey had a visceral sense that a Scranton victory would be unfair: he hadn't done anything to earn it; he was being handed the governorship just because of who he was and what he'd inherited. But Bill Scranton was moderate and pro-choice, exactly the kind of Republican Pennsylvanians tended to elect.

Once again, the positive spots got us somewhere, but not far enough. We never assumed they would. Carville was eager to attack. We tied Scranton's thin record to his privileged background. After college, the ad said, his family bought him a chain of small-town newspapers—and the photo of a long-haired Scranton filled the screen—"but he stopped going to work and the newspapers failed." Then as lieutenant governor, he'd missed meeting after meeting of the state commissions he was on—one of his only real duties in that office. The spot concluded: "They gave him the job because of his father's name; the least he could do was show up for work." The line had just popped into my mind as we were writing the script. It was the flip side of the Casey message: He was hardworking; he grew up without the wealth and connections that mean you don't have to work. The most powerful negative is always the reverse of the positive case.

The race was tied in October, or, Caddell reported, a little better than that. Then, at a televised debate two weeks before the election, Scranton announced that he was pulling his negative ads off TV. They'd had a negligible effect anyway, but the press applauded his move—and he obviously hoped Casey would be forced to follow his lead. Casey didn't even consider it. We were nervous about the fallout; maybe voters were as repelled by the negative ads as the press said. Still, we had no choice but to stay on track.

Scranton got a bump from his all-positive pledge. But it wasn't our decision to hold to the negative course, it was something Casey himself said that almost caused the bottom to fall out. He'd been advised that he should stand his ground on abortion without sounding extreme; as governor, he'd be constrained by the ruling in *Roe v. Wade*, able to seek only limited restrictions. But then in the debate, he answered a smart reporter's hypothetical question. If the courts permitted it, he would sign a bill outlawing abortion. "Jesus Christ!" Carville screamed into the phone I was holding away from my ear. Casey's opposition provided no exceptions, even for rape and incest, and proposed laws also included a cutoff of funding to family planning clinics that provided abortion counseling. Scranton was out on the campaign trail assailing Casey as "a one issue-candidate." We had threaded the needle to this point, but soon we were 7 points behind.

We had to claw our way back with one last and nuclear attack on Scranton. We had discussed and rejected the option of an ad about his past drug use. I hated the idea; it was too risky. Instead, Caddell and I scripted an ad that skirted the line, but didn't go over it—except visually. Scranton had been a devotee of TM (transcendental meditation) and had traveled the world with the Maharishi Mahesh Yogi. TM might be harmless, but it didn't sound that way to voters in the blue-collar precincts of mainstream Pennsylvania. With our editor Tony Peist, I was at Modern Video adding in Ravi Shankar–like sitar music to accompany the side-by-side pictures of the long-haired Scranton and the long-haired Maharishi when Carville walked in the studio to look at the spot. He and our campaign finance chair were going to dinner; they'd be back afterward. Before he returned, the phone rang: Ed Rendell, now campaigning for us, was telling the press that I was making an ad about Scranton's drug use. The phone rang again: now the story was that I had been doing just that until Casey had vetoed the idea. I tracked down Carville. He told me to be calm, he'd be right over. I was incandescent when he explained that he and Casey's fund-raiser were Rendell's sources; they'd asked him not to tell anyone, knowing that he promptly would. Then Carville could make Casey look good by putting out the word that he'd ruled out any spot about drugs, while getting the drug story into the papers without Casey getting blamed. I'd take the hit. I said I was goddamned pissed. Still there was nothing I could do but finish what would become known as "the guru spot."

Casey was skittish about it. He was on the road. There was no way to show him the finished ad. I described it to him. He fretted that it might seem like we were bringing up drugs. The script never mentioned drugs, I said; I didn't say that the look of the spot could evoke the drug issue without mentioning it. To defend the ad's relevance, I went on, we had included a Scranton quote that he wanted to bring transcendental meditation to state government. Casey asked me to call one of his daughters who, like most of his eight children, was now grown up; she was worried sick that the spot would defeat her dad and destroy his reputation. As we talked, I realized that there were other Caseys on the call. I said bluntly that if we didn't run the ad, her dad was going to lose. Was I sure the spot would work? one of the Caseys asked. No, but it was our best shot. Would I take responsibility for it? Yes, I said, knowing that if Casey lost, his "unscrupulous" consultants would be excoriated anyway.

Casey would have a lifelong aversion to hearing about "the guru spot"—and especially resented statements like one in Wikipedia that it "depicted Scranton as 'a dope-smoking hippie.' " It didn't, but that was a technical truth. I'd be called "a master of negativity" in the years ahead and then be blamed for not being negative enough in the 2004 Kerry campaign. But I've never accepted the argument that all negative ads are wrong; the standard should be whether they are relevant and truthful, although the fine points inevitably tend to get lost in a 30-second spot. Is it really "wrong" for voters to be told, for example, that someone opposes the minimum wage? There's too much easy cant and too little precision in the critiques of negative advertising. But the "guru spot" did skirt the line.

As much as Casey didn't want to hear it, the negatives would make the difference. They would be decisive in the Cranston campaign, too. Alan Cranston, a senator not made for the television age, was reelected because of television. He looked "cadaverous," as the focus groups put it, because as a runner he was out there every day trying to keep himself fit. One winter morning, I even opened my door at the O'Hare Airport Hilton in Chicago to encounter someone pounding out wind sprints up and down the hall. It was Cranston; I didn't even know he was at the hotel. But the way Californians reacted to his appearance left us with a conundrum in a state where voters might not care so much about the age of their politicians— look at Reagan—but expected them to be minimally mediagenic. What was a media consultant to do? We produced a batch of positive spots in which Cranston was an apparent presence, but his face was seen for only a few seconds. In one, for example, the camera focused from the knees down on someone in a sweatsuit running through a park while the narrator explained, "He's always ahead of the pack"—and then, without using the candidate's name, reeled off a list of achievements. Only at the end, as he finished the run, did we cut to a brief shot of the smiling candidate's face as the narrator, for the first time in 30 seconds, referred to "California's Alan Cranston."

We had a surprise in store for the winner of the Republican primary. We planned to launch a negative assault the day afterward. We had no illusion that Cranston could be reelected unless we succeeded in "disqualifying" his opponent. But that had another implication, as I explained to the candidate at a one-day campaign retreat in a beach house perched on a hilltop above the Pacific: We'd go on the air June 4 or 5; except for brief pauses, we'd have to stay on—and keep up the pressure—all the way to November. Or as Caddell put it: "Keep our foot on the other guy's throat." This would be the most expensive political ad buy for any candidate in California history (a record that would be shattered four years later); Cranston would have to raise an average of $75,000 a day, each and every day, until the election. It sounded impossible as I said it. Cranston matter-offactly replied that if that was what it took, he could do it.

The opponent we didn't want was Ed Zschau, a former high-tech executive and moderate congressman from the Bay Area whose own media blitz featured an arresting sound effect teaching voters how to pronounce his last name; it sounded like the first syllable of "shower." He had one vulnerability, although the press wasn't making much of it. To make himself acceptable to Republican primary voters, he'd tacked to the right. After the primary, we were sure, he'd move back to the center. But the tactic had left him on the record taking opposite sides on a number of critical issues. We sent a crew to tape him speaking at an event. He apparently assumed they were from the local news and obligingly asked them if they had enough footage. They did. We edged it to make it look like a strip of film, and the frames sped by and then intermittently stopped and flipped as we assailed him for flip-flopping on issues. The specifics didn't matter that much, because the flip-flops were designed to raise doubts about Zschau's character. You could smile—and we often would—at the tone of this spot and a series of sequels captioned "Zschau Flip-Flop Update."

When we held a screening for reporters a day after the primary, they sounded confounded by our unorthodox strategy. On the surface, Cranston was well ahead in the polls. Why was he attacking first and this early? It was, we did concede, an unusual move; and we relied on that old political chestnut—Cranston was taking nothing for granted. But Zschau and his top campaign staff were taking a few days off after their grueling primary battle. By the time he returned and their new ads went on the air, we'd gone a long way toward defining Zschau before he could redefine himself as a moderate. Zschau persisted with positive image-building ads, but they had little impact; people occasionally called the Cranston headquarters and asked when the next Zschau Flip-Flop Update was coming.

Marylouise came to Washington late in July; the *L.A. Times* national bureau was offering her the chance to write her column from the road during the 1988 presidential primaries. She was thrilled and I planned on taking her to celebrate at an expensive Italian restaurant a block from the K Street lobbying kingdom. This time, I announced, I was going to pay, not the *Times*. Once we sat down, we were joined by Bob Giuliano, a lobbyist for the Hotel and Restaurant Workers Union. He selected the very fine wine; I never even saw the bill. Then he tagged along as I walked Marylouise back to the Jefferson Hotel. We were sitting in the bar and she excused herself for a minute. I said: "Bob, it's time for you to go"—which he obligingly did. Marylouise was a little surprised that Giuliano had to leave, but then told me that her friend Stacey, Henry Winkler's wife, was looking for the right man for her to date. I don't know why—it was uncharacteristic—but I didn't hesitate: "How about me? I love you." The next morning, as I left the hotel, I had to slip quietly past the bar, now transformed into a breakfast room, where Marylouise was having a coffee with Muffie Brandon, the former social secretary in the Reagan White House. Back in Los Angeles, Marylouise informed her managing editor George Cotliar that she was involved with me. He responded: "But wasn't he a good source?" She was done writing about the Cranston race—and she'd never go on the road to cover the '88 presidential primary season because I'd have a client who was a candidate. This was still a few years before James Carville and Mary Matalin got people accustomed to the idea that two people in a relationship could have opposite views, or that one could be a partisan and the other a journalist.

After Zschau switched in September to negative ads indicting Cranston for opposing the death penalty and missing votes on drug enforcement, our artificial lead steadily melted. To make matters worse, President Reagan was coming to California for the last weekend of what he was calling his last campaign to ask his home state to "win one more for the Gipper" by electing Zschau to the Senate. Doak and I had hired a young associate, Joe Trippi, a restless veteran of the Kennedy and Mondale races, gifted with a supercharged, original mind. Cranston needed one more jolt, I told Joe, one striking way to refresh the flip-flop message and poke fun at Zschau; it had to draw enough attention to partially offset Reagan's impact. Couldn't we satirize an ad that was already on television, something people were familiar with? Joe asked if I'd ever seen the K-Tel Records commercials, where an announcer hawked a compilation of old songs as the titles floated across the screen. We bantered back and forth, imagining and writing a spot we named "Hits." The song titles included "Do the Zschau Bop Flip-Flop"; "I'd Send the Bucks to Nicaragua"; and "Both Sides Now." The script even aped the extras the K-Tel commercials threw in: "And we'll send you additional Zschau Flip-Flops for free . . ." It would be a 60-second spot, doubling the already stratospheric costs of running an ad in the megamarkets of California. It was, I confessed to Cranston, kind of a wacky idea; he'd never seen the K-Tel commercials, he admitted, but if it might break through, then try it. In the homestretch of a tense race, he was a candidate who would rather be reelected than reassured. We hastily put the spot together with a record album jacket featuring a two-faced Zschau as our narrator sang the song titles to the cobbled-together music. The broadcast time we paid for was dwarfed by the coverage we got. The "Hits" ad broke the mold—it was in the news, right up there with the stories about Reagan barnstorming for Zschau. One station even held its own focus group at a record store, playing the ad and then showing the store's young customers commenting and laughing.

I made a deal with Marylouise, and with fate. Doak and Shrum had four statewide races that November: Casey, Cranston, Mikulski, and David Walters for governor of Oklahoma. My deal with Marylouise was that if we won at least three of our four races, we'd go to Italy for a week; two of them, and we'd go to the Napa Valley; one, we'd meet in Kansas City—and none, I'd hide out in her house in L.A. There was no danger of that; Mikulski was far ahead. But the other three races were tight—and in each case, the conventional wisdom was that they would be decided by the television ads. "TV will do it," Mervin Field, California's leading independent pollster, told the press. Depending on the outcome, Doak and I would either have a booming business or be out of business.

On Election Day, Carville called me in Washington; he was beside himself. The early exit polls in Pennsylvania were bad; Casey was running points behind. James ordered everyone who was driving to Scranton for election night to turn around and join the get-out-the-vote effort in Philadelphia. Carville had poured his soul and manic talent into this one race, which, if lost, might be the last campaign he'd have a chance to lead and win. He was compulsively superstitious. He hadn't changed his underwear for days; I didn't understand why that meant good luck, and didn't ask him.

Early in the evening, I stopped by an election party in Georgetown. It was an upbeat gathering. Democrats were on course to recapture the Senate. The networks announced Barbara Mikulski's victory early. But David Walters was behind; Oklahoma counted votes fast and early. He lost by 2 percent.* Bob Casey's race was too close to call. And California, well, it would come in hours later. I couldn't join in the happy mood yet, and maybe not at all. For me that night, all politics was too local. I retreated to my apartment, where Steve McMahon, a young press aide I'd hired in Kennedy's office who would soon become an associate in my firm, and my closest friend Tom Rollins, who had now become Kennedy's staff director on the Labor and Human Resources Committee, found me sitting in bed, pulling the covers over my head, and intermittently turning the television on and off. They stayed as I alternated calls with Doak, Carville, Marylouise, and the Cranston staff.

Casey made it in a squeaker—by just 73,000 votes. I thought to myself, the guy from the valley finally beat the guy on the hilltop. And the abortion issue would come full circle in the Democratic Party with Casey and his son. As governor, Bob Casey would be

---

* We'd work for him again when he ran and won in 1990.

banned from the speaking platform at the 1992 Democratic Convention, while his pro-choice Republican opponent in his reelection campaign would be invited on stage. But by 2006, national Democrats would recruit his son Bobby, almost as pro-life as his father, to unseat the third-ranking Republican in the U.S. Senate. A presidential possibility still has to be pro-choice to be nominated by the Democrats. But like the Republicans who tolerate Rudolph Giuliani, despite his record on *Roe v. Wade* and gay rights, Democratic leaders and pro-choice voters have decided that the party's tent has to be big enough for pro-life statewide and congressional candidates.

That night in 1986 was a long one that stretched into morning. Marylouise phoned; she was at Cranston's election night headquarters in Los Angeles and the candidate wanted to talk to me. He thanked me for "a great job"; while the numbers were tight, he thought we'd be okay. Marylouise said she would phone again when the Cranston race was decided. By morning, it was. Cranston's margin was only 116,000 votes out of 7 million cast. Doak and I got a lot of credit that year. But in elections as close as Cranston's, Casey's, and Walters's, where winners get all the credit and losers all the blame, John Kennedy's words express the reality: "Victory has a hundred fathers and defeat is an orphan."

The day after the 1986 midterms, I was invited to lunch on the Georgetown waterfront with Pamela Harriman and Janet Howard, the director of her PAC, "Democrats for the 80s," which had collected millions of dollars for Senate and House candidates. I had gotten to know Pamela and her husband, Averell Harriman, well in the past few years. They'd met in London during World War II when the twenty-two-year-old Pamela, then married to Winston Churchill's son Randolph, had captivated the far older Averell, who was serving as FDR's special envoy. Thirty years later, shortly after Harriman's wife and Pamela's second husband, Leland Hayward, both died, they were brought together again by *Washington Post* publisher Katharine Graham. He was eighty; she was fifty-one. They took up where they'd left off and were married within weeks.

On their twelfth anniversary, he toasted her and said it was "really the fortieth."

Over coffee, the first time I'd seen them together in 1979, Harriman was daunting, alert, and inquisitive. He quickly shifted from politics to the world stage. What did I think of Pope John Paul II, who'd just been elected a few months before? I responded that he might be too conservative, too much like Pius XII. You didn't like Pius XII? he asked almost incredulously. I didn't, I replied—and Harriman interjected: "I did. He was a friend." I was taken aback; I didn't think of popes as potential friends, but after all this *was* Averell Harriman. When the Marshall Plan was pouring aid into Western Europe to thwart a Communist takeover, he'd spent time with Pius XII, who, he informed me, mixed an excellent martini.

Pamela was beautiful, compelling and complex—someone who had captured, often briefly, many of the twentieth century's most powerful men. Her detractors were wrong that her charm was a substitute for intellect and insight; she was widely read and mostly self-educated—since she'd married Randolph Churchill at the age of nineteen. She was a loyal friend. Each winter, and sometimes in the summer, she invited me—and later Marylouise—to the coral stone home she'd bought in Barbados. I was introduced to her neighbor up the beach, Claudette Colbert, who had hosted two other former movie stars, Ronald and Nancy Reagan, for a presidential visit. Colbert's most vivid memory, she said, was swimming with Reagan inside a ring of Secret Service agents, with naval ships a little farther offshore. She'd asked him if he'd liked being president. He plunged underwater, then surfaced and answered her with a big grin on his face: "It's the greatest part they ever gave me."

On a trip to Barbados in 1985, I had a sense that the increasingly frail Averell Harriman would never return again. He died in July, at the age of ninety-four. After the funeral, I went to Birch Grove, the home Pamela had shared with Leland Hayward in the green hills an hour north of New York City. We read through the condolence notes and telegrams. Janet Howard was sorting them into two stacks, one for people Pamela knew and another for those she didn't. I quickly sifted through the second stack until I came to a telegram signed "Francis Albert." Was this who I thought it was? Yes, it was. And as we walked the grounds of the house, Pamela recounted how Frank Sinatra had suggested they marry in the 1950s; she'd said no. That was one relationship she wasn't getting into.

In the years after Averell Harriman died, before Bill Clinton sent Pamela to Paris as the U.S. ambassador to France, she was often reflective about her life. She wasn't apologetic about the men she'd enthralled: Harriman; the pioneering broadcaster Edward R. Murrow; and Roosevelt's top aide, Harry Hopkins. The war was a time, she remembered, when you never knew if you'd survive the next bomb and see the next day.

She fondly remembered John Kennedy's return to London as a young congressman in the late 1940s. JFK was then painfully thin, almost emaciated, the price of his service in the South Pacific. He got sick in London; his fever was so high he had to be taken to a hospital. Pamela sent her housekeeper there every day to bring him the homemade soup he preferred to the dreary hospital meals. When he was well enough to travel, Pamela and the housekeeper went to see him off. As he was lifted onto the ship on a stretcher, the housekeeper said: "I'm afraid we'll never see that poor boy again." Pamela shared that verdict years later with JFK—and in 1960, as president-elect, he called to ask for the housekeeper's address, so he could send her an invitation to the inauguration. She was still in Britain; but, he said, he wanted her to know that "that poor boy" had made it.

Behind her back, of course, some of those who wanted to frequent Pamela's salon derided her past. It was all right for men to live as she had; for them, there was not just acceptance, but a kind of macho admiration. But not for a woman; and even worse, there was a sense of envy about how it had all seemed to turn out.

On my trip to Italy with Marylouise, I thought about what I'd learned in 1986 during my on-the-job training as a media consultant. Creativity mattered, as long as it wasn't an end in itself, but a vehicle for a message. The best strategy was often the cold-eyed recognition of necessity—seeing your only chance and taking it. The interplay of personalities and rivalries was inevitable, at times bitter, but probably inescapable when any single decision could make all the difference in a campaign. I had learned to rein in my debater's capacity to win an argument and instead listen to colleagues like Carville, Doak, Trippi, and, yes, Caddell. Any of them could have the idea that would turn a race. I had also sensed how hostile the press was to negative spots and political ads in general, in part because they shifted the balance of power over voter perception away from the media and toward the paid political class.

Off our 1986 success, in the run-up to the next presidential contest, we had at least three potential clients. Our firm's strongest competitor, Bob Squier, had forsworn presidential primaries. He believed, as his associate and soon to be partner Carter Eskew said, that you could make more money focusing on Senate and governor's races. That often was and is true. Temperamentally, I couldn't stand aside from the national campaign. Doak assumed that we would enlist with Joe Biden. I wasn't so sure. Our relations with Caddell were sour—and he wasn't just Biden's pollster, but in his mind, Biden's guru. But Biden, who'd imposed a truce on the three of us for 1986, was determined to have all of us with him in 1988. He summoned me to another meeting in his Senate office. I said we weren't the problem: Pat didn't want us anywhere near his campaign. That was about all I said because Biden then talked nonstop for almost two hours; it was a high-energy combination of reassurance, reminiscence about John and Robert Kennedy, and a discursive survey of his own reasons for running. But at the end of this torrent of words, we were no nearer to dealing with the difficulty we'd started out to "discuss."

Mario Cuomo phoned; he certainly wasn't committed to running, but he at least wanted to think through 1988. We met in his governor's office at the World Trade Center. We spent perhaps two hours together, but it wasn't all about politics or the presidency. He launched into a back-and-forth about the differences in our respective Catholic educations: I'd gone to "elite" Georgetown, and then Harvard Law School; he'd gone to St. John's for college and law school—and then scrambled to find a job in a New York law firm. He'd been taught by Vincentian Fathers; I'd been taught by the Jesuits. He was more Augustinian, closer to St. Augustine's notions of sin and evil and Plato's view of a world that fell short of its ideal form, than to the Jesuits, with their practicality, their capacity to rationalize, their elaborate systems of logic and metaphysics. Sometimes, they seemed to be a church of their own. I mentioned Teilhard de Chardin, the Jesuit paleontologist who'd argued that human beings, too, were in a constant state of spiritual evolution toward an "omega" point. Cuomo said he had read all of his work—and clearly he had; but, of course, the Jesuits and the Church had silenced Teilhard. I'd never engaged in this kind of conversation with a politician. We ranged over theological issues and swapped references to scholars like Hans Kung and Karl Rahner. Cuomo had learned from Rahner, he needled me, even if he was a Jesuit. On an issue like abortion, he worried that the Church was moving away from a reconciliation with the democratic process, although he personally got on with Cardinal John O'Connor, who wouldn't give him the grief he'd bestowed on Gerry Ferraro in 1984 if Cuomo ran for president this time.

And so at last we came to the subject of our meeting. I'd already glimpsed something more than Cuomo's depth; for all his eloquence, there was in him a tinge of sadness, an almost palpable sense that we lived in a broken world that needed to be set right, but never fully would be. His first question about 1988 wasn't about strategy and tactics but the grounds of his decision. I don't know whether he meant it, but he asked whether he was up to being president. Compared to what? I replied, George Bush—or even Reagan—or the rest of the field? But Reagan, he said, had been an effective president, even if he disagreed with him. That's because he governed from first principles, I argued; so would Cuomo. He didn't need to search around for his beliefs. He pushed back: he was a governor; he lacked foreign policy experience. But it was governors who generally got elected—and if you were governor of New York or California, Americans assumed you were ready for the White House. Cuomo corrected me: it wasn't governors who were elected, but ex-governors; the last sitting governor to win was Franklin Roosevelt in 1932. And that was his concern. He had to do his job in New

York. How many days would he have to be away on the campaign trail—say in Iowa? Not as many as most candidates, I answered; they'd spend 100 or 140 days in Iowa; he could get away with 60 or something short of that. He turned to message. If he ran, he'd talk about poverty; he was opposed to the death penalty; he wouldn't trim his sails. Could this work? He was a New Yorker through and through and he didn't know the rest of America all that well. Yes, he could win, I said, but it wasn't a sure thing. His toughest opponent would be Gary Hart, who had yet to embarrass himself out of contention; they would be the two large figures in the race, but this time, Cuomo would be the new voice. If he spoke for ordinary Americans, for the middle class—if he spoke to their anxieties and hopes, and he could do it probably better than any other candidate—they'd get past his views on the death penalty. And in any event, once he'd won the Democratic nomination, he'd get to take on Bush. I underestimated Bush all the way to the fall.

We wrapped up as Cuomo ticked off a list of Democratic operatives and asked what I thought about each of them. He was mulling over his decision, he said, but he'd soon decide whether to take the first step toward running by setting up an exploratory committee. A few weeks later, on his weekly radio show in New York, he announced that he wouldn't be a candidate. He phoned me afterward to say he'd told a number of people that one of his reasons was that I'd told him he had to spend so many days in Iowa. He hoped I didn't mind—he wasn't trying to blame me, but, well, he had used me a little. I was glad to be of service, I said. After all, following our meeting, he'd called me "close to genius" in the *New York Times*. I added that Marylouise (Cuomo had met her at an event in Los Angeles) had ordered two custom T-shirts, one for her stenciled GENIUS and the other for me stenciled CLOSE TO.

Soon after that January 1987 session with Cuomo, I was in California for the Democratic State Convention. David Doak wasn't ready to give up on Joe Biden—but I listened to Biden's speech with a sense of recognition and dismay. It had been rewritten on the plane west by Biden and Pat Caddell, who was intent on proving that he could not only do the polling but the speechwriting and the ads as well. As Biden wowed the convention, John Emerson, a Californian who was one of Gary Hart's top advisers, walked over and asked me: Didn't those words sound like Robert Kennedy's? I had already realized it because the lines were lifted and not attributed, intentionally or unintentionally, from two of RFK's most famous speeches. In South Africa, RFK had said: "Few will have the greatness to bend history itself. But each of us can work to change a small portion of events, and in the total of all those acts will be written the history of this generation." Only two incidental words in the passage were different in Biden's speech. There was another lift as well: The gross national product does not, both the Kennedy and Biden speeches proclaimed, "measure the beauty of our poetry, or"—Biden's text omitted the "or"—"the strength of our marriages, the intelligence of our public debate, or"—the "or" was again excised—"the integrity of our public officials." The crowd was swept away; Bob Burkett, Biden's national finance chair, was pumping his fist in the air. He was a friend of Marylouise's, and I took him aside and told him what was happening. Biden couldn't do any more of this; he'd get caught.

This was what happened when Caddell decided to write speeches, Doak commented. Doak was still attempting to negotiate our way into the Biden campaign with an assist from Tim Ridley, Biden's chief of staff. Meanwhile, I was trying to avoid another set of negotiations with another potential candidate, House Democratic Caucus chairman Dick Gephardt. No House member had been elected president since James Garfield in 1880. At first, I regarded Gephardt, a founder of the "centrist" Democratic Leadership Council, as too conservative for me—and for Democrats in presidential primaries. For a long time, he certainly had been on one issue: abortion. Gephardt had first run for Congress in 1976, in the first white heat of controversy over *Roe v. Wade*; he had endorsed a "right to life" constitutional amendment. But he explained to me that he'd taken this position without thinking much about it. As he prepared his presidential bid, he shifted; he now believed government should neither favor nor oppose abortion. On the one hand, a woman should decide; on the other, public money shouldn't be used to pay for abortions. He would never convince a skeptical press that his change of view on the issue wasn't just a conversion of convenience. I suspected that his original stance was the expedient one; anti-abortion feelings ran deep in his congressional district.

In the fall of 1986, my fellow veteran of Kennedy's presidential campaign, and noncampaigns, his political director Bill Carrick, sought my advice about an offer to be Gephardt's campaign manager. I said this one was a long shot, but since no one expected Gephardt to win, what did Bill have to lose? When Carrick's appointment hit the press right after New Year's, twelve months before the Iowa caucuses, Gephardt was at 1 percent in the polling there. Carrick, who lived a block away from me in Georgetown, was a pal. I'd traveled to the Cipriani in Venice with him and his marvelously named girlfriend Bee Gee Truesdale six months before. Bill was now relentless as he sought to enlist Doak and me for his newfound candidate. As Gephardt was readying his formal announcement, Carrick pressed me; at least, I could help him with the speech. It wouldn't commit me to anything else, but it mattered to Bill. I talked to Gephardt again and drafted the speech.

The signature policy dealt with foreign trade: America's workers should not "be sacrificed on the altar of a false and rigid free trade ideology." We "cannot live in a global marketplace in which Americans are free to buy but not to sell. . . . The next President must be as tough in negotiating the terms of trade as this President [Ronald Reagan] has been in negotiating with the Russians." I wasn't busted for writing the remarks, although E. J. Dionne in the *New York Times* detected that they "resonated with ideas drawn from John F. Kennedy's oratory." (Of course, that was and is commonplace; the Democratic Party by now has been living off the legacy and memory of a president lost nearly half a century ago, before the majority of today's Americans were born.) But after we formally signed on with Gephardt in the late spring and as the campaign went on, I'd be assailed for its populist tone, referred to in *Newsweek* as a "body snatcher" who'd manufactured a protectionist Gephardt. In truth, to this point, I'd hardly thought about the trade issue; the position came from him, and was strongly held.

I reiterated to Carrick that Doak had a prior commitment to

Biden, and he and I were going to honor it. Carrick was sure it would never work out, as he told me afterward. And that's the word Doak got from Tim Ridley in Biden's office. There was no way forward. Caddell wouldn't hear of it—and Joe was unwilling to make him back down. Even if he tried, there was no reason to believe he'd succeed. Caddell might just walk out. Doak's reaction was low key; we'd both seen this coming. Go ahead, he said, call Gephardt and Carrick; if you're ready to go there, so am I.

There were other recruits, too, the farm team of the future. The chief fund-raiser, Terry McAuliffe, was a callow, fast-talking businessman who could sell anyone anything; he was the chairman of a bank before he was thirty. Donna Brazile, an intense, self-deprecating African-American organizer from Louisiana, had decided that she didn't want to be with Jesse Jackson this time. Joe Trippi, who'd left our firm to work for Gary Hart, had spent the final days of that campaign with the besieged Lee Hart and then the candidate at his ranch outside Denver, Troublesome Gulch. Carrick was wary of Trippi: he was uncontrollable and inseparably wedded to his own views. But I responded that Trippi was also imaginative, a fount of ideas. To me, he was like JFK's description of one of his advisers. Joe had ten new ideas a day; three didn't matter; five were disasters; two were brilliant or even transformative. The trick was to figure out the right two.

In the summer of 1987, the presidential campaign was overshadowed by a titanic constitutional struggle over the confirmation of Robert Bork to the U.S. Supreme Court. He was the doctrinaire conservative who had carried out the "Saturday Night Massacre" during the Watergate investigation; he had executed Nixon's order to fire Special Prosecutor Archibald Cox after the U.S. Attorney General and his deputy resigned rather than do it. Bork's legal writing was acidly hostile to basic Supreme Court precedents, and even appeared to question the *Brown* decision that declared racial segregation in public schools unconstitutional.

As the Senate prepared for the Bork hearings, Larry Tribe, a likely Supreme Court nominee in a future Democratic administration, called me from his office at Harvard Law School. He'd been asked to testify against Bork. He was inclined to say yes—and if he did, he'd portray Bork as out of step even with generations of conservative justices. I gave Larry an honest warning. If he played this part, the right would never forgive him—and it might cost him any chance to ever sit on the Court himself. He'd just have to live with that, he replied; Bork would be catastrophic as a justice. Tribe testified, and a few years after Bork was defeated, the conservative columnist George Will observed to me that the confirmation process had become a demolition derby. Wouldn't the country be better off with both Bork and Tribe on the Court than with neither? Were we establishing a precedent that the leading constitutional scholars who'd pushed frontiers of thought on both sides were to be banned, never even nominated for fear of what would follow?

As chairman of the Senate Judiciary Committee, Biden would take center stage at the Bork hearings. But first, he was on stage for an August debate at the Iowa State Fair. More and more, Biden was touching an emotional chord with crowds; Gephardt, who was doggedly moving around the state day after day, gaining and even leading in some polls, was coming to the conclusion that Biden was the real threat. In the run-up to the debate, the political analyst Bill Schneider—these days, he's on CNN—showed the Biden campaign a videotape of British Labour Party leader Neil Kinnock's speech to his party conference. He also played it for me and left a copy behind—and he'd given it to the Dukakis staff as well, although I didn't know it. In it, Kinnock asked why he was "the first Kinnock in a thousand generations to be able to get to University." He spoke of his ancestors' long hours in the mines. Why didn't they get a chance? "Was it because all our predecessors were thick?" No, it was "because they had no platform on which they could stand." Biden started to quote the material in his stump speeches, or so the later explanation went. But standing on the platform at the Iowa State Fair, his entire closing statement was the Kinnock language—this time, without crediting it to Kinnock. Some of the phrases had been Americanized, but otherwise it was a word-for-word copy. I was thunderstruck when I heard it. After warning Biden's finance chair about the earlier appropriations from Robert Kennedy, I'd assumed no one in Biden's campaign would let anything like this occur again. I told Carrick and Gephardt the story—and that I had a copy of the Kinnock tape. Gephardt responded that under no circumstances was I to do anything with it; put it in a desk drawer and leave it there.

That's what I did, but the storm that was about to break would almost destroy the Gephardt candidacy—as well as Doak and me. A tape that combined Kinnock's peroration and Biden's reached the *New York Times*, NBC, and the *Des Moines Register*. It was front page in the *Times*; the *Register* reported that the source of the tape was one of Biden's rivals. Two stories now picked up steam: Biden's alleged plagiarism and the identity of the opponent who played the "dirty trick" of revealing it. The Dukakis operatives, the real culprits, went for a "twofer": having fed the press the tape, they now fueled the reports that Doak and I had done it. We denied to Gephardt and Carrick that we'd sent, delivered, or shared the tapes with anyone else. We were at the campaign headquarters when we received a call from our office. ABC World News Tonight was about to go on the air explicitly identifying Doak and Shrum as the source of the Biden tape. Doak called Hal Bruno, the network's political director, who told him the report was solidly sourced. Doak gave his word that the story was untrue; he added that he was speaking for both of us. I was prepared to get on the phone. Peter Jennings agreed to kill the report—for now. But if he found out we'd lied, we'd pay dearly for it.

It was a reprieve, but what rescued us from the swirling rumors was an unusual step by the *New York Times*. As reporters told me afterward, Craig Whitney, the Washington bureau chief, felt the paper was in a dilemma: he knew the tape had come from the Dukakis enterprise, which was now blaming us, and his reporters were filing copy to that effect. Generally, the *Times* wouldn't state who *wasn't* a source because that would narrow the range of possibilities and in effect help identify who *was*. But by not saying anything here, the *Times* could become party to a disinformation campaign. I was told it was a controversial decision inside the paper, but Whitney finally issued a statement that no one associated with

Gephardt had planted the story with the *Times*. But, with the media sleuthing in high gear, events could have gone wrong for us anyway if the focus of the questioning had reached beyond the tapes themselves. In fact, I had talked with the *Times*'s Maureen Dowd when she was following up her initial story on Biden and Kinnock. She'd heard that at the California State Convention, he'd "borrowed" the speeches of Robert Kennedy. A Reagan White House aide had phoned the *Times* and pointed out the similarities. Had I noticed at the time? She'd been told I knew past Democratic speeches almost by heart. I said I couldn't be cited in any way, but I confirmed the lift from RFK and another one in a different Biden speech from Hubert Humphrey. Dowd asked if I had a hard copy of the Humphrey remarks, from the 1976 Democratic Convention. I did; she borrowed and then returned it after her follow-up story ran. In it, Dowd offered the Biden campaign's defense for the failure to credit RFK: "The writer of the speech, Patrick Caddell, had re-created the passage subconsciously."

Then it wasn't just about the speeches anymore. Biden was accused of plagiarizing a paper in law school; he replied that the incident wasn't "malevolent." A C-SPAN tape showed him claiming, incorrectly, that he'd graduated in the top half of his law school class, had a full academic scholarship, and had earned three degrees in college—when in fact he'd double-majored in history and political science, but only had one B.A. In another context, it might have been dismissed as political puffery, or not even noticed. But now everything Biden had ever written or said was being raked over just as he was presiding over the Bork hearings. Down the hallway from the Senate Hearing Room, I bumped into Tom Donilon, not only one of Biden's most trusted political advisers but a first-rate lawyer, a former member of the *University of Virginia Law Review*, who was counseling Biden on both the Bork nomination and the presidential campaign. He said he wanted to talk to me for a minute—in private. Ted Kennedy was at the Bork hearings, so we sat in his office.

Did I see any way, Donilon asked, that Biden could get through the firestorm without damaging the prospects of defeating Bork? Biden might survive, I said, but a protracted controversy about plagiarism had to help Bork; conservatives were already questioning Biden's fitness to sit in judgment on the nominee. I had no idea what else was out there, what other paragraph could be picked over, and I could hardly be seen as a source of disinterested advice. But if someone cared about Biden and his future role, I added, maybe it was time to tell him he should withdraw and focus on the Bork hearings. At least that gave him a good reason for leaving the race; for Biden, Tom responded, this was a reason that really mattered. It was clear that Donilon's mind, at least, was made up.

Biden convened a meeting in Washington as he moved toward a decision. Caddell was immovable and angrily insistent that Biden had to remain a candidate; as Donilon recounted it, Pat said Biden couldn't get out—he, Pat, had been waiting to run for years. It was hard to get anything resolved in this environment, so it was decided to resume the discussion later that day at Biden's home in Delaware. They'd go up on the Metroliner. Caddell was intentionally given the wrong time, so that he'd miss the meeting. On September 23, Biden ended his presidential campaign. He'd made "mistakes," he said; they were "exaggerated," but they were obscuring "the essence of his candidacy." He had to choose between his own ambition and the "battle" to save the Supreme Court: "I intend to attempt to bring that battle to victory"—and along with Ted Kennedy, most Democrats, and a few moderate Republicans, he did.

It was a presidential year that hadn't officially started. But two candidates—Hart and Biden—had already been knocked out. The aftershocks kept coming. Iowa Democrats were mad at Dukakis—and Gephardt; despite the fact that we'd been absolved, the accusation stuck. Iowans just knew that we'd done something wrong. A frustrated Gephardt called from the road: Do I have to deny this at every stop? Our polling showed a sharp decline that lasted through the fall. Dukakis managed to arrest his own drop by using his considerable resources to finance an early television buy. But he was behind Paul Simon, the bespeckled, bow-tied senator from Illinois, an expert on Lincoln, whose nonpolitical image suddenly appealed to

Iowans as the ideal counterpoint to a campaign that appeared mired in mud. Indeed, Simon's most memorable ad featured his bow tie. He was proud to be a traditional liberal: "I am not a neo-anything. I am a Democrat." The candor probably counted as much as his positioning, but by late autumn, Simon was in first place, as high as 40 percent in some polls.

But with Simon, the message was the man more than anything he said, or any vision he had for the future. In that sense, he was like Dukakis, who was running on "the Massachusetts miracle" of growth and jobs, without specific proposals to replicate the achievement nationally. Simon was the prairie progressive. Their candidacies, while different, were both fundamentally personal. Gephardt had something to say on foreign trade, a controversial and, we thought, compelling message; his ads could build on his story—his life experiences and his record—not rest on it. But we couldn't afford to go on television through the fall and into December without jeopardizing our capacity to compete just before the January 1988 Iowa caucuses. Gephardt, who had spent a hundred days on the ground in the state, was just fading away.

Doak and I probably waited too long to film as we honed the Gephardt appeal with our pollster Ed Reilly and debated and tinkered with the scripts. We were in Iowa, cameras rolling, late in the season; to ward off the bone-penetrating chill, the candidate had to slip into an overcoat between takes at an outdoor location with a factory in the distance. We almost didn't capture Gephardt on camera for what would become the most notable and notorious spot from any candidate in the primary campaign; by the time we filmed it, the sun, already low in the sky, was beginning to set across an orange-rimmed horizon. Doak had scheduled the taping of this script last because he was dubious about it. I pushed the crew—Stop fooling with the setup and the makeup, just film. We got a few takes; one of them would have to do; the light was now gone.

I was invested in this ad, but it wasn't just mine. Gephardt and I had been talking about using examples to bring the trade issue down to earth; what would a specific American product, one everyone was familiar with, cost overseas after all the tariffs and taxes imposed on it in a foreign country? We had some research that calculated costs on items from pens to personal computers. Gephardt was on the road as a few of us brainstormed in my condo. What about an American car—say a Chrysler K-Car? Americans would be stunned by what it cost in Japan. We couldn't use Japan, I replied; Gephardt was already being blasted as a protectionist. Bashing Japan, the classic target of anti-foreign trade forces, would make things worse. How about Korea? Joe Trippi said. The United States had gone to war to save it from a Communist takeover; that country was now exporting a low-cost vehicle called the Hyundai into the American market. He scratched out a script and handed it to me. We edited and timed it, and edited again. The spot was straightforward, not sensationalistic; in that sense, it was a natural fit with Gephardt. But it also conveyed a presidential strength that transcended the trade issue itself. By the time Korea was through with nine different duties and fees, Gephardt would say, a $10,000 Chrysler K-Car cost $48,000 there. Unless that was changed, if he was president, the Koreans would be left "asking how many Americans are going to pay $48,000 for one of their Hyundais." Gephardt later gave me a toy Hyundai that I still have on my desk; it cost a lot less than $48,000.

Once we had this spot, and others in the can, including a 60-second bio, we had to decide when to go on the air. Should we launch a week or two before Christmas, take a break, and then return right after the New Year? All the campaigns would be off the week between Christmas and New Year's; viewing patterns were unpredictable; you missed a lot of the audience because, as someone exaggerated, "everybody went to Florida that week." I interjected: "Not our everybody." Not the blue-collar, union, and rural Democrats who were our likely caucus supporters. They couldn't afford to go to Florida; they were at home, in the snow. Even when they visited friends or relatives, the TV was on. Why not throw out the rules of the road and launch the day after Christmas? We'd have a week of unimpeded advertising with no other political spots on the air.

Gephardt went along with this, although he'd pretty much given up as he limped along at 2 to 4 percent in the polls. After his workaholic months in Iowa, he took a break with his family to ski out

West, explained that things looked bad—but he'd given it his best shot, and so had they. Iowa was likely the end of the road. But while he skied, voters were watching his ads. On the way back, he landed in Des Moines for a campaign event. He phoned me right after he'd gotten through the airport and to the headquarters. For more than a hundred days, he said, he'd crisscrossed the state, introducing himself to people, telling them he was running for president. They'd listened politely; an encouraging number had signed up; many had drifted away after the Biden tape. Today at the airport, however, he'd been mobbed: everybody had recognized him. Suddenly, the phone banks were harvesting more and more Gephardt commitments. "Bob," he said, with a mingled sense of wonderment and excitement, "it's *all* television." It wasn't, of course; he'd built a strong organization. But without air cover, the ground troops had been stalled. They hadn't been able to gain ground in the face of the post-Biden fall-out or the image of Gephardt as a young political hack. He'd even been compared to the satirical "Congressman Bob Forehead"—a vapid, Ken Doll–like figure from the comic strip *Washingtoon.*

The Gephardt spots upended the race in a matter of days. Iowans suddenly viewed Gephardt as someone who'd come from an ordinary background and genuinely cared about people. The Hyundai ad touched a raw nerve; this *was* their fight, too, and he looked like the right choice. We dispatched every spare body from the Washington headquarters and most of the staff from other states to Iowa. Gephardt jumped from 2 or 4 percent to 14 percent in two weeks, and then just kept gaining. There was now one other move Doak and I wanted to make that we couldn't afford—broadcast the 60-second bio in New Hampshire for a couple of weeks before a victorious Gephardt arrived there from Iowa. New Hampshire voters didn't really know him, although he'd campaigned there, too. And after Iowa, we'd only have eight days to catch up with Dukakis, who was in first place in the polling in the Granite State.

On caucus day, Doak and I had had breakfast with the columnist Bob Novak, who for all his conservative ideology was a bottom-line reporter who worked hard to get his predictions right. We told him we thought Gephardt was going to win; by now, worrying about expectations was beside the point. Novak, a free trade true believer, said that Gephardt was wrong on that issue, but he was also the Democratic nominee Republicans feared most. Gephardt finished first, with over 30 percent of the vote. Dukakis was almost 10 points back, in third place; but it was time for the Winter Olympics and he salvaged a small victory in the sound-bite war when he exulted: "We won the Bronze." After all, he had New Hampshire to fall back on. But that wasn't the reason we were concerned—Paul Simon had come in second, and he pledged to go on. (When I consulted for his Senate reelection campaign in 1990, he'd say he wished he hadn't— Gephardt might have beaten Bush.)

So Gephardt had a victory no one had predicted that conferred none of the advantages we had anticipated. We wouldn't have a two-way race in New Hampshire. We didn't get the expected bounce from Iowa because the press and the political world were irresistibly drawn to the stunning story that on the Republican side, Vice President Bush had lost not only to Senator Bob Dole but to televangelist Pat Robertson. Our best chance for the nomination, a sweep in both Iowa and New Hampshire, was evaporating. Our best hope was to chip away at Dukakis in New Hampshire and get the silver medal there, while holding off Simon and maybe driving him out of the race.

That, too, was suddenly in jeopardy Wednesday night, six days before the voting. Andy Rosenthal, who was covering political advertising for the *New York Times*, tracked me down at our state headquarters. Did I have any comment on the new Simon ad that was about to go on, attacking Gephardt for changing his positions on Social Security, nuclear energy, and certain weapons systems? I didn't tell him, but until that moment, I had no idea anything like this was coming. Simon had promised to be positive. His campaign, in previewing the spot to the press, had inadvertently let us in on it. I gingerly parried Rosenthal's questions to elicit more details about the attack. I observed to Mark Longabaugh, our New Hampshire campaign manager, that we couldn't afford to return fire at Simon and leave Dukakis unscathed; he would benefit from a negative exchange that left him above the fray. Dukakis hadn't run any negative ads, but I asked Longabaugh if there were free press stories in which Dukakis had criticized Gephardt. If so, in our response ad to Simon, we could accuse both him and Dukakis of being negative because they were afraid to run on their own records—and then we could go after them, especially Dukakis, on tax increases, the issue where he was most vulnerable in taxaphobic New Hampshire. The spot, on television by Friday, reminded voters that Dukakis was "one of the biggest tax raisers in Massachusetts history."

We held Dukakis to under 40 percent. We did come in second— and Simon was effectively out of the race. Maybe we could now pick up some momentum, and offset some of Dukakis's fund-raising lead, with a quick victory in South Dakota, which came a week after New Hampshire and two weeks before a truly Super Tuesday, when almost all the southern states would vote on the same day. So we boldly announced: "On to South Dakota." We sent Ed Reilly into the field in that state for a fast polling snapshot to identify our best issues. The bad news came back: Dukakis was almost 20 points ahead. We had just a few days to turn the numbers around, or our bonus state could become a backbreaker. The clearest chance, Doak and I decided as we scrounged through the negative research, was to convince South Dakotans that Dukakis was an outlander who didn't understand them. And the material we found made him sound way out of touch to anyone who lived on the Great Plains. It was a quote from 1986, when Dukakis had advised farmers in trouble to "grow blueberries, flowers, and Belgian endive." In the spot we scripted, that advice was *the* Dukakis agriculture program. Doak came up with a *coup de grâce*: at the end of the spot, the narrator would incredulously repeat, "Belgian endive?" There was a 30 percent shift in South Dakota in four days. Gephardt racked up a double-digit win over Dukakis, and the conventional wisdom was now moving our way. After South Dakota, *Newsweek* named Gephardt "the smart money pick for the Democratic nomination." Doak and I were "the hottest media consultants."

But the seeds of a Super Tuesday defeat had already been planted. Gephardt's appeal on trade, his populist sense of fighting for "you," had real resonance in the South. But voters there knew little else about him. Tennessee senator Al Gore, making his first run for president at the age of only thirty-nine, had fled both Iowa and New Hampshire in the face of rock-bottom poll numbers, and retreated to his regional base. In a debate in Texas, he decided to fill in the blanks about Gephardt. He was on message—and on the attack. Gephardt had made "a 180 degree reversal" on abortion. Gephardt had supported "Reaganomics." Then came the exchange that left Gephardt all but speechless. In an earlier debate, he had accused Gore of moving to the right as a conscious political strategy: "You've been sounding more like Al Haig" (Richard Nixon's chief of staff) "than Al Gore." Gephardt now wheeled out the Al Haig reference again—and Gore was waiting for it. He leaned forward and shot back: "That line sounds more like Richard Nixon than Richard Gephardt."

I was angry at myself; while preparing, we'd almost cavalierly decided to recycle the old line. Used one-liners almost never work in debates; the opponent has heard, been hurt, and is ready. It's the flip side of another reality of political debates: In the glare of the limelight, with so much on the line, candidates tend to fall back on what they've been saying on the campaign trail. We never should have given Gore the opening he was waiting for.

The debate was bad enough, but things were about to get worse due to Tad Devine, Dukakis's chief delegate hunter. Up in Boston, he argued that aside from winning some of the South, say Florida and Texas, where Hispanics were strong, Dukakis's fundamental strategic objective had to be to drive Gephardt out of the race on Super Tuesday. This March 8 showdown came just three weeks after New Hampshire, and two weeks after Iowa. If Gephardt survived as a serious candidate, Devine calculated, he could beat Dukakis in industrial states like Michigan and Pennsylvania. Gore had far less potential there—and could be disposed of later. We now faced an onslaught of millions of dollars in negative ads. I saw the most corrosive one—from Dukakis—in my hotel room as I was traveling with Gephardt. A gymnast with comically dyed orange hair dressed in a suit was trampolining and tumbling forward and back and forward again as the narrator described Gephardt's flip-flops. Together, Dukakis and Gore were now spending two or three times as much attacking Gephardt across the southern states as our entire advertising budget for Super Tuesday. The trade message might help with voters but, as Terry McAuliffe said, it made fund-raising a bear with virtually every traditional source of political money except the unions—and they hadn't endorsed anyone yet.

Reilly was polling, and we were still ahead as we arrived in San Antonio for a rally, appropriately in front of the Alamo. We'd been holding our own; but at some point, wouldn't the throwweight on the other side begin to matter? It did. As new numbers came in, Gephardt's lead dissipated in state after state—and disappeared in several of them. You didn't have to be a pollster to know which way this wind was blowing. On the Sunday before Super Tuesday, Gephardt and I watched television for an hour in Dallas in between events. We saw three Gore and three Dukakis spots and none of our own. Awash in a tide of negative advertising, without the resources to counterattack while airing the Gephardt biography or the Hyundai spot, Gephardt carried only his home state of Missouri. It was a miserable night in the St. Louis hotel where the crowd that had gathered to celebrate straggled out of the lobby into the rain. I walked past the Secret Service agents who would soon be leaving us and into Gephardt's hotel room. By the end of March, he was running for re-election to Congress.

After we lost, the Gephardt campaign was criticized for betting too heavily on Iowa and New Hampshire. Carrick, Doak, and I had all agreed on the strategy. The best chance—maybe the only chance—for the unknown and underfunded Gephardt was to go all-out in the first two contests, in smaller states with affordable media markets. Whatever he didn't spend there, or in Iowa and South Dakota, would be a drop in the bucket on Super Tuesday. What we underestimated was the nearly universal establishment antipathy to the trade message that left us even more underfunded—at the moment when we were most under constant assault. Yet without that message, Iowa never would have been won.

So Gephardt was denounced—and after he lost, dismissed—as

an opportunist and a protectionist. It didn't matter if he explained that he wasn't trying to put up walls, but level the playing field. By the fall, Dukakis would appropriate his theme and even the trade issue as he finally gained ground against Bush at the end. Gephardt also had a long-term perspective; he told me in 1988 that in the years ahead, it wouldn't just be blue-collar jobs that would be lost; white-collar jobs would go, too. And whatever the merits of the solutions he proposed then, the Gephardt of that campaign was not a throwback, but ahead of his time in seeking to temper the effects of a globalizing economy. By 2004, you could hear echoes of Gephardt in every serious Democratic presidential candidate who campaigned against outsourcing; whether you agreed with him or not, the imprint Gephardt left on the party would be more enduring than any legacy left by Dukakis.

Marylouise and I had gotten engaged in the early months of the Gephardt campaign. I was with him in L.A. when I asked her out to dinner. She, of course, could always get the usually impossible reservation at Spago, the restaurant that made Wolfgang Puck the most celebrated chef in America. When we arrived, we ran into the filmmaker George Stevens sitting at the bar; he was going to grab a quick supper alone. Marylouise instantly asked him to join us. Every year after the political season, Stevens produced and I wrote the script for the Kennedy Center Honors for CBS. Most of the time I liked to have dinner with friends, but not the night I planned to propose to Marylouise. We had a long meal, with Puck sending over a series of dishes and Stevens picking out the wines. I remembered that I'd had to ask someone else to leave when I'd told Marylouise I loved her fourteen months earlier in a bar at the Jefferson Hotel in Washington. So while she was off chatting with Puck, I told George that I had to talk about something private with her and asked if he'd mind excusing himself. When she returned, I just blurted out: "I think you should marry me." She didn't say anything at first; she couldn't talk, and Puck rushed over. He looked as if he was about to give her the Heimlich maneuver. Was everything all right? She murmured that we were getting married. Puck broke out champagne for all the customers still left in the restaurant.

After we toasted each other, Marylouise asked: "When?" Right after the election, I replied. I meant the general election in November 1988. So she scheduled the wedding right after the California primary in June, five months earlier. There were three hundred guests, her Hollywood, Reagan, and antiwar friends and my political ones. Three memories stand out. At the rehearsal dinner, my about-to-be stepson Michael delivered a pitch-perfect impersonation of me. He explained that while people assumed I liked history, literature, and art, the secret truth was that my favorite pastime was guzzling beer and watching Sunday football. Rosemary Clooney had offered to sing at the ceremony; every head in the church snapped around when her first notes rose from the choir. I'd invited Larry Tribe to read the Old Testament passage during the mass without letting the priest know that Larry wasn't Catholic but Jewish. I wasn't asked so I didn't tell—because I wasn't sure it would be permitted. Marylouise and I watched an elderly priest who was assisting at the altar force communion on Larry not once but twice, even though he was shaking his head "no." It was, unintentionally, in the eclectic, ecumenical spirit of the occasion. At the reception afterward, amid all the recognizable faces, I saw someone whose presence said a lot about my wife's spirit and character. There, standing near Pamela Harriman and Warren Beatty, was June, the checkout clerk from the Beachwood Market who'd been Marylouise's pal for years.

As we saw it, Marylouise and I had thrown a wonderful party, the prelude we hoped to a wonderful life. For all practical purposes, however, we were broke. In the next eighteen years, she would earn more from buying and selling houses—while writing novels on the side, including two mysteries with Barbara Mikulski—than I would from political consulting. But at this point, after paying for the wedding and the honeymoon and making a down payment on a home in Los Angeles that fit what Ted Kennedy described as my "edifice complex," we were scraping by on her *L.A. Times* paycheck and waiting for my post-presidential campaign earnings from other political clients. Some of them had decided to hire Doak and me only after Gephardt had dropped out—or, in a few cases, earlier because

they'd assumed he'd be out of contention long before their own races
heated up.

I assumed the presidential campaign was over for me. That wasn't
entirely true. After the Democratic Convention, I was asked to help
prepare Dukakis's running mate, Texas senator Lloyd Bentsen, for
the vice-presidential debate. Doak balked; we had our paying clients
to take care of. I told Tad Devine, who was now running the Bentsen
operation, and Tom Donilon, who was in charge of the prep, that I
could only give them a couple of hours, and took a taxi to the Ritz-
Carlton on Embassy Row where they'd taken over a series of conference rooms. The first thing Devine and Donilon wanted me to do
was review the briefing books and, for the most likely questions,
draft shorter versions of responses and rebuttals. Bentsen was complaining that he was drowning in too much material. When I finished and the longhand drafts were typed, I said I probably better
go; maybe I could come back later after spending some time in my
office. Devine objected: Have something to eat, and then stay for a
session with Bentsen. Over a cheeseburger and a glass of red wine, I
asked if Bentsen was ready for the off-the-wall question. What
would he say if a charge was leveled about Dukakis and he didn't
know the facts? Try it and see how he reacts, Devine suggested.

   We were sitting around the conference table with Bentsen practicing Q and A. I popped the surprise: Did he agree with Governor
Dukakis that the CIA should end all covert operations and be
confined to information gathering? He looked stricken, and then
broke out of the mock format, responding in a distressed voice: "He
said *what?*" Bentsen couldn't know everything about Dukakis's
record—and maybe the charge was believable. After all, Dukakis
had already been pilloried for taking a series of improbable positions. Usually, the truth was more complicated; for example, he
didn't oppose the Pledge of Allegiance, but forcing schoolchildren to
recite it. But nuance, as it usually is, was overwhelmed by the headline. We reassured Bentsen that, no, Dukakis had called for reining
in CIA abuses, but never for abolishing covert action. We gave him a

rule of thumb: If his running mate was accused of espousing an absurd policy, he should deny it and move on.

I'd come to the prep with an idea that occurred to me as I watched
George Bush's hapless vice-presidential pick, Indiana senator Dan
Quayle, defend his comparative youth and lack of experience. In late
August, I'd read Maureen Dowd's *New York Times* story on a
Quayle press conference where he'd said: "I'm very close to the same
age as Jack Kennedy was when he was elected—not Vice President,
but President." What an opening, I thought then. Now, at the conference table, I predicted to Bentsen that, when the issue of experience was raised, as it inevitably would be, Quayle, under pressure in
a high-stakes debate, was likely to rehash what he'd been saying and
invoke JFK—in terms of their similar ages, or the number of years
they'd served in the House and Senate. Had Bentsen known JFK?
Yes, he had served with him. Did he feel comfortable, if the chance
came, telling Quayle that he was no John Kennedy? Sure. The moment was worded, practiced, and polished in the mock debates.
Bentsen went into the encounter with Quayle armed with a devastating rhetorical polyptych: "Senator, I served with Jack Kennedy. I
knew Jack Kennedy. Jack Kennedy was a friend of mine. Senator,
you're no Jack Kennedy."

As it turned out, Bentsen almost didn't have a chance to deliver
the blow. I watched the debate on television with anticipation—then
apprehension. Bentsen was doing well, but Quayle was surviving.
Three times, Quayle was asked about his experience and each time
he avoided any reference to JFK. Finally, Tom Brokaw pressed him
again: "I don't mean to beat this drum until it has no more sound"—
but do you have the experience it takes if you suddenly have to succeed to the presidency? I'm convinced that during his own debate
prep, Quayle had probably been warned that the comparison to
Kennedy was a step too far—and that he'd consciously avoided it to
this point. But he'd run out of things to say, although in situations
like this, candidate are best off repeating themselves no matter how
hard the questioners probe. Quayle fumbled around, talked about
assembling a good cabinet, cited his communication skills—not his
best case, in light of what was about to happen—and then reaching

down into his rhetorical DNA, closed by saying he had "as much experience in Congress as Jack Kennedy." Bentsen looked right at him and leveled him. The Texan's timing was perfect, and as soon as he finished with: "Senator, *you're* no Jack Kennedy," the auditorium erupted in thunderous applause. Quayle compounded the disaster by complaining weakly, "That was uncalled for," and Bentsen spontaneously drove the point home: "You're the one who made the comparison—and I'm the one who knew [JFK] well."

Near the end of the race, with Dukakis far behind, I was drawn in again to script a series of 5-minute spots in which he would take his case straight to the country on national television. But I set one unusual condition because I'd been through this before with the candidate. I'd been asked to draft his Labor Day kickoff speech. The text I sent positioned Dukakis as a fighter for the middle class and working families. It needed a tagline. I said that it should be along the lines of the slogan we were using in Howard Metzenbaum's Senate race in Ohio: "On Our Side." Obviously it couldn't be precisely the same words. I was called a few days later with a thank-you, and the news that Dukakis didn't like the speech. It wasn't him, and he couldn't give it. Now, with the campaign in its final weeks, I didn't want to waste my time again, so I said that while the 5-minute television speeches were obviously the candidate's, and he could change them, would he agree to talk with me before he did that? He would and he did, tracking me down in the editing studio in Philadelphia before he recorded a broadcast that dealt with foreign trade. Surprisingly, he didn't want to soften the argument; not surprising, given what I knew of him, he wanted to make it more precise. He was almost cheerful on the telephone.

In those closing days of the campaign, Dukakis was combative, publicly confident, and a tribune of Democratic beliefs. Oddly, for someone previously allergic to a populist tone, he sounded completely comfortable with it. He took on "influence peddlers," "sleaze merchants," "dishonest contractors and polluters." In a line that would be appropriated, presumably unintentionally, by Howard Dean in 2004, Dukakis called on his growing and enthusiastic crowds to "take back America." At virtually every stop, he announced, I'm "on your side." An agitated Howard Metzenbaum called me to complain that the beleagured Dukakis had kidnapped his slogan—and I'd probably been party to the deed. I told Metzenbaum it didn't matter; he was 14 points ahead. The Dukakis campaign was now telling its own story of a comeback, even a surge—and the Bush margin that had ballooned to double digits would close to 7 points by Election Day. How much of his final quasi-populist case Dukakis actually believed is unclear. But on the day of his unscripted declaration that he was a "liberal," which he said on his own, without advice, I suspected that there were more deeply rooted convictions inside him than he had expressed during most of his failed run for the White House.

That his strategists and Democrats in general were appalled when he used the "L" word exposed a long-term, debilitating weakness in the party. Democrats have cast around for phrases to describe themselves, from Mario Cuomo's preferred euphemism "progressive" to the contentless "centrist" to a resolute lack of resolution—the claim, which I myself have participated in making, that "labels don't matter." The Republicans have taken the opposite tack. But it wasn't always so. Dwight Eisenhower was explicitly cast as a "modern Republican." On the verge of his presidential nomination in 1960, Richard Nixon had conceded "liberal" platform planks to New York governor Nelson Rockefeller in what relatively powerless conservative Republicans denounced as the sell-out "Pact of Fifth Avenue." That year, it was politically far better to be called liberal than conservative; in fact, John Kennedy flourished his identity explicitly in a major speech in New York: "I'm proud to say I'm a liberal." But for the past quarter century, while Democrats have fled that word, Republicans have embraced, defended, and rehabilitated the term "conservative." When they tried it in 1964, Barry Goldwater was annihilated. But Ronald Reagan renewed the call. The Republicans have convinced the country that they have a governing philosophy and a plurality of Americans have come to identify themselves, in poll after poll, as "conservatives."

Dukakis, of course, could not have reversed the long Democratic retreat in the war of words even if he had used the "L" word day after day. He would have paid a political price—as Republicans did in the early stages of their openly conservative manifestation. But they stayed at it, and for three decades, there has been only one Democratic president, Bill Clinton—and he won with 43 percent of the vote, largely as a "remainderman," when the first President Bush was doomed by recession. This may happen again; after Iraq, Hurricane Katrina, and the second Bush's malaprop presidency, voters may move away from "conservatism." They may decide, for the moment, that you can't govern the country if you hate the government.

Republicans put a gloss on a label they will never surrender, as in 2000 with "compassionate conservatism." But there is no sign that most Democrats have the stomach to engage in any long-term effort to reclaim and rehabilitate "liberalism." The battle may be too long neglected and too far gone, the identity that Kennedy confidently asserted too tarnished. So the other side will continue to use "liberal" as a political profanity, speaking the word far more often than Democrats, who will seek to get by with euphemisms and a collection of proposals, many of them liberal in effect, but generally accompanied by a nod to the right.

After Dukakis lost, I wrote an op-ed column for the *New York Times* describing a way forward, arguing that "we have to be willing to stand for something, for people, for a set of economic ideas that can be broadly described as populist. . . . [This] can be the spark that rekindles the Democratic flame, that gives life to a relevant and powerful liberalism that dares to speak its name." I received a handwritten note from a newly elected senator, Joe Lieberman. My column was, he wrote, "a great piece . . . it described my campaign here in Connecticut this year." Lieberman would be part of another presidential campaign I was involved in—one that would be both won and lost. By then, he would be studiously nonliberal. The word itself would be consigned to memory and Republican attack ads, and after the Florida recount, I would be reading stories criticizing me for losing successive presidential campaigns by being excessively liberal. But that wasn't the verdict in 1988. Following Dukakis's makeover at the end of that race, the November 21 *Newsweek* awarded me an "up" arrow: "[C]onsultant's patented populism failed Gephardt but helped Dukakis."

The next two years brought victory, defeat, and for me enduring lessons.

We signed on to the long-shot New York City mayoral candidacy of David Dinkins, who ousted Ed Koch in the primary and then squeaked by Rudolph Giuliani in the general election. Helping to defeat Koch settled an old score for me that went back to his pettiness and hostility toward Ted Kennedy during the 1980 campaign. I also took some pride in working for the first African-American mayors of Los Angeles, Chicago, and New York, as well as the first Hispanic mayor of Denver.

Paul Simon, the Illinois senator who'd derailed the Gephardt strategy, was a surprise client in 1990. I was chatting with him at a pre-dinner reception before one of Washington's traditional incestuous springtime gatherings of press and politicians, when Bob Squier interrupted us, telling me with a half-serious laugh to leave Simon alone: "He's mine." Squier had handled his 1984 Senate race. Simon, whose mild demeanor could be misleading, countered: "I'll decide who my consultant is." Soon after, Doak and I had the assignment. Simon was a prime Republican target; Roger Ailes, the architect of Bush's dismantling of Dukakis, was the media consultant for Simon's opponent, Congresswoman Lynn Martin. We launched an advertising campaign that tagged her spots as negative—and then explained that she had voted to cut Medicare and Social Security. Simon was delighted after one of our polls came in: "We're killing her—and the voters think she's the one who's being negative."

A frustrated Ailes flew to the state and called Simon a "weenie" and "slimy." I couldn't resist taking a swipe at Ailes. What could you expect, I said, from the man who was responsible for the racist Willie Horton ad during the Dukakis campaign? The infamous ad had attacked the Massachusetts prison furlough program for letting a murderer out on the weekend to kill again. It played on the worst of stereotypes, focusing on the bearded, menacing-looking face of Horton, who happened to be African-American. Ailes always vehemently denied responsibility for the spot, claiming it was the product of an independent expenditure group. This is a game Republicans have played over and over again. A Republican operative warned me that I'd made a mortal enemy. After the election, which Simon won by 30 points, I had my first and only meal with Ailes, not at a visible Washington spot but a restaurant across the Potomac in Pentagon City. It was a polite, slightly strained evening during which he told me he was tired of political consulting. Six years later, when he was running the Fox News Channel, Ailes approved hiring me as a part-time political commentator; I even appeared on the network's '96 election night coverage. After a year, I refused to re-up with Fox because I decided I was being used as token balance in a conservative propaganda machine.

The 1990 election demonstrated the power of some emerging and emotionally charged issues. Conservative Oklahoma elected a Democratic governor, David Walters, who campaigned for term limits for state officials. I didn't agree with the idea; but as a nonpolitician who'd barely lost four years earlier, he was an ideal vehicle for the message. We produced a wickedly effective commercial with Walters striding across an empty state legislative chamber telling voters that the seats here "belong to you, not to them." We hadn't shown any official the script when we requested permission to film in the chamber. We were now told we could never film there again. We didn't need to; Walters won in a landslide.

In Georgia, the big issue was the lottery. The campaign manager was James Carville and the candidate was Zell Miller, who'd once served as executive secretary to an arch-segregationist governor, Lester Mattox. In sixteen subsequent years as lieutenant governor— no term limits here—Miller had morphed into a born-again progressive. He had four primary opponents, but he was the only one who favored a lottery, supposedly a third rail in states like Georgia where fundamentalist ministers excoriated it as gambling. They had unlikely allies on the editorial boards, who characterized it as bad policy, a tax on the poor, a way to evade tough choices about how to raise revenues. Carville called this "elitist shit"—and the voters agreed. Miller romped to the nomination.

He was a handful as a candidate; he was mercurial and his mood swings came on unexpectedly. Carville observed that Zell Miller was almost two different personalities. Before one of the debates, Doak and I called in from Washington to a briefing. Miller seemed to be primed and ready. But after the debate, Carville reported that there had been one very strange moment. Just before he went on, Miller announced that he couldn't do this, he wasn't up to it, maybe he just shouldn't run. Carville all but pushed him onto the stage. In the run-up to the election in November, James phoned me with a different worry. An Atlanta TV station wanted to film our get-out-the-vote operation. We didn't have one; we'd put all the money into television. James and I discussed an idea: couldn't we just go out and get some unused phones? We already had some in the back room, Carville said. He could just spread them around tables in the big room at the headquarters, put people on them to pretend they were making calls, and pack them back up after the television crew left. We laughed about it after Miller was elected governor.

Miller's moodiness concealed a level of resentment that could be directed equally, and randomly, to either side of the political spectrum. He carried Georgia for Clinton in 1992, took on the old-boy politics that had spawned his career in a vain effort to remove the Confederate battle emblem from the Georgia flag, and was almost defeated for reelection. Afterward, he set off on a journey to the right. He was pro-choice, then pro-life. As a senator, he sponsored a constitutional amendment to outlaw even domestic partnerships for gays. His other proposed constitutional amendment was odd and antiquarian—to have state legislators, not voters, elect U.S. senators. He was prickly with his colleagues, but had an apparently friendly relationship with John Kerry, who said that at first Miller sounded well-disposed toward a Kerry run for president. Miller then endorsed George W. Bush—and spewed out a manic, hate-filled attack on Kerry at the 2004 Republican Convention. Afterward, when MSNBC's Chris Matthews questioned his facts, Miller exploded on national television and said he wished he could challenge Matthews to "a duel." One side of his divided personality had won out: The sometime progressive of 1990, whose populism had always had an angry tinge, was now a screeching right-wing demagogue. He will become a lasting footnote in what the historian Richard Hofstadter called "the paranoid style in American politics": a feeling of being "dispossessed" that feeds a "heated sense of exaggeration, suspiciousness, and conspiratorial fantasy." In 1990, Zell Miller was a win for us, but I'm sorry I ever worked for him.

A spectacular defeat in another race taught me a painful lesson: Listen to your own instincts, not the consensus of the political class. In the run-up to the 1990 gubernatorial campaign in California, I'd decided that the best potential Democratic candidate—in the primary and the general election—was Dianne Feinstein, the mayor of San Francisco. Hadley Roff, my compatriot from the Muskie campaign who'd been slapped with a wet towel by the candidate in the back of the plane, had gone on to serve as Feinstein's deputy mayor. Hadley and I had lunch with Feinstein and her husband Dick Blum at Trader Vic's. I was a little taken aback at how nonpolitical Feinstein was; she ventured that if she did run for governor, maybe she should run as an independent. She was reputed to be brittle and difficult— and maybe she is. But we hit it off, and when Roff asked for a plan, I sent a strategy memo suggesting that her first ad focus on the awful night she'd become mayor, when her predecessor had been assassinated by an anti-gay retired police officer. With grace, self-possession, and empathy, she had pacified a saddened and agitated crowd of thousands gathered at night outside City Hall. And it was all on film.

The last candidate the California Democratic establishment was contemplating was Dianne Feinstein. The consensus choice and the prohibitive favorite was John Van de Kamp, the state attorney general. I talked with Roz Wyman, the veteran Democratic power broker who as a young city councilwoman had famously brought the Dodgers to Los Angeles. She was a friend of Feinstein's and of ours, who'd opened her Bel Air mansion to Marylouise and me for our wedding reception. Her reaction was instantaneous: Van de Kamp is our candidate; don't do this to Dianne; she'll just end up hurting herself. Most of the big fund-raisers and most members in the political elite of the state agreed, and Doak and I were offered the Van de Kamp campaign. My wife was a lone and stubborn hold-out: She thought Feinstein would be the stronger choice and it was time for a woman. Doak left the decision to me. I made the wrong one. We agreed to go with Van de Kamp. Even worse, when Dick Blum heard rumors and started calling me, I didn't return his calls—or Roff's. We had never signed anything with Feinstein, but I was afraid to face the music. Feinstein won the Democratic nomination, then barely lost the governorship that November. She was elected to the U.S. Senate two years later. In 2004, she endorsed John Kerry for president early on and never walked away during the dark months of the pre-primary period. As Kerry was sweeping up the primaries, I found myself sitting in a holding room in Oakland with her and Blum. You are always better off doing what you think is right, she archly observed.

The hardest lesson of 1990 was that sometimes it is wrong to work for a candidate—not because he can't win but because he doesn't deserve to. Jim Mattox, the attorney general of Texas, was running for the Democratic nomination for governor against the state treasurer, Ann Richards, who'd garnered national fame at the 1988 Democratic Convention when she'd derided the first George Bush as "poor George. He can't help it. He was born with a silver foot in his mouth." Mattox was rough around the edges, a hardscrabble fighter who early in the race questioned Richards's fitness to serve because she was a recovering alcoholic. And he suggested that she'd used hard drugs. James Carville, who was also consulting for Mattox, was apoplectic when he called me. I flew down to Austin to tell Mattox that if this was where his campaign was headed, then we were all quitting. But the charge, he feverishly said, was true. He knew people who'd done cocaine with Richards. I said I didn't want to hear it ever again. He promised to hold his tongue.

In the runoff primary for the nomination, Mattox was behind. He ordered up a question in a poll: Would Texans vote for a candidate who had used cocaine? The answer, of course, was no—from, as I recall, about 80 percent of the voters. Suddenly we were in our conference room in Washington writing a spot. I was dubious: The question in the poll was hypothetical; why would people believe the charge, especially when it came from Mattox? There was no proof. The ad would probably damage us more than our opponent—and it was also wrong in principle. But I wasn't prepared to risk a rupture within our firm. Doak said we had an obligation to the client; we just had to write the script carefully. I'm convinced he thought it was fair. I didn't walk out of the room, and so I shared responsibility for a disgraceful ad that posed a McCarthyite question: "Did she use marijuana, or something worse, like cocaine, not as a college kid, but as a forty-seven-year-old elected official sworn to uphold the law?" Once on the air, the ad exploded in our faces. The race hit bottom for me a few days later when I turned on *Face the Nation* the Sunday before the election. There was an unblushing Mattox angrily issuing an unequivocal smear at Richards: "We're not talking about pot. We're talking about cocaine." Asked for evidence, he defiantly reprised the accusation. I said to Carville, who had now gotten as far removed from the Mattox campaign as he could, "How did we get into this?" He said the best answer we could give was to deny that we were ever there.

After the primary, in which Richards captured over 56 percent of the vote, a *Boston Globe* editorial excoriated "Doak and Shrum," called the ad "a hoedown of dirt and calumny," compared it to "Willie Horton," and pointedly noted that I had been a "speech-writer for Sen. Edward Kennedy." Why was he being "notably silent?" I soon heard from him. He sent me a copy of the editorial and wrote across the bottom: "At least they spelled your name right—Ted." I was often accused of being a maestro of negative campaigning. But this time, I'd gone down a slippery slope with a client I didn't believe in who crossed a line that I might not be able to define but knew was there. I asked a friend to tell Richards I was sorry. The next time I saw her, she acted as if nothing had ever happened.

There was one last lesson of 1990, a happy one even though it came in a losing campaign: Some candidates are bigger than their defeats. When we were first hired, I didn't imagine that Bill Nelson's prospects were bleak in the Florida governor's race. He was a moderate six-term congressman who'd flown on the space shuttle Columbia. He was unopposed for the Democratic nomination. But the campaign all but ended long before primary day with the surprise late entry of retired Senator Lawton Chiles, the legendary "Walkin' Lawton" who'd traveled the length of Florida on foot in his first Senate race twenty years before. Chiles was tired of being retired; he'd been out of office just over a year. I took the first flight from Washington to Orlando. The safest course, I bluntly said to Nelson, was to drop out of the gubernatorial contest. Chiles had name recognition and popularity, and he'd have the editorial boards. Nelson could run again for his seat in the Congress. He'd win another term and live politically to fight another day. But Nelson was determined to stay in. He'd give it his best shot, but if anyone wanted out of the campaign, he'd understand.

On election night, after Nelson conceded in the ballroom of an Orlando hotel, I was nursing my hurt in the lobby. He and his wife Grace came in, sat with me for a while, and said we'd all done our best. Over the next three years, we talked occasionally. One day, Bill Nelson said he assumed we didn't do down ballot campaigns, but what if he was a candidate for state treasurer and insurance commissioner? Would we make an exception for him? It's rare that defeated candidates ask consultants back. I worked as hard as I ever have in any statewide contest. Nelson won and was reelected four years later. But he had no way to run for higher office—until the incumbent Republican senator Connie Mack announced out of the blue that he wasn't running in 2000. Nelson phoned that morning and all but declared his candidacy that day. He stayed with us, as our other clients did, after we signed on with Al Gore's presidential campaign. Nelson won by 300,000 votes and in 2006 was reelected by a margin of more than 1 million, humiliating Katherine Harris, who as Florida's secretary of state helped pilfer the state for George W. Bush six years before. It was a payback I particularly savored.

We'd made some of our own difficulties in 1990. But with victories in five out of six general election races, the consultants' trade magazine *Campaigns and Elections* named us the top Democratic media firm. Marylouise and I went to Rome with Carville and a beautiful woman we'd introduced him to who'd been Marylouise's colleague at the *L.A. Times*. By now, Marylouise had left the paper and was writing her first novel. Carville was insatiably curious about every basilica, art gallery, and ruin; we spent hours in the Roman drizzle exploring the stone arches and stairways of Trajan's Market. I knew James was the best person in the Democratic Party to manage the next presidential race. He told me didn't want to—in a way that conveyed just how much he did. And who'd ask him, anyway? he wondered.

But first, Carville and I were about to get involved in an unexpected statewide race that looked like a long shot. Our victory there would set the table for the 1992 presidential campaign and hand Democrats a signature issue in that contest, one that would dominate the first two years of the Clinton presidency.

6

MY BRIDGE TO THE TWENTY-FIRST CENTURY

On April 4, 1991, in a sunlit noontime sky over Philadelphia, a private plane with Republican senator John Heinz on board collided with a helicopter flying close by to check if the plane's landing gear was down. Heinz was killed. There would now be a special Senate election in November to fill his seat, to be held only months after the U.S. victory in the Gulf War with George Bush and the Republicans still presumably riding high. As governor, Bob Casey would name an interim appointee likely to be the Democratic candidate in the special election.

Within days, it was clear where the Republicans were headed for their nominee. Casey's predecessor as governor was now Bush's U.S. Attorney General, Dick Thornburgh. Most observers agreed it would be an uphill battle for any Democrat. But Casey dithered, not settling on a choice until five weeks after Heinz was dead. Harris Wofford, Casey's secretary of labor and the once young New Frontiersman who'd initiated JFK's election-winning call to Coretta Scott King when her husband was in a Georgia jail, avidly pursued the appointment. I'd known him a long time. He asked me several times to talk to Casey, and I did. I reported back that there wasn't much Wofford could do but be patient.

Wofford got the nod only after he reassured Casey on the issue of abortion. I asked him what he'd said. He was evasive. He and Casey had talked it out; the governor understood he wasn't a standard pro-choice Democrat. (More than a year later, Casey, tapping a finger on his desk, told me he had a letter inside from Wofford pledging to be pro-life. He wasn't during his time in the Senate. Not only was Casey anti-abortion, but to him, that was a litmus test; and Wofford, who saw one last chance at the brass ring of high elective office, rationalized his way past it.)

We were so far behind in the polls that Democrats in Washington reacted with a kind of embarrassed pity when they heard that Carville, Doak, and I were working for Wofford. We started our search for a message in a focus group run by Mike Donilon, Tom's brother, Caddell's former partner and my future one. When he mentioned health care to the respondents, there was a spontaneous combustion of frustration, anger, and a demand for change. When Donilon tried to move on, they refused. Paul Begala and I were watching behind a two-way mirror. Mike came in after the first group left, and I said we probably had our issue; it wasn't, in honesty, the one we expected to find. And the issue was bigger than itself: it was a metaphor for rising economic anxiety as the lingering Bush recession took its toll in lost jobs and slow growth.

Donilon fielded a poll that confirmed both the conventional wisdom—and the potential to confound it. Wofford was behind Thornburgh 67 percent to 20 percent; only 15 percent of voters even knew who Wofford was. But when Donilon's poll described both of them—Thornburgh as a former governor and cabinet member who supported President Bush, and Wofford as a Democrat who'd worked for JFK and Casey and who would fight in the Senate for health care, jobs, and fairness to the middle class—the race closed to a virtual tie. I was convinced Wofford could win in 1991, and that Bush's standing was so fragile, he could lose in 1992.

To put it mildly, a belief in Bush's vulnerability was not widely shared. As we were developing the Wofford strategy, Dick Gephardt convened a session in his House Majority Leader's office to decide whether to run for president again. Paul Maslin had conducted a set of caucus, primary, and general election surveys. It was clear, he reported, that Gephardt could capture the nomination. But the research was equally clear that no Democrat could beat Bush. Bill Carrick, the media consultant who'd managed the Gephardt campaign in 1988, weighed in on the same side. So did virtually everyone in the room—except Doak and me. I had my usual argument to a presidential candidate on the edge of withdrawal: If you can get the nomination, take it; no one can be certain this early what it will be worth—and no one who can win it now can be certain that it will be there the next time around. And I had another argument. The afterglow of the Gulf War was fading; the 1992 election was likely to pivot on the economy and domestic issues like health care. I was seeing the first signs of it in Pennsylvania. But Gephardt said he'd made up his mind: He wasn't running and he was going to announce that publicly.

As his advisers were filing out of the room, I still wasn't prepared to give up. I stayed behind to reiterate my case and added that 1992 was Gephardt's best chance; he had a base of support, built in 1988, that would steadily erode over time. He interrupted me. He didn't yell, but he noticeably raised his voice: "Bob, if you want to run for president so goddamn bad, why don't you run yourself?" I'd never heard him swear before. I said that he obviously felt strongly and there was nothing more to say.

We were about to make our first ads for Wofford when he called me. Consultants have to listen to their candidates, not just script them with poll-tested language. Wofford told me that a friend of his had asked what kind of country was it that provided lawyers for criminal defendants, but not health care for people who needed it? Could we get that into a spot? We sure could. We filmed Wofford in a doctor's office. The words weren't formulaic; they weren't "pol speak"; they sounded the way people talk: "If criminals have the right to a lawyer, then I think working Americans should have the right to see a doctor when they're sick." True to his lawyerly sense and his commitment to civil liberties, Wofford objected to that last line just before the cameras rolled. They weren't criminals, he observed, until they were convicted; couldn't we call them, say, "accused criminals" or just "defendants"? I replied that the spot started with him saying, "The Constitution says those accused of a crime have a right to a lawyer"; we didn't have time to reiterate a qualifier in the punch line. I thought to myself it was fine if voters heard Wofford as more hard-line on crime than he really was.

While we were broadcasting spots with bite, Thornburgh's ads sounded as if he was on his way to a coronation: "Some folks have asked me why I'm running. . . . It's simple. I love this state." By the end of September, a public poll showed Thornburgh's lead down to 12 points—and the momentum was all moving Wofford's way. Newspaper endorsements came one after another, and contributions rolled in. We had the resources to close out the race with a 60-second biography—a piece of expensive airtime that we couldn't remotely afford early on—along with a "comparative" spot that hit Thornburgh one last time. Doak and I were in a conference room in Philadelphia reviewing scripts with Carville, who proposed to change one line. Doak resisted; Carville persisted. Doak got mad, told Carville off—he didn't know anything about ads—then shoved a file cabinet and stalked out of the room. There was a long, tense moment of silence. Carville was about to walk out, too, when I said, let's just get the ad fixed; we can iron out the language. Doak and Carville never again had more than a passing relationship. Doak, who'd played a big role in bringing Carville into the Casey campaign in 1986, seemed to regard James as a kind of protégé. But Carville was too big for that now—and after Wofford won, he was about to become a lot bigger.

On election night in Philadelphia, I was elated as Wofford racked up a 12-point victory. I boarded a Metroliner back to Washington to be with Marylouise—and confidently awaited the results of the other off-year campaign where Doak and I were the media consultants.

Ray Mabus was the first governor in Mississippi history to run for reelection after the one-term limit was repealed. He had defied the conventional wisdom about Mississippi when he won the first time. He was young, progressive, and had gone, of all places, to Harvard Law School. He was even pro-choice. Legislators had passed his sweeping education reform, but then, spurred by the state's churches, blocked a lottery to fund it. When they did pass a bill to permit riverboat gambling, he quipped to me: "I guess they think it's holier."

Mabus had thought about skipping a reelection race and gearing up for a White House run. Nationally, he wasn't well known, but potentially he was emblematic of the "New South." It was 1990 when he mentioned the possibility. I told him we couldn't work for him for president; we were committed to Gephardt. But I conceded that the notion was appealing. Why risk a 1991 campaign for governor? With the national economy in trouble, so was Mississippi's, and he could be blamed for the state's downturn. As the campaign unfolded, his Republican opponent railed against welfare cheats, racial quotas, the Voting Rights Act—and the fact that Mabus was "Harvard-educated." It was the "old" Mississippi reasserting itself, but for months the polls seemed to say it wasn't working. The phone calls that election night grew increasingly anxious. Finally, Mabus called to report that he'd lost, not by much; he was devastated. He asked if Marylouise and I could visit him and his wife Julie before they left the governor's mansion.

The mansion's household staff consisted of trustees from the Mississippi State Penetentiary, whose manner belied their violent crimes. As they served us drinks and dinner in the upstairs study, we discussed the impending presidential campaign. Mabus said if Mario Cuomo didn't run, there were only two real choices: Bill Clinton and Bob Kerrey, the independent-minded senator from Nebraska who'd lost his leg in Vietnam and won the Congressional Medal of Honor. We probably needed a southerner, Mabus said, with a resigned smile. But he worried whether Bill Clinton could withstand the scrutiny. Everyone down here, he continued, knew that Clinton had a woman problem. They'd seen it at regional meetings and governors' conferences.

Clinton had announced in October and stories like this, accurate or not, were everywhere with political insiders and the press. Pamela Harriman told me she'd always liked Clinton, admired his political skills, but frankly, he had "a zipper problem." She recalled how he'd stayed over at her Georgetown home several times, and on one occasion come in late with a woman and they spent the night together. Pamela was hardly a prude, but she was angry with Clinton: it was reckless, just the kind of thing that had destroyed Gary Hart. She knew Hillary well and she didn't like her own home being used that way.

Carville and Paul Begala were interviewing with both Kerrey and Clinton. Carville told me that he just had a sense that Kerrey was too scattered, too unfocused. Clinton would be the better bet—and the better candidate. Once the pick was made, *The Washington Post* headlined: "Clinton Wins the Carville Primary." (In 2004, in a reprise I hated, the press would be writing about the "Shrum Primary.")

I'd seen Bill Clinton a few times in the years since the McGovern campaign. In 1980, after he was defeated for reelection as governor of Arkansas, he came to Washington to drum up support for a bid for chairman of the Democratic National Committee (DNC). He met with Ted Kennedy to assure Kennedy that if he got the job, he'd be attentive to his wishes about the nominating process. He started to explain why, after delivering a stirring introduction for Kennedy's 1978 midterm convention speech challenging Carter on health care, he felt he'd had to support his fellow southerner in 1980. Kennedy cut him off—or let him off a painful hook. The future was what mattered, he said, not the past. And the future was the subject I raised as I took the subway with Clinton from the Senate Office Building to the Capitol. Why did he want to run the DNC? I asked. It was a dead end, the gateway to a subsequent career as a Washington lawyer or lobbyist—or maybe a job in a future Democratic administration. Clinton was down, depressed, almost shattered by his loss. What else was he going to do? He could run for governor again, but he didn't know if he could win. But the DNC, I replied, would be the end of his national ambitions. At least in a 1982 election in Arkansas, he wouldn't have the burden of Carter at the top of the ticket. At the end of the subway ride, we stood and talked for a while. I argued, quietly, that he just had too much potential to give up and become another Washington fixture.

Clinton had been back in the governor's office for more than eight years by the time he and Doak shared a long car ride across Arkansas in 1991. David had worked with Hillary in the Carter campaign in 1980 and we were hoping to become Clinton's media consultants in his next reelection bid. We had no chance, Doak said to me back in Washington. We were seen as Gephardt's guys—and Clinton, quite reasonably, wanted someone who would stick by him if he ran for president in 1992. He hired another media consultant, Frank Greer, who headed one of the three media firms that, along with Squier's and ours, were the big players on the Democratic block. Clinton also hired a professor turned pollster named Stan Greenberg, someone I'd later partner with in races from Britain to Israel to Al Gore. But in 1992, Greenberg hardly knew me.

Later that fall, I had one of my periodic lunches with *The New Yorker*'s Elizabeth Drew. She asked for a reality check on her own assessment of the Democratic field as she stood in between courses to ease her chronic back pain. Afterward, I took her outside to find a cab. If we'd left 30 seconds later, the next year and decade might have taken a different turn for me.

But as she was being driven away, I ran into Don Sweitzer, a Democratic operative who was close to DNC chairman Ron Brown. Naturally, we started talking about the coming presidential race. He told me that at a recent party confab, Bill Clinton had spied Ron Brown's daughter in the audience, didn't know who she was, and tried to pick her up—or as Sweitzer put it, "hit" on her. I had no idea whether this story was true, although I'd heard that earlier one from Pamela Harriman. Some of America's best presidents hadn't been faithful to their wives. But by 1992, the times and the rules had changed. Sweitzer said the party couldn't afford another sex scandal. He thought Clinton was a "risky" nominee. (Once Clinton had the nomination in hand the following spring, Sweitzer would be named the campaign's liaison to labor and then in 1994 political director of the Democratic National Committee.)

Sweitzer's story was just another one of many oft-told rumors swirling around Washington when George McGovern phoned and asked if we could have dinner at the Jockey Club, the wood-paneled restaurant where lobbyists, high officials, and the well-heeled of

Washington gathered for crab cakes and conversation. We sat in one of the banquettes and the topic again predictably turned to 1992. McGovern had a rooting interest in his onetime staffer Bill Clinton. But he was concerned that Clinton was the choice of the centrist Democratic Leadership Council, which he saw as a kind of inquisition determined to purge any stray "McGovernism" from the party. I replied that in my view, Clinton was using the DLC at least as much as it was using him. He also had a host of advisers from McGovern's 1972 campaign—Sandy Berger, for example. McGovern wondered how much truth there was to the reports about Clinton's personal life. I said that, yes, they were everywhere—and off-handedly cited what Sweitzer had said about Ron Brown's daughter. But I didn't see how they would ever become a public issue. Who was going to tell? This exchange had taken about two minutes and I didn't think twice about it.

In December 1991, I took a trip that was a first step down a road Doak and I had not expected to take—to the presidential campaign of Bob Kerrey. Tom Donilon, the Carter whiz kid who'd then run the Bentsen debate prep along with Tad Devine, was getting married in one of the Victorian-era mansions that dominate and define Newport, Rhode Island. His brother Mike had left polling and become a partner in our firm after the Wofford victory. They had grown up in blue-collar South Providence, where their father had served on the local school committee and their mother had been a clerical worker in a local school. The Donilons' boyhood friend Tad Devine had been raised in a housing project and his father had been a sidewalk inspector. As I looked around this mansion, so lavishly decorated for Christmas, the wedding struck me as a celebration of how far they had all come.

At the reception, Tad told Jim Johnson that he'd been contacted by Bob Kerrey. Kerrey, a favorite when he announced in September, and described in the *Boston Globe* as perhaps "the party's most attractive candidate since John F. Kennedy," by December seemed trapped in a directionless campaign without a focused message. Partly that was a reflection of Kerrey himself. I would come to see him as the most existential politician I've ever known, a Walt Whitmanesque character who, in effect, could happily say to voters: "Do I contradict myself? Very well." Now Kerrey was mulling the reinvention of his campaign. He'd asked Devine, a veteran of three presidential races, to consider taking over. Johnson responded why not, what did Tad have to lose? Everybody knew the trouble Kerrey was in, and Tad might rescue the enterprise. But he had to insist on having his own people in critical slots. Tad said it was probably a long shot that he'd do the Kerrey race. But he turned to me and asked whether Doak and I would sign on if he did. I replied that Kerrey already had a media consulting firm, and my relationship with him consisted of only a few handshakes over the years.

There is nothing more hazardous in politics than assuming strategic control of a presidential campaign late in the game; in this case, it would occur just seven weeks before Election Day in New Hampshire, when Devine, as Kerrey's new campaign chief, asked us to fly there for a session in which the candidate could get "comfortable" with us. The meeting proved to be uncomfortable and unwieldy. Doak and I had brought three other partners into the firm and they all insisted on coming along.

Each of us tried to get a word in as Kerrey "got acquainted" for the first time with a team of strategic consultants to whom he was about to entrust the most important chapter in his political career. He was alternately despondent and challenging: What could he do now, what do you guys think we should do? Clinton was for a middle-class tax cut as a way to spur the economy and provide immediate relief to middle-class families. But Kerrey had been equivocal on the issue; he told us he thought the tax cut was "pandering." His economic plan, Kerrey said—and he repeated this in our office just across the Potomac from Georgetown a few days later—was his health care plan. It would save businesses billions of dollars and lift a load of dead weight off the economy. This was true, but not exactly easy to explain to voters, who were looking for something more than a long-term answer to the acute short-term pain of the downturn.

Even worse, Kerrey, who'd made national health reform the centerpiece of his campaign, had been tarnished when the *New York Times* published a front-page report that there was no health insurance for the employees at the restaurants he'd opened in Nebraska after he left the Navy SEALs. At a focus group in the final, heated run-up to the primary in New Hampshire, Devine would witness the corrosive impact of the *Times* story. One participant gave Kerrey credit for being the first candidate to raise health care (he'd been running on it even before Wofford had). But others dismissed Kerrey as a hypocrite—if he cared so much about the issue, why didn't he give health coverage to his own workers? By then, the first Clinton sex scandal had erupted, the charge that he'd had an affair with a lounge singer named Gennifer Flowers. A woman in the focus group dismissed the scandal as others nodded. Clinton wasn't preaching fidelity, she said; Kerrey was preaching national health insurance, but denying it to his own workers. Kerrey, Devine concluded, had his own character problem—one more relevant to the voters' own lives.

Moreover, Kerrey wasn't the only one for comprehensive health reform. After the Wofford election, Clinton, who until then had paid little attention to the issue, enthusiastically embraced it. Health care was no longer a defining difference between Clinton and Kerrey. Kidnapping your opponent's best issue is a time-honored technique in politics, a tactical move to neutralize the other side's appeal. Thus, in 1992, Clinton pledged himself to what would become the driving cause and biggest defeat of his first two years in office largely to deprive Kerrey of an advantage on a question that was decisive for Democrats. If you were for national health reform, you could now vote for Kerrey—or Clinton.

After Devine persuaded a dubious Kerrey to hire us, we were fully and frantically engaged in a rescue mission, writing and producing a round of spots just days before they were to go on the air. One of them had to deal with health care; we couldn't just concede the issue to Clinton, although our research never identified a way to get Kerrey off the hook for hypocrisy. But we had to address the economy more directly. Unfair foreign trade was potentially a more powerful issue in the depressed New Hampshire of 1992 than it had been for Gephardt in the prosperous New Hampshire of 1988. We thought we had a powerful visual to go with the words. Maybe Kerrey, who ran several miles a day on his artificial leg, could also ice-skate. Doak and I explained the concept for a spot, but said it would only work if he was willing to be tough on trade. Kerrey answered that he believed in opening up trade; but sure, he thought there ought to be a level playing field—and we ought to protect America's economic interests. It was hard to know what he meant by this or what his real policy was. But we were desperate to find a place to stand in this race. So was he. And so "the hockey ad," as it was instantly christened, was filmed and on television in a matter of days.

Kerrey didn't skate, but walked across the ice rink to a hockey net. He said: "What's happening in the world economy is like a hockey game where others guard their goal to keep our products out, while we leave our net open. . . . It's time to play a little defense for a change. We're becoming a low-wage nation, and all George Bush does is go to Japan and beg for a few concessions. I'm Bob Kerrey and if I'm President, the time for begging is through." The spot commanded attention and sparked instant controversy. In retrospect, we shouldn't have made it and I shouldn't have tempted or persuaded Kerrey to put it on. As he'd soon announce publicly, it wasn't who he really was. But at first, it seemed to be just what we needed. As Elizabeth Kolbert wrote in the *Times*, "This is the new Bob Kerrey: direct, plain-speaking, politely pugnacious. . . . [The ad] has already, even advisers to other candidates say, perceptibly lifted the Senator's standing." In a stroke of unanticipated good fortune, it hit the airwaves the same night the network news showed George Bush throwing up at a state dinner in Japan. It felt as if we were in the race.

Doak, who had directed the shoot, told me that Kerrey had fussed all through the filming. And he was being criticized in the press as a creature of his consultants; Shrum had just taken the Gephardt clothes and draped them across his shoulders. At times, in his speeches on the campaign trail, Kerrey all but quoted from the ad. At other times, he fled from it, numbing audiences by talking technocratically about his other economic policy—not middle-class tax cuts but, for example, an "Industrial Extension Service." The ambivalence was resolved when *Newsweek*'s Howard Fineman pushed him on the discrepancy between his record on trade and the hockey ad. Fineman called me to report that Kerrey had just denounced the hockey ad, saying, "I would describe it, looking at it right now, as a mistake." Nothing in my experience had prepared me for this. It was damaging to Doak and to me. But even more important, in the most authentic way possible, the candidate had just proclaimed his own inauthenticity; candidly, he'd proved that he wasn't candid. Devine threatened to quit unless Kerrey agreed not to do it again and to stay on message. But the spot was contaminated, useless, and Kerrey was soon sinking in the polls. And one of his loyalists, who'd opposed hiring us, weighed in publicly; Paul Johnson, our New Hampshire state director, told the *Boston Globe* the hockey ad had turned off voters; he found it "refreshing" that Kerrey could criticize it. Press secretary Mike McCurry tried to spin the flap as proof that Kerrey was "brutally honest." Kerrey now added that the ad "wasn't a mistake—it was just cold in there," in the hockey rink.

The one thing that doesn't succeed in politics is public squabbling about strategy. In addition, faced with money constraints, the initial pop from the hockey ad had faded as our media buy diminished. Devine had told me we had a million dollars when he took control of the campaign. He soon discovered that he was about $800,000 off; so we weren't buying time on Boston television. Then the candidate's own verdict on the hockey ad, amplified by some of his own advisers, deepened the doubts about him just as Clinton's character was coming under assault because of Gennifer Flowers's allegations and the revelation of a letter to an Army officer in which a young Clinton had explained why he wasn't keeping his ROTC commitment. To me, the letter, while overwrought, actually appeared to support Clinton's account of events; but in the onrushing maelstrom of campaign news, it was treated as further proof of his duplicity.

Kerrey talked to Tad about switching to an all-out negative assault on Clinton; he raised the idea again with me. The difficulty was that there was another candidate in the top three. Former Massachusetts senator Paul Tsongas, a deficit hawk, a well-balanced Ross Perot before there was a Ross Perot, was gaining so fast that he might run away with New Hampshire. Kerrey's best hope was to squeeze past a troubled Clinton for second place, but he couldn't do it by overtly attacking Clinton because he'd anger Democrats and drive them to Tsongas. Kerrey's numbers had stabilized and he had a chance to nudge them in a debate the Sunday night before the Tuesday primary. He was engaged and disciplined as he prepared; he told me as he left the room: "Wouldn't you like to know what I'm really going to go out there and say?" Kerrey turned in a first-rate performance. The next day, Clinton's polls showed Tsongas far ahead, Clinton dropping to 18 percent, and Kerrey at 14. Our own data showed Kerrey as high as 17 percent.

To worried Democrats in Washington, Clinton now looked wounded; Tsongas was ultimately implausible as the nominee; and Kerrey was so inconsistent and potentially self-destructive that Dick Gephardt was conferring with Bill Carrick and other advisers about a late entry into the race to "save" the party. I believed that Kerrey could inch up to 20 percent—and if he did, he'd be sufficiently re-deemed that there would be no room for a latecomer like Gephardt. We'd be on our way to the nomination, even if the ride, inevitably with Kerrey, would take some abrupt and surprising turns. But at the same time Clinton was fighting back hard, appearing with Hillary in their famous *60 Minutes* interview, attacking the "smears," and talking passionately about the economy, empathizing in what would become his trademark way with the pain people were feeling, emphasizing that this election wasn't about him but them. I was struck by his public resolve when his back was against the wall. I didn't quite realize that for voters, he was validating his character in a way that transcended personal scandal and questions about his con-duct during the Vietnam War.

That issue cost us our lead pollster. Harrison Hickman had anonymously faxed information about Clinton and his draft status during Vietnam to Walter Robinson at the *Boston Globe*. Robinson read the return number at the top of the fax and fingered Hickman. When Devine and I heard about the story, we rushed to see Kerrey. All Kerrey needed to say was that the fax was unauthorized and Hickman had been taken to the woodshed. But by that time Kerrey was already finishing up, and Mike McCurry grabbed us as we arrived backstage and said: "My God, you can't believe what he just did." Kerrey had labeled his longtime pollster and friend "Harrison Hitman," charged that he had "violated a personal trust," and announced that Hickman didn't work for him—"not at this moment." It was on the news and then in the papers on Monday morning as I rode around the state with Kerrey. That pre-primary day didn't feel right; it was clammy and dark when we stopped at a bar and Kerrey spoke to a half roomful of Vietnam vets, to halfhearted applause. No matter what happens here, one of them defiantly said to me, he's the best. We stopped at a bowling alley; Devine reported some new preliminary numbers from our backup pollster. Kerrey at 16 or 17, neck and neck with Clinton. I thought, well, we might actually get to 20.

Election days can be a long wait for a diagnosis that can spell political life or death. Across New Hampshire, voters decided that in the end, it was a two-person race between Tsongas, the leader in all the polls, and Clinton, who'd slipped behind but fought back to sustain himself against a sea of sludge. Kerrey—well, he had high favorables now, but he was the third man. Instead of picking up undecideds and some Clinton defectors, we lost some of the vote we thought we already had.

That night, as Tsongas took 34 percent—less than expected—and Clinton 26 percent—far more than expected—Kerrey limped in with 12 percent. Other candidates were further back. Our candidate was in no mood to talk; he informed Devine that he just might drop out of the race then and there. Tad and I scribbled some talking points on a yellow pad. He borrowed Dukakis's post-Iowa line about the Olympics four years before and slightly rewrote it: "We may not quite be golden yet, but bronze ain't bad."

Clinton turned silver into an unalloyed triumph as he named himself "The Comeback Kid." The candidate and his wife, and Carville, Begala, and George Stephanopoulos, had navigated some of the most treacherous waters in modern American politics, and reached the shore. Clinton's political position was now close to ideal. Few thought Tsongas could win the nomination; no one thought Jerry Brown, back for yet another quixotic try, was a plausible nominee. Kerrey was, but he was on his last legs—although after a reporter asked him about that during the next week, he quipped to me: "I'm always on my last leg." If anyone but Kerrey beat Clinton, or another scandal engulfed him, the likely beneficiary would be someone like Gephardt or Cuomo, who weren't even running—unless Kerrey won in South Dakota and then, without a base in the South, somehow brought Clinton down in the southern primaries. Kerrey did win South Dakota big—40 percent of the vote to Clinton's 19 percent—with the help of an ad charging that Clinton's "top economic adviser" had called for an end to farm subsidies. He wasn't actually on Clinton's staff and that wasn't Clinton's position, but the charge was enough to turn the race.

Devine had assigned me to fly to South Dakota with Kerrey to get him on message and keep him there. The days on the road with Kerrey were alternately tense and engaging as the conversation ricocheted from his political frustration and resentment to rambling literary discussions in which he advised me to read *The Moviegoer*, a novel by his favorite author, Walker Percy. I was finally back in Washington as the candidate headed for Georgia—an absence that didn't save me from getting into trouble with Clinton. I'd drafted remarks making a carefully stated case that Democrats couldn't afford a nominee who was vulnerable to an all-out negative assault from Bush. Kerrey looked at the draft on the plane to Atlanta, then furiously turned out his own hammer-and-tongs version. He summoned Devine and McCurry to look it over. Their reaction, as Tad told me, was that this was way over the top. Kerrey was ready to say that the people Clinton really owed an apology to for Gennifer Flowers were "Hillary and Chelsea." Devine and McCurry managed to excise the most pungent prose and deflect the candidate from any comments about Clinton's personal life. But Kerrey could barely contain himself—and in the end, he didn't. At a speech after he landed, he was memorably endorsed by a state representative, "Able" Mabel Thomas, with a blast at Clinton's Vietnam record: "We want a commander in chief, not a commander in chicken." Backstage, she'd also given Kerrey his own matching memorable line. Not content with suggesting that Clinton couldn't win—that his Vietnam-era record was a "weakness" that "the Republican

Party knows how to exploit"—Kerrey angrily added that Clinton is "going to get opened up like a soft peanut." Months later, the post-election *Newsweek* book flatly reported that the "devastating sound bite" was "from the pen of Bob Shrum." That was certainly what Clinton believed, as I would soon learn.

Kerrey not only lost Georgia to Clinton but finished behind Jerry Brown and lost all seven contests that day. It was time to call it quits. There was no money left and nowhere to go. I met Devine in the corridor outside Kerrey's Senate office. Kerrey was pecking out his own withdrawal statement—all he said to me was that it was all his, he wrote it, and it was damn good. It was. It was a call for fundamental change—"not timid change, not change at the margins"— that should have marked the beginning rather than the end of his campaign. He compared his run to the Jamaican bobsled team, which had gamely been routed in the Winter Olympics.

There was hubris in what Doak and I tried to do with Kerrey— coming in late with no chance to build a real relationship with him, manufacturing a message that didn't reflect the candidate's genuine convictions, and never figuring out how to navigate his often self-destructive spontaneity, if that was possible. Although I would come to know Bob Kerrey after 1992, enjoy his company, and respect his restless intellect, I've never been sure what kind of president he would have been. He not only thinks out loud; he would have governed extemporaneously. He has a philosopher's skepticism about ideas, even his own, and a tendency to whir from position to position—at times, I thought, merely because an opposite idea momentarily strikes his fancy. Thus the champion of national health reform, who pushed Clinton to embrace it by his presence in the race, would tell me that the Clinton plan was flawed because it was "big government"; then, when it failed, he criticized Clinton for abandoning it: "I'm not elected to give up. I'm not elected to read the polls and say the public wants us to give up." Once the Clinton plan was defeated, Kerrey would speak up for federally financed universal national health coverage based solely on ability to pay—the biggest government solution of them all.

All the political leaders I've encountered have been shaped by a formative lesson that, consciously or not, seems to inform their choices at critical junctures. I'm convinced that for Kerrey, the most important lesson was, Don't follow the plan, because when he did, in a nighttime action in Vietnam where the intelligence and the maps were wrong, he nearly lost his life. He saved himself and his men and won the Medal of Honor by improvising; I doubt that he's ever again fully trusted authority or trusted a plan. But he's just one example, a vivid one, of the different touchstones that make politicians who they are. For Bill Clinton, the guiding lesson, brilliantly displayed in that 1992 campaign, throughout his life, and in his presidency, is that he can talk his way out of anything. A former Senate colleague of Al Gore's described Gore's life maxim this way—that his father, also a senator from Tennessee, taught him that the way to become president was to be the smartest person in the room, which led him at times to puffery and condescension, and his over-aggressive attitude toward George W. Bush in their first debate. And perhaps the root of this Bush's stubborn refusal to admit mistakes or change course is seeing his father's presidency shattered after he reneged on "Read my lips: no new taxes." When the going gets tough, leaders fall back on what's most basic in themselves.

After the New York primary, when Clinton had the nomination securely in hand, I saw George Stephanopoulos and Paul Begala in Washington. They told me that I had a big Clinton problem—not just with him, but with Hillary, and not just because of Kerrey's burst of overheated rhetoric in Georgia. Instead they mentioned "some dinner" with McGovern. I remembered it. They told me that someone sitting nearby had overheard us and reported to Hillary that I was trafficking in tales about her husband's sex life. I described what I'd actually said and George and Paul suggested that I write the Clintons a note that was both explanation and apology. I couldn't bring myself to do it—in part because I didn't think I had done anything wrong and I wasn't sure it would work anyway. The Kerrey campaign had left me bruised, and now I had to deal with this?

I should have tried, because the enmity, I discovered, was very real. When Carville suggested that I be brought on board after Kerrey's withdrawal, Hillary had responded with an angry no and then stopped talking to him for several days. "James was sent to Siberia," Begala told me afterward. And when Clinton selected Al Gore as his running mate, Pamela Harriman called to say she'd just talked with him and he wanted to know if I'd draft the acceptance speech. Absolutely, I said, with a sense of relief. She phoned back a few hours later: Absolutely not, the Clintons had responded when Gore mentioned the idea. Pamela was surprised at the vehemence of the response: What had I done?—the Kerrey campaign was months past.

Meanwhile, Carville called Mike Donilon and then me: Could Donilon join the new media team the Clinton campaign was putting together? We'd get a fee, even if it wasn't much. I could advise Mike on spots and strategy—from a safe distance nearly 1,000 miles away from Little Rock. The other two members of the team were Carter Eskew, Squier's partner, and Mandy Grunwald, who had worked for another pioneer of political media consulting, David Sawyer. Carville now had enough control of the campaign to chart the course he wanted, within limits. And what he wanted was to downgrade the media adviser Clinton had started the campaign with, Frank Greer. With a drawn-out drawl, Carville referred to him as "Frank the Truth" for Greer's habit of inserting "the truth is" into every response spot. James was consigning Greer's firm largely to the role of buying the spots.

Carville's invitation to Mike Donilon provoked a tense discussion with Doak. He said all of us had to be hired or none of us could participate. But the Clintons didn't want me; and while I didn't say it bluntly, Carville didn't want Doak. I argued that Clinton was probably going to win anyway, that we shouldn't stand in Donilon's way, and that we couldn't: he could just pick up and leave if he had to. To me, the pragmatic case was clear—better to have a tangential part in a possible Clinton victory and a partner who would be associated with it. Doak grudgingly conceded that if I felt that strongly about it, Donilon could go to Little Rock, but he had to pay attention to our other clients, too. This proved to be hard, unless Donilon was working with me, because Doak barely spoke to him for the rest of the campaign. There was a distinct chill when they passed in the hallway.

I soon suspected that our firm would lose Mike Donilon if Clinton won. Marylouise and I had told Mandy Grunwald about a house for sale two doors down the street from ours in Georgetown. She bought it. One night, as we stepped onto our front porch to go to dinner, we saw Mike and Mandy getting out of a car in front of her house. We said hello and I wouldn't have thought much about it; they were probably just working on some scripts, but Mike acted awkward and embarrassed. I tried to make things gentler between him and Doak, but to no avail. The day Mike received his bonus check in December, he cashed it, resigned, and formed a new firm with Eskew and Grunwald.

One other—and unlikely—person talked to me about joining the Clinton campaign. The young Republican pollster Frank Luntz had kicked over the traces by aiding conservative pundit Pat Buchanan's attempted primary coup against President Bush and then by signing on briefly with the independent candidacy of Texas billionaire Ross Perot. In the summer, I traveled with Luntz for two days to Slovenia, a newly independent breakaway from the former Yugoslavia, to talk with a group of reformers about upcoming elections there. Luntz asked if I could put him together with the Clinton people; he said he had more in common with Clinton than I might think—and I was certain that for his own business reasons, the thing he feared most was a Bush back in the White House. I thought Luntz's offer was a bad idea. I mentioned it to Donilon, who agreed. The Buchanan tie alone was enough to disqualify Luntz. In 1994, after he designed and polled the "Contract With America" for Newt Gingrich, and field-tested the language for the GOP campaign that captured both houses of Congress, it occurred to me that it might have been a benefit to extricate Frank from Republican politics. Working for Clinton would have been a Rubicon he couldn't have recrossed; but at the time, it was a nonstarter.

* * *

As Donilon and I discussed Greenberg's polling data, we decided that the Bush strategists had made a fatal error. They had two lines of attack against Clinton: on his character and on his time as governor of Arkansas. That time had its good points and its bad points, but there were enough of the bad to fuel good negative spots. Instead the Bush managers chose to launch on Clinton's character, which proved to be persuasive only with the woefully insufficient base Bush already had. With the wider electorate, the advertising eroded the credibility of future attacks on Clinton's record. When the spots criticizing his performance as governor hit the airwaves, they met a wall of skepticism. At the same time, Bush failed to offer a convincing rationale for a second term, any sense that he had a plan for the future. His message, to a country seeking hope, was an appeal to fear: The voters might be unhappy about him, but Clinton was worse.

Meanwhile, Carville was obsessed with keeping the Clinton campaign on message. That was easier with the ads than the candidate. A pledge to "end welfare as we know it" reassured voters in the middle. The point of the lance was economic: Clinton had an economic plan, a health care plan; Bush didn't and you couldn't trust what he said anyway. But it was hard to channel a candidate who was a policy prodigy. Clinton's broad reading and interests sometimes led him to break out of the message box of his own campaign. I was on the phone with Carville one day when he said he had to hang up; the road was calling in. He was agitated when we talked a little while later. Somewhere in the Midwest, he said, Clinton had suddenly launched into a soliloquy on nuclear nonproliferation. There wasn't one goddamn vote in it, Carville shouted at me—a warning he had already delivered, a little more respectfully, to his contrite candidate. When James put up his famous sign in the war room—"It's the economy, stupid"—it was not just an admonition to the strategists and to the staff, but to one very smart former Rhodes Scholar named Bill Clinton. He'd never won one of those fancy scholarships, Carville told me on vacation after the campaign, but it didn't take a genius to know what this election was about.

With just two weeks to go, I was talking with a Carville who was anxious, agitated, nervous about every straw in the wind. Doak and I were the strategists for John Glenn's Senate reelection campaign in Ohio. What did the polls there show? Carville demanded of me, and he didn't mean about Glenn. Clinton was ahead; it was close, I admitted. But I was certain that nationally the fundamental contours of the race favored Clinton. Perot had a ceiling; so did Bush—and Clinton could win with a popular vote in the low to mid-40s. I was trying to reassure Carville, but his job was to worry, and he took to it with a vengeance. I even joked with Donilon about when James would stop changing his underwear.

Marylouise and I were planning to take refuge in Italy the night before the election; there was nothing to do on Election Day but fret and worry. (I'd find out that wasn't necessarily so as the 2000 presidential returns came in.) Carville called to say he was joining us on the trip with Mary Matalin, the Bush adviser who felt as fiercely about her candidate as she did about James. When they were first dating, he'd brought Mary to a dinner party at our home. Marylouise and I stayed up all night in Venice watching the returns in our room at the Cipriani, the best place in the world to celebrate a victory or cushion a defeat. The victories rolled in that night—for our House and Senate candidates and for Democrats generally. Over a very early morning breakfast from room service, we watched the president-elect and Hillary, Al Gore and Tipper, and their families walk out onto the floodlit platform in front of the governor's mansion in Little Rock. We finally went to sleep. When the phone woke us, it was a jubilant James Carville: He and Mary were stopping in Paris and then boarding the Orient Express to Venice.

When they arrived, Natale Rusconi, the manager of the Cipriani, soft-spoken, elegant, and the consummate hotelier of his generation, was with us to greet them and offer them an upgrade—to a luxurious suite like the one the Reagans had stayed in during the G-7 Summit five years before. James was already a household face, even overseas. On the launch from the Cipriani to St. Mark's Square, fellow passengers asked to take a photo with him. People pointed at him in the narrow labyrinth of lanes that crisscross that city of canals, often stopping him to say how happy they were that Clinton had won. Mary hung back, and Marylouise would talk with her; a few times, she cried, and then James would hold her hand as we strolled toward a museum, a church, or a trattoria. Over a pre-dinner drink in the living room of their suite, James observed that this was a long way from where he'd started in the bayous of Louisiana. It was a happy time for him, a bittersweet one for her, but somehow they shared it. They could get through anything if they'd made it through 1992 on opposite sides; in fact, it turned out to be practice for their permanent roles as indelible personalities united in unrelenting public combat.

The last night they were there with us, James allowed he wasn't going to work at the White House; he was too smart for that. He could stay close to Clinton anyway. He was way up the mountain, maybe at the summit; he didn't believe that could last forever—maybe for a few years. Maybe he'd fall off or be pushed off the mountain, but he was sure as hell going to make the most of it and enjoy the ride all the way. Mary interjected: "But next time we're going to beat you, James."

Clinton's 43 percent was the lowest popular vote for a winning candidate since Woodrow Wilson eighty years earlier. But it did feel like a triumph to starved Democrats. Ironically, post 9/11, it's hard to imagine a governor of Arkansas with no foreign policy experi-ence—or for that matter, the George W. Bush of 2000—being elected president. But 1992 and the two presidential elections that followed it occurred in another world, during an interregnum be-tween the end of the Communist empire and the new terrorist threat.

The Clinton win created both a legacy and a mythology. He did present himself as "a different kind of Democrat," a phrase from a spot Mike Donilon worked on that highlighted his support for both welfare reform and the death penalty. And once he had the nomina-tion securely in hand, Clinton had had his "Sister Souljah" mo-ment—an in-your-face appearance in front of Jesse Jackson's Rainbow Coalition, where he rebuked an African-American hip-hop performer for apparently inviting blacks to stop killing each other and go after whites instead. But there were two strands to the

Clinton message: a defensive one that took the edge off stereotypes about Democrats, and a central argument that was rooted in Democratic values of economic and social justice. As the campaign's slogan phrased it, it was time to "put people first." One draft of Clinton's acceptance speech reflected the Democratic Leadership Council's centrist approach, emphasized his less liberal credentials, and offered the sounds of reassurance, with its call to a "New Covenant." Another, largely the product of Paul Begala, emphasized Democratic themes like tax fairness and health care. Clinton didn't choose; he had them stitched together. The long section on the "New Covenant" almost felt like a separate speech.

What became lost in memory—and this affects the debate Democrats are still having about themselves—was that fundamentally Clinton didn't run or win in 1992 by sounding less Democratic. He called for national health reform. He explicitly proposed increasing taxes on the wealthy. He appealed to the "forgotten middle class" and scorned a government "hijacked by privileged private interests." But the Clinton lesson was rewritten in retrospect to erase the core of a 1992 message that was populist in both effect and vocabulary. The retroactive mythology would emphasize the "triangulation" of his 1996 campaign—the tactical expedient of stealing the other side's clothes while disguising or discarding your own true colors. So, by 2000, when Al Gore spoke of "the people, not the powerful," Clinton partisans and Clinton himself would complain that it was class warfare and bad politics. This difference will be fought out again in the presidential campaign of 2008, although it's worth noting that on the eve of the 2006 midterms, Carville and Clinton's onetime pollster Stan Greenberg advised Democrats that other than the Iraq war, their most effective criticism of Bush and the Republicans was that they were "working for big corporations and the privileged, not the people or the country."

The weekend before the Clinton inauguration, Marylouise and I decided to give a party for a few Washington friends and out-of-towners who were arriving to celebrate the Democrats' return to power. We might as well celebrate, too, even if the Clinton I'd first met in college wasn't so well disposed toward me now. The event ballooned from an expected 20 guests to 125—Clintonistas who had nowhere else to go that night as the Clintons and Gores prepared to finish their procession to Washington with a bus ride from Jefferson's Monticello. More and more potential guests heard about the event from others and called to announce that they were coming. Marylouise and her sister Jane stood in the kitchen cooking endless amounts of pasta, surrounded by a throng of happy Democrats. Everyone there assumed I shared their joy. In fact, I was ambivalent. I certainly preferred Clinton to Bush. Clinton was perhaps the most talented Democratic leader in a generation and our best chance to achieve big changes like national health reform. But for the second time in my career, I now faced the prospect of being on the outs with a Democrat in the White House. I'd just have to make the best of it.

One thing I was doing, along with my wife and Tad Devine, who'd joined Doak and Shrum after Mike Donilon left, was advising the gay community in an effort we'd named the Campaign for Military Service. Short of money near the end of the primaries, Clinton had appeared at a massive gay fund-raising event in Los Angeles where he'd been introduced by David Mixner, his friend since the antiwar movement and his most prominent gay supporter. Mixner would have preferred that Clinton endorse the proposal already before Congress to protect gays and lesbians from job discrimination; but Clinton shied away from that, in part Mixner believed, because if he fell short in 1992 and returned to Arkansas to prepare for a second presidential try in 1996, he didn't want to be forced to deal with the issue at the state level. Instead, he promised to end the ban on gays and lesbians serving in the armed forces, which was a purely federal question. But it was also something that, in theory, a president could accomplish with a direct order and a stroke of the pen.

Now Clinton was president and he had to act. He could issue an immediate executive order and almost certainly see it overturned by Congress; if he had taken that course he would have suffered an early defeat, but at least gays in the military wouldn't have dominated the early months of his administration. Or he could consult with the Joint Chiefs of Staff and try to negotiate a way—maybe a two- or three-year transition period—to implement the idea. Instead, he found the worst of both possible worlds. As someone still close to the Clintons told me afterward, he'd in effect communicated to the Joint Chiefs that he didn't care all that much, explaining to them that this was a campaign promise he'd had to make—but, of course, he didn't want to do anything to hurt the armed services. Once it was put that way, whatever chance there was to bring the military along—to invite its leaders to fashion a policy, however gradual, to end the ban on gay service members—was gone.

We didn't anticipate that when the first meeting of the Campaign for Military Service gathered in our living room in Georgetown. In the early days, Paul Begala was around as an unofficial representative of the administration. But he was noncommittal about how to raise money and a possible television ad strategy.

Soon, we were no longer graced with his presence or advice. When I next saw Paul, he cautioned that it was important not to back the president into a corner. Tom Stoddard, an idealist who was running the Campaign for Military Service, a teacher at NYU Law School and the architect of New York City's law banning discrimination against gays, informed me that we had just a million dollars to spend on advertising—and that was with Marylouise and others beating the fund-raising bushes full time. We created two spots and made a limited cable buy. One told the story of a soldier named Joe Zuniga, a veteran of Desert Storm and recipient of the Kuwaiti Liberation Medal, who'd been named "Soldier of the Year." It almost looked liked a recruitment ad. It carried the unsuspecting viewer along until the end when the announcer identified Zuniga as "soldier, patriot, gay American." Zuniga was discharged for admitting he was gay—a practice that continued under the "don't ask, don't tell" compromise that Clinton finally announced in July 1993.

Eleven days after the Clinton compromise, Mixner was arrested during a protest in front of the White House. This wasn't his first White House arrest. During a demonstration about AIDS in the Reagan years, the police who hauled off him and others were wearing rubber gloves, a conspicuous and superstitious precaution against the impossibility of contracting the disease from touching the protestors. They had responded by chanting: "The gloves don't match the shoes." This time, the police were on better behavior. Mixner heard that Clinton was furious at him. Five months later, Clinton, whose anger tends to fade over time, invited his old friend, with whom he'd shared an apartment for a month in 1970, to visit him in the Oval Office.

The signature proposal of the 1992 campaign—health care—was on legislative hold. There's a first rule of presidential leadership: If you want a big change, push for it at the start of your administration. Lyndon Johnson had done it with the 1964 Civil Rights Act. Ronald Reagan had done it with his 1981 tax cut; George W. Bush would follow the same path in 2001. But the choice of Hillary Clinton to lead a task force would not only result in a late, complex, and contentious legislative proposal, but sacrifice the opportunity for early if imperfect action. Early on, Republican moderates like Senator John Chafee and leaders like Bob Dole, who was wary of being seen as an obstructionist, were in a mood to compromise. I told a friend in the administration that delay was dangerous. He agreed, but he'd also been involved in the transition. This was the assignment Hillary had "asked for"; the president had no choice but to give it to her after the way she'd stood up for him during the campaign. It was her bailiwick, and no one else's; she was setting up shop in the West Wing. By the time the health care legislation was finally ready, months after the White House's self-imposed deadline, the Republicans would be emboldened to oppose it by their near defeat of Clinton's economic plan, which would be approved in both the House and the Senate by a 1-vote margin, without a single vote from the other side.

Clinton was in the early stages of that battle when I passed a television in Chicago's O'Hare Airport and stopped in my tracks to watch the Branch Davidian compound burning in Waco, Texas. The FBI assault on the headquarters of a cult had killed almost everyone inside, including children it was supposed to save. I boarded my plane for the short flight back to Washington where Marylouise and I were scheduled to attend a birthday dinner for Larry Lawrence. She had known him for years as the proprietor of the landmark

Hotel del Coronado in San Diego. He was a big-time Democratic fund-raiser who was in Washington to collect his reward. He'd soon become Clinton's ambassador to Switzerland after he barely scraped through his confirmation hearings. When my cab from the airport pulled up to the restaurant, I knew who one of the "friends" at the party was. On the street was a phalanx of Secret Service and I had to identify myself as I went in and headed for the room where I expected to see dozens of people at a full-blown celebration. But when I walked in, there were just nine or ten, sitting around a table, where the chair next to the president was empty. Larry's wife Sheila asked me to sit there.

I hadn't had a conversation with Bill Clinton for years. I doubted he wanted to see me—and I was surprised to see him just hours after Waco. Clinton acted as if nothing special had happened that day. I guessed that maybe he was in a state of denial. The next day he would have to defend himself from the charge that he was blaming Waco on Attorney General Janet Reno. Waco must have been on his mind; it was the subject on everyone else's that never came up. Clinton was casual and jocular. He bantered with me about the time we both worked for McGovern. He asked what I thought about the prospects for his economic proposal. He had to win; his whole presidency depended on that—and on health care. As he left to go back to the White House and the aftermath of the crisis, I could only say to myself that at the worst of times, presidents need a break. After the bloodiest Civil War battles, Lincoln had gone to the theater. But I couldn't stop thinking about those children at Waco; I suspect neither could Clinton, though he had to try for a little while. I also had a selfish reaction. Perhaps this Democratic president, whom I'd met nearly three decades before, had put aside my past "offenses." At some point, I might get the chance to work with him.

By 1994, there would be times that I was asked to provide some advice and contribute some words—starting with a request to help on the State of the Union message and followed later by an unexpected invitation to sit down with Hillary Clinton as the assault on her ethics, and the president's, was escalating. The charges about an Arkansas land deal known as Whitewater were front and center in the mainstream press; Hillary's law firm had handled legal work for the deal, in which the Clintons had invested when he was governor. One afternoon, I was expounding on how she should handle Whitewater to a table of Clinton-connected guests at a brunch at Jim Johnson's house. Vernon Jordan and his wife Ann were there. In the 1970s he had been one of the nation's most prominent civil rights leaders as head of the Urban League; he was now one of the president's most trusted friends—a golfing buddy and a heavyweight lawyer who had told me that no way, ever, was he going to let Clinton persuade him to take a post in the administration. He didn't need one to be listened to; nor did Ann, a former professor at the University of Chicago who sits on numerous corporate boards. As I was holding forth, she left the table, returned a few minutes later, and then took me aside and said Hillary would like to have lunch with me.

The Hillary Clinton I met with was anything but cold and remote. She reminisced about Marylouise and Bill and their years together at Yale. But she was also depressed and defiant about the accusations over Whitewater. I never understood the fine points of this so-called scandal and neither did most Americans; the Clintons lost money, the allegations never came to anything legally, but the protracted investigation would lead, in a roundabout way, to Monica Lewinsky and impeachment. I said that whatever papers Hillary had, she ought to release them as soon as possible; if she didn't, the stories would feed on themselves and her refusal to disclose, pounding away at the notion that she had something to hide. She replied that the documents were being searched out—but observed, correctly, that making them public wouldn't satisfy the critics. I was struck by her bitterness toward the press; and although I was determined to get along, I dissented when she said that the media had tried to destroy Bill during the '92 campaign. I said that looking at it from the other side of the primary contest, I thought the press had treated the personal stuff responsibly, dismissed or backpaged it, and enabled Clinton to put the charges behind him. Most reporters I knew liked and respected the president—and her.

She listened, but probably thought I just didn't see, or didn't want to see what was happening. I believe now that in one sense, her reaction was right, but misdirected. The media were investigating and reporting, of course, sometimes on their own initiative, but constantly spurred on by right-wing Republicans who regarded Clinton as an illegitimate president; from the moment he first emerged, they couldn't stomach the idea that someone who'd protested the Vietnam War and in their view evaded the draft could ever sit in the White House. (On the second count, they changed their mind when it came to George W. Bush.) Then, when Clinton actually won in 1992, conservatives were ready to go after him in what became a nonstop, eight-year campaign to destroy his presidency. Everything was fair game in a witch hunt on a tireless search for an offense. The search almost succeeded, unfortunately with an assist from Clinton's own foolish transgression with Monica Lewinsky. But she was still at college, not yet a White House intern, when the tremor that would ultimately lead to Clinton's impeachment first rippled across the National Conservative Political Action Committee's conference in February 1994.

As Larry Horowitz would have put it, it was "beyond belief," but I was scheduled to speak at the conference's "Presidential Banquet"—a roast honoring the conservative columnist Bob Novak. There are people who don't understand our friendship since we agree on virtually nothing; but you can't pick all your friends on the basis of politics. Bob and I even talked occasionally about religion. A few years later, Marylouise and I would sit in a pew as he was baptized into the Catholic Church and received his first communion; in that church we were, as Pat Moynihan put it, the "liberal remnant." The rest of the congregation was packed with the right-wing establishment, from the *National Review*'s Kate O'Beirne to Pat Buchanan. On the way out of church, I was walking down the aisle next to Novak when I turned to him and said: "Now at least you have to care about the poor." Without missing a beat, he shot back: "No, I don't; Buchanan doesn't."

I had a lot of fun at the roast. I announced that like my fellow speaker on the program Gordon Liddy, the Watergate burglar, we both had "*broken into* national politics in 1972." I observed that

Novak, a CNN commentator, and Jane Fonda "have one thing in common—they're both supported by Ted Turner." In Washington, I concluded, "Presidents come and go, but Novak remains."

There was an undercurrent of excitement in the conservative tribe that night that they had the scandal that just might bring Clinton down. For the real highlight of that conclave wasn't the Novak roast, but a press conference featuring Paula Jones, a former Arkansas state employee who accused Clinton of pressuring her to have "a type of sex" with him when she was summoned to the governor's hotel room at a Little Rock conference in August 1991. The true believers were excited. But when I mentioned the allegation to Novak, he sounded skeptical; it was embarrassing, but how would anything ever be proven?

The mainstream press all but ignored the allegations until Jones filed suit on the last day before the statute of limitations expired. Clinton hired Bob Bennett to represent him. Bennett was another friend of mine of over thirty years who'd been a debater at Georgetown before me. He would perform a singular service for Clinton by carrying an all but hopeless appeal to the Supreme Court arguing that presidents were immune from civil suits like Jones's. The appeal would delay the proceedings—and the depositions that surfaced the affair with Monica Lewinsky—until after the president's 1996 reelection.

A year after that, as the Whitewater investigation morphed into a sex scandal, it occurred to me that this never would have happened if the Clinton administration hadn't pushed for a renewal of the statute that provided for independent counsels, appointed by a special panel of three federal judges, to investigate alleged wrongdoing by high officials of the executive branch. The statute had expired in 1992; as the Whitewater charges hit, Attorney General Reno, on her own authority, appointed a special counsel. At the same time, Congress was considering reviving the law. The Republicans opposed this in principle, or so they said; an independent counsel had brought down Nixon and scourged Reagan during the Iran-contra scandal. There were Democrats who privately believed it was best to let the law die permanently. House Speaker Tom Foley told me that the bill, which was prized by "reform" groups like Common Cause, could be killed by peeling off enough Democrats to vote with the Republicans—who would bear the brunt of the blame for its defeat. Clinton could say he was for it and then lose; why plant this land mine for himself? But the White House was immovable, Foley said: this was a "reform" administration and they wanted the legislation to pass. After Clinton signed it into law, the special three-judge panel led by David Sentelle, a protégé of Jesse Helms, dismissed Reno's choice to investigate Whitewater and named someone new, Kenneth Starr. Foley would be proved right; the system could spawn an out-of-control attack engine, too easily triggered and manipulated by a president's enemies. When his Whitewater investigation ran dry after three and a half years, Starr would persuade Sentelle's three-judge panel to widen his mandate to include possible perjury charges against the president related to his relationship with Lewinsky.

The 1994 State of the Union was the first speech I worked on for Clinton. Finally, I thought, when I was asked. In a premonitory stroke of triangulation, proposals included a tough crime bill to balance the centerpiece of his legislative agenda—which was, of course, health care. The plan had at last been sent to Capitol Hill in October 1993, and the crime bill that balanced it ideologically was itself a balancing act, with something for everyone—gun control and an expanded federal death penalty, along with funding for 100,000 new police. As I looked over the drafts before going to the speechwriting office in the Old Executive Office Building next to the White House, I handwrote an insert on health care that made it into the final speech with a few edits; with Clinton, there were always at least a few. The words were designed to draw a line in the legislative sand; they were dramatic and dangerous. Clinton would hold up a pen as he said that he would "take this pen" and "veto" any bill that "does not guarantee every American private health insurance that can never be taken away." I warned George Stephanopoulos that the language, while powerful, would box Clinton in. He shouldn't say it unless he meant it. I wasn't privy to the discussions or rehearsals in the White House theater where Clinton incessantly rewrote and his inner circle debated rhetorical flashpoints like this. I wasn't rehabilitated to that degree—yet. The veto threat, reinforced by Clinton flourishing his pen, was the most memorable moment of the 1994 State of the Union. Clinton afterward thanked me for helping out— I'd made a host of other suggestions and edits—but the line that created that defiant image was the one that mattered most.

I'm not sure I did him a favor. A line can sound too good not to be used: JFK's "pay any price, bear any burden . . . support any friend, oppose any foe"; the first Bush's "Read my lips: no new taxes." Rhetoric can outpace reality.

By midsummer, with the nonstop airing of the health insurance industry spots featuring "Harry" and "Louise" sitting at a kitchen table, worrying about big government dictating their health care, the Clinton plan was on life support. The Democratic ads designed to defend it were overwhelmed by the spending and the distortions on the other side. Doak and I got a call; would we meet with the president and the first lady to discuss making some new and different spots? We waited for them in the early evening in the Map Room in the White House basement while they finished watching a movie in the theater down the hall. I stepped out into the corridor for a minute and saw the president and his wife far down the hall walking arm-in-arm with her head on his shoulder. It was entirely real; they didn't realize that I was standing there. I was struck by the scene. The two of them together, in private, bore no resemblance to the caricature being concocted by right-wing polemicists. Despite what I'd heard in the past—and would hear again—about his personal transgressions, I had no doubt that there was a deep bond between them.

They saw me, broke out of their reverie, and picked up the pace. We all sat down in the Map Room. Clinton was weary. He said he knew the odds he now faced on health reform. No one understood his proposal; it had been buried under a mountain of mud. The other side had lied, lied, and lied; he didn't know whether he could win this thing and the DNC didn't have much money left to spend on ads. But he wanted, before the fight was finished, to explain the plan clearly, simply, straight to the American people. We agreed to script and then film a series of 2-minute spots, with Clinton in the Oval Office speaking into the camera. The major networks wouldn't sell us 2-minute slots, but that was an academic issue anyway. With the money that was available, we could just afford to run a series of spots on successive nights on CNN. I wasn't naive enough to believe that this would really make a difference. Even if we generated free press, most Americans would never see the ads.

When we returned to the West Wing for filming, we met downstairs with a polite but unwelcoming Stan Greenberg and an unhappy Mandy Grunwald—without her partners Carter Eskew or Mike Donilon. Stan and Mandy wanted a few edits; we accepted some of them and then trooped upstairs to film the president. When Mandy walked into the Oval Office, Clinton was warm, almost effusive; I think he felt guilty about displacing her for this project. As he looked over the scripts, he asked her and the rest of us if we had any other suggestions. Uncharacteristically, he quickly cut off the discussions, tinkered with the text himself, and tried out his changes on us. They were good; he once said to me that if he could get away with it, in a post-presidential career, he might like to be a media consultant. (Informally he often is; he just can't help himself.)

In a few takes, Clinton delivered each spot in the conversational tone that makes his speaking style so distinctively effective. He sounded as if he was taking Americans into his confidence: "Many of you still have doubts about reform and I sure can understand why. I see the same TV ads you do. Never in the history of the Republic has so much money been spent to defeat an idea." He then answered the doubts—and in spot after spot, laid out the plan in plain language.

The ad campaign sparked a small burst of press coverage, but by mid-September, the Republicans were taking no prisoners and making no deals. The Democratic leadership couldn't even bring the bill up for a vote. Instead of being defeated, health care reform simply died. Clinton said he was glad we'd made this last-minute effort to talk plainly to the country; at least he was on record—and, he laughed, he'd done it "without charts," the ubiquitous props deployed by Ross Perot during the 1992 campaign.

Being made up for an appearance on *Face the Nation*. I had no idea I was preparing for this as a debater at Loyola High School in Los Angeles and then at Georgetown.

2

During the 1972 campaign several of us made a quick side trip to Disneyland while George McGovern was delivering a speech. We surprised him on the campaign plane afterwards. With me are my fellow speechwriters Sandy Berger and John Holum, the candidate, his assistant Pat Donovan, and our assistant, Nancy Howard.

3

After McGovern conceded, Holum, Berger, and I were commiserating with him in his suite when he laughed: "There they are: the men who wrote the words that moved one state."

4

With two leaders of principle who shaped my life in politics, George McGovern and Ted Kennedy, on the night before Kennedy's 1980 convention speech.

5

More miles on the campaign plane in 1980 with Kennedy and my friend and fellow speech-writer, Carey Parker. Kennedy could make us smile even when things were tough.

6

With the historian Doris Kearns Goodwin we reviewed a speech draft on a flight to Los Angeles. That night, I met my future wife Marylouise.

7

Checking out the podium at the 1992 Democratic Convention in New York. Ted Kennedy didn't care that I was in exile from the Clinton campaign, and I helped write a score of speeches, including Senator Barbara Mikulski's nomination of Al Gore.

I had great partners as a political consultant. Tad Devine and I celebrated at a party at Lynne Wasserman's home after Al Gore's acceptance speech at the 2000 Democratic Convention in Los Angeles.

8

9

My partner, David Doak, and I visited the Dead Sea on a trip to Israel in the 1980s. At this point, our partnership was very much alive.

A happy moment with Carter Eskew and Mike Donilon. In the shifting realm of political consulting we were once rivals, but became partners and close friends.

James Carville took up Italian cooking after one of our trips to Italy—and some helpful hints from my wife. We're in the kitchen as he prepares dinner at his and Mary Matalin's Virginia farm after the 1992 campaign.

12

Marylouise snapped this photo in St. Mark's Square in Venice when we were on vacation with Dick and Jane Gephardt. His 1988 presidential campaign left me labelled, for better or worse, a "populist."

13

On location in a wheat field in eastern Washington to film House Speaker Tom Foley's ads in 1994. I had temporarily lost a lot of weight—and Foley lost narrowly that year as a casualty of the Republican midterm landslide. I saw a poster in one store window in his district accusing him of "treason" for supporting the ban on assault weapons.

14

At our home in Washington, I saw a different side of Alan Greenspan than congressional committees did. We had a lot of fun—and an ongoing argument about the virtues of the minimum wage.

15

Marylouise and I leaving for a costume party to mark Ted Kennedy's birthday. You were supposed to go as someone from the '60s: I was Pope John XXIII and she was the Flying Nun.

I have no idea what
Marylouise has just
said to the president
in our front hallway
or why he's laughing.

16

17

Bill Clinton prepared for his State of the Union messages in the movie theater in the East Wing
of the White House. He's in the midst of an edit with Communications Director Don Baer
while pollster Mark Penn and I stand ready with the next suggestion.

18

After Ehud Barak won the Israeli election in 1999, his consultants Stan Greenberg, James Carville, and I shared what all of us thought was an extraordinary moment in history with him and the president during an official dinner at the White House. All of us thought peace was now possible.

19

After I had lunch with my father and my sister Barbara in the White House Mess, the president sent for us. It wasn't on his schedule, but after the photo, he took the time to talk to them and show them around the Oval Office. My father couldn't believe he was actually there.

20

Al Gore has just scored a knockout victory over Bill Bradley in the January 2000 *Des Moines Register* debate in Iowa. He's with his daughter Karenna, consultant Bill Knapp, Carter Eskew, adviser Laura Quinn, and speechwriter Eli Attie. I have my overcoat on because I'm about to go out to TV interviews and claim victory.

21

Donna Brazile became Gore's campaign manager when we moved the headquarters to Nashville in November 1999. She and I are having an impromptu discussion with Gore's trusted young aide Mike Feldman and campaign chair Tony Coelho, who would be gone by June 2000.

We knew the acceptance speech was a home run even before the postconvention polls came in. Right after the speech, Gore and I celebrated in a backstage room at the convention hall with his mother Pauline and my stepson Michael.

22

23

On November 27, 2000, I monitored the TelePrompTers as Gore announced from the next room at the vice presidential residence, in a nationally televised address, that he was contesting Florida secretary of state Katherine Harris's certification that Bush had carried the state. It was two weeks before the U.S. Supreme Court stopped the recount and handed the election to Bush.

24

The bus was our rolling office during the no-chance days leading up to Iowa and New Hampshire. John Kerry didn't have a lot of would-be advisers. I would just lean across the aisle and decisions would get made.

25

My fifty-fifth birthday party in 1998 offered a glimpse of the future. I chatted with John Kerry and Jim Johnson, one of Washington's best-connected wise men, who would run the Kerry vice-presidential search in 2004.

26

Kerry tossed a football to staff and reporters as I looked on after his triumph in the January New Hampshire primary. We were 30,000 feet in the air and a long way from the political depths of the previous November and December, when Kerry was being written off and I was being blamed.

27

Mary Beth Cahill came in as campaign manager when Kerry's prospects were at their darkest. The nomination was in hand when Kerry won Virginia and Tennessee on February 10, and we then made a poll-driven decision to start muting the populist rhetoric of recent months.

A happy moment in the snow during Kerry's sweep of Iowa and New Hampshire. I wish I'd looked and felt that way in November. Ohio, Ohio . . .

As the mid-term election approached, the antigovernment mood that Perot had capitalized on was reinforced by an economic recovery that was still not seen that way, a failure on health care, and an economic plan that Republicans had successfully depicted as little more than a tax increase. I didn't anticipate that the Democrats could lose both houses of Congress for the first time in more than forty years—it couldn't be that bad. But at a Democratic Senate retreat a year earlier, I'd worried out loud that if health care was lost and the other side successfully positioned us as the "pro-tax party," 1994 would be an "election where we just struggle to hold on."

My firm had its own roster of challenging races, but there was no doubt that one client, Herb Kohl, would cruise through his Senate reelection in Wisconsin. He was closer to Doak and his former campaign manager Michelle Carrier, now our partner, than he was to me. And after almost ten years, our firm was coming apart, even if Doak and I didn't acknowledge it yet. We had differences of temperament and style, including his persistent tendency to ruminate over strategic choices or over even a single word in a script. For better or worse—and at one time or another, it could be either—I tended to reach a conclusion sooner and was impatient with sessions spent massaging a clause or phrase. I was an increasingly public presence, quoted in the press and on talk shows like CNN's *Crossfire*. Doak avoided most of this, and he and Carrier took me to dinner one night to say I should, too. It was bad for business—a criticism that made no sense to me or Tad Devine, who had joined the firm when Mike Donilon left.

The fissure between Doak and me was widened when we were hired by Paul Sarbanes, a low-key former Rhodes Scholar, the senior senator from Maryland, but decidedly junior in personality and visibility to his irrepressible colleague Barbara Mikulski. Sensing an opening in a difficult year for Democrats generally, the Republicans had recruited their former national chairman, Bill Brock, to run a well-financed campaign against Sarbanes. A former senator from Tennessee, he was now a Washington lobbyist and resident of Maryland. In Baltimore, we met with Sarbanes's team of advisers. Our firm was Sarbanes's choice on one condition: I had to be the one closely involved in the race, not Doak. David was angry—more it seemed at me than at Sarbanes. I believe it was just a case of comfort level: Sarbanes was familiar with my work for Ted Kennedy and both of us had gone to Harvard Law School. He saw me, rightly or wrongly, his chief of staff explained, as a political operative who actually knew and cared about the substance of issues. I said to Doak that if the tables were reversed—as they already were with Herb Kohl, who looked to him and Michelle Carrier—that would be fine with me.

The Brock campaign sought to portray Sarbanes as the senator who wasn't there. We wanted to characterize him as a quiet hard worker who didn't brag on himself. Unfortunately, it was true. He almost rejected the first set of scripts—which asserted, for example, that he'd successfully fought to increase the minimum wage—because, he said, "Those weren't really my bills, they were Teddy's." All he'd done was co-sponsor or vote for them. Kennedy, who was in his own tough reelection, said he was happy to share credit with his colleague. Each day, Sarbanes drove himself forty miles from his Baltimore neighborhood to Capitol Hill and back. In an effort to show him working hard, not just say it, we filmed him pulling up to his home, parking his car, and walking to the front door. After the first take, I said it was pretty good and offered a couple of suggestions for the next one. He looked at me and said—and he sounded serious—that he couldn't do it again; it wouldn't be real; he only came home once a day. I was dumbfounded. His wife Christine intervened: Paul, just go back and do it as often as they need you to—and he did, with a shrug and an expression on his face that said he couldn't believe what you had to do in politics.

I'd been warned there was something else he wouldn't do, but when the time came, he was ready to go negative on his opponent. Brock said he was disgusted with Sarbanes and his handlers, but his complaint was hardly a matter of principle. His own attack ads barely dented Sarbanes, and Brock lost by almost 20 points.

We were also consulting for one of the most vulnerable Republican targets, Virginia senator Chuck Robb, the son-in-law of Lyndon Johnson and the state's former governor who'd served in Vietnam and then entered politics after law school. Tales of sexual misconduct and drug use had simmered and just barely surfaced during his 1988 Senate campaign. At the time, Robb had inartfully explained: "The only person I have loved, emotionally or physically, is my bride, though, like any other red-blooded American, I have some fun from time to time, but I don't think that's either disqualifying or inappropriate." But the stories then were few and far between, and Robb won with 71 percent of the vote.

The explosion came in 1991, when Robb preempted an NBC report by admitting that he'd spent time alone with a former Miss Virginia, Tai Collins, in a hotel room, but the only thing that had happened was a massage. (Focus groups found this incredible, even laughable; men reacted by suggesting that there must be something wrong with the guy if that's all he did with a beauty queen. But he earnestly held to that explanation and if you knew him, it was possible to believe it.) Robb did have one piece of good fortune. His opponent was Oliver North, the linchpin of the Iran-contra scandal, a right-wing hero who was so far right and so tainted by scandal that the state's Republican senator, John Warner, refused to endorse him. We could win this on issues; we told Robb the last thing he should talk about in this campaign was personal scandal.

Unfortunately Robb had an irrepressible impulse to exculpate himself. By mid-December 1993, he'd written reams of explanation and counterattack and dispatched the material to our office. Tad Devine, then working closely with Doak on the Robb campaign, and I agreed on a method to deal with all this: stall, rewrite, cut, and play for time. Doak was home on his family's farm in Missouri over the holidays. I was sitting in my living room in Georgetown when Robb called from the LBJ ranch on Christmas Day. He was flying back to Washington. Could I meet him in the office to review what he'd written? When we got together, he handed me a jeremiad that would have hurt him more than his targets.

Larry Sabato, the University of Virginia professor and frequent TV commentator, whom Robb had previously derided as "Dr. Dial a Quote," had "suspicious motives" and was "creating a feeding frenzy"; to stick the knife in, that played on the title of Sabato's most recent book. *The Washington Post* was running stories that were the kind "expected of tabloids, but not of a leading national publication . . . lurid insinuation . . . dated regurgitation." We needed the *Post*'s endorsement; this was perfectly if inadvertently designed to prevent it. NBC News and Tom Brokaw had engaged in "a hatchet job"; the producer's "demeaning interrogation . . . began in the gutter and proceeded downhill from there." How would Brokaw react to this? Robb had contacted "libel lawyers" to sue "NBC News and various publications" for reports that "were categorically false."

I did my best to quibble and delay. Doak and Devine weighed in—and the process dragged on for weeks. In the end, Robb insisted on putting out a letter, but it was stripped of inflammatory passages, whittled down to a denial of drug use, an apology to his wife and family, and a denial of any "criminal wrongdoing" in another head-line scandal, the taping of former Virginia governor Doug Wilder's phone conversations.

As tensions mounted between us, Doak made it clear to me that Robb was his client, though the candidate would check in with me by phone. Doak, as I told him, had exactly the right strategy—dis-member Oliver North. Robb scraped by with a 50,000-vote margin out of 2 million cast. I saw him occasionally in the years ahead, after Doak and I split up, and I admired Robb's unwillingness to bend with the political wind. This was a man, on the eve of the political fight of his life, who had spoken out across Virginia in favor of gays in the military because he'd served with them in Vietnam and be-lieved it was wrong to discriminate.

Devine and I had plenty of other work to do—for two of the most prominent Democrats in the country, who suddenly found them-selves in trouble: Senator Ted Kennedy and House Speaker Tom Foley.

For me, Kennedy's 1994 Senate race began in a hotel room in London in 1991. I was there on one of my periodic stints consulting for the Labour Party. The phone woke Marylouise and me. Kennedy's nephew, Willie Smith, had been arrested on a rape charge during an

Easter weekend trip to the family's Palm Beach home with the senator and his son Patrick. Ultimately Willie would be acquitted, but in the weeks and months until then, Kennedy himself was engulfed in a tide of sensationalist press that recycled past charges and rumors about his own private life. In Massachusetts, our polls, which had registered a nearly 70 percent rating for Kennedy before Palm Beach, plummeted into the low 40s. With his nephew's trial about to begin, we had to stem the tide. Kennedy couldn't talk outside the courtroom about his own memories of that night in Palm Beach, but he had to say something that acknowledged the voters' concerns and conveyed a sense, as the *New York Times* put it, that he would "mend his ways."

Just a week before the trial, he spoke at the Kennedy School of Government at Harvard. The speech focused on public policy, but one brief section was personal. I talked with him, drafted language, and we refined it. It was simple and straightforward:

> *I am painfully aware that the criticism directed at me in recent months involves far more than honest disagreements with my positions, or the usual criticism from the far right. It also involves the disappointment of friends and many others who rely on me to fight the good fight. To them, I say: I recognize my own shortcomings—the faults in the conduct of my private life. I realize that I alone am responsible for them and I am the one who must confront them. I believe that each of us as individuals must struggle not only to make a better world, but to make ourselves better too.*

It didn't satisfy all the critics; and it was a hard passage for someone who doesn't easily talk about himself. But the polls stabilized and inched up, and the issue faded as the country turned to the 1992 presidential primaries.

In July of that year, Kennedy married Vicki Reggie. He'd found what he'd told me I had and he hoped for when he had advised me to marry Marylouise—someone you really love. Vicki was a lawyer, funny and strong-willed, the thirty-eight-year-old daughter of a prominent Louisiana political family; her father had supported civil rights and JFK at a time when that took courage in the Deep South.

She was politically astute and she'd become a real force in the 1994 campaign in which Ted Kennedy would face his toughest opponent for the Senate in thirty years. Mitt Romney was a wealthy venture capitalist, a self-described moderate Republican. The Romney of 1994 proclaimed himself unequivocally pro-choice. He was untried as a politician, but young and telegenic.

When Romney announced in February 1994, the message was distinctly nonideological: Kennedy was out of date. But he included one conservative zinger: the way to end "the welfare crisis" was to stop "paying children to have children" by denying additional help to welfare mothers when they had another child. On a conference call with Kennedy, we urged him to go along with the idea—or at least not oppose it—for the duration of the campaign; the poll numbers were clear. I laid out the case. Kennedy exploded. He couldn't believe he was hearing this from me. He was rich—and he wasn't prepared to keep his Senate seat by taking food out of the mouths of poor children. If that was the price, well, they needed the help a lot more than he needed the Senate.

It had been a long time since Kennedy had run serious political ads in Massachusetts. The *Boston Globe* might cover him; in Washington, he might be seen as one of the great senators, but at home the undecided and "soft" voters who might decide the election knew surprisingly little about him other than the personal stories—which, they now said in a focus group, they didn't mind as long as Kennedy was doing a good job for them. But when the moderator asked about health care, Kennedy's trademark issue for almost a quarter of a century, the participants hemmed and hawed and said they weren't sure where he stood. Finally, one of them remembered a photo of Hillary Clinton on his sailboat, taken while the Clintons were vacationing on Martha's Vineyard in the summer of 1993: Hillary probably wouldn't have gotten on the boat if Kennedy wasn't for health care.

We were on television in the summer months before the election, with a $600,000 media buy; the Republicans said it was a sign Kennedy must be in trouble. But by late July, the public polling had him 16 to 20 points ahead—and so did our own data. Michael Kennedy, the senator's nephew and campaign manager, called me and said it was time to go off the air; we'd advertise again in September. I argued back—and then appealed to Kennedy—that it was risky to leave the airwaves to Romney. Kennedy was unusually curt; the decision was made. After the election, he explained why he'd discounted my concerns: Yes, I was his friend, but I was also the media guy, and I made a commission on the ad buys.

Romney commanded the airwaves for the next six weeks—not just with positive spots, but with an unrelenting attack on Kennedy as out-of-step and out-of-date. Just ten days before a token Republican primary, where Romney would romp, we had no idea where we stood because the campaign had made a decision to put polling as well as media on hold. Our pollster Tom Kiley finally went into the field. His voice was sepulchral when he found me in Washington; we had to get together with the candidate right away. Kiley was blunt: Kennedy was 1 point behind; his favorable and unfavorable ratings were almost identical. Romney was well liked and well ahead on a whole series of issues and attributes. The electorate, as I summed it up, was ready to give Kennedy a gold watch and retire him. I offered one suggestion for tampering just a little with the data we were about to review with Kennedy and Vicki in their Back Bay apartment: Re-weight the sample to make it slightly more Democratic and show him 1 point ahead. It didn't really matter, but maybe psychologically it would be easier for him to take.

After we assembled in their living room, Kennedy and Vicki were uninterested in regrets or recrimination. When I amplified Kiley's polling presentation by bluntly stating what he was gently implying—that this had happened because we'd been off the air— Vicki glared at me. Kiley finished and Michael Kennedy said the first thing we had to discuss was the budget implications of all this. Kennedy interrupted. That wasn't relevant; the budget was now whatever Bob said it was. Kennedy had never run a negative ad in Massachusetts, but the question now was how we were going to attack Romney, he said as he turned to me. We should start, I suggested, with a spot that could be quickly produced in an editing studio, based on the second most effective argument in Kiley's poll—that while Romney had made over $11 million in two years, "his largest company denied health insurance" to "thousands" of "its employees" while providing coverage to their "workers overseas." Vicki understandably asked why start with the second-best attack? What was the strongest one? I said it was explosive, but we had to do some on-location filming. Our opposition research team had discovered a firm called AMPAD that Romney's venture capital firm had acquired in Indiana, laying off workers, cutting wages and cutting off health insurance, and then rehiring some of the employees at lower pay. We could have a narrator tell the story—or the workers at the AMPAD plant could speak for themselves.

Tad Devine flew to Indiana to interview them. He had a script I'd written in case they had trouble telling the story in 30 seconds; several of them could read it off the prompter and we'd cut back and forth between them. Tad called me from the shoot exulting that he'd thrown away the script; these folks were unbelievable. We ended up with five 30-second gems; instead of picking among them, we ignored two of the most durable canons of political advertising—put maximum firepower behind one spot, and make certain every spot you run has a minimum number of rating points, say 800 or 1,000, so that the average viewer sees it eight or ten times. We put all five of what became known as "the worker ads" on the air in rotation. It was a political mini-series that looked like no other ads I had ever made or seen before.

On camera, the workers destroyed the foundation of the Romney campaign: the claim that he'd created 10,000 jobs. A woman who'd been laid off said: "I don't like Romney talking about creating jobs. He took all ours away." Another worker said: "He cut our wages to put money in his pocket." Then: "We had no health insurance, we had no rights anymore." And from a packer who had been laid off after twenty-nine years, the kicker: "I would like to say to Mitt Romney—if you think you'd make such a good senator, come out here to Marion, Indiana, and see what your company has done to these people." Almost instantly, the spots were the talk of Massachusetts— and incidentally, Indiana. We were defining the race and redefining Romney. His campaign spokesman charged that we'd put "words in people's mouths." The *Boston Globe* checked this out and dismissed it. Thank God, the script I'd drafted had been discarded.

Now the Romney campaign also had to deal with a busload of AMPAD workers who traveled to Massachusetts from Indiana to dog his footsteps. For days, he refused to meet with them; when he did, he said only that he'd consider their comments. Romney's favorable was now just 40 percent, his unfavorable 31—and Kennedy's was 57–38, a huge swing in just two weeks. Michael Kennedy said he saw why Romney was being hurt, but why did negatives against him make voters more positive about Kennedy? Because, I answered, by taking up the AMPAD workers' cause, Kennedy was saying something about himself, too.

We hit one bump in the road during this period. In mid-September, Kennedy's nephew, Massachusetts congressman Joe Kennedy, called Romney a member of a "white boys club," and added that his Mormon Church "has a belief that blacks are second class citizens . . . women are second class citizens . . . you ought to take a look at those issues." It was an attack we didn't need to make and had forsworn all along. Joe Kennedy is decidedly his own man, one of the most straightforward people I met in politics. But he's also a realist, and he agreed to do something uncharacteristic for him— back down. He called Romney to apologize and publicly said he hoped religion would play no further role in the campaign. The tempest was about to die when a reporter baited Senator Kennedy by asking what he thought of Joe and what he'd said. The candidate, in an excess of familial loyalty—his nephew would have forgiven a little disloyalty here—answered that it was fair to question Romney about his Church's record on African-Americans. Predictably, Romney called a press conference, cited JFK's pleas for tolerance during the 1960 campaign, and tried to goad Kennedy further by saying he had betrayed his brother.

On a hastily convened conference call, I said we had to nip this in the bud or it could dominate one news cycle after another. For a while, there was some thrashing around in an attempt to find a middle ground. I argued that the only viable option was unqualified retreat. Kennedy was both frustrated and irritated: "Are you saying that I should walk off the field with my tail between my legs?" I didn't pause—or I might not have put the answer quite this way: "No, I'm saying you should put your tail between your legs and run off the field as fast as possible." There was a long silence. Then the candidate said to get a short statement ready reiterating his original position banishing Romney's religion from the campaign. He phoned back a few minutes later. Sometimes, he said, he felt like firing me. But JFK had advised him that he always had to have "two or three sons of bitches" around who weren't afraid to disagree.

With this mess behind us, our media assault continued and our poll numbers kept rising. So I felt confident when Marylouise and I went to dinner with columnist George Will and his even more conservative wife Mari, once a top official in the Reagan White House. In mid-meal, the maitre d' said he had a call and I should pick it up in the office in the back. It was Ranny Cooper, Kennedy's ex-chief of staff, who had returned as a full-time volunteer when the campaign got into trouble. Our strategy of avoiding debates with Romney had just been undone. The *Boston Globe* and the *Herald*, normally crosstown rivals, were now demanding a debate, and they had their own proposal—dates and places. We'd lose the *Globe* endorsement, Cooper said, if we didn't agree. When we did, the Romney campaign went into a premature victory dance—another proof that in politics, you have to be careful what you wish for. The press set low expectations for Kennedy, which worked to our advantage.

For five days before the debate, we carved out hours a day to practice in an office just around the corner from the Four Seasons Hotel in Boston. Kennedy knew how he wanted to prepare. I posed questions to him and to David Smith, another former staffer who had mastered Romney's arguments and even some of his mannerisms. After 15 or 20 minutes, we broke off, and then Kennedy made me answer the same questions he just had. I also knew that Romney believed he'd found a silver bullet. Under attack for his own business practices, his campaign had leaked a story about an alleged sweetheart deal that had landed the Kennedy family a prime piece of commercial property in Washington, D.C. Kennedy didn't even know about it; the parcel had been purchased through a blind trust that benefitted the third generation of the family. But as Romney harped on the issue, I decided the details weren't important; whatever else they thought of Kennedy, Massachusetts voters wouldn't credit the idea that he was corrupt. I was certain Romney would make the charge in the debate, I said to Kennedy during our practice—and there was a devastating response. He might be reluctant to make it because it unmistakably referred to his brothers' assassinations, but he decided that in this context, it was right. We practiced the line a few times: "Mr. Romney, my family did not go into public service to make money—and quite frankly we've paid a price."

Kennedy spent the afternoon before the debate sitting by himself at the JFK Library. "He's communing with ghosts," said Dave Burke, Kennedy's top aide during his early Senate years and later president of CBS News, who, like other alumni, had rallied to their old boss's side when he was in trouble. Meanwhile, we were leaving nothing to chance. Romney's ads had featured graphic footage of an overweight Kennedy struggling to rise from a park bench. We didn't want his image during the debate to remind viewers of that visual, which was designed to reinforce Romney's charge that a tired Kennedy's time had passed. But the slender, unobtrusive podiums selected for the encounter at Faneuil Hall would do just that. We found a way to swap podiums. Eddy Martin, who went back with Kennedy to the beginning of his political career, was puckish, wily, and well connected. Workmen, who obviously looked like they belonged there, went into Faneuil Hall and replaced the original podiums with alternatives so imposing and so large that all the audience or the cameras would see were the candidates' heads and upper chests—and their hands if they made a gesture. Just to be on the safe side, Eddy had the original podiums shipped to an undisclosed site on the other side of the state.

We did no last-minute cramming. Kennedy was ready for an exchange that was watched, as it turned out, by 3 million people in Massachusetts—an incredible viewership that outdrew the state-wide audience for most Super Bowls. As usual, I paced in the hallway at the back of the auditorium as the debate unfolded. Romney was defensive about his business record and assailed Kennedy for his ads attacking it: "When will this end?" In response, Kennedy cited the Romney ad accusing him and his family of profiting from the Washington land deal: Romney hadn't brought the issue up in the debate yet. So Kennedy did, paused for a moment, and then delivered—and improved—the punch we'd planned: "Mr. Romney, the Kennedys are not in public service to make money. We have paid too high a price." The ignition of applause almost blew the roof off Faneuil Hall. Romney was on the defensive; he was, Kennedy said, "not pro-choice, but multiple choice." The other great line was entirely Kennedy's, and entirely spontaneous. When it came time for the candidates to question each other, Kennedy asked Romney about the cost of his health care plan. Romney fumbled around and then said he couldn't be expected to come up with an estimate. Kennedy shot back: "But that's exactly what you have to do as a legislator."

Kennedy, who had stood on the precipice just weeks before, trounced Romney on Election Day 58 percent to 40 percent. Unlike many other Democrats in 1994, he hadn't run by running away from the party's principles. He'd campaigned for national health reform, and against "the laissez-faire notion that all government has to do is get out of the way and . . . private interests and power will see to it that prosperity trickles down to ordinary people." Kennedy didn't blame others or second-guess strategy when things got tough. And he didn't hold a grudge: Twelve years later, he would work with Mitt Romney, then governor of Massachusetts and a Republican presidential possibility, to make that state the first in the nation to provide universal health care.

Kohl, Sarbanes, Robb, and Kennedy survived the Republican tide of 1994. Few forecast how sweeping it would be, but when I was in St. Louis to shoot reelection ads for Dick Gephardt, I witnessed how apprehensive Democratic leaders were as the election approached. We were ready to film when Gephardt had to break off for a conference call with Bill Clinton and Tom Foley, the Speaker of the House who was also our client. Gephardt told me to listen in on an extension in the den. The two congressional leaders were worried about the gun control section of the pending crime bill that banned assault weapons. They calculated that this could cost the Democrats fifteen or twenty congressional seats in districts where the gun lobby was strong. Foley and Gephardt pressed Clinton to consider an alternative proposal—strip the gun provisions out of the crime bill and let the House vote on them separately. With health care dead in the water, Clinton wasn't prepared to back down on another highly visible, hot-button issue. He said he didn't think guns would hurt that much; his own polling showed big support for the assault weapons ban. Gephardt replied that the national numbers missed the local realities. Foley agreed with him. Clinton didn't. He needed the bill the way it was; anyway, there'd be a backlash from the gun control folks if it was changed. They didn't have anywhere else to go, Gephardt argued. But Clinton wouldn't budge. The crime bill, originally intended to reverse or at minimum neutralize a longtime Republican advantage on law and order, instead became a Republican weapon aimed straight at vulnerable Democrats.

One of them was Tom Foley, who for thirty years, with a combination of statesmanship and shrewdness, had held on to a district in the eastern part of Washington State that was far more conservative than he was. He and his wife Heather often spent long evenings at our home and visited us on the Jersey shore, where we'd bought a house for Marylouise's parents. I had never worked in Foley's campaigns before; it had been a long time since he faced a real challenge. Now he was in trouble in 1994. He was the face of the political establishment in a place that had given nearly a quarter of its presidential vote to the antipolitician Ross Perot. And the flip side of that liability—his clout as Speaker, his ability to deliver for the district—wasn't what it seemed. To some extent, the disgruntled voters of 1994 didn't care. Unbelievably, a significant minority of them believed that whoever represented the Fifth District would be the Speaker of the House—they thought they could get rid of Foley, but keep his clout. And in the rural expanses outside Spokane, he was weakened by his association with Clinton and his failure to block the passage of gun legislation.

Before we filmed, Heather and I drove the expanses of eastern

Washington for two days, from the Grand Coulee Dam through some of the richest wheat fields in America. We stopped for lunch in a small town. A store next to the café had a large poster in the window: WANTED FOR TREASON — THOMAS S. FOLEY; he was guilty of depriving people of their Second Amendment right to keep and bear arms. Just after the September primary, a public poll told the political world what we already knew: Foley was in danger, nearly terminal. He was 14 points behind his Republican opponent, who favored a term limit of six years for members of Congress—and promised that's all he would serve, a promise which he, of course, broke when his time was up six years later.

We fought back to a tie and even on some days in the tracking polls a slight lead as Foley campaigned nonstop and our advertising assailed his opponent for saying the federal government should "get the heck out of education"—which would jeopardize $34 million that came into the district for schools, college loans, and disabled children. Then came another piece of bad news: Bill Clinton was ready to campaign in Spokane. For the first but not the last time in my political career, I said we had to keep him out. As the *Portland Oregonian* put it, Clinton was "widely unpopular in Foley's district." So, the White House responded, Clinton would go to Seattle; would Foley be there to greet him? No, I told the Speaker and Heather, we couldn't do that either; the picture of the two of them would dominate the paper and the local news—and the Clinton visit was just two days before the election.

Foley fell short by a handful of votes and the morning after conceded quietly and with class. He was the first Speaker to lose reelection since 1860. It had been a bad year for Democrats and a great year for our consulting firm, but Foley's defeat broke my heart.

Not long before the '94 election, at the Kennedy School at Harvard, I debated Frank Luntz, the young Republican pollster who took credit for the linguistic legerdemain of the GOP's "Contract with America," the document that drove their campaign. Frank, who deserved at least some of the credit he was claiming, predicted a Republican sweep, an outcome that at the time was still generally considered improbable; the GOP, he said, had the phrases, and they'd soon have Congress. This explanation became the political equivalent of an urban legend as the notion that words mattered more than reality morphed into the other enduring legacy of 1994. For example, conservatives would now call for repeal of the "death tax," not the estate tax; they would denounce "partial birth abortion" instead of campaigning for their real aim—to outlaw most if not all abortions.

Campaigns have always been a war of words as well as ideas. The belief that Republican mastery of that game was key to their success in 1994 spurred Democrats into a search for their own sleight of tongue that goes on to this day. The architecture of a message matters; but this exercise has been carried to the point where it can become a substitute for thought and persuasion. One expert, George Lakoff, who regularly instructs Democratic senators and members of Congress at their retreats, has urged progressives to make income taxes more palatable by calling them "membership fees" and trial lawyers less controversial by labeling them "public protection attorneys." The national debt piled up by Bush, he says, should be rebranded the "baby tax." Most of this hasn't been tested rigorously; some of it is transparent and needless. Isn't "debt," as in "national debt," a negative enough phrase? But 1994 left some Democrats thinking that they didn't really have to prosecute the battle of ideas, just find the nomenclature to repackage them—as the second George Bush would when he sold an ideologically driven tax cut for the wealthy as a commonsense tax cut for families.

After a 1994 outcome that staggered his authority and threatened to make him a one-term president, Bill Clinton didn't try that kind of trick. He developed a different one. He discarded policies like national health reform instead of relabeling them. The riskier course, on which he would have had to bet his reelection, would have been to renew the battle for a simpler plan and make it a fundamental dividing line. That's a lot to ask of a president staring into his own political grave. For Clinton, it was better to give up the possibility of historic achievement than to risk giving up the Oval Office. So

Clinton's reelection would be fueled by bite-size ideas and a tactic masquerading as a strategy—triangulation—designed to disarm the other side. In fact, while the word "triangulation" was coined in the Clinton era, Richard Nixon was the original triangulator. During his first term as president, he imposed wage and price controls, signed the law establishing the Environmental Protection Agency, mandated affirmative action in federal contracts, and approved anti-hunger programs—many of them the signature domestic issues of his Democratic rivals. His design was not only to co-opt their issues before his 1972 reelection, but to give himself a freer hand in Vietnam and foreign policy.

Clinton's version of triangulation, whether it was responsible for his 1996 victory or not, assured that it would be a victory without a mandate. The shift also left me once again in exile from the Clinton White House, because along with a change in strategy, there was a changing of the guard. By early 1995, Stan Greenberg was out as Clinton's pollster, replaced by a political switch-hitter named Dick Morris, with his whispered confidence that he had a playbook to transform Clinton's game. Morris started out as a young West Side liberal in New York City, then became ideologically indifferent, polling not only for Clinton when he was governor of Arkansas but for Republicans across the country. He had picked his way back into Clinton's favor through the debris of the 1994 defeat. Morris brought along his version of triangulation, and also Doug Schoen and Mark Penn, two other New York–based pollsters who believed the party had to tack in a more conservative direction, although, unlike Morris, they never would have advised right-wing senators like Jesse Helms and Trent Lott. In the upheaval, Carville was sidelined, too, but less visibly. He maintained the public perception of a special relationship with the White House. Clinton, who liked to cover his bets, never knew when he might need James again.

I didn't hear about it until afterward, but there was some talk of bringing Doak and me in as media consultants. But early in 1995, the Doak, Shrum partnership came to an end. Without telling me, Doak had fired Chip Smith, a talented young associate whose offense appeared to be that he was too close to Tad and me. That was only a manifestation of the deeper causes of the split. I had simply ignored David's request to end my television appearances and mute my willingness to talk with reporters. Our working sessions were less frequent and more strained. I didn't feel any animosity; but after ten years, our time was up. The tensions had leaked beyond our conference room door. *New York* magazine had reported in late November that we were splitting. I refused to comment; Doak only said: "Not that I know about." Tad and I sent Doak a letter drawn up by our lawyer, dissolving the firm. There was no public acrimony—and maybe a sense of relief on both sides. After a few days in a makeshift office in the kitchen of Chip Smith's apartment, we rented space in a new and oddly designed building in upper Georgetown; the single elevator, for example, labored its way to the third floor and didn't even go to the fourth. (When Joe Lieberman showed up in our conference room during the 2000 campaign, the Secret Service was upset that there was only one way out.)

Steve Pajcic, the defeated candidate for governor of Florida whom we'd lost as a client during our earlier breakup, with Caddell, had become my friend. He now brought the first race to the new firm of Shrum & Devine. It looked like an impossible one. Nat Glover was attempting to become the first African-American sheriff in Florida since the Reconstruction era, running in a heavily white county that included Jacksonville. The retiring sheriff had said he respected Glover, but a black man just couldn't get elected. In our ads, we decided to confront the prejudice head-on without mentioning it: Glover, a graduate of the FBI National Academy with three decades of law enforcement experience, was the "best qualified" person for the job. The race was a test of whether Jacksonville could rise above race. It could, up to a point. Glover served two terms as sheriff and then was defeated for mayor. A former rival, a white Republican, who endorsed Glover in that mayoral campaign, saw his business spraypainted with the epithet N_ _ _ _ _ LOVER.

Doak, Shrum wasn't the only partnership that had broken up. Carter Eskew was leaving Mike Donilon and Mandy Grunwald to go into commercial advertising. At lunch, Donilon told Devine that he wanted to come with us but feared I was mad at him. Nothing could have been more off the mark. He'd done the right thing for himself when he left Doak, Shrum after the '92 Clinton campaign. I saw political consulting as a place where those already at the top could take some satisfaction in developing talent, but couldn't keep people down. It was a free market and they had every right to set up on their own. For example, Joe Trippi and Steve McMahon, Howard Dean's future advisers, had been associates in my firm. Later on, frustrated by the absence of African-Americans in the front ranks of consultants, I would try to recruit Donna Brazile as a partner.

For the '96 campaign, Clinton turned to Bob Squier, who was more than willing to get involved this time. Clinton might be in a political bind, but he was the incumbent and there was plenty of time and money to fix what ailed him. Squier and his partner Bill Knapp were the ad makers, but the strategy and content of the advertising were dominated by Morris, Schoen, and Penn, and the president himself, who occasionally wrote his own 30-second scripts. The strategy of triangulation was brutally simple and effective. For example, if the Republicans had a popular idea like welfare reform, steal it, even if this ultimately meant accepting a draconian version that in some cases could deny welfare benefits altogether to poor mothers. Blame the other side when they made a mistake—the colossal blunder would be House Speaker Newt Gingrich's decision to shut down the government during an impasse over the budget. But avoid any dividing line based on the Democratic theme that the president and the party were "on your side" and would "put people first." So in his 1996 State of the Union speech, Clinton even gave the opposition a taste of their own elixir: "The era of big government is over." Flummoxed Republicans had no choice but to applaud.

That line was poll-tested—and so was virtually every other proposal and phrase offered during the permanent campaign that Clinton waged in 1995 and 1996. Polling and focus groups can measure how best to sell voters ideas you believe in. But here the survey research was used to decide not how but what. The proposals that scored 70 or 80 percent became the Clinton program. Not surprising, this process had a built-in bias toward the inoffensive, the modest, and the symbolic. Thus the president pushed proposals like school uniforms, a V-chip for parents to censor the television their children were watching, character education, and right-to-know laws requiring polluters to disclose emissions. Whatever you thought of them, they weren't going to change the world. But there were also targeted tax cuts to neutralize the Republicans—along with the highest scoring of traditional Democratic proposals like raising the minimum wage. All this was amplified by the attacks on the tobacco industry, which was poisonously unpopular. The congeries was held together by a poll-tested mantra: "Community, opportunity, responsibility." Clinton could crown an otherwise unambitious program with his ambitious summons to "build a bridge to the 21st century."

It was a disciplined strategy, a strategy of personal presidential survival, which achieved that much and no more. Clinton pursued and on election eve presumed he was about to attain the goal of winning over 50 percent of the popular vote, something only two other Democrats had achieved in half a century. On Air Force One, Penn didn't bother to take the president aside to tell him the numbers had shifted. In front of other advisers and friends who were reminiscing with the president on the last flight of this campaign, Penn just matter-of-factly announced that Clinton was going to fall short of his cherished goal. He got up and went into his bedroom. On Election Day, his total was 49 percent, well ahead of Dole. But he had another Republican Congress, one that would have enough votes to impeach him. Nixon's 23-point margin over McGovern in 1972 had been called "a lonely landslide" because Republicans picked up just a handful of seats in the House and lost two seats in the Senate. Clinton's 1996 victory was just as lonely. He would enter his second term without a mandate for big ideas that might have led to the legacy he coveted. He'd rescued himself, but built no lasting foundation for a Democratic comeback.

I had been far removed from the Clinton campaign, focused on our candidates for the Senate and the House. Then unexpectedly, one of them, Joe Kennedy, asked me to meet with Dick Morris in the summer, before the Democratic Convention. We were producing ads for Joe's reelection—which was hardly in doubt. They were intended to lay the groundwork for 1998, when he planned to run for governor of Massachusetts. He said he understood I wouldn't like the idea, but Morris had called him, and so had some of Clinton's people, and I needed to hear Morris out. He was right about my reaction, and not just because Morris and I were at opposite poles of the Democratic Party. Unlike the DLC centrists and Clinton's self-effacing but immensely capable domestic adviser Bruce Reed, who sincerely believed in moderating the Democratic message, Morris, to my mind, was simply an acolyte for his latest polls—which were often designed to evoke an adverse response to what he regarded as overly Democratic ideas.

I dutifully showed up in Joe Kennedy's office, where I promised to listen with an open mind and hold my tongue. I didn't have to say anything; Morris said more than enough. He was late. When he arrived, he sat down in a large leather armchair, his feet barely touching the floor, and triumphantly explained his tardiness. He had been with the president, who had vetoed two earlier welfare reform bills and now had to decide whether to sign another one that contained many of the same provisions he'd objected to before. Clinton was ready to sign it. Morris bragged that *he* had just won the 1996 election for Clinton. He'd been the one who'd pushed the president to give in to the Republican bill. Clinton—"the dumb s.o.b."—was bothered by the softheaded objections from some of the liberals on his staff, but Morris had beaten them back. It occurred to me that in front of Joe Kennedy, it wasn't a good idea to describe Democratic presidents this way; his uncle had been one of them. I thought the tryout was already over as we turned to the specifics of the governor's race. I don't recall much of what Morris said—I was still quietly awestruck by his initial remarks—until he articulated a central recommendation. Joe had to distance himself from Ted Kennedy, who was out of step even with Massachusetts. Joe glanced at me and I just said to Morris that we'd probably disagree on that—and I knew the state pretty well. Political consultants talk about pitching clients; the performance that day was an anti-pitch. Joe said he had to go to the House floor for a vote. The meeting broke up, and he told me to wait until he got back. "Thanks for going through that, pal," he said when he returned. He'd stick with Tom Kiley, Ted Kennedy's pollster and his for more than ten years.

In the summer of 1996, Senate and House Democrats were fighting for more than a lonely Clinton victory. From the start, Dick Gephardt, who'd succeeded Tom Foley as the House's top Democrat, had been determined to take on the Gingrich Revolution of huge tax cuts for the wealthy and a rollback of the social safety net. Not long after Gingrich took the gavel, Gephardt and I discussed the options in a conference room down the hall from his office in the Capitol. After the decimation of their ranks in 1994, a lot of House Democrats were afraid to oppose any tax reduction, no matter how regressive. For a moment, I think a surprised Gephardt wondered if I was too when I switched the subject to the proposed Republican cut in Medicare. How much was it? $270 billion. Couldn't we put the two proposals together, I asked, and attack the other side for financing $250 billion of tax breaks for the rich by slashing health care for the elderly? Republicans would claim the equation was unfair—that in absolute dollars, the amount of Medicare spending would go up; they were just restraining its projected growth. This was one case where the battle of vocabulary did matter. Democrats could and did win the argument—by pounding away at "a $270 billion Medicare cut," while making a wholly reasonable case to reporters on substantive grounds that if there were more seniors and fewer dollars and fewer benefits for each of them, that was a cut. This response, combined with Clinton's offer of more modest tax relief targeted, for example, to help middle-class families pay for college tuition, gave Democrats the upper hand. Clinton could threaten to veto both the Republican tax cut and the Medicare cut. The battle not only culminated in the government shutdown, but Republicans got all the blame for it after reports that Gingrich had put through a budget bill Clinton would have to veto in revenge for being assigned to sit in the back of Air Force One on the president's flight to the funeral of the assassinated Israeli prime minister, Yitzhak Rabin.

While Democrats wouldn't take back the House—they would gain only two seats in 1996—the episode was the real turning point for Clinton's own fortunes.

On the Senate side, Devine, Donilon, and I were working again for some of the most threatened incumbents and in two races for open seats—one a toss-up, the other relatively safe.

Jack Reed, a West Point and Harvard Law graduate and three-term Democratic congressman, wouldn't have hired us if he'd heard me describe his chances in Rhode Island as "relatively safe." He would roll up 64 percent of the vote. Reed had told me that he'd always been committed to public service. He said he'd decided to leave the military and go to law school and then into politics after a general who was a friend advised him that while he had the talent to reach the top ranks of the Army, at 5 feet, 6 inches, he was too short for the military culture and he'd never make it. Today, as a member of the Senate Armed Services Committee, he asks the questions that the men who were tall enough to become generals have to answer. (For women in the military, the barriers are presumably different.)

The toss-up contest was in New Jersey, where onetime basketball legend Bill Bradley announced his retirement after three terms. Bob Torricelli, a hard-driving congressman and prodigious fund-raiser who was almost as intelligent as he thought he was, interviewed us in his office. He told me afterward that he'd already pretty much decided to hire us because he knew how cocksure he could be and he also knew I wouldn't be afraid to talk back to him. I wasn't—and I had to. He was nominated without opposition; but as we prepared to go on the air in September 1996, Donilon called me after a brutal conversation with the candidate. Torricelli had just looked at our spots, said they were terrible, and asked if they were made in the basement on a Movieola. He'd ordered the cancellation of the dial groups scheduled to test them, where participants could register their reactions second by second by turning a dial up or down.

I phoned Torricelli and said first of all, he couldn't yell at Mike Donilon; he was smart, and we needed him. Second, Torricelli was wrong about the ads—and we had to test them. But he hated them, he shouted; they wouldn't work. I realized that he was bothered by the fact that he himself wasn't speaking directly into the camera, that he was just on film with a narrator doing a voice-over. Torricelli thought of himself as a great speechwriter and orator; but on television, he tended to sound stilted and over-rhetorical. He grudgingly agreed to let the focus groups decide on the spots. When he arrived for the dial group, he introduced someone who was with him to Mike by saying, with a touch of sarcasm, "This is the guy responsible for these things." The spots tested about as well as any ads could. They ran for several weeks, followed by scathing attacks on the Republican candidate on abortion rights and gun control.

I'd warned Torricelli that he'd be driven to distraction by the methodology of our pollster Mark Mellman, who was burly, experienced, in command of details—and immovably resolved, unlike other pollsters, to offer respondents an explicit choice of "undecided" when asking the initial question about voter preference. This inevitably results in a higher number of undecided voters and races that can look closer than they are. Mellman's last survey showed Torricelli in the mid-40s, ahead by 4 or 5 points. I assured the candidate he'd win by seven or more, but he was frantic when he called me on Saturday. He had a Republican informant, Roger Stone, a veteran Reagan operative and Washington lobbyist. Stone had just warned Torricelli that the Republican numbers were showing a last-minute shift to his opponent. He had to do something big to stop it. I was skeptical of the source—and convinced this made no sense. In our polls, the "undecideds" looked likely to break to Torricelli. Rolling the dice with some untried and untested attack was a gamble we couldn't afford and didn't need. Just calm down, I said, and finish out the campaign. The candidate was unhappy. He told me that if he won, it was his win; if he lost, it was my loss. I said I'd live with that. I was wrong about the final margin. On Election Day, he won by 10 points.

Torricelli didn't hire us the next time around, in 2002, when he was being investigated on charges of accepting illegal gifts. Maybe, I said to Donilon, Torricelli will do all the talking in his ads this time. With the ethics allegations taking center stage, he fell behind; as the storm mounted, so did the pressure on him to withdraw. Just before he did, Torricelli called me for the first time in a year and acted as if we'd been conferring all along. What did I think? He should get out, I said. Was there anything else he could do or say? No. How could he explain his decision? Be honest and don't brag about his accomplishments—which is exactly what he would do anyway. One last thing, he explained to me. He had informed both the governor, who would pick his replacement, and his Senate colleague Jon Corzine that he'd go, but on one condition. The replacement candidate couldn't be Frank Lautenberg, who'd retired from the Senate in 2000. Torricelli had a long-running feud with him. Within a few days, we were producing the ads for Lautenberg, who handily disposed of the Republican who had been leading Torricelli.

Tom Harkin, an unabashed liberal from Iowa, was in one of the toughest races we handled in 1996. Carter Eskew, who was out of politics but still close to his former client Harkin, proposed that we collaborate on the campaign. It was surprisingly smooth sailing until the final week, when the Republican nominee, a six-term conservative congressman, launched an anti-abortion ad featuring a retired Catholic priest wearing his Roman collar. Harkin, the priest charged, favored partial birth abortion. The tracking polls turned grim. The ad was hurting Harkin badly because it was peeling away Catholic voters who tended to support Democrats on the basis of bread-and-butter issues—any issue but abortion. Democrats in Iowa just tried to avoid it or survive that. Any other course was unthinkable.

But the only thing I could think of was the unthinkable. On a conference call with Harkin and his Iowa staff, I said we had no choice but to respond and the material was there. Harkin could point out that he favored Iowa's state law banning third trimester abortions; this would counter the charge on partial birth abortion. Then Harkin could go after his opponent for opposing choice even in cases of rape and incest. There was consternation on the other end of the phone; this was really risky. But as Harkin finally said, the campaign couldn't just stay a course that wasn't working. To modulate a potential backlash from Catholic Democrats, we'd have the ad sponsored not by Harkin but by the state party. Harkin's numbers stabilized and he survived by 6 points because he'd done something too many pro-choice Democrats are afraid to do: He refused to let the other side define the issue, broadened it beyond a buzz phrase like "partial birth abortion," and painted his Republican rival as the one with the extreme position. The anti-choice strategy can't be defeated if it isn't confronted. But given the instinctive caution of candidates, and the misreading of the 2004 presidential contest, this may not happen nationally unless and until the right wing gets its wish and a packed Supreme Court reverses *Roe v. Wade*—which would set off a pro-choice tidal wave in the next election.

For me, the first step toward the 2004 presidential race was another close 1996 Senate contest, one we came to late in the game. Bill Weld, the popular Republican governor of Massachusetts, was challenging John Kerry's reelection. I'd been a casual friend of Kerry's for years and written speeches for him at Democratic conventions. He'd recently married John Heinz's widow Teresa; I liked her and so did Marylouise. After Weld entered the race, Kerry was constantly casting around for the best strategy, concerned that his campaign wasn't finding a way through. In the downstairs library of Teresa and John's Georgetown house, he asked me if we'd be willing to partner with the media firm he'd used in the past to make the spots—and shape the strategy. I said yes, but nothing happened. Soon after, Kerry invited me over again and said he was having trouble working out the arrangement. I responded that was fine; we should just stop talking about it. But could we talk about the campaign as it went on? he said. Sure, I answered.

After dinner with John and Teresa one summer night, he showed us a reel of his spots. One of them, featuring Kerry Rollerblading in spandex across a bridge over the Charles River, was intended as visual proof that he was a leader, someone who was always in the forefront of the issues. But visually, I said, Kerry actually looked a little odd, goofy. Marylouise was less polite; this would make Kerry a laughingstock. He couldn't appear on television in spandex. (She was right on the mark: If the spot had run, it would have been the "windsurfing" of 1996.)

I was in Boston in early September filming commercials for Joe Kennedy's jaunt through a congressional reelection toward a governor's race that would never happen. My office called: Could I see John and Teresa that night at their home on Beacon Hill? As I got out of the car and crossed the cobblestoned street, Teresa opened the door, nodded her head, and said: "Come right in." We sat in the kitchen—where I'd spend many hours during the 2004 campaign, from the announcement to the concession—and Kerry asked if my firm would take over responsibility for strategy and television ads in the Senate race. He had only one condition: I had to be able to get along with Ray Dooley, a laconic, shrewd master of the Massachusetts political landscape who was now directing the campaign. That was no problem. I respected him, and so did Tad Devine.

Kerry handed me his latest private poll. He was a few points behind Weld; more ominously, he was behind, mostly by big margins, on fourteen out of fifteen attributes like "strong leadership" and "cares about people like me." The only attribute he led on was "protecting the environment." What should our first ad be? Even before we filmed him, I said, we'd make a spot going after Weld on the minimum wage and get it on the air right away. Kerry agreed, a little reluctantly. I'd soon find out why.

Teresa intervened. She's smart and decisive. Since John Heinz's death, she's run one of the largest philanthropic enterprises in the country. She now told Kerry that he couldn't fuss with the ads. He could see them or at least the scripts before they aired, but the campaign had to get moving, and moving fast. The minimum wage spot was quickly out of the editing studio and on TV. Ted Kennedy, who I'd learned had pushed Kerry to hire us, called me with a chuckle in his voice. He liked the ad—a lot. But it was more than a little ironic. Kerry had almost ended up on the wrong side of the issue. In 1995, as he was attempting to define his own political space, separate from Kennedy and distinct from the stereotype of a Massachusetts liberal, Kerry had stood up in a closed Democratic caucus and suggested that the minimum wage was an "old" idea whose time had passed. Kennedy had roared back that anybody who said that wasn't much of a Democrat—and Kerry backed down. It was a good thing that clash never made the papers, Kennedy now said, or our first anti-Weld spot would have been a nonstarter. With it, we set about the business of overturning Weld's image as a moderate—soon tying him to Newt Gingrich and tagging him for cutting help to Social Security recipients in state nursing homes. He'd proposed to confiscate all their benefits except for a dollar a day. We branded him "Dollar Bill."

In this race, the ads could only begin to reshape the parameters of the battle; the decisive front line was a relentless procession of debates with Weld. Facing a tight contest, and under pressure from the news media, Weld and Kerry had agreed early on to an unprecedented series of eight debates. The exchanges commanded national attention and big television audiences in Massachusetts. The initial ones had also reflected the essential weakness in the Kerry campaign: despite some good, even a few great moments for him, they had been fought out on Weld's turf.

Kerry and I took a trip alone in his speedboat to prepare for the next debate. The reason Weld was gaining ground, I said, was that he was focusing on "crime, welfare, and taxes," and Kerry was taking the bait. He was almost stubbornly on the defensive, insisting that he was tougher and better on Weld's preferred issues. I told Kerry: "If the question is taxes, the answer isn't you." Crime was a similar trap; Kerry was a former prosecutor, but he was against the death penalty. The best we can do, I said, as we cut through the waves of Nantucket Sound, is neutralize these issues; we have to move them off center stage. We couldn't continue to play Weld's game, sending voters the message that questions like crime and welfare should be the deciding factors. The most critical strategic imperative was to bring the debates and the campaign to Democratic ground—to education, the environment, the minimum wage, and Social Security. Then we could not only bolt Weld to the Gingrich Congress, but torture him by asking, for example, whether he'd vote for Jesse Helms as chairman of the Foreign Relations Committee. If he said no, he'd alienate the small corps of Massachusetts conservatives he might need to win; if he said yes, he was no moderate.

Kerry executed the strategy flawlessly. In the first debate after our boat ride, he drummed at the theme: "My opponent likes to talk like a Democrat, but he votes like a Republican." Weld had even vetoed a cigarette tax increase to finance health coverage for 165,000 Massachusetts children. Who, Kerry asked the voters, do you "trust" on health care? Kerry was now gaining ground in the debates and the television ad wars. But the race was no sure thing; at times, the tracking polls rattled Kerry, but he never showed it publicly. As Election Day neared, the wise guys, the Boston pols who'd assumed he was doomed, started to change their tune. He just might make it. They might think he was aloof, but our closing "positive" spot confounded that notion—and it was also a devastating attack on Weld because it seemed anything but negative. Our camera crew caught Kerry answering questions from a young schoolboy holding a pad who was reporting for a "kids" newspaper. What, he asked Kerry, are the differences between you and Governor Weld? Kerry ticked them off, then smiled as he got to the minimum wage. Weld was against it, Kerry said; but he himself was for it, so that "they" will pay "you" enough—and he touched the young man's shoulder—when you grow up and do this for a living. He laughed, and as he walked away, said: "See you later." The spot tested through the roof in a last-minute focus group. Kerry was, for once, the happy warrior.

For me, it was a happy campaign—and not simply because Kerry came back from his near collapse to win by 7 points, but because what had been a casual friendship with him became a bond of trust in times of tension, punctuated by a capacity that too few others have seen in him to laugh at himself. Before one debate, we conducted a regular prep session; but then Kerry decided that we'd finish on a small plane flying to an event in the state's second largest city, Worcester. When we got on the plane, he sat in one of the two pilots' seats. I looked at him and asked: "Who's flying this thing?" Kerry replied: "Me. What, are you worried that I can't learn and fly at the same time?" One thing he never needed to learn was the facts; he knew too many. He could debate and "win" a point even if it was in his interest to slide off it and turn to more advantageous ground. But once he was comfortable in a "message box," he was as good a debater as I've ever encountered in politics.

Just a week before the election, there was another moment that tested him, and predicted the future, when a *Globe* columnist charged that instead of being a hero in Vietnam, he'd been awarded the Silver Star for a "war crime"—finishing off an enemy soldier who was no longer resisting after being wounded. Flanked by veterans and his crewmates, he blasted the account. Admiral Elmo Zumwalt, the Chief of Naval Operations during the Vietnam War, denounced the allegation as "such an absolutely outrageous misinterpretation of the facts" that, despite his intention to stay out of partisan politics, "I felt it was important to be here." In the end, the episode hurt the columnist, not Kerry. Unfortunately, when the smearing of Kerry's war record was recycled in 2004, Zumwalt wasn't there to defend him (he had died four years before). And in 2004, some of the vets—but none of his crewmates—who had stood up for him in the Senate race switched sides and changed their stories, for reasons they wouldn't explain and that probably had more to do with their political preferences than with what had happened during the war.

Finally in 1996, I signed on to an initiative campaign that would engender vehement criticism of me from the right wing that continues to this day. Ward Connerly, an African-American on the University of California Board of Regents who posed as a moderate but was a darling of conservatives, spearheaded a California ballot initiative, Proposition 209, to end affirmative action in public institutions and state programs. The measure, misleadingly labeled the "California Civil Rights Initiative," had a seemingly insurmountable lead in the polls; voters didn't understand what it would actually do. There wasn't much of a fee for us here, but my partners and I were determined to create ads exposing 209's real impact. The anti-209 manager called me in September to report that David Duke, the Ku Klux Klan leader who'd become nationally notorious as the Republican nominee for governor of Louisiana, had agreed to debate in favor of 209 at California State University at Northridge. I said we'd send a camera crew and the campaign should get the film to us as soon as possible. The resulting spot was dramatic and controversial. It began with film of a Klan rally and a burning cross; then cut to Duke walking onto a stage at the university wearing a suit and tie as the narrator said: "He's not just another guy in a business suit. He's David Duke, former head of the Ku Klux Klan. And he's come to California to support Proposition 209." The spot sparked an uproar, but it almost turned the tide. The proposition passed with 54 percent of the vote—not enough to give Connerly the needed momentum to carry his anti–affirmative action cause across the country—until a similar measure passed in Michigan in 2006.

But for me, the aftermath began even before the votes were counted. A *Wall Street Journal* editorial, without a shred of proof, scorched Shrum, Devine, and Donilon for inviting David Duke to California. I wouldn't have known how to contact him, didn't ever want to talk to him—and why would he listen to me? But the charge was right out of the right-wing playbook and it's lived on ever since. After the 2004 election, Ann Coulter, the conservative propagandist who loves to hate liberals, called me a "swine" for making the anti-209 commercial. But I suppose I regard it as an honor to be trashed for this by Ann Coulter—just as it's an honor to see it cited as one of the reasons for including me in the *100 People Who Are Screwing Up America* by Bernard Goldberg, an ex-CBS reporter who invented a new career for himself by labeling the network where he'd worked for twenty-eight years as "biased." I have trouble understanding how, in the right-wing worldview, I'm screwing up America and simultaneously responsible for Gore and Kerry losing. Did the right wing want them to win?

I hoped Clinton's second inaugural would transcend the instrumental nature of his reelection race—that it would provide a framework of conviction and vision for a second term. It ought to speak to the next four years and to history, not just to the next round of polls. But that wasn't my business. I had an inaugural assignment of my own related less to my political experiences than to my occasional moonlighting as a writer for the Kennedy Center Honors and other nationally televised awards shows. Gary Smith, the Hollywood producer who was in charge of a starry inaugural gala—Michael

Douglas, Whoopi Goldberg, Candice Bergen, Kenny G—drafted me to script the evening. I was backstage afterward when I saw almost everyone pressing in one direction, toward the president, who'd stopped by to thank the performers and crew. I saw no reason to push to the front of the crowd. Then someone came into the area where I was packing up my papers and said the president wanted to see me. He wasn't happy with his inaugural address, he said; this deal tomorrow is really important to me. Was I willing to rework the speech with him? Of course, I said. Marylouise and I were supposed to go to a party at the Jockey Club, but she could go without me. Well, he replied, he and Hillary were going to the same party. They'd stay briefly, and then we'd go back to the White House.

Crowded into the restaurant were two hundred people, almost all of them recognizable, from the worlds of politics, power, and entertainment. I warned Marylouise that I'd have to leave early. Somewhere around 2 A.M., I was ready to give up. Clinton grabbed me and said we'd talk early in the morning. It was 6 A.M. when the phone rang. "This is Bill," the president said; he was sending over a copy of the speech. He had to go to a church service with Jesse Jackson. But that would be relatively brief; he'd call back right afterward so we could get together. The idea of editing an inaugural address just hours before it was to be delivered struck me as nearly unbelievable coming from anybody but Bill Clinton. He had endless energy and a ceaseless impulse to tinker—which, of course, could actually damage the final product; but he never seemed to feel that the best could be the enemy of the good. The draft I read was far from perfect. I inserted some new lines and marked a few others for deletion; the only conceivable course was modest, hopefully judicious edits, not a wholesale rewrite.

I watched the service on television. The praying and singing went on and on; in his sermon, Jesse Jackson instructed the president that he'd been reelected by the poor and commissioned the first lady to renew the fight for universal health reform. That, I said to Marylouise, is one thing that's not going to happen in the next four years. The time was draining away—and when the president finally called, there was almost none left. He had to have coffee with the congressional leadership at the White House and then motorcade to the Capitol for his swearing in. There wasn't time to do much, he said; did I think the speech was okay? I thought to myself: He has to give this within the next hour. I'm not going to offer last-minute criticisms that would shake his confidence. And anyway, the words he spoke invariably sounded better than they read on paper. So I told him the speech was "fine" and then I decided I had to do better than that and added that it was "excellent"; he'd do very well. Was I sure? he asked. Yes, I answered—and he said he'd call me afterward to see what I thought.

I left the house to make my way through the crowds to Fox News; it was the year I was under contract as a Fox commentator— and I now had to opine on the inaugural address I'd already read, and the prospects for Clinton's second term. I praised the speech; I would have done it even if I hadn't had that back-and-forth with the president over the previous 12 or 13 hours. The speech wasn't one for the history books, but I was surprised by the harsh tone of the reaction, and not just from Republicans. Usually, a president gets the benefit of the doubt on his inaugural day. George W. Bush's call in his second inaugural for universal democracy was only mildly questioned at the time, perhaps because the language had an almost antique eloquence. But Clinton's 1996 performance, said Tom Brokaw on NBC, "lacked great passion or memorable phrases." The normally Clinton-leaning columnist Margaret Carlson judged the speech "full of platitudes." *The Washington Post*'s liberal doyenne Mary McGrory summed up the din of criticism that filled the airwaves in her next column: "Why would a man willfully choose to make a mediocre speech?"

Rereading it now, some of the speech is more fascinating than it sounded then. The Clinton of the 1996 inaugural brims with pre-9/11 confidence that's both painful in retrospect and foreshadows Bush's hubristic promise of global democracy:

We will stand mighty for peace and freedom and maintain a strong defense against terror and destruction. Our children will sleep free from the threat of nuclear, chemical, or biological weapons. Ports and air-

ports, farms and factories will thrive with trade and innovation and ideas. And the world's greatest democracy will lead a whole world of democracies.

Yesterday's platitude is today's most elusive hope. At the time, it didn't even occur to me to cut this language, although I would have suggested making it an explicit summons—"Let us build," rather than an apparent certitude, "We will."

Early in the evening, Clinton phoned again. I'd just told Todd Purdum from the *New York Times* that I was "very pro the speech," but I wasn't about to tell the president that Purdum's article was likely to be pretty tough on him. Clinton, though, was well aware of the verdicts that had already been rendered on television; he was especially hurt that William Leuchtenburg, a benchmark historian of the Progressive Era and the New Deal, had pronounced the speech "the most banal address by an American President I have ever heard." Surely it wasn't that bad? Clinton said. I was amazed that he had either seen or heard about the coverage in this kind of detail. And he had heard what I'd said on Fox. He thanked me and observed that I'd been a pretty lonely voice. The speech, he added, wasn't very good; he knew it himself—and he wished we'd had time to reshape it. Could I help him out, early on, with the State of the Union message that was scheduled for February 4?

I received a form letter from the White House speechwriting office asking me to forward any suggestions I had. So that was that; I put it aside. I'd been too involved myself for too long in the speechwriting process, placating people who wanted to help presidential candidates by telling them to send their ideas in. They usually went nowhere. Clinton phoned a few days later: Had I done a draft? Had I talked to Michael Waldman, the chief speechwriter—who soon would become a friend and collaborator on speeches like this? No, I replied; all I had received was that request to send in some ideas. The president said he didn't care what "they" wanted; he wanted as much of a draft from me as I could manage before he started editing and rehearsing in the White House theater. He'd get me a list of the speech's major proposals right away. For most of that night and the next day, I wrote as usual on my yellow legal pad, then had the draft typed and sent off to the White House.

When I went to the first speech prep with the president and the staff, I wasn't sure the speechwriters were happy to see me—and I understood that. Waldman confirmed the impression in his memoir about the Clinton years: Just how disruptive was I going to be? As it turned out, Waldman wrote, it worked out smoothly. But it didn't start off on the right foot. I read through the draft that was handed to Clinton; at first glance, there was almost nothing there that I had sent. Clinton glanced up and asked if Shrum's stuff was in here. They'd put in a few lines, he was told. Well, where is his draft? Back in the speechwriting office in the Old Executive Office Building. Okay, then go get it, and Bob and I can have a cup of coffee while you do.

The language I had crafted was incorporated into the text the president soon read on the TelePrompTer screens while standing at a podium in the White House theater. He revised out loud during each run-through over a period of days. Erskine Bowles, the multi-millionaire businessman from North Carolina who'd become Clinton's new chief of staff just two months earlier, enforced a rule apparently developed during the prep sessions for the 1996 debates with Bob Dole. Two people in the ranks of advisers and staff were the designated "talkers," in this case, Clinton's pollster Mark Penn and I. Others could write their comments on notes that we'd quickly look through; they didn't talk unless the president directed a question to them, usually about substance. Waldman, who controlled the text through incessant rounds of revision, could intervene—and he did so sparingly. At times, Clinton would open up a few minutes of general discussion at the end of a run-through. It was a disciplined method for a process that otherwise could have spun out of control and into the endless back-and-forth that Clinton reveled in.

In all my years, I'd never experienced anything quite like the president's rolling process of editing out loud. Clinton could read a passage and then rewrite it on the spot in complete sentences and often in nicely balanced phrases. He appreciated rhetoric—up to a point—and as he cut or toned down certain lines, he looked at me and allowed that while that might be a great phrase, it just wasn't him. But he did buy into the naturally turned phrase that didn't call too much attention to itself: "My fellow Americans, the state of our union is strong. But now we must rise to the decisive moment, to make a nation and a world better than we have ever known before." Clinton excised the last word, "before"; it wasn't needed. "We must be shapers of events, not observers. For if we do not act the moment will pass—and we will lose the best possibilities of our future"—a phrase I had used before, but no one had a patent on it.

The beginning was intentionally short, and with the first proposal, he again occupied the traditionally, if inaccurately, Republican ground of fiscal responsibility: "Let this Congress be the Congress that finally balances the budget"—which could bring both sides of the aisle to their feet. The president, who a year before had proclaimed that "the era of big government is over," then offered a series of smaller initiatives that in the area of education added up to a more than modest agenda driven by government. He'd been reelected by triangulating; he wasn't abandoning the approach, but his second term had to be about something and he was trying to build his bridge not just to the twenty-first century, but to his own legacy. After Clinton finished each rehearsal, we adjourned to a suite of offices in the Old Executive Office Building to work late into the night. I was no longer the outsider to be feared, and I was intent on being cooperative with the staff because I realized how I'd feel in their position. Some of them I'd collaborate with in future campaigns.

Clinton took much of the ending I'd written and reworked it with the speech writing staff and Penn. It was time to build a foundation for this new century: "Money cannot buy it, power cannot compel it, technology cannot create it. It can only come from the human spirit. America is far more than a place; it is an idea"—a phrase, I told him, that while not exactly the same, was a linear descendant of something McGovern had said in 1972. He didn't mind that, but he was determined not to explicitly invoke his "bridge to the 21st century." That campaign mantra was tired—and he wished he hadn't recycled it for the inaugural address. In the end, the word "bridge" appeared in the speech only twice; there was a graceful leavetaking of the phrase as he descibed "a bridge to a land of new promise."

As the president left for Capitol Hill, I went home to watch on TV. This reflected my usual phobia. I had no desire to stand there—in this case, on the House floor—while a speech I'd worked on was being delivered. As Clinton was finishing, the verdict in the O.J. Simpson civil trial was about to be announced; the networks bannered the news while staying with the president until he'd uttered the words "God bless America," then cut immediately to the courtroom in Santa Monica. Some critics wondered if this blunted the effect of Clinton's speech. To the contrary, Penn told me when he had his poll results, the impending news pulled more Americans into the audience and they gave the State of the Union high marks. One commentator described it as "a grand vision of thinking smaller." Clinton might have ventured more the next year; but by then, the question wouldn't be his proposals but his prospects for survival. Even then, he'd be able on the basis of the economic news and a declining federal deficit to reaffirm, amid the clamor of scandal, that the state of the Union was "strong"—and then audaciously repeat the phrase in 1999, when he emphatically told me he wanted it in the speech. When the storm of scandal came, he understood the key to his survival: Whatever Americans thought of his transgressions with Monica Lewinsky, they gave him credit for the prosperity that marked his presidency. It was a form of cognitive dissonance—low marks for his character and personal conduct, high job approval ratings—that would shore Clinton up, but ultimately sour his relationship with Al Gore and disable him as the effective advocate for Gore that Clinton and his partisans still insist he could have been.

The day after the 1997 State of the Union, Pamela Harriman died in Paris and Clinton enlisted my help to write his eulogy for her funeral. Five years earlier, at Thanksgiving, she had organized a day at her weekend home in the Virginia countryside for my stepson Michael, who'd come down from Brown University for the weekend. She heated up the swimming pool in the late autumn chill and served roast beef with Yorkshire pudding, because, she explained, "That's what keeps young men strong." She and I went for a walk through the woods discussing what everyone expected, but she hadn't yet been explicitly told: that the newly elected Clinton would name her ambassador to Britain or France. She didn't want Britain; the tabloid press would have a field day about her personal life. France, on the other hand, was a place where the media, and the culture, accepted and even admired her kind of adventurous life—although usually when lived by men. For Pamela's swearing in a few months later, she asked me if we could collaborate on one last speech. Looking out at the hundreds gathered in an ornate room at the State Department where Al Gore administered her oath of office, she invited everyone to come and visit her in Paris—"Just not all at once."

Marylouise and I took her up on her offer. It was January 1994 and I'll never forget both the penetrating dampness I felt standing on the stone floors at Notre Dame and the steaming hot chocolate that was brought to us as soon as we walked back into the embassy residence. Along with Pamela's other paintings, Van Gogh's *White Roses* was on display over the mantel in the vast first-floor sitting room. Despite what she told me was a Japanese collector's offer to buy it for over $50 million, she had promised to donate it to the National Gallery in Washington. That's what Averell had wanted. He once told me that he didn't understand why more people hadn't bought paintings like this when he had; it had cost a few thousand dollars in the 1930s ($72,000, I later discovered). But a few thousand dollars, I replied, was a fortune to most people then.

Pamela tempered the instinctive anti-Americanism of French leaders like President François Mitterrand and she skillfully maneuvered through the byways and backrooms of French politics. I was in Paris again in 1995 as Mitterrand was retiring and Jacques Chirac was in a neck and neck race with the Socialist candidate for president, Lionel Jospin. Pamela sent me to see Chirac's media advisers and offer advice about his upcoming debate with Jospin. Chirac had been a mediocre debater in the past and this encounter could be decisive. I'm not sure I made any difference, but the new French president knew that she'd tried to help—and Jospin would never have known if he'd been elected.

Pamela's most powerful confidante on the embassy staff was her longtime political aide, Janet Howard. Howard was almost her alter ego, and a friend of Marylouise's and mine. A few months after our January 1994 stay in Paris, Howard told me on the phone that rather than being financially secure, Pamela was being pressed by the Harriman family over investment losses in the trust fund that she nominally oversaw. The money was actually directed by the legendary Clark Clifford, his law partner Paul Warnke, and Bill Rich, who had long run the Harriman money day to day. Rich had decided to invest heavily in a former *Playboy* resort in Great Gorge, New Jersey; good money had been sent after bad—and the trust fund was depleted. I reminded Pamela of what her husband had said on his last trip to Barbados, that she should just let Clifford, Warnke, and Rich handle the money after he was gone. That memory was no consolation. Selling *White Roses* would have been the easy way out, but it was off limits. By February 1995, to fend off a lawsuit and more of the ugly stories that could stain her ambassadorship, she was consigning three other paintings—by Picasso, Matisse, and Renoir—to be auctioned at Christie's.

Pamela was in Washington for Clinton's second inauguration. Her term as ambassador was ending, but she had a few more weeks in Paris before her successor arrived. She invited Marylouise and me to her Georgetown house for an informal lunch, just the three of us, after the swearing in. The lunch was sweet and a little melancholy. After we left, Marylouise said she was worried about Pamela; she looked pale and was too thin.

Two weeks later, Sandy Berger, another of her close friends and now Clinton's national security adviser, phoned me. Pamela had suffered a massive stroke while taking her daily swim in the pool of the Ritz Hôtel. She never regained consciousness and when she died, the president sent a plane and a delegation headed by former Speaker Tom Foley to bring her body home. Janet Howard organized a bus with a police escort to ferry her friends to Andrews Air

Force Base. I could hardly believe, I said to Berger on the tarmac, that the person I'd just laughed with on inauguration day was in that box.

The funeral was in the soaring National Cathedral, where Woodrow Wilson was buried. It was fashionable to dismiss Pamela as a courtesan who had lived, in her decidedly unauthorized biographer Sally Bedell Smith's phrase, a life of "reflected glory"—and then at the end contrived an A-list moment of her own in Paris. Neither Clinton nor I wanted her to be remembered in a one-dimensional way. So the eulogy not only acknowledged her "luminous presence that could light up . . . even the city of light itself"; it gave her something she had craved most of all, credit for a substantive contribution, "four years of singular service and achievement, earning the confidence of France's leaders [and] the respect of its people." The conclusion implicitly acknowledged and, with a touch of defiance, approved of the road she had taken. "What a journey it was," Clinton said, "and well worth making."

Soon after there was another contact from the White House; chief of staff Erskine Bowles asked to see me in his office. Marylouise and I had come to know him pretty well in the first Clinton term, when he'd served as director of the Small Business Administration. We chatted for a while and then he popped the question: The president wanted to know if I would consider joining the White House staff—not just to work on speeches, but on politics and policy. It was what I'd dreamed of two decades ago. And that was the problem: I was in my mid-fifties. I'd made no money until I was forty-three, and Marylouise and I were finally building up some savings. I replied that I was honored to be asked and it was painful to say no, but I just couldn't afford it. Bowles pointed out that he'd made a financial sacrifice to return to government. But Erskine, I answered, you already have—I don't know—$50 or $100 million. I'm just trying to achieve some financial security—and I have to do it now. But I'll be happy to help out whenever the president wants me to. With the Clinton administration, I was finally—if not permanently—in from the cold.

Marylouise and I now received our first invitation to a state dinner at the White House, for Prime Minister Chrétien of Canada. We had no connection with Canada, there was no remote reason for us to be there, except that it was the next state dinner on the schedule and Clinton was saying thank you. The day of the dinner, the White House social secretary rang Marylouise. She was to be seated at the president's table, with Mrs. Chrétien and five other guests, ranging from Dan Aykroyd (the comedian had been born in Canada) to NBC News correspondent Andrea Mitchell. I was seated five or six tables away. At the dinner, Clinton was still on crutches, recovering from a knee injury after stumbling on a stairway at golfer Greg Norman's Florida home. But he was anything but subdued and not particularly interested in talking about matters of state. Marylouise brought up the Employment Non-Discrimination Act, designed to protect gays and lesbians, a bill then (and now) before Congress. The bill, she said to the president, should cover transgendered people, too. "Oh," he interjected, "you mean like the movie *Priscilla, Queen of the Desert?*" She answered, "Not really": two of the main characters were transvestites; only one was transgender. "What's the difference?" Clinton wondered. "Accoutrement," Marylouise responded. As Clinton and my wife discussed the taxonomy of sexual orientation, Mrs. Chrétien listened in stunned silence. Aykroyd said to Marylouise: "I didn't think this is what we would talk about at a state dinner."

Clinton's table was casual and free-flowing, not stiff and formal. Andrea Mitchell passed around photos of her recent wedding to Federal Reserve chairman Alan Greenspan—and plotted with Marylouise about how to shoehorn a honeymoon into her workaholic husband's life. Maybe they could find four days in June, after an international conference Alan was attending in Switzerland. Go to Venice, Marylouise advised, to the Cipriani; she'd help arrange it. After the formal toasts, musicians from the Marine Band strolled in, playing Canadian tunes from movies and Broadway musicals. From my table on the other side of the room, I could hear—and so could everyone else a couple of voices warbling the words slightly off key. Clinton had said to Marylouise: "Do you still know all the words?" At the end of the evening, with Clinton about to hobble out of the state dining room and head upstairs, I listened as he and

Marylouise harkened back to their time at Yale, when he'd been one of the few law students to own a car and had lent it to her weekend after weekend so she could drive to Philadelphia to visit her sick father. I still wished Clinton was bolder and more progressive, but power is magnetic; he was a Democrat, someone I'd first met in college, only the second Democratic president during my political career and the first one that I was getting along with.

Improbably, we went on the Greenspan-Mitchell honeymoon—along with Marylouise's sister Jane and our twelve-year-old nephew John. The dates Andrea gave us for their time in Venice overlapped the week we were already scheduled to be there. We were prepared to shift our trip, but she said no, it would be fun if we were all together. As we plied the canals to see the Jewish Ghetto, the first one in history, and the great medieval Franciscan Church of the Frari, with its Canova sculptures and Titian's *Assumption* above the altar, I was intrigued by the depth of Alan's knowledge about architecture and Renaissance painting—both of which, of course he pointed out, reflected fundamental mathematical concepts of proportion and perspective. He gently tutored my nephew, as averse to math as I had been at his age, in the beauty and logic of numbers.

Our friendship with Alan and Andrea came about because of my wife, who was as much a force of nature in Washington as she had been in Los Angeles. In his book excoriating political consultants, Joe Klein writes that Marylouise transformed me from a rumpled, socially dysfunctional political activist into part of the Washington establishment. There is some truth in that, although I never abandoned the notion, which she shared, that Democrats were in politics to stand up for "the people, not the powerful"—a position that would earn me plenty of establishment criticism when I was blamed for fastening it to Al Gore. I spent evenings at dinner happily arguing the minimum wage with Greenspan, who opposed it in principle. At our dinner table, Greenspan and Gordon Brown, the British chancellor of the exchequer—and with Tony Blair, the architect of New Labour's return to power—began a dialogue on how to combat Third World poverty, which bore fruit in some important changes in international financial institutions. Lally Weymouth—

whose mother, Katharine Graham, liked to function as Marylouise's sous chef in the kitchen—once half-seriously arraigned my wife for infecting her mother with dangerous left-wing ideas.

If "Oatsie," as she was known to everyone, was running a salon, it was an informal one based on risotto, roast chicken, and an alternating cast of guests—from government and journalism, even some Republicans, and old friends like Tom Rollins, who'd left Kennedy's Senate staff to start a business we invested in that, like Marylouise's real estate dealings, would ultimately earn us more than I ever did as a consultant. We really liked the people who belonged to what the NBC producer Tammy Haddad named "the meal plan," but it contributed to a kind of consultant lore that the gatherings gave me an unfair advantage in recruiting clients. Maybe they helped, but most of our guests were already clients or friends, and some like House Democratic grandee John Dingell, who spent Christmas Eves with us, had hired other consultants. Marylouise was a great hostess and cook, but she was also an activist; recruited by Hillary Clinton as part of a delegation to violence-scarred Northern Ireland, she returned again and again as a driving force in a community-based effort to build peace there.

There was one unequivocally political event at our house during Clinton's second term. The White House asked us to host a lunch with the president for contributors who, we were told, pledged to raise at least $300,000 for the Democratic National Committee. What kind of meal, Marylouise wondered, do you give fifty people in return for $300,000 each? Fried chicken! The president mingled and then kept glancing at the food as he sat in a chair in the living room answering questions. He was finally preparing to leave, holding a foil-covered plate in his hand. He waved a piece of fried chicken at us as the motorcade sped off.

The month before the 1998 State of the Union, the one that he would have to deliver amid the Monica storm, Clinton nearly stopped talking to me again. I was blamed for a speech Dick Gephardt gave at Harvard positioning himself for a presidential run against Gore in 2000. I had edited the speech and added lines criticizing Democrats "who set their compass only off the direction of others, who talk about the political center but fail to understand that, if it is only defined by others, it lacks core values." But the line that really stung, directed straight at Gore, investigated for his 1996 fund-raising at a Buddhist temple, was: "We need a Democratic Party that is a movement for change, not a money machine." Clinton took this as a direct slap not at Gore, but at him. I admitted to Paul Begala that I had worked on the speech, but unbravely refused to take responsibility for any specific line.

In early December, I discovered that I was caught in the fall-out during my annual stint writing for the Kennedy Center Honors. George Stevens, the producer of the show, handed me a copy of the president's proposed remarks for the event. Stevens wasn't happy. Was this text what I'd sent to the White House? No, it wasn't, I answered, and called the speechwriting office. Waldman explained that an angry Begala, saying he was acting at the behest of an angry Clinton, had forbidden the use of anything I wrote about anything. That night, Marylouise and I saw Mickey Kantor and his wife Heidi, a former correspondent for the *Today* show. He had resigned as secretary of commerce, but was still close to the president. It was natural for him to ask about the Honors show that weekend, and I explained what had happened with the White House. I guessed I was back to square one with Clinton, I said, and I'd just have to live with it. I heard from Mickey later that night. He'd talked with Clinton, who said he didn't know anything about this. He was the president and he'd decide who he wanted to talk to, what drafts he wanted to see, and who he got along with. My surmise was that Clinton had exploded not only about the Gephardt speech, but about me; but as it often did, his anger quickly cooled. Begala had just taken him too literally.

Bowles called to make sure I'd be available for the 1998 State of the Union. I saw and recast some early material and sent some of my own to the White House. The process seemed pretty much under control. Then I arrived for a pre-rehearsal meeting with Clinton on the most chaotic and depressing afternoon of his presidency. As I hurried down the driveway from the northwest gate, I steadily picked up speed to move past the ranks of reporters ranged along the driveway shouting questions. "Shrum, Shrum" was ringing in my ears as the Marine Guard opened the door to the West Wing. The breaking story of Clinton's affair with a twenty-two-year-old intern was sending the press into a frenzy.

When we convened in the Cabinet Room, Clinton seemed subdued and distracted. State of the Union drafts were on the table, but it was almost as if he wasn't there. The man who normally loved to talk didn't have much to say. We were told we'd reassemble the next day. As the session was breaking up, I asked Clinton if I could see him for a minute. Someone informed me afterward that staff members—or at least most of the staff—weren't supposed to just collar the president for a conversation. But I wasn't the staff—and even if I'd known the rules, I don't think it would have deterred me.

Clinton invited me into the Oval Office and said he just couldn't believe "this" was happening. I responded that I didn't really want to talk about the allegations. I just wanted to say that next Tuesday, when he went before the Congress and the nation, friends and enemies—and the American people—would watch as they never had before. If he could command that chamber, if he looked and sounded presidential—well, that was a critical test he had to pass. What I didn't say explicitly, but believed, was that the country would decide whether he could still be president. So, as hard as it was, I continued, even as he dealt with the allegations, he had to engage in and focus on *this* speech. For more than a few hours every day, he had to put everything else aside. He was pretty good at that when he had to be, he said. I told the president I'd be there the next day and went downstairs to Sidney Blumenthal's office.

Ensconced in his windowless space next to the White House communications shop, Blumenthal was a fierce partisan, a political intellectual, and a graceful writer with whom I'd spend a lot of time in the cauldron of the following week. When I stopped in, he was on the phone telling someone—I don't know whether it was someone in the press or another staffer—that Monica Lewinsky was unreliable; she had a bad reputation around the White House; she'd been obsessed with the president; she was a stalker. I didn't think this was a good idea and was about to say so when Clinton's secretary, Betty Currie, summoned me back to the Oval Office. Mark Penn was there, too. We talked about the State of the Union briefly and then Clinton turned to the scandal. He'd heard what I said earlier about the speech and thought it was good advice. But he just wanted us to know—he wanted me to know; we'd known each other almost thirty years— that "I did not do this thing." I didn't notice how carefully his denial was worded and I doubt the wording was even conscious. I was asked months later whether I was mad that the president had "lied" to me. I'd said on television that he'd denied the charge, and where was the proof? It was a tack I had to abandon after Lewinsky produced the blue dress with his DNA on it. My answer was simple: Why would he have told me or anyone else the truth?—except maybe his lawyer or his wife, although his reluctance to face the marital music would continue for months. It was ridiculous to think Clinton would create witnesses against himself—and it would have cost me a fortune in legal bills. I wouldn't have been able, in the early months of the scandal, to cite his denial in the constant combat of the cable TV coliseum.

I did say two things to Clinton before I left the Oval Office for the second time that day. First, I thought it was important for people around him not to trash Lewinsky; what she said could have a big impact on him. She shouldn't be led to conclude that the president regarded her as an enemy. Second, I was worried about e-mail. I didn't think the White House staff should be e-mailing each other or anyone about this. The e-mails could become grist for the special counsel's mill. I don't know what Clinton did with either piece of advice.

In the days ahead, the president was preternaturally disciplined as he prepared for the State of the Union. The scandal must have been on his mind, but most of the time none of us in the White House theater could detect that. I'd brought him a Cuban cigar. Hillary wouldn't let him smoke. But during a break between sessions, he chewed on it as he walked with Penn and me in the East Wing corridor outside the theater and we then ducked into the wintry Sculpture Garden outside. He betrayed his anxiety for a moment: Was he going to survive this thing? Yes, we both said; the first critical step was the speech and we were getting it into good shape.

In the meantime, he had to answer questions about the scandal. In an interview with the PBS anchor Jim Lehrer, his initial response was too clever by half: "There *is* no improper relationship." Clinton may have expected—or hoped—that because Lehrer was a "serious" journalist, proud of focusing on substantive issues, he might stop there. He didn't. Clinton said it differently: "There *is* not a sexual relationship." The answers were instantly parsed by a skeptical press; here it really did depend on what the meaning of "is" is. Why didn't Clinton just say there *was* no sexual relationship? The Lehrer interview had only added fuel to the fire. So Clinton, counseled by his longtime friend Harry Thomason, the television producer, did shift to the past tense. While we were down the hall waiting for him in the theater with just two days of practice left before Tuesday night's State of the Union, Clinton was emphatic but awkward as he met with reporters in the Roosevelt room: "I did not have sexual relations with that woman"—pause, was he trying to remember her name, or did he want it to seem so?—"Miss Lewinsky."

Thomason would be criticized for giving the president bad advice; but if survival was the goal, Thomason got it right. It's common and often correct in a scandal or crisis to tell the principal to get everything out right away. But not this time. Never mind the cost of confessing to Hillary; "getting everything out there early" might have forced the president out of office in a matter of days. The *New Orleans Times-Picayune* editorialized: "IF TRUE, RESIGN." Some congressional Democrats were nervously wondering, off the record, if they had to go down to the White House and push Clinton to go—as Republicans had with Nixon. The *New York Times*'s journalistic mandarin R. W. Apple, no enemy of Clinton's, likened the case to Watergate. And George Stephanopoulos, the senior adviser who'd left the White House staff the year before, said that if the charges were accurate, we might be headed for impeachment. As Americans learned in stages what had happened, as partisan lines were drawn and partisan loyalties reasserted themselves, Clinton was able to survive. But he would have faced a very real danger of losing his presidency if he had slapped the country and the Congress in the face with the unvarnished truth from the start. Then Clinton prematurely might have been history, and Gore, after assuming the presidency, almost certainly would have won in 2000.

There were only a few Democrats willing to speak up publicly for Clinton at the outset of the scandal. As we finished one prep session, he said we'd get together for the next one at seven thirty that evening. I noted I was supposed to be a guest on *Crossfire*, but I'd cancel. Clinton said "no, no" he wanted me to do the show—he knew what we'd be arguing about—so we'd just start again on the speech a half hour later. On the show, I received a mock compliment from the conservative agitator Laura Ingraham—"I give Bob an enormous amount of credit for coming in today because a lot of President Clinton's friends haven't come forward." Then she pushed me into a corner, and I had to claim that "no one" at the White House was saying that Lewinsky was a stalker. I at least believed it wasn't happening anymore, anyway not in conversations with reporters—and what else could I say?

As we worked it over, the speech was becoming a consciously strategic document that transcended triangulation: while the target audience remained as always the broader public, for the first time in years, the imperative was to reach out to congressional Democrats. In short, Clinton had to prove to the country that he could be president and he had to hold his base. So, the first substantive section of the address celebrated "the first balanced budget in 30 years"—and swiftly moved to an issue that moved Democrats: the surplus should be set aside, "100 percent of the surplus . . . every penny . . . [to] save Social Security first." We had to get Democrats on their feet early, and embarrass as many Republicans as possible into joining them in a visual validation of the Clinton presidency. This imperative also led to a call near the top of the speech calculated to rouse Democrats again—a proposal to "raise the minimum wage." We broke our prep format and had a brief free-for-all to argue the idea. One economic adviser worried that this wasn't central to the president's domestic agenda and shouldn't be a lead-off item. I said what was central to the speech was getting all the Democrats on our side as soon and as often as possible. Americans had to see a president who was leading, in charge, validated by the reaction in the House chamber. Clinton said leave the minimum wage right where it is—right after Social Security.

The appeal on Social Security, the minimum wage, and then education was cast in a thematic framework that subtly but clearly backed off the claim of 1996 that "era of big government is over." The phrase never sat well with a lot of Democrats; they saw it as a repudiation of progressive politics. Clinton told me that he had been misinterpreted. He now redefined his position in a way that was music to Democratic ears but still stole the Republicans' clothes: "We have moved past the sterile debate between those who say government is the enemy and those who say government is the answer. My fellow Americans, we have found a third way"—this phrase, borrowed from the British Labour Party, was a particular favorite of Blumenthal's. "We have the smallest government in 35 years, but a more progressive one."

For Clinton, this was good offense, but there was one piece of defense that made no sense. It was obvious and the press speculated it might be coming. Some of Clinton's friends outside the White House, and a few advisers inside, urged him somehow to address the scandal directly. Say something at the beginning of the speech to get beyond it. Clinton showed some suggested language to Penn and me in the hallway outside the theater the day before the State of the Union. We both agreed that it was a terrible idea: Instead of a speech that showed him as presidential, this kind of preamble would define his presidency in terms of the scandal. No one would hear anything else—the balanced budget or the minimum wage. The strategic purpose here was to rise above the frenzy, not feed it. Clinton said Hillary saw it that way, too—and the decision was made. More Americans than ever might watch the State of the Union because they were fascinated with the Lewinsky story, because they wanted to see how Clinton stood up to the pressure, but they wouldn't hear a word about the allegations.

Finally, if Clinton had to bring the Democrats to his side at the beginning, he had to position himself at the end as a president speaking for the whole nation. John Glenn, in his last year in the Senate, was about to retrace his historic 1962 journey orbiting the Earth by flying on the space shuttle. So came the perfect penultimate grace note: "Godspeed, John Glenn." Both parties would cheer. And we shaped language to build on the applause: "John, you will carry with you America's hopes and on your uniform, once again, you will carry America's flag, marking the unbroken connection between the deeds of America's past and the daring of America's future."

Hillary said she wanted me to be the last person to talk with the president before he left for Capitol Hill and, this time, go up to the House Chamber as well. I replied that I had to leave as soon as the president did because I had a long-scheduled meeting in North Carolina early the next morning with a client, John Edwards, who was running for the Senate. If I was late, he would conclude that I was shortchanging him to play around at the White House. What I didn't add was that at this moment, Edwards wanted to keep distance between himself and Clinton—a preference he'd later reverse, to his peril. He didn't particularly like the idea that I was working on the State of the Union. So I said I could see Clinton before he departed for the speech and then rush to National Airport to catch the last flight to Raleigh. I was waiting in a room in the White House basement with the motorcade lined up outside. My assignment was reassurance; I could offer it because I believed in the strategy behind the speech—and beyond that, now more than ever, I knew Clinton's confidence would count as much as the content. The president and Hillary walked in, and as the few staff with them held back, the three of us stood there and I told Clinton how good the speech was, how ready he was, how well he'd do. It was a kind of *sotto voce* pep talk. He asked whether I really thought this would work. Listen, I said, this is going to be terrific.

When I got off the plane in Raleigh and got to the airport exit next to baggage claim, I paused to listen to Clinton, who was about to finish. I heard the roar as he saluted John Glenn. Democrats were now confidently with Clinton; they'd come to their feet time and again as he spoke. And the reaction that would build over time and save Clinton in the end surfaced in a *New York Times* story on reaction to the State of the Union that quoted a forty-eight-year-old mailman: "I just hope the President's dilemma passes under the rug and he can go on and lead the country." Once again I received a copy of the State of the Union inscribed by Bill Clinton—the most significant one I'd be involved in, a speech that was a high-stakes test not of this president's program, but of his very fitness to hold the office. However else he is judged, Clinton that week and that night passed an unprecedented test with flying colors—and, Penn informed me, rising poll numbers even as the scandal rolled on. The president would endure to fight another day.

When I saw Edwards, he said he was amazed that Clinton had pulled it off. But I would never do what he did, Edwards commented. Maybe he didn't do it, I answered. Edwards was skeptical; a Clinton sex scandal was a big problem in North Carolina.

I'd first met John Edwards when I went to Raleigh the year before to pitch him for the Senate race. Unknown to the public, he had amassed a fortune as a trial lawyer. He told me about his life—and then asked me about mine. It was unusual; potential clients generally want to know how many races you've won, not where you come from. His father, as the country was to hear over and over again in 2004, had been a millworker; he seemed intrigued that mine had been a tool-and-die maker—and somehow I'd gotten to Georgetown and Harvard. I liked Edwards instantly. I wanted to do this campaign, so I stopped talking about myself and pushed the discussion to strategy. His real advantage, I said, wasn't just a financial one; it was that Republicans couldn't stereotype him as an urban, out-of-touch Democrat. His life story was his inoculation. He was a high school football player from the small mill town of Robbins, North Carolina, who'd gone to the local Baptist church every Sunday and worked his way through college. That story, I said, had to be the heart of the first ad—and it would be. The other spots we ran during the campaign would consistently reinforce this narrative with a single memorable image of Edwards in a blue workshirt in front of the water tower in Robbins.

Edwards sounded like a natural populist. He said he spent his career standing up for ordinary people against powerful corporations. He told me he'd never taken a class action case, and he spoke vividly about some of the children and families he had represented. One of them, Valerie Lakey, had a large portion of her intestines sucked out by a defective swimming pool drain. She required medical care every day, 12 to 14 hours a day with a tube feeding her through her chest, for the rest of her life. Edwards took the case on a contingency; he earned nothing unless he won it—which he did, with a $25 million verdict.

He was concerned that after law school, he'd briefly been on the side of the insurance companies, at a law firm in Nashville. He didn't like the practice; he left it and returned to North Carolina with his wife Elizabeth, whom he'd met in law school. She was at the table listening to every word—and filling in the blanks with her own. Did I see a problem with his background as a trial lawyer? No, with him, it was an advantage. He shouldn't wait to be assailed for it; he should trumpet it in his own ads and preempt the attack by telling voters about the families he'd fought for.

He admitted he hadn't voted in some elections—about half, as it turned out. How would I handle that? By having him look straight into the camera, say it was a mistake, and he wasn't making any excuses; he should have voted. But there were reasons he'd missed voting, he said. He'd had to be out of town; he'd been in an important trial. If you debate this, I answered, you lose the argument. Just say plainly that you were wrong. That kind of answer could stop the questioning dead in its tracks: if reporters pressed him, Edwards could simply reiterate that he should have done the right thing and wouldn't try to explain the mistake away.

I was supposed to be pitching a potential client for the Senate. I suddenly realized there might be even more there. Edwards was a "natural," and Elizabeth was compelling. We had a common bond, she joked; we both worried about our weight. She wanted me to know that she had some pretty strong opinions of her own. So, I said, did my wife. Elizabeth would speak her mind during the campaign, and she and I would sometimes disagree. But not this day. She asked how I thought they should deal with the death of their son Wade. I knew the story already from Edwards's pollster, Harrison Hickman. Wade had been killed in a freak traffic accident at the age of sixteen just after he'd returned from Washington, where he had been a finalist in a national high school essay contest on "What It Means to be an American." My answer was that we shouldn't deal with this at all—no mention in ads, no reference in speeches. If asked, John should say it was a private family tragedy and that it had nothing to do with the campaign. Later, Elizabeth told me it was the right answer, different from what they'd heard from some other consultants, and one of the reasons I was hired.

I'd seldom encountered anyone with as many innate political gifts as John Edwards. He didn't know much about the issues; but the values he spoke about and the life he'd led made him someone who could convincingly tell people that he was on their side. He struck me as a genuinely charismatic figure with a potentially limitless political future. In the airport waiting for the plane back to Washington, I called my partner Tad with startling news: "I think I just met a future president of the United States."

Edwards and the camera were made for each other. He could read a script off the TelePrompTer flawlessly the first time; after two or three takes, he didn't need the script at all. He could take the gist of an idea, ask how long he had—"Twenty-five seconds . . . twenty-seven?"—reframe it in his own words, and hit the mark almost precisely. It looked effortless. In fact, the only problem he had was effort. We discovered as we reviewed the issues that he hadn't bothered to read the briefing books. What was second nature to most candidates who'd spent years in politics was foreign to him—for example, basic knowledge about economic policy. Instead of reading, he seemed to absorb material by talking it through. There's nothing wrong with that, I thought; FDR was a listener, not a serious reader.

More troubling was an exchange we had one afternoon as we were throwing around questions and answers in his law firm's conference room, with the usual box of Krispy Kreme doughnuts on the table. "What is your position, Mr. Edwards, on gay rights?" I asked. "I'm not comfortable around those people," was how he began his answer. You can't say that, I interjected—and I was hoping he didn't mean it. Running in North Carolina, and after his time in a Bible study group with one of Jesse Helms's advisers, he was only looking, I hoped, for a way to identify with socially conservative voters. Elizabeth reacted sternly, almost angrily: "John, you know that's wrong." She was more liberal than he was, and had been a major force in the evolution of his political views. We then shaped an answer—a kind of generalized opposition to discrimination—that he said he could live with in the state, while not undermining his future as a "national" Democrat. John and Elizabeth, once in Washington, would become good friends with leaders in the gay community like Hillary Rosen, the lobbyist for the record industry, and her partner, Elizabeth Birch, the head of the Human Rights Campaign, the most influential of the gay political groups.

Edwards manifested a visceral reaction against poverty and racial prejudice. Before and during his 2004 presidential campaign, he talked about civil rights and affirmative action to largely white audiences as well as African-Americans. The issue was personal to him, he told me after another briefing session during the Senate race. As a young man, he'd remembered siding with black classmates who were protesting the continued segregation of the homecoming court at his recently integrated high school. But his reluctance on gay rights would stay with him. As John Kerry's running mate, he would be averse to saying that he was for civil unions as an alternative to gay marriage.

(Once he entered the 2008 presidential race, Edwards would tell a New Hampshire town meeting that he had "a lot of personal struggles" with same-sex marriage: "I'm not there yet"—leaving the impression that he might get there, but for now preferred "civil unions or partnerships." He had a balancing "but": his twenty-something daughter favored marriage equality; the crowd applauded that. So when I first asked him about gay rights and he said he was uncomfortable with "those people," he was probably being genuine. He would evolve over the next decade, driven by a change in society and himself, or by the political exigencies of satisfying Democratic presidential primary voters, or by a combination of both.)

Edward's opponent in the 1998 Senate race, the incumbent Lauch Faircloth, was a pale clone of Jesse Helms. Faircloth was afraid to debate. When he accidentally bumped into Edwards at a local barbecue, Faircloth refused to be photographed shaking hands with him. It was a good day for us in the press. In midsummer, I was in New York for Gerry Ferraro's underfunded 1998 try for the Senate, when Edwards called to ask what I thought of accepting Bill Clinton's offer to come down and campaign and fund-raise for him. Clinton, in the midst of the impeachment crisis that the Republicans would overplay, was in bad shape in the North Carolina polling, and I told Edwards the visit was a bad idea. "But I already told him to come," he confessed. How much money will he raise? I asked. About $400,000 or $500,000, Edwards figured. Great, I said, because we're going to need it to make up for the political damage.

In the fall, Faircloth, whose campaign was relentlessly negative, broadcast an ad featuring footage of Clinton and Edwards together at that earlier event, and branding both as lying, "liberal lawyers." Our answer featured Faircloth—with, of all people, Bill Clinton. He had voted with Clinton hundreds of times (they were mainly procedural votes, but we didn't say that). We showed them side by side in our response spot, noted how often Faircloth had supported the president, and then asked the preposterous question: "Is Lauch a liberal?" The voters were now laughing at Faircloth. "Liberal Lauch," as the ad was known, must have been the only Democratic commercial that put Clinton alongside the *Republican* candidate. "Liberal Lauch" won a prize as the best political commercial of the year; more important, it sealed the race. Edwards won in what was hailed as an upset. Early on, most people in Washington had been skeptical when I talked about the race. How could he possibly make it in North Carolina? Democrats were getting killed all over the South. You don't know Edwards, I replied—but you will. The margin on Election Day was only 4 points, but Edwards was an instant Democratic star.

Two other 1998 races were high profile—one a come-from-behind victory; the other a famous, or infamous, defeat. The victory came in Maryland, where we were drafted in September to rescue the faltering campaign of the state's incumbent Democratic governor, Parris Glendening. We were recruited by his lieutenant governor, Kathleen Kennedy Townsend, RFK's daughter, and Barbara Mikulski, who herself was cruising to a 71 percent reelection. In California, Al Checchi, the co-chairman of Northwest Airlines, received more attention for the money he spent in the gubernatorial primary—over $40 million—than the positions he advocated. It was, to date, the most expensive statewide campaign in American history—and the most expensive loss.

My partners and I got slammed in the press for the money we'd made. One reporter even pursued a story that we'd "stolen" from the Checchi campaign by overcharging for editing at a studio we "owned." We didn't own it and it hadn't overcharged; but I had to call an editor I knew to keep it out of the paper. We were the poster boys for greedy consultants—and Checchi was now a byword for the proposition that rich candidates couldn't buy their way into office. It was a misreading of the reality. Money is an advantage, a big one, but not dispositive; the contours of the race matter and so does the temperament of the candidate. Checchi tended to assume that his success in business translated into political acumen. In contrast, during the 2000 New Jersey Senate contest, when I offered former Goldman Sachs CEO Jon Corzine a piece of tactical advice he didn't want to hear, we argued it out and then he yielded: "All right, I'll do it your way. But I just want you to know that I'd never let you invest my money." Checchi would have been a better governor than he was a candidate. And he was a class act who, in the midst of the nasty aftermath of the race, defended me to reporters.

Nationally, the 1998 midterm was suffused with the Lewinsky scandal, the Starr investigation, and the prospect of impeachment. Monica Lewinsky had produced the blue dress with its irrefutable DNA, which she had saved as a souvenir. This was stunningly unpredictable proof of Marx's dictum that history repeats itself, first as tragedy, then as farce: Nixon caught by words on tape, Clinton by a stain on a blue dress. By mid-August, the special counsel was bringing his grand jury to the White House, to question the president. Marylouise and I were spending a couple of days in Sun Valley visiting Jim Johnson and his wife Maxine Isaacs, the press secretary in the 1984 Mondale presidential campaign, now a political scientist with a cold-eyed view of the interplay between the press and public opinion. Clinton's pollster Mark Penn called: The president was going to make a brief nationally televised statement to the country after his grand jury testimony. Would I take a shot at it? "This better be good," Maxine said. In fact, the draft was easy to write: it had to be plain, straightforward, and in my view genuinely apologetic. But I knew it wouldn't be easy for Clinton to deliver it. And he didn't. Battered and angered by the questions from Starr's staff, he instead gave a speech that acknowledged the relationship, but then assailed Starr and in effect said the episode was "nobody's business" but his family's. Mickey Kantor, who was there, later told me that maybe they should have put the speech off for a day to give the president time to cool down.

The version I'd sent in was a dead letter as far as I was concerned. Then, while Marylouise and I were changing planes in Denver on our way back to Washington, I checked in with my office, which relayed an urgent message to call John Harris at *The Washington Post*. I punched in the numbers to dutifully defend Clinton. Harris had something else in mind. He had a copy of what I'd drafted. He wouldn't say where he'd gotten it; but he did tell me that "some" White House aides regarded it as "undignified," "groveling," something that would weaken Clinton domestically and overseas. I refused to comment and phoned Penn to tell him what was happening—I didn't want to be blamed for this, and asked how in the hell could this leak possibly help the president? And why did anyone on the staff want to go after me? I wasn't the one who was going to be hurt here. Penn was nonplussed and said he'd call me back. I was getting on a flight, I responded, and we wouldn't land until later that night.

The next morning in the *Post*, Harris offered an inside account of the writing of Clinton's speech—and the rejection of my version, which was now floating all over Washington. According to Maureen Dowd's column, it was "nicknamed the 'Shoot Me' draft at the White House" because it contained an apology to Monica Lewinsky and her family. This was a mess I didn't want to be in. But while I still wouldn't comment, I wasn't going to lie to reporters and deny what I'd written. One of them read the whole brief text back to me:

My Fellow Americans:

No one who is not in my position can understand fully the remorse I feel today. Since I was very young, I have had a profound reverence for this office I hold. I've been honored that you, the people, have entrusted it to me. I am proud of what we have accomplished together.

But in this case, I have fallen short of what you should expect from a President. I have failed my own religious faith and values. I have let too many people down. I take full responsibility for my actions—for hurting my wife and daughter, for hurting Monica Lewinsky and her family, for hurting friends and staff, and for hurting the country I love. None of this ever should have happened.

I never should have had any sexual contact with Monica Lewinsky. But I did. I should have acknowledged that I was wrong months ago. But I didn't. I thought I was shielding my family, but I know that in the end, for Hillary and Chelsea, delay has only brought more pain. Their forgiveness and love, expressed so often as we sat alone together this weekend, means far more than I can ever say.

What I did was wrong—and there is no excuse for it. I do want to assure you, as I told the Grand Jury under oath, that I did nothing to obstruct this investigation.

Finally, I also want to apologize to all of you, my fellow citizens. I hope that you can find it in your heart to accept my apology. I pledge to you that I will make every effort of mind and spirit to earn your confidence again, to be worthy of this office, and to finish the work on which we have made such remarkable progress in the past six years.

God bless you and good night.

As the process now rolled on toward impeachment, I agreed to talk about the speech on television. My real purpose was to make the best case I could, as I said on NBC's *Meet the Press*, that following his initial reaction, Clinton had "tried to find ways to say this"—to express genuine remorse. Tim Russert put excerpts from my draft up on the screen as he read them. "Are those your words?" he asked. I ducked slightly: "It's rather odd to get so much attention for a speech that wasn't given." But I stood by it: "I think the President would have been better off had he taken that spirit."

By now, I had a good reason to know that Clinton wasn't blaming me for writing or leaking this speech that was never spoken. Not only had he edged toward its tone, but I'd had another call from the White House after the president had ordered the bombing of suspected terrorist installations in Afghanistan and Sudan that were part of a network headed by Osama bin Laden—the first time, I think, that the name registered permanently with me. Chief of staff Bowles said the president was flying back from his post–grand jury two-week vacation in Martha's Vineyard to meet with his advisers and address the nation on television. He was dissatisfied with the draft and hoped I'd look at it while he was in the air. But, Bowles said, this was a sensitive document, closely held by the National Security Council staff. He would fax it over, and could I get suggestions quickly back to him? I did.

There was no way Clinton could avoid the skepticism of a press corps that gleefully noted that as he was leaving the Vineyard the movie *Wag the Dog* was playing on a television in the press tent. Critics who later would blame Clinton for not doing enough to get bin Laden now sneered that the bombing was nothing more than a diversion from the Lewinsky scandal. After a few hours in Washington, Clinton returned to Martha's Vineyard to finish out an unhappy vacation with his wife and daughter. Mark Penn said to me: "He would have been better off staying here" (in Washington).

In the fall, Clinton was energized by the midterm elections and frustrated with the Republican focus on scandal and impeachment. So was a billionaire named Danny Abraham, the owner of Slim-Fast, a big contributor to Clinton and someone I'd come to know in the run-up to the Israeli election. Stan Greenberg, James Carville, and I were consulting for Ehud Barak, Clinton's future partner in the process that almost made peace. Abraham was convinced we had to go after the Republicans for their fixation on impeachment. He was willing to pony up several hundred thousand dollars of his own. The president himself wanted ads and he called me to "suggest" his own formulations. By the Wednesday before Election Day, the commercials were on the air in critical districts. "This is no ordinary time," one of them began, and then indicted the Republicans for wasting millions on endless "investigations." Shouldn't America be focusing on the things that matter—Social Security, education, health care? Wasn't it time to "move on"? The Republicans were unintentionally amplifying the message with ads that highlighted the president's transgression; their irrepressible enmity toward Clinton drove their strategy into a ditch. On Election Day, Democrats didn't recapture the House, but gained five seats; it was unprecedented for the party holding the White House to pick up congressional seats in the sixth year of a presidency.

Undeterred, the Republicans in the House impeached the president and the Senate prepared for a trial as we prepared the 1999 State of the Union message. The Senate verdict was a foregone conclusion; there was nothing close to the two-thirds vote required to expel the president from office. The besieged Clinton of 1998 was, by 1999, more concerned with achievements that could bring him a last bite at history's apple than with the denouement of the scandal. I made one minor deviation of my own from the standard preps at the White House; I didn't offer the president a cigar to chew on. I assumed it would be awkward after some of the testimony in the Lewinsky case. Without a hint of self-consciousness, he complained to me: Where was his cigar? I showed up with a Cuban the next day.

After Ehud Barak won the Israeli election in May 1999, Marylouise and I were invited to another White House dinner. Clinton, an immensely talented president who longed for a legacy, was visibly exultant, perhaps because one seemed within reach that night. I was sure he had an Israeli prime minister who was ready to make big compromises for peace. A little more than twenty-four hours after Barak's victory, Greenberg and I had met with the prime minister—elect in the wee hours before we left for the Tel Aviv Airport. He said he was serious; he was going to go the last mile to find out whether the Arabs would make peace. It had to be done now: "The balance of power in the region is likely to shift against us in the next ten years." He was hardheaded about the issue—after all, he was the most decorated soldier in Israeli history. But beneath that, he had more than a touch of idealism. It touched me, leaving me almost speechless, when he told Greenberg and me that people who would never know our names might live because of what we had helped to do in that election.

The peace process was a metaphor for a Clinton presidency where high achievement was sometimes close, but in the end elusive. Clinton contributed to progress in Northern Ireland, but fell short in the Middle East and on health care—either of which would have been a history-making breakthrough. He achieved a balanced budget, but that is a legacy easily squandered, and his successor would throw the surplus away. He was a president with bad luck, some of it made by himself; some of it sown by the inveterate hatred of his partisan foes; some of it—I think he would say—due to the absence of great challenges like the civil rights revolution or the Cuban missile crisis. He was the Comeback Kid who lost and never brought back his party's majority in Congress. His strategy of tactics reelected him, but failed to build a strong sense of Democratic purpose and left too many in the party intent primarily on finding the next expedient. He was a great politician—for himself, if not always his party or its principles—but he wasn't what he most hoped to be: a great president. He is a Pied Piper for Democrats. His bigger than life political presence has overshadowed the nominees who succeeded him—and often outshines his wife, a potential nominee the next time. In the end, his legacy is nostalgia, not high achievement.

Nor did Clinton measure up to what seems to me to be the other test of presidential greatness: whether a president has renewed and enriched America's idea of itself. This is a greatness as enduring and often more so than a list of specific bills passed and crises met. Unlike Franklin Roosevelt, John Kennedy, and Ronald Reagan— whatever one thought of their policies, however one read their legislative scorecards—Clinton's framing of America's purpose will not be a touchstone for future generations. Lincoln was the quintessential president who met and in some sense even set both standards—great deeds and a lasting and animating contribution to national self-definition. Harry Truman, not conventionally eloquent and resistant to self-reflection—he never had a sleepless night, he said, about Hiroshima—is remembered and invoked because of his doughty demonstration that long odds could be overcome and an "ordinary" man could be president. One reason, aside from the Vietnam debacle, that Lyndon Johnson has faded both as memory and inspiration is that, even when he could call on JFK's speechwriters for moments of eloquence, he never added to the wellspring of American self-consciousness. I once asked Joe Lockhart, Clinton's former press secretary, what words from Clinton would be carved in stone on a memorial wall because they had left an indelible impress on the country's history and living heritage. He replied ruefully: "I guess we can't very well use 'I did not have sexual relations with that woman, Miss Lewinsky,' or 'the era of big government is over.' " The words reflected a reality. For Clinton, survival itself was his great achievement.

7

AN INCONVENIENT CAMPAIGN

I never thought I would be part of Al Gore's 2000 presidential campaign. He was inheriting Clinton's strategic team, pollster Mark Penn and ad maker Bob Squier—and, hopefully for him, some of the Clinton charisma. Bill Clinton was a great politician, even if he wasn't a great president. Al Gore might have it in him to be a great president, but he wasn't a natural politician.

For Gore, the 2000 campaign would be an inconvenient one, in which he came across as more earnest than at ease, stiff and self-consciously serious. This picture of Gore as a man uncomfortable in his own persona was "conventional wisdom." When John Kenneth Galbraith coined the phrase in 1958 in *The Affluent Society*, he was referring to economics. But the coin of the realm in politics is perception, and how Washington—and the world—viewed Al Gore was a preconception that would prove hard to escape.

On the basis of exaggerated stories about his claims to "inventing" the Internet and "discovering" Love Canal, the toxic site near Niagara, New York, that led to the Superfund law—claims he hadn't actually made—he would be cast early in the campaign as an "exaggerator" and then devastated by the stereotype after he made a few minor misstatements in his first debate with George W. Bush. Sometimes, Gore did skate close to the line; partly, I believe, this reflects a southern political tradition of casually inflated claims and attempts to please the immediate audience—a political tendency by no means confined to the South. And then there was his ingrained temptation, to which he too often yielded, to prove he was the smartest person in the room. All this would damage him considerably, even if it had little or nothing to do with his considerable capacity to be president.

But the real inconvenience was that for much of the campaign, Gore was trapped in a role that wasn't authentically his. As Carter Eskew, his friend and former colleague at the *Nashville Tennessean*, the adviser Gore most trusted in 2000, described him to me, he was in reality "a futurist populist." He was in tune more than any other political leader of his time with the speed and span of technological and environmental change, steeped in it and fascinated by it. But also, at least in his inner self, Gore had never lost touch with the populist roots of his early Tennessee politics, the belief that the role of leadership was to stand up for people against entrenched interests.

That had to be sublimated during the Clinton years—and Gore the competitor was mesmerized by Dick Morris when Morris was riding high. As the 2000 election approached, Gore took the course of least resistance and apparently greatest promise by initially positioning himself as an ideological clone of Clinton, a sanitized acolyte of Clintonian triangulation.

Tad Devine, Mike Donilon, and I were busily lining up clients with a pledge that seemed all too easy to keep—that we wouldn't be distracted by the presidential contest. When I, and later Devine, unexpectedly assumed major roles with Gore, Mike Donilon would have to do a lot of the heavy lifting in our seven Senate races. Six of the candidates would win. On balance, it would have been an impressive year for our firm even without a presidential contest.

I'd had intermittent contacts with Al Gore during the Clinton years. In 1994, he'd asked to see me and requested a favor. Rachel Carson's *Silent Spring*, the landmark 1962 exposé of the poison of pesticides, was being reissued and he'd been invited to write the introduction. Determined to do it himself, he'd started on it a few times, but now the deadline was looming. Would I draft the introduction for him? It wasn't a subject I knew, except superficially. He loaded me down with a series of articles, monographs, and books, which I hauled to Boston where I was filming the commercials for Ted Kennedy's reelection struggle against Mitt Romney. Each afternoon, as soon as the shoot finished, I holed myself up in my hotel room with the Gore materials—and he sent more and more. I stayed up for most of two successive nights and stayed an extra day to scrawl out an introduction. I included a lighthearted reference to the first President Bush's attack on him: "Having been labeled 'Ozone Man' during the 1992 campaign, a name that was probably not intended as a compliment but that I wore as a badge of honor, I am aware that raising these issues invariably inspires a fierce—and sometimes foolish—reaction." When I sent the finished product to Gore, he called to thank me and then said—I think tongue-in-cheek—that it was almost as good as if he'd done it himself.

After I had worked with Clinton and Gore on the environmental section of the 1997 State of the Union, the vice president occasionally invited me to confer with him in his West Wing office and in his official residence at the Naval Observatory—NAVOBS, as everyone shorthanded it. When he gave me a ride to my office in his motorcade after breakfast one morning, he was paging through the daily national intelligence briefing and announced in mock frustration there was nothing in here that you couldn't find in the *New York Times*. We discussed politics in general terms; but the conversations gravitated toward one subject: Carter Eskew. With Squier in charge of Clinton's media in 1996 and set to do Gore's in 2000, the vice president had fallen out of touch with Eskew. After Squier and Eskew split up in 1994, the hard feelings hardened as the years went on, and Gore said he was frustrated by the situation. He knew I worked with Eskew on Tom Harkin's Senate campaign in 1996 and now on Joe Lieberman's. How was Eskew? What was he thinking about the presidential race? I told Carter about Gore's inquiries and he replied that he just didn't see Gore calling him or bringing him in; Squier would never stand for it.

I wasn't sure this was right, but I was busily reassuring prospective clients of something I *was* certain of: Tad, Mike, and I weren't going to do a presidential campaign, period. I offered that reassurance one more time not too long before it turned out to be untrue. I was in Israel making ads for Ehud Barak, slamming the incumbent prime minister Benjamin Netanyahu, when the phone rang in my room in the Dan Hotel and someone introduced himself as Jon Corzine. He was the former co-chair of Goldman Sachs and he was thinking of running in the Democratic primary for the Senate in New Jersey. He wanted me to come to a meeting in two days. But I was in Tel Aviv, I said. Well, couldn't I just fly to London, catch the Concorde, go to the meeting, and take the Concorde back? When I reached the University Club in midtown Manhattan, a phalanx of Jersey pols was assembled to wait for the prospective candidate. Doug Schoen, Mark Penn's partner, had taken a poll, and he led me into the old-fashioned members' bar to give me the bad news. There was no way Corzine could defeat former Governor Jim Florio for the nomination. I told Doug we ought to send the pols home and chat with Corzine.

Corzine arrived and read the poll, which had positioned him as a centrist agent of small-bore change. But this isn't me, Corzine said; if he was to run, it would be to fight for big and progressive ideas. I said we ought to poll again and test what Corzine actually believed; it might have the additional virtue of making him nominatable—and electable. Schoen had new numbers during my next trip home from Israel: Corzine, the progressive, could win.

Corzine hired us to handle strategy and media—after I reaffirmed that Shrum, Devine, and Donilon would definitely not be involved in a national campaign. By the time Corzine repeated this back to me, my statement was, in Nixon press secretary Ron Ziegler's unforgettable phrase, "inoperative." But Corzine believed I had meant it when I said it—and he'd decided to stick with us anyway as long as we were still there when he needed us.

I had first sensed that we might also be there with Gore when he explicitly asked me: Would Eskew and I be willing to work with Squier? Certainly, I said, but I wasn't sure Squier would be willing to work with us. Eskew and Gore were finally talking when I stopped briefly in Washington after the Barak victory. It had been two long hard years—the campaigns of 1998, without the customary low-key off year that usually followed, then the Israeli campaign, a 5,000-mile-away, 18-hour-a-day proposition. Now I'd promised to take Marylouise on a June driving trip around France and into Italy. "Taking" her was a misnomer, since I don't drive; she was the driver and I was, as we joked, the "navigator" who more often than he admitted misread the maps. Before we left, Eskew said something was about to pop with Gore, so enjoy the trip; I'd have a lot to do when I got back.

A speech draft arrived for me on a fax machine in a hotel bar in rural France. Gore had directed his young speechwriter Eli Attie to check in with me about the remarks announcing his presidential candidacy. I would work closely with Attie, a gifted, Harvard-educated scribe who, when he couldn't reach the real West Wing with Gore, would migrate to Hollywood to write for the liberal *West Wing* on television. He was for me an invariably agreeable colleague, although his subordinates on the speechwriting staff complained after the campaign, as one of them put it, that he "kissed ass up, and kicked ass down." That's not uncommon in politics—or probably in Hollywood. The faxed draft was a well-written recitation of Penn's latest national poll, with an emphasis on "values of faith and family" and "moral leadership." I was in no position to redraw the architecture of Gore's announcement at the last minute on the fly in the French countryside—and that wasn't my mandate. I offered some edits. The speech was too obvious; it signaled that Gore was running in an uneasy combination of continuity with and contrast to Bill Clinton. The *New York Times* headlined the story: "Embracing Clinton at Arm's Length." Gore had compounded the problem and contaminated the press coverage of his announcement when he responded to a question by telling ABC's Diane Sawyer that in the Lewinsky scandal, "what Clinton did was inexcusable and . . . as a father, I felt it was terribly wrong. . . . You can imagine how I felt."

Gore told me a few weeks later that he "hated" questions like this about Clinton. There was no good answer. That first day of the campaign revealed the unhappy dilemma that would stalk Gore to the end: His strength inside the Democratic Party was that he was

Clinton's vice president, but Americans generally had reservations about rewarding Clinton with a third term. The dilemma was evident in the almost guilty ambivalence expressed in the high job ratings and low personal ratings they gave Clinton in the polling. (In a Greenberg poll just before the Democratic Convention, "warm" feelings toward him were 36 percent and "cool" feelings 52 percent.) Gore would grapple endlessly with this reality while taking heat from Democratic loyalists who assumed that what he needed to prevail was Clinton constantly stumping on his behalf. And Tipper Gore would express the frustration one day in the dining room at NAVOBS when she angrily observed that with the problems that Clinton had, he probably wouldn't have won in 1992 without the family values exemplified by the Gores. So Gore suffered from the downside of Clinton as Bush relentlessly pledged to restore "honor and dignity" to the White House; but he reaped only limited benefits and even a backlash when he tried to gain some credit—and some political points—for the economic prosperity of the Clinton years. Our numbers showed that voters gave a lot of credit to Clinton, Federal Reserve chairman Alan Greenspan, and even former Treasury Secretary Bob Rubin—and very little to Gore.

The announcement was a hobbled start, and Gore was entering three turbulent months of setbacks and changes. He'd already named former Congressman Tony Coelho as his campaign chair. Coelho, who'd resigned his post as House Democratic whip and his seat in Congress under an ethical cloud, struck some reporters as a strange choice when he was tapped in May, but he had a reputation as a no-nonsense political operator. He'd been given the authority to "shake up" the Gore operation, but it was the candidate himself who would drive the process. When I returned from my vacation, Eskew informed me he was going to do the Gore campaign—and so was I. Carter had phoned Bob Squier to set up a meeting, but Squier wouldn't return the calls. Then, on July 9, came a front-page *New York Times* story based on a long interview with Squier at his Virginia farm. Eskew's hiring, the paper said, "looked like a sure sign of panic." Squier accused Eskew of having engaged in "deeply unprofessional behavior" when their firm split up, and added that he hadn't called Carter back and he preferred to talk to the reporter. The story questioned Gore's sense of "loyalty."

For Eskew, Squier's broadside was painful; Bob had been his mentor. But for Gore, it was more than enough; his media adviser had gone after him on the front page of the nation's newspaper of record. Squier was gone from the campaign. As we put together a new media strategy team, Carter asked me if I had any objection to including Bill Knapp, Squier's partner, who was an innocent by-stander in this debacle. I wasn't about to object—and Knapp proved to be a genuine collaborator who, like Mike Donilon, was always pushing the envelope of our assumptions, both in the Gore cam-paign and later when he joined the Kerry effort in 2004. In a consult-ing field that was voluble and hardly ever self-effacing, I joked to Eskew that if we left Knapp and Donilon in a room, they might not say much, but a great script would emerge.

(Squier's departure had a sad epilogue. He soon discovered that he had colon cancer, and it hadn't been caught in time. In early 2000, Carter Eskew and I were at his memorial service at the National Cathedral. It was very public; for me, and for Carter, it was a chance to honor the man who'd brought both of us to Washington. Bill Clinton delivered a eulogy. Al Gore was sitting there stoically; he wasn't asked to speak. After we left the cathedral, Carter turned to me and said: "Sometimes, I hate politics.")

On Saturday morning, July 17, 1999, *The Washington Post* carried another story about the troubles in the Gore campaign—this time about money: Gore was spending his campaign funds "at a far faster clip" than either the leading Republican, Texas governor George W. Bush, or Gore's Democratic challenger, former New Jersey senator Bill Bradley. But that was one bad story that claimed almost no at-tention as it appeared on the same day the news broke that John Kennedy, Jr.'s, plane had gone missing on a Friday night flight to Martha's Vineyard. I had an occasional and easy relationship with him—from helping with his remarks introducing "Uncle Teddy" to the 1988 Democratic Convention to discussing his plans to start a new political magazine called *George*. He'd taken on my stepson Michael as an intern there and commissioned me to turn out an instant tribute to Pamela Harriman when she died just as the magazine was about to close its next issue. With the check he sent me for my 750-word piece came a handwritten note: "Now if you could only get Teddy to pay you by the word."

There's a well-practiced drill that instinctively takes hold when something tragic happens—again—to the Kennedy family: You check in; you see if there's anything you can do; you fend off reporters. I had a request to appear on *Face the Nation* that I was going to turn down. I told Ted Kennedy's office about it and the word came back that it was up to me, but maybe I should do the show. The airwaves were filled with too many self-professed friends sharing their thoughts about John as the search off the Vineyard went on. I could go on the show—and I did; say the right thing; and then the Kennedy office could tamp down the repeated, painful process of endless commentary, at least from real advisers and friends.

A few days later, Ted Kennedy told me there was no hope; I should work on the eulogy for a memorial service. I'd done this before, but it was harder now. I had a note John had sent me after the services for his mother, where he'd thanked me for drafting the intercessions, the prayers in the middle of mass, and then added: "We all know Uncle Teddy wrote that eulogy, but . . ." For all the pain, the words this time almost wrote themselves. There was a poem in *Words Jack Loved*, Edward Kennedy's privately printed book, that the ambassador of Ireland had recited to John's mother and father when he was born. It concluded: "And at the end of all loving and love / May the Man above / Give him a crown."

It was a sunny, humid day in New York City as Ted Kennedy continued: "We dared to believe in that other Irish phrase, that this John Kennedy would live to comb grey hair." I sat in the church hoping this man who had shepherded his family to gravesides so often could make it to the end of his remarks. He did—just barely. We all walked up the closed-off street on the Upper East Side to a subdued reception. Then I flew back to Washington and the Gore campaign.

* * *

As we struggled to accommodate the contradictions in the public mood reflected in Penn's data, I came up with an unwieldy slogan we would use for a while and then discard: "Al Gore—Change That Works for Working Families." But in the campaign itself, other big changes were in the offing. One was substantive—and hotly debated internally through the dog days of August. Bill Bradley was about to announce; his linchpin issues were political reform, poverty, and health care. The third was the one with the most potential bite for Democratic primary votes. Around the long table in Gore's dining room, political and policy advice clashed. Gore himself was unrelenting in the push to get a health care plan out before Bradley, who was preparing to campaign on universal coverage. Couldn't we somehow preempt that, I asked, without plunging into the pitfalls of the Clinton plan? No way, said Elaine Kamarck, the keeper of the centrist flame in the Clinton-Gore White House. Anyway, there just wasn't enough money. She said instead we could cover all children, let parents enroll in the same program if their children were covered, and let people buy into Medicare—a series of steps that would cover 12 million or so of the 44 million uninsured Americans. But Bradley, I argued, could kill us if Gore said that's all he was doing and nothing more. Sarah Bianchi, a whip-smart young staffer who'd been the Harvard roommate of the candidate's daughter, Karenna Gore, said we could make a bigger claim if we talked about "access" and not "coverage." After the meeting, I sent a memo to Kamarck, putting the notion of access together with a step-by-step approach. Gore could say: "As President, I will commit this nation to a series of steps to achieve universal health care . . . in the first decade of the 21st century." This formulation sounded good without providing more specifics, and it was pretty much where Gore ended up.

The campaign, as the press and most Democrats saw it, was still uninspiring, uncertain about how to handle Clinton and plagued by constant references to Gore's literally legendary "overstatements" about the Internet and Love Canal. "Goddamn," he exploded to me, "I never said either of those things." It didn't matter. Late night comedians could have fun with the charges and reporters could repeat them as accepted fact. One veteran political reporter told me that too many journalists thought they'd been conned by Clinton; they were going to be extra tough on Gore. The myths were taking hold—and laying the foundation for Bush's caricature of Gore as a serial exaggerator.

We convened at NAVOBS for a "message" meeting where Mark Penn was to present his latest polling data on a PowerPoint projected onto a screen at the front of the dining room. Gore was in a waspish mood. There were no compelling theme; he grudgingly went along with "Change That Works for Working Families," noting that it wasn't exactly a powerful frame. He'd been through some unpowerful ones like "practical idealism," which had more truth, but less appeal, than "compassionate conservative," already the trademark phrase of the Bush campaign. One question above all others was on his mind. How were we going to deal with "Clinton fatigue"? Penn, who was standing in front of his screen while the rest of us, including Gore, were sitting around a table, pumped his arms as he gave an uncharacteristically exuberant answer: "Clinton fatigue, Clinton fatigue—there is no Clinton fatigue." I glanced at Eskew—this was a perilous route for Penn to take—and then at Gore as his pollster cited findings at odds with most other surveys. Clinton had not only high job ratings, Penn said, but high personal favorables. Gore snapped that this was not what he was seeing or sensing as he traveled the country. The meeting ended on this discordant note. I commented to Penn that he had to come up with something more than dismissing Gore's concern out of hand; the guy was vice president of the United States—and the candidate.

Within days, Eskew walked into my office and said the vice president wanted a new pollster. Penn was close to Clinton and, through the Democratic National Committee, was polling for him as well. Gore wanted numbers untainted by divided loyalties. This was a problem for my firm; we were doing other business like Corzine's campaign with Penn and Schoen—and in the incestuous precincts of consulting, it's always prudent to avoid alienating fellow consultants who can recommend you to potential clients. I called Penn after he was given the word and said that it wasn't our decision. I have no

idea whether or not he believed me. There's a natural desire to conclude that the principal, especially if he might be the next president,
isn't the one responsible for your firing; it has to be the result of campaign infighting. In reality, candidates at this level are generally
strong enough to decide for themselves, but calculating enough to let
someone else deliver the bad news. I asked Stan Greenberg whether
he'd be interested in taking on Gore's polling; he demurred—for the
moment. We settled on Harrison Hickman, who was acerbic, often
sarcastic, and a bit of a loner. But I trusted his numbers. Gore knew
Hickman and felt comfortable with him. To the vice president, it
was an asset and not a liability that Hickman, the pollster who'd
been caught faxing the press derogatory information about Clinton's
draft status in 1992, was hardly a White House favorite. At least,
Gore observed, he won't tell me there's no such thing as Clinton fatigue.

In the early fall, there was a lengthy *New York Times* deconstruc-
tion of Gore's faltering campaign, citing "top advisers [who] second-
guess early moves." Gore was infuriated by the leak and the
anonymous sources; he was hypersensitive about the press, especially the *Times*. (A reporter there told me after the campaign that
Gore's repeated calls to editorial page editor Howell Raines about
the paper's editorials had achieved near-storied status among *Times*
staff. George W. Bush, he said, had never phoned Raines once.)

Through all the shifts in the Gore enterprise, then and later, there
was one constant: Carter Eskew. While he and Gore had similar
backgrounds, their personalities were very different. Gore was
earnest even if he could be funny; Eskew was funny even when he
was serious. Intellectually, Gore was methodical and deductive;
Eskew sometimes could leap across four or five steps to a succinctly
stated insight. And unlike Gore, Eskew didn't care who got credit as
long as the job got done. The vice president was intrigued by the apparent ease with which Eskew moved through life. He is a physical
fitness fanatic and a connoisseur of fine wines. He is a writer who as-
pires to finish his novel—someday; an engaging personality who's
chosen to have very few close friends; a free spirit who is a successful
hard-nosed businessman and a creative ad maker. He and I were

close—and he shared his strategic role with me throughout the Gore campaign.

As Penn departed, Gore implemented a recommendation advanced by Tad Devine to get the headquarters out of Washington—where the campaign had leased a vast expanse of space in an office building on K Street, the flagship symbol of lobbying and insider politics—and move to Nashville, which, Devine noted, had the additional advantage of reshuffling the staff without a high-profile series of firings. The news would be the move. The staff left behind could say they hadn't been fired; they just couldn't relocate to Nashville. Tad, who didn't want the job of campaign manager himself and didn't want to move to Nashville, also had a nominee: Donna Brazile. She was an African-American from Louisiana; I'd first met her when she was a field organizer for Dick Gephardt in 1988.

Early in October, Gore announced her appointment and opened our headquarters in Nashville in a vacant car dealership. At least there was a lot of parking, Eskew joked, as he prepared to make the trek to Nashville and leave behind Faith, the woman he was settling down with at the age of forty-five after many years as a happy bachelor. I had bet a skeptical Al Gore ten dollars that Carter and Faith were about to get married. It happened a month after the move to Nashville. Carter called me in London, where I had a long-standing commitment to spend a few days with the Labour Party. He and Faith were inviting a few friends over for a farewell party before he settled into an apartment in Nashville; it was actually a surprise wedding—and now I was going to miss it. The day after the wedding, I found an envelope under my hotel room door with the American Embassy's name and address embossed on the corner. I opened it to find a ten-dollar bill and a faxed note from Gore: "You win." It had been hand-delivered courtesy of the U.S. ambassador. I had to swear to Gore afterward that when I made the bet, I had no inside knowledge.

The move to Nashville was a tactic designed to signal a fresh start. The press coverage, the inside baseball about a faltering Gore and a surging Bradley, was now behind the curve of events. We were actually getting our act together. The first decision was about advertising: We'd go on early—and we'd be positive. Our polling showed that voters, even Democratic activists, knew little about Al Gore other than that he was Clinton's vice president. We had to tell his story. If we were lucky, Bradley would let us have the airwaves to ourselves for a few weeks—which is exactly what he did. Gore, who insisted he wanted to run as an "underdog," would draw contrasts with Bradley primarily in the debates. And we had to change the prevailing thematic, which, we told the vice president in another meeting, cast him as an "insider, incremental, phony" and Bradley as "outsider, big ideas, genuine." There was no way Gore could be the outsider, but as the meeting notes recorded it, there was a difference that could rally Democrats to us: "Gore fights . . . Bradley makes speeches. There have been seminal fights . . . and [Bradley] has not been around" for them; he'd announced he was leaving the Senate in 1995, at the height of the Gingrich ascendancy. He might claim to have "big ideas"; Gore had to position himself as the champion of "Democratic ideas."

We had a place to launch the strategy—at the Iowa Democrats' Jefferson–Jackson Day Dinner on October 9. Most events in a campaign are skywriting; they come and go with little discernable effect. Not this J-J Dinner. One of our direct-mail consultants, Larry Grisolano, came up with a catch phrase for the Gore-Bradley contrast: When health care, gun safety, Social Security, and education were at risk in the Gingrich Congress, the right thing to do was "stay and fight." That's what Gore had done; Bradley had walked away. On each issue, as Gore repeated the line "Stay and fight," the crowd chanted it over and over. Our field staff had planned it that way— and planted ringers around the hall to trigger the response. Bradley, in a choice that would mark his campaign and mar his chances, disdained engagement. He was, as the *Boston Globe* said, "professorial and low key," and the verdict, for a change, was good news for Gore: He "blew the roof off" the place.

Presidential campaigns have turning points, but the polls don't turn in a day. Gore, Hickman reported, had a "large lead" in Iowa, although a public poll set it at only 3 points. New Hampshire was closer and in one survey, Bradley was slightly ahead. We were now advertising heavily in the Granite State. Bradley still wasn't on the air—and he wouldn't be for another three weeks. Our spots touched on Gore's motivation: he'd seen his father defeated for the Senate because he supported civil rights and opposed the Vietnam War; then they recounted Gore's military service, his time in divinity school, and his decision to enter politics; finally they laid out the Democratic ideas he'd fight for as president. One was health care, and this was key to our next chance to confront Bradley—in a debate at Dartmouth College at the end of October.

To prepare, eight or ten of us gathered with Gore in a conference room at the Wayfarer Hotel outside Manchester, a place that had seen many famous primary nights but was now fading into genteel senescence. Carter and I were running the debate prep; Naomi Wolf, the feminist author and a secret adviser to Dick Morris in Clinton's 1996 run, was there. Her presence in our campaign was becoming another distracting sideshow. No matter how we dressed it up, the truth was that she had advised Gore to dress in "earth tones" and distance himself from Clinton; Gore, the "beta male" to Clinton's "alpha male," had to become the leader of the pack to become president. Or at least this was how I understood it. To me, it was a case of life imitating satire, that could and did make Gore an object of ridicule. But Gore valued Wolf's advice, for the moment. The press was obsessed with her, reported that she was being paid $15,000 a month, and "cited" offputting and distorted quotes from her writings, such as the claim that she advocated teaching teenagers how to masturbate. The heart of the storyline was that Gore the phony was letting a "mystery" guru reinvent him.

Carter and I noted that for all Wolf's protestations that she wanted to be anonymous, she'd leave the secure area screened off for debate prep by the Secret Service and parade across the Wayfarer lobby when journalists were there. Gore was determined to hear her out during the prep, but most of her suggestions dealt with calibrations in vocabulary, some of them minute. She did offer one zinger:

that Bradley's health plan would consume so much of the federal budget that it would "shred the social safety net"—a salvo that would be widely quoted in press reports of the debate.

But something else happened during the debate that much of the press missed or discounted at first. Sarah Bianchi was working with a health care policy expert from Emory University to dissect the Bradley proposal. First, because of its overall cost, Bradley set aside no money to keep Medicare solvent. Second, low-income Americans who relied on Medicaid would instead receive $150 monthly subsidies to cover the costs of buying insurance. We quickly agreed to attack Bradley for leaving Medicare high and dry. But Gore was skeptical when I said we ought to simplify the Medicaid point and charge that Bradley was replacing the program with a $150-a-month "voucher"—a toxic word among Democratic activists because it usually described public subsidies for students to attend private schools. Gore, the supposed exaggerator, was reluctant to stretch this far. Was it fair, could we get away with it? He wouldn't deploy the voucher attack in this first debate, but it would soon become a standard refrain that defined and undermined the health care plan that was the centerpiece of the Bradley campaign.

We motorcaded north from Manchester to Hanover, the New England hamlet where Dartmouth is located, with a single imperative in mind: to shift the issue away from which candidate would cover the most Americans. We'd also inched up our own estimate of the number of Americans covered under Gore's plan from 85 percent to 90 percent, which didn't sound significantly lower than Bradley's 95 percent. But above all, we had to highlight the weaknesses in our opponent's approach. In retrospect, I realize that this echoed the strategy that brought down Clinton's national health reform: We were, in effect, making people—in this case, seniors and Medicaid recipients—afraid of what they were going to lose.

As soon as we drove onto the Dartmouth campus, Gore took a tack that he'd thought up himself. After plunging through the crowd, he went on stage 15 minutes early and invited the audience to pose some pre-debate questions; he stayed 90 minutes after the debate to keep answering more of them. It was his way of breaking out of the trappings of office and, in a word that was overused that year, "connecting" with people. Both in the informal give-and-take and in the debate itself, he asked people their names and how the issue they'd raised affected themselves or their families. That we had planned during the prep. The staff was in a holding room, a locker room with cement floors, watching the debate on television, when Gore responded to an innocuous question about confidence in government that never even mentioned Clinton—in fact, the questioner blamed the "Republican Congress"—by bringing up the Lewinsky scandal himself: "I understand the disappointment and anger you feel toward President Clinton. I feel it myself." I was pacing in and out of the adjacent bathroom; I hit my fist against a cinder-block wall. Carter spread his hands and asked, What does he think he's doing? But then Gore did exactly the right thing as we had rehearsed it: Bradley would "wipe out Medicare and wipe out the chance to save Medicaid." He might cover a few more people in the short run, but Gore's alternative reached "almost ninety percent of Americans."

One of our runners informed us that reporters in the press room were groaning or jeering at Gore's tactics. I went there to claim victory. It wasn't just spin; Gore had confounded the central rationale of the Bradley campaign—that he was the candidate of big ideas and the proof was health care. Under assault about Medicare and Medicaid, Bradley had barely responded. Most of the press corps was having none of it. The columnists Al Hunt and Mark Shields, both of them old friends of mine, let me know in no uncertain terms that what Gore was doing was "ugly." Gore should be making an argument for himself, not tearing down Bradley. But I was looking at the contest from a different perspective: I wanted to win—and we couldn't afford to cede health care to Bradley. He never fought back and his plan became our piñata. Two months later, in a debate in Iowa, where the candidates could ask each other questions, I recommended to Gore that he continue to press Bradley on where he was going to get the resources to save Medicare. My God, Gore said, that's dangerous; the guy must have a response by now. I had a prediction I was willing to bet on: Bradley would stubbornly refuse to answer the question directly. Either he didn't have an answer or he was too proud to give one.

There were two other events in this period, one of them little noticed, that had a large impact on the outcome of the primaries. The first was the AFL-CIO's decision to endorse Gore early—something big labor had never done before for someone who wasn't already president. The other decision—to hold to the existing primary schedule—was made during the latest chapter in the perennial, arcane exercise of rewriting the party rules. The schedule as it stood provided a five-week gap following the first two contests in Iowa and New Hampshire. Winning both of them, I believed, was our best chance to avoid a long, drawn-out contest. Devine said if we did that and Bradley had nowhere to redeem himself for five weeks, he was finished; he'd be wandering around giving speeches without any votes or victories to validate his candidacy. But if it was Gore who faltered in one of the first contests, the five weeks would give him time to draw on his institutional strengths as the incumbent vice president, raise money, and target the primaries where he could prevail. Several states were anxious to fill the void, Michigan in particular. Some Gore advisers thought maybe we should compromise on the schedule. Tad was adamant; so was I. Eskew and Coelho bought our analysis. We had the votes on the Rules Committee to maintain the five-week gap, and Gore now had a pivotal advantage in the primary campaign. Oddly enough he hadn't even met Devine, who'd made his case on this—and the pivotal move to Nashville— in memos.

Bradley finally went on television on November 17, nearly a month after Gore. The ads perplexed me—and the focus groups we showed them to. They featured two retiring senators, Bob Kerrey and New York's Daniel Patrick Moynihan, the Senate's resident intellectual. Moynihan was largely unknown to voters in Iowa and New Hampshire; Kerrey was yesterday's news. The spots had a tagline—"It can happen"—obviously intended to imply that Bradley could win, in the primaries and the fall, but the focus groups didn't get it. Bradley's ads were the product of a team heavily dependent on Madison Avenue. The younger, more political staff in his campaign regarded the spots as too ethereal and argued that Bradley had to defend himself against Gore's assaults. He had to go on the offensive.

But he didn't, and both campaigns ground along on the same script all through the month of December—with two attention-grabbing exceptions. First, Bradley suddenly cancelled campaign appearances because of an irregular heartbeat that his staff then said had "righted itself." It would happen again, but it had little if any impact on the primary race—maybe because Bradley never seemed to get that close to the nomination. The second exceptional event brought together a Democrat and a Republican, Bradley and Arizona senator John McCain, Bush's principal challenger. They signed a joint pledge to forgo large, unregulated campaign contributions to their national committees if they were nominated. At their joint appearance, Bradley took a swipe at Bush, and McCain said Gore needed "a controlling legal authority"—echoing the unfortunate phrase the vice president had used to defend himself during the investigation into his 1996 fund-raising. The event commanded the cameras; it was, the instant wisdom went, a boon for these two reformers. But after talking with Devine, Eskew and I told Gore that in reality, it was an unexpected break for us. Independents in New Hampshire could vote in either the Democratic or the Republican primaries. They preferred Bradley to Gore, but they were falling fast for McCain. If Gore won Iowa, making Bradley look less likely to win the Democratic nomination, his lovefest with McCain had just signaled even liberal-leaning independents that it was all right to vote for this Republican. And the end, they would, letting Gore eke out a narrow victory in the Granite State.

The image of Gore as a dominant if not always fair debater was reinforced in early January 2000 as Iowa and New Hampshire neared.

The morning before a prime-time debate at the University of New Hampshire, we committed big news with the biggest endorsement we could secure—Ted Kennedy's. He had enduring appeal to the Democratic faithful. The first time he stumped in Iowa for Gore after the endorsement, Michael Whouley, the laconic, bottom-line

Boston operative who was overseeing our organization there, said he'd never seen anything like this. Could we just bundle Kennedy onto a plane and send him back every day? But Kennedy's nod was singularly important for another reason. He was "Mr. Health Care," the person Democrats trusted most on the issue. As we discussed a possible endorsement, I was honest with Kennedy: The press was going to ask him why he wasn't for Bradley, who had a plan for universal health care. The answer, Kennedy and I decided, was obvious: The Bradley plan was impractical and it did shortchange Medicare. Besides, Kennedy added, he'd been fighting to pass health reform and tackle poverty for years. Now Bradley was running on the issues, but he'd never done anything about them while he was in the Senate.

In the University of New Hampshire debate that followed the Kennedy endorsement, Gore wheeled out the senator's imprimatur on health care while Bradley gritted his teeth and then in effect assailed both Gore and Kennedy for being trapped in "the Washington bunker." Going after Kennedy was not the best way for Bradley to defend himself on health care. The "bunker" reference also gave the vice president an opening he could exploit relentlessly in the days ahead: Yes, he'd been in the Washington bunker—"I stayed and fought against the . . . Gingrich Congress"—while Bradley had shrugged and walked away.

As Donna Brazile and I walked across the darkened campus of University of New Hampshire toward the press room, she was frantic about an impending media squall of her own making. In an interview, she'd said that African-American Republicans like Colin Powell were just tokens: Republicans would "rather take pictures with black children than feed them." Did I think she had to resign? For God's sake, no, I said. Sure enough, a Republican official demanded that Gore fire Brazile for "racist" remarks. I regarded what she said as true. So did Gore, he told me. He just wished she hadn't said it. They both talked to Powell, and I took every press call I could to defend Donna and downplay the incident. Things like this make headlines, but they're just a sideshow for voters, who tend to focus on real issues unless a campaign gets trapped in the quicksand of controversy.

The next debate was in Iowa on January 8, where Bradley had been tempted to make an all-out effort, apparently by the October poll that showed him only 3 points behind Gore. It was a reasonable temptation given the history, which John McCain was about to repeat, that candidates who skip Iowa don't get nominated. We played along, warning reporters that Bradley was a genuine threat in the state. We wanted him competing there. But that spin was pretty wobbly by the morning of the debate. The *Des Moines Register* now showed Gore ahead, 54 to 33 percent. The debate was about to administer the final blow.

Gore of course would pound away at Bradley's health plan, but he had another, literally more graphic attack prepared—one that much of the press would regard as patently unfair. We reviewed it and Gore rehearsed it in his hotel suite where he'd just climbed off an exercise machine and was having breakfast. In the Senate, Bradley had opposed a disaster relief bill for farmers after floods had inundated their fields in 1993. We had invited a farmer to sit in the audience. When Gore had his chance to question Bradley, he would say: "Let me introduce a friend to you. Chris Pederson is here. Could you stand up, Chris? Why [Senator Bradley] did you vote against the disaster relief for Chris Pederson when he and thousands of other farmers here in Iowa needed it after those '93 floods?" How in the hell was Bradley going to reply? Gore asked. Well, sir, our issues director David Ginsberg answered, there was something he could say and so there was a risk here. There had been two measures—the original bill that Bradley supported, and a supplemental amendment that he opposed. Well, Gore worried, maybe he had to give up this question. What else did we have? I interrupted to push Ginsberg: Didn't farmers need both provisions? Yes, probably—and if Bradley defended himself by pointing to the first bill, Gore could still win the overall argument. It just wouldn't be as clean a shot. But there was something else, I continued: Bradley almost never deigns to respond, and he probably won't even remember the vote anyway. Gore decided to take the chance.

In the holding room with Eskew and Bill Knapp, I watched Gore pop the question—and a flustered Bradley fall apart. All he could say was: "This is not about the past. This is about the future." Reporters seldom call a political debate on the spot, but this one was different, even if they thought Gore's shot was underhanded. Backstage afterward, Gore was almost giddy; when Eskew and I came in the room, the candidate and his daughter Karenna were grinning from ear to ear. I was carted off to do some post-debate interviews.

We had one more face-to-face confrontation in Iowa: the "Black-Brown Debate," to outlanders a surprising event in what they assumed was a white-bread state. Democratic caucus goers were activists who cared about civil rights—and there was a modest but growing minority community in the state. On Air Force Two, flying back to Iowa from the Martin Luther King, Jr., holiday observance in Atlanta, we briefed Gore on the challenge we assumed Bradley would make: Why hadn't Bill Clinton signed an executive order to outlaw racial profiling at the federal level? Gore could respond by promising to do that as president, and then say that Clinton didn't need a lecture from Bradley or anyone else about standing up for civil rights. Gore then had to take the offensive. Why hadn't Bradley spoken up when New Jersey State Police were found to be arresting people for "DWB" (driving while black)? We had invited Newark mayor Sharpe James to the debate to back Gore up: after the debate, James would conveniently claim that he had asked Bradley to take on the issue and Bradley had done nothing.

Buried in most of the post-debate stories was a reference to an event that would have a shaping, even a decisive influence on the ultimate outcome in 2000. Both Gore and Bradley were asked about Elian Gonzalez, the Cuban child whose mother had drowned while fleeing with him to Florida. His father was demanding that Elian be returned to Cuba. Both candidates said the father ought to come to the United States where he could freely express his wishes. The question didn't strike anyone as a political trip wire.

There are times in campaigns when the outcome seems sealed. Even the taciturn Michael Whouley now predicted that we'd win Iowa comfortably. Defying my long-held superstition, Eli Attie and I didn't even bother witing a concession speech. With Eskew, we took the victory draft to Gore in the late afternoon of caucus day,

January 24; the wan light outside the hotel window was fading and the caucuses would soon gather and divide into Gore and Bradley supporters. Where's the other draft? Gore wondered with a half-serious tease in his voice. I admitted there wasn't one; write it, he said. We didn't. At a raucous celebration in a cavernous hall at the Iowa State fairgrounds, Gore was soon thanking the state's Democrats for "the biggest victory in the history of the contested caucuses here in Iowa." The man who'd written off the state during his floundering 1988 campaign had just buried Bradley 63 percent to 35 percent. Bradley's lame explanation was that he'd bettered Ted Kennedy's 31 percent against Jimmy Carter. When I next talked to Kennedy, he tartly observed that that wasn't exactly a famous victory.

We flew to New Hampshire in the middle of the night and Air Force Two landed just ahead of a snowstorm. As Gore went off to his first stop, Eskew and I checked out a hall we'd rented for debate prep, then headed down the street to a Dunkin' Donuts. Soon we were in the midst of a full-scale blizzard. The staff that hadn't been on Air Force Two, including our issues staff, wasn't going to make it to Manchester for at least two days. We shifted debate prep to a makeshift setup at the hotel where we were staying. We could practice whenever Gore wasn't being plowed through the snow to campaign stops. Attie would take and type the notes. Eskew would play Bradley. As usual, I'd moderate the mock debates, and this time, ask all the questions. We had to scrawl numbers on the yellow legal pad pages we held up to indicate how much time was left to finish an answer. I joked to Gore that we didn't have to worry about the trappings of the vice presidency now. It was just four or five of us in a room. We anticipated that a different Bradley might show up this time—otherwise, why bother to rehearse at all?

But I was surprised when Judy Woodruff of CNN, a longtime friend of mine who nonetheless came down hard on candidates I worked for, opened this debate with a brutal question. She suggested that Gore had distorted Bradley's health plan and then chal-

lenged him to respond to the charge that "you will do almost anything to win." Gore insisted that he'd said nothing that was "untrue." In what was more than a role reversal—Gore had gone after
Bradley's positions, not his character—Bradley repeatedly bashed
the vice president's honesty and ethics. Our game plan was for Gore
to defend his integrity; hold his ground on the issues—don't give an
inch, for example, on health care—and call out Bradley when he
stepped over the line. At one point, Gore shot back: "If you want to
talk about a higher standard, you need to live by it." The high drama
reached its lowest level when Bradley, who'd been reluctant for so
long to engage at all, compared Gore to Richard Nixon. The candidate's wife Tipper, who was watching the debate in a glass-
partitioned cubicle next to the one we were in, was beside herself. I
said we were going to be fine.

The aftermath was predictable in one sense: the press celebrated
the new, more aggressive Bradley. But in the larger sense, we had to
hope that we were right about voter reaction—that this Bradley not
only sounded like the conventional politician he'd claimed he
wasn't, but that the tone of his assault on the party's likely nominee
would alienate Democrats. At first, this seemed right on the mark.
Harrison Hickman reported that through Thursday night, 24 hours
after the debate, Gore, riding the momentum from Iowa, was leading 53 percent to 38 percent in New Hampshire. But Hickman had
an important caveat: "While Gore's personal ratings among undecided voters are fine, most look more like Bradley voters in terms of
their overall opinions, especially toward Clinton." Moreover, he
warned, the survey had been completed Thursday night—prior to
the State of the Union speech that would weld Gore and Clinton's
images together on every television screen in America.

Before Gore left Manchester to fly to Washington for the speech,
I told Carter Eskew that I wished there was another blizzard that
would ground the plane. When Tony Coelho had gleefully informed us weeks before that he'd arranged with the president to
schedule the State of the Union to give Gore a boost just before New
Hampshire, we'd asked him if that was definite. Thinking we were
worried that it wasn't, he'd reassured us that it was all set. All we

could do now was hope for the best—and the general reaction the day after was that the event had been an unalloyed blessing for Gore. Clinton had singled him out for praise five different times after mentioning him only twice the year before.

Then the tracking polls started to come in. Gore was slipping and the double-digit lead was suddenly around 7; the debate played some role and so did Bradley's continuing attacks. And the Gore who in recent months had become his own man had looked like a second-fiddle Kewpie doll bobbing up and down at the State of the Union. As Eskew put it, the image had "reinfantilized" him and turned him into a Clinton surrogate just as soft and undecided voters who gave Clinton low personal marks were making a final decision about how to mark their ballots.

Gore went into a nonstop campaign blitz, and I called Ted Kennedy in Hyannisport to ask if he'd return to New Hampshire this last weekend. He'd thought this thing was done and won, he said. It wasn't—and I described the trends. We needed his help. Once Kennedy's with you, he's there all the way. He showed up Sunday for a huge rally in a barn in a town called Somersworth. He delivered a compelling comparison of the Gore and Kennedy families' commitment to public service and progressive values. It was a call to tribal loyalty, and when Kennedy introduced him, Gore seemed to catch the charisma gene. He fired up the crowd with a spontaneous and passionate speech about his vision for the country and an unrelenting indictment of the devastating effect of Bradley's health plan on Medicare and Medicaid. Without Kennedy's imprimatur on health care and all-out advocacy, Gore probably would have lost a primary that was now too close to call.

(I saw a vivid demonstration of Gore's feelings about Kennedy months later during a convention planning session. Someone suggested that Kennedy was too liberal, too much of a lightning rod, to be accorded a speaking slot in the sharply limited prime-time network coverage of the convention. I was about to say that this was ungrateful, unacceptable, and I don't know what other words would have tumbled out, when Gore, his voice rising a notch, settled the issue: We might not be sitting around this table, he said, with the nomination secure, in complete control of the convention, if it wasn't for Teddy. He was speaking; he was speaking in prime time—and that was that.)

Our collapsing polls in New Hampshire were political purgatory, but Election Day itself felt like hell. The early exit polling showed Bradley beating us pretty comfortably. I got word that CBS pollster Dotty Lynch had concluded there was something wrong with the "exits"; after analyzing the demographic breakdowns, she'd cautioned her own network that the New Hampshire electorate didn't "look like the mailing list for the Nieman-Marcus catalogue." But we weren't taking any chances. Gore was out there on a campaign bus scheduled to return in the early afternoon to the turreted, Disneyland-like hotel where we'd been ensconced for the week. We phoned the bus, told Gore about the exit polls, and kept him on the road. Tim Russert called me with more bad news: the second wave of exits was holding for Bradley. We were going to lose. What were we going to do? I could hear the excitement in his voice—not because he was against Gore, but because he loves a good political fight.

Then Michael Whouley came up with a last-ditch scheme: send Gore into areas of southern New Hampshire where there was a lot of Bradley support among more upscale voters and commuters who worked across the border in Massachusetts. Many of them cast their ballots late in the day after driving home. Gore's motorcade—candidate, press, Secret Service, and police—could snarl traffic and keep some of the commuters from ever getting to their polling places or even trying to. We were prepared to try anything. But we didn't share the rationale with Gore; we just sent him on his way. Soon Whouley heard from an irate vice president. He was causing a massive traffic jam and it was time to call off this last-minute foray. Whouley was reluctant to tell him the truth, instead explaining that we still had to fight for every last vote. But voters, Gore snapped, were having trouble getting to the polls. Whouley cleared his throat: "But sir, they're mostly Bradley voters." He didn't need to say anything more. Gore got the point and continued on, although there wasn't enough time to go on to the last stop Whouley had planned. The traffic was just impossible.

Gore was back in the hotel for a few minutes, then we all left for the 25-minute drive to the Holiday Inn and Convention Center in Manchester where our "victory" celebration was being held. Marylouise and I were in a staff car with Carter and his wife Faith. His cell phone brought us the word that the last wave of exit polls was in—and Gore was going to lose, probably by 5 points. We glumly repaired to the hotel's executive offices. The vice president and Tipper were in a room off to the side. A few of us gathered and fretted in the larger, desk-filled space just outside: Karenna Gore and her husband Drew were there; so was Marty Peretz, Gore's mentor at Harvard and the owner of *The New Republic*, with his wife Anne. We listened for any hint in the tone of Whouley's usually deadpan voice as he trolled the telephone for real results.

John Kerry unexpectedly materialized, virtually the only outsider that night who made it past the checkpoints and the Secret Service. Gore was grateful to him; he'd given his endorsement even before Ted Kennedy had, at a low point in November with Bradley moving up in New Hampshire. When Kerry and I had discussed it, he had expressed one big concern: Were we really in a position to pull this thing off? I replied that we were already turning the race around; the press just didn't see it that way yet. I was also aware that Kerry wanted to be the vice-presidential nominee. His chances would have been better if he had come nowhere near the back room that night.

Like everybody else, Kerry had heard about the exit surveys— which were withheld from the public until the polls closed, but were the common currency of political insider trading all through Election Day. When Kerry arrived, Gore came out to greet him and promptly got an earful, as Kerry expounded on why Gore was losing in New Hampshire. The stump speech didn't work; he didn't have a clear focused message—the critique went on and on. Tipper took me aside and told me to somehow get Kerry out of here. I interrupted him to say that we had to make him available for television interviews as soon as possible; he needed to go up to his room and shave. Tipper didn't forget that night and that moment—and when the time came, she was distinctly unenthusiastic about picking Kerry for vice president.

We were tossing a football around in the outer office anxiously glancing at Whouley, glued to the phone. Suddenly, he finished a call, matter-of-factly said that he now had enough real results from bellwether areas, and we were going to win—as it turned out, by 6,000 votes, or just over 4 percent. The exit polls had simply been wrong, even if the networks didn't know it yet. Tipper embraced her husband, and then Gore sat at a desk in the thin light of the adjacent office, reviewing his victory statement with Eskew, Attie, and me. For the most part, I didn't care what Gore said now. For all intents and purposes, the contest for the nomination was over. The upside of Tad Devine's calculus was about to be proved right. Bradley, defeated in both Iowa and New Hampshire, was now entering a five-week-long political limbo with nowhere to bounce back. John McCain's New Hampshire upset over George W. Bush left Bradley in a media limbo, too. The next step was a Republican primary in South Carolina seventeen days away, and that would suck up all the press oxygen.

Gore was now the first Democrat in twenty years to win competitive contests in both Iowa and New Hampshire. On March 7—Super Tuesday was getting earlier and earlier with each cycle—he routed Bradley in all sixteen states, including California and New York. Gore would become the only nonincumbent in either party ever to sweep all the primaries and caucuses. On the Republican side, McCain won a few more contests, but Bush, too, had the nomination wrapped up. His campaign had smeared McCain's war record, a pretty daring move for a draft evader—and anonymous sources in South Carolina had spread the tale that McCain had a black child. (He and his wife had adopted an orphan from Bangladesh.) We hadn't won pretty, either. Gore had shredded Bradley, but at least he'd done it on issues and in open debates against an opponent who, we discovered early on, was too "principled" or just too proud to respond.

But now, on the crest of victory, we had a problem that was the one great failing of our primary campaign and in part my fault: we had failed to lay down a foundation, a thematic predicate, for the battle with Bush. Like Clinton in the general election in 1996, we'd prevailed in the primaries with a strategy of tactics, adopted at a time when Gore was in deep trouble. We'd had to dismantle Bradley. But as Carter Eskew put it, what was Gore going to say now? Our campaign was about to enter a fog of missteps in which Gore would increasingly lose ground to his opponent. He would have a brief comeback in July, then fall 17 points back following the Republican Convention.

We didn't start out there. After Super Tuesday, in a curious meeting room that featured a spiral staircase to nowhere at the Loew's Hotel in Nashville, we held our first post-primary strategy session. Sitting on one of the steps, I listened to Hickman report on the latest polling. Gore was ahead of Bush—by only 2 to 4 points, but he was ahead. There were issues we tested in the polling that worked against Bush and for Gore: Social Security, where Gore would use the surplus to shore up the trust fund and Bush favored privatization; Medicare and prescription drug coverage for seniors; the Patients' Bill of Rights to guarantee that people could pick their own doctors. Implicitly, there was a larger theme here, a very Democratic one—that Gore was standing up for the majority of American families and Bush was for special interests. But there was wariness about abandoning the received orthodoxy of Clintonian centrism. I didn't share it, and Gore sometimes wandered on his own into more progressive territory. Bush's big tax cut, he soon charged, was designed to benefit "special interest donors"; it was "completely different from the agenda of the American people."

There was another idea that intrigued Eskew and me. With Gore getting very little credit on the economy, Bush was constantly repeating a clever line that was sinking in—that the prosperity had been created by the American people, not government. Hint, hint—not Clinton, not even Greenspan, certainly not Gore. Why couldn't we carve out an advantage on the economy as our issue not by running on past achievements but by setting out an economic strategy for the future? It wouldn't be easy; after a while, people tend to take good times for granted—and Bush was doing his best to reassure them that, except for a tax cut, he wasn't all that different on the economy. Gore shouldn't, and couldn't, let him get away with it. So we had to move on issues and set a message framework. We had to decide.

But Gore already had. He cut into the discussion to declare that he intended to spend the next several weeks focusing on campaign finance reform. Almost everyone in the room was taken aback. This was playing to weakness, to Gore's greatest vulnerability on a field where his credibility was tattered by the continuing probes into the 1996 campaign. I said this was the wrong road to take; so did Eskew and others, but Gore was immovable and abrupt. I later said to Eskew that Bradley had lost the nomination, but captured Gore's head. The vice president resented the charge that he had engaged in shady fund-raising; his resentment was amplified because, as he saw things, it was Clinton who had sent him off to do it. The unfortunately unforgettable image was Gore's visit with contributors at a Buddhist temple—roll the videotape, and television stations frequently did. Gore had been a political reformer in the Senate and he was determined to reclaim that status, to get his reputation back. He planned, he announced at our post–Super Tuesday session, to focus on campaign finance for two weeks and then advance a new reform plan of his own. He ordered us to get the plan—and a speech—ready.

To launch his push and to push back against his own skeptical campaign staff, he almost immediately gave an interview to the *New York Times* proclaiming that "he would make overhauling the campaign finance system a central theme of his presidential bid." The story, predictably, noted that "he brushed aside fresh questions about his own conduct." He even made a visit to independent Minnesota governor and former pro wrestler Jesse Ventura to talk about how to reform the system. In the midst of all this, he had another inescapable task: to raise money, in large amounts and large contributions, for the Democratic National Committee, which could broadcast ads on his behalf. Without that, he'd be unilaterally disarming himself against a Bush campaign that had spurned federal funding for the primaries and so could spend unlimited amounts until the Republican Convention. But when Gore appeared at high-profile fund-raisers, he was accused of hypocrisy. He wanted stories trumpeting his commitment to reform, yet there was hardly one that didn't rehash the allegations against him. In essence, we were running against ourselves.

Coming up with a reform plan was equally painful. We spent hours around the dining room table at NAVOBS, surrounded by flip charts, as Gore X-ed out options and drew arrows to connect different proposals. In the end, what we had was an endorsement of the McCain-Feingold bill to ban the very money Gore was raising for the DNC, along with something entirely new—an endowment, to be funded by tax-deductible corporate and individual donations that would provide public funding for Senate and House candidates. Bush attacked it. Gore didn't pick up votes; in fact, he was losing them. But he got something else he coveted: Common Cause praised his plan. Fair or not, Gore as the tribune of campaign finance reform didn't ring true.

The damage was clear when we held our next strategy discussion with the candidate on April 3. Gore, we reported, had "slipped" in the polls; Bush had "gained." We had to "focus on issues that matter to people—education, Social Security, health care . . ." To placate Gore, the PowerPoint added that this "doesn't mean ignoring campaign finance reform; [it] means smart targeting." This was a euphemism for letting the issue drift away. Gore pounced on it. Well, he retorted, I'm not giving this up. In the weeks ahead, he mentioned campaign reform less and less.

At the meeting, we proposed a defining contrast for the campaign, although I added that we didn't yet have the right words because the ones we did have were worn and overused: "Gore is on your side; Bush is not on your side." I knew that, even if we found a fresh phrase, it would be hard to implement this. For me, it represented the fundamental difference between the parties and the candidates. But others in the campaign thought we had to replicate Clinton's nonideological appeal. Our recommendation reflected that ambivalence as we temporized by suggesting that "on your side" might play better in industrial Pennsylvania, Ohio, and Michigan—and "W [stands] for wrong" might be more effective in "new economy" states like California. We were hamstrung by our own internal politics—and I felt constrained by the stereotype that I was always pushing a populist line. "W stands for wrong" had a short rhetorical life; it was heard publicly from Gore only a few times. The first time he heard it, Gore winced; he didn't like it. It was juvenile to attack someone's name. We had to raise the stakes, not lower them. The idea behind "on your side" might be right, Gore said; but for God's sake, we couldn't say it that way; "on your side" was Dukakis. In the weeks that followed, we did move on—but not to a coherent message and our strongest issues. Instead, we plunged deeper into the fog.

The numbers we'd reviewed on April 3 showed our "primary halo" had "worn off" because "we've talked about campaign finance"—and "Elian." But at least campaign reform had been a choice the candidate himself had made. The arrival of a six-year-old Cuban boy in Miami was a matter of fate. And the way Gore handled the controversy about sending him back to Cuba became more proof, in a Bradley phrase that the Bush campaign soon picked up, that Gore would "do anything to get elected." Gore didn't romanticize the Castro regime or blame the United States for isolating it. In the Senate, he'd been an arms controller, but also a hard-liner toward the Soviet Union and communism in general. At one point during the Elian firestorm, he asked me: Would we have sent a child back to East Germany after his mother died trying to get him across the Berlin Wall?

The honesty of Gore's position was in doubt because a bright thread of expedience ran through the fabric of his public image. He was in fact less expedient than a lot of politicians—and stubborn in pursuing politically charged causes like global warming. But he could come across as transparent and incredible, explaining, for example, that he missed some of the FBI's most damaging questions about possible White House fund-raising violations in 1996 because he was drinking a lot of iced tea during the meetings and was often in the bathroom. We cringed when we heard that. The Bush campaign skillfully exploited every such episode to reinforce the

argument that Gore was untrustworthy, artificial, an untruthful exaggerator. Coming from Bush today, those words would sound
purely self-descriptive. But Gore's position on Elian, however principled, represented a hard case that would leave a lasting impression
in the public mind—ironically, without achieving the political purpose that was imputed to him. I have little doubt that if Clinton
hadn't sent Elian Gonzalez back, enough additional Cuban-
Americans in Florida would have voted for Gore to send him to the
White House despite the voting irregularities.

The view of Gore as crassly political was underscored by an accident of timing. Tad Devine had been making the case that the pun-
dits who concluded that Florida was a lost cause were wrong. Gore,
who yearned to be competitive somewhere in his native South,
bought Devine's analysis, even though he still had yet to meet him.
So, in an unfortunate coincidence, Gore announced in mid-March,
just as the Elian issue was building to a boil, that he intended to go
after Florida's 25 electoral votes.

Elian Gonzalez's fate would play out on cable television and then
in the streets of Miami, with the drama heightening the juxtaposi-
tion of Clinton and Gore on opposite sides of the issue. Tony Coelho,
who was in contact with leaders in the Cuban exile community, reported that to satisfy them, Gore had to issue an unqualified call to
keep Elian in the United States. He did. Eskew and I realized there
would be media backlash, but believed that on balance it was the
right political move. Donna Brazile had her doubts: Didn't the child
belong with his father? That feeling was widely shared among
African-Americans. George Bush took the same position as Gore;
but he got a free ride. Everyone expected him to side with a Cuban
exile community that was heavily Republican, but had recently
elected one of its own, our client, as the Democratic mayor of Dade
County. Three weeks later, the surprise raid that whisked Elian out
of his great uncle's home and onto a plane to Cuba enraged Miami—
and let the Bush campaign mock Gore, who claimed to be the most
influential vice president in history, as "ineffectual."

For us, April was a wasted month, dominated by the ugly stories
about Elian, another Justice Department interrogation of Gore

about campaign finance offenses in 1996, and a series of Bush speeches and events that dominated the dialogue on big issues. For example, Gore was frustrated when Bush grandly pronounced that he was committed to making health care accessible to every American, but then, as Gore groused, proposed a "piddly" $3 billion for community health centers. Why, he asked me, was the press letting Bush get away with this? It wasn't a health care plan; it was a hoax. I replied that it was because the press was consumed—and we were trapped—in the coils of the sexier news about Elian and fundraising scandals. And while we had a communications team, we hadn't settled on what to communicate consistently.

Coelho came to our office in Washington to discuss firing our press secretary Chris Lehane, a wiry thirty-two-year-old fast-thinking, even faster-speaking veteran of the Clinton White House. Lehane had become known for damage control and counterattack during the Whitewater investigation. He was inexhaustible and cocksure—or, as Coelho complained, unpredictable and uncontrollable. Carter Eskew didn't want to let him go, and neither did I. Coelho had a point—and the sharp end of it would hit me later in the Gore campaign and especially in 2004 with Kerry. But I pointed out now that Lehane was good at planting negative stories, and packaging and branding a round of campaign events. For example, Gore would soon embark on a "Progress and Prosperity" tour. Sure, Lehane wasn't deferential to Coelho, Eskew, me, or sometimes even the vice president of the United States. But we promised we'd work to keep our press secretary in-bounds. So instead of firing him, while he traveled with Gore, we hired a new communications director in the headquarters—Mark Fabiani, someone I'd judged in college debate who'd made a name for himself defending the Clintons during the spin wars that surrounded the Whitewater investigation. It took some persuading to pry Mark out of La Jolla, California, where he was now in business, and onto a plane to Nashville; the last time I'd recruited him was for Al Checchi's campaign. Was this going to be another disaster? he asked me. It was typical of him. He was dour, often downbeat, not a happy warrior; but when he wanted to be, he was a first-rate communications planner and crisis manager.

Still, communications planning can too easily become a substitute for setting a strategic course and sticking to it. That's what Bush was doing. He said he would restore honor to the White House; gave the impression that he wouldn't endanger the economy, that we should share the proceeds of prosperity in the form of a tax cut; he promised to strengthen the military but pursue a "humble" foreign policy. He was, in short, a safe pair of hands—not a hard-shell conservative but a compassionate conservative, not a risk but comfortable change. Gore instead spent the spring of 2000 ricocheting from gimmick to gimmick. He couldn't win as Clinton. He couldn't be the un-Clinton; Bush already was. And we couldn't forge a consensus inside the campaign to kick over the traces and move beyond Clinton's nonideological 1996 model to an edgier message that reflected Eskew's description of Gore's authentic identity as a "futurist populist." It might have been there inside him, but we weren't getting it out. We moved from "School Days"—where Gore spent an entire day in a single school, visiting classrooms, conferring with teachers and parents—to "Working Family Days," seasoned with periodic policy announcements to pick up the pace.

Our firm and Knapp's were collaborating on DNC ads that would be aired in early June. The first one focused on prescription drug coverage for seniors. The issue was a real contrast with Bush, even if it still left us without an overall thematic framework. But that was the heart of the matter. Each time I flew to Nashville, I found Eskew increasingly restless and dissatisfied. We were a collection of issues, he complained, a succession of campaign weeks branded with one label after another.

Our failure on message was compounded by a more comprehensive sense of a campaign in disarray. New questions were being raised about Coelho's financial dealings as the U.S. ambassador to an international exposition in Portugal. A May 15 *New York Times* story reported, accurately, that we'd "drifted and lost focus." Gore was "trailing Bush in almost every demographic category"; Coelho was also constantly at loggerheads with Brazile. One anonymous "senior campaign official" put the blame on the candidate: "Gore obviously has to step up his game . . ." Gore, who detested process stories like this, called me and asked: "Do you really think this thing is work-ing?" Not yet, I said honestly, but we'd get there.

One palliative was to hold weekly meetings in Nashville of our top advisers and consultants. But there was a more radical treatment in store. After the *Times* story, Eskew called me and said the vice president was going to be at the next weekly session and wanted me to bring Tad Devine along. The site this time wasn't going to be the headquarters, but a skybox in the empty off-season stadium of the Tennessee Titans. Twelve or fifteen of us—less a strategic core than a strategic squad—waited around for almost an hour; people were joking and chatting casually to disguise their apprehension. What was Gore going to say—especially after that lousy story in the *Times*? He was down the hall where he'd asked Coelho and Brazile to join him and Eskew for a private talk. I assumed Gore was con-ducting a no-holds-barred dissection of why his campaign was melt-ing down. When he finally strode into the skybox, he looked at us one by one and greeted each person by name. At a certain point, he saw someone whose face he didn't recognize, although he knew per-fectly well who he was. Devine, a former college basketball player, stood and introduced himself: "Hello, Mr. Vice President, I'm Tad Devine." The room filled with laughter and the tension broke.

Gore was both self-possessed and deadly serious as he delivered a combination pep talk and verbal head banging. This was the great-est campaign team in the world. He wasn't going to make any changes. But some people were responsible for leaks that were hurt-ful and self-destructive. He wasn't singling anyone out, just saying the leaks now had to stop. He had no doubt we were going to win. But to do it, he added in an unspoken but unmistakable reference to the *Times* story, we all had to raise our game.

He left, the meeting ended, and once we were alone, Carter had a one-sentence description of the preliminary session with Coelho and Brazile: "Oh God, it was brutal." There weren't going to be any changes; well, not really. Eskew and I now had a task—to persuade Devine to take over the management of the campaign. The three of us went to dinner at the Sunset Grill, one of the two or three places we frequented in Nashville. We broached the subject with Tad. No, no, he said, he couldn't do it; he couldn't leave his wife and family alone in Washington for the next five months. I reminded him that he was the one who had suggested moving the headquarters to Nashville. "But I didn't want to move myself here," he said. Anyway, Gore had just met him, didn't really know him. Carter answered that Gore had been impressed by his ideas during the primaries. Tad had the experience and capacity to run a national campaign. We were in a mess—both organizationally and strategically, where we couldn't reach consensus. He had to take the reins. By the time we were leaving, he said he'd talk with his wife, think about it, maybe he could do it for a month or so. "He'll do it," I said to Eskew, as Devine headed for his hotel room.

Friday of Memorial Day weekend, the two of them went to NAVOBS to see Gore. They sat down on the bandstand porch at the front of the residence and the vice president asked Devine to take on the campaign; he knew it was a sacrifice for Tad's family—Gore had been well briefed by Eskew—but Devine had to do this for the country. Tad said he would accept the job and move to Nashville on one condition: He had to have authority; he couldn't go into a situation where he was fighting with others for control. Something could be worked out with Donna Brazile. Gore agreed that Coelho had to go.

On Memorial Day, Gore told his campaign chairman. Coelho had to have some time to find a reason to resign. He got his reason two weeks later when he was in a hospital for an inflamed colon and cited medical concerns as he stepped aside. The night before, Gore had called Devine, who told him that, in terms of both the party and the press, the strongest choice to replace Coelho as campaign chair was Commerce Secretary Bill Daley. He had waited through the first Clinton administration for his appointment to the cabinet; now we were about to ask him to give it up. Devine advised Gore that he needed Daley to sign on now—so we could announce his arrival and Coelho's departure simultaneously. If he had to, the vice president should ask Clinton to intervene with Daley. The next afternoon, Gore and Daley were standing side by side in Ohio as Gore introduced his new campaign chairman.

Donna Brazile agreed to travel full time on the plane with Gore;

she would keep her title as campaign manager and have a voice in major decisions. She and I would end up writing and editing most of the African-American advertising together. She would also push field organization hard—and that would make a difference on Election Day. She was someone I cared about and I knew the change was hard for her. But I was honest with her: It made no sense to leave; and she mattered to the campaign. Finally, she could emerge afterward as a national personality in her own right. What I said was true, and I admired Donna for swallowing hard, moving on, and giving Gore everything she had.

The changes were in place, but so was the scheduled "Progress and Prosperity" tour, the last chapter in our message timidity. Although he offered some new proposals, the overall sense was of Gore giving himself credit that the voters didn't for the economic achievements of the past eight years. This rankled him, he told me two months later when we were finalizing the acceptance speech, because he had stiffened Clinton's spine when the president was wavering on his economic plan in 1993. But this was hardly an argument Gore could make publicly. After the tour, a new "Battleground" poll showed Gore 12 points back.

I wasn't around for nine or ten days of this period because I was on "vacation" in Italy—which was a subterfuge. This was the year the post-election *Newsweek* account, in referring to the trip, noted that I owned a villa in Italy. (I'm still waiting for the magazine to send me the keys.) I went to the medieval town of San Gimignano to write a first draft of the acceptance speech. Before I left, sitting next to his swimming pool, Gore and I sipped iced tea—he actually did drink a lot of it. He had ideas of his own about his convention speech. He wanted to talk about his family and his roots in Tennessee. He wasn't sure what to say about Clinton. But he was intrigued with a story about the quadriplegic Cambridge University scientist Stephen Hawking, who communicates through a voice synthesizer. I'd heard him tell the Hawking story before; maybe, he said, he could use it in the acceptance address. It was a long anecdote about a visit they'd had in the White House, which concluded with Gore asking if you'd just seen Hawking, who would know that this

was the smartest man in the world? I thought the story was complicated, obscure, and might sound elitist; but I said I'd fit it in.

I did a preliminary outline on a legal sheet that reflected what we
had to accomplish strategically in the speech, and then sat for five
days, putting lines or paragraphs on to several hundred 3-by-5 cards.
I then organized the cards to fit and reshape the outline. When I returned, I showed the draft to Eskew, Devine, and Eli Attie. We
wrote through it again—the first of many times. But while there was
a long process ahead, the central elements of the acceptance speech
were already there.

Gore had to stake out the future, not cling to the past: "I speak
tonight of gratitude, achievement, and high hopes for our country."
Later, on the economy: "The election is not a reward for past performance. I'm not asking you to vote for me on the basis of the economy
we have. Tonight, I ask for your support on the basis of the better,
fairer, more prosperous America we can build together." I surmised
that if he didn't try to seize the credit, voters just might give some to
Gore. The economy was also the way to pay tribute to Clinton: "For
almost eight years now, I've been the partner of a President [in the
final version, "a leader"] who led [in the final version "moved"] us
out of the valley of recession and into the longest period of prosperity in American history . . ." Gore also had to respond to Bush's
claim that the good times were due solely to the American people.
Gore said that was true—up to a point. A few years before, under
the last Bush administration—although he didn't have to say that
explicitly in the speech—the people were working hard: "But your
hard work was undone by a government that didn't work . . . didn't
put people first . . . and wasn't on your side."

Gore then had to pivot quickly and separate himself from Clinton in a way that, unlike some of his earlier attempts, was natural
and confident, not strained or critical: "We are entering a new time.
We're electing a new President. And . . . I stand here tonight as my
own man and I want you to know me for who I truly am." As his
own man, he could set out his own plans for the future, in the process
draw contrasts with Bush, often without mentioning his name.
Thus he could cite his own targeted tax cuts for the middle class and

compare these to the opposition's proposal, which would lavish benefits on the wealthy while giving the average family enough money "to buy one extra Diet Coke a day." Similarly, Bush's plan to privatize Social Security was "Social Security minus." Gore's plan was "Social Security plus."

Gore could tell the personal stories of a series of people he'd met during the campaign who exemplified issues like prescription drugs for seniors, the Patients' Bill of Rights, education—and I left some blanks for other issues. And instead of the common ritual of accepting the nomination at the start of the speech, or more rarely at the end, he could do so in their names—and "in the name of all the hardworking families who are the strength and soul of America." He could capture the word "values" and define it in Democratic terms like health coverage for children: "To me, family values means honoring our fathers and mothers, teaching our children well, caring for the sick . . . respecting one another. . . ." And "honor" was not something Gore would cede to an opponent promising to restore it to the White House: "To me, [honor] is not just a word, but an obligation. And you have my word . . . we will honor hard work by raising the minimum wage so that hard work always pays more than welfare." He would offer the obligatory praise for welfare reform—a nod to the center—and pledge to protect the right of sportsmen and hunters to own guns. The populist would also be a futurist, with a call to "reverse the silent, rising tide of global warming."

Of course, there were paragraphs on foreign policy and national security—brief because that was a decidedly secondary concern in 2000. Gore would cut one that has a haunting ring in light of the subsequent events and his own passionate opposition to the Iraq war: "I have news for Saddam Hussein: if I become President, our policy toward you is going to get even tougher. It is time for you to go"—an intentional echo of his most famous line at the 1992 convention. Today, the words about Saddam Hussein sound quintessentially Bush-like. That I penned them so casually says volumes about the fact that the issue was an afterthought at the time. That Gore excised the words reveals both his aversion to bombast about war and peace and a temperament and sense of judgment that would have made him the right president post-9/11.

I had struggled with how to temper Gore's supposedly wooden personality or turn it into an asset. Something I didn't predict and no one planned would come along to help—the passionate kiss with Tipper before the speech. But there were words as well: "As Americans, we all share in the privilege and challenge of building a more perfect union. I know my own imperfections. I know that sometimes people say I'm too serious, that I talk too much substance and policy. Maybe I've done that tonight." Gore himself came up with a powerful clincher: "But the Presidency is more than a popularity context. It's a day by day fight for people. . . . Sometimes you have to be willing to sacrifice your popularity to pick the hard right over the easy wrong."

Before Eskew and I showed the draft to Gore, I squeezed in the reference to Stephen Hawking. At this point, it looked as if it could be short because the candidate was hoping to have Hawking appear on the convention podium the night before the acceptance speech. Gore said that while this draft was good, he wasn't sure it was him— or that it was exactly what he wanted. He'd take it, and then develop and show us his version. As we left, Eskew told me not to worry; we'd get to the right place: "Just stick with me." Gore, he added, wants to write his own speech. We're just going to have to go through a painful process to get back to pretty much where we already are.

But Devine had already raised another, very different objection: This was the right speech, but like the candidate's remarks on the road, we still needed a single line, a memorable phrase that summed up Gore's message. People had to know what this guy was all about. He was about standing up for people, I said—and especially on issues like the environment and taxes, standing up against entrenched interests. He was moving in that direction on his own on the campaign trail. But we needed a phrase to make it come alive; it couldn't be "fighting for us" or "on your side," or some other worn-out line. We didn't have any polling on it, Tad said, but you've already come up with the phrase and maybe we ought to just adopt it. It was from a one-minute biographical spot in Ted Kennedy's 1994 campaign, which featured a breathtaking list of legislative accomplishments and then lifted the argument to a thematic level: "At the heart of it all are simple but fundamental ideas—to stand up for your beliefs . . . to serve the people and not the powerful." How about that, Tad said, "the people, not the powerful"?

We tried it out on Carter Eskew—who liked it. Then Devine blurted it out on a conference call with Gore, who seemed to take almost instinctively to the line and started to roll it out immediately in the first week of July. He initially mangled the phrase slightly: "The question is whether you're for the people or for the power." Thus was born what would become the most controversial line of the Gore campaign. Almost as soon as the line first came out of Gore's mouth, the press caught the drift. "Populist Themes Set Gore Apart From Clinton" was the *Times* headline—and the story noted that this was consistent with his own record in Congress. Clinton advisers grumbled, anonymously, that a populist appeal couldn't get a Democratic nominee above 50 percent of the vote—which, of course, Clinton hadn't attained when tacking and triangulating four years before.

Eskew and I heard the argument full force when we went to see Clinton's pollster Mark Penn later in July. Bill Daley was dissatisfied with Hickman—and intent on bringing in Greenberg, who had turned me down ten months earlier. But Penn had been calling and Eskew said we at least ought to hear him out, although he'd be a hard sell not just to Daley but to Gore. Penn had just completed a national survey that, on the face of it, ranked the "populist" message higher than the blander Clintonian approach. But he proceeded to explain why the numbers were misleading: the populist argument, in the end, wouldn't get Gore over 50 percent—the same assertion we'd read in the *Times*. When Eskew asked for more data to prove Penn's point, Mark merely said it was clear from the overall numbers and reflected his overall experience in the last four years. In essence, he was recommending that we rerun Clinton's 1996 campaign. But we weren't running against Dole, and Gore wasn't the incumbent. Eskew, to my surprise, ended the meeting early, explaining that we had to go see the vice president. When we got into the cab, he turned to me and said: "Bullshit." After the election, Penn wrote a piece asserting that Clinton's mantra of opportunity, responsibility, community "consistently" scored higher than "the people, not the powerful"—which he amended in his question to the "people versus the powerful," a slight change that may have made a substantial difference. When I read the piece, I remembered Clinton's 1992 acceptance speech: "Our people are pleading for change, but government is in the way. It has been hijacked by privileged private interests." That year, Clinton wasn't Clinton—at least by Penn's lights.

Stan Greenberg was ready to go. He and Hickman would run parallel national polling operations until the Democratic Convention, when Daley decided we should fire Hickman altogether. Devine saved him—he didn't want to ruin his reputation—and Hickman stayed on in a lesser role running the polling of individual states. Greenberg reviewed all the data we had and quickly dispatched a memo. Gore, he wrote, should be the candidate "fighting for ordinary families, not the wealthy special interests." But his "guess" was that we should soften the way we said it—even moving away from "working families" to just "families." His research would push us in that direction and away from "the people, not the powerful." The last time it was intentionally uttered by Gore was in one line in the acceptance speech. Greenberg would insist that the banners prepared for the post-convention Gore boat trip on the Mississippi— THE PEOPLE, NOT THE POWERFUL—be taken down. I went along with this—we all did—because the tamer variants tested marginally better. But they were also less memorable. Voters answering a question on a poll have just heard a phrase; that doesn't mean it stays with them as a definitive, motivating rationale for a candidate and a campaign. Maybe this sounds like a political fine point, but it may have determined the outcome. As I said to Greenberg afterward, I wish I'd fought to hold to "the people, not the powerful." We would have had a better chance to carry a populist state like West Virginia— maybe even Missouri—and it wouldn't have cost us any state that was close. We became too much a prisoner of our own polls. If Gore ever ran again, a friend of his told me in 2006, he might do it without taking any polls and simply say what he believes.

But in 2000, even as he was emerging as his own man, he was still intent on pleasing his immediate audience. Marylouise and I saw a vivid demonstration of that one night at our home when the audience was just three people: Kay Graham, her son Don, who'd taken over as publisher of *The Washington Post*, and Don's wife Mary. Gore had called Marylouise with a request to invite Kay and Don to a dinner party with Tipper and him. Marylouise wasn't about to pretend that this was her idea so she told Kay that it was the vice president's.

We also invited Marylouise's sister Jane, who lived with us and staffed higher education issues for Senate Democrats. She had worked with Don Graham on a special project to develop a college tuition-aid program for Washington, D.C., students. The conversation over crab cakes at a table in our kitchen was as much about that as about politics. We were surprised to discover that Gore and Don Graham, who'd attended St. Alban's School at the same time, had lost touch while Gore was vice president. Graham had graduated three years before Gore from both St. Alban's and Harvard. They'd seen each other over the years, but hardly at all since 1993. Gore was trying hard, too hard, to reestablish a bond between them. In the living room after dinner, he reminisced about their common bond of serving in Vietnam. Then he casually suggested that, despite all the opposition at the time, as the years passed, history might judge that the Vietnam War made some sense after all. I was taken aback, but suspected that Gore didn't mean it; he was only trying to identify with Don, who after returning from Vietnam, had spent a year and a half as a D.C. police officer. He had a reputation as a a political moderate. Marylouise, characteristically, had a blunt response to Gore: But what about the 55,000 dead Americans? What about the hundreds of thousands of dead Vietnamese? For what? Don quietly said he didn't agree with Gore, who quickly backpedaled. Most politicians strive to please; after two or three elections, it is a reflex. At times like this, however, I felt that Gore was his own strongest opponent. He was prodigiously informed, in truth principled, and wryly humorous. But too often, he left people, even those who were for him, wondering what makes Al run.

His next big decision was picking a vice-presidential nominee. He was intrigued with the unexpected, the unconventional, the breakthrough idea. He didn't want to make the "usual" vice-presidential choice, and he didn't think he could afford to. He'd been 12 points back in late June in a public poll; after a month of "the people, not the powerful," he'd cut that deficit to 6 points in the ABC–*Washington Post* survey and just 3 points in Hickman's data. But as the Republican Convention ended in early August, he was again far behind. He sensed the need to throw a long ball and I could tell that he relished the chance.

That's how John Edwards not only got considered after less than two years in the Senate, but nearly got the nod. Warren Christopher, the congenitally cautious former secretary of state, was in charge of the search process; he thought Edwards was untested, unprepared, a reckless gamble. Edwards himself had first broached the long-shot possibility of being Gore's running mate with me early in 1999. John and Elizabeth lived only four blocks from Marylouise and me and we would get together for casual dinners. The night he first raised the subject of the vice presidency with me, I hadn't yet gone to work for Gore and I still didn't expect to. But I replied that the case for picking him was clear: Clinton and Gore had shown that two southerners constituted a strong, maybe the strongest, Democratic ticket. Gore might conclude that Edwards's lack of experience was offset by his capacity as an advocate. And that was his calling card.

John Kerry called me repeatedly as Gore neared his choice. Should he come back from Sun Valley, where he was taking a few days off at Teresa's home? No, I said, that wouldn't make any difference. I couldn't tell him that Gore, running double digits behind, was determined to make an out-of-the-box choice—and that it was coming down to Edwards and Connecticut senator Joe Lieberman, who would be the first Jewish candidate on a national ticket. Kerry was a backup, a safe haven, in case they both faltered in the final lap. And there was also a second backup. Gore asked Tad Devine to talk to Bob Kerrey, who hadn't even been through the vetting process.

John Kerry also had no idea that he had undermined his prospects months earlier with his well-meant but badly received lecture on the tense election night when Gore seemed to be losing the New Hampshire primary. That episode—and Tipper's reaction to it—wouldn't have stopped Gore from choosing Kerry if he thought it made political sense. But Kerry came from a state we were going to carry anyway, Gore calculated. He tended to discount the importance of Kerry's proven skills as a debater; he thought Edwards and Lieberman would do equally well in an exchange with George Bush's newly self-nominated running mate, Dick Cheney, who'd been in charge of the vice-presidential selection process.

After one of their meetings Edwards reported to me that Gore told him: "Whether I pick you or not, I think you're going to be president someday." But Gore was bothered about the press reaction if he chose someone so inexperienced. Several of us countered that it might be a rough couple of days, but that would rebound in our favor when Edwards performed well in the first, inevitably tough press conference, and if he then outdebated Cheney. With Gore on the eve of decision, campaign chairman Bill Daley told Edwards he was close to being tapped. The press was now camped outside his house. Marylouise went shopping with Elizabeth, as they often did, this time to buy a couple outfits for the convention. Afterward, she dropped Elizabeth off; the reporters saw them, and took it as a signal of Edwards's impending selection.

But Gore was troubled by the report—ironically compiled by someone who had worked for Edwards but was now our campaign's research director—that as a lawyer, Edwards had taken the legal but potentially controversial step of incorporating himself to avoid paying Medicare taxes. It had come up in the 1998 Senate race, and we'd beaten it back; but it now gave Warren Christopher an opening to renew the case against Edwards as too callow, too uncertain, too far out of the box. He pressed Gore. How could he risk his reputation by making such a choice? Almost simultaneously, Democratic National Chairman Ed Rendell, a future governor of Pennsylvania and himself Jewish, told reporters on Saturday that the country wasn't ready for a Jewish vice president: "If Joe Lieberman were Episcopalian, it would be a slam dunk." Gore was incandescently angry. He was drawn to the idea of making history and appalled by the premise that he would yield to prejudice. I looked at the press reports and told Eskew, who was Lieberman's stalwart advocate, that Rendell had just done him a big favor.

Hickman had polled on the possible choices. Most of them weren't well enough known to register nationally. By Sunday night, Gore had made up his mind. The result was the safe unorthodox pick: the Orthodox Jew Joe Lieberman, who had the added virtue, as Gore saw it, of having rebuked Bill Clinton for his personal transgressions in a celebrated speech on the Senate floor. Edwards was just a reach too far. Gore called five or six senior staff together for a final and transparently pro forma discussion. John Kerry got a passing mention, and John Edwards—well, he had a big future. But Gore focused on the historic nature, the instant impact, of selecting Lieberman; he knew him and trusted he could be president. Devine worried about Lieberman's nonconfrontational style; the vice president is supposed to be the cutting edge of the campaign. Our running mate had to go after Cheney hard in a debate. Yes, he argued, Lieberman would be an instant hit now, but now wasn't what mattered: "Mr. Vice President, you need Mr. October, not Mr. August." After Tad finished, I pushed the point and Gore bristled. We adjourned to Donna Brazile's room for a drink. As soon as the door was closed, I said, "It's over. It's Lieberman."

The weekend before the VP selection, Eskew and I flew to Gore's borrowed vacation retreat on North Carolina's Figure Eight Island for the next session on the acceptance speech. By now, Gore had written his own version—some edits of the draft we'd given him, but reams of new material. The reference to Stephen Hawking, who couldn't travel to Los Angeles to speak at the convention, was morphing into a disquisition. I recognized my own pride of authorship—and more critically, Gore's all-but-certain refusal to bend on the most important speech of his life unless we had some objective measure to gauge what worked and what didn't. I took the problem to Stan Greenberg, who was in the first stages of conducting polling and focus groups for the campaign. What if we put all the material together, in as coherent a draft as possible, filmed Gore delivering it, and then tested all of it in a dial group where participants could register their reactions by dialing up or down all throughout the speech? We couldn't trust the results, Stan explained, if the dial group had to react too long to a single piece of material. Why not record the speech, cut it into one- or two-paragraph segments, and test them a few at a time in different dial groups? This was even better, I said: we could actually compare the effects of alternative language and passages that substantively said the same thing. But to do it this way, we'd need lots of groups, and that would cost hundreds of thousands of dollars. Devine paused, then said it was too important not to spend the money.

Gore bought into the process. It was high-tech and it yielded definite answers—and for all his own pride of authorship, he knew he had to get this speech right. His changes and additions had doubled the length of the original draft. In front of a camera in the room with the spiral staircase at Loew's Nashville, he rolled through the 12,000 words Eli Attie and I had cobbled together. He did it in one take. We hadn't bothered with transitions or been bothered by overlaps since the tape would be sliced into dial group–sized pieces. The exercise offered us an unexpected bonus. I noticed that as Gore pushed his way through the text rapidly, the excruciatingly measured, undulating cadence that could make him sound phony simply disappeared. As Gore practiced with Michael Sheehan, a consultant who'd worked with Clinton for years, we both told the candidate that the right pace was one that felt a little too fast for him. Don't milk the applause, surf it; as soon as it starts to diminish, speak up and speak over it. The speech might sound fast in the Convention Hall, but it would sound natural and forceful on television where the cheering faded for viewers even while the speaker and the delegates were still hearing it. With all the interruptions—120 of them, the cheering and chants of "Go, Al, Go"—Gore would still deliver the 5,670 words of what one commentator called "the speech of his life" in just 51 minutes.

But reducing the text to that length consumed Eskew, Attie, and me. We met with Gore each night to edit and practice on his journey west to the convention in Los Angeles. Greenberg or his staff would fax or phone in the results from the latest of the focus groups: this line was effective, that one failed or even hurt; this section went off the charts, that one was a downer. We had numerical scores, but Gore soon adopted a bottom-line approach: Just tell me what should go, what should stay. The process had its funny moments. One night, the candidate walked into the meeting room where we were waiting, sat down at the long folding table with the speech materials spread around it, and as I started to review the focus group results, said with a self-deprecating shrug: "I know, all your stuff worked and all my stuff didn't."

We had scheduled Clinton to speak Monday night—as far removed as possible from Gore's appearance on Thursday. Originally, the White House had suggested that the president speak Monday night, followed by Hillary on Tuesday. We replied that they'd both have to speak Monday. We don't want this thing to be a Clinton show, Donna Brazile said; we have to shift the attention to Gore. That was easier said than done. After his speech, the president was to leave Los Angeles and pass the torch to Gore at a rally in Michigan. But on August 10, four days before his convention speech, the president stole the spotlight with an appearance before 4,500 ministers in Chicago. His remarks were supposedly an effort to help Gore. Clinton said he was "in the second year of a process of trying to totally rebuild my life from a terrible mistake I made . . . I had to come to terms with a lot of things about the fundamental importance of character and integrity." And it was unfair to "blame" Gore, Clinton added, for "any mistake" he'd made. Clinton had been forewarned that he'd be asked about the Lewinsky scandal during a question-and-answer session. When he heard that, Gore's reaction was: Well, why did the president have to do the event in the first place? Gore, a Grateful Dead fan, called Tad Devine and said: "What a long, strange trip it's been."

It was a little strange for me, too. Chris Lehane was telling the press that Gore was writing the speech himself—which was what the candidate wanted him to say. And by Wednesday, enroute to Los Angeles, Gore was describing to reporters how he'd scribbled ideas on poster-sized sheets of paper on an easel; he had, but that wasn't where most of the text came from. "This is a speech I have written," he said, "and I will deserve the credit or the blame." The day before, someone from the *New York Times* had tracked me down on the road with Gore. I knew what the candidate was saying and now I had a choice: either to positively affirm Gore's version of events or to let him be accused of lying, which would be bad for the campaign and, given his likely reaction, bad for me. So I assured the reporter that Gore was "literally, truly and unquestionably . . . writing his own speech." The day of the speech, Eskew found a more artful way out. He simply answered: "Everything in the speech reflects what he wanted in the speech, if you know what I mean." All this was inside baseball, not worth the exaggeration about Gore's authorship; no one in the voting public cared. Eskew gave me the right advice— just grin and bear it. And in fact, the way we put the speech together, with Gore's constant, intimate involvement, if not necessarily all his words, meant that he would genuinely own it by the time he mounted the convention rostrum.

On the Thursday morning of the acceptance speech, at about 6 a.m. west coast time, Marylouise and I were awakened by a phone call from Washington. I was now being lobbied by a would-be penultimate editor, the president of the United States. He hadn't seen the acceptance, he said, but he had heard that it was too populist. He was concerned. The best theme was still opportunity, responsibility, community—his theme. I replied that Gore had to use his own words. Clinton conceded on that—reluctantly. I tried to damp down his anxiety as he made more suggestions, then asked the real question: Was "the people, not the powerful" all over the text? No, I said; we had other language (by now I was paging through the draft) like "I've taken on the powerful forces. And as President, I will stand up for you." I added that "the people, not the powerful" only appeared once; but Gore had to say it or it would look like he was backing away. Was welfare reform in there? the president asked. Yes. Clinton pointedly noted that no one had ever shared the draft with him—and I wondered how Gore would react if he knew I was reading parts of it to the president. He finished the call by telling me that he hoped I had this right; his tone wasn't all that hopeful.

Our advance staff had constructed an exact physical replica of the convention podium in our hotel. On Thursday afternoon, leading Gore through a final drill, we were having one last disagreement with the candidate—and we were losing the argument. The section on Stephen Hawking was now a lengthy excursion near the end of the speech. Greenberg's people hadn't bothered to test it because, as he apologetically reported to me, they just assumed that it would never make the final cut. But it had become the equivalent of Gore's last stand. Tipper came in and asked Eskew and me if everything was in good shape. Mostly, I said, but we couldn't get the Hawking passage out, and I was afraid it would drain the force of the speech as Gore powered toward his ending. She walked over to the podium, and said: "Al, take Hawking out." He said to her, half-serious, half-laughing: "You too?" The cut was made.

We left the hotel late and roared across Los Angeles in the motorcade. There was another rehearsal room at the Staples Center, right next to the cubicle with the TelePrompTer operators. There was no time to practice again, but Gore had a few more fixes. As he sat with one of the operators and made them, he turned to me and said: "Just don't argue with me." I had no intention of doing that, but then he inserted a line about signing the renewal of the Voting Rights Act during his first term as president. But did we know, I asked, when the act was due to expire? I'd get hold of our research director, David Ginsberg, and check. Gore strode down the corridor toward the back entrance to the convention floor to meet his Harvard roommate, the Oscar-winning actor Tommy Lee Jones, who was going to

walk with him down the aisle through the cheering delegates toward the podium. Gore brought Eskew, Attie, and me along. We
could walk a few paces behind him.

The convention was a sea of anticipation, concern, and obligatory
applause—the delegates were hoping for the best—as Gore started
up the aisle after Tipper introduced him. A correspondent stopped
me, asked if I'd written the speech, and could I do a quick interview.
I turned around and fled; Eskew and Attie would see the speech
from a platform off to the side of the podium. I wouldn't—and as
usual, I was too nervous anyway. From the opening at the back
of the curtain, I watched Gore grab his wife for that famous
kiss, which I knew hadn't been planned, at least by any political
strategist. I retreated to the prompter room to watch on television—
and it was a good thing I'd returned. Ginsberg reported that
the Voting Rights Act didn't expire until 2007; could we get the line
out? It was risky to try because Gore was already speaking, but
the specter of exaggeration always hung over this campaign. I ordered a terrified prompter operator to switch to the backup copy
during an early ovation; the screens from which Gore was reading
would be blank for a second at most. I cut the reference to voting
rights in the primary copy of the speech—and then had the operator
switch back during another ovation. Gore, who knew the speech so
well by now that he probably could have delivered it from memory,
picked up on the change, and teased himself and me afterward: "I
guess I got that one wrong."

From the practice room, I talked with Greenberg, who was monitoring his dial groups. They were off the charts. Afterward, Gore
and his family, including his mother, were in a room with a bar and
a buffet celebrating with their friends. He was smiling from ear to
ear and he clapped me across the shoulder. He knew it hadn't always
been easy, he said, but it had come out all right. Most of the commen-
tariat hadn't delivered a final verdict yet, but I was certain that the
"bounce" was coming—and it would be a big one. For the first time
in the campaign, America had seen Gore straight on, unmediated by
an often skeptical media. The country had seen him not as Clinton's

number two but as a potential president. If the Greenberg data were accurate—and I had no doubt they were—this was a new election. Gore had a slight lead just after the convention that soon opened up to 5 points nationally. With the Lieberman selection, the kiss, and the speech, he had achieved, depending on what polls you cited, a turnaround of between 16 and 22 percent.

As I left the convention, I looked back on a day in July at NAVOBS when Gore had stopped working on the speech, left the room, and reentered with a flourish carrying a birthday cake for Eskew and me (our birthdays are days apart). Next year, he said, we'll do this at the White House. The Gore I had come to know was both brittle and big-hearted, idealistic and calculating. He was more comfortable now because he was not only proclaiming but also becoming his own man. He was an inveterate tinkerer who sometimes got the little things wrong, but got the big ones right. Unfortunately, in 2000 with a press corps largely disillusioned with Clinton and convinced that Gore was "phony," the little things—the overclaiming, the exaggerations, the miscues of tone and tactics—would become the biggest factors of all.

That was never more true than in the debates with Bush. Jim Johnson, who had recently retired as chairman of the mortgage giant Fannie Mae, was in charge of negotiating with the Bush campaign. The first crucial question, it seemed, was whether the debates would happen at all. The Bush representatives were proposing alternatives—joint appearances on *Meet the Press, This Week, Face the Nation*, or some combination of the Sunday talk shows. I had no doubt that under this scenario, the broadcasts would be shifted to prime time, but they gave Bush two things his negotiators were demanding. First, he wanted to sit during the debates. Second, he wanted to avoid the town meeting format, already scheduled for one of the three encounters planned by the official Commission on Presidential Debates. The format had devastated his father in 1992 when he came across as tone-deaf about the economic pain of ordinary

Americans and stared at his watch, signaling his impatience with having to answer their questions.

Bush the second was coming across as "afraid" to debate and his side finally yielded after securing an agreement to sit in the second debate and to set the town hall as the final, and therefore presumably least important, event in the series. Johnson told Eskew and me that the Bush negotiators were intransigent about one demand: Cheney and Lieberman had to sit when they met face to face. (Looking at Lieberman, anyone could know this wasn't about height.) While I was convinced the other side had genuine concerns—for example, a belief that Bush was more casual, more likely to perform well in a seated, conversational setting—Johnson and I also thought that the foot-dragging was a deliberate, strategic feint to lower expectations. Gore had constantly warned that the campaign should never boast about his abilities as a debater; we had to contain expectations as much as possible. I told him that it was tough to do this against Bush: in a debate with Gore, Bush was almost bound to get more credit for doing less.

We also had to decide what kind of prep we were going to have— the elaborate, heavily staffed entourage of the Clinton and Gore "debate camps" in 1996, or the leaner model we'd followed in the primaries. Eskew and I favored the latter, and I explained to Johnson that with Gore, candor and criticism would go down easier if he didn't have a big audience looking on. Later we were told that Bush had his own rule for the preps: six people in the room; if another person came in, someone had to leave. But Gore was sure that he wanted to replicate 1996 with all the bells and whistles; the advance staff would even retrieve the mounted shark that had hung on the wall at debate camp that year and put it back up for the 2000 sessions.

Before debate camp, a Gore campaign that was cruising along drove into another cul-de-sac of puffery. In the midst of an assault on the big drug companies, Gore pointed out that his mother-in-law had to pay more for her arthritis medicine than it cost to treat the family dog with the same pills. The reporters pushed for some proof. Why couldn't we give it to them? I asked Eskew. After all, a congressional study had revealed the prevalence of disparities like this. But that's all we had, Eskew replied; Gore's mother-in-law was getting the medicine for free, and probably against the rules, from the White House physician—and we sure didn't want that to become known. As this latest apparent exaggeration seeped into public consciousness, Greenberg reported that Gore had been nicked in the polls.

We had a practice Q-and-A session before we left for Sarasota, Florida, for the mock debates to be held in an old warehouselike building next to a ship canal. Former congressman Tom Downey was slated to play Bush, but he had to be replaced after Bush's own prep materials were mysteriously mailed to him. We turned them over to the FBI and recruited Paul Begala, who'd known Bush well in Texas, as the new stand-in. In this early, less formal give-and-take, the candidate was a little ragged. He winced and made notes when I said that an answer he'd just given on education was so long-winded he hadn't had time to fit in a comparison with Bush. In general, his language had to be more economical, with fewer windups. As he moved along, he got steadily better—and Carter and I told him that his answer on Medicare was precisely what he needed in content, tone, and pace.

In Sarasota, I played Jim Lehrer, the host of *NewsHour,* who would be the questioner in all three of the presidential debates. Of the twelve topics on which he would pose questions in the first debate, we guessed well enough to cover ten; the other two were issues Gore could answer in his sleep—a "litmus test" for judges and what to do about Serbian dictator Slobodan Milosevic. Carter Eskew sat at the table with me facing Gore and Begala. Everyone else, as many as twenty or sometimes thirty people, were in chairs on the floor below the stage. Following each mock exchange, Eskew and I would comment, then Greenberg, and others if they felt they had to. Johnson—along with Daley and Devine—did everything they could to limit the chatter. Our research director, David Ginsberg, was there to keep the facts straight. And our first guideline for Gore was, Don't cite any fact you're not sure of.

The mock debates revealed problems we tried to guard against— and one difficulty that we didn't foresee. In the one on October 1, Gore had a tendency to sigh as he was about to rebut Begala, a.k.a.

Bush—and in one case, he did it while "Bush" was talking. He occasionally tried to protract the discussion—to get in another lick—when the moderator wanted to move on. Afterward, Eskew and I said he shouldn't react to Bush—just take notes on a yellow pad if he needed to occupy himself—and *never* quarrel with Lehrer. This first time around, Gore referred just once to the "lockbox"—his plan to prevent the Social Security Trust Fund from being spent for other purposes. That was a little light, I commented; we have to make sure the concept gets through, since one of Bush's biggest weaknesses was his proposal to privatize Social Security.

That last piece of advice was the kind Gore didn't need. One of his strengths is message discipline; but carried to excess, it could become a weakness, conveying a sense that he was an automaton. In the next mock debate, the day before the real encounter with Bush, he took the advice I gave him to heart—and mentioned the lockbox five times. We should have advised him not to go overboard; then *Saturday Night Live* couldn't have turned his seven mentions of the lockbox in the real debate into classic political satire. But there were other issues that were bothering me and clearly troubling Eskew. Gore was reacting more visibly and more frequently to Begala, sighing audibly during seven of his mock opponent's answers and when launching into his own rebuttals. He was still grimacing—which in the practice room itself was more noticeable than the sighs would be on television. Gore wondered if it mattered that much; under the rules, the camera wasn't supposed to be on the candidate who wasn't talking. Eskew warned that the networks wouldn't necessarily follow the rules. Assume the camera's on you all the time.

We had one disappointment on the debate prep team. Begala suggested that Bush could be rattled if Gore invaded his space; the vice president should come out, assertively stride across the stage, and push Bush back with his handshake. Carter and I were trying to tone Gore's atmospherics down, not ratchet them up, but he liked Begala's ploy. I commented that Gore had to be careful here; he couldn't carry this too far. More bluntly, I told Devine that the tactic was a distraction, maybe even a danger. It was Alpha male-plus. Eskew and I ended with our mantra—Don't react to Bush, don't quarrel with the moderator, and at least don't make it obvious that you're invading his space.

Unfortunately, the advice was to become a how-to primer in reverse. As Air Force Two flew toward Boston, the site of the first debate, I felt good about Gore's prospects. He had his strategy and his answers down cold. We had hammered away at something else throughout the practice—accuracy. He couldn't use a statistic, a fact, or a story unless he was certain it was true. During the flight, he showed us a note from a father complaining about school overcrowding, along with a news report and a photo of his daughter standing in a Sarasota classroom because she didn't have a desk. There it was in black and white; no one bothered to check it further. Gore already had his education answer and his examples. But he also had a soft spot for the latest and most telling anecdote. We had a massive roster of "real people" who, we told the press, were briefing the candidate. Reporters regarded it as a gimmick; Gore was serious about it.

Gore left late for the debate at the University of Massachusetts. The broadcast staff was insisting that they had to get him to the side of the stage as a rushed makeup artist frantically powdered his face. She'd be blamed for his "orange" tint. But it wasn't her fault; she didn't have time to do her job. Gore gulped down four or five diet colas and bolted down several protein power bars. It was a recipe for hyperaggression.

Gore barely got away with his stride and his handshake, although after the third debate, a well-primed Barbara Bush would try to stoke the issue by complaining: "I thought he was gonna hit George." Bush was awkward, often uncertain and pedestrian during their first encounter; but he turned in a tolerable performance. On substance, Gore dominated the night; the people in the hall hardly noticed his sighs, but on television they were an annoying sideshow. Outside the auditorium, in the trailer where we were watching, there was a moment two-thirds of the way through the debate when Bill Daley pleaded, "Stop, stop!" at the screen—and then groaned when Gore didn't. Both candidates had been asked to cite a decision they had made that validated their capacity to handle "the unexpected, the crisis under fire." Gore talked about his role in the Balkans and the peacemaking process there. Bush, perhaps triggered by the word "fire" in Lehrer's question, inexplicably talked about dealing with a local fire and then floods in Texas—and mentioned the Clinton administration's FEMA director James Lee Witt. On this comparison, it would have been game, set, match for Gore. But Lehrer asked a follow-up about a potential financial crisis—and after Bush bumbled his way through an answer, essentially saying he would ask Alan Greenspan what to do, Gore decided to one-up him. Instead of just describing his work during the 1994 Mexican peso collapse and the 1998 financial crisis in Asia, Gore felt compelled to add that as vice president, he too had been to a forest fire— and with James Lee Witt. Daley, looking at the screen, said: "Reel him in."

As I headed for the press room, I held to the comforting thought that Gore, while a little over the top, had clearly won almost every exchange. After a few minutes with the press, I noticed that the Bush troops weren't talking about substance, but about style and Gore's "misstatements." At this point, the instant polls were rolling in: Gore had won all of them handily, except for ABC's, where his margin was only 3 percent. That judgment would change as the Bush campaign changed the subject, magnifying sighs and exaggerations into the prevailing story. In an election where, at least to many, Bush seemed unthreatening and the stakes didn't seem all that high, the spin about sighing and lying, as I heard one Bush partisan put it, reversed perceptions about the outcome of the debate— not so much with those who'd seen it, but with the millions who learned about it through news and commentary.

Gore was vulnerable on exaggerations and he knew it going into the debate. His offenses were minor. He had gone to that fire, not with James Lee Witt but with another FEMA official. He'd invoked the young woman in Sarasota in the overcrowded classroom; she had a desk now, and her defensive principal explained that even if she had been standing before, there was a lab stool to sit on. Bush had his own misstatements—for example, that Gore had outspent him in the campaign. One of them was even more serious. Bush had denied Gore's charge that his prescription drug plan wouldn't help middle-class seniors in its first years when in fact it gave them nothing at all until their drug bills were above $6,000. But the Bush miscues provoked barely any criticism, no matter how hard our campaign pushed them. Gore, already caricatured as the Internet-inventing, Love Canal–finding candidate, was the one in the media bull's-eye. This deprived him of what could have been a decisive victory in the debate. In retrospect, it's astounding to me that sighs may have determined who was president on 9/11.

But I still thought Gore had won when Eskew, Greenberg, and I traveled the next morning to the Lieberman-Cheney debate site in Kentucky. We landed, picked up a rental car, and stopped for lunch. The cell phones started ringing. We were in real trouble amid an intensifying storyline focused on Gore's gaffes. Devine, Fabiani, Ginsberg, and Lehane had their hands full trying to stem the tide. We needed a quick turnaround and the Cheney-Lieberman debate the next night was the best chance. The grim Cheney was the least popular of the four candidates in our data—and everyone else's. He was ideal—for us—as an unappealing Bush defender or an unconvincing Gore assailant, or so we thought. And he could be a target himself. We met with Lieberman and his debate prep team and then had dinner with him. Our message wasn't complicated: Lieberman had to stand up for Gore, go after Bush on the issues, and make sure Cheney didn't break out of his special-interest Halliburton box. This wasn't Lieberman's nature, but it was our necessity—and we thought we had agreement on it when we left for Washington.

I watched the debate at home while Eskew was at his farm in Virginia. Minutes into the encounter, when Lieberman announced he was going to be "positive tonight," he proved it. He offered a rote tribute to the Clinton-Gore years and then mildly criticized the Bush tax cut not as unfair, but as unaffordable. Cheney kindly corrected him: there was a surplus, and Bush and Cheney weren't using all of it for tax cuts. With each passing minute, Lieberman was laying a velvet glove on Bush and an unscathed Cheney was growing in stature. Eskew called me: "Can you believe this?" He called again: "Oh, God." Then came the shoot-me moment. Lieberman suggested that Cheney himself was proof that the Clinton-Gore economy was good: "I'm pleased to see from newspapers, Dick, that you're better off than you were eight years ago too." Without missing a beat, Cheney responded, to laughter and applause: "I can tell you, Joe, the government had absolutely nothing to do with it." That was a lie and I thought to myself: "Hallelujah, this is the big fat one." But instead of pointing out that while Cheney was CEO of Halliburton, it received billions of dollars in federal and defense contracts and loan guarantees, Lieberman proved his opponent's point: "Gee, I can see my wife, and I think she's thinking, 'Gee, I wish he would go out into the private sector.' " Then came the crushing blow—and it was from Cheney: "I'm going to try to help you do that, Joe." Eskew called again: "Oh God, oh God"—and then just hung up. Cheney was avuncular, reasonable, witty, and competent. Soon, he emerged as the most popular candidate on either ticket, with a net favorable rating that was 13 points higher than Gore's—and 6 points higher than Bush's.

We gathered again in Sarasota, and the prep session for the second presidential debate started with a sermonette from Gore. The gist of it was that mistakes the first time around weren't anybody's fault but his. It was a decent gesture, but as we quickly found out, he didn't really mean it. I was concerned that the first debate had so emphasized domestic issues that Lehrer would focus on foreign policy in this one. Foreign policy should have been our strong suit and a weakness for the untried Bush, whose only high card was that he had surrounded himself with his father's advisers. But Gore was close to unwilling to deal with substance, devoting minimal time to practicing or even discussing how to capitalize on this advantage. Instead, he stared at videotapes with Michael Sheehan in an attempt to learn how to be nicer and more user-friendly. Eskew showed him the *Saturday Night Live* segment on the lockbox—which guaranteed that the word would never be heard again. The purpose of showing him the skit was to loosen him up; it was obvious that seeing it just made him more uptight.

So, when he faced Bush again at Wake Forest University in North Carolina, Gore, as usual, was a message machine—but this time, driven by an obsession with tone. This was the debate where he and Bush were sitting side by side, and Gore was almost meek; he used the word "agree" twelve times. For example, he agreed with Bush that America should be a "humble" nation and that the United States couldn't allow itself to get overextended overseas. Just once, Gore mildly noted that he didn't "think" he agreed with his opponent—on the question of nation building. In our holding room, we were talking back to the television, pleading with Lehrer to move to domestic issues. But when he finally did, nearly halfway into the debate, Gore announced that he and Bush agreed on a federal law to ban racial profiling and even on some aspects of gun control. Then for good measure, he added: "And I agree with a lot of other things the Governor has said." Bush went out of his way, especially on foreign and security issues, to mute most potential points of conflict with Gore. And Gore obliged. At one point, when he tried to make a comment, and Lehrer said it was time to move on, Gore elicited an all-too-knowing laugh from the audience: "Far be it from me to suggest otherwise." After Bush reproved him for his exaggerations, the vice president didn't fight back by pointing out Bush's or by assailing his opponent on the merits. Instead, he sheepishly apologized for his own misstatements and then defensively tried to explain them away. The first debate had been a defeat where style mattered more than substance as the Bush forces won the spin wars. They didn't need much spin after this second encounter. It was another loss on style, but in a different way. The candidates may have been sitting, but Gore was in a crouch. We took a hit in Greenberg's polling, and public polls had Gore behind by as many as 5 points.

We had one debate left—at Washington University in St. Louis. Instead of repairing once more to Sarasota for prep, we were at a corporate retreat in the Missouri countryside. Gore whiled away time in his suite and with the "real people" who'd been brought in to brief him. The shark, thank heavens, had been left behind. When Gore finally showed up for a prep session, he was in a sour mood. He allowed me, just barely, to show him the imaginary line that he shouldn't cross in order to invade Bush's space. But we quickly realized that he'd immersed himself in the strategy memo and question-

and-answer document we'd given him. He was primed to nail Bush on Social Security privatization with a clear, simple explanation of how the Bush plan spent the same trillion dollars twice—to pay current Social Security benefits and to finance the transition to private accounts. You couldn't do both; the trust fund would be insolvent. As it turned out, in the debate itself, Gore had to get the argument out in response to a question that wasn't exactly on point; but Bush created the opening by referring to his privatization plan when he didn't have to. Gore also hammered away at the fact that the Bush tax cut mostly benefited the very wealthy. As one newspaper report described it, Gore returned to "those 'people, not the powerful' issues that buoyed him in the polls" after the Democratic Convention.

He was combative, but not overly aggressive; he'd almost found the right balance. He did marginally trespass across the imaginary line that marked off Bush's territory. And he broke the rules only once, asking a teacher who was questioning him what grade she taught. Lehrer stopped him; stung by the 1992 town hall debate with Clinton, when a woman pursued the first Bush about whether he had felt any personal impact from the nation's economic difficulties, the second Bush's negotiators had been obsessed with preventing any audience interaction in 2000—and we had agreed to rule it out. But I didn't care about Gore's minor violation of that rule. Not only did Gore pin Bush on Social Security, but pushed by Gore and then Lehrer on whether his tax cut went primarily to the top 1 percent of Americans, Bush had blurted out: "Of course it does." We cheered in the holding room. And Gore had sounded his strongest populist note on prescription drugs for seniors. "If you want someone who will spend a whole lot of words describing a convoluted process and then end up supporting legislation that is supported by the big drug companies," he said, referring to Bush, "then this is your man . . . I want to fight them—[I] will fight for you." The polls, in which Bush was leading by up to 9 points, mostly awarded the debate to Gore. He had laid the groundwork for a comeback in the homestretch. Within two days, Greenberg's polling showed us only 1 point behind.

* * *

The battleground states, seventeen or twenty of them, would decide the race. Since 2004, we've heard talk about a "50-state strategy," calling on Democratic candidates to compete nationally, everywhere in America. But that's financially impossible at the presidential level as long as nominees accept federal funding, which limits their spending. At the headquarters in Nashville, we had to make hard decisions about where to spend advertising dollars and candidate time; which states to take for granted—although no one ever put it that way; and where to give up the ghost. Some of the calls were easy; even with unlimited resources, it would be futile in a presidential campaign for Democrats to target Idaho and Wyoming—or Republicans to go after Rhode Island or California. But in 2000, Karl Rove not only said that the Bush game plan included California, but, ultimately, the campaign sent the candidate there and poured in millions of dollars. We assumed at first that this was a trick play—and Devine was apoplectic about the notion of spending any of our money in California. If we did that, he relentlessly insisted, we'd be short elsewhere, and we didn't have a margin for error; we had to carry most of our targeted states. We experienced a brief and phony October crisis when California governor Gray Davis insisted that *his* polling showed us only slightly ahead and losing ground. I was convinced that he wanted the extra resources to boost the prospects of his local candidates. Bill Daley came into Devine's office and asked if we could afford just a couple million dollars for California. Devine said he'd quit before he conceded that; it was malpractice. We commissioned a poll, found we were about 10 points ahead, and the issue died. On Election Day, Gore would carry California by 1.3 million votes.

The trade-off between Florida and Ohio was the most painful choice. Gore consistently trailed in our Ohio polling by 5 to 7 percent. In Florida, he trailed marginally, and then pulled 1 or 2 points ahead as we slowly won the advertising war on issues like prescription drug coverage under Medicare for senior citizens who dominate that state's electorate. We had gone off the air in Ohio on October 10. Later in the month, we ventured one last whack at winning the state with spots on Social Security and Bush's record in Texas. But we stayed 4 to 6 points back in the nightly Ohio tracking—and cancelled our TV advertising there a week before the election. Bush was lavishing money on Florida and we needed every cent to fight back. After the election and the fiasco of the Florida recount, there was plenty of second-guessing about the Ohio decision. But if we'd divided our resources between the two states, we almost certainly would have carried neither. Targeting Florida and holding to it, an audacious strategy first promoted by Devine, was what almost made Gore president—and would have done so if the butterfly ballot hadn't tricked thousands of traditionally Democratic Jewish voters into inadvertently casting their ballots for ultraconservative Pat Buchanan, who regularly questions America's close ties to Israel.

For the last two and a half weeks of the Gore stretch run, Eskew and I alternated traveling with the candidate. I took the first segment; Carter took the second. Gore was unflappable when I had to tell him, after one stop, that the daily CNN tracking poll showed a big swing to Bush. It made no sense, he commented; there was no event that could explain it. Maybe he'd just never talk about polls again—but what did ours say? Depending on the track, night to night, we were just ahead or just behind. Finally, Gore had broken through on the economy with a 12-point advantage over Bush. When we tested the candidates' attacks on each other—Gore was "arrogant . . . a big spender . . . untrustworthy" and Bush won't "fight for the average person . . . had a poor Texas record and [has] risky Social Security proposals"—Gore was preferred 49 percent to 42 percent. He had his game plan, his argument, and we were sticking to it.

With one exception: Gore was determined to give a blunt speech on global warming, and to do it in Michigan. The issue didn't have the same power then, the warnings didn't have the same credibility then that they do now—and this was a third rail in the automotive state of Michigan, which we had to carry. Just before a rally, Gore told me he knew Carter and I and all the rest of us were against a climate change speech in Michigan. He was right. I had talked to Chuck Campion, the classic Boston pol who had been parachuted in to help save the state—a quadrennial rescue mission he'd take on again in 2004. He is one of the wittiest and bluntest political operatives in the business; he said if we gave that speech, he might as well just go home. But Gore announced to me that he didn't care, he was going to say his piece anyway. He ordered me to confer with Katy McGinty, his chief environmental adviser, on the cell phone while he was at the rally. I phoned her from a sunny lot outside where the motorcade was parked. McGinty is a spontaneous soul, who says what she thinks and used to show up for meetings at NAVOBS carrying a six-pack of beer because she didn't like the brands that Al, as she always called him, usually served. When I reached her on the cell phone, she said, Was Al out of his mind? This was the nuttiest thing she'd ever heard; he'd lose Michigan. She'd rather have a president who did something about global warming than a defeated candidate who'd given some "goddamned noble speech" about it. And Carter and I certainly couldn't think this was a good idea. Tell Al, she said, to call her. When I reported her verdict to a disbelieving candidate, he phoned her, listened for a couple of minutes, and then he did budge. He said to me with resignation, "Well, I guess that's that."

I handed off to Eskew and spent the final days in Nashville; each one never seemed to end and yet moved at warp speed. With polling reviews, ad planning, message shaping, and my constant television interviews in a makeshift studio in the barnlike, low-rise office building to which we'd moved the headquarters, I was up from dawn till nearly midnight—and living mostly on adrenaline. With Devine, Daley, and Greenberg, we were in conference calls with Gore and Eskew from the road several times a day. And Daley was handling Bill Clinton, who was more than eager to give his advice and campaign all-out in the critical states. He had raised a mountain of money for the Democratic National Committee, but even though Gore had become his own man, the president was convinced that the country yearned for a third Clinton term.

We also had to deal with what I referred to as "the Tennessee mess." Voters in Gore's home state were decidedly negative about him. One focus group report put it this way: "Most of the men clearly relish the opportunity to stick it to Gore as a payback for what they see almost in terms of personal betrayal. They see him as a phony, acting almost as if he is from Tennessee." No matter what spots we tested, even those designed specifically for Tennessee, no positive claim about Gore moved voters. The only realistic option was to raise doubts about Bush. We did, but Bush's favorable rating was 10 points above Gore's; and while he was seen as "too conservative" and too close to special interests, Gore was "too liberal" and too close to Clinton. Still we couldn't give up and move advertising resources to a state like New Hampshire—which we would barely lose—and which would have tipped the outcome even without Florida. Gore never would have permitted us to go dark on television in his home state, and we never proposed it. Yet all we had to say there were words on the wind.

Internally, we had to resolve a pitched battle about the cutting edge of the case against Bush in the final week. Greenberg's November 1 poll showed that while Gore was leading by only 2 percent, an astounding 54 percent of people agreed that Bush "seems in over his head"—and only 43 percent disagreed. The number was slightly deceptive; just a quarter of voters thought this described Bush "very well." Lehane and Fabiani argued that Gore should pound away at the already rooted perception that Bush wasn't up to the presidency—or as Lehane put it, that he was "stupid"—although even he allowed that Gore couldn't say it quite that way.

Greenberg, Eskew, and I didn't believe that Gore could say it at all; the idea was out there, taking hold on its own. Gore, who was seen as "a little too arrogant" and willing to "say anything to win votes" by approximately 60 percent of Americans, was in no position to advance an explicit argument that would sound so condescending. Daley and Devine backed us up. Fabiani just shut his door in protest; but Lehane never gives up when he has a scythe in his hand. The two of us had a shouting match: he told me, in effect, that I was going to be responsible for losing the election. Greenberg calmly said the opposite: the voters would recoil from a patronizing Gore instructing them that it would be dumb to vote for someone as dumb as Bush. From the plane, Eskew said don't bother with it; it isn't going to happen. Gore had already had to sit there during one of the debates as Jim Lehrer recounted how Fabiani had publicly called Bush "a bumbler."

Gore's last push was set, and Bush generously offered us some additional firepower when he denied that Social Security was "some kind of federal program." This was the kind of thing that implicitly fueled the qualms about whether Bush was in over his head. Gore roared from the stump: "Yeah," Social Security is a federal program, "and a damn good one, too." We rushed a television ad into production and aired it heavily in Florida, where the latest Zogby Poll had Gore leading by 5 percent.

At this point, the campaign was briefly overwhelmed by a sudden media squall about Bush's arrest years before for drunken driving in Maine. The Bush team had known about it all along; in 1996, they'd dispatched Alberto Gonzales, later Bush's choice for U.S. Attorney General, to extricate him from jury duty so he wouldn't face the possibility of answering a question under oath about whether he'd ever been arrested. But we had no idea about the DUI and, as far as I knew, nothing to do with getting it to the press. It had been leaked by a maverick former Democratic candidate for governor of Maine, someone with no connection to our campaign. When I first heard about it, I nearly fell over. Daley presciently commented that we'd be better off without this thing. Events seemed to be moving, ever so slowly, our way; we didn't need a wild card on the table just now. After Bush initially acknowledged and apologized for "mistakes in my life," his strategists sent him out to call the story "dirty tricks." It was obviously an attempt to play into the perception that Gore would do or say anything to win. Eskew, who didn't give on-camera interviews, did one with the traveling press to deny any Gore involvement. Devine and I sat down in the TV studio in our headquarters to repeat the same denial—over and over. Greenberg reported that the DUI had no discernable impact in the polling; it had been a long time ago and voters were willing to let the subsequently born again Bush off the hook. In fact, it was a bad story that diverted media attention from Gore's push on Social Security.

The perennial problem of what to do with Bill Clinton became acute in the closing days of a close election. I became caught in the controversy and was still facing Clinton's ire a year later. The idea that Gore or any of us, out of pique or jealousy, would have sacrificed victory to avoid relying on Clinton is absurd. Gore had waited too long, I had waited too long, and all of us cared too much; we were ready to do what we had to, to call on anyone who could help us win. And personally it wasn't easy to keep spurning the president of the United States. We did it precisely because the data, nationally from Greenberg and state-by-state from Hickman, overwhelmingly showed we had no other choice. We didn't know what Mark Penn was telling the president, but we had to confront what our polling was telling us:

— In late September, Clinton's "thermometer" rating—the percentage of Americans who had a favorable view of him personally versus the percentage who were unfavorable—was negative by 7 percent. Gore's was positive by 12 percent—and consistently, Clinton's highest unfavorables were among the undecideds and the soft voters who hadn't settled on a candidate once and for all.

— By the end of October, Clinton was still net negative, and, even though Gore had a 2-point lead, 50 percent of voters thought he was too close to the president.

— In focus groups of soft and undecided voters from Florida to Iowa, there was a deluge of complaints about Gore's association with Clinton—

- "Some of the stuff that Clinton has done; [Gore] was holding back and knew about it. He's a liar."
- "He didn't stand up and say 'This is wrong.' "
- "He should have spoken up about the moral fiber of the White House."
- "Will he be like Clinton? . . . might sweep things under the carpet."

—In Arkansas, where Clinton did campaign the last weekend, his favorable was 43 percent and his unfavorable was 48 percent.

—In Iowa, as an October polling reporter explained, "Clinton's personal ratings have always been the worst of any battleground state, especially among swing voters." His standing there was as bad or worse in our final survey.

This last finding threw me into a collision with my client Iowa senator Tom Harkin. He caught me on a cell phone in a car the weekend before the election. Iowa was close, he exclaimed, and the only thing that could save it was a visit from Clinton—who could fire up the troops. I matter-of-factly replied that in terms of the votes we were still fighting for and trying to hold in Iowa, this would be counterproductive; we already had the faithful that Clinton could fire up. Harkin was having none of this. He knew the state. If I wouldn't help get Clinton on the ground for a big rally, well, goddamn it, Harkin exploded, then I'd never work for him again. We had decided not to share numbers on Clinton outside the campaign; there was enough tension already with the White House. Clinton wanted to be seen as an asset we mistakenly failed to deploy, not as a damaged president whose presence had to be rationed sparingly. But now, I snapped. I read Harkin the data from the latest Iowa survey—after he pledged not to share them with anyone else. Gore and Bush were tied in the state; Clinton had a good job rating there, but that wasn't what counted; more people agreed that it was "time for a change" than that "we should continue with a Democrat in the White House." Most disturbing, Clinton's Iowa favorable was 39 percent and his unfavorable 47 percent—and the deficit was cavernous with the voters we were barely winning. Gore, by contrast, was 10 percent net favorable, and trending up. We had battled back to a tie with Bush on values. Now, I asked, did Harkin really want a Clinton starburst in Iowa? In a subdued tone, he asked: How about one last stop from Lieberman? Gore would carry Iowa—by 1 point.

In other states, Clinton's favorable was mostly in deficit and seldom better than even, no matter how his job performance was rated.

This national case of cognitive dissonance had reached a new stage; it was almost as if Americans felt appreciation for the prosperity they'd enjoyed, but guilty for the price they had paid—a scandal in which their children had heard and asked them about the graphic words and details on the evening news. Except from Clinton loyalists, every piece of data we had said that his all-out presence on the campaign trail would be a liability among the voters who would swing this election.

Just five days out, Clinton told a national radio talk show targeted at African-Americans that Gore was the "next best thing" to a third Clinton term. The comment, of course, made news far beyond the African-American community; as Gore acidly said, that was a helpful way to put it. Then Bill Daley brought me directly into the Clinton question and set in motion the events that put the bull's-eye on my back. He appeared in Devine's office, where we were reviewing final advertising decisions, and said he needed to see me. Was I aware, he reported as we stood outside, that Clinton was now scheduled to campaign in New Jersey on the last weekend? It didn't matter much to us, Daley continued; we were double digits ahead in the state. But what about my client Jon Corzine, who was in a tight race for the Senate? He was the one who had invited Clinton. Did I really think this was a good idea? I called Corzine's pollster, Doug Schoen, Mark Penn's partner. I half-expected him to say the Clinton visit was fine. He said we had to stop it. The race was too tight. African-Americans were already going to turn out heavily for Gore and Corzine; but Corzine needed some of the normally Republican-leaning moderates he appealed to as a businessman—and anyway he'd win if he stayed the course. We couldn't afford some new big event that would have an unpredictable effect.

So now I phoned Corzine, who explained that the invitation hadn't been his idea. Clinton had contacted him to say that he was stumping for Hillary in New York, and had some time to cross the Hudson and campaign for Corzine. What, Corzine asked me with a rare note of irritation, was he supposed to say? "No," I answered—and explained why. Call the president back and tell him it just won't work out; a scheduling conflict, whatever, something. An unhappy

Corzine agreed to stiff-arm the president of the United States. Corzine was nervous on election night—he was behind in the early returns. When I talked to him from Nashville, I reported that the folks in charge of the network exit polls were certain that he'd win by 3 or 4 points—and he did. What I didn't realize was that Corzine—or someone in his campaign—had conveyed the message that I was the one who didn't want the president in New Jersey.

Over the next few months, I heard again and again that Clinton blamed me for keeping him off the road for Gore—I was guilty of that, but I wasn't the only one—and for what he regarded as Gore's misbegotten populist message—guilty again, although I didn't believe it was misbegotten, but actually underplayed. And I was told he was mad about Corzine. Washington was my livelihood; I had to get clients in this town again. I was under no illusion that Clinton would recommend me, but it was only prudent to say something to him. Beyond that, whatever my judgment about the middling record of his presidency, I liked him. I didn't regret our decisions about him in 2000; we had to do what was right for Gore. But I understood how Clinton felt. I wrote him in September 2001 to explain the Corzine situation as gently as I could. In December, he sent me a handwritten reply:

> Dear Bob,
> Thanks for your letter of September 17th—Corzine didn't lose, so no harm done—I believe a different strategy would have produced a victory for Al Gore but no one discussed it with me after I talked with Joe Lieberman the day his selection was announced.
> We are where we are. I will always be grateful for your help on the State of the Union speeches.
> Best to Marylouise.
> Bill Clinton

Clinton's situation wasn't the only factor that made the 2000 election close. Gore made his own mistakes. But precisely because the outcome was so close, it mattered that Clinton was disarmed in campaigning for his successor; it mattered that Gore was punished by some voters for their conflicted feelings about someone else's conduct. The Republicans, of course, had sought to tarnish and disable Clinton from the start; but he himself had provided stunning proof. My college classmate and lifelong friend George Thibault, director of the Academy of Harvard Medical School and a Clinton supporter, said it reminded him of F. Scott Fitzgerald's words in *The Great Gatsby* about "careless people," who "smashed up things and then retreated back . . . into their vast carelessness . . . and let other people clean up the mess they had made."

In 2000, Gore had to pick up the pieces, and overcome his own political awkwardness, his need to be the brightest person on the stage, and a nearly $50 million spending advantage held by Bush and the Republican National Committee from the conventions to the end. In Florida alone, the Gore campaign and the DNC were outspent by $10 million. That was inconvenient, too. But by Election Day a candidate who wasn't a natural as a politician had apparently persuaded the American people, just barely, that he was the right choice. He had come back from a 19-point deficit against Bush in January and a 17-point deficit in July to the point where, according to the afternoon and then the evening exit polls, he was the president-elect.

My first memory of Election Day is an early morning call at the Nashville headquarters from my sister Barbara Craig, who was living in Boca Raton, Florida. She'd just voted, she said, and the Palm Beach County ballot was confusing. She'd had to study it for a few minutes to make certain she was voting for Gore, not Pat Buchanan. Some seniors were marking their ballots twice just to be sure they were counted for Gore. I told Devine; he'd already heard from some other locals, he said, and we had lawyers on it. It wasn't clear what we could do, but I didn't waste a lot of time thinking about it.

Carter and Faith Eskew and Marylouise and I went to lunch. Gore had said that he and Tipper would try to drop by. They were at their "farm" an hour outside Nashville; the one-story, low-ceilinged house there was decidedly ordinary, a far cry from Gore's image as a scion of privilege. They might arrive in Nashville in time for dessert. When they didn't, we wandered down the street to a used bookstore. Almost simultaneously, we heard from both Gore and someone from the campaign ringing us with the first round of exit polls. Gore happily recounted the results: He was going to carry the states we had to, including Pennsylvania, Michigan, and Florida. The first west coast numbers weren't in yet, but none of us was worried any longer about the outcome there. Eskew and I hugged each other; we were going to win. And I was crying when I embraced Marylouise. I still can't put what I felt completely into words—and I had no suspicion that in four years, I'd relive it again.

The Gore campaign had been hard, unrelenting, at least twice on the verge of collapse, doubted before the primaries and pronounced doomed in the general. Gore could be difficult, and the last thing I wanted was to work for him in the White House. But he belonged there—and Bush didn't. Gore could hurl himself into trouble, but then he'd rise to the occasion. He could give us grief, and sometimes it was deserved; but he could be as hard or harder on himself. Yes, when he equivocated and pandered, he always got caught. But politicians generally play that game—Clinton, for example, more than Gore, but more skillfully, too.

When I was with Gore on election afternoon in the hotel room where we'd set up a podium to practice his victory speech—and that's what we now all thought it would be—he seemed almost liberated. He could leave the pettiness of the campaign behind, the constraints of being vice president, and govern and lead. I had no doubt global warming was on the agenda. Clearly, I had my own personal stake in the outcome. I'd been trying to help elect a president for the better part of three decades. I didn't know if I could ever bring myself to try again. Now I believed, I wouldn't have to.

Gore went over his speech draft—and then went to see his family. I told Eli Attie that, yes, we had to have the other statement or it would be bad luck. Just before the first returns started to come in, Gore was back to look at his remarks. They were fine, he said, as he put them aside; he didn't need a text for this one. He'd look at it later. And, he laughed: "I just might wing it." He'd arranged for a distributor of BlackBerrys, the electronic device I'd always refused to carry, to set up shop with the newest models in a room down the hall. Gore sent me there to get one; it could be useful during the transition, when I got back from my usual trip to Italy. Instead, I would use it constantly during the grinding battle over Florida, and then throw the hateful thing away. Some of the top staff—Tad Devine, Michael Whouley—were at the headquarters to monitor the returns on banks of computers and phones. More and more people gathered in the practice room in front of the television set that was there. Anyone and everyone we could find in the media—and they were constantly calling us, too—was confirming the exit polls. So was the early vote count. Around ten minutes of eight, the networks called Florida for Gore. We applauded. Gore went to dinner with his family in their suite; and a big tableful of us—Daley, Brazile, Carter and Faith, Marylouise and I, and a few others—adjourned to the steakhouse on the first floor of the hotel for a celebratory meal.

Someone jokingly wondered what George was saying down there in Austin to his brother Jeb about Florida; even more interesting, what in the world was Jeb saying back? That must really be a pleasant dinner. As we bantered and chortled, I fleetingly thought about the cruelty of politics; whatever I felt about Bush, this had to be painful. But it was pretty fleeting; we were on our way, and it never occurred to me that the cruelty was about to turn. In the background, one of the anchors said his network was about to call Tennessee. I stood up, walked closer to the set, and saw the outline of the state go red as he said, "Bush." It was disappointing, but it didn't matter as long as we carried enough of the close battleground states—from Wisconsin and Minnesota to New Mexico and Oregon—and in the end, we would. None of us contemplated the possibility that the Florida call would be withdrawn. Some of the reporters told us that Rove was protesting it. How could he be so sure that the call was wrong, that the exit polls were this far off the mark? At that moment, I remembered the New Hampshire primary, but reassured myself that this was a far bigger state, with a far bigger sample in the exit polls.

Just before 10 P.M., the networks reversed themselves; Florida was suddenly too close to call. The practice room was jammed. Marylouise and Faith had nervously retreated to the room next door. Enough of the dominoes were falling our way—if Florida finally came through or if we carried one more small state like New Hampshire. But as the clock moved from 1 A.M. to 2 A.M., the actual vote totals in Florida seemed daunting. Was Dade County out? Or which parts of it? And what about heavily Democratic Broward County? Election nights are mazes of rumors that constantly turn in on themselves. But Whouley told me that if the numbers he was seeing were correct, Bush was too far ahead, and we couldn't catch up.

Gore was in jeans and sandals, stretched out on the floor watching television, when my cell phone rang again shortly after 2 A.M.: Turn on one of the networks—I'm pretty sure it was CBS; they were about to call Florida and the presidency. We didn't trust Fox, which had moved first, at the behest of John Ellis, the consultant in charge of the network's team analyzing exit poll data. Ellis, a one-time friend of Marylouise's, was Bush's cousin; he had been on the phone frequently to Austin that night. But CBS—that was a different story. As I put down my cell phone and started to get out of the chair to change the channel—someone else must have had the remote— Gore fired a one-word question at me: "What?" All I could do was repeat the number of the channel I'd been told to change to: they were declaring the winner. Gore knew who it was as he pushed himself off the floor, switched channels, and stood there silently watching a cheering crowd gathered outside the Texas State Capitol, with cannons booming and the voice and graphics proclaiming the presidency of George W. Bush. There was hardly any time for the moment and the sorrow to settle in. The vice president of the United States clipped out an unmistakable command: "Let's get this over with." He set off for his suite, that "other" speech draft in hand, to dress, collect his family, and be driven to our own outdoor throng, gathered in a steady drizzle at the Nashville War Memorial.

I collected Marylouise and we went to our room to pick up our raincoats. Inside, she broke down and I sat holding her hand. On television, I suddenly saw the motorcade pulling away from the hotel, but decided that it didn't matter whether I was there or not.

My cell phone rang again; it was a senior network correspondent who assumed I was in the motorcade and warned me: The Florida numbers are wrong; don't let him concede. I frantically tried to reach Eskew riding in a van with Daley a few places behind Gore's limousine. They had just heard the same thing, he said. And by the way, where the hell was I? Well, I'd missed the departure. Somehow, he responded, you better get your ass over here and fast.

My young assistant Austin Brown drove me at breakneck speed through red lights to the security perimeter set up blocks away from the War Memorial. Meanwhile, Eskew and Greenberg had no success in reaching Gore, who was presumably paying no attention to the beeping of his BlackBerry. But David Morehouse, the no-nonsense trip director from Pittsburgh's blue-collar north side, would be the first person to see the vice president when he reached the War Memorial. He did answer his cell phone—and was told that under no circumstance could he let Gore go straight up on stage; no matter what, take him to the holding room. Something was wrong with the results. There wasn't a lot of time to tell him why after Gore pulled up, determined to hurry directly to the podium with Tipper and his family. He'd already called Bush to concede after the networks called the election. Morehouse, always respectful but never afraid of the vice president, blocked the path to the stage and insisted that while he didn't know the details, Gore couldn't speak yet: "You're going to the holding room." A simmering candidate, who'd just seen his dream crushed and really did want to get this over with, reluctantly followed Morehouse down the hallway.

I had jumped out of the car that was rushing me to the site at the first security checkpoint, and ran through the metal detectors, huffing and sweating, pointing at my Secret Service pin as the alarm buzzer sounded and the Secret Service agents waved me through. I fought through the crowd to a wall around a raised garden that abutted the memorial. An agent I knew glanced down in surprise and pulled me up to the top of the wall. I raggedly trotted to the end, jumped down, and took the pathway that led to the corridors and rooms under the stage. Bush's 50,000-vote lead in Florida little more than an hour before had collapsed to 930 votes as the totals were recalculated—and there were more ballots to be counted. As I walked in, Gore had just hung up on Bush after revoking his earlier concession. Gore glanced at me as I puffed for air and allowed that he was glad I could make it. He had the sardonic humor of someone who'd just been retrieved from the gallows, but didn't know if it was only a temporary stay of execution. We all agreed that Gore should return to the hotel—we weren't sure exactly what he should say at this point. He asked about sending legal swat teams into Florida. They were ready, he was informed, and a charter plane would soon have them on their way. But someone had to speak to the crowd. Eskew and I told Daley he was nominated. When he announced the election wasn't over, the thousands who'd ridden the roller coaster of the night from victory to defeat to confusion detonated into whistles and clapping, the reborn sounds of hope mingled with an underlying apprehension.

An inconvenient campaign was about to become an inconceivable one—a second campaign that in drama and daily twists and turns all but overshadowed the original one, a bitter battle that culminated only when the U.S. Supreme Court acted like a packed ward committee and stopped the real votes in Florida from being counted, "electing" George Bush president by a literal margin of 5 to 4.

We began the battle with a mistake. After a meeting in the war room where Gore's former chief of staff Ron Klain briefed us on our legal options and described the troops of lawyers we were deploying to Florida, the Gore high command, weary after one of the most intense days and nights any of us had known, agreed that this had to be positioned primarily as a question of law, not politics. In part, that was right; the initial network call for Bush would create a public impression that he had won and Gore was trying to reverse the results. In Greenberg's post-election polling, Americans were split on who should be president, but by more than 3 to 1 thought Bush would be inaugurated in January. You could sense this coming even in the thin hours of the morning after. There was a feeling that we had to persuade the public that we were fighting on principle. In larger part, treating the dispute as nonpolitical—and in fact acting that way—

376 I ROBERT SHRUM

was a mistake, one the Bush forces never duplicated; if they needed raw political force, including a near riot to stop the Dade County recount, then so be it. Anything to win. The damage could be repaired later, after Bush was in office—or more likely, Americans would just move on. But the "say anything, do anything" candidate Al Gore was hobbled by a higher sense of duty; determined as he was to prevail, he was equally and even in private vocally determined not to "tear the country apart."

I also suspect Gore welcomed the prospect of seeing his case made publicly by "distinguished" lawyers and scholars, not by the political consultants and operatives he had tolerated all these months. We simply stopped giving television interviews. The campaign recruited—and I regret my part in advancing the idea—Warren Christopher as our public face for the recount. This bright idea provoked the Republicans to a brighter one, their own "distinguished" former secretary of state, who also happened to be a consummate politician, James L. Baker III.

As we headed down the corridor to confer with Gore at noon the day after the election, there was an elegantly suited, stick-thin figure in front of us pulling a small suitcase on wheels; Christopher had just arrived from Los Angeles on a private jet. The legal issues were complex. But the moral issue should have been simple—count every vote. Why, Eskew wondered, in our meeting in Gore's suite, couldn't we just call for a ballot-by-ballot statewide recount? Because, the lawyers informed us, that wasn't what Florida law provided for. The first recount would just run all the ballots through the voting machines again. Then we could request recounts in specific counties. This might have been the only legally mandated procedure, but it could—and would—be characterized as a legalistic maneuver to shop for a selectively favorable outcome. The political voices were muted. We had done our part—if not enough. Eskew and I still had our reservations, and Ron Klain would come to share them. But Gore, with the presidency so close and yet so far, was as comfortable as he could be with the course we were on—and with Christopher's role. After a hurried briefing, Christopher was front and center at a press conference that afternoon. It was not a stellar performance—he didn't know the legal issues all that well. Eskew and I paced behind the blue curtain at the back of the ballroom.

The twists and turns of the month-long battle that ensued have been described elsewhere again and again. One moment I will never forget came when Joe Lieberman was asked about the "military ballots" on a November 19 Sunday talk show. These absentee ballots were cast by service members overseas; no one disputed that many of them had arrived without the legally required postmarks and over 1,500 of them had been disallowed, although Republican-dominated counties had counted theirs. Whouley, who was in Florida with Klain, suspected that some of the military ballots had been cast after the election, maybe even at the behest of unit commanders. Challenging military votes was bad p.r., but it was an option we couldn't afford to discard. Without the questionable ballots, Bush would lose Florida—and Gore would win the presidency. Lieberman knew this, but on *Meet the Press*, he went his own way: "My own point of view, I would give the benefit of the doubt . . . Al Gore and I never want to be part of anything that would put an extra burden on the military personnel abroad." Gore asked me if I knew Lieberman was going to say this. Did Carter? Neither of us did. Gore sighed and said, "Why?" Within 24 hours, Florida's attorney general, a Democrat, caved in as well and said that local election boards should count military ballots even without postmarks. Whouley and Klain both commented that there went one of our best chances.

We were living an endless, grinding succession of days around the vice president's dining table at NAVOBS, listening to reports on events in Florida, rehearsing, refining, and sometimes revising strategies, legal and political. From inside the residence, we could hear Bush demonstrators down the hill and across Massachusetts Avenue chanting: "Get out of Cheney's house." Gore irritably demanded that we marshal counterdemonstrations. He was intent on keeping this nonpolitical, but only up to a point. And he was increasingly convinced that the other side was nakedly stealing an election he had actually won. But we were never ahead in the actual vote counting, and never certain we could get all the votes accurately counted. One afternoon in late November, a discouraged Christopher made a carefully couched, implicit argument for weighing the merits of surrender. There comes a time, he said to Gore, when you have to consider your "reputation" in history. I'm seventy-five, but you have a future. Gore was visibly taken aback: he was looking for advice on how to succeed, not fail. Soon after, Christopher returned to Los Angeles for a while, and the very political Bill Daley became our principal spokesman. Gore himself made periodic public statements; in one he finally called for "a single, full, and accurate statewide count."

The Bush team was on the offensive everywhere—from Florida secretary of state Katherine Harris's office, which acted like a branch of the Bush organization, to the Florida legislature, where members threatened to ignore any additional vote counting and certify the Bush slate of electors. The Bush campaign had already gone to the federal courts to challenge the Florida Supreme Court's right to set recount procedures as a violation of both Florida law and the U.S. Constitution, as an unacceptable usurpation of the state legislature's power, and as a violation of the U.S. Constitution's procedures for selecting presidential electors.

As the case headed for the U.S. Supreme Court, Ron Klain and I pressed his mentor at Harvard Law School and my old friend Larry Tribe to argue for Gore. It was no secret Tribe was a liberal; but he was a commanding figure on the heights of constitutional law, with an enviable record of success before the Court. The law clerks used to joke that instead of the custom of assigning one of them to prepare questions, when Tribe was the counsel, some justices enlisted two or three of their clerks. At first, Tribe pleaded that he was busy with teaching and writing; he had other cases; he didn't really know Gore—and he didn't want to get caught up in internal campaign intrigue. We'd protect him, Klain and I promised—and Ron urged me to push my old friend hard. It was the case of a lifetime, I urged Tribe on the phone, in its effect if not constitutional principle. The entire future of the country was on the line. Gore was a little skeptical. Wouldn't Tribe alienate the moderate and conservative justices?

Klain answered that Tribe had often carried the votes of justices who didn't agree with his philosophy.

The case reached the U.S. Supreme Court for the first time in the last week of November. The Bush campaign asked for a drastic remedy: an order to halt the vote counting ordered by the Florida Supreme Court. In the argument on December 1, the one discordant note was a furious barrage of questions thrown at Tribe by Chief Justice William Rehnquist and the Court's conservative avatar Antonin Scalia, whose right-wing views on constitutional issues would be permanently marginalized if Gore were to appoint the next several justices. Three days later, the Court denied Bush's request to stop the vote counting, although neither side could claim an unequivocal victory. The case was sent back to Florida's highest court with a mandate to explicitly set out the standards for their decisions, clarifying one statutory and one constitutional point. "If the state court follows the road map set out for it," the *New York Times* reported, "the case might no longer present a federal question for the justices to review."

David Boies, another of America's "uber-lawyers" and a brilliant former aide to Ted Kennedy, was representing Gore at the state level. The Florida Supreme Court reheard the case and on December 8, on a 4 to 3 vote, ordered both an immediate hand recount of 45,000 disputed ballots and the addition of 383 votes to Gore's December total, cutting the Bush lead to 154 votes. I wasn't absorbed by the legal fine points, but the opinion appeared to satisfy the U.S. Supreme Court's mandate. That night, we were back at another steakhouse, the Washington Palm, celebrating again. We should have known better. Daley, Eskew, Jim Johnson, Donna Brazile, and I toasted the certainty of a vote count and the probability of a victory. That's still debated, depending on the criteria of different postinaugural counts. But except for the labored rationalizations of one conservative apologist, a federal judge who served up his "unofficial" musings in a book, there's hardly any dispute that the butterfly ballot alone robbed Gore of Florida.

The next afternoon, December 9, the world turned upside down again. The U.S. Supreme Court, with a bare majority invoking the fear that the ballots couldn't be counted in time to meet the proscribed date for appointing the presidential electors, issued a stay ordering that the votes not be counted at all—until the Court heard the constitutional arguments again. This struck me as patently contradictory—delay as a remedy for the shortness of time—and I feared that the fight was over except for the formalities. Gore decided that for this argument, Boies would replace Tribe. We were told that Gore had been warned both by his brother-in-law and by one of Tribe's scholarly rivals that he was "too liberal." This had been raised before, and Klain and I thought it had been settled. Now we had to handle Tribe. He's a proud man; but he swallowed hard and sat down with Boies and conferred with him on the intricacies on which the case now hinged.

It probably wouldn't have mattered who argued the case on December 11 before a Supreme Court that was divided into "red" justices and "blue" justices, although Steve Breyer reportedly hoped to persuade Justice Anthony Kennedy to accept a compromise that would have let the vote counting continue. As it got later and later that night, we concluded that there probably wouldn't be a decision until the next day. I went home and flicked on the television in our bedroom to see Breyer driving out of the Court. I knew what was coming. The post-midnight ruling halted the recount, period—and made Bush president by judicial fiat.

My first call was with Tribe, who characterized the decision as both "strange" and "watertight." The core of the majority, usually the most unyielding advocates of states' rights, had invoked federal power with barely a rationalizing gesture toward their professed principles. So embarrassed were they that they disclaimed any future precedent based on their decision. And the decision was watertight, Tribe continued, because there was no recourse left for us, nowhere we could go—no judicial form, no legal argument—that had any prospect of success. When Gore convened a middle-of-the-night conference call, he asked if there was anything else we could do. Without citing Tribe—this was now a delicate subject—I said, "No, this is it." He interrupted irritably: Did I mind if he relied on the lawyers who actually knew what he was talking about? No, I responded, I didn't mind, but he'd get the same answer. Let's see where we are in the morning, he finished, and we all hung up.

The next night, from his ceremonial office in the Executive Office Building on the White House grounds, Gore brought an unprecedented campaign to an end with an eloquent leavetaking. Dick Goodwin had drafted the remarks and faxed them in from Concord, Massachusetts. Eskew, Attie, and I looked at the text and made almost no changes because it was nearly pitch-perfect. Neither did Gore. Afterward, as we descended the long outside staircase of the EOB toward the West Wing, and the glare of television lights that ironically turned the night into high noon, I thought to myself that it would be a long time before I walked this way again.

Gore had been determined to do big things as president. "I'm not interested in school uniforms," he once said to me. And while Americans all but discounted foreign policy during the 2000 campaign, there's little doubt in my mind that a nation that saw the danger of 9/11 coming would never have come close to trusting its security to the untried hands of a one-and-a-half-term governor of Texas who had traveled abroad hardly at all. After 9/11, as we blundered or were bamboozled into Iraq, I started to doubt Bismarck's aphorism that God looks after fools, children, and the United States of America. If that were true, Al Gore would have been president as we faced a global war with terrorists. And I remembered how, as we shaped and reshaped his acceptance speech at the Democratic Convention, he insisted, against the advice of those of us who told him voters didn't care, on a reference to "the challenges of terrorism [and] new kinds of weapons of mass destruction."

Gore supposedly flunked the beer test, the measure of "likability" that in today's culture is treated as a predictor of votes: Which candidate would you rather sit and have a beer with? I'm not sure there's much hard evidence for the decisive influence of this test—and in fact, Gore was fun to sit and have a beer with. Obviously, the question was purely metaphorical in the case of the teetotaling Bush. But the real test, more real to me now than then, is: Who do you want sitting behind that desk deciding whether to send young Americans to war? Elections do matter. In 2000, an inconvenient campaign ended with an implausible result and still incalculable consequences. After he was denied the presidency he won, Al Gore within a few years became a prophet with honor—an early voice against the Iraq war and a globally influential voice against global warming. It then became fashionable to celebrate "Gore unplugged"; that, the conventional wisdom now declares in its latest iteration, is Gore at his best. Eskew noted that the more accurate formulation is "80 percent unplugged." Otherwise, Gore can make the kind of provocative appearance he did on the cover of *Vanity Fair* in 2006 next to a headline that called global warming "A Threat Graver Than Terrorism," coupled with his own apparent agreement inside the magazine, where he described the problem as an "unprecedented danger." All this is arguably true, but politically fraught; Gore would have been attacked for subordinating the terrorist threat if he was in the midst of a presidential campaign. The cover was a highly visible boost to his environmental agenda—but Gore could have protected himself, cover headline or not, with a slight seasoning of political acumen by writing in his own essay that climate change was the "other" great threat to our future.

Gore has to live every day with his belief that he was elected but not inaugurated. No one else can fully comprehend how this feels. Four years on, the day before the Bush-Kerry election, David Morehouse was reading our final poll numbers to Gore. We were ahead in Pennsylvania, ahead in Michigan, tied in Ohio, and plus 3 in Florida. "It looks like we'll win Florida," Morehouse said. Gore responded, drawing his words out in his slow southern drawl: "That'd be good, that'd be good." Then he paused. "But what would be better is if Florida ends in a tie and they catch Bush cheating and they put him in jail."

8

THE 9/11 ELECTION

By now, I knew that presidential campaigns are accidents waiting to happen. It wasn't just the butterfly ballot in Palm Beach County, without which Gore indisputably would have carried Florida and the Supreme Court never would have had a chance to pick the president. In 1960, if Martin Luther King, Jr., hadn't been arrested, if John Kennedy hadn't then called King's wife Coretta—or maybe if Richard Nixon had—the outcome would have been different. ("Daddy" King, Martin Luther King, Sr., had endorsed Nixon because he feared a Catholic president; he switched his endorsement after JFK's call. Kennedy was amazed when he heard about his earlier stance: "Imagine Martin Luther King having a bigot for a father!") If Gerald Ford hadn't rhetorically freed Poland in the second presidential debate in 1976, with the incredible denial that it was under Soviet domination, Jimmy Carter probably wouldn't have been elected; the Republicans would have been blamed for the economic and geopolitical woes of the late 1970s— and Ted Kennedy, not Ronald Reagan, might have won the presidency in 1980.

Ten months into the accident of the Bush presidency on a sunny September morning, James Carville, Stan Greenberg, and I were confidently briefing a breakfast session of national reporters about Bush's parlous poll numbers. Then, to my annoyance, my cell phone rang with a call from my office. I had told my assistant not to interrupt me during the breakfast, but the news was urgent: a plane had crashed into the World Trade Center. The reporters fled to their bureaus. The Bush presidency was transformed; politics was suspended and then upended; war was coming. The midterms would be a 9/11 election—and so would 2004.

I'd been involved in enough presidential campaigns that fell short and I'd helped elect more than two dozen senators, so I knew it was easy to get blamed for a loss and hard to get credit on the crowded stage of victory. I also knew all too well that political strategists are not masters of the political universe. Candidates matter more than consultants, and both are fallible and susceptible to crippling miscalculation. A third of a century had taught me that you can't see around every corner, especially in a presidential contest—that to succeed you first have to survive and, at some point in the long march to the nomination or Election Day, walk through the valley of political death.

So I knew what I was getting myself into if I saddled up once more. Carville asked me why in the world was I thinking of doing this? The odds were long for any given candidate—and why did I want to make myself a target again? But Carville had "won"; I hadn't. Even more, I was appalled by the Bush policies and irresistibly drawn to the game. Four of my clients were serious about running for president: John Edwards, Dick Gephardt, Joe Lieberman, and John Kerry. My partners and I said we wouldn't go to work for anyone until after the midterms, so the press started to write about the "Shrum Primary" as the first test of the 2004 race. I wouldn't answer a single question about the Shrum primary. For me the decision was personally complicated and painful enough without playing it out in public. It says something about the rise of consultants, and the lack of real events to report during the doldrums of the permanent campaign for presidency, that a story like the Shrum primary had any legs at all.

I thought Lieberman was too conservative to win the primaries—and too conservative for me. He stood proudly, not reluctantly, with Bush for war in Iraq. At lunch with him, I suggested that he at least find some major domestic initiatives where he could work with Ted Kennedy or Hillary Clinton. He couldn't be so monochromatic, I said; he had to widen his appeal. I knew he wouldn't do it. Joe is what he seems, the Republicans' favorite Democrat.

I saw Gephardt in his House Minority Leader's office in the late summer or early autumn of 2002. He was definitely running for president. I told him, as respectfully as I could, that he shouldn't; he wouldn't get the nomination; I didn't put it this bluntly, but his time had passed. He said that for him, "it's up or out," the presidency or private life; he didn't want to spend the rest of his years in the Congress. This was a hard meeting for me, and I wanted it to end. I wished him luck, he thanked me, and I left.

For me, the choice was between John Edwards and John Kerry.

A few months after the 2000 election, Kerry told me in his Georgetown study that he wanted my firm to do the ads and strategy for his upcoming Senate reelection, but there was a condition: He was running for president the next time, and I had to agree to be with him. I said we couldn't make a commitment until after the midterms. I also believed we owed it to Al Gore to wait for his decision. I never thought he would run and he might not hire us again; but I didn't want it to look as if those who had worked for him in 2000 were scattering before he made up his mind.

In the months ahead, I chatted with Kerry several times and had dinner with him and Teresa. He knew his campaign manager to be, Jim Jordan, didn't like me. I had no idea why, but Kerry said that if I was part of his presidential campaign, he'd make things work out. Jordan had run the press operation in Kerry's Senate office until Kerry opted against running for president in 2000. Jordan had then decamped to the Democratic Senate Campaign Committee, where he became staff director. He remained close to Kerry; as a native North Carolinian he balanced off the patrician New Englander's Boston-dominated core of longtime advisers. But as his influence grew, Jordan had largely marginalized them. He was close to Jim Margolis, the media adviser he'd recommended to Kerry for the 2002 Senate race. But Margolis, Kerry assured me, had been hired for that race—with no commitment that his firm would handle the presidential campaign, at least, as Kerry added months later, on an exclusive basis.

I had barely met Jordan, a barb-tongued thirtysomething, when Paul Wellstone, the senator from Minnesota, called my office early in 2002. He wanted us—specifically, Mike Donilon—to make the campaign ads for him that the Senate Campaign Committee was paying for; but Jordan was a roadblock. I called Kerry and said I didn't mind that Jordan was never for us. I did mind when he actively tried to stop clients from hiring us even when they wanted to. Kerry said, "Oh Christ," and that Jordan would be over to our office in half an hour to straighten this out. He was. We sat down and he shot a challenge across the conference room table: "How dare you call my boss and try to get me in trouble?" I said that we should just get Kerry on the speakerphone and settle the issue then and there. Jordan changed his tone and agreed that we could do the Wellstone work. We shook hands because we had to, and he left; it was a preview of my first few months in the Kerry presidential campaign.

During this period, I saw Edwards more than I saw Kerry. At an all-day session at his house, I heard one prominent trial lawyer say he could raise millions of trial lawyer dollars if Edwards ran for president. We spent some of that money early. His Senate seat wasn't up in 2002, but we produced ads featuring him boosting Democratic candidates in North Carolina; not coincidentally, it was also an image-boosting buy that spilled over into South Carolina, which would hold one of the early 2004 primaries. After a day of filming at Edwards's summer home on Figure Eight Island in the Outer Banks, we went out to dinner. Afterward, while Elizabeth drove the car home, John and I headed back on his boat; as the darkness closed in, we got lost in the tall grasses of the shallow waterways. He finally found the channel; and back in his living room, we talked about the likelihood of war in Iraq. Edwards said no one had yet made the case to him.

That fall, as a vote loomed on the resolution giving Bush authority to go to war, Edwards convened a circle of advisers in his family room in Washington to discuss his decision. He was skeptical, even exercised about the idea of voting yes. Elizabeth was a forceful no.

She didn't trust anything the Bush administration was saying. But the consensus view from both the foreign policy experts and the political operatives was that even though Edwards was on the Intelligence Committee, he was too junior in the Senate; he didn't have the credibility to vote against the resolution. To my continuing regret, I said he had to be for it. As I listened to this, I watched Edwards's face; he didn't like where he was being pushed to go. The process violated a principle I'd learned long before—candidates have to trust their own deeply felt instincts. It's the best way to live with defeat if it comes, and probably the best way to win.

The meeting we held in the Edwardses' family room did him a disservice; of course, he was the candidate and if he really was against the war, it was up to him to stand his ground. He didn't. If he had, it almost certainly would have been Edwards and not Dean who emerged early on as the antiwar candidate. But Edwards didn't want to look "liberal" and out of the mainstream; he was, after all, the southern candidate and thought of himself as Clintonesque. He valued the advice and prized the support of the centrist Democratic Leadership Council. I had my own concerns: If he took the antiwar route, I knew I would have been characterized as a malign force moving him to the left—which wasn't true, although I wish it had been given that I now regard the Iraq invasion as one of the great mistakes in the history of U.S. foreign policy.

Kerry was a different case: he had long-standing national security credentials and no one could attack his commitment to defend the country—or so it seemed at the time. He'd voted against the 1991 Gulf War when Saddam Hussein invaded Kuwait; the case then looked more urgent and less ambiguous than it did now. But I'm convinced that this earlier opposition to the Gulf War was now having a subtle, unspoken effect on him and most Democrats. The United States had prevailed swiftly and overwhelmingly in 1991; the Iraqis had fled Kuwait and were in pell-mell retreat when the first President Bush and Colin Powell decided that occupying Iraq would be a quagmire and called a halt to the forces rolling up the open road toward Baghdad. If victory this time was as quick and even more complete, Democrats worried, wouldn't Bush cement his image of strength and those who stood against him cast themselves as hopelessly weak in the post-9/11 world?

On the eve of the October 11 Senate vote on the war resolution, Kerry told me he was skeptical of the Bush administration's claims about weapons of mass destruction. After an eleventh-hour meeting in his Senate hideaway office, Kerry phoned again to ask my view on the politics of the vote. He thought the resolution was being rushed through before the midterm elections to scare Democrats into supporting it. Moreover, there was no evidence that Saddam Hussein had anything to do with 9/11; his government was secularist, opposed to fundamentalist forces like al Qaeda. Kerry added he didn't trust Bush to give the diplomatic route a real chance—and if he didn't, America might have to carry the burden of war almost alone. He feared that Bush, Vice President Dick Cheney, and Defense Secretary Donald Rumsfeld would treat the weapons inspection process as window dressing and refuse to give it enough time. But—and this was where he wanted to get my opinion—would he be a viable general election candidate if he was in the small minority of senators who voted no? Jordan was insisting that he had to vote with Bush. Nancy Stetson, a Kerry foreign policy adviser who'd argued the other side, later told me that Jordan had hammered Kerry: Go ahead and vote against it if you want, but you'll never be president of the United States. I thought that was wrong. Unlike Edwards, Kerry wasn't a first-term senator short on national security experience. On that count, he had the freedom to do what he wanted. So I told him it was impossible to predict the political fall-out if we went to war. No one could be certain what the ultimate costs and consequences would be, or how Democratic primary voters, who detested Bush, would react. The safest vote was whatever he thought was substantively right. On the Senate floor before the roll call, I later learned, Ted Kennedy buttonholed Kerry and passionately contended that even if it looked like good politics now, siding with Bush was wrong on the merits—and even politically.

The irony is that the man who became the 2004 Democratic presidential nominee, and perhaps his running mate, too, were actually against the Iraq war, but voted to let Bush start it—although Kerry insisted then and labored the point all through 2004 that there was a distinction between giving the president the authority to use force and the wisdom of the way in which he chose to use it. The votes that Kerry and Edwards cast reshaped the Democratic contest. Howard Dean, who had set out to run as the fiscal conservative, now had the opportunity to reincarnate himself as the antiwar candidate. He would move from obscure long shot to rallying point and then frontrunner. If Kerry had defied the conventional view and opposed the Iraq resolution, the Dean candidacy would have been left without political oxygen. Grassroots activists, in what would become the antiwar majority of Democrats, would have moved to the more experienced Kerry faster and in even greater numbers than they would have to an antiwar Edwards.

The midterm elections were near, and so was my own decision about the presidential campaign, when Marylouise and I spent an unseasonably warm fall day visiting Ted and Vicki Kennedy in Hyannisport. We were sitting on the porch, looking out over the harbor, when he turned to me and said, "Look, I can't tell you what to do. But I think you should work for John Kerry." Ted and Vicki—and my wife, who was Kerry's strongest advocate despite her disappointment about his war vote—pressed the case. I was a little surprised—not that Kennedy was for Kerry; he almost *had* to endorse his Massachusetts colleague, but that he felt so strongly about it.

There was an assumption around Washington that Kennedy was secretly for Edwards. Not only had he and John McCain accorded Edwards a high-profile role as one of three principal sponsors of the Patients' Bill of Rights, but it was Edwards, Kennedy told me later, who kept a moody McCain from jumping ship. In a meeting in McCain's office, the Arizona Republican told them maybe he had to stop being a cosponsor because Edwards was just giving too much away to the trial lawyers. Edwards offered to fix the problems then and there. McCain said they had to get more staff recommendations. Edwards responded that they should see how far they could get on their own. McCain was abrupt: "I have to leave." But he said that his two staff members, obviously steeled to resist the blandishments of

Kennedy and Edwards, could stay. Kennedy sat back and watched Edwards operate—smoothly, persuasively, and logically. After a little over an hour, the McCain staffers told their boss on the phone that they had a deal. Kennedy, himself a master of senatorial give-and-take, was impressed.

The political class, in Boston and Washington, also "knew" that Kennedy and Kerry didn't get along very well. It was true that the "other Senator" from Massachusetts invariably had trouble operating in Kennedy's shadow. The Kennedy staff and the Kerry staff had their rivalries and collisions; but whatever the tensions, there was an offsetting sense of cordiality, even friendship, between the two men. Kerry was one of the few senators invited to the periodic Kennedy birthday parties where his family and friends had to wear costumes from a particular period. For example, the theme one year was classic movies: Marylouise put my leg in a cast and we went as James Stewart and Grace Kelly in *Rear Window*; Kerry, dressed up as Lawrence of Arabia, was considerably more comfortable than I was. But to Kennedy, the 2004 election was more than personal—and about more than routine loyalty to his Massachusetts colleague. Kerry, he concluded, was the best candidate in the field and the best candidate to beat Bush.

I owed it to John Edwards to talk with him; I half hoped he wouldn't run. I was coming to believe he wasn't ready; he was a Clinton who hadn't read the books. I sat down with John and Elizabeth at their home in early December. John told me he still hadn't decided; but if he did run, he assumed we'd play the same role in the national campaign that we'd played in his 1998 Senate race. He asked whether I believed he could run for president and reelection to the Senate at the same time. I told him that was a bad idea—that he'd look like he doubted his own presidential prospects and the press would hammer him endlessly. Elizabeth said there was something she was worried about—that I could be too visible and dominant a force in the campaign, "the elephant in the room," as she put it; I'd have to downplay my role and hide behind Mike Donilon. It was a stunning moment to me—and not just because of my lifelong struggle with weight. After a lifetime in politics, I wasn't hiding behind anyone. I defensively told Elizabeth that most voters couldn't care less who the advisers were. The conversation was a tipping point; it reinforced my growing doubts about working for Edwards. I shared them with David Ginsberg, soon to be his communications director. And I spoke to John and Elizabeth once more before they left for Christmas, over a cup of coffee in their kitchen. She said they were going home to North Carolina to mull over the decision by themselves.

On New Year's Day, 2003, Edwards called me to say he'd made up his mind: he was announcing the next day. A few days later, I picked up *The Washington Post* and found the "elephant in the article." Edwards's pledge to be a "champion for regular people" was reminiscent, the reporter Dan Balz wrote, of Gore's 2000 pledge to serve the people, not the powerful: "It smacked of Democratic strategist Bob Shrum."

My partners and I had two more discussions with Edwards in his Senate office. In the first, Tad Devine candidly told him he hadn't done the right substantive preparation to run for president. In the second, Edwards asked us to take charge of the media and strategy—and said we'd report directly to him. He also offered us "7 or 8 percent" of the media buy, which was more, I knew, than we could earn from a split arrangement with Margolis in the Kerry campaign. We said we'd think about Edwards's offer. Not long after that, I called from Chicago and told him that we'd decided it was best—for him and for us—if we didn't work for him in 2004. But were we going to work for someone else? Yes, I responded, John Kerry. He was angry: "I can't believe you would do this to me and my family. I will never, ever forget it, even on my deathbed."

We had decided to go with Kerry, but it hadn't been easy—or expected. Most of Kerry's advisers, as he told me, had assumed all along that Tad, Mike, and I would join the Edwards campaign. But Kerry never accepted that; neither did Teresa. He had checked in regularly to discuss the political lay of the land. The phone rang again in mid-December. Gore had now announced he wasn't running in 2004; Kerry asked if we could sit down and talk in the next week or so, before Christmas. Could Marylouise and I come over for dinner? I answered: Why didn't he and Teresa come to our house?

First we had a conversation that was more personal than political—Kerry's daughter Alex and my stepson Michael were classmates from Brown. We discussed their exile in Hollywood; she was embarking on an acting career, he was now a television writer. Then John pressed me about the campaign. He said that whatever misgivings he had about Bush's course, the Iraq war, if it came, probably, almost certainly, would be over by the primaries. He didn't see Howard Dean as a real threat; but both John and Teresa were seriously focused on the engine that, unbeknownst to us, would soon supercharge the Dean campaign: the Internet. For the first of many times, I heard Kerry insist it had to be a central part of his own effort. He would repeat this often in the months ahead, sometimes angrily, because Jim Jordan would dismiss the Internet as a sideshow.

I said again that Jordan didn't want my partners or me involved in the Kerry effort. The candidate interrupted me, "But I do." By now, we were sitting in the living room having coffee. Teresa was leaning into John on the couch; he had his arm around her. I looked at him and said we'd have to work out a tolerable relationship with the campaign. I had no idea how hard that would be. He and Teresa were leaving for Sun Valley for Christmas; we said we'd get together in January. It was still an ambiguous situation.

We worked out the details in February and Jordan grudgingly accepted what would become an uneasy arrangement because, as he said, "My boss wants it." We formed an ad hoc company with Jim Margolis and agreed to split the fees for buying television media. The standard commission is 15 percent; no one pays that in a presidential campaign. We agreed that Margolis's firm and ours would each be paid 4.5 percent. (It is, of course, settled knowledge that media consultants make out like bandits. In fact, if their candidate wins the nomination, they do well, although not nearly as well as the press generally presumes. And Republican media consultants, one of them bragged at a 2004 post-election conference, worked for a flat fee in the presidential race. They could make up the difference with the corporate contracts sent their way.)

My firm was now fully engaged—not always with a campaign manager who hadn't wanted us, but with Kerry himself. As the Bush administration ramped up preparations for the war, Kerry in private obsessively rehashed what he thought the president was doing wrong: the international inspectors needed more time; the United States needed more time to build an international coalition. At this point, I think he was conscience-stricken about his vote on the war resolution and about the prospect of sending a new generation of young Americans off to what he thought might be a needless or futile war. On March 20, 2003, the day the Bush administration launched its invasion, the campaign had to put out a statement in Kerry's name. He rejected the pro forma version drafted and re-drafted by the campaign and Senate staffs. He wrote his own lengthy piece, full of reservations and criticisms. And it was one of the few times early on that Jordan called me: This was a disaster, he said. Kerry had to be clear that he was supporting Bush.

It was a more important moment than I realized, probably Kerry's last chance to go with his own doubts and oppose the invasion as premature and unjustified, given the state of our intelligence, the lack of major allies—the only one with us was Great Britain—and the fact that the inspectors looking for WMDs hadn't finished their work. Kerry invoked all these concerns in the statement he wrote. Had he gone with it, he might have been able to argue more persuasively in the months ahead that his vote to give the president the *authority* to use force if necessary wasn't necessarily a vote for a war that shouldn't have in fact been waged. That, too, would have been nuance, but at least it would have been more credible. Kerry asked me if he'd be criticized if he issued his own draft because it seemed at odds with his earlier vote. Sure, I said, and he argued that it really wasn't. I told him he should say what he believed—which, if it had happened, would have precipitated a blowup between Jordan and me. "We have to stay together on this," he had warned me. Jordan leaned heavily on the data from our pollster Mark Mellman that showed overwhelming popular approval for the war. So, while expressing his reservations in muted form, Kerry gave in; buried in the press release the campaign issued in his name was a statement that, with American troops committed to battle, it was important to support the war and win it. This was just enough to convey the sense that Kerry did back Bush's decision although, technically, the statement never said that.

Over the next eight months, the Kerry campaign almost fell apart in a gradual process that accelerated to near warp speed by the fall of 2003. The first sign came during an early April meeting of Kerry and top staff in the second-floor dining room of the Phoenix Park Hotel, a few blocks from the Capitol Building. Amid the self-consciously Celtic surroundings, there was a lot of happy talk about fund-raising. The first-quarter reports were about to be filed with the Federal Election Commission and Kerry's total, Jordan said, would be almost $7 million, far more than any other candidate's. Edwards wouldn't hit $5 million; Dean's total would be negligible. Jordan's handheld then buzzed with the news that Edwards had actually outraised Kerry, with a total of $7.4 million; Dean had raised $2.6 million. Jordan's estimate that Edwards couldn't possibly do this again only stoked the candidate's ire. I asked if most of Dean's money came from the Internet—and if so, fueled by his antiwar stance, why wouldn't he be able to collect even more the next time around? Jordan replied that the Internet was an adjunct, a way to talk to people who were already with you; no way could someone raise tens of millions of dollars online. Kerry jumped in: "I disagree." The Internet was key and it had to stop being treated as secondary. Kerry called me after the meeting and said: "I think we're in trouble."

He was a front-runner, but a fragile one, with a shallow base. And Iraq, despite the immediate success of the invasion, was a storm about to envelop our campaign. Howard Dean was the rider on the storm. He was gaining ground on the eve of the first candidate debate at the South Carolina Democratic Convention in early May.

Our debate prep session, in a cramped conference room off the Hampton Inn lobby in Columbia, was exactly wrong—too many facts with no sense of strategy and no one in charge. At one point, South Carolina's acerbic Senator Fritz Hollings, whom I'd first met forty years before at the Democratic Convention, stepped into the room. He teased Kerry and me: "John, if you've got Shrum here, how you gonna win?" We all laughed. I'd helped Hollings out at a crucial point in his previous reelection, and for years we had joked and jibed back and forth. Within a few days, someone in the Kerry staff gave the story to *The Washington Post*, which treated Hollings's comment as serious criticism. When Hollings called about it, I told him not to worry: "Stuff like this just goes with the territory."

The real problem with the debate was that Kerry himself defaulted reflexively to a negative strategy: attack Howard Dean. It's often his first instinct to deal with a problem frontally, as he initially had on issues like crime during his 1996 Senate race against Bill Weld. I had advised that he could rebut Dean, but shouldn't initiate an attack. Instead, he went out of his way to confront Dean—for example, on an obscure point about his record on children's health care as governor of Vermont. It went down badly with the audience and the press; the effect was to elevate Dean. Afterward, I ran into Dean's campaign manager Joe Trippi at the airport. He was eating a breakfast sandwich from a fast-food counter and, in between bites, poor-mouthing his campaign's chances. Kerry had all the endorsements, the institutional advantages, he said; the Dean campaign had some grassroots, but that wasn't enough. Trippi looked like the cat that was swallowing the canary; he had a strategy and he believed it was working. As our conversation was ending, I asked him if Dean ever read a prepared text. "No," he said, "we kind of think that's old politics." Walking toward the gate for my flight, I thought how risky it was to leave a guy out there on his own all the time. If Dean continued to rise, he'd be heard by a nation, not merely by roomfuls of activists.

The mood inside the Kerry campaign was rancid. Jordan took to attacking his own candidate in e-mails. Even worse, his e-mails were vicious about Teresa; when she was scheduled for an interview with the *New York Times*, he wrote: "what are the odds—take this as I mean it pls—that she won't fuck this up . . . wallow in victimhood. . . ." She didn't. Jordan also complained that "she thinks it's her prerogative . . . to stop and talk to reporters . . . there's always a chance she'll say something stupid. This has to stop." I told him that Teresa was going to have to talk to reporters: the answer wasn't to trash her but to help her. But sources in the campaign were describing her on background as a liability and reporting that we were trying to figure out how to shut her up. That period shaped an image, a caricature, that dogged her all the way to November 2004. She could never be a stick-figure spouse saying nothing and smiling fixedly while her husband stood at a podium. As an engaging if unorthodox campaigner, in living rooms across Iowa, she would be critical to her husband's success there. She's smart about politics: she saw the Dean threat and the potential of the Internet before almost anyone else in the campaign. But she hardly got credit for any of this, and until late in the game, she never received the backing and assistance she should have had. She was left vulnerable to Bush campaign attacks exploiting stereotypes about her wealth and her immigrant's accent. Teresa had been born and raised as a doctor's daughter in the Portuguese colony of Mozambique. She often publicly recalled her father's service to the poor there. Her distinctive presence could be invoked to prove her "foreignness," as great an offense as the fact that Kerry could speak French.

Teresa refused to come downstairs to join our next big strategy meeting at her home in Nantucket over the Fourth of July weekend. We experienced a repeat of our April session in Washington, only this time it was worse. Kerry asked for a full briefing on the use of the Internet; he didn't like what he heard. We had supporters like our California fund-raiser Mark Gorenberg who were players in the Internet universe. Why weren't we calling on them? Kerry's mood darkened as he was taken through a rote PowerPoint that was more a substitute for strategy than an expression of it. There was a sense of wrenching division around that table in Nantucket—between the Bostonians Kerry had invited back in and Jordan and his allies, who wanted to exile them from the campaign.

Through a painful accident of timing, the quarterly federal fund-raising reports were coming out again. Jordan said he was sure that everything was financially on track—that we'd beat Edwards, and be far ahead of Dean. Then the numbers hit: Kerry did nose out Edwards, but Dean had soared into first place with nearly $8 million in the past three months. It was an Internet tidal wave. Kerry rounded on the staff. Do you people ever know what you're talking about? Jordan replied that Dean couldn't possibly duplicate this next time. I said that he could surpass it, raising $10 to $15 million in each of the final two quarters of the year. Then, I continued, he would refuse to accept federal funding for his primary campaign, which meant he wouldn't have to observe the spending limits in the early states. At that point, we couldn't possibly compete with him unless we went outside the system, too. I added that at least with no limit on overall pre-convention spending, a successful Kerry candidacy could fight back against what I was sure would be a Bush negative onslaught that would rage from the day after the Democratic nomination was in hand until we received federal funding following our convention in July.

There was something I was conscious of that I didn't say—that if he declined public funding for the primaries, Kerry himself would be pressed financially. Unlike Dean, we didn't have a broad enough base of support; we were relying on high-dollar donors, and the take from them would dwindle as Dean looked like the winner. And contrary to a widespread assumption, I knew that John Kerry, unlike his wife, didn't have the kind of fabulous wealth that could indefinitely sustain a presidential campaign; his net worth, as I was told a few months later, was around $12 million—and he'd have to risk a lot of it just to get through Iowa and New Hampshire because under the law, he couldn't use any of Teresa's inherited Heinz fortune.

I wasn't sure how Kerry would react to the suggestion that he reject public funding. Jordan, Margolis, and their allies at the meeting dismissed the scenario I outlined. Dean wouldn't go outside the system; he couldn't possibly raise enough to do it. Kerry had always been for campaign finance reform—how could he turn his back on it now? But, I responded, what if there was no other way to win?

Kerry listened in silence for a while, and then said that he wasn't prepared to go there—yet.

Before the session started, I had run into Ron Rosenblith at the bare-bones motel we were all staying at across the street from Nantucket Airport. He'd been an advance man in the McGovern and Kennedy campaigns and then the manager of Kerry's upset victory in the 1984 Massachusetts Senate primary. Although Rosenblith and his wife lived in Washington, Jordan saw him as one of the "Boston boys" to be excluded from the campaign. He was only at the meeting because Kerry insisted on it. Ron and I sat in the sunny motel courtyard and chatted while waiting for the van that would drive us to Kerry's house. This was just after we heard about Dean's fundraising breakthrough, and Ron said you could see his candidacy moving like lightning on the Internet. We, by contrast, were moving backward. "This thing is all fucked up," Ron said. After our two-day meeting, he remembered how someone on the staff had responded all but contemptuously to a Kerry grilling about the Internet: "He doesn't even like John. He hates him. What's he doing here? He ought to be fired." He paused and then said, "Actually, it's Jordan who has to be fired."

Before I left Nantucket, I sat in Teresa's upstairs library and briefed her about the downstairs meeting she had declined to attend. She said she would do what she had to; she'd work hard, but she thought the campaign lacked two things—good strategy and good management. I realized how skittish Kerry was about shaking up a campaign; he'd done it in 1996 only after prodding from Ted Kennedy, and only after his longtime pollster Tom Kiley, a former seminarian who's both personally gentle and intellectually rigorous, had forcefully warned him and Teresa that he was on the verge of defeat. In the run-up to the 2004 presidential race, Kiley had been pushed aside for Mellman, Jordan's favorite pollster. I had urged Kerry to bring Kiley back, and he, too, was at the table in Nantucket.

We left Nantucket without finding or defining any clear way forward. We were feeling the pressure of Dean's momentum while

Kerry was plodding through a conventional schedule, Dean was blitzing the country with his "Sleepless Summer Tour." Maybe, it suddenly dawned on a lot of Democrats, he was not only viable but unstoppable—at least by anyone already in the race. So Wesley Clark, the U.S. Army general who had commanded NATO in the late 1990s and ran the successful air war to stop the Milosevic genocide in Kosovo, was now preparing to announce his own candidacy. "He's the only hope," my friend Victor Kovner, a liberal activist who'd been close to Gore and Clinton, told me when I saw him in New York. Kerry was fizzling out. Exacerbated by the sense that it was all slipping away, the lead-up to Kerry's formal announcement of candidacy in September was protracted and bitter. The process fed the perception that we were divided and doomed as the fissures inside the campaign broke into the open.

First, there was a confrontation about schedule. Chris Lehane, the former Gore press secretary who had agitated to close the 2000 campaign with an argument that Bush was too stupid to be president, was Jordan's handpicked choice to be Kerry's communications director. For now, he was doing it part time, commuting from the west coast. He was a master of snappy one-liners, but his sense of strategy was instant political gratification—get the hit you can today and then worry about tomorrow.

He and Jordan had that kind of announcement plan. We had all agreed that Kerry would deliver his announcement speech on successive days in Iowa, New Hampshire, and South Carolina, the sites of the first three contests. We'd end in Boston, but hadn't decided where to start. Lehane and Jordan were fixated on South Carolina, with Kerry standing in Charleston in front of a mothballed aircraft carrier, the *Yorktown*, to highlight his military service. My partner Mike Donilon and I argued for Iowa and then New Hampshire, where we needed maximum impact; if we won the contests there, the fight for the nomination would be all but over. Those two states were Kerry's opportunity for a quick kill, or the places where his candidacy could die a quick death.

I thought Jordan and Lehane's response would be that a South Carolina kickoff would showcase Kerry as a "national" candidate.

But they didn't argue that. Their rationale was the photo op at the aircraft carrier. In a round of conference calls, I suggested that we could get the photo op by going to Charleston after Kerry had announced elsewhere. Lehane replied that if we went to South Carolina second, third, or last, we wouldn't get the picture. What if it rained in Charleston or was too hot? I asked. Jordan brushed the question aside. Kerry had his own preference. In thoughts he tape-recorded on the announcement, he envisioned a "start in Iowa in the morning," but once again he allowed himself to be persuaded to go against his own instincts.

Writing the announcement speech itself was chaos. Kerry and I discussed what to say, and he told me to do a draft, and then share it with his brother Cam, with Jordan, with both his pollsters, Mellman and Kiley, and with his longtime Boston adviser, John Marttila. Them and no one else—Kerry said he wanted the draft closely held. One complicating factor was that Kerry was uncomfortable with the slogan Jordan and Mellman were pushing: "The Courage to Do What's Right for America." He thought it sounded like he was bragging about his own courage; so did his sister Diana. Mellman tested alternatives, but I wasn't surprised when he and Jordan came back and reported that their initial preference had been right all along. In an effort to get along, I said we could thread the line into the speech in a way that conveyed the sense that Kerry was appealing to the American people's courage, not applauding his own. The candidate reluctantly bought it, but he said that, Damn it, he didn't want to see any signs that just said something like "Kerry and Courage."

The dustup over the slogan represented more than a semantic dispute. At this point, the Kerry pudding had no theme; he couldn't be the antiwar candidate, although he was alternatively worried and disdainful that Dean had now claimed the most potentially powerful ideological ground in the Democratic Party. The case for Kerry, that he was the candidate who could and should be president, would ultimately prove to be compelling to Democrats determined to defeat Bush. But this would only emerge later, in tune with the natural rhythms of politics, when caucus and primary voters finally faced the reality of choice. Even then, as the weeks before Iowa showed, the argument would have to be inferential rather than frontal, leading voters to reach that conclusion themselves rather than hitting them over the head with a blunt-force winnability argument that could backfire if they were instructed they had no alternative.

In the absence of a coherent message, the announcement speech had to be compounded out of Mellman's issue polling, seasoned with references to Kerry's own genuinely felt concerns like the environment. Kerry was constantly on the phone about the speech; he faxed in sheets of handwritten pages. Like him, I don't type, so I wrote the draft in longhand, and faxed it from my home on the Cape to my office in Washington, where it was typed and then sent on to Kerry and e-mailed to Jordan. He passed it on to Mellman and to Lehane and our speechwriter Andrei Cherney. I didn't know Andrei very well; he'd worked on Al Gore's White House staff, but had left before I arrived on Gore's 2000 campaign.

I assumed or hoped that the process of reviewing and editing the draft wouldn't be poisoned by the other tensions surrounding the announcement. Partly this feeling was based on what I'd just experienced in my day job, writing and filming television ads. The filming took place in the colonial home of a supporter in Concord, New Hampshire. Jim Margolis and I directed the shoot and the two of us were to start with an interview of an unscripted Kerry. But the candidate arrived late and unfocused. We wouldn't get much of anything useful from an interview, I said; we had to rely on the scripts. Kerry, whose ease in reading from the TelePromPter had surprised me in his 1996 Senate race, powered his way through a dozen or more spots. He'd do a take. I'd critique it—and we usually had a "keeper" by the third try. The shoot was rushed, but it went smoothly, as did the collaboration with Margolis. I talked about the announcement draft with Jim. He said it sounded on target, and I told him that like Mellman, he could get a copy from Jordan as soon as it was finished.

When it was—and because driving, like typing, is a skill I've never mastered—I took the commuter bus from the Sagamore Circle, which abuts the Cape Cod Canal, to South Station in Boston. In a skyscraper across the street, in a conference room in Cam Kerry's law office, I sat with him, Kiley, and Marttila as we went through the draft page by page. Kiley said: "It's the right speech, the best we'll do with the data and situation we're in." Then an alternative draft, an entirely different version, arrived on the fax from Lehane and Cherney. I would later learn that Cherney was just trying to get on the winning side of a gathering civil war inside the campaign. The first line of the draft—"Spring training is over"—was preposterous, a defensive concession of Kerry's apparent stumbles and decline. The draft featured a series of veiled but blunt-force blasts at Howard Dean. That tactic had failed spectacularly in the South Carolina debate. I was convinced that a direct negative assault on Dean would damage us, conceivably boost him, but most likely let another candidate like Edwards move ahead while Kerry and Dean battered each other.

When he saw the alternative draft, Kerry reacted to it bluntly: "I am not going to say *this*." But trying to keep a fragile peace, he phoned me on the Cape and asked me to find and insert a few lines from what he called "that other speech." Doing this pushed a draft that was on the verge of being too long over the edge. He called again and asked if Marylouise would drive me back to Boston so that we could sit at his kitchen table and come up with a final version. The Heinz-Kerry kitchen is in the chapel of the former convent that became their Beacon Hill town house, but the all-nighter that followed was anything but blessed. We spent hours rewriting and trying to shoehorn in several more phrases from "that other speech." Kerry rejected most of them, said he was tired and needed to sleep, and asked Cam and me to stay up and keep at it. We did—for almost the whole night, a tortured process because Cam, unlike his brother, has no natural feel for the power of language. He tends to write literally and legalistically and engage in protracted arguments about single words or phrases.

I caught two hours of sleep in a guest bedroom upstairs. Marylouise drove to Boston again with a suitcase full of clean clothes for me; we were about to fly out of Logan Airport for the announcement tour. We got to the airport in a drizzle. As we headed into the small building that led to our chartered plane, Kerry drew me aside under the overhang of a wooden porch and told me that as soon as the announcement was over, he was going to deal with the Jordan problem.

I said nothing, and after boarding the plane, Kerry, his brother, and I went back to cutting a draft that was still too long. The whole process had been a microcosm of what would always be wrong with the campaign: When his back was plainly against the wall, as it soon would be, Kerry was bold and decisive. At other times, he tended to second-guess, revise, fiddle, confer with anyone in sight, and try to placate everyone around him. For him, I think the easier days in the White House might have been harder. But in a crisis, I believe Kerry would have shown the right stuff as president; he was the young naval officer who didn't think twice about turning his boat around and heading back into enemy fire to rescue an American soldier stranded in the water.

We stayed overnight at a hotel in Charleston near the *Yorktown*. By the time we motorcaded the few hundred yards to a platform in front of the aircraft carrier, the sun was blazing in a hot September sky. John and Teresa paused in a holding area under a small tent. It was the last patch of shade they would see for well over an hour. Even though I took refuge there through the entire event, my shirt and suit jacket were soon soaked through. The candidate, his wife and family, and his supporters, including fellow veteran and former Georgia senator Max Cleland, who was introducing him, were on a griddle, not a stage. Cleland was a triple amputee as a result of his Vietnam wounds; he'd been driven from office in 2002 by a disgusting campaign questioning his patriotism that featured ads picturing him alongside Osama bin Laden. That morning in South Carolina, I sensed the coming debacle as Cleland, a fiery speaker, a striking presence in his wheelchair, vainly tried to stoke up a wrung-out crowd. The advance team had distributed hand-held fans and when Kerry spoke, the rows of spectators sitting (or imprisoned) in folding chairs had to choose between cooling themselves at least a little and clapping at the applause lines. But we got our photo op—sort of. Only part of the aircraft carrier was visible; you couldn't tell exactly what it was and the networks didn't oblige us with many wide shots.

What viewers mostly saw was Kerry with his coat off, sweating in front of some American flags.

Afterward, the reporters were soggy and hopping mad. The *New York Times*'s Adam Nagourney walked up to me and asked, "How could you guys do this?" I gamely responded that it was a great announcement, a great visual—but I had no doubt that the bad stories were coming. Ivan Schlager, a friend of Kerry's and mine who'd worked for Fritz Hollings before becoming a top Washington lawyer, knew what I really thought. Schlager told Hollings, who was blunt: "Boy, I'm glad to know Shrum's not that crazy." He said anyone with a "pea brain" knows you don't do a big, formal speech outdoors in Charleston in the heat and humidity of early September: "Hell, boy, it's still summer."

On the bus back to the airport, and then on the flight to Iowa, Cam and I, and then the candidate, shortened the speech by three or four minutes. As our motorcade was rolling into Des Moines, Jordan's handheld was beeping again; he jumped out of the SUV, and it was the last I'd see of him for several hours. The event was held indoors, in a packed ballroom on top of a multistory former Masonic temple. As Cam and I ascended in the elevator, a young press aide explained to us that Kerry would be better this time; he'd gotten rid of that "bad" speech from South Carolina—the one, I thought to myself, I was responsible for. This would be a good event because Kerry would get it right this time, she added. I knew she wasn't putting out this spin on her own. I soon discovered it was what Lehane had fed the press on the plane as Teresa was feeding them chocolate chip cookies.

In reality, the two speeches were almost identical. A thousand Iowans packed into the room gave Kerry a rousing ovation. One reporter said to me, This was a great event, why in the world didn't you guys start here? Back in Kerry's suite at the venerable Hotel Fort Des Moines, I told him what Cam and I had heard on the elevator and what I was hearing from the press. I said I was tired, frustrated, and angry about being a punching bag. How could we let campaign insiders take the infighting public and damage him to win turf battles and settle personal scores? They probably thought they were right. But we could never win this way—and personally I was damned if I was going to make my best case to him when there were disagreements, then do what he decided and get publicly trashed for it. He said again that he knew what was happening, was sick of it, and he was going to fix it. Just hold on, don't react, don't fight back in the press. So for months afterward, I wouldn't take most reporters' calls, and until the final weeks of the campaign, I stopped doing television interviews to argue the Kerry case. We needed to be talking about the candidate, not me.

I told Kerry I wanted to take a shower, literally and metaphorically, and put on a fresh shirt. Then I stopped by the staff office and a young volunteer handed me a draft press release unequivocally reaffirming that Jordan was and would be the campaign manager. Why in the world were we putting this out? I returned to Kerry's suite, where Jordan and Margolis were buttonholing him in the living room. They seemed surprised by my sudden arrival. It turned out that Jordan had hastily abandoned the motorcade on the way into Des Moines when he'd suddenly been contacted about rumors that he was going to be fired. They were now all over the press corps; left unchecked, he and Margolis said, they would overwhelm the announcement story. Jordan wasn't heated and he didn't sound angry. But he insisted that there was no choice but to back him up in the clearest possible terms—not just for now but permanently. Kerry was annoyed and distinctly unenthusiastic about the idea. If we had to say anything, why not just put out a simple response that there was no basis to the story? That, he was told, would be a nondenial that would just feed the speculation. Kerry persisted—there had to be another way; why did we have to be talking about this at all? Margolis, who was now doing the talking, replied that Lehane was already briefing the press. We couldn't pull back—that, too, would make things worse.

Kerry asked what I thought, which was, although I didn't say it, that he'd been sandbagged, that Jordan had sensed Kerry's dissatisfaction and orchestrated or exploited the leak to head off his own demotion or dismissal after the announcement tour. What I did say was that if Lehane was out there briefing the press, then trimming or reversing course would bury the announcement in a landslide of stories about indecision and disarray. I was half-wrong. Kerry would have been better off getting the gain as well as the pain by dismissing Jordan on the spot. That didn't happen. Jordan assumed, I think, that the candidate was locked in. Kerry was resigned to the box he was in—for now.

The next day in New Hampshire, we had scheduled a rally, a conversation with voters in a diner, and press interviews, but no replay of the formal announcement address. For the climax of the tour, late that afternoon, Kerry would reprise it to a crowd of thousands gathered outside Faneuil Hall in Boston. He decided that for this event, we should reverse the domestic and foreign policy parts of the speech. Until then, we'd consciously started with national security to send a signal that Kerry was ready to compete on what was regarded as Bush's high ground. Now we could push harder on issues like the economy and health care. But preparing to board the caravan for Boston, Kerry bristled as he approached the buses lined up in the parking lot. The one he was supposed to ride on with Vietnam vets, including his former crewmates from the small Swift boats that plied the rivers of the Mekong Delta, was emblazoned with the words KERRY and COURAGE. It was exactly what he'd said we wouldn't do—go around proclaiming that he was courageous. He looked at me and said: "I'm not getting on that thing. You guys ride in that one and I'll take the staff bus." But the state troopers were saddled up and their motorcycles were ready to go. He asked if I knew about the signs and I said no, but we couldn't fix this now, and the vets who were traveling with us were already on board "his" bus.

After his speech outside Faneuil Hall got a raucous reception from his hometown crowd, Kerry was reaching through the police lines to shake hands when one of the fund-raisers, Bob Crowe, his close friend and neighbor on Nantucket, said to me: "This thing's a mess—Jordan's got to go." He went on to say that Jordan never talks to the fund-raisers, he's alienated them, he can't explain a coherent strategy for winning, and we're headed in the wrong direction—politically and financially. I wearily replied: "That's up to John," and returned to the hotel. I was having a drink in the bar with Marylouise when Chris Lehane walked in. I stood up and said hello, but he just stalked by. Within days, he left Kerry to flack for Wesley Clark, who was the flavor of that month. Lehane would counsel his newfound candidate to skip Iowa. Clark wouldn't have won there, but he might have drawn enough votes from Kerry to deny him victory and perhaps lived to fight another day. So Lehane might not have been working for our campaign anymore, but his advice was working for us.

In the weeks ahead, the Kerry campaign limped along—and downward. Only the Herculean efforts of our finance chair Lou Susman and his fund-raising team—with Lou, a top executive at Citigroup, calling in every chit he had—kept us solvent, just barely. We were still nowhere on the Internet. And the campaign was still deeply divided about how to deal with Howard Dean. Jordan, Margolis, and Mellman pressed constantly to go after Dean with negative ads; but in Mellman's Iowa surveys, none of the negatives raised very serious doubts for more than a relatively small fraction of the voters, less than 30 percent. Yet Kerry, the once fragile front-runner steadily falling behind, was emotionally drawn to attacking Dean. As he turned away from the microphone following a press conference, assuming his voice was no longer being picked up, he looked at his press secretary David Wade and angrily spat out: "Dean, Dean, Dean." But in contentious meetings in the conference room at our cramped headquarters, the town house on Capitol Hill that had been Woodrow Wilson's headquarters nearly a century before, Mike Donilon and I kept responding that a TV blitz against Dean would doom us, too, and help a third candidate. It really wasn't a strategy but an act of desperation—and how could we go down this road just because we couldn't think of anything else?

There was another road, I constantly argued. Look at the history of the Iowa caucuses. The polls in the months before didn't mean much. Gephardt had come from nowhere in December to victory less than six weeks later. Bush had upset Reagan in 1980 and Dole had upset Bush in 1988, and then nearly lost in 1996 when he was the front-runner. And even Gore in a two-way race had held on to his lead not with negative ads, but out in the open, with tough debate tactics that nonetheless seemed fair—at least to the voters if not the press. Caucus goers in Iowa tended to get serious around the first of the year, I said. And this time, when they started to ask what would be the decisive question for Democrats in 2004—who had a chance to beat Bush, who was the most believable presidential choice?— Kerry had to be there to meet them. He had to look like the answer, not a panicked mud wrestler down in the pit with Dean. Sometimes the best strategy is to accept and act on stark necessity. There were certainly things I was wrong about in the Kerry campaign, but not how to deal with Dean and Iowa—a battle I would ultimately win only after the campaign itself underwent traumatic change.

The pressures for change were mounting as I traveled with the candidate to New York, where I had dinner in late September with Lou Susman and his wife Margie. The fund-raising, he said, was in crisis. The contributors disliked Jordan almost as much as he seemed to dislike them. Lou was seeing John and Teresa later that night to say a change had to be made. Veteran advisers like John Marttila and Ron Rosenblith, still largely cut out of the operation, were also talking with Kerry, with me, and I don't know who else in the campaign, about replacing Jordan. The candidate seemed tempted to move, but he was afraid of the fall-out. He asked me: Wouldn't the press coverage be a disaster? It would be pretty bad, I said, but if he was going to let Jordan go, better in the fall than in January.

Kerry was clinging to the hope that he wouldn't have to do it. He'd found a September compromise, a buffer to hold the factions together: Jeanne Shaheen, the former Democratic governor of New Hampshire. He had persuaded her to take the newly created post of campaign chair, a big risk for her; when she accepted, we were in trouble everywhere, notably in her home state. In her new post, she was only in Washington a couple of days a week, but she did her best to bridge the divisions. We bumped our way through October and downward in the polls.

Preparing for the mid-November Iowa Jefferson-Jackson Day

Dinner, the event where Gore's performance had flummoxed Bill Bradley four years before, we all agreed that we had to spend a lot of our dwindling resources buying up big blocks of tickets. Dean and Kerry were the only candidates who would do that. But we disagreed about what Kerry should say. Jordan and Margolis urged that we stay where we were, with the basic theme we already had: "The Courage to Do What's Right for America." But in a conference call, our state manager John Norris said that Larry Grisolano, the direct-mail consultant and organizer who had come up with "Stay and Fight" as a slogan to attack Bradley four years earlier at the same dinner, had been hit with another burst of creativity. He was proposing that we shift gears and position Kerry as "The Real Deal." I immediately liked the idea: it was a first cut at implicitly making the argument that Kerry was the guy who could win—and Dean couldn't. Jordan objected that the signs we had ordered to plaster around the auditorium were already printed. I replied: "Print new ones." Shaheen agreed, and while Kerry at first was lukewarm about "The Real Deal"—it wasn't perfect, there had to be something else, he said—he agreed to try it out. He was anxious to move on, not just thematically but organizationally.

Jordan would be gone before Kerry mounted the stage at that November 15 J-J Dinner. Kerry had felt out John Sasso about coming in as campaign manager. Sasso, the architect of the Dukakis nomination strategy in 1988, told Kerry he couldn't afford to give up his lucrative corporate consulting business and tried to figure out ways to make the campaign work without removing Jordan. Kerry talked to another possible replacement, my partner Tad Devine, who so far hadn't had much to do with the campaign. The downside of Tad was that he *was* my partner. A change in campaign leadership would be tough enough for a lot of the staff Jordan had hired; it wouldn't help if it looked like I'd triumphed and taken control through Devine. I thought Kerry had overcome that concern when he asked Devine to sit down with his brother Cam. But Cam's offer was hedged and complicated; maybe there had to be some role for Jordan. And Cam wanted a bigger role for himself. Tad said no.

I had been talking with Ted Kennedy's chief of staff, Mary Beth

Cahill. The Massachusetts congressional delegation felt it wasn't being consulted or deployed effectively; after discussing the complaint with Kerry, I asked Mary Beth if she'd be willing to coordinate the "Mass delegation" for us. She said no, not under present circumstances. It would have been a small job for a person with a big résumé. Mary Beth had run Emily's List, the most powerful women's political action committee in America. Soon Kerry was thinking of a bigger job for her. Kerry called me on November 9 and said Jordan was on his way to Boston; he was going to tell him that Mary Beth was taking over. He asked me: Please don't talk to the press, don't attack Jordan. I said I hadn't; I promised I wouldn't; and I didn't. Kerry's hope was to make the change with as little recrimination as possible.

That was unrealistic. As they sat in his living room in Beacon Hill that afternoon, he asked Jordan to resign. Jordan said he would have to be fired. He was, and he flew back to Washington to meet with the staff at headquarters. Many of them were loyalists—more to him than to Kerry. They were ready to mutiny. After Jordan left headquarters, Margolis performed the vital service of quieting the turmoil. Kerry talked with the staff on the speakerphone, answered some rough questions, said it was his decision, not one that I had made for him. I was asked to avoid the headquarters that night. Kerry didn't criticize Jordan and asked everyone on the staff to stay, a request Mary Beth would repeat the next day.

The news stories, predictably, were hideous, especially because the firing just looked to reporters like the next chapter in Kerry's inexorable slide. Unnamed staff members expressed their anger in blind quotes; they even assailed Kerry for eating while he had been on the speakerphone. He told me it wasn't true, but it became a neat metaphor for an unfeeling candidate just going through the motions of reaching out to his aggrieved troops.

Kerry, who'd been ready for a brush fire, kept hoping against hope that the firestorm would go out. He didn't want anyone fanning the flames. He clamped down on any criticism of Jordan. This was sensible—he wasn't running against Jordan; but the result was a one-sided battle in the press. Two of Jordan's loyalists quit, prompting a second round of bad stories; to replace one of them, Mary Beth brought in Kennedy's communications director, Stephanie Cutter. She would become a scapegoat later in the campaign; but she was a feisty operator in her mid-thirties, who quickly picked up the pieces of a shattered communications operation. Of course, because of her Kennedy provenance, her hiring just fueled the spin about a Shrum coup. Then the next shoe dropped: on me. Just days after Jordan's departure, *New York Times* reporter David Halbfinger called to interview me for a profile. I told him I wouldn't cooperate; we were past the infighting and I wasn't going to respond to anything anonymous sources were saying about me. On the morning of November 12, Marylouise picked up the papers outside our front door. I heard the distress in her voice: "Oh God, you have to read this."

I bolted out of our bedroom and met her halfway down the stairs. I hadn't expected a good story. I'd already been pictured as the secondary villain in the initial pieces on the Jordan firing, when the *Times* had recycled the controversy surrounding the announcement speech and reported that I "went to Mr. Kerry's home" to get my way when in fact I'd been summoned there. But now, complete with a front-page photo, I was the centerpiece in a tome about the "Shrum Curse" and the succession of presidential campaigns I was supposedly responsible for losing. Actually, except for James Carville, no strategist had been in the driver's seat of a successful Democratic campaign for the presidency in three decades. Some of the charges in the article were accurate. I *was* older than Jordan and most of the other players in the Kerry enterprise and I *did* oppose their insistence on an all-out negative bombardment against Howard Dean. But the implication was that because I had prevailed in that argument, Kerry was doomed; unnamed and unhappy Kerry aides were eager to state that now I would have the "dominant" say on strategy. Once Kerry was winning, that spin would change: we were, I read to my surprise, just executing the strategy Jordan and his allies had left behind.

I couldn't blame Halbfinger; there was no lack of sources ready to go after me. But that morning, I remembered what one of the candidates to whom I had so blithely dispensed the advice to ignore a bad story once said to me: "That's easier advice to give than to take." Kerry phoned and said he was sorry about the *Times*, but it was absolutely critical for me not to respond in any way. I agreed again, even though I realized that if I didn't fight back, I'd be a defenseless target in the press. But something bigger was at stake: Kerry and the presidency.

The early phases of the Kerry effort and some of the later ones were messy—at times even brutal. But there's a myth about campaigns, nourished by a book I learned from and loved, Theodore White's groundbreaking *Making of the President 1960*, which portrays a master plan masterfully executed to secure an improbable nomination and then prevail in a wafer-thin election. I've heard Ted Kennedy laugh about the once common references to "the well-oiled Kennedy machine." It *was* extraordinary by the standards of its time. But the best campaigns are smart—and lucky. All campaigns have "accidents"—and some of them even become assets. When you're winning, everyone claims credit. When you're losing, someone or something inside the campaign gets blamed, although never the candidate, unless the election is over or the advisers who've been forced out speak out. To see inside campaigns as they really are is to be reminded that the sausage always looks neater than the sausage-making.

But at this point in the Kerry effort, both process and product looked bad. And things would continue that way for a while, at least in the nearly unanimous judgment of the political world, even as they started to get better. The weekend after the shake-up, Kerry would appear at that Jefferson–Jackson Day Dinner. "The Real Deal" signs were printed and ready. But Kerry didn't like most of Cherney's speech draft. So the day after the story about the "Shrum Curse," with calls for comment flooding my firm's office on the Georgetown waterfront, I ignored them, took out my legal pad, and in about an hour, came up with a different version.

My adrenaline was flowing; I knew what Kerry had to say. He was comfortable with the text—and committed most of it to memory. On the surface, the speech was directed at Bush, not Dean. The message was that Kerry could go toe-to-toe with Bush—on national security and domestic issues like health care; implicitly, that did strike a contrast with Dean and Edwards, both inexperienced in foreign policy. In my mind, Edwards, although pretty much written off by now, was a real threat. Kerry went after Bush for the way he went to war in Iraq and his "Mission Accomplished" photo op after a stunt flight to an aircraft carrier. Kerry couldn't attack frontally since he had voted for the Iraq resolution—although, he repeatedly explained to us, not for Bush's unilateral rush to war. But the fine distinctions didn't matter that night as Kerry unveiled a smackdown that Andrei Cherney and I had been discussing and toying with for weeks. It played off Bush's chest-thumping challenge to the Iraqi insurgents. If the president wanted to have a debate about security, then Kerry had "three simple words for him: 'Bring It On.' " Kerry had to repeat the line three times to break through the applause that rolled across the hall. (As with most good lines, it wasn't the first time this one had appeared in American politics. In 1965, Jack Burby, the press secretary to the Democratic governor of California, Pat Brown, scrawled a comment across an article about a movie actor named Ronald Reagan who was contemplating a race against Brown: " 'Bring him on' is our motto.")

Reporters discounted Kerry's performance at the Iowa dinner. After all, we had packed the place by buying up tickets. Hillary Clinton, who'd introduced the candidates, was portrayed as the non-runner who'd won the evening. Dean was still riding high on a flood tide of Internet money. But that mid-November speech, when it almost felt like midnight in the Kerry effort, gave heart to our Iowa troops; they stayed with us, and by the time of the caucuses, although no one knew it until the returns came in, we had the strongest organization in the state.

Kerry faced three critical strategic decisions in those final months of 2003. His whole future as a candidate depended on making the right one every time.

Even before he had unleashed "Bring It On," he'd made the first decision, with some help from Howard Dean, to decline federal matching funds for the primary campaign. While Kerry could never hope to match Dean in Internet fund-raising prior to Iowa, he could afford to put enough of his own money into the early stages of the process, Devine argued, to make a potentially decisive difference. It could be fatal to give up that option, and he certainly would have to opt out if Dean did just to stay competitive. Devine said something else equally compelling, which I repeated to Kerry again and again, to the point where he was clearly annoyed: A candidate who was in the system and secured the nomination would face a Bush campaign flush with funds from the end of the primaries to the conventions. Under the new McCain-Feingold law, the Democratic National Committee could no longer run a massive advertising blitz directed by the presumptive nominee—as it had done for Gore in 2000. The DNC could run ads; but under the law, enforced with new criminal penalties, they had to be truly "independent." The Kerry campaign couldn't control, produce, or place them.

Kerry bought into the notion that he'd have to opt out if Dean did. So did Lou Susman, which surprised me because it would be tough to raise money to supplement what Kerry himself could spend, and Lou would have to carry the brunt of the burden. He conferred in Boston with John, Teresa, and her lawyers to figure out how to convert Kerry's assets into campaign cash. The best way was to mortgage Kerry's half interest in the Beacon Hill home purchased when they got married. Their other homes—on Nantucket, and in Sun Valley and Pittsburgh—had been Teresa's before they were married.

During the messy days when Kerry was preparing to ask Jim Jordan to leave, Dean was polling his supporters on the Internet to let them decide whether he should opt out. The minute Dean announced the ploy, I told Kerry it was clear what their answer would be: Dean would turn down the matching funds and free himself from the spending limits. He did it on November 8. This gave Kerry the cover to do the only thing that could now rescue his prospects. On Mary Beth Cahill's first day as campaign manager, after what couldn't have been more than a 5- or 6-minute conversation, she told me: "There's no other choice—opt out or give up." And so Kerry, at his best when things were toughest, decided to bet on the long shot that he could win the nomination and then pay himself back with contributions from latecomers jumping on a bandwagon that might never roll. Kerry would now "loan" the campaign $6 million or so, although we wouldn't publicly announce the exact amount. If he didn't score in Iowa and New Hampshire, the campaign would be broke, and the candidate who'd wagered the lion's share of his personal assets would have no way to recover them.

The decision was interpreted in the press as a sign of desperation by a campaign in terminal condition, but we moved on to a second critical strategic choice. Later in November but still early in her tenure, Cahill convened a meeting in the narrow, dusty conference room at headquarters where we settled, once and for all, the debate about whether to use our upcoming television advertising to launch negatives against Dean. With data projecting from his PC onto the wall, Mellman, with earnest thoroughness, reviewed the rank order of the negative arguments. Again, none of them did real damage to Dean. I said I'd been to this movie before with far more effective negatives in the arsenal—in multi-candidate Senate races where one candidate had scorched another on television, the target had responded, and amid the mutually assured destruction, a third choice had moved up from the back of the pack and won. The most likely beneficiary if we yielded to this temptation now, I said as I saw some surprised faces around the room, was John Edwards. But I plowed ahead: maybe we could even be the beneficiary of someone else's demolition derby if we didn't start one ourselves. If we didn't go after Dean on television, which on the basis of Kerry's all too evident resentment toward him was what most insiders assumed we'd do, someone else in the field would probably feel the pressure to do it. I repeated that we could clash with Dean in the debates that were coming—Democratic voters expected that; there wouldn't be a backlash. We might even be able to trigger a moment where Dean himself showed that he wouldn't have a remote chance to make it through a general election against Bush.

Andrei Cherney, who was sitting near the end of the long conference table, spoke up: But didn't negative work, didn't we have to bring down Dean? Look at what Clinton did to Dole, he said, tying him to Newt Gingrich in the 1996 campaign. I was about to reply when Cahill spared me by asking: "Andrei, who invited you to this meeting?" There was a moment of silence and he stood up, then squeezed through the narrow space behind the other people sitting at the conference table, and left the room. It was tough, even though Mary Beth hadn't raised her voice. But it was also a stark signal that this campaign was going to be different now. In a businesslike way, we finished thrashing out the issue with a corps of advisers that included Mellman, Margolis, and Donilon—and came to a conclusion.

Negative ads against Dean were off the table if we could now convince Kerry. He was intellectually if not emotionally persuaded. And he went with his head, not the heat of his feelings toward Dean. At the end of my conversation with him, Kerry only asked: "Are you sure about this?" I said yes—not because I was sure our strategy would work, but because I was certain the alternative wouldn't.

The third crucial choice was a lifetime in politics away, a month in the future. But what had already happened was a harbinger of what the Kerry effort would now become—until we locked up the nomination. In one sense, all the good campaigns are the same and all the bad campaigns are the same. Kerry's went from bad—divided and strategically unresolved—to good, and then the best in the Democratic field—disciplined, energized on the ground, immune to the gloomy press and polls, and relentlessly strategic. Being written off as dead was even something of a blessing in disguise—although it seemed at times, as Winston Churchill once said, "very well disguised indeed." Because it was widely assumed Kerry was a dead-weight loser, we weren't plagued with the host of ad hoc advisers to whom Kerry tended to give a hearing on balmier days. As long as our cause looked hopeless to everybody but us, we could crisply discuss an issue with Mary Beth and other key advisers at the headquarters, and reach a decision. Then I could just lean across the seat in the SUV, or the aisle in the bus, confer with Kerry, and close the deal.

It can take a long time to turn a presidential campaign around, and even as the ship is righting its course, it can still look like it's heading for an iceberg. Our lowest point came during a relentlessly painful trip to California in early December; we were there to collect some scarce cash and to pump Kerry's foreign policy credentials with a speech at Stanford. In our little motorcade in San Diego, the noxious smell of backed-up exhaust fumes started filling the cab of the candidate's SUV. Teresa was hanging out one window and I was hanging out another as we sputtered our way up the hill to a modest fundraiser. On Pearl Harbor Day, the commander of a local naval base refused to let Kerry bring the press along on a visit to a rusting Swift boat memorial. Kerry went ahead anyway because a group of fellow vets had gathered to join him for a brief ceremony. Afterward, he spent 20 minutes showing me around the old land-bound Swift boat that was sitting up on blocks on a scruffy patch of grass.

Kerry, his press aide David Wade, and I sat in a cramped small plane and rewrote the speech he was about to deliver at Stanford. Once we got there, we had trouble printing the new draft. A mid-level administrator—I don't know her title—ruled that we couldn't use a campus office, computer, or printer for political purposes. So we locked her out of her own office and by the time a higher authority arrived, we were finished printing and perfectly agreeable to leaving. The auditorium was filled—and our luck on this trip seemed to be changing. The speech was as close to a home run as you could have in front of an academic audience.

Then we promptly hit bottom. At a fund-raising lunch at a restaurant near the Stanford campus, a few of us standing in the parking lot suddenly caught the scent of a genuinely big story as our cell phones started to ring. There was a rumor that Iowa senator Tom Harkin was about to endorse Dean. Actually, it was worse than that; it was Al Gore, a reporter told me in a call a few minutes later.

As Kerry was working the tables inside, David Morehouse, the former Gore aide who at our November nadir had resigned a position at Harvard to run our road show, headed into the restaurant to get Kerry. We stood with Kerry in the sun-dappled parking lot and told him what was about to happen. He was incredulous and then angry. Damnit, he'd endorsed Gore—I remembered because I'd helped persuade him to do it—when Gore was at his low ebb in New Hampshire in 2000. Kerry wanted to talk to Gore right now. Morehouse and I both had Gore's cell phone number. Kerry dialed it and a few seconds later said: "Al, it's John Kerry." The line went dead. When Kerry redialed the number, Gore's phone was turned off.

Back in New Hampshire, the state's firefighters were our CPR. Their international president—a brawny, tireless guy named Harold Schaitberger—traveled with us day after day. More than political calculation had brought the firefighters to Kerry. He'd stood with them on a series of issues. They weren't the kind that make headlines—except when a fire in Worcester, Massachusetts, had killed six firefighters in 1999, and Kerry had abandoned a trip overseas to come home and comfort the families. And the firefighters were the best kind of supporters to have; despite what they read in the polls and the papers, they were with Kerry first, last, and always. So we drove town to town in New Hampshire, fire station to fire station, for rallies that featured Kerry and a chili feed. Sometimes, we had chili three or more times a day; it was hard to keep track after a while. Each station had its own distinctive recipe.

The polls were shifting in New Hampshire—in the wrong direction. While Kerry's favorables were high, Dean was far ahead and Wesley Clark was moving up. Kerry couldn't get traction because on the national stage he was seen as a loser—and he seemed to be nowhere in Iowa. He now had to face the third big strategic decision—a tough one for a senator from neighboring Massachusetts—to abandon New Hampshire for Iowa. The idea had been germinating for weeks. With Tad Devine fully involved in the campaign once Mary Beth took over, he pushed his concept that the presidential primaries weren't just sequential but synergistic. What happened in the first contest in Iowa always reshaped the field in New Hampshire. Kerry couldn't make a comeback in either state by spending time in New Hampshire; the breakthrough had to come in the Iowa caucuses. That was a genuine possibility, I said once again—if you believed, as I did, that caucus goers rethink their choices after New Year's. In Mellman's data, Iowa Democrats liked Kerry even though he was in third place; he was what they were looking for, even if they didn't know it yet. With the season for psychic satisfaction over, Dean, who was already on the knife's edge of doubt about his electability, could suddenly become the wrong choice.

So we recommended to Kerry that for most of January, he should abandon New Hampshire and focus on Iowa. If we came in second there, we'd be the alternative to Dean. But first place, I said only to Kerry, Mary Beth, and a few others, should be our real aim. Most observers would have regarded that as delusional. The course we were urging would reverse the campaign's long-held assumption that New Hampshire was our firewall, the place we could go to restore our viability when no one else would take us in. Kerry was torn about our recommendation; politicians, and presidents, prefer to have more options, not fewer, and not just one. It was the last in a series of make-or-break choices. Kerry bought into the strategy. Only once during our exile from New Hampshire did he reimagine the state. Maybe, he ventured, we could "sneak back" for a night and be back in Des Moines the next morning. Cahill and I said no. That was the answer he expected.

Our Iowa organization was elated, scared, and motivated. "It's all up to you," I teased our Iowa campaign manager, John Norris, a young Democratic star in the state who'd barely lost a congressional race in 2002. On the other hand, our New Hampshire organization was demoralized, a little rebellious, but resolute. Sue Casey, the operative who'd spearheaded Gary Hart's 1984 New Hampshire victory, understood the logic. But she worried that Kerry might drop so low in the relentless drumbeat of daily tracking polls in New Hampshire that only an outright victory in Iowa could bring him back in the Granite State. I told Ken Robinson, our talented, beleaguered young press secretary in New Hampshire, who had to take the brunt of the calls as Wesley Clark surged and Kerry collapsed, "Just hold on." That, too, was easier advice to give than to receive.

Kerry's Iowa rallies in early January 2004 had good crowds and genuine energy. One day, our meager press contingent, consisting of a few reporters and the network technicians and "imbeds," young novices who were the cost-cutting way to cover the campaign, was "big-footed." I first heard the term during the 1980 campaign. The *Boston Globe*'s Tom Oliphant explained how a corps of the regular Kennedy beat reporters coined it when Drummond Ayres from the *New York Times* was temporarily displaced by one of the paper's mega-journalists, Hedrick Smith, who had unusually large feet. When CBS anchor Walter Cronkite made his apparition on the campaign plane, T. R. Reid of *The Washington Post* nicknamed him "ultrafoot." With Kerry now on his do-or-die trek through Iowa, *Washington Post* columnist David Broder and the paper's top political reporter Dan Balz showed up. After Kerry fired up the audience in a crowded room, Broder talked to me as I stood against a back wall. He's often portrayed as the repository of conventional wisdom, but his instincts and his sure sense of events on the ground have set a standard for political journalism. He told me maybe "something was going on here" that the press and the polls hadn't picked up yet. Balz, too, said he was surprised by what he was seeing; maybe Kerry was competitive.

We also escaped a stray bullet that would have at least nicked us. At an early morning event, I spotted Peter Yarrow of the sixties folk group Peter, Paul and Mary crossing a parking lot, guitar in hand, outside a fire station where the local fire and police unions were endorsing Kerry. Peter was a longtime friend of the candidate's and a tireless activist. He'd written a song for the Kerry campaign—"an anthem"—and after talking with the candidate "the other night," he'd climbed on a plane to premiere it in Iowa. Once the union officials were finished and Kerry had thanked them, Peter strode to the microphone and a slightly startled Kerry introduced him. His anthem was classic sixties, a protest ballad that denounced Bush, and the firefighters and police appeared to like it, or at least the tune.

Then he got to a line denouncing police brutality. The members of the audience stared sideways at each other and the press began telling Wade they wanted to chat with Peter, who was only too happy to oblige following his performance. As he started into an impromptu "press avail" where his comments on the war made him sound like a Dean partisan, I asked Wade to go over, collar Peter, and tell him we had to leave. Peter was irritated with Wade for interrupting his session with the reporters—and irritated again in the bus when David Morehouse and I said it would be better for us if he rewrote the anthem a little or just stuck to his old standards.

Unfortunately, he did. At an evening house party, he was performing "Puff the Magic Dragon" when Kerry, standing in the back of the room, mimed puffing on a joint. Most of the people there didn't see it—and neither did I; I'd retreated back to the bus to make some calls. When Wade stepped onto the bus and sat down next to me, he was beside himself as he recounted what had just happened. As we drove away, Kerry denied it. Wade said it was on tape. Kerry responded that, well, it was just a joke. Wade went to the back of the bus. We were lucky, he reported when he returned. It was late Saturday night, the camera crews didn't all have it, and most of the network imbeds didn't think it was a big deal. We were told later that a CBS crew got the tape to Washington in time for *Face the Nation*, but that Bob Schieffer's reaction was, Not on my program. I never asked Schieffer about this. I'd first come to know him when we shared breakfast tacos in Austin during the 1972 campaign and I earnestly explained how McGovern could carry Texas. I could credit the idea that Schieffer refused to take a cheap shot, but I thought it was best to let a sleeping toke lie. It did—except for a down-story mention in *The Washington Post*.

As Kerry stalked caucus goers morning to late night, in between stops he did periodically inhale something—prodigious take-out meals that Marvin Nicholson, his 6 foot, 8 inch personal aide-de-camp, obtained from the "best" restaurant in whatever town we were passing through. Usually, Marvin would pick up three take-out meals so Kerry could have a choice and a couple of us would end up with better than the stale sandwiches loaded onto the bus a couple times a day. Occasionally, Kerry would pass a half-finished plastic plate of spaghetti and meatballs across the aisle to me. Well into my customary campaign weight gain, I didn't need it, and I marveled at Kerry's metabolism. Like Al Gore, a constant infusion of food got him through a succession of 18-hour days, but unlike Gore, Kerry had to work hard not to lose weight. He also had a hacking cough that for weeks on end hit him hard after nearly every event. No one in the press knew it, but he had low-grade pneumonia. His doctor's remedy, he told me, was to rest his voice. Fat chance, but he never coughed his way through a speech or broadcast debate; somehow he held it in. In the telling, this all sounds like a hard slog, and it was. But we smiled and bantered a lot with Kerry. We'd tell him the stump speech was too long; he had to hold it to 15 or 20 minutes. He'd say: "Time me." Then he'd board the bus after an event and we'd look at him and say something like "Thirty-one minutes." No, that can't be. Oh yes, it was. He'd laugh and so would we, and then we'd press him again. Gradually, but not consistently, the speeches got shorter.

Dean, of course, still appeared to be coasting along. He'd won some of the biggest prizes among the union endorsements—the public employees and the service employees. Their leaders had decided that Dean was going to win and climbed aboard. So had Tom Harkin; as the only Iowa Democrat ever elected to the Senate more than twice—he'd won four times—he was regarded as a powerful influence on the caucus attendees who tend to come from the activist ranks of the party. At times, it was only natural to feel that our hill was just a little too steep to climb. Late one night, Kerry and I were sitting in the dark at the front of the bus when he said: "Look, if I get knocked out, I'm just going to support Gephardt." I had my own doubts and sometimes I thought about them as I went to sleep at night. But I also envisioned a victory celebration on caucus night; I could see it in my mind's eye. It might not come, but my job was to ease, not reinforce, Kerry's worries. We had a strategy, we had to stick to it—and we had powerful ways to advance it and amplify what Kerry was doing on the road.

The January 4 *Des Moines Register* debate brought a chance to zero in on Dean in the right way. Kerry arrived late for debate prep the night before in a Des Moines hotel meeting room; his day on the road had stretched on and on, beyond midnight. In between coughs, he kept venting about the schedule. We weren't going to get any prep done this way, so I interrupted him: "Look, John, you're right, but it doesn't matter." With Kerry calmed down a notch or two, we reviewed the debate format, which gave each candidate a minute to question one of the others. Mike Donilon and I were convinced Kerry had to direct his question to Dean, but it couldn't be argumentative or arcane. And he had to let Dean indict himself with his own record or words; the question had to sound "fair" to Democrats, not like a personal assault—and it had to deepen the doubts about Dean's prospects in a general election. In short, the question had to suggest, not state, that Dean couldn't win. Donilon pointed out that just after Christmas, Dean had made a statement, little noticed in the holiday press, that could be turned into stark, even startling evidence he was just unelectable. Mike asked me what I thought and we distilled the question down to 15 seconds or less: "Governor Dean, you recently said that you wouldn't presume that Osama bin Laden was guilty—or that he deserved the death penalty. What in the world were you thinking when you said that?"

Dean's own words *were* the attack; there was no good answer, whatever he said. And it wasn't just the specific issue that mattered, as incendiary as it might seem; voters would conclude that someone who said something like this couldn't possibly win in November. In the debate, Kerry added a discursive preface—he just couldn't stand giving up that much of his allotted time—and then asked Dean the question, while leaving out the reference to the death penalty (which Kerry opposes, with an exception for terrorists. He didn't want to inject that nuance into the press coverage.) Dean tried to explain the statement, yet had to own up to it. The press stories were bad but not catastrophic for him; the important thing was that potential caucus goers saw the debate. The sense of Dean as a risky choice was taking hold.

It was now time to bring Ted Kennedy back into Iowa full force and full voice. I had been discussing this on and off with Cahill and

Michael Whouley, who had returned to Iowa to repeat his organizational magic for his longtime friend John Kerry. This one, he observed, was tougher than Gore. Whouley insisted in his quiet monotone that nothing would fire up Democrats like Kennedy stumping with Kerry. Months before, when I'd suggested that Kennedy's campaigning could be critical for us, Jordan had responded that being too close to Kennedy could make Kerry look too much like a Massachusetts Democrat. But our problem in Iowa was the opposite: antiwar Democrats, disappointed in Kerry's vote for the Iraq war resolution, were drawn to Dean.

Kennedy had led the fight against the resolution, but his impact transcended that. His early January appearances across the eastern half of the state were like a magnet for Iowa Democrats; a lot of them didn't arrive at a rally as Kerry supporters, but a lot more of them were when they left. Kennedy brought the crowds to their feet as he draped Kerry with the Democratic mantle. Over the years, Kennedy had become more comfortable in referring publicly to his brothers. So he teased the Iowans that JFK had won the state's delegation in 1960, while he himself had lost the caucuses in 1980; but they could make up for it now—they could do a favor for "old Kennedy" by standing with Kerry this year. He hit Bush hard: Democrats had to beat him—and Kerry was the candidate to do it. Kerry couldn't put it quite that way, but Kennedy could say it for him. I hitched a ride on Lou Susman's plane taking Kennedy back to Washington. He looked at us and said, "I think everybody's wrong about this thing. I think you've got a real chance."

Another piece of the strategic puzzle fell into place as attack ads filled the airwaves. With Kerry staying positive on television, Gephardt felt he had to go negative to beat Dean back. Gephardt was "expected" to win Iowa after his 1988 victory there. Dean had to retaliate. It was the predicted dynamic. Both combatants were hurt; and while the press saw them as the two front-runners all the way to the weekend before the caucuses, Kerry was steadily gaining ground. Our ads were a glove-tight fit with the strategy of presenting Kerry as presidential. He spoke straight to the camera outlining what he would do as president—for example, his plans on health care and the economy.

National security, however, was key, and one spot had more impact than any other, inadvertently setting up one of the defining moments of the Iowa campaign. Mike Donilon said to me: How about having one or two of Kerry's crewmates talk about what he did on that Swift boat, and not just in general terms but about a specific incident? We had too little time—or money—to film again, but Jim Margolis said he had some footage of interviews he'd conducted for a campaign documentary produced before my partners and I had signed on. He and Donilon could look at that. The result became known, and celebrated once we'd won Iowa, as "the Del ad." Del Sandusky, a mustached, husky vet, spoke plainly, in his own words, at times over black-and-white footage of a Swift boat plowing a Vietnamese river delta. Del vividly recounted how when the boat was under fire, Kerry "saved our lives."

The spot was on the air when, almost 2,000 miles away, a retired Los Angeles deputy sheriff, now a world-renowned expert on orchids, was browsing through an Oregon bookstore and picked up a copy of historian Douglas Brinkley's *Tour of Duty* about Kerry's service in Vietnam. He leafed through it, and in the index saw his own name, misspelled. Jim Rassman hadn't been on Kerry's crew; he'd been one of the men the Swift boats ferried through the rivers and dropped off on intelligence missions. On the morning of March 13, 1969, when Rassman was knocked off the stern of one of those boats and found himself in the water with bullets spraying all around him, Kerry ordered his own vessel to turn around and plow through enemy fire to rescue Rassman. A wounded Kerry knelt on the deck, leaned over, and pulled Rassman out of the water. They hadn't seen each other since that day thirty-five years ago. Rassman, a Republican, phoned our headquarters in Washington. Was there anything he could do to help? There certainly was; we soon had Rassman on a plane to Iowa. Kerry was told he was coming just forty minutes before; as Rassman told his story, the candidate fought to hold his emotions in check. They embraced, and the photo and the story drew blanket coverage. Rassman became a celebrity in his own right in the closing days of Iowa and during his subsequent appearances in New Hampshire and other primary states. His arrival was one of those campaign accidents that become an asset—in this case, a powerful one. You have to hope for luck in a campaign. But "the Del ad" had laid the groundwork so Rassman's sudden appearance had maximum force. After the Iowa caucuses, I congratulated Doug Brinkley and told him he was the other winner. His book, on which he had spent several years, would have faded away quickly if Kerry had lost early. Now he had a best-seller. Doug laughed and said: "Yes, but I'm the one who found Jim Rassman."

Finally, we had a long-shot endorsement of our own. Whouley had been conferring on and off with Iowa's governor, Tom Vilsack, who said he wouldn't endorse anyone, but Michael just kept the conversation going. A week before the caucuses, he thought Kerry should sit down with Vilsack for a final push. When the candidate and Whouley arrived, Vilsack and his wife Christie were waiting. They'd made a decision—or rather, she had. The governor had to keep his promise to stay neutral. But Christie had decided to come out for Kerry. And there was no deal; there was no quid pro quo. She thought Kerry would make the best president and she was worried about what a Dean nomination would do to the party. The endorsement was one of the few times a secret actually held until the last minute, in part because there were only a few hours between the decision and the event. The next morning, a genuinely surprised press corps watched Kerry and Christie Vilsack descending the statehouse steps toward a bank of microphones.

Her decision was big news. She was popular with Iowa Democrats in her own right, and her intervention sent a powerful signal: It was time to get serious. She had done that, at some political risk to her husband. So should caucus goers. Suddenly it was conceded that while he wasn't winning, Kerry was back from the dead. But Edwards, too, had come alive at last with a surprise editorial endorsement from the *Des Moines Register*.

After a meeting in Washington to discuss election night strategy and New Hampshire, I was on a Midwest Express flight back to

Iowa for the final push the weekend before the Monday night caucuses. Also on the plane were James Carville, who was commenting
for CNN, and Tom Harkin's wife Ruth, who'd held a high post in
the Clinton administration. The three of us gathered in the aisle.
Carville was intense—no surprise—and said: "You gotta pull this
off." Dean was a "fucking disaster." I said I thought Kerry had real
momentum. Ruth, who has her own finely honed political sense of
the state, said that's what she was hearing, too; she exclaimed that
she'd told her husband not to endorse Dean.

These last days were a journey to victory tinged with quiet worry.
Everywhere Kerry went, you could feel the tide moving toward
him; but would it get there in time? At a joint appearance of all the
candidates that was nothing more than a succession of stump
speeches, Kerry seemed to sweep the room. Edwards, too, was eliciting some fervor. One night, as we walked through the lobby of the
Fort Des Moines heading for the elevators, Kerry spotted Dean
manager Joe Trippi pacing back and forth, cell phone glued to his
ear. He always seems to be there on that phone whenever I come in,
Kerry observed as the elevator doors shut; if he's spending all this
time talking to reporters, who's running the Dean campaign? A
shocked and still largely disbelieving political world heard Saturday
afternoon, January 17, that Sunday's *Des Moines Register* poll would
show Kerry in first place, with Edwards in second. We couldn't
worry about Edwards at this point; we just had to maximize our
own vote when the caucuses convened on Monday night.

On Sunday, with Kerry on a last-minute dash across the state,
Mary Beth and I walked through the frigid winds whipping the
streets of Des Moines toward the Kerry headquarters, a former auto
dealership and showroom. When we couldn't take the cold anymore, we found temporary refuge in a non-Starbucks boutique coffee shop along the way. Inside, we saw tables of Dean volunteers
wearing the trademark orange woolen caps their campaign had issued to them. We saw more and more orange on our final lap toward
the headquarters; it was all over Des Moines and all across Iowa,
adorning an army of thousands, largely from out of state. I speculated that this would turn off Iowans. They're proprietary about

the caucuses, I said to Cahill; they don't like outsiders telling them what to do.

The caucuses started gathering between 6 and 7 P.M. Monday. I was driven out to meet Kerry, victory speech in hand, at a reception in a suburban Des Moines home. We were so close now, and I couldn't bring myself to scrawl out an alternative draft in case we fell short. Kerry climbed on the bus with our press corps in tow. One of the young imbeds came up the aisle and tapped me on the shoulder. He handed me the Fox "entry" poll, which measured the voters' preferences as they walked into the caucuses, where they would separate into different clusters around the room to "caucus" with those who supported the same candidate they did. I'll never forget the first line on that scrap of paper: "Kerry—29%," an 8-point lead. I don't even remember the exact order after that, just that Dean and Edwards were close to each other and Gephardt was far behind. I reached across the aisle and tapped Kerry on the sleeve of the barn jacket he usually wore to keep warm on the bus. I held out that piece of paper. What is it? he asked. "The Fox entry poll" was all I could manage. I wordlessly passed the numbers to him. Maybe we should have been skeptical or cautious, but we weren't. We'd been through too much; we reached across the aisle and embraced each other. A sense of relief and then elation spread through the handful of staff sitting around us.

We had to force our way through a chaotic throng in the hotel lobby on the way to Kerry's suite. It was the same one we'd stayed in on the announcement tour—a political lifetime ago. As we watched the television coverage, he sat on the couch, his arm around Teresa, with one of his daughters on the floor and the other on the arm of the sofa. The early returns were fragmentary and inconclusive. Edwards was surprisingly strong, powered by a deal with the otherwise irrelevant campaign of Ohio congressman Dennis Kucinich, who agreed to move his supporters to Edwards in precincts where Kucinich didn't reach the required threshold of 15 percent. We were ahead, but could Edwards catch up? A fidgety Kerry asked me a question I'd heard from him before: "Are you sure about this?"

I walked down the hall to the war room where we were gathering returns from our own team of caucus watchers across the state. Whouley was at the phone, then at the computer screens, as the results were loaded in. Whouley and Norris had created a faster reporting system than the state party—just as under the radar they'd put together the best field organization in Iowa. One of the Boston pols who'd arrived to help out in the closing days took me aside and told me not to worry; it was all over. But I wasn't the one who was worried, I said to him and then to Whouley, who'd just left the computer screens to join us. What could I tell Kerry? "We won," Michael said, his deadpan expression completely intact. "*You* have to tell Kerry," I responded. Whouley didn't like leaving the war room with the numbers still pouring in. "Come on," I insisted. We went to Kerry's suite, its dining room and hallways now clogged with friends, fund-raisers, and supporters. (It's amazing how crowded the candidate's suite is when you're winning and how sparse the crowd becomes if victory ebbs away.) Off to the side, we talked with Kerry—and I let Whouley do the talking. I knew Kerry was convinced when he turned to me and said, Let's look at this victory statement again.

But suddenly we broke off to watch in awestruck disbelief as Dean, who was headed for a distant third place, "conceded" in what became known as the "scream" speech. People who heard Dean give it in person, including some members of the press, later said it didn't sound that bad in the room. But what's seen and heard on television can be more real than reality. On screen, Dean was yelling his way through a roll call of coming primaries with a manic grin on his face. As usual, he had gone on stage without a prepared text, but this time under the pressure of defeat; he'd torn off his coat, handed it to a startled Tom Harkin, and simply ignited. Harkin gamely smiled and applauded. He was in that room, I thought, but he knew what was happening on television. An awestruck silence descended across the celebration in the Kerry suite.

Later, Steve McMahon, Dean's media adviser who'd been my intern in Ted Kennedy's office nearly a quarter century earlier and then an associate in my firm in the late eighties, told me that caucus night had been a nightmare. The Dean campaign, like all the others, had canvassed caucus goers and rated them 1, 2, 3, or 4; 1 meant they were certain to vote for Dean, 2 meant they were likely. But Steve recounted how, in place after place, the Dean organizers had gotten their 1s and 2s to the caucuses, only to watch them walk across the room and join the Kerry and to a lesser extent the Edwards forces.

What Dean had to do that night would have been difficult for any candidate; what the world was witnessing on television was the result of trying to do it without a script in the midst of an emotional maelstrom. Aside from Kerry's victory, the big news out of Iowa would be Dean's "scream." It was instantly legendary, some of the best political material the late night comedians had been handed in years. But while the scream would be remembered as a defining moment, Dean was already beginning to weaken in New Hampshire, and the outcome in Iowa would accelerate the process, just as Devine had predicted. Dean had raised $40 million, but incredibly spent virtually all of it. Within days, the flow of funds would shift toward Kerry, and Trippi would be gone from the Dean enterprise, ensconced back on his farm in Maryland.

After our victory rally, we were at the Des Moines airport in the middle of the night, boarding a plane for New Hampshire. It was the same trip, under the same circumstances, as it had been four years before—with one difference. Gore had been the vice president flying on Air Force Two. But Kerry, like all other passengers on this charter, had to stand in line for a security check. That phase of the campaign was ending; the Secret Service was about to arrive. Kerry was now the front-runner—the dreaded title no one wants until the voting actually starts. Instead of sitting down in the front compartment of the plane, I wandered into the back. Our squad of press had become an entire platoon. As we neared Manchester, I chatted off the record with a gaggle of reporters. Mostly I just wanted to hear what they had to say. The big story—and the big question—was clear to them: Could Dean make a comeback?

It was an ideal storyline for the Kerry campaign. It cast New Hampshire as a two-candidate contest: if you didn't want Dean—and more and more Democrats were afraid to nominate him—you gravitated to Kerry. He was a "winner" now and the New Hampshire voters, who all along had given him high favorables in the polls, could vote for him. Wesley Clark had enjoyed a free ride while Kerry was confined to Iowa. Clark's strategy had been to present himself as *the* alternative to Dean, but now there was someone else who'd actually beaten Dean, and done it convincingly. And Joe Lieberman was simply out of the Democratic mainstream—and out of contention; he seemed to be running as an unalloyed cheerleader for the Iraq war. There weren't many New Hampshire Democrats who responded to that. "He's running in the wrong party," one of our field organizers said.

In the two-dimensional race the press would report and the voters would buy into, it was hard to see how Edwards could get traction; despite repeated visits to the Granite State, his folksy style had never resonated with the state's flinty electorate. The headlines about Kerry's Iowa victory and the obsessive replays of the Dean scream were crowding out a third story about Edwards's unexpected showing in the caucuses. He had dealt himself in, but not in New Hampshire; he would have to wait for the South Carolina primary.

We landed at dawn at the Manchester Airport to a rally in a hangar packed with an army of Kerry partisans who had materialized overnight. To catch a nap, we then drove to our no-frills hotel near the airport—no restaurant and no coffee shop, just a coffee machine and a cold cereal buffet each morning in the "lobby." Very early one morning, I woke to a staccato pounding on my door. I opened it to find a frazzled John Kerry in a T-shirt, socks, and khakis, wondering if I had any hot water; there wasn't any in his room. We turned on my shower; the stream of water was icy. The hotel had lost all its hot water, and might not get it back for 12 or 24 hours. We barnstormed through a long day hoping that our deodorant held.

The hotel was a metaphor for the risk Kerry had taken. The folks who worked there were uniformly nice and eager to please, but we were there because we were at the end of our financial tether. We had just enough money to get through Iowa and New Hampshire.

We had put aside no resources to survive beyond that. Contributions were now pouring in, especially on the Internet, but they weren't banked or budgeted yet. Kerry had bet the store—or rather, his house—and now he was on the verge of running the table, all the way to a quick nomination.

With each passing day, Tom Kiley's tracking poll showed Kerry steadily moving up. The audiences at our rallies spilled out the doors into the snow-covered parking lots. We were rolling to victory—or so we thought until Election Day. Kiley's last survey had Kerry 12 points ahead of Dean, a landslide that would effectively knock Dean out of the race. But when the first network exit polls were leaked to all the campaigns, they showed a narrow Kerry win, barely outside the margin of error. We heard that the *Los Angeles Times* had its own exit poll in which Dean actually held a 1-point lead. Maybe this was four years before all over again; I remembered the exit poll data that had called Bradley over Gore. My reaction was that if the exit polls in New Hampshire were wrong then, they were wrong again; they just didn't seem to model the state right.

With the real polls about to close, I went back to our hotel, where Teresa had joined her husband in the "suite." She was worried. Jim Margolis and I were sitting there, sipping some very fine wine she'd brought along out of the motel's paper cups, as the television screen constantly updated the returns. Kerry had a lead in the raw vote; Teresa kept fretting, but the lead held and then grew to between 10 and 15 points. Kerry was in the shower when the race was called. Teresa let out a whoop and shouted: "Honey, you won." The bathroom door was open and Kerry came around the corner with a bathrobe wrapped around him and a big grin on his face. Two weeks before, Dean had led the field by double digits in New Hampshire—and Kerry wasn't even in second place. Now his final margin over Dean was 13 points—almost exactly what Kiley had predicted. I went over the victory draft I had brought with me as Kerry donned his shirt and tie; he sat down on the bed to pen in some changes in his distinctively vertical, almost indecipherable handwriting.

Our motel had no public space remotely big enough for an election night party, even if only for a concession. So with hope and a prayer, Cahill had sprung for a ballroom in downtown Manchester. We made our way toward it though a jubilant back hallway of politicians, staff, the faithful like Jeanne Shaheen—and a sudden apparition, the legion of the newly converted. I turned the corner and there was Marylouise, who'd spent the last couple nights with me and gotten up early to share some cold cornflakes before I left each day. She'd been on her own mission, struggling to drum up new big-dollar contributors for Kerry; by the time of the convention, she'd help raise $8 million. I kissed her for a long time amid the jostling crowd and then stood in the open doorway that was just behind the stage. A multitude of reporters, cameras, and lights ranged on a riser in the back. The room was hot and electric and Kerry's speech was one of the best of the entire campaign. I retreated to the hallway to do what else?—pace back and forth. Kerry thanked his crewmates and the other vets who'd stood with him in the lonely months leading to this night. He called them his "band of brothers" and said: "We may be a little older, we may be a little grayer, but we still know how to fight for our country." Kerry challenged Bush again, but this time Democrats across the nation heard him clearly. He was prepared for a battle on national security; he welcomed it: "Bring it on."

The passage about his Vietnam service was central to the narrative that had moved Kerry this far, and we believed it would be crucial to defeating Bush in November. Kerry's war record was a powerful story. It had been attacked in the 1996 Senate race by right-wing veterans enraged that he had protested the Vietnam War after coming home. The attacks had misfired then. In honesty, that night and for months to come, none of us thought Bush could successfully recycle the tactic. When I mentioned what had happened in the Senate race to James Carville, he spat out: "No way can that draft dodger go after Kerry."

The morning after New Hampshire, a relaxed Kerry started tossing a football back and forth with staff and reporters on a plane to St. Louis; photographers snapped him standing in the aisle next to me as I watched, leaning over my seatback. The photos were everywhere in the press the next day. It was, for the moment, a bookend to all the Kerry-bashing of the previous fall—and for me, all the stories about the "Shrum Curse." They, too, would return, of course, but I wasn't thinking about that on this happy flight.

Of the seven primaries or caucuses that were scheduled for February 3, just a week away, Kerry won five, including a landslide victory in Missouri. We had tried for a knockout in South Carolina. If Edwards couldn't win there, he was out of the race. I was back in Washington for what proved to be a tense election night. Early on, Edwards trounced us in South Carolina—and not just because of his southern appeal. It was increasingly clear that Democrats genuinely liked him. What was holding them back was the fear that as a one-term senator, he just wasn't ready for the presidency, and couldn't win it in an election dominated by 9/11 and the war in Iraq. He almost overcame that doubt in Oklahoma, and if he had won there as well, he would have surfed a media wave generated by a press corps naturally eager for a closer race. We had nothing going in Oklahoma except two great young organizers who were sent in with just a week to go: Josh Galper, who'd helped elect the state's Democratic governor in 2002; and Chad Clanton, a young perpetual-motion protégé of Carville's, who hailed from Waco, Texas, and sounded like it. Thank God, we also had Wesley Clark. Along with Cahill, Devine, and others, I kept shuffling up and down the rickety staircase connecting the three floors of our 14-foot-wide headquarters, monitoring the Oklahoma returns. It was a close three-way race, but we were headed for third. We were pulling for a Clark victory, which was all that mattered to us now. He squeaked into first place by a margin of a few hundred votes over Edwards. Kerry was just a little further behind. It was virtually a three-way tie, but Edwards hadn't prevailed.

The question now was whether Kerry could carry a southern state. The notion of the southern primaries as a test of a candidate's potential appeal in a general election, which is how the press generally frames the story, has always struck me as a cliché that works only one way: for the most part, the Democrats who vote in the primaries are a dwindling percentage of the southern electorate; they're hardly a bellwether unless you *can't* carry them. But a week after he faltered in South Carolina and Oklahoma, Kerry "proved" he was a national candidate with a southern appeal in the next two contests, Tennessee and Virginia. What really drove his vote was that he was now the apparent nominee, and in Virginia, Kerry topped 50 percent, beating Edwards by 25 points. Tennessee was big, too—a 14-point win; but Clark's last-gasp presence may have saved us there because he collected nearly a quarter of the vote. As one of the news magazines was photographing the candidate with Cahill and me before he went out to give his victory speech, Kerry said: Okay, so I've shown I can win in the South; when's Edwards going to show he can win outside the South, somewhere besides the one southern state where he was born?

In politics, be careful what you ask for. The next week was Wisconsin, where Kerry started with a comfortable 18-point lead. Edwards was now reaching out to liberals by focusing on poverty and to worried blue-collar workers with a new emphasis on fair trade. He hadn't been in the Senate when NAFTA was voted on, so he could claim that as a private citizen, he'd opposed it. But events more than issues were to shape the outcome. What looked like an easy ride for Kerry suddenly stopped with red-light alert on the *Drudge Report* alleging that Kerry had had an affair with an intern working in his office. The story was traced to Wesley Clark. Just days before he withdrew, when the traveling press asked him why he was still in the race, he said there was something personal, Clinton-like, that could bring Kerry down. His words were supposedly "off the record," but something like that never is. Lehane was accused of spreading the charge or filling in the details. Who knows? Chris is the kind of lightning rod who gets blamed even when he isn't guilty.

Kerry was on the Don Imus show when the Drudge alert hit and he had to answer questions about it before any of us had a chance to talk with him. Imus, who'd tagged him as a "tall can of hairspray" during the 1996 Senate race, had subsequently become Kerry's agreeable on-air sparring partner. When he was asked about the intern, Kerry off-handedly dismissed the charge. His answer could be construed as condemning the rumor but not denying its truth. In the hours that followed, the sense that there might be another Monica here steadily gathered force. As Kerry spoke at an event in Wisconsin, I stayed in the holding room on the phone with Cahill and headquarters. No one knew if we could deny the story unequivocally or if there was anything else that might pop up. We had to know the facts. When Kerry and three or four staff members returned to the holding room, I took our trip director David Morehouse aside and said: "We need to get everyone but Kerry and me out of here."

Once we were alone, I told Kerry that I had to ask him if there was any basis of any kind for the report about the intern—and much as I didn't want to, the follow-up that could readily come from a reporter in this post-Clinton world: Had he been faithful to Teresa throughout their marriage? Kerry looked straight at me across the windowless, cinder-block space. He said he wasn't mad at me for raising the question, but he resented what was happening; it was the right-wing attack machine in action. Yes, he knew the intern, who was in her twenties. He'd had a casual drink with her, but there had never been a relationship. And while her name had not been published, it probably would be and that was goddamned unfair to her. He added that, as I knew well, he'd been involved with a number of women before marrying Teresa. But never since then. She'd kill me, he said, in a brief flash of humor. He'd been faithful—period. We were safe in flatly denying the Drudge story—and we did. The former intern, who talked with our lawyer, issued her own denial after the press tracked her down in Africa.

By election night, our earlier 18-point lead had dwindled to a 6-point margin over Edwards, who benefited not only from the intern story but from an unexpected endorsement by the *Milwaukee Journal Sentinel*. But for Dean, Wisconsin was the last primary. The state's famously liberal Democratic electorate had dismissed him as irrelevant. Shortly after he withdrew and went home to Vermont, I had another glimpse of the cruel coldness of politics. Kerry called Dean's cell phone, got no answer, and left a message. When Dean called back, he apologized. He didn't have staff anymore; he was taking a nap, his cell phone had fallen under his bed, and he couldn't get to it in time.

But Edwards had just enough plausibility to last two more

weeks, to Super Tuesday, when ten states, including California, Ohio, New York, and Georgia, cast their votes. From Iowa on, he had captured the imagination of many in the press who still couldn't believe they'd been so wrong in writing off Kerry—and at least subconsciously still wanted to be right. A contrast was developing between Kerry and Edwards—and the downside for Kerry would be set in concrete by November. Kerry was viewed as remote, complicated, unexciting. In contrast, Edwards's weekly concessions made him sound both high-minded and down to earth, naturally eloquent and accessible. Delivered without notes, they had an energy that eventually wore thin after constant repetition; but they made him, in that season, and perhaps it will happen again, a charismatic spokesman for Democratic values. In the run-up to Super Tuesday, I believe Edwards could see where the path was leading, even if he didn't explicitly admit it to himself. Almost to the end, he ran the kind of nonconfrontational race that made it look like he was actually campaigning for vice president.

His continuing presence was helping us, as long as he didn't stay too long. The simulacrum of a race guaranteed constant media coverage. Edwards's case against unfair foreign trade also pushed Kerry to refine his own position: he was, Kerry argued, for free *and* fair trade, with labor and environmental safeguards in every trade agreement. Then at a rally at Macalester College in Minnesota, Kerry and I stumbled across a statistic that would become central to his economic argument in the fall. In every presidential campaign, young researchers at headquarters work late into the night assembling "trip books" with page after page of political, demographic, and economic background on each of the candidate's scheduled stops. They often wonder whether these tomes really get read. That day in Minnesota, while waiting for the audience to pass through the Secret Service magnetometers into the gym, Kerry and I were paging through the briefing book. A statistic caught my eye: The new jobs that were being created in Minnesota paid thousands of dollars less than the jobs that had been lost under Bush. I said to Kerry that this had to be true in other states, too. It was. The stats had been in earlier briefing books; we just hadn't made much of them. But this line of argument was essential because it let Kerry campaign on the economy, not just the unemployment rate, tapping into the anxiety that more and more Americans were feeling about their standard of living. Soon, Kerry started using a simple line to cap off the statistics. In dial groups, we tested videotape of him delivering it: "People are working nights, they're working weekends, they're working two jobs, three jobs—and they still can't get ahead." In the second-by-second response of participants, the line scored off the charts. And the argument about wage decline was an insurance policy—not enough of one in Ohio, as it turned out—if the Bush administration finally could point to some job creation as the election approached.

There was a companion argument I was convinced we had to make—the outsourcing of American jobs—that distressed some of our business supporters like former Clinton treasury secretary Bob Rubin. He thought it was irresponsible to stoke populist fires about outsourcing; it was part of the natural churn of a globalizing economy. Natural, I said to Kerry, unless you happen to be the skilled worker who's told his job is being packed off to China, and you're being pushed out to look for something at McDonald's. I knew outsourcing wasn't the heart of the problem, I told Gene Sperling, who was now advising us on economics. But it was a powerful symbol of Bush's indifference and there had to be some acceptable way to talk about it. Sperling sculpted the language. Despite Rubin's aversion to any appeal that could be construed as class warfare, he does have a genuine commitment to economic fairness and he agreed to introduce Kerry for a major speech in Ohio that included an attack on outsourcing. I don't think he was comfortable with it, but Kerry was. It became a staple in our campaign, a vivid, human way to discuss the economy for a candidate accused of dealing in abstraction and complication.

The final debate before Super Tuesday was in New York City. Until now, we'd prepared for a confrontational Edwards who had never showed up. It was late in the game, too late for Edwards, but this time, he came with guns blazing. I sat in a dank, windowless room near the studio watching Edwards's scattershot assault: Kerry had a bad record on trade and was trying to have it both ways. His economic and budget plans would drive the country "deeper and deeper" into deficit. Kerry's ideas were "the same old Washington talk"; confronted with a tough issue, Kerry had a "Washington committee . . . studying" it. Kerry artfully parried his opponent's jabs. Edwards had been in the Senate five years; "that seems to me to be in Washington, D.C." He ignored Edwards's provocations to all-out battle and kept banging away at Bush. But he was seething when he got back to the holding room: "That guy just eliminated himself as vice president."

Presidential nominees often resist or reject their strongest possible running mates because of grudges over past rivalries or clashes. Reagan put that aside when he narrowed his choice to Gerald Ford or George Bush. JFK picked Lyndon Johnson, who was anathema to his campaign manager, his brother Robert—but Kennedy wouldn't have won without LBJ. On the other hand, Johnson himself ruled out RFK, in effect leaving him out there as a potential rival in the primaries four years later. And the first George Bush settled on, of all people, Dan Quayle. I didn't want Kerry to take a similar path. I asked David Ginsberg, Edwards's communications director, what had happened to the nice guy who seemed to be auditioning for second spot on the ticket? What had gotten into Edwards in the New York debate? The staff hadn't been for any of that, he replied. But Edwards *was* frustrated as a race where he had come near to breaking through was coming to an end; he had been determined to go after Kerry this time, and Elizabeth had agreed with him. Four days later, when he withdrew, Edwards was gracious. Kerry, who doesn't hold a grudge when the fight's over, would put this one aside.

On Super Tuesday, Kerry swept every contest except Vermont, which cast a sentimental vote for Dean. As the primaries rolled to a conclusion, the down-and-out man of the previous fall carried all but three of the fifty-four states and territories, and two of those he lost were the home states of his opponents. He was the first Democrat in modern times to win the nomination without having the most money in the bank as the pre-election year ended. What lay ahead was daunting: an attempt to defeat an incumbent president, secure in his own party and base, in a time of war. It had never been done before. But a lot of Democrats, blinded by their hatred of Bush, didn't see that and don't see it to this day. The assumption was and is that Bush was ripe for the taking in 2004. I never shared this assessment; I knew getting to the White House would be an even more formidable challenge than resurrection in the primaries.

Marylouise and I, Mary Beth, and a brace of others were with John and Teresa waiting to go downstairs for his Super Tuesday victory statement in the mall of the old Post Office Building on Pennsylvania Avenue in Washington when a call came in from just two blocks away. It was George W. Bush congratulating Kerry, who recounted their brief conversation: the president said he was looking forward to a good, clean campaign. I didn't think so. We were facing the gang that was willing to do anything to snatch Florida and the 2000 election. The negative ads were already in the can and they were soon on the air—after a round of commercials that focused on Bush and 9/11 (the subject of the only positive advertising in which the Bush campaign invested substantial dollars all the way to November because the only positive case they could advance was about 9/11 and the fight against terrorism, not jobs, or health care, or even Iraq). The Bush forces didn't care when they were criticized for exploiting the images of 9/11; they just continued to do it. But the heaviest throwweight of their advertising would blast Kerry as too liberal, as a tax raiser, and increasingly, as a flip-flopper.

Within days of Super Tuesday, with anti-Kerry ads reverberating across the battleground states, a drumbeat within the Democratic Party called on us to respond, respond, respond. But we had only a couple of million dollars in the bank; if we reacted, we'd have to do it in dribs and drabs. I argued that with money coming in, we needed to accumulate enough to go on the air with a massive buy. We had to wait and take the hits. And when we put up our advertising, we had a first-stage priority to build up Kerry, to insulate him from the attacks, to give people a reason to vote for him. The independent expenditure committees and the DNC advertising, which we couldn't direct or control, would have to do a lot of the negative work against Bush, at least early on, but obviously they could figure that out.

It was another risky decision; on the politics of winning the election—if not the internal politics of the party—it was the right one. By May 3, when we launched a $25 million ad buy, at that point the largest single one in presidential campaign history, the Bush offensive hadn't inflicted serious damage—and we quickly reversed it. By the end of the buy, Kerry was in the lead. But that was later. For now, the press couldn't figure out why we were asleep at the wheel. Anonymous quotes from Democratic sources suggested that we didn't know what we were doing. We had to offer a rationale—and I got sloppy, telling reporters on background that the negative attacks, for example labored charges about raising taxes, wouldn't connect with voters in a post-9/11 world. I'd been portrayed in the past as an avatar of negative advertising; I didn't and don't have a quasi-theological objection to it. But I believed that early on we could absorb the Bush barrage, then counter it and come back; anyway, we didn't have any other choice. But my spin just stoked the apprehension among Democrats: Couldn't somebody over at the expansive new Kerry headquarters on 15th Street do this one right? And there were plenty of people ready to try.

The doubts about Kerry were compounded at a "Unity Dinner" in Washington that Clinton pal and Democratic National Committee chairman Terry McAuliffe had long ago scheduled for the spring. When I found out about this and saw the program, I said at one of our staff meetings: If we can't cancel this, can we at least have Bill Clinton speak first, before Jimmy Carter and the defeated 2004 primary candidates, instead of introducing Kerry? No, it wasn't our event; it was set in DNC stone. And it set up a one-on-one speech contest with Clinton, which Kerry was bound to lose. Clinton can show up anyone; he can't help himself—as Hillary would find out two years later at Coretta Scott King's funeral. Her remarks sounded pallid when she spoke right after her husband. At the Unity Dinner, Clinton sent ripples and then waves of excitement across the room as he spoke. He had a compelling construct, invoking a line from Scripture, and applying it to Kerry: whatever the problem, war or health care or jobs, Kerry was summoned to the task and his answer was: "Send me." Each time Clinton repeated the phrase, a roar of applause rolled across the high-ceilinged expanse of the National Building Museum. Behind the stage, before he went on, Clinton showed me his notes and asked if what he was going to say was all right; he had taken his speechwriter's draft and recast it with this line from the Bible. The speech would bring people to their feet, I answered. But I worried it would do more for Clinton than for Kerry.

And so it did. It was as if Clinton thought subconsciously that he should be the one leading the party. Clearly, so did much of the Democratic establishment assembled in that room. They loved Clinton; they were ready to accept Kerry, but not because he was their favorite. He'd seized the nomination, for the most part without their help. Kerry was intimidated by the performance that was supposed to introduce him. He sounded rote, formulaic, almost apologetic that his own speech wasn't very good. It wasn't—and that was the campaign's fault. An enterprise that had defied predictions of doom by constantly taking risks was now becoming cautious and focus group–driven.

The night Kerry had triumphed in Virginia and Tennessee, Mary Beth told me we had to start moving away from the tough rhetoric we'd been using—for example, Kerry's warning that if he was to win the White House, the oil and energy lobbyists were being thrown out, and "don't let the door hit you on the way out." Even Kerry's challenge to Bush on the national security issue—"Bring It On"—had to be banished to the deep freeze. The campaign had data to back up the shift. Our third pollster, Diane Feldman, had been conducting focus groups among undecided voters. They didn't like edgy arguments that scorned Bush or sounded "negative." Kerry should just talk about what he wanted to do as president; he should be "positive." It was a cliché we would hear for months. The fault wasn't Feldman's; she was reporting accurately what she was seeing. But our method was wrong—and very different from the Bush campaign's. Their focus groups, as we discovered after the election, talked to "soft" Kerry and "soft" Bush supporters because they were better informed than the outright "undecideds," who tended to pay little attention to the election until the end—and then if they did cast a ballot, tended to break the same way as the soft voters did. It was in focus groups like this that the Bush team discovered the potential power of a "flip-flop" attack on Kerry, although it would prove to be a thin edge at first, until Kerry's own unforgettable words gave it a cutting edge.

I muted my reservations about our shift in tone and message. My doubts were instinctive, based not on hard data but hard experience. The lesson of the Gore campaign, and my other years in politics, was that you have to let candidates be who they really are. Kerry was itching to go at Bush at the very moment when he was being told to temper his rhetoric. But I felt partially disabled by my own reputation as too ideological, too left, too populist—or, as my critics would put it, too prone to class warfare.

I should have just taken the heat, argued for the tougher language, and been ready to hear the charge, "There he goes again." But I don't think I would have won the battle. Gone was the tight strategic team of the winter months. If victory has a hundred fathers, it also brings forth a hundred advisers. From being political poison ivy, Kerry had become the only flower in the field, and they all just buzzed around him.

The most prominent new counselor, of course, was Bill Clinton. Less than a year after the 2004 election, Kerry would tell me, "The only thing the Clintons care about is themselves and power." But in that post-primary spring, and for months afterward, he prized the calls from Clinton; they were a certification of his success and his coming presidency, even if most of the advice was boilerplate—for example, reach out to the middle. But not always: Clinton, Kerry reported at the time, did suggest blunting Bush's appeal to cultural conservatives with a reprise of Clinton's Sister Souljah moment in 1992 when he'd denounced her call for violence against whites—and done it as conspicuously as possible in front of Jesse Jackson's Rainbow Coalition. Kerry, Clinton ventured, should consider defying Democratic interest groups by endorsing the Bush proposal for a federal constitutional amendment banning gay marriage. The notion was also a replay of a Clinton tactic in his second presidential race in 1996, when he'd signed the Defense of Marriage Act, providing that no state had to recognize a same-sex marriage performed in another. At the time, Kerry had been the only Democrat running for reelection in the Senate who'd voted against the bill; he'd denounced it as "gay-bashing on the floor of the United States Senate." Clinton, Kerry told me, had advised him that maybe he could now disarm his opponent on an issue that Karl Rove was exploiting to mobilize the religious right.

This was a flip-flop too far for Kerry. When he mentioned it to me, my reaction was that it was wrong in principle—and bad politics. Kerry already had taken his position: he was for civil unions, not same-sex marriage; but the states should decide the issue and the U.S. Constitution shouldn't be misused as a political football. Still, an anxious Kerry understood Clinton's advice even if he decided he couldn't take it; he couldn't believe that the controversy over same-sex marriage had burst into the campaign because of a decision by his own state's Supreme Court. "Why couldn't they just wait a year?" he said to me. Kerry was frustrated by what he regarded as the nearly indefensible nuance of his position on civil unions, and by what he saw as the inevitable political fall-out of the issue. Tell me again, he asked, what the difference is between what I'm for and marriage?

Kerry and the other candidates grappling with gay and lesbian rights aren't much different from political leaders in earlier generations who faced demands for equality that defied the old order and roiled large segments of the public, especially older generations set in their ways. Lincoln crabbed his way toward emancipation, downplaying the question of slavery until events, which he skillfully manipulated, opened the path to a bolder course. John Kennedy, fearing the loss of the Democratic South to the Republican Party, temporized on civil rights until the issue became irrepressibly urgent; then he did what was right—and as he feared, ever since, Democrats have paid a heavy political price in that region. Kerry, too, wished the question hadn't come to him, and certainly not now.

He tried to tiptoe his way through it—as do most progressives who aspire to the presidency.

Over time, I said to Kerry, the gay marriage debate will resolve itself. All the surveys show that younger people are for it; they don't really care who marries whom. I cited my longtime belief that culture is more powerful that politics. *Will and Grace*—the hit series whose gay characters are engaging and sympathetic—counted more than a hundred political speeches. Twenty-five years from now, or even sooner, everyone would look back, as we now do to the angry fight over interracial marriage, and would wonder what all the fuss was about. This was cold comfort to the candidate. "I know it," Kerry responded. "It won't be a big deal then. But it is now."

For Kerry, same-sex marriage was one thing; he wasn't troubled by it except as a political problem. But surprisingly, for someone who boasted that he'd always been pro-choice, abortion rights presented a harder case. He is a believing, not a nominal Catholic; during the Ohio primary, on Ash Wednesday, he ordered an unscheduled stop so we could get our foreheads crossed with ashes in the cathedral in Cleveland. This was no photo op. Kerry and I and a few other staff members had the smudges on our foreheads before the press corps rushing off the buses ever reached the sanctuary. At the urging of advisors, including me, Kerry had catered to primary voters by pledging to appoint only pro-choice Supreme Court justices. But now, with the nomination sewed up, the issue was heating up. As some bishops announced that they would deny him communion, Kerry was angry and distressed to find himself publicly at odds with vocal members of the hierarchy in his own Church.

When he learned that he was scheduled to give an interview to two *Time* reporters on religion and its impact on his private and public life, he exploded in his hotel room. The last thing he wanted to do was stoke the fires of this controversy. His cell phone was out of juice, so he borrowed mine. Cancel the interview, he told the Washington office. But the two reporters were already in the air—and this was his chance to talk about his own religious grounding—not an argument that persuaded him. He had a kind of New England reserve about wearing his faith on his sleeve. He hurled my cell phone the length of the living room into a far corner of the suite. He did the interview, which predictably contrasted his Catholicism with his views on abortion and stem cell research.

Kerry the Catholic would lose the Catholic vote, which Gore the Protestant had carried, and in the aftermath, panicked Democrats would scramble to flourish their own "moral values," even if that meant muting their convictions. Some of this took the form of ducking, bobbing, and weaving on a woman's right to choose during the 2006 confirmation hearings on Samuel Alito's nomination to the Supreme Court. I doubt that Democrats can become winners by not being who we are or not standing up for what we believe. In 2004, we didn't frame our argument as clearly or consistently as we should have in terms of the values Democrats can claim—values like fairness, equity, and the common good. Inside the Kerry campaign, we focused too narrowly on religion per se. But for John Kerry, or any other Catholic Democrat who's running for president, that's understandable. The Church's hierarchy doesn't arraign a non-Catholic candidate for being pro-choice; Clinton and Gore never faced the opposition Kerry did from within his own Church—and from bishops who concluded that he had to be brought to heel precisely because he was Catholic. If that attitude persists, the implication is clear: it will be risky for Democrats to nominate a Catholic, because any Democratic nominee will be pro-choice, no matter how the issue is downplayed or qualified. Forces within the Catholic Church itself could return us to the pre-JFK era so that no Catholics need apply, at least in the Democratic Party.

As the Kerry campaign's circle of advisers grew, it also shrank by one person, Jim Margolis. Cahill wanted to lower the commissions the campaign was paying for the media buy. Devine, Donilon, and I were ready to compromise with a split of 4 percent for the three of us and 3 percent for him. Instead, Margolis abruptly decided to leave the campaign. Reporters who didn't know the figures assumed the change represented a grab for money, although we had had no intention of driving Margolis out. He was replaced by Bill Knapp, who had partnered with us in the Gore effort four years before. According to *Time* columnist Joe Klein, Margolis sensed that Cahill, my partners, and I had been determined to get rid of him. In fact, we were surprised when he left and all of us sought to avoid a replay of the turmoil of the previous fall.

Klein himself was trying to play many parts. He was not only reporting on the campaign and preparing to write a book about consultants; he was also a constant critic and yet another sometime adviser. After the Kerry appearance at the Iowa Jefferson–Jackson Day Dinner, he told David Wade: "Great speech, but it's too late"— then turned around and stalked away. With Klein, it was almost always too late for us, in part because we didn't always take his persistent advice. He would chastise Kerry on the phone when he didn't like a speech, counseling both Kerry and me about what the candidate should say and what our strategy should be. He argued to Kerry, for example, that his health care plan should call for an individual mandate, requiring all Americans to buy health insurance. Rejecting his advice was uncomfortable for Kerry, who liked Joe, craved his approval, and worried what his columns would say when we didn't take his recommendations. It was uncomfortable for me, too. Joe had disagreed with me for years about politics and policy. He was a neo-liberal who once suggested to me that inner city public schools should be run by Catholic nuns; the bad news, I responded, was that the supply of Catholic nuns had run short. He was also close to Marylouise's confidant Anne Wexler. Anne, whom I'd known since the 1972 campaign, tried to make peace between Joe and me, which led to several long evenings at Joe's house where he importuned me with his ideas for the Kerry campaign.

Joe, to his credit, had done this in our darkest days. But in the preconvention season, new ideas and advisers were coming at us from everywhere. One of them took a crack at a less confrontational stump speech. Paul Begala, James Carville's sidekick on CNN's *Crossfire*, who let it be known later that he'd be willing to step in as campaign manager, wrote a memo to Kerry that he asked me to sign with him. In it, he agreed with the "overall framework of 'stronger at home, respected in the world' " and warned: "Scale . . . back the populist rhetoric. The media will kill you if you sound too much like Dick Gephardt or John Edwards." In a later book, *Take It Back* (2006), Begala criticized the Kerry campaign for doing what he had originally recommended. Promoting the book on *Meet the Press*, he told Tim Russert, "Here's what they called a message: J-HOS. It stands for jobs, health care, oil, security. . . . Without a message, Democrats were, if you'll pardon the expression, J-HOSED." I was startled by this when I heard it because in his memo to Kerry, Begala had noted that the stump speech he was proffering "follows the J-HOS formulation"—which he helped invent and which was never intended or presented as a message, but simply as an organizational mnemonic to keep Kerry from wandering all over the issues terrain. A month later, Begala reiterated his view. "We need one theme: Stronger at Home, Respected in the World," he wrote, "and four issues: economy, health care, energy independence, and security"—in short, J-HOS.

After Begala's performance on *Meet the Press*, Wendy Button, who'd written speeches for Hillary Clinton, John Edwards, and then Kerry, reacted in an e-mail: "Begala helped write the J-HOS stump speech. How could he . . . not disclose that? . . . I know, I know . . . this is D.C." She had seen the Begala memo, which massaged Kerry's ego as well as his message: "The plan aspect is critical. . . . You are going to win. You are going to be President. . . . You need [to] build support for an agenda on which you can govern." After Kerry didn't win, Paul assailed him for doing too much of that.

There would be successive waves of advisers, including a cacophony of ad hoc ad makers. At Kerry's request, Ari Kopelman, a social friend of his and Teresa's and the former CEO of Chanel, organized a group of Madison Avenue pros to weigh in. Their first cut was a slogan: "Truth. Fairness. Leadership." Kopelman suggested that the first two words could be dropped "down the road"; after weeks of cogitation, his group settled on: "John Kerry. Responsible Leadership." Kerry was disappointed when he heard it, but said test it in our polling along with a battery of slogans. "Responsible Leadership"

scored well. But we settled on the one Begala had endorsed—
"Stronger at Home, Respected in the World"—because it not only
tested well but was about the voters and not just the candidate.

In the fall, Kopelman's New York group would come up with an
inventive and intriguing anti-Bush idea. I flew to New York to see
Kopelman and two other advertising legends, Peter Georgescu, the
former chairman of Young & Rubicam, and Keith Rinehart, famous
for branding companies like McDonald's. They presented a series of
concepts and scripts. The one that stood out called for an elephant—
a real, live one—sauntering around a china shop, smashing fine
crystal, glassware, and pottery as the narrator recounted Bush's failings. It could have cost a million dollars or more to produce—and
then it would have to be tested to see if it worked. We were tight financially; under the law, I couldn't tell the three of them to take the
concept to the DNC, or some other independent group. If we'd had
more money, I would have pushed to produce it and show it to a dial
group.

I had to deal with someone else whose casual offer to pitch in was
welcomed by Kerry, the fashion designer Kenneth Cole. He's famous for clever riffs that push his products by reaching beyond
them—for example, for shoes: "What you stand for is more important than what you stand in." Find out if he has some great ideas,
Kerry said, and even if he doesn't, talk to him. Cole was a contributor to our campaign, and Mario Cuomo's son-in-law. His stream of
consciousness poured in day after day, e-mail after e-mail, phone call
after phone call. But were we really going to run an ad—better in
print, Cole suggested—that said: "There is only one man that can
Kerry us forward"? Or use the slogan: KERRY. ON. IN '04? Nor were
we going to proclaim: "All work and LOW pay makes every Johnny
part of our middle class." Before and after the convention, the calls
and e-mails kept coming. The high point was a "joke" in August as
Kerry was under fierce attack: "As many of you heard, I did take a
few days off from the campaign last week and yes I did wind-surf. It
was very interesting, in case you heard. I saw following me 'The
Swift Boat Surfing Veterans' for Truth.' . . . On a board that I think

was bought for them by a company called Halliburton something." Cole cared. He was indefatigable. But by the fall, I just didn't have any more time to keep him happy.

Bill Knapp, our fellow political ad maker, told me how glad he was that I was the one who got to handle another high-powered, high-profile volunteer message maker: Steve Jobs. For Jobs, the documentary filmmaker Errol Morris had created high-profile television spots with people explaining why they were switching from PCs to Apples. Jobs wanted Morris to duplicate that appeal for Kerry, with Republicans explaining why they were switching from Bush to Kerry. The difficulty was that they weren't and they wouldn't; except for a dwindling remnant of moderate Republicans, who were coming to Kerry anyway, Republicans weren't our battleground.

Kerry kept asking me if I was talking with Jobs. I was. He had an idea for an unconventional national convention that I passed on to the candidate. He thought Kerry should forgo the usual acceptance speech and use the occasion to debut the Jobs-Morris advertising campaign, standing before the delegates and the country as he introduced, showed, and commented on a series of "switcher" spots. I regarded this as the political equivalent of a corporate product rollout that would have made Kerry look like a pitch man, not a president. At a moment of maximum visibility, instead of offering his vision for the country, his message would have centered on the things Americans claim to hate most about politics: political ads. Kerry was taken aback by the idea—This is what he had been waiting for?—and he instantly rejected it.

Jobs seemed to take it for granted that he could do for Kerry what he had done for Apple. But while political advertising is sometimes too poll-driven, there is a fundamental difference between it and product marketing. Product advertising is a success if it moves market share a few points—for instance, from 5 to 7 percent, a move that can translate into millions of dollars in profits. But political spots have to help candidates reach 50 percent—or something less, if there's a third choice in the field—in a short time period and by a certain date.

* * *

No strategist or adviser, from any quarter, could have prevented the long-lasting disaster, seeded in the spring, which the Bush forces would harvest all summer and fall. The candidate's own words, provoked by a clever Republican ploy, then exploited by Bush's ad makers, would etch the image of Kerry as a flip-flopper indelibly on the public mind.

Early on, the Bush forces didn't have the material to make a persuasive case for that charge; voters weren't moved much by the notion that Kerry had opposed the first Gulf War but voted for the Iraq resolution. And he had an answer he'd given over and over to the charge that he'd opposed an $87 billion appropriation for military operations in Iraq: It should have been paid for by repealing the portion of the Bush tax cut that went to the wealthiest Americans, and the legislation should have included provisions holding the administration accountable to Congress for its future conduct in Iraq. Kerry had favored an alternative bill which did that while providing funding for our troops; he just didn't want to give the president a blank check. This was one issue where nuance was a strength, not a weakness.

With Kerry scheduled to appear at a veterans' event in West Virginia, the Bush campaign created an ad targeting that media market and criticizing Kerry for opposing the $87 billion appropriation. A veteran in the audience asked Kerry about his vote. He was succint and clear—as he would be again in the debates with Bush. But this was a moment for complication, not conciseness. Instead, the candidate was devastatingly memorable. Kerry, a politician intent on placating his immediate audience and a decorated war veteran who resented the suggestion that he would abandon soldiers on the field, responded by reassuring his fellow vets that "he actually did vote for the $87 billion" before he "voted against it." The Republicans had footage—even better footage than they could have hoped for—and would immediately weave it into their existing attack ad. In our polling, no previous formulation of the flip-flop argument had done serious damage to Kerry. But this was credible, a single phrase that seemed to prove the whole case against Kerry—and it had come right out of the candidate's mouth.

Immediately after Kerry's appearance, Cahill pulled me into her office: Had I heard what John just said? I sat there in disbelief. Then, with a sense of resignation, I commented that we had to do our best to explain the statement, defend it, and move beyond it as fast as possible. I knew it could haunt us for the rest of the campaign.

At first the impact was muffled as our big ad buy ran its course. Our own polls showed us moving up and then ahead. Stan Greenberg was conducting national surveys for the Democracy Corps, a group I'd founded with him and Carville that regularly circulated polling results and strategy memos to Democrats and the press. To avoid any conflicts with federal campaign law, I'd withdrawn as an active participant in the Democracy Corps when I'd signed on with Kerry. But under the law, Greenberg and Carville could regularly brief us, as long as we didn't offer suggestions or directions for their research. Their data showed us a point ahead in mid-June, halfway through our ad buy, and then showed Kerry with a 3- to 5-point advantage in the first part of July. We had come out of the first air war of the general election, as Greenberg wrote, with Bush "faltering" and "in grave danger of defeat." The second survey was taken just after the selection of John Edwards as Kerry's running mate. This was one of the two pre-convention decisions that mattered most. The vice-presidential pick, as usual, commanded the media spotlight; the second, perhaps more fateful decision—to accept federal funding and spending limits for the general election—was forged in private, in heated debate, with just a flicker of press attention.

Kerry had asked Jim Johnson to head up the vice-presidential search. Jim, my friend stretching back to the 1972 campaign, was one of Washington's best connected "wise men"—at times successively, and at times simultaneously, not only chairman of the giant mortgage company Fannie Mae, but of the Kennedy Center and the Brookings Institution; he had been Gore's chief debate negotiator in 2000, and was a likely treasury secretary or White House chief of staff in a Kerry administration. The candidate was obsessed with keeping the veep process closely held to prevent the speculation and leaks that had embarrassed him when he was on Gore's final list in 2000. This worked—until the last hour.

One option, the one that would have sealed the election, was off the table. John McCain's political strategist John Weaver had talked earlier with Cahill and said he needed to see Kerry about McCain. According to Kerry, when he met with Weaver and Cahill, Weaver said McCain was serious about the possibility of teaming up with him. Kerry had then sounded out McCain, who rejected the idea. McCain, I told Kerry, was running—but for president, in 2008, against Kerry if he was elected, or after a second Bush term. This meant he'd have to prove his loyalty to Republicans; and we couldn't expect much if any help from him if Kerry was slimed by some "independent" Republican group. It didn't matter that Kerry had rallied across party lines to McCain's defense when he was smeared in the 2000 primaries. Kerry nonetheless clung to the hope that if his service record was questioned, being a member of the "band of brothers" would be more important to McCain than party ID. But I didn't expect much "straight talk" from him this time around.

With McCain off the list, I walked from my house to Johnson's, which was next door, on a spring afternoon. The obvious vice-presidential choice, we agreed, was John Edwards; in the primaries, he'd emerged as a first-rate campaigner—and I told Jim that despite thiness on substance, I thought, as I been in 2000, that he could handle Cheney in a debate; We couldn't afford to repeat the Lieberman mistake. But there were two other clear possibilities: Dick Gephardt and Hillary Clinton. Kerry was ready to partner with Clinton if it was the way to win, but he doubted it was. He liked Gephardt, was confident he was up to the job of being president, and hoped he might help carry Missouri, which could make the difference in a close election. But both he and Teresa worried that Gephardt was a gray choice who wouldn't light any fires. While Edwards might, they were both uneasy with him. I'd said to Kerry early on that all I cared about was picking the strongest choice—personal feelings had nothing to do with it.

Johnson had compiled a list of about twenty-five "serious" candidates—and some others besides—and we reviewed it in his living room. In addition to Edwards, Clinton, and Gephardt, it included New Mexico governor Bill Richardson and some "out-of-the-box" choices, like Nebraska's maverick Republican senator Chuck Hagel, a kind of McCain surrogate. Hagel, who I guessed wouldn't accept and didn't know his name was on the list, was a nonstarter because he had a zero rating from the League of Conservation Voters. Richardson's prospects were shadowed by alleged womanizing. Publicly reluctant, he coveted the publicity of being considered, but withdrew before the process was finished.

A quiet round of polling helped guide the search. Hillary Clinton had high negatives—she would hurt the ticket; Dick Gephardt apparently didn't help in Missouri—in fact, Edwards's numbers were decidedly stronger there. When I heard this, I should have questioned whether the numbers actually reflected the ultimate impact of a Gephardt pick. As Kerry's running mate, Gephardt's campaigning and the institutional forces in Missouri might have given us a chance in the state, and he might have boosted us a little in Ohio, maybe just enough. But the process was evolving to where it had started—perhaps not in Kerry's mind, but in the conventional wisdom and the will of the Democrats across the country. When I handed Johnson a memo about advertising to be rolled out right after the choice was announced, I included a contingency for "a VP selection . . . from outside the present battleground states." Johnson and I both knew that meant North Carolina—and Edwards—but Kerry and Teresa still weren't there.

Kerry talked with several potential picks, including Gephardt and Edwards. He was comfortable after his conversations with Gephardt, but even queasier about Edwards after they met. Edwards had told Kerry he was going to share a story with him that he'd never told anyone else—that after his son Wade had been killed, he climbed onto the slab at the funeral home, laid there and hugged his body, and promised that he'd do all he could to make life better for people, to live up to Wade's ideals of service. Kerry was stunned, not moved, because, as he told me later, Edwards had recounted the same exact story to him, almost in the exact same words, a year or two before—and with the same preface, that he'd never shared the memory with anyone else. Kerry said he found it chilling, and he decided he couldn't pick Edwards unless he met with him again. When they did, Kerry tried to get a better personal feel for his potential number two; as rivals for national office since 2000, shortly after Edwards had entered the Senate, the two men hadn't spent a lot of time together. Kerry also wanted a specific reassurance. He asked Edwards for a commitment that if he was chosen and the ticket lost, Edwards wouldn't run against him in 2008. Edwards agreed "absolutely," as Kerry recalled him saying. If Kerry had shared this at the time, I would have told him what I did later: it was naive to think he could rely on a promise like that. Unlike Joe Lieberman, who'd been plucked from relative obscurity by Gore, Edwards had made his own mark in the primaries. He was ambitious—and if he saw his chance the next time, he was likely to go for it.

At the beginning of July, I was at Teresa Heinz's farm outside Pittsburgh, where Kerry would announce his pick in a couple of days. She sounded at peace with the idea of Edwards. It was very early on July 7, the morning of the announcement, when the story finally leaked. The day before, Linda Douglass from ABC had called me from her home on Cape Cod Bay, just up the beach from ours. I'd refused to say anything, except to tell her that it was a good idea to get herself back to the network's Washington bureau. The first leak came after midnight. "GEPHARDT," blared a special edition of the *New York Post*. We were told later that someone had given Rupert Murdoch the inside scoop—why would anyone in our campaign leak to him?—and he ordered the paper to go with it. The headline ignited a media frenzy. Andrea Mitchell from NBC and Linda Douglass both phoned me in rapid succession: Was this true? I was determined not to be a source, no matter how far off the record. But Andrea and Linda were friends and after a few seconds of back-and-forth, I only said: "I wouldn't go with that story if I were you." I refused to go any further. I realized they would conclude that if it wasn't Gephardt, it was Edwards. They did, and somehow found confirmation. Mitchell, and then just minutes later Douglass broke the news on the morning shows. I rationalized that this would steal any of Kerry's thunder; it was too late for that. The press conference was about to be held on the lawn of Teresa's farm on a sparkling summer morning.

Afterward on the phone, Edwards and I talked for the first time since I had informed him of our decision to work for Kerry. He said he knew I'd helped and he was grateful. I told him that I welcomed the possibility that we might be friends again, but that wasn't the reason for my preference. I believed it was the right move for Kerry. (Kerry's relationship with Edwards would sour after the election—and mine would simply fade away. When Elizabeth discovered she had breast cancer, John and Teresa reached out to help the Edwardses find the best doctors they could. Marylouise and I called—but afterward, never heard from John again. Maybe we shouldn't have expected to. Kerry told me that the Edwardses simply stopped returning calls or talking to him and Teresa. Within months, Edwards started preparing for a bid in 2008. Kerry said that he wished he'd never picked Edwards, that he should have gone with his gut.)

The other decision-making process, already under way, on whether to take federal funding for the general election and thus live within a federally mandated spending ceiling, was contentious and messy. After turning down public money in the primaries, which would have limited the campaign to spending $45 million prior to the convention, we would ultimately raise nearly $250 million by then—incredibly, approximately the same amount as the sitting Republican president. For us, million-dollar days of fundraising on the Internet were not uncommon. If both candidates now accepted federal funding for the general election, they'd each have $75 million to spend. But it wasn't an equal $75 million. Bush, whose convention came in early September, had to make the money last for just eight weeks until Election Day. But with our convention at the end of July, we faced a nearly thirteen-week campaign. In August, the Bush forces could spend another $50 million or $60 million in primary funds on a massive flight of advertising to attack Kerry. Legally, we couldn't respond with money raised for the primaries once Kerry accepted the nomination, so our only option, if we accepted public funding, would be to absorb the punishment or draw down the resources we needed to be competitive in the homestretch to November 2.

Tad Devine and Kerry's longtime adviser Ron Rosenblith argued relentlessly that the only solution was to reject the public money and the spending limits; we could raise far more—and we wouldn't have our hands tied in August. I personally witnessed the eagerness of people to give and give to get Bush out of the White House when I did some fund-raising myself—for example, picking up tens of thousands of dollars at an event organized by my stepson Michael for his fellow TV writers at Henry and Stacey Winkler's home in Los Angeles. With anyone who would listen to him, Rosenblith shared his estimates of the money we could put together, from both the Internet and traditional contributors. I was convinced; so were our Internet experts, although a number of them later felt pressured to change their minds. But Cahill and some others were fiercely opposed to taking the gamble. The federal money was certain; what if we hit a down-draft in the polls and our contributions dried up? But I believed that if we were in trouble, we'd actually need *more* money and we could go get it; the anti-Bush feeling wasn't opportunistic; people were giving to a cause. The next objection was that we'd have to divert Kerry, Edwards, and their wives from the battleground states to fund-raising events in safe states like New York and California. But I replied that we could do that at night. Then came the warning that Bush would follow our lead and might then outraise us. But, I responded, we'd stayed even with him so far; the Internet was revolutionizing politics. Why give him a $50 million or $60 million advantage from the end of July to early September? Finally, we were cautioned that Democratic candidates for the Senate and House would be aggrieved because we were depleting their potential sources of funding. When Jon Corzine, now the chairman of the Senate Campaign Committee, heard about this, he called me and said it was crazy for Kerry to stay within the federal contribution and spending limits and that Democratic candidates would live with a decision to opt out.

The lawyers came up with a loophole in the law that might let us have it both ways. We could hold our convention; Kerry and his running mate could give their speeches—with one small excision: they wouldn't utter the ritualistic words formally accepting the nomination until September, when Bush did. Then technically we could keep spending primary money to counter the other side. There were only a few of us who were aware of this far-fetched ploy. But, of course, it leaked. *The Washington Post* blasted us and added: "We do look forward to [Kerry's] non-acceptance speech."

We backed off and the question was now inescapable: Would we take the federal funding or opt out? Waves of clashing memos, e-mails, and financial projections flew across the campaign. Rosenblith concluded one of his missives: "There is no choice here." I drafted talking points for Kerry to explain opting out: "This is a fight for working families and the middle class . . . and I'm going to ask the American people to continue to sustain this campaign in the unprecedented way they have in the past few months. So go to John Kerry.com and join in our effort." (When Kerry mentioned our Web site in his acceptance speech, $5 million would pour in in one night, but because we'd accepted public funding, we wouldn't be able to spend it in the general election.)

Something else flew around the campaign: the charge that I was for declining public money so that the campaign would spend more on television and I would make more on commissions. So without telling my partners or Bill Knapp, who shared the commissions with us, on June 18, I clambered onto our newly chartered 757 to talk with Kerry on a flight from Washington to Nantucket. I told him that the media consultants would cap our earnings at the amount we'd make if he took public funding. If he opted out, and the campaign spent more, we'd be paid nothing more. (In reality, we ended up with less; we quietly gave up most of our commissions for the final weeks, over a million dollars, to try to win a close race.)

I thought I'd persuaded Lou Susman that we should opt out. But he told me that as our finance chair, he saw it as a close call, and he felt he had to stand by Cahill. The final conference call with Kerry was protracted. Different estimates of what we would have under either scenario had been put on the table, debated, derided, and defended. I tried to cut through all the numbers by emphasizing that we'd only gotten to where we were by not playing it safe. If he'd accepted public money in the primaries, Kerry wouldn't have won the nomination; and if somehow he had, we long since would have hit the legal spending cap and been left with no resources to respond to the Bush onslaught. As usual, Tad Devine was blunt. He told Kerry that the stakes couldn't be higher: "This may be the most important decision you'll make. The wrong decision can lose you the election." Maybe we didn't see the Swift boats coming, but something would. One thing we all agreed on—and explicitly told Kerry: If he didn't opt out, we'd have to be off television in August. Inevitably, we'd face attack ads; our only recourse would be to respond in the free media.

Kerry consciously chose the cautious option. He informed me later that he was startled to discover that we had $50 million in our coffers after the convention that our campaign couldn't spend in the fall. Rosenblith had predicted correctly that we'd raise tens of millions of dollars that July. After he lost, the candidate was angry at those who had advocated staying within the public funding system; they'd low-balled the figures, he complained, badgered others to support their recommendation, and not given him all the information he should have had. But, I replied, you did have an alternative set of figures—and I don't doubt the motivation of Cahill or her allies in this debate. They were determined to win the election, too, and they thought opting out was just too dicey. It was Kerry who decided; in this case, the bucks literally stopped there. If he had the chance to do it over, he never would have accepted this unequal playing field.

We developed the acceptance speech much as we had with Gore. I wrote a first draft, and we had reams of paper besides, suggestions from outsiders and from our speechwriting staff. Andrei Cherney had been pushed out—at Cahill's behest, not mine, on the grounds that he couldn't get along with the new recruits to the speechwriting shop. It was now headed by Terry Edmonds, who'd done the same job in the Clinton White House. He had developed a riff for Kerry based on Langston Hughes's call to: "Let America be America again." Kerry and I both thought it was superb; it might make a spellbinding conclusion to the acceptance speech. Unfortunately, it fell victim to literal-minded focus group participants who bristled: "But isn't this already America?" Wasn't the line somehow unpatriotic?

With Josh Gottheimer, the young Clinton veteran who was taking time off from Harvard Law School to wordsmith for Kerry on the campaign plane, I liberally larded the original version I'd written with the material we'd received from others. We then videotaped Kerry delivering all of it and sliced the tape into short pieces, so Mellman could duplicate the Greenberg process from four years before and test the language in dial groups. As we honed the draft, I met up with the candidate on the road and then in Nantucket, where he took a few days' "break" to prepare for his final pre-convention journey from Colorado, through the Midwest, and then up the Atlantic seaboard, where he would arrive at the convention in Boston on July 28, the day before he delivered his acceptance speech. I'd fly in commercially—to places like Norfolk and Philadelphia—and get to Kerry's suite before he and the press arrived at the hotel. When sessions were finished, I'd sneak out a side door to a waiting car. To me, this was a lot of wasted motion that wouldn't fool anybody into thinking Kerry had written the entire speech himself. He had written material of his own for the section about his mother and father. And a lot of what he wrote was original and fresh—the story of riding his bike into Communist East Berlin when his father was a diplomat and he was twelve years old. There was one memory that had to be tweaked: Kerry had described how his father "had done things a boy remembers. He gave me my first sailboat." I said most boys in America didn't have that kind of memory; it would just confirm the image of Kerry as privileged and elitist. So I changed sailboat to "baseball mitt." Kerry expanded the phrase to read: "my first model airplane, my first baseball mitt, my first bicycle." Really, who could question this anyway?

I had another assignment—to help Teresa prepare for her convention speech. After all the criticism, she was resolved to make sure it was primarily about her husband, not herself or her own views. In Nantucket, she asked whether I thought she had the balance right. I said yes—and she did, but I was wrong about the reaction she'd elicit. What would command attention was not the bulk of her remarks, which focused on John Kerry, but the bright red dress she wore and her brief defense of her right "to speak my mind, to have a voice, to be what some have called 'opinionated.' . . ." The day before she took to the podium, she'd publicly told a reporter for a right-wing Pittsburgh newspaper to "shove it." That clip, played over and over, was the context that now imprisoned her for the rest of the convention. The Bush operation did its best to keep her there. In their narrative, she continued to be the "foreign" wife of the "French" Kerry. As she wryly observed to me—thankfully in private: "They're attacking John because he speaks French. Well, Bush doesn't speak French—or English."

To separate Clinton's convention speech as far as possible from Kerry's, we'd slotted it for Monday night, for 25 minutes, just before the end of the prime-time network coverage. He went just one minute over. The next night featured Teresa, Ted Kennedy, and Barack Obama, the Democratic Senate nominee from Illinois. His keynote address would make him an instant star and presidential possibility himself. But when we tapped him for the keynote, we couldn't foresee his full impact or what the speech might mean for the future; in any event, for us, the future was now. When I saw Obama's draft, I was struck by its eloquence; this was a politician who could write. He was also, I discovered, a politician who wasn't self-absorbed. I asked that he cut one of his best phrases because word for word it was already in Kerry's acceptance speech. Some in this country, both Obama and Kerry intended to say, want to divide America into red states and blue states: "I see . . . one America—red, white, and blue." Obama didn't hesitate. To conclude his riff, he came up with other words: "There's not a liberal America and a conservative America. There's the United States of America."

In the practice room at the Convention Hall, Kerry sounded didactic during a run-through. I got Morehouse to clear the room and Michael Sheehan, there as he had been with Gore to coach the candidate on delivery, repeated the advice he'd offered in 2000: Kerry had to surf the applause; what counted was energy on television, not milking the enthusiasm in the hall. The candidate picked up the pace in the next run-through as a dozen of us mimicked the clapping and cheering of the delegates. We had a speech. But we also had the debris of unused drafts and phrases requested by Kerry. JFK's adviser Dick Goodwin had been actively involved; a week and a half before, I'd asked him to drive to my place on the Cape to do a semifinal edit. But the other legendary Kennedy speechwriter, Ted Sorenson, had only the shadow of a contribution in the speech, a single line, used in a different sense than it was intended. Someone had to tell him. I reminded Kerry that he should call Sorenson—or have Cahill do it. I wasn't going to. The situation was embarrassing and unfair, and I'd made it clear from the start that I hadn't wanted to put Sorenson in that position. But it was a busy day and, as far as I know, no one told him in advance.

As we left the practice room, Max Cleland rolled down the hallway in his wheelchair. He was scheduled to introduce Kerry to the convention. Shrum, he said to me, I have a great last line: "John Kerry, report for duty." I told Cleland it *was* great, but would he mind yielding it to Kerry? So we had a new start to the speech— "I'm John Kerry, and I'm reporting for duty"—a line that blew the roof off the Convention Hall, but within weeks would be cited as a mistake that left the candidate more vulnerable to charges about his military record. If this was a mistake, it went far beyond that speech. The convention, which spotlighted Kerry's crewmates and fellow Vietnam vets, was consciously designed to emphasize Kerry's commitment "to fight for America"—and in the process, provide evidence of his bona fides on national security. That's why from the first draft on, the speech started with national security to show it wasn't an afterthought, an issue Kerry was afraid to run on but had to cover. Then he could turn to domestic issues like health care, wage stagnation, and the export of American jobs. That section was striated with populism. Kerry, for example, denounced "another windfall . . . [for] the big drug companies." (And at this convention Clinton denounced the Bush tax cuts for benefiting the wealthy.) In the end, just less than half of Kerry's speech—and less than that of the prime-time convention coverage—was devoted to Iraq, terrorism, and national security.

Greenberg told me a month later that this didn't matter; the images had focused too much on Kerry as warrior and not enough on bread-and-butter issues. By then, Kerry seemed to be in trouble, and the convention was one convenient explanation. Right after the acceptance address, however, Greenberg had called my cell phone: The speech was "a home run"; so was the convention. That night, the bar of the Four Seasons Hotel became the site of an impromptu party. We were celebrating what we were convinced was a great week; most of the journalists there seemed to share that verdict. Then came the stories that the convention hadn't produced much of a bounce for Kerry, although the ABC–*Washington Post* poll showed an 8-point turnaround for him from the figures a week before. Most public polls didn't agree. Our own data—from Mellman—had Kerry moving from a 1-point deficit to a 7-point lead in the battleground states. But whatever the numbers, we had never expected a bounce like Gore's in 2000, when he'd been so far behind as his convention neared. I said to reporters, and believed, that this was a tight race in a closely divided country where only a small fraction of the vote was in play. No matter what, Kerry was going to get 45 percent and Bush was going to get 45 percent; we were fighting for the rest. This made every little bit count more. The Bush White House understood that with ruthless clarity.

The Sunday after the Democratic Convention, the national terror threat level was raised to "orange"—the second-highest level. Perhaps this was another coincidence; but the coincidences invariably seemed to be convenient for the president. The threat level had also been raised just after Edwards had been picked for vice president—and before that, just as we were launching our big springtime television ad buy. It was another tilt of the playing field that we had to live with. We had no proof that the alerts were manipulated, and Kerry would get shredded in the press and the polls if he denounced them as political. Indeed, we fell sharply in our overnight tracking polls when Kerry extemporaneously ridiculed Bush for continuing to read out the children's book *The Pet Goat* in a Florida classroom after being informed of the 9/11 attack. We couldn't politicize the terrorist threat, but Bush could. Our challenge was to separate 9/11 and Iraq in the public mind. After the post-convention alert, our bounce, whatever it was and for whatever reason, simply stopped.

Immediately after the convention, Kerry left Boston for a train trip across the country. This was when the campaign really began to go off the rails. Our debate prep team boarded the westbound train in La Junta, Colorado, for a preliminary discussion with the candidate. Bush still hadn't agreed to debate at all. Maybe, I suggested, it was the old rope-a-dope to lower expectations, but that was tougher for him than it had been in 2000: He was now the president.

I was in one of the parlor cars on the train when Jamie Rubin, Madeleine Albright's former spokesman, confessed that he was concerned about an interview he'd just given to *The Washington Post*. He was traveling with the candidate to handle foreign policy on the road, and he said maybe he'd gone too far in defending Kerry's vote on the Iraq war resolution. How far? I asked. It was hard getting a straight answer but he guessed that, well, it wasn't that bad. Our press secretary, Stephanie Cutter, was worried—and it *was* that bad, as I discovered over breakfast with a distressed Rubin and a blind-sided Cutter in Albuquerque the next morning. Rubin was quoted in the *Post* story as saying that even knowing what he did today, Kerry would still vote for the Iraq war resolution. I had pressed several times for Kerry to raise a similar question on his own and offer an unequivocal no—of course, he wouldn't have supported the invasion of Iraq knowing what he did now. Our national security staff headed by Rand Beers, who'd resigned from the White House staff to protest Bush's policies, worried that if Kerry went that far, some of the generals endorsing him would draw back. He had to refuse to respond to the "hypothetical," said Beers, and instead insist that the issue was the future. Now a campaign staffer had answered a hypothetical—and even worse, Rubin had said that "in all probability" Kerry as president would have gone to war in Iraq, as Bush had, to remove Saddam Hussein.

I was certain that was untrue—and a political disaster. I said to

Rubin and Cutter, this is nuts; how in God's name had Rubin decided to say this? He was clearly afraid his tenure in the campaign would be short-lived. (It was—at least traveling with the candidate; but disposing of him altogether would lead to another story, and why kill him that way when he could just stay in the headquarters?) I predicted to Rubin that we'd somehow have to repudiate his words; to that extent, we'd have to throw him under the bus—the press bus, to be precise. He'd have to say he misspoke. Cutter had a more immediate concern. Kerry was scheduled for a "press avail" that day, an informal press conference. What was he going to say? Nothing, I answered; just cancel it. I was supposed to go back to Washington. I grabbed Kerry when he returned from Sunday mass and said we had a problem; we'd have to put off the press avail. What was the problem? he pressed. I didn't want him to lose it in the driveway of the hotel, standing beside his Secret Service vehicle, with reporters within earshot if he raised his voice. I answered that he had to stay calm, but Rubin had gone too far in describing his position on Iraq; we had to postpone any avail until we had worked out an answer. A barely contained Kerry suggested that maybe I should go on the next leg of the train trip. I answered that I had to get back to work on the debate prep and the September advertising. We'd send the needed talking points out that night or the next morning. What I should have done is just urge him to cut the Gordian knot then and there, disavow Rubin's remarks, and say that of course he wouldn't have favored the war knowing what he knew today.

Once again, we were caught in the flypaper of Kerry's Iraq vote. If it was, as he had said, "the wrong war in the wrong place at the wrong time," then why would he have launched it? The Bush campaign gleefully spread the word that Kerry's position on Iraq was the same as the president's. If that wasn't so, Bush said, "the American people deserve a clear yes or no answer." We couldn't settle on one back at the headquarters; our national security staff said we still had to hold the line against responding to a hypothetical. I couldn't yet force a different decision. So the guidance we dispatched to the train as it rolled toward an event at the Grand Canyon, where Kerry was supposed to talk about the environment—oh sure, that would make news—was to walk the same ambiguous line and challenge the president on faulty intelligence and postwar planning. But the time for that was over—and the notion that Kerry could continue to duck the question was an unsustainable illusion after the Rubin episode. Kerry finally held the press avail at the Grand Canyon on August 9, where he said he still would have voted to give the president "the authority" to invade; but he evaded a definitive statement about the war itself.

It was a nuance that led to stark headlines—for example, in the *Boston Globe*: "Kerry Says He'd Still Vote to Authorize Iraq War." If we didn't get to a simple, straightforward position, I said to Cahill, Kerry's apparent inconsistencies and inexplicable nuances would dominate and destroy him in the first debate with Bush. The president would chase him around the stage demanding an answer. We couldn't be against the war and for it; we'd already been there and done that with Kerry's vote on the $87 billion to fund the conflict. I told our national security staff we didn't have a choice anymore. We had to answer the hypothetical—and before the first debate. Kerry would do it in a speech at New York University on September 20, announcing that on the basis of what he now knew, he would not have supported the Iraq war.

Kerry took the heat for all this. But with a few exceptions, too many other Senate Democrats had suppressed their doubts and had been bullied into voting with Bush, overcompensating for their fear that otherwise, the party would be seen as weak on national security. Virtually none of the party's foremost foreign policy advisers had argued the other side. By 2004, they were trapped in their own counsel and a conventional mind-set within the foreign policy establishment; for all the criticism he faced, Kerry in the end actually went beyond what most of them would have advised when he said that it was, at least in hindsight, a mistake to go to war. I recalled a story Ted Kennedy had told me about his brother. Sitting on the Truman Balcony at the White House in the summer of 1963, JFK said he had one piece of advice if his younger brother ever ended up in the Oval Office. The men with medals, stars, braids, and résumés would troop in sure of their recommendations—as they had before the Bay of Pigs disaster. But the credentials didn't matter; they were no guarantee of wisdom or good sense. You had to ask the tough questions. Forty years later, on the Iraq war, the bloggers were more right than the experts.

Of course, Kerry had all the Democratic experts with him as the nominee and the potential president who could appoint them to high office. One of the amusing sidelights of the conference calls that brought them together to offer advice was an ongoing implicit audition for secretary of state. Joe Biden, the top Democrat on the Senate Foreign Relations Committee, would be making a point, often at length, and then Dick Holbrooke, Clinton's former UN ambassador, who saw Biden as his foremost rival for State, would interrupt him or try to top what he had said. Those of us who were listening to the call would smile and on one occasion Kerry intervened: "Dick, let Joe finish." I don't know who would have won the beauty contest for secretary of state.

At the heart of Kerry's prescription for future policy in Iraq was a call to involve more of our allies in the postwar that was increasingly becoming a continuing war; this prescription was dismissed by Bush as something his administration was already attempting to achieve. Kerry answered that after alienating so many other nations, Bush couldn't pull it off—that his only answer was "more of the same." And Kerry also had a secret plan that he told me he couldn't reveal during the campaign. As president, he would communicate in confidence with France, Germany, and other allies that had economic interests in Iraq and a stake in Mideast stability. They would have a choice: If they didn't send enough troops to form a true multinational force, one not dominated by the United States, then we would withdraw our troops in three to six months. It might have worked— and I suspect that for some Europeans, there was disappointment but perhaps also a sense of relief when Kerry lost. Bush was their easy excuse to avoid involvement. Kerry was also right that he couldn't have disclosed his plan publicly as a candidate. Reluctant allies would have felt politically compelled to reject the ultimatum. And at home, Kerry would have been accused of "cutting and running"—the charge Democrats were dealing with by 2006—and even worse, with giving the now demonized French a veto over our national security. Kerry's notion was the kind of policy that can only succeed once you are already president, as a similar move did when the newly inaugurated Dwight Eisenhower hinted at a nuclear strike to force a truce in the Korean War. It wasn't something you could propose in a campaign.

While Kerry was at the Grand Canyon, the so-called Swift Boat ads, financed by an independent group with close ties to Bush contributors, had already been on the air in three states for five days, slandering Kerry's service in Vietnam and disputing the Bronze Star he had won for valor. The warnings about the consequences of accepting federal funding were about to become too true; if we hoped to be competitive with Bush in the fall, then, we had agreed, August for us had to be the month without advertising money. Otherwise, we would have heeded our first instinct—to hit back hard. I never understood the criticism that we preferred to let an attack like this go unanswered, even in a limited number of media markets in a few battleground states. I recalled the *Boston Globe* editorial that had once called me a master of "dirt and calumny." Nor was I inclined to accept either from an opponent. Kerry himself was on the phone constantly. His honor was being stolen, his good name, and he wanted to get it back. I tried to calm him: What we wanted to get was the presidency—and Mellman was reporting another "reality," that in his nightly tracking, the Swift boat spots weren't having any impact. Kerry reached a boiling point—and Democrats in general were openly incredulous—before Mellman finally warned after almost two weeks that, well, it now looked from his latest data like the ads were hurting us. They had triggered a flood of coverage on cable news, with a big ride on Fox. Soon an Annenberg Survey would find that almost half of Americans had heard of the attacks, although they were on the air in just a few places and at relatively low levels.

Five or six of us—Cahill, the media team, and Mellman—convened in a windowless conference room at the headquarters and called Kerry, who was in Boston. He was scheduled to address the firefighters' convention there the next day. I argued that he had to take this on in his speech, and we had to produce a response ad, put it on the air, and put the onus on Bush for a third-party front group that was doing his dirty work. Kerry was relieved, and he was angry that we hadn't listened to him and struck back sooner—and that he hadn't just ordered us to do it. No one dissented from doing it now except Mellman. He was concerned that we were just escalating the battle; this would make it a big story on the network news. It *is* a big story, Kerry retorted; he didn't want to hear any more debate about this. And he didn't understand why the Democratic National Committee or one of the independent groups on our side hadn't figured out that they should have been broadcasting ads defending him.

The firefighters' speech was drafted and e-mailed to Boston. We scripted, produced, and shipped our first response spot; the DNC caught the drift and released an ad with the former Air Force Chief of Staff endorsing Kerry. We followed up with another spot comparing the Swift boat ads to the tactics Bush had used against John McCain in 2000 and challenging the president to denounce the smear. McCain, the man Kerry had defended in 2000, said that if we didn't stop invoking him, he'd denounce Kerry. We cut McCain from the ad. Karl Rove, who studiously denied any connection with the smear, knew the Hobson's choice we faced in August: Spend now and run short later, or hold off and get hurt. Either way, Bush would benefit.

The first round of Swift boat attacks on Kerry sparked a debate about his Vietnam service that increasingly hinged on the details of specific battles more than thirty years before. Kerry had or hadn't been on or across the Cambodian border on Christmas Eve, as he claimed. I read the records our research team had laboriously compiled; he'd been there all right, if not on Christmas Eve, then that winter. The lowest point was the vile charge that Kerry, who had also been awarded the Silver Star, the nation's second highest military decoration, had self-inflicted or faked one of the three wounds for which he had received Purple Hearts (under the regulations in effect at the time, it was the total of three wounds that got him sent home from Vietnam before his scheduled year-long tour of duty was up). We were facing—and now fighting back against—an unproven set of shifting slurs, lie after lie. Some of the men who had defended Kerry in his 1996 Senate campaign now took the other side; none of them had been crewmates on Kerry's boat.

The real grievance, I told the candidate, wasn't his war record in Vietnam, but his antiwar record after he came home. Kerry was anxious to confront that, too; and my former client, Bob Kerrey, now president of the New School University in New York, ghosted a biting defense of the young John Kerry's protests during the Vietnam War—to be delivered by the candidate, in an in-your-face way, at the American Legion National Convention. Mellman said this would be a blunder: People in the focus groups couldn't grasp the notion of Kerry the war hero opposing the war he fought in; it confused them. Kerry and Kerrey, another hero who'd protested Vietnam after coming home, both thought this was ridiculous. But Greenberg reported that his data showed that voters didn't see Vietnam as "relevant"; they "want to hear" about the future.

Kerry was deflected from offending the American Legion—maybe he should have—and instead gave every candidate's conventional speech. But he was restless and anxious to protract the battle and reclaim his reputation. He wanted the DNC to commit millions of dollars to more response ads, to be produced by a group of vets, led by his former brother-in-law David Thorne. I don't know how he legally communicated the request, if he ever did, and why it never happened. But he was still intent on using that Bob Kerrey draft. He would raise the issue with the Clinton acolytes who soon joined the staff and then in a conversation with Clinton himself as the former president was lying in his hospital bed just before his emergency heart surgery. They were unanimous: it was a bad idea. In hindsight, I'm not so sure Kerry's agitation was misplaced. In an election where the switch of one close big state like Ohio, or two close smaller ones, would have reversed the outcome, voters who were left with doubts about whether Kerry's service was "honorable" may have made the difference.

I am certain that we—and I—made indisputable mistakes in dealing with the Swift boat lies. We took the polling too seriously for too long; we should have known better than to credit comforting numbers that conveniently fit our resolve to conserve resources. The consensus that we had to be off the air in August was too iron-clad. Kerry's service was the indispensable foundation of his credibility on national security. The mistake, in my view, wasn't that we showcased this at the Democratic Convention instead of devoting even more words and time to concerns like health care, but that we didn't fiercely and instantly protect the defining truth of Kerry's life when it came under attack. One bad decision—to take public funding—explained but didn't justify the other—to let the Swift boat attacks plow ahead for nearly two weeks without a response.

By the end of August, we had a campaign on the verge of upheaval because we had a candidate in near panic—as I discovered during our next debate prep session, this one on Nantucket. We should have expected to lose ground that month. The Bush campaign was spending tens of millions of dollars on its own negative ads. But the Grand Canyon gaffe exacerbated our problems, and so did the tragic and unexpected overture to the Republican Convention in New York, a convention choreographed to play on Bush's one high—his response to 9/11. Just as the Republicans were gathering, Chechen rebels who were engaged in a series of terror attacks against Russia seized a school in Beslan, a town half a world away that most Americans had never heard of. The crisis there was brought home to the United States—and into the election—by a constant stream of television coverage. As the siege mounted and then the rescue attempt left 344 people dead, including 186 children, Mellman warned that Bush was gaining in the tracking polls night after night. In the afterglow of the Republican convention, Kerry would fall 7 points behind in the battleground states in our data—and some public surveys would show the national margin at 10 or more. This bounce, too, would fade; within two weeks, Mellman would have the gap down to 4 points and then 1.

But Kerry wasn't waiting to see his ads back on television full force, or for the post–Labor Day engagement with Bush we'd already planned. He was distracted and late during our scheduled Nantucket debate preps. He'd been on the phone with Bill Clinton.

Then on Monday, as the Republican Convention was gaveled to order, he gifted the other side with priceless footage for their commercials. When he announced to us that he was taking a break to get some exercise, Mary Beth Cahill told him: "John, don't go windsurfing." He promised not to; we asked him afterward why he had. He said that he'd thought he'd given the press the slip and there were no cameras around to film him. But there were. Voters in the battleground states would see the image over and over in a spot reiterating Kerry's comment about voting for the $87 billion before he voted against it. The spot ended: "John Kerry. Whichever way the wind blows."

We were about to go into another debate prep when Cahill told me we had to talk on the lawn outside. She said we were going to make some "additions" to the campaign. She was distressed and, I thought, worried about her own status. It was the first I knew of what would become a wholesale infusion of former Clinton aides. The story was about to break—and former press secretaries Joe Lockhart and Mike McCurry were about to arrive, along with Greenberg, who had just severed his ties with the independent expenditure groups. There were other Clinton veterans, too, and in addition to them, John Sasso—the Bostonian who'd been Kerry's first choice to replace Jim Jordan—would now travel full time with the candidate. All this would soon become fodder for critical stories about me; but one aspect of it was particularly unfair to someone else. Stephanie Cutter, our communications director, was blamed for our bad press in August. In reality, Lockhart, McCurry, Karl Rove, and Shrum together couldn't have put a positive spin for Kerry on the cruel month of August. The problem wasn't the communications shop, but rather the real events that were being communicated.

Cahill's position was in theory unchanged but in reality shaky. I didn't know what mine was, although Kerry soon told me that it was unchanged. That, of course, wasn't true—for a time. Kerry and Sasso had a conversation from the road each morning with Cahill and Lockhart about our communications objectives for the day; I was in an odd spot because Kerry would frequently call me afterward to see what I thought. I'd promptly close the loop with Cahill and Lockhart. This jerry-built process would wax and wane until mid-October, when Kerry told me to get on the plane with Sasso and then became increasingly dismissive of the morning calls.

On September 4, one of the recruits from the Clinton camp described our "new" message to a staff meeting at the headquarters: "It's very simple. Bush has taken us in the wrong direction. . . . If you want a new direction, John Kerry and John Edwards." One anonymous senior aide—not me; I was doing my best to hold this enterprise together—sarcastically told the *New York Times*, "That's really groundbreaking." It was straight out of a poll—from Greenberg, who was now sharing a tiny side room with Lockhart. The formula of "right direction, wrong direction" was elevated to the status of a silver bullet, so sacrosanct that on September 7, Lockhart sent around a censorious e-mail: "JK has inserted in today's speech the phrase 'it's time for a change.' . . . Thoughts on whether we want to throw ourselves in front of this train?" I shrugged to Cahill and Lockhart that it meant the same thing. Kerry could and would vary the language sometimes; we weren't clerics guarding the fine points of doctrine. Greenberg objected that the country was afraid of "change" so we couldn't say it quite that way. I replied that if voters weren't willing to change, I didn't see how we'd ever win—and I said the same thing to Kerry. All this was symptomatic of a time-consuming exercise where we'd eventually arrive pretty much back where we'd started. As Greenberg phrased it:

> . . . *We need to move in a new direction.* . . .
>
> [Reassurance] *For sure that means a strong military and I will battle the terrorists who threaten our country.* . . .
>
> "[Define strength at home] *To be strong at home, we must have a strong middle class.* . . . *While CEOs are doing fine, the middle class struggles with scarce jobs, stagnant incomes and skyrocketing health-care costs.* . . .
>
> [Closer] *Vote Bush to continue in the wrong direction. Vote for Kerry and Edwards and a new direction.*

474 | ROBERT SHRUM

It was pretty much what Kerry had been saying for months. But this version was words, words, words, not a narrative. The message ribbon around all of it—"right direction, wrong direction"—was transactional, not aspirational. It almost took the edge off the message, and perhaps that was its purpose. It would be a sufficient Democratic appeal in the protest election of 2006; but 2004 was a knife's-edge contest and Kerry's appeal needed its own edge. We never settled on a single, simple phrase to sum up his appeal. That was everybody's fault, including mine—although I would have preferred just to say what Kerry was, a fighter "for us," or what he was for, with a summons invoking that risky word "change."

On the night of September 4, Kerry, along with a handful of us from the reconfigured command structure, held a conference call with Clinton in his hospital room. The day before, the candidate and the former president had a chat of their own, "for 90 minutes," as the instant leak to the *New York Times* reported. When he read a summary of Clinton's remarks, Joel Johnson, another one of his former staff members who'd come to the campaign, e-mailed back: "Just classic." Clinton's advice was mostly sensible if unspectacular, as we all heard for ourselves on the phone with him the next night. Bush had made "bad decisions." It was "okay" to talk about Vietnam, but not too much. "Have a field day with compassionate conservatism." Deal with attacks by responding that the reason for them is that Bush "can't talk about the last four years or the real differences. . . . Do a lot of 'there he goes again.'" Have surrogates attack Bush directly: "On national security, we haven't stabilized Iraq." There was even a populist tinge: "Bush fights for Halliburton, John Kerry fights for kids." It was Campaign 101; but it was also an amazing performance from someone as sick as Clinton was.

Unfortunately, there was a moment during this call where I had to explicitly disagree with him—on a recommendation he'd already made to Kerry that was all too tempting to our frustrated candidate: Kerry should go after Bush as the bigger "flip-flopper" in the race. This, I replied to Clinton, wouldn't work; it would be a futile effort to scale the vertical slope of public perceptions about Bush. People might see him as wrong, might blame him for mistakes, but they had a settled and almost unshakable belief that on the most critical questions, he was all but immovable. They even believed it might be a fault—that Bush was too stubborn. We couldn't counter that by quibbling with his record on education or the environment, as Clinton suggested. The more Kerry talked about flip-flops or charged that Bush was "more nuanced than I could ever be"—the phrase Clinton offered—the more salient the flip-flop issue would become. Like it or not, Kerry, the man who had voted for the $87 billion before voting against it, had provided far more vivid proof that he was a flip-flopper than anything we had on the president. We couldn't afford to echo and magnify Bush's message that flip-flopping was the basis on which voters should decide. I knew that Kerry didn't like hearing this, but Clinton was either half-persuaded or weary. He said he saw the point; the bottom line was that Bush was "wrong." (I was startled after the election when Clinton and some of his allies diagnosed the failure of the Kerry campaign as insufficient attention to national security. The whole burden of his conversation that night was, yes, holding Bush accountable on Iraq and Osama was necessary but not the heart of the matter. Kerry had to switch the focus to domestic issues. That was Lockhart's constant mantra, too, until the final week, when he found and flogged a tactical opportunity in press reports of an unguarded and looted Iraqi weapons dump.)

After the Clinton conference call, I had to fend off questions from reporters who'd "heard" that I'd had a furious row with a sick Clinton—or alternatively, that he'd told me off. The conversation had been civil and comfortable, our one back-and-forth calm and rational. I simply denied that Clinton and I had quarreled, and Stephanie Cutter, who'd been on the call, managed to kill the story. But we were now awash in self-serving and blame-placing leaks. As evidence of the transformative effect of the Clinton infusion, one newspaper cited "a combative" Kerry denouncing the shipment of jobs overseas and the fact that in Pennsylvania they were being replaced with jobs that paid $9,000 a year less. In reality, Kerry had been hammering at this for months; now it was proof, as a headline writer put it, that he had been transformed by Clinton's advice: "Forget Vietnam—it's the economy, Clinton tells Kerry." I smiled at that, but not at reports like the one in *The Washington Post* that Cahill and I were being singled out by "Kerry himself" for the campaign's travails. Kerry, who could have quieted this with a sentence or two, said nothing. My wife was sad and enraged; referring to the story of how Kerry had turned his boat around under fire to rescue Jim Rassman in Vietnam, she said: "Bob, he's left you in the river."

My political ethos held that the candidate shouldn't have to defend his advisers. It should be the other way around. And I would never ask Kerry to say a word. But when he didn't talk to Ken Auletta for a long profile on me that was about to be published in *The New Yorker*, Auletta phoned. His editor said he had to ask about the swirl of rumors. Would I be gone by the time the profile came out? No. Was I reduced to a cipher? No. The profile was balanced and, on balance, generous enough that my father said he liked it. I was relieved and grateful to those, inside and outside the campaign, who defended me to Auletta. John Sasso sounded a note of solidarity after I got slammed. On a call from the road, he joked about one of the lines that appeared in *The Washington Post*: "Shrum is now handling ads, some speech work and debate preparation, but less strategy." So what else is there to strategy, he said, the schedule?

Our polls improved as Bush's convention bounce faded. Our advertising was back on the air full force. By mid-September, Greenberg's numbers showed just a 2-point gap nationally. The race was returning to where it naturally had been before both conventions—too close to call. With a different August, with a Kerry competitive with Bush instead of strapped for resources, he probably would be president today. But there was no time then, as the debates approached, to mourn what might have been.

There was a Clinton confidant who made a big difference, our chief debate negotiator, the civil rights leader turned Washington power broker Vernon Jordan. I had written Cahill a memo in May that, after my Gore experience, recommended "a relatively small" prep. We had to persuade Kerry that we couldn't afford to "turn what should be a targeted prep into a seminar"; "policy advisers"—they all wanted to be there and ultimately most weren't—would have to confine themselves to "prevent[ing] JK from making an error" on substance, not offering "strategic or tactical advice." Kerry accepted this and told me that I had to play essentially the same role I had in the run-up to his 1996 debates when Massachusetts governor Bill Weld was challenging him for reelection to the Senate. Along with Ron Klain, the former Gore chief of staff, I would run the preps and control the critiques after the mock debates. (Cahill enforced this with a soft-spoken iron will.) I got one thing wrong in the memo. I worried that acting as a chief negotiator wouldn't "deeply engage Vernon's interest." Instead, he took his mandate, ran with it, and made decisions, upsetting Cahill and surrendering one of the Kerry's biggest demands—to the candidate's annoyance and his ultimate benefit.

After he met privately in mid-September with the Bush negotiator, Jim Baker, who said he wanted the two of them to work things out quietly and privately, Jordan reported back to Cahill and me—and Kerry—that the Bush side was pushing for two changes in the format designed by the Commission on Presidential Debates. As predicted, they were wary of the town hall meeting; they preferred just two debates, with journalists posing the questions. They were also demanding that the first debate focus on foreign policy, not domestic issues. Baker might have been bluffing, but he said this one was a deal breaker. His reason seemed obvious: 9/11, terrorism, national security were all Bush had; he sure as hell couldn't run on health care. But I suggested to Vernon and Mary Beth, and then to Kerry that maybe foreign policy first was actually better for us; we could take the risk that Kerry at least could fight to a draw here, come across as presidential, and prove that he could be trusted on national security. And if Kerry "won" when Bush was dealing his strong suit—this was the one area where the expectations game favored Bush—then we'd have him on the run. It was, I said, the president who was taking the risk here. Jordan thought so, too. Cahill bought into the analysis, and Kerry went along—with two provisos.

The town hall meeting had to happen—that was nonnegotiable. And so was a period of open-ended discussion between the candidates.

Cahill and I were at a routine meeting when we got the word that Vernon now had a deal with Baker. Mary Beth was furious: he was supposed to bring it back for our approval, not sign off on it himself. She didn't hide her anger as she told Jordan that; his response was icy—and their relationship never recovered. Jordan had accepted strict time limits, enforced if necessary by a buzzer, with no free-form exchange, in return for securing a third debate. It looked like we had given in. In fact, Jordan had outfoxed Baker and his own candidate, who didn't see it that way until after the first debate, despite the argument I made: the time limits were "our friend." The Bush campaign believed in their stereotype of a prolix Kerry, who couldn't live within them and would be humiliated if he exceeded the time limits three times and a buzzer blared that reality to all of America. But the constraint, I said, could work for us. It would keep Kerry disciplined and his answers direct. "Exactly, my man," Jordan said, when I repeated the point to him—and anyway, in return, he'd achieved everything else we wanted. A grumpy Kerry had no choice but to go along.

We had set up discrete units to prepare the debate books; to insulate them from day-to-day events, they operated outside the campaign structure. Jonathan Winer, for years a Kerry foreign policy adviser and a deputy assistant secretary of state under Clinton, recruited two of the best young associates in his law firm, Alston & Bird, for the project. Greg Craig, a legal superstar and foreign policy expert and my friend of thirty years, did the same at Williams & Connolly, one of Washington's landmark firms. Ron Klain and I met regularly over the summer with the two teams to identify the most likely questions and draft, review, and revise the answers and rebuttals. But the challenge wasn't simply to turn out a list of questions and responses; it was to tie them to a strategy and identify "moments" that could turn the debates. The polling offered some guidance, but this was fundamentally a creative exercise. Klain and I constantly updated the strategy document for both the prep team and the candidate. Before the actual preps, we sent Craig into exile—in effect, traded him away to the other side—because we decided he was the best person to play Bush in the mock debates. He was so adept at the role that we heard almost every line from him that we ultimately heard from Bush himself. The only difference was that Craig was a lot better Bush than Bush was.

The first mock debates were held in a barn at a resort in rural Wisconsin, 1,000 miles from the debate site at the University of Miami. Early on, Kerry got the personal venom toward Bush out of his system. Lying on the floor after one practice, he said he knew he had to pick his shots, not fire away wildly. He'd get it down—and he did. We not only covered every question in the actual debate, but Kerry also mastered a series of "moments." On the $87 billion, for example: "I made a mistake [in] how I talked about funding Iraq. President Bush made a mistake in invading Iraq. Which was worse?" He delivered it almost word for word in the first debate. And lines he didn't use there, he would deploy in the next encounter—for example, referring to "the President's weapons of mass deception in this campaign." After each practice, Klain and I gathered comments from the small number of advisers who were there and then critiqued Kerry. Cahill reinforced the rule that others were to talk sparingly, if at all, by her own example, chiming in only a few times. John Sasso had just one central point to make before each debate: in the first one, talk the language of patriotism and national strength; in the second, on domestic issues, talk values and not just programs. He was restrained, but so persistent that I nicknamed him "Bones" because, as I teased him, once he had a bone in his teeth, he never let go of it. I promised him a set of silver dog-bone cufflinks from Tiffany's.

We flew to Miami the night before the September 30 debate—and the next day, after a last informal run-through around a glass table in Kerry's suite, learned anew that in this campaign, anything could leak. As we tossed questions and answers back and forth, Kerry was getting a manicure—a fact that promptly reached the press. It looked like more proof that he was elitist. Kerry was mad; there weren't many of us there. How, he raged, did this get out?

Probably, I told him, from the hotel staff talking to each other and then to their friends. It was small beer anyway and he had to keep his eye on the main chance.

Speeding to the debate site that night with Kerry and Teresa in the Secret Service SUV he preferred to a limousine, we passed competing groups of Bush and Kerry partisans. Kerry happily gave a thumbs-up to both friends and enemies as the lights of the motorcade flashed across their faces. I said to myself: This guy is ready, not just substantively but psychologically. After he headed for the stage, I sat in the cavernous holding room with Cahill, Sasso, and a few others. I had plenty of room to pace. I was puzzled by the boxy bump on Bush's back, under his suit coat, unexplained to this day; surely, it wasn't some kind of device to let his handlers coach him as he went along? Bush did sound distracted. Early on, he blurted out: "Of course, we're after Saddam Hussein"—who was already in prison awaiting trial—"I mean bin Laden."

The time limits that were supposed to hurt Kerry worked against the president instead. On the one hand, his answers were sometimes glaringly short, and the green, yellow, and red lights installed on each podium at Jim Baker's insistence made that unmistakably clear. On the other hand, Bush went over time—or came perilously close to it—far more often than Kerry did and still couldn't complete his answer. He alternately sounded out of his depth and almost plaintive in the foreign policy area he was supposed to dominate, tripping over his tongue as he inexplicably responded to a question about capturing bin Laden by referring to the Philippines: "The Philippines—we've got help—we're helping them there to bring—to bring al Qaeda affiliates to justice there." He seemed almost overburdened by the presidency as he kept pleading: "It's hard work . . . it's hard work." (I told Cahill there is a great retort for Kerry to use when Bush says this in the next debate: "If it's such hard work, I'd be happy to take it off your hands." Unfortunately, Rove and company cleaned the "hard work" line out of Bush's head before he debated again.)

The highlight for Kerry came as he dealt with what we had identified as a decisive challenge: he had to break the connection, assiduously promoted by the Bush campaign, between 9/11 and the Iraq war. Klain and I had given him a memo the week before that suggested "a simple rule of thumb" to drive home the difference: "He says Saddam, you say Osama." Kerry was relentlessly prosecuting the argument in the debate itself when Bush gave him the ideal opening; he justified the invasion of Iraq by saying "the enemy attacked us." Kerry hit Bush square on with the rule of thumb: "Saddam Hussein didn't attack us. Osama bin Laden attacked us." A discombobulated president irritably conceded the point: "Of course, I know Osama bin Laden attacked us. I know that." So Bush said Saddam; Kerry said Osama—and he separated 9/11 from the war in Iraq in a plain-spoken and convincing way. We cheered in the holding room.

The lowlight for us came right afterward. Kerry said that America's use of force had to pass "a global test." Where had *that* come from? We'd spent rehearsal after rehearsal making sure the candidate would insist that no other nation could have veto power over U.S. military decisions. When I heard "global test," I threw my cell phone across the room; this time, it broke into pieces. I noticed a photographer for one of the news magazines who kindly decided not to take a picture. "Global test" was a mistake that didn't count because we developed a quick defense: that America had to make the best case it could to justify its policies, but the ultimate power to act was ours and ours alone. The debate was so one-sided that we didn't have to spin it as a win; it indisputably was one. And Kerry ended on a grace note that I'd first scribbled out on the back page of an earlier speech draft when I was thinking about his closing statement. "President Bush and I both love this country," Kerry said. "But we have different convictions about how to lead it."

We climbed back into the SUV with a pumped Kerry. You didn't need a poll to know what had happened. But the polls were better than good. For example, in a *Newsweek* survey, there was a net 8-point swing to us in the vote. Kerry was now ahead and *Newsweek* concluded: "Debates don't always shake up a presidential race, but this one did."

Klain and I had to go join John Edwards's prep session in

Chatauqua, New York, the quaint Victorian village that provided Amerca's pre-television, pre-movie entertainment in the form of lectures and shows, with performers roaming the country on the Chatauqua circuit. I frightened Edwards's six-year-old daughter Emma Claire when I began a briefing by saying that after what had happened in Miami, Cheney had to take out a machine gun to try to "kill" Edwards in the vice-presidential debate. Emma Claire started crying and fled into her father's arms as I carefully explained to a six-year-old that this was just "a metaphor." She looked mystified and the room broke into laughter. Elizabeth Edwards had a better answer. Bob, she said, didn't mean that—and we went back to work.

What did concern me as I listened to the mock debate after we arrived was that Edwards came across as unsure and nervous. He was interrupting answers to check them or ask for more information. At this point, he wasn't the debater I'd urged Gore and then Kerry to select as vice president. We adjourned early so he could go to his room with his briefing books. He'd be fine if he had the material down—and he did the next day. I felt cautiously confident when I left him in Cleveland, the site of his debate, and flew to our next session with Kerry outside Denver. Kerry told me later that Edwards called him before the debate in a state of "panic." He was worried; maybe he wasn't ready; could he pull this off? Kerry, who thought Edwards was suffering a peculiar but baffling case of stage fright, told his running mate that he'd heard he was in good shape. He'd do a great job.

I watched the Cheney-Edwards contest with T. R. Reid, now *The Washington Post*'s Rocky Mountain bureau chief. I was surprised when he was so sure Cheney had won. In his own smooth way, Edwards had been tough and aggressive, unlike the quiescent Lieberman of 2000; at least this time, the outcome in the public polls was a split decision. Edwards had done much of what we'd asked of him, defending Kerry at the cost of shortchanging his own self-defense. He had even been modestly confrontational. This was a departure from his day-to-day tone on the trail. Despite the material constantly dispatched from the headquarters to Edwards, both Cahill and I were frustrated with how reluctant our vice presidential nominee

was to go after Bush or Cheney. Amid the postelection recriminations, he would blame his restraint on the campaign, which in reality
was pleading with him to be tougher.

When I saw Kerry after the VP debate, he said it was "okay," but
not all he hoped for. I responded that the encounter hadn't stopped
the momentum of the race; it was still with us. I added that the one
thing I didn't like in Edwards's performance was his reference to
Mary Cheney as a lesbian; he had complimented the vice president
on his "love" for his daughter. He'd gotten away with it, even garnered some positive comments in the press. But it was a gamble he
hadn't needed to take.

Bush showed up for the second debate, at Washington University
in St. Louis, without the suspicious box under the back of his suit
jacket. The town meeting format he so despised turned out to be
friendlier to him because the audience provided something of a
buffer between him and Kerry. And there was an actual DMZ, a
demilitarized zone, between the two candidates; after Gore's
encroachment in 2000, the Bush campaign had negotiated a guaranteed separation. While Bush when asked couldn't bring himself to
admit that he'd made any mistakes as president, the expectations for
him were now so low that he had a modest rebound in public perception. He still wasn't the "winner": public polls registered a closer
Kerry victory. But the third debate five days later was a rout in the
instant surveys. In Greenberg's data, more Americans now credited
Kerry, not Bush, with having "clear plans on what he wants to
achieve." Kerry couldn't entirely erase the flip-flop image, but he'd
mitigated it—and he had opened up an 8-point advantage when
voters were asked which candidate is "on your side."

After the third debate, Cahill urged me to appear in the spin
room. I went in and took questions on the record, on television—for
the first time in many months. As I confidently proclaimed victory, I
discovered in between interviews that the Bush surrogates were
hardly arguing substance or style. They were suddenly harping on
what they damned as Kerry's cynical exploitation of Mary Cheney's
sexuality. The vice president and his wife would soon weigh in.
"This is not a good man . . . [this was] a cheap and tawdry political

trick," Lynne Cheney said. It was a calculated effort to blunt the effect of Bush's stumbling performance, a reprise of the 2000 spin about Gore's sighs and exaggerations. I tried to insist that both Kerry and Edwards hadn't been playing politics when they'd referred to Mary Cheney, that their comments were well-meant, not mean-spirited and manipulative. But the second time around, this was harder to believe. Even worse, Kerry's words were directed to Bush, not Cheney, and they were gratuitous, in answer to a question about whether homosexuality was a choice, not genetically determined. Tired of the other side's exploitation of gay marriage, it looked as if Kerry had yielded to a foolish temptation to level the playing field a little with socially conservative voters.

A *New York Times* focus group found that undecideds regarded Kerry's reference as out-of-bounds. We took a 2-point hit in our nightly tracking in the battleground states, then climbed back to 50 percent, with Kerry 4 or 5 points ahead of Bush. But the moment hurt because it blunted the cumulative effect of the three debates; there now was an alternative storyline to a Kerry "sweep."

I caught a commercial flight back to Washington with Lockhart, but I wasn't there long. Kerry summoned me back to the road to discuss strategy for the stretch run and review the speeches we were planning to put domestic issues front and center alongside Iraq and national security. I didn't take a suitcase with me; it was to be a quick one-day trip. When Kerry, Sasso, and I finished, I told Kerry I'd see him later. Where was I going? he asked. To Washington. No, he'd decided that I should just get on the plane and stay. I called Mary-louise and told her to FedEx clothes to the hotel we were staying in the next night. And I checked in with Cahill: Kerry might be building his own ad hoc team on the plane, but we all had to work together. She said fine, but there was something else I had to do while I was traveling with the candidate. With the exception of commenting after the third debate, I'd been electronically silent ever since the campaign upheaval prior to the primaries. Now, she said, I had to do network Sunday talk shows—from the road. (On one of them, I made a bet with Ken Mehlman, Rove's designated hitter as Bush's campaign manager, that Kerry would win with over 300 electoral votes. He's never collected the dinner—but he did get the White House.)

For the next two and a half weeks, Sasso and I sat across from each other on the plane, and usually rode with Kerry to his stops in the Secret Service SUV. We prosecuted a strategy of holding Bush to account on Iraq while focusing as much as possible on domestic issues and the defining Democratic theme that Kerry was fighting for people, while the president stood for special interests. Sasso, who had repositioned the faltering Dukakis campaign with a last-minute invocation of "on your side," was with the program. But because we never settled on a single phrase to sum up Kerry's appeal, he cast his argument in shifting words. For example, in Wilkes-Barre, Pennsylvania, he told a packed theater that Bush's "four-year spending spree on tax giveaways for millionaires has undermined the hopes of middle class families and . . . put Social Security on a dangerous road." We seemed to have a consistent if imperfect message, one that tested powerfully in Greenberg's national polls. On our morning calls, Greenberg continuously emphasized that this was "a remarkably stable race" that Kerry was likely to win.

On October 21, we were sidetracked by a pitifully obvious excursion designed to placate blue-collar Democrats worried about Kerry's position on gun control. Kerry in truth was a hunter, and he was enthralled with the idea of going hunting in front of the cameras and bagging a goose outside Youngstown, Ohio. As the hunting party set out, I commented to David Morehouse that while he looked fine in his fatigues, our candidate looked odd in the neatly pressed camouflage clothing that he was wearing. Predictably, Bush made fun of this when Kerry returned, as a reporter wrote, "his hand stained with goose blood." Camouflage was not the ideal metaphor for a candidate accused of being intentionally unclear. But the real flaw was the notion that Kerry could prevail by showing voters that he was a regular guy, one of them. He wasn't. Neither was John Kennedy in 1960: JFK appealed in West Virginia, for example, not by an artificial effort to come across as someone who resembled West Virginians and shared their culture, but as a leader who cared about them. Now one of our two press secretaries, Mike

McCurry, had to explain to skeptical reporters that, no, Kerry's coming photo opportunities wouldn't include windsurfing: "It's too cold this time of year."

It was a hiccup—some of my fellow travelers at the front of the plane would have said it was a great success—in a crescendo of events that carried us toward Election Day. On October 25, Bill Clinton, just out of the hospital, spoke to a crowd of 150,000 or more that stretched back twelve blocks in Philadelphia; at his side, Kerry was hitting his stride and on message: "Are you ready for a president again who is a champion of the middle class?" Jon Bon Jovi was an opening act for Kerry to audiences of tens of thousands. And in Madison, Wisconsin, Bruce Springsteen and Kerry attracted 80,000, close to half the population of the entire city. On election eve, they would bring more than 50,000 people to the waterfront in Cleveland.

In the stretch run, we had gigantic crowds—and a message I thought we'd agreed on, something I had believed in all along. As Greenberg and Lockhart expressed it in another one of their memos, Kerry was a "president who will both defend our country and fight for the middle class." Then we went off track again. The latest headlines revealed that an unguarded munitions dump had been looted in Iraq. Lockhart viewed it as a breakthrough for us. One day on the issue might have been useful; by the second and third day, Sasso and I were restless, worried that we were backing ourselves into a corner, that the tactical was getting in the way of the strategic. Half of our message—the fight for the middle class—was being drowned out. Lockhart's instinct as a former White House press secretary—to ride the wave of the day's news—was getting in the way of Kerry making the news we needed. On the plane, we decided to dump the munitions dump; it became a brief reference and then disappeared.

The candidate was back on message at an outdoor rally in West Palm Beach the Friday before the election. I was backstage behind the band shell when we heard the first news about a bin Laden tape warning Americans not to reelect Bush. (I thought the tape evidenced a shrewd grasp of American politics. Bush was al Qaeda's best recruiting tool.) I shuddered at this late October surprise. We had to handle it right—and right away. We couldn't wait until we flew on to the next stop. We grabbed Kerry as soon as he was off stage; we squeezed into the SUV with him as we headed for the airport. As usual, in a tight spot, Kerry was cool. I dictated a brief statement and we handed it to him. He waited in the SUV as the press corps was assembled on the tarmac, making a few notes on the statement. Then he put it aside. He knew exactly what he wanted to say: "Let me make it crystal clear—as Americans, we are absolutely united in our determination to hunt down and destroy Osama bin Laden and the terrorists. They are barbarians, and I will stop at absolutely nothing to hunt down, capture or kill the terrorists wherever they are, whatever it takes—period."

We didn't want this to be *the* issue. But then Kerry went a step too far when we reached Milwaukee, criticizing Bush for letting bin Laden escape when he was cornered in the Afghan mountains. It was true, and he'd said it before and the argument had scored—but why did he have to raise it now? McCurry moaned. Because he's tired, he's frustrated, he's human, I replied; all candidates are. Mike replied that it was a bad day to be human. Bush pounced on the remarks to keep the bin Laden tape center stage. Kerry and I both wondered whether or how far in advance the president had known the tape was coming. Bush had started his day with a speech focused on 9/11. And the Republican Party was also running an ad at saturation levels in Ohio featuring a father and daughter whose wife and mother had died at the World Trade Center. Bush had been introduced to the child, taken her in his arms, and comforted her. She now expressed, in the most affecting way, the only effective positive the Bush campaign had: "He's the most powerful man in the world and all he wants to do is make sure I'm safe." It was the most powerful spot of the entire campaign. We had fought for months to keep the contest from simply being a 9/11 election. Now that's what it would become.

(There was another piece of news that we wouldn't know about until the monthly jobs report came out three days after the election. But it already was a daily reality in the lives of people looking for work. Kerry had long held a decided advantage on the economy, but in October, it had produced a burst of 337,000 new jobs. They might not pay as much as the jobs that had been lost, but economic fear was easing as people went back to work.)

I was relieved to read Greenberg's report that last weekend. It was "a dead-even race where the undecided will play the final role . . . they almost always break heavily against the incumbent . . . [and] leaned toward the Democrats by two-to-one. . . . The tracking for the Kerry campaign . . . including Friday night"—after the bin Laden tape had hit—"show[s] Kerry with a clear and stable lead." We were also slightly ahead in Florida and in Ohio, according to our polling there. We seemed bound to win one of them—and the presidency. Or so we wanted to believe. And so we would hear as the exit polling results started rolling in on Election Day.

After our massive election eve rally with Bruce Springsteen in Cleveland, where he handed Kerry his guitar pick and told him to take it to the Oval Office, we squeezed in a last stop in Toledo. A thousand people waiting in an airport hangar after midnight cheered, whistled, and stomped as Kerry shouted, "I don't know if George Bush is at home in bed in Crawford, but I am here fighting for every last vote." As we walked down our motel hallway that night to grab a little rest before flying to Boston, even the self-contained John Sasso was guardedly optimistic; the numbers looked good. Neither of us knew that Mellman had taken a one-night sample showing Kerry just 1 point ahead in the battleground states, a decline of 4 points since the bin Laden tape on Friday.

I'm sure that if Kerry had won, victory would have had a hundred fathers. Once he lost, most of them were content to leave the orphan of defeat at the doorstep of others—especially mine. After the election, I accepted this as inevitable, and I wasn't about to run away from my role in the campaign. But change the outcome in Ohio and the jostling for credit would have filled the stage.

Democrats hated Bush so fiercely—and "hate" is the right word—that they assumed Kerry should have beaten him. For many months afterward, Kerry contributed to this view, and hurt himself, with a series of lamentations about campaign mistakes, often delivered up to groups of his supporters. I had urged him to pursue another storyline, especially if he wanted to run again. He had received more votes than any other Democratic nominee in history. He'd lost, closely, in a 9/11 election to a wartime president who wrapped himself in that tragedy. Kerry's resolve now should be to speak out, lead, and fight back. I sympathized with Kerry's consuming fixation on the past. He'd almost been to the mountaintop; he'd thought briefly that he had reached the summit; now he was at the bottom again. After the theft of the 2000 election, Al Gore had simply withdrawn, traveled the world, and grown a beard; he didn't come roaring back until 2005. After 2004, John Kerry traveled the country, too often wringing his hands in meetings with fund-raisers and fellow Democrats. It wasn't the path to his future, but it suited the purposes of many of the latecomers to his campaign. They'd been poised to reap the benefits if he prevailed. Now, intent on moving to a candidate who commanded their real loyalties, another Clinton, they were happy to wash their hands and point fingers at Kerry and others who couldn't, or wouldn't, walk away.

We all made our share of mistakes in 2004, candidate and advisers alike. That's the way campaigns are and life is. It is clear that Kerry should have voted against the Iraq war. He wasn't good at defending a convoluted rationalization he never really believed. He colossally misspoke on the $87 billion. We should never have accepted federal funding in the general election; but then I and others should have ignored the consequences of that and spent the money to hit back early and hard at the Swift boat attacks. And we should have put the focus group results in perspective instead of trimming the harder-edged, progressive language of the primaries. In the debates and by the end, Kerry was fighting for the middle class and against special interests, yet staying away from a powerful phrase to sum up that cause.

If Democrats are afraid to say what we are about, if the party doesn't stand for something more than a set of poll-tested programs and a carefully engineered set of tactics to win office, we are likely to lose unless the Republicans hand us victory on a platter of indisputable failure or perceived economic crisis. And then what will we have to show for our power but time in office, modest or symbolic change, or achievements like the Clinton deficit reduction that don't stand the test of time?

Indeed, when Democrats won in 2006, taking the House and against long odds even the Senate, the slogan was "new direction," but the substance was populist. Candidates not only ran against the Iraq war, but in race after race, appealed on the minimum wage, Social Security, and taking on the big drug companies. The one strong Senate challenger who had a chance but lost, Harold Ford in Tennessee, was also the one who relied most on Clintonian "centrism." He was an African-American in a southern state, and the Republicans' sleazy racist ad hurt him; but so did his own emphasis on telling voters what he wasn't—a liberal—at the expense of telling them what he would fight for on their behalf. The chairman of the Democratic Congressional Campaign Committee, Rahm Emanuel, a convinced disciple of triangulation as a young aide in the Clinton White House, proclaimed after the Democratic victory in 2006: "Prescription drugs, gas prices, and economic populism are no longer associated with blue-collar downscale voters. Office park workers can be just as populist as industrial workers." Aside from Iraq, the hot-button issues the next time seem likely to be national health care reform—people are increasingly demanding sweeping change—and energy independence, with a corresponding crackdown on the oil industry and polluters. Kerry prefigured this in 2004, eliciting an almost visceral response from audiences every time he said: "I want an America that relies on its own ingenuity and innovation, not the Saudi royal family."

Despite our mistakes, there were things to be proud of in a Kerry run that fell just short. He shook up his campaign when he had to; he soldiered on in the gloomy days of late 2003. He held to a strategy that brought him to a comeback in Iowa and a triumphant march through the primaries. We held our fire when Bush launched his first wave of negative ads in the spring, waited until we had enough resources for a massive ad buy of our own, and saw Kerry move ahead as we entered July. Amid the debris of the Swift boats and his own tangled position on Iraq, he finally let go of his caution and announced that given what he now knew, he wouldn't have gone to war. He dominated the debates, with only one slipup that mattered. (I know, when an election is this close, every slipup matters; but the Mary Cheney reference aside, no one could have expected more from any candidate than Kerry's performance debating Bush.)

A year later, I met Kerry for a drink at the Yale Club in midtown Manhattan. We hadn't talked in months, and I launched into a random excursion across the political landscape. I was about to discuss Jon Corzine's race for governor of New Jersey, my last campaign, the one I'd signed on to before my decision to leave political consulting, when Kerry interrupted me. He had something he'd come here to discuss. He wanted to apologize for some of the things he'd said and allowed others to say about me since the election. Even on the Swift boats, he said, I was probably right that the root of the error was the choice to accept public funding. And he added that a lot of the criticism directed at me was unfair. I replied that I'd heard about some of the negative comments and just ignored them. In politics, losing doesn't buy you any love. What was important now— whether or not he intended to be a candidate again—was for him to focus on the future, and especially the unfinished business of Iraq.

He confessed that he did want to run again; explained his anger at Edwards, who himself seemed to be preparing to run, no matter what Kerry decided; and said that he just didn't see how Hillary could win. What states was she going to carry that he and Gore hadn't? And against John McCain?

He turned to Iraq. He was making yet another speech on the war in late October at Georgetown University. Would I look at it? When I did, it sounded like he was still caught in the coils of the past. I urged him to call for a straightforward deadline for withdrawal. For Kerry, the war was now an unequivocal mistake: he was ready to demand benchmarks and the withdrawal of some troops; but a deadline was still a step too far that he wouldn't take for another few months. Early in 2006, he told me about the words of a U.S. pilot who'd flown him during a recent trip to Iraq: "Senator, whatever you do, don't make me tell my grandchildren this was in vain." Kerry, however, finally brought himself to tell the truth he believed in an op-ed piece in the *New York Times*, followed by a Senate floor speech and an appearance on *Meet the Press*. American combat forces, he said, should leave Iraq by "year's end." Kerry's aide David Wade sent an e-mail thanking me for my input. *Newsweek* columnist Jonathan Alter, someone I have known and liked for a long time, explained on the Don Imus show that Kerry was better now because he'd gotten rid of all the consultants.

Kerry raised millions of dollars for Democratic House and Senate candidates in 2006 and was campaigning across the country when he fractured a bad joke about Bush's intellectual seriousness in a way that let the other side claim he was disparaging the educational achievement of American soldiers—that they were in Iraq because they hadn't done well in school. In the end, the episode didn't hurt Democrats and may have intensified the salience of the Iraq issue just as Election Day approached. Kerry himself was the real casualty of his own verbal misfire. He was criticized not only by the usual Republican suspects, but by prospective rivals for the 2008 nomination. After a year when he had largely moved beyond recriminations about 2004 and emerged as a leading antiwar voice, a few seconds at the start of a routine speech seemed to count so much that Democratic Senate and House candidates didn't even want to be seen with him. Whatever presidential hopes he still had were undone by another gaffe that painfully reminded Democrats of his self-destructive one-liner about the $87 billion for Iraq. A single casual word or phrase, as I learned across the years, can count more than all the careful calculations.

Politics is often unfair and seldom fits the precise contours of the prevailing narrative. To know and write about political leaders candidly is to reveal their jagged edges; even the best of them are flawed heroes. Al Gore and John Kerry are both complex figures, at different times their own best advocates and their own worst enemies. In short, they're human beings. They each would have had bad moments in the White House, but they would have been good presidents. Gore the "exaggerator" never would have claimed that we could cut taxes massively and still have a federal surplus. Kerry the "flip-flopper" would have pursued a steady course to rebuild America's alliances and standing in the world. They both had core convictions—and at times their consultants, advisers, and fellow officeholders did them a disservice by urging them onto apparently softer, safer, more cautious ground.

You can rake over the regrets, but you have to live with the reality and, as George McGovern said on election night 1972, "get on with life." After the upside-down result in 2000 and the near miss in 2004, I decided to accept an offer to teach and write at NYU. It was time, after more than a third of a century, to leave the campaigns to others. Our Washington friends—and we treasured them—would continue to be our friends even if they were a few hundred miles away. We sold our home—to a member of the Bush cabinet. The night before we left, Ted and Vicki Kennedy threw a party for Marylouise and me that spilled across the first floor of their Washington residence. I couldn't help smiling when I saw Bob Novak, a stranger here in this strange Democratic land. Many of the senators I'd worked for were there as well; I hoped that a small portion of their records was part of my record in politics, too. The highlight of the party was a song Ted and Vicki wrote and performed to the tune of "Camelot," as friends—my partners, my clients, so many others—gathered around a grand piano:

> *It's true, it's true, Bob has made it clear*
> *That he and Oatsie true are leaving here*
> *They've spent so many moons among their friends here*
> *Doing politics—so cool and so hot*
> *And their friends in turn have spent a lot of dough, dear*
> *[My clients laughed]*
> *In Shrum-a-lot*
> *To see Bob pace and chew that Nicorette gum*
> *As he orders all to give the best they've got*
> *Shrum-a-lot, Shrum-a-lot*

I know it gives a person pause
But in Shrum-a-lot, Shrum-a-lot
Progressive values are a noble cause . . .

To hear it from Edward Kennedy, in that wonderful Irish rumble that evoked both memory and hope, reminded me of why I'd started out on this road long before. The life I'd led gave me the chance to bend history in the direction of my beliefs. I only wish I had succeeded in bending it a few more inches.

A NOTE ON METHODS AND SOURCES

This is a memoir, based on memory and on material kept over the years, a collection that surprises me in its scope and variety: speech drafts, memos, notes I made, videotapes, letters, and e-mails. I have used direct quotes only if I vividly remember or made a note of what was said. I have resolved any questions about exact expression by relying on paraphrase.

I have engaged in a process of fact-checking, including an extensive review of contemporaneous sources. I have benefited from the help of remarkably capable research assistants. Any responsibility for errors is, of course, mine, but I must record my debt to them.

Jed Seltzer is a gifted writer and intellect, a tireless researcher, and a candid critic. I could not have finished this book without him. Sam Carter did an outstanding job; he has an uncanny knack for tracking down the most obscure secondary sources to check a date or a speech quote. Carolyn Koo thoroughly—and I mean thoroughly—reviewed several chapters. Vanessa Silverton-Peel, who knows more about politics at twenty-three than anyone has a right to, researched, double-checked, and also typed and retyped most of the manuscript. Jon Herczeg, my immensely able assistant during the Kerry campaign, stayed with me for the early stages of this project; he assiduously organized files, boxes, and discs of material before he decamped for NYU Law School.

Though the first draft of the book discusses virtually every campaign I was ever involved in, for editing reasons the finished product does not and could not do so. I have omitted most overseas campaigns. I have focused on races, won and lost, most relevant to this story of American politics. The candidates I worked for mattered to me and almost all deserved to be elected, even the ones who weren't.

ACKNOWLEDGMENTS

I want to acknowledge the following candidates, friends, and associates whose names do not appear in this book as a result of the editing process, but were very much part of the story: Art Agnos, Bertie Ahern, Kara Kennedy Allen, Tom Allen, Roger Altman, Alan Arkatov and Mary Leslie, Mike and Carol Berman, Tom Bradley, Dan Brewster, Dale Butland, Heather Campion, Joe Cerrell, Jack Corrigan, Mark Dayton, Debbie Dingell, Jack English, Patricia Ewing, Alan Fleischman, Wilson Goode, Jim Gerstein, Dan and Rhoda Glickman, Ted Greenberg, Jane Harman, Peter Harris, John Hempelmann, Leo Hindrey, Fred Hochberg, Kathleen Hall Jamieson, Edward Kennedy Jr., Henry and Charlotte Kimmelman, Sarah Kovner, Richard Leone, Ken Lerer, Jack Leslie, Jeff Link, Nick Littlefield, Bill Lynch, John Macks, Kelly McMahon, Melody Miller, Tom Miller, Luis Moreno and Gabriela Febres-Cordero, Melissa Moss and Jonathan Silver, Mike Naylor, Michael Nussbaum, Wayne Owens, Andres Pastrana, Gary Pearce, Federico Peña, Joe Pichirallo and Mary Rainwater, Alex Pinellas, J. B. Poersch, David Quarles, Charlie Rangel, Edmund and Doris Reggie, John Reilly, Connie Rice, Anne Roosevelt, Marvin and Janet Rosen, Caroline Kennedy Schlossberg, Arnold Schwarzenegger and Maria Shriver, Donna Shalala, Tom Shea, Louise Slaughter, Liz Stephens, Teresa

Vilmain, Setti Warren, Harold Washington, and Wallace and Martha Wilkinson. I owe a special debt of gratitude to Eunice Kennedy Shriver and Sarge Shriver for decades of friendship.

The following journalists, not mentioned by name in the book, were notably part of my campaign trail: Bob Ajemian, Mike Allen, Gloria Borger, John Chancellor, Eleanor Clift, Adam Clymer, Richard Cohen, Jim Doyle, Michael Duffy, Rowland and Kay Evans, Gwen Ifill, John Harwood, Bob Healy, Pat Healy, Walter Isaacson, Peter Kaplan, Mickey Kaus, Michael Kinsley, Michael Kramer, Christopher Lydon, Jim Naughton, David Nyhan, Deborah Orrin, Bill Press, Jim Rutenberg, Joe Scott, Richard Stout, Karen Tumulty, John Walcott, Margaret Warner, and Tom Winship. I didn't always like their stories, but I mostly like the people who write and report. I will always be grateful to the late Meg Greenfield, not only a good friend, but a great ideological sparring partner.

I have worked with and against several Democratic political consultants who don't appear in these pages, but who show that politics can be an honorable profession: David Axelrod, Bill Hamilton, Paul Harstad, Peter Hart, Celinda Lake, Ed Reilly, and Mark Squier. Alex Castellanos, Bill McInturff, Mark McKinnon, Mike Murphy, and Ed Rollins are among the Republican adversaries not mentioned by name whose ads and strategies have influenced political consulting.

In each of the preceding categories, I am certain that I have omitted the names of other individuals I should have singled out.

I happily thank patient and talented assistants during my years in politics, who all went on to better things: Dan Baum, Austin Brown, Dana Hill, Nancy Howard, Josh Leahy, Patty McHugh, Jon Michel Picher, Julia Norton, Jay O'Brien, Phil Press, Brooke Rosen, Adam Strasberg, and Sandra Walker.

I owe more than I can say to those who encouraged or helped as I wrote this book, whether or not they agree with some or all of the views expressed here: Ellen Bennett, David Bohnett and Tom Gregory, Peter Burleigh, Linda Douglass and John Phillips, Joe Duffey and Anne Wexler, Nancy and Loren Dunlap, Carter Eskew,

Michael Fleming and Luis Lavin, Paul Goodrich, Kerry Green, Jill Halverson, Omar Hendrix, Steve Holloway, Jim Johnson and Maxine Isaacs, Eric Klinenberg, Chris Matthews, Greg Minoff, Andrea Mitchell, David Mixner, David Morehouse, John O'Leary, Betty Ann Ottinger, Ira Reiner and Diane Wayne, Vicky Radd Rollins, Michael Singer, Anna Strasberg, Barbara Thibault, Phil and Joan Vasta, Marco and Joan Weiss, and Henry and Stacey Winkler.

Tammy Haddad is a great political television producer who said I had to write this book. So did Lou and Margie Susman. John Sexton, the president of New York University, and his late wife Lisa Goldberg, the president of the Revson Foundation, did so much to make the book possible; I know that neither of them would share a number of its conclusions. Not a day goes by that Marylouise and I don't think of Lisa. I am deeply grateful to my colleagues at the Robert F. Wagner School of Public Service at NYU, especially Mitchell Moss and Dennis Smith, and to Dean Ellen Schall, who provided support, enthusiasm, and two superb research assistants, whose indispensable contribution is described in the note on methods and sources.

I thank Tad Devine, Kathleen Hendrix, Tom Rollins, and George Thibault for reading the manuscript. Their insights were invaluable, as is their friendship.

I am blessed with an agent, Philippa Brophy, full of laughter and sass, a wise counselor and a powerful advocate. I thank her assistant Sharon Sketinni and also Mary Krienke for their help. At Simon & Schuster, I have benefited from the advice of David Rosenthal and the experience of Lisa Healy, Victoria Meyer, Tracey Guest, Kerri Kennedy, Jane Elias, and Chris Carruth. I think Ann Adelman must be the best in the world at copyediting manuscripts. Roger Labrie's editorial judgment, his rigor and patience, made this a better book and made it possible for me to meet my deadlines.

It was an honor and my great good fortune as a first-time author to be in the hands of the legendary editor Alice Mayhew. She lives up to the legend. I am indebted to her peerless sense of structure, pace, and language. She had a massive impact on the architecture of this book.

I thank the political leaders who have let me share their causes and hopes. Above all else, I thank my family: my mother Cecilia Welsh Shrum and my father Clarence Shrum, who has lived into his ninety-fourth year. Their brave decisions made a new life for me and my sister Barbara and her sons Robert and Chris. My sister-in-law Jane Oates has been a sustaining presence during this endeavor and in our lives. She lived with us for eight years in Washington and allowed me the privilege of helping to raise my nephew, John Lichman, whose passion is writing. My stepson Michael Oates Palmer, today a Hollywood writer, was, from the age of twelve, with me in spirit and heart in every success and every adversity; he gave me a gift I will never forget in his Brown commencement address when he spoke of his "three parents." My wife's parents, Elinor and Ray Oates, embraced me and sometimes my politics.

Marylouise, described in these pages, inadequately, as an activist who's changed the world and my world, a columnist and author, is not just the woman I love, but the ground of my being. It is only right that I have dedicated this book to her because I couldn't have lived it without her.

INDEX

Bush, George W., 300–493
  advisers of, 358
  approval rating of, 383
  campaign spending by, 356, 456–59
  as conservative, 197, 309, 332, 443, 474
  in debates, 351–60, 365, 451, 464, 466, 471,
    472, 476, 483, 484, 491
  Democratic opposition to, 439–40, 488–89
  draft record of, 234, 326, 433
  drunken driving arrest of, 365–66
  economic policies of, 298, 327–28, 332,
    337–38, 356, 357, 360, 437–38, 462,
    487–88, 493
  foreign policy of, 333, 338–39, 355–56,
    359, 386–88, 406, 477, 480
  Gore compared with, 300, 305, 306, 309,
    326–82, 383
  Iraq War leadership of, 92, 197, 228, 338,
    381, 382, 384, 386–89, 392, 393–94, 400,
    413, 424, 431, 434, 440, 451–52, 463,
    464–68, 475, 479, 480–81, 484, 485, 489,
    490, 491–92
  Kerry compared with, 396, 397, 400, 413,
    415, 424, 433, 439, 451, 464, 466, 471,
    472, 491
  negative attacks by, 440–41, 451–52,
    458–59, 468, 471, 472, 490–91
  as president, 55, 93, 228, 231, 270,
    310
  presidential campaign of (2000), 55, 204,
    222, 227, 300–382, 440, 469
  presidential campaign of (2004), xii–xiv,
    200, 382, 383–493
  Social Security privatization by, 354,
    356–57, 358, 360, 361–62, 365, 366
  tax cuts by, 253, 327–28, 332, 337–38, 357,
    360, 451, 462, 485, 493
Bush, Larry, 134
Buthelezi, Gatsha, 150, 151
butterfly ballots, xv, 362, 383
Button, Wendy, 448
Byrd, Robert, 115
Byrne, Brendan, 126
Byrne, Jane, 98, 100–101

Caddell, Pat, 33, 45–46, 50–51, 57, 59, 60–61,
  63, 67, 68, 70, 77, 128, 130, 136, 140–42,
  144, 155, 157, 158–60, 164, 167, 174,
  176, 177, 179, 182, 183, 255
Cahill, Mary Beth, xi, xii, xiii, 409–11,
  414–15, 416, 418, 419, 423–24, 427–28,
  432–33, 434, 435, 436, 440, 442, 446,
  447, 452, 453, 457, 458, 459, 462, 466,
  468, 472–73, 476–77, 478, 479, 480,
  482–83, 484
California Civil Rights Initiative, 267–68

California Democratic primary:
  of 1972, 37–38, 41, 43–44, 46
  of 1980, 109–12, 114
  of 1984, 145
California governor's race:
  of 1990, 201–2
  of 1998, 293
California Senate campaign (1986), 154, 157,
  159, 166–70, 171
Cambodia, 19, 64
"Camelot," 493–94
campaign finance laws, 144–45, 167, 293,
  317, 327–28, 329, 330, 361, 397–98,
  414–15, 440–41, 449, 452, 456–59, 468,
  471, 489, 491
Campaign for Military Service, 229–30
Campaigns and Elections, 205
Camp David peace accord (1978), 69
Campion, Chuck, 363
Carey, Hugh, 115, 116
Carlson, Margaret, 270
Carrick, Bill, 178–79, 181, 190, 208, 218
Carrier, Michelle, 239
Carson, Rachel, 301–2
Carter, Amy, 130
Carter, Jimmy, 76–131
  approval ratings of, 108
  economic policies of, 91, 93, 98–99, 102,
    108, 113, 115
  "malaise" speech of, 77
  media coverage of, 77, 96–97, 113
  as president, 76–77, 132, 211
  presidential campaign of (1976), xvi, 25,
    60–71, 87, 127–28, 129, 155, 383
  presidential campaign of (1980), 28, 63,
    67, 69, 74, 76–131, 136, 155, 212, 321
  Shrum as speech writer for, xvi, 60–71, 73
Carville, James, 146–47, 162–63, 164, 165,
  168, 170, 174, 199–200, 202, 203, 205,
  207, 209, 211, 219, 223, 225–27, 228,
  254, 296–97, 383, 384, 411, 427, 433,
  434, 447, 452
Casey, Bob, 156–57, 160, 162–66, 169–71,
  206–7, 209
Casey, Bobby, 156, 171
Casey, Sue, 419
Castro, Fidel, 330
Catholic Church, 1–2, 4, 8, 9–13, 62, 84, 138,
  172, 174–75, 192, 234, 262–63, 383,
  445–46, 447
CBS, 15, 191, 249, 373, 421
CBS News, 249
Centers for Disease Control and Prevention,
  U.S., 134
Central Intelligence Agency (CIA), 139, 193
Chafee, John, 231

PHOTO CREDITS

ABOUT THE AUTHOR

ROBERT SHRUM has been a major force in American politics for more than three decades. He was involved in Democratic presidential campaigns from 1972 to 2004, most recently as senior strategist to Al Gore and John Kerry. He has helped elect more than thirty U.S. senators, ten governors, and the mayors of major American cities. He lives on Cape Cod and serves as a senior fellow at New York University.